ISBN 978-1-332-02264-9
PIBN 10270441

MEMORIAL

OF THE

WALKERS

OF THE

OLD PLYMOUTH COLONY,

EMBRACING

GENEALOGICAL AND BIOGRAPHICAL SKETCHES

OF

JAMES, OF TAUNTON;
PHILIP, OF REHOBOTH;
WILLIAM, OF EASTHAM;
JOHN, OF MARSHFIELD;
THOMAS, OF BRISTOL;

AND OF

THEIR DESCENDANTS,

FROM 1620 TO 1860,

BY

J. B. R. WALKER, A. M.,

MEMBER OF THE OLD COLONY HISTORICAL SOCIETY.

"Look unto Abraham your father, and unto Sarah that bare you: for I called him alone, and blessed him, and increased him." ISAIAH 51: 2.

NORTHAMPTON:
METCALF & COMPANY, PRINTERS.
1861.

CONTENTS.

PREFACE.

It is the custom with some persons to depreciate, and even to ridicule, genealogical inquiries and labors. The study of pedigree, seems to them, not only tedious, but profitless. They have no reverence or love for the past, and it is a matter of indifference, who their ancestors were, or whether they ever had any. This is sometimes an eccentricity,—sometimes a proud independence, which ignores ancestry, in order to increase its own importance, and show that its heights and honors have not been attained through the wealth, patronage or name of progenitors. But a more fruitful cause of this low estimate, has been the boasting and arrogance of some, with reference to their distinguished ancestors. There is a false and foolish pride of lineage, which deserves censure and ridicule. It was such conceit that prompted the retort of Cicero, when a patrician said to him, "You are a plebeian." "I *am* a plebeian," replied the eloquent Roman orator, "and the nobility of *my* family *begins* with me, but that of yours, will *end* with you." The vain reliance upon remote and doubtful pedigrees, and the arrogant assumption of place and honor by reason of distinguished descent, without corresponding merit, was well ridiculed by Lord Chesterfield, when he placed among the portraits of his ancestors, two old heads, inscribed—Adam De Stanhope, and Eve De Stanhope. It has been justly observed, "all that a man can rightfully lay claim to, is his own name; the embellishment should be his own, not that of his defunct predecessor." This thought has been expressed by Chapman, with great felicity and force in these lines:—

'Tis poor, and not becoming perfect gentry,
To build their glories at their fathers' cost;
But at their own expense of blood or virtue,
To raise them living monuments; our birth
Is not our own act; honor upon trust,
Our ill deeds forfeit: and the wealthy sums,
Purchased by others' fame or sweat, will be
Our stain, for we inherit nothing truly
But what our actions make us worthy of.

There have been so much conceit and arrogance, in respect to lineage, that even wise and good persons have been led to underrate the importance of the subject. Thus, the excellent Rev. William Jay, of Bath, in his autobiography, (vol. 1, 19th p.) says :—"I have not to trace a long and proud lineage. If any great and illustrious individuals have been found among my ancestors, they have not been ascertained in my family, in my own time. But were I mean enough, to feel any mortification here, I could not console myself. When one of Lord Thurlow's friends was endeavoring to make out his relationship to the Secretary Cromwell, whose family had been in the county adjoining Suffolk, he replied, 'Sir, there were two Cromwells in that part of the country, Thurlow the Secretary, and Thurlow the Carrier, I am descended from the latter.' We have read of a man, who in prospect of his promotion, being asked concerning his pedigree, answered 'he was not particularly sure, but had been credibly informed, that he had three brothers in the ark.' But one of our most distinguished poets surpasses this, in his epitaph :—

'Princes and heralds, by your leave
Here lie the bones of Matthew Prior,
The son of Adam and of Eve,
Can Nassau or Bourbon go higher?' "

Bishop Chastel was one of the most learned divines of the 16th century, bishop of Orleans, and great almoner of France. Francis I. asked him, 'Whether he was born a gentleman?' Chastel answered, 'That he was not perfectly certain from which of Noah's three sons he was descended.' Every genealogist, in his appeal for information, has doubtless sometime met a response like the following :—"The answer which you seek of me, O illustrious friend and joy of my liver!" wrote an eastern Cadi, in reply to M. Layard's inquiries about certain antiquarian statistics, "is both difficult and useless to be given." But while there is danger of our setting too high a value upon our pedigree, yet it is well to remember our ancestry, nor is it wrong to recount and rejoice in, their achievements and worth. Inspiration recognizes the intimate connection between ourselves and our ancestry, when it asserts "children's children are the crown of old men ; and the glory of children are their fathers." Parents and children, ancestors and descendants, reflect honor or dishonor upon each other. Virtuous and godly children are as gems in "the crown" of a venerable and virtuous old man, and in filial honor, they in turn, cherish him as their "glory." So too, such as have good blood in their veins, yet have no analogous excellence in their characters, dishonor those who bore them.. And this law unites successive generations in a common life and history. Clever has well stated this mutual relation. "A good root," says he, "maketh the branches to flourish, by virtue of the lively sap that it sendeth up. And flourishing branches win praise to the root, for the pleasant fruit which they bring forth." They who transmit a good name, noble examples, and a pure faith, lay their descendants under sacred and lasting obligations of gratitude for, and emulation of, ancestral faithfulness and piety.

The more one studies history, and races, and families, the more must he be convinced of the marked and permanent influence of BLOOD. Despite all the crossings by intermarriages, every genealogist has marked, and marvelled at the continuance, from generation to generation, of some particular type of character, that was visible in the earliest known ancestor. This fact has been strikingly illustrated in the descendants of many of the early Pilgrim, or Puritan colonists. To read aright the lesson of human history, to reach wise and safe generalizations, one must not forget the law of descent, and the force there is in blood or race. "Religion does not run in the blood of that family," said an aged but observing man, as a vicious youth passed him. "I have known the family for several generations, but I have never known any among them who gave evidence of piety."—The qualities and forces of the character do "run in the blood," and whether good or bad, are propagated, and pass down through successive generations. In some families, the parents, and the ancestors, back to an early period, have been marked by moral and christian excellence. The family of the elder Edwards is an illustration of this law and force of Blood. His ancestors, for many generations, were eminent for religious worth. And his numerous progeny have, with few exceptions, "flourished by reason of the lively sap sent up from the good root." Wherever they are found, they are characterized by the moral qualities, and illustrate, in no small degree, the spirit of their illustrious and godly ancestor. And this force of Blood, is just as visible in the transmission of evil qualities, giving to some families, through long periods, "a bad eminence," perpetuating a type of character, with which, religion or intelligence are rarely, if ever, united.

It is argued, by such as underrate genealogical research, that every claim upon the esteem of others, is founded upon character, and that this embodies every quality that can justly command the affection and reverence of men. But as character is not altogether isolated from, nor independent of ancestral fountains, from which, the native impulses, the mental and moral tendencies and forces, have come, the subject of pedigree belongs, clearly, to the history of every man's mind and life. Our ancestors live in us. Though dead, they speak. In nature, below man, the various orders of being, animate and inanimate, do little more than repeat ancestral forms and habits. Man also, is a derivation from the past, and ought to be considered and weighed in connection with it.

The study of genealogy, therefore, has important scientific and moral uses. It summons the Past, to interpret the lives of men, with respect to physical, mental and moral character. It shows how the Past has poured itself into our present life. It embalms in the memory of the living, the lessons, examples and obligations, of an honorable lineage, and as the Romans when emigrating to foreign climes, took with them the carved images of their fathers, and set them in the choicest places of their new homes, so it sets the images of our ancestors before us, to be an inspiration and benediction to our life.

MATTERS PERSONAL. ORIGIN OF THE WORK, &c.—Seven years since, in a respite from professional labor, the subscriber undertook what had been a long cherished purpose, viz., to trace his descent from James Walker, one of the first settlers of Taunton, Mass. The materials thus gleaned, respecting the ancient Walkers of T. induced him to extend his plan and compile a complete genealogy of the Family. It was soon discovered that they were allied with the Rehoboth Walkers, and the plan was enlarged, so as to include this more fruitful Branch. As the ancestor of the Eastham Family emigrated to this country in the same ship with James of Taunton, it was supposed that they were related, and accordingly his descendants were traced. At length, in view of the fact of there being no less than 14 of the name of Walker, ancestors of distinct branches, in the country even before 1650, and the wide extent and frequency of the name at the present time, it was determined to limit the work to the Walkers of the Old Plymouth Colony. and their descendants. This plan required the addition of the Families of John of Marshfield and Thomas of Bristol. The compiler has been successful in obtaining information respecting all the lineal descendants of these early settlers, with a very few exceptions, and especially those of Taunton and Rehoboth lineage. It is thought that in no similar work, equal in size, have fewer branches been left incomplete. The publication of the work has been deferred, that every measure which promised success, might be taken, to trace every male line down to the present time, and include every descendant named Walker. The fulness of these Genealogies in this respect, may be seen by reference to pages 420, 21, of the Appendix. They embrace the period between 1618 and 1860.

One who has had no experience in genealogical inquiries, can form no just idea of the amount of labor required, to collect and arrange the names and materials of the biography of the widely scattered and numerous descendants of the early settlers, through a period of two centuries and a quarter, the labor of extensive correspondence, examination of town and state records, histories, ancient wills, and deeds; labor greatly increased also, by the delay, and in some cases, refusal of those from whom information was sought. His labor arising from these latter sources, delay and indifference, the compiler has reason to suppose, have not been greater, than what is usually the experience of a family historian. But no complete and accurate Genealogy can be prepared without an expenditure of time, and money, for which no adequate remuneration can be expected, save in the pleasure attending such pursuits, and the consciousness of doing something, in grateful reverence, to enshrine in a permanent Memorial, the lives and virtues of one's ancestors and kindred—a Memorial, which, while it may be no mean offering to their worth, may also be to the descendants, full of inspiration to piety and patriotism, as they trace their lineage from the self-sacrificing founders of civilization, and the brave and steadfast defenders of freedom in this New World. The compiler has spared no pains nor expense to secure thoroughness and accuracy. Records have been examined and re-examined, and all correspondence, some of it illegible and with its facts badly arranged, has been carefully compiled and copied. As the highest merit in a Genealogy is correctness, this has been sedulously labored for, and if persistent efforts to verify dates, harmonize conflicting statements, and make a Memorial complete and reliable, can accomplish the object,—this work is a success. If any do not find so full an account of themselves and families as was anticipated, it is because in most instances no more was furnished. To some extent there has been a condensation of the materials, but generally in respect to those who have evinced no interest in their publication, as justice demanded that subscribers and their families should have the largest space consistent with the plan of the book. Various traditions obtain in some branches of the Family respecting their ancestors, and the time of their emigration to this country. But what is stated in this work concerning their advent, is sustained by abundant and incontestable proofs. None of these traditions reach back far enough into the early history of New England.

ABBREVIATIONS AND EXPLANATIONS.—ae. for aged; abt. for about; b. for born; bapt. for baptized; bef. for before; chil. for children; d. for died; dau. for daughter; dec'd for deceased; Bap. for Baptist; Cong. for Congregationalist; Meth. for Methodist; Pres. for Presbyterian; Epis. for Episcopal; m. for married; unm. for unmarried; m. ch. for member of the church; In'y and Inv'y for Inventory; (Ins.) for Inscription on tomb-stone; grad. for graduated; pub. for published; rem. for removed; Rec. for Records; Prop. Rec. for Proprietors' Records; Plym. Col. Rec. for Plymouth Colony Records; Rep. for Representative; Res. for residence; res. for resides; w. for wife; wid. for widow; yr. for year; Coll. for College; N. S. for New Style; O. S. for Old Style. The names for towns are abbreviated, as Mid'o for Middleboro; D'n for Dighton, and the initial letter only is frequently used, when the name has been given in full just before. Dates since 1800 are sometimes abbreviated thus, '29 for 1829. There are other abbreviations, of such common use, that the meaning will be obvious.

A name in parenthesis, thus, Sarah Richmond, dau. of Wm. and Anna (Gray) indicates the *maiden* surname of Anna, w. of Wm. Richmond. (See 34th p.) An interrogation mark (?) implies doubt, or want of absolute certainty. Sometimes two dates of the same event are given, the authority being so nearly equal, that the compiler could not determine which is the correct one. Where town and family records, as in some instances, disagree, or members of the same family have reported different dates, and insist upon their accuracy, both are given, one of them being placed in brackets. If discrepancies between the dates given here, and those of their ancient family records, are discovered by any persons, such should consider whether the difference between Old and New Style will not harmonize them. Undoubtedly in a few instances, where no family records exist, names and dates have been furnished from memory, and errors may be discovered. But these will be found only among the living or later generations, and for them, the compiler is not responsible. As the orthography of names varies in different families, the compiler has reproduced the spelling which was furnished him, except where there were obvious errors. Birthplaces are not always stated where the dates of birth are given, but they can be ascertained by reference to the person's father, and his residence at the time of the birth.

OLD AND NEW STYLE.—In computing time, the solar year is reckoned 365¼ days, but this is too much by 11 minutes and a fraction. If this excess be neglected, in the course of centuries, the 1st of January would fall back towards midsummer, and in 1582, the time of Pope Gregory XIII., it was found that the vernal equinox which in A. D. 325 happened on the 21st of March, actually occurred on the 10th of March. For the purpose of rectifying the calendar, the Pope ordered that 10 days be dropped from that year. This was called "New Style" and the former calendar, "Old Style." The new calendar was soon adopted in all Catholic countries, but in England and her colonies, it was disregarded till 1752, when the error of the old calendar amounted to 11 days, and by an Act of Parliament, they were dropped from Sept. of that year. Some persons may not understand the double dating, like Feb. 9, 1684–5, on p. 23, No. 9. The real date is Feb. 9, 1685. The civil or legal year in England, formerly commenced on the 25th of March, and was so reckoned till 1752, when the new or Gregorian calendar was adopted, which makes the year commence on the 1st of January. But before that period, as some other nations had adopted the New Style, it was usual for English and American writers to designate both years, if the event occurred before the 25th of March. If the year commenced the 25th of March, the date would be Feb. 9, 1684, if the year began the 1st of January, the date would be Feb. 9, 1685, and changed to New Style by addition of 11 days would be Feb. 16, 1685.

ARRANGEMENT OR PLAN OF THE BOOK.—The plan adopted, is that recommended by the Genealogical Register, and which after examination of published genealogies, appeared to the compiler, the most intelligible. Experience has confirmed his choice, and no other plan, yet devised, is so simple and so easily comprehended, by persons not familiar with genealogical works.

The numbering is enumerative, the numerals at the left of the page giving the whole number of Walkers down to any period or generation. The small figure over a name at the right, thus James,^{6} indicates the generation to which this person belongs, reckoning from his earliest ancestor in this country. A few moments attention to the directions which follow, will enable the reader to ascertain the pedigree, and find the descendants of any person whose name is given in Part I. of the Index. The figure at the right of a name in brackets, thus, "CHILDREN OF LIEUT. JAMES WALKER,^{4} [10]" on p. 30, refers backward to No. 10, 24th p., where an account of this James^{4} will be found. He is one of the "Children of James Walker,^{3} [5]" and by referring to No. 5, 21st p., an account of his father may be found. And James, No. 5, is one of the "CHILDREN OF JAMES WALKER,^{2} [2]" and referring to No. 2, 4th p., it will be seen that he is descended from the 1st James^{2} of Taunton, son of Widow Walker^{1} of Rehoboth. Reversing the method, in order to trace descendants, the figure at the right of the name in parenthesis, thus, JAMES WALKER,^{2} (5) on 4th p., refers to what follows at No. 5, 21st p., and shows where the children of James, No. 2, may be found. In No. 5, James,^{3} (10) on 21st p., the 10 in parenthesis refers to No. 10, on 24th p., where the children of James, No. 5, may be found. No. 10, James,^{4} on 24th p., has 27 in parenthesis, thus, (27) which indicates where this James' children may be found. (See 30th p.) No. 27, James,^{5} (59) on 30th p., the 59 in parenthesis refers to No. 59, on the 37th p., where the son of James, No. 27, is found. This line terminates here, the descendants of James, No. 59, if he had any, having baffled all research, and accordingly he has no reference number. But No. 61, Eliakim, on the same page, has the reference number (121) for which see the 50th p., where Eliakim's children are found, and by observing these directions, it will be easy to trace Eliakim's grandchildren and descendants, or those of any other person. The children and descendants of the females are not carried forward to the next generation, but their names and all that pertains to them, appear in connection with their Walker mothers or ancestors, though in smaller type. In some instances, these sketches embrace several generations, as with the descendants of Mehetable, No. 15, on 25th page.

A copious Index is furnished, so that the names of all the Walkers, and of all persons who have married Walkers or their descendants, if mentioned in this Memorial, may easily be found, and whatever account is given of them, be referred to. A full and valuable Summary may be found in the Appendix, pp. 415, 16. It will be well for the reader also to examine the ADDITIONS and ERRATA, on pp. 417—420 and 451, and by some mark on the pages where they properly belong, indicate a reference to them, especially those which relate to themselves, or kindred.

Some persons bearing the name of Walker and descended from other early settlers, may imagine that this work, purporting to be a

Genealogy of the Walkers, contains an account of themselves and families. Such will be disappointed, as those only are included who are of Old Colony lineage. They will however find much pertaining to the History of the name, that will interest them, and possibly may find the root from which they are sprung, in the Appendix, (p. 401—407,) which contains the names of the other Walkers in New England previous to 1700.

It may perhaps seem needless for the compiler to say, that he has been gratified by the interest evinced by the members of the different branches of the Walker race, especially those of Taunton and Rehoboth origin. It is impossible for him to mention here the names of all, who by words of encouragement and by prompt and full correspondence, have done so much to bear him through an enterprise demanding such unlimited patience, and in which, completion can be achieved only by years of labor. Without forgetting his obligation to any, he cannot forbear however to publicly and gratefully acknowledge the services and hearty co-operation of George Walker and Richmond Walker of Taunton, Abel B. Walker of Andover, Rev. Horace D. Walker of East Abington, the late James O. Walker of Swanton Centre, Vt., Abel Walker of Whiting, Vt., Hon. Zuriel Walker of Ferrisburgh, Vt., Hon. John A. Walker of Pittsfield, Thomas Walker, Esq. of Utica, N.Y., Hon. Edward C. Walker of Detroit, Mich., Prof. Charles M. Walker of Indianapolis, Col. Amasa K. Walker of Hampden, Me., Joseph Brown of Seekonk, John W. Higgins of Eastham, and Miss Maria Thomas of Marshfield. He is also indebted to those who so readily responded to the request to furnish the portraits which embellish the book, and which render it far more valuable as a Memorial of the Walkers. Several were constrained to withdraw their pledges to this effect, but others and a greater number have supplied their places, so that but one of the many Family histories now published, equal in size to the Genealogies of the Taunton and Rehoboth Branches, is so abundantly illustrated with portraits.

The descendants of these Old Colony Families, have generally belonged to the agricultural and mechanical classes, and have been characterized by good sense, sound judgment and christian excellence. None have achieved celebrity in literature or statesmanship. They have mostly helped swell the ranks of the honest and pious yeomanry of New England and the West. It is interesting to trace the transmission of the Puritan faith, to see the streams, originating in the piety of the good Dea. Philip Walker of Rehoboth, and James of Taunton, the honored magistrate, coursing down the centuries and over the land, yet maintaining their purity, and bearing moral fertility wherever they have gone. The compiler has added a feature to this work which has not generally been introduced. He has endeavored to ascertain the religious sympathy and church relation of each person. It has seemed to him, that for the highest use of a Genealogy, it is important to know whether a person is "born of God" as well as "born of the will of man." The biography of multitudes may be summed up in the statement of the author of Euthanasy, "born upon such a day—died upon such another, with an utter blank between." But with a religious birth to fill this "blank" of some unhonored and lowly man or woman, with steady and attractive piety, the life becomes useful, even noble, answers "life's great end," and is worthy of a record here, as it has a record on high. Of such, it can never be said they were

> "Fixed to one peculiar spot
> To draw nutrition, propagate, and rot."

With a name on which no stain has ever rested, with an ancestry not often great, but always virtuous, filling, with fidelity and honor, the stations they were called to occupy, one may justly be proud of his lineage. It is the hope of the compiler, that all who by means of his labors, find that such are their name and ancestry, may be grateful for the "glory" they have in "their fathers," and learn from them, that "the richest bequest which any man can make, for the benefit of posterity, is that of a shining and spotless example."

HOLYOKE, MASS., Jan. 1, 1861.

INTRODUCTION.

Walker. Origin and meaning of the Name.—Surnames have originated from various sources, such as localities, occupations, offices, social relations, and personal qualities or peculiarities, character and history. Others are Norman names, dating from the Conquest. Two other classes are derived from the Christian names of father or mother, and from the animal, mineral or vegetable kingdoms. Local English names constitute the most numerous division, and unlike those of occupation, do not indicate the condition, or social rank of those who first bore them.

The custom of assuming or applying names from the various pursuits of life obtained at a very early period. Among the Romans, many and even those of the highest rank, had such names. "These names became hereditary in England next in order, after the local names, about the 11th and 12th centuries, and form a large class. They had a prefix *le*, as Stephen le Spicer, le Bakere, &c. in records of 12th and two succeeding centuries." Walker, says Lower in his "Surnames," signifies either (Anglo Saxon *wealcere*) a fuller or an officer whose duty consisted in walking over or inspecting a certain space of forest ground. In the North of England, a fulling mill is still called a '*walk*-mill,' and at Alfrich, Co. Worcester, there are some thin strata of unctuous clay of a whitish hue, still called Walker's clay. The same custom obtains in the South of Scotland, where the Walkers are numerous. There is a string of names, Lower adds, derived from occupation, which sounds right odd, when placed in juxtaposition, and which *prima facie*, would appear to be fully as applicable to the equine as to the human species, viz., Traveller, Walker, Ryder, Ambler, Trotter, Hopper, Skipper and Hobler. Ryder means another forest officer, a superintendent of the Walkers, a ranger who derived his name from the circumstance of being mounted, and as having a larger district to supervise. From this, it is clear that Lower leans to the opinion that Walker is a name of occupation. Arthur, in his work on the Etymology of names, gives it the same signification. The Anglo Saxon Dictionary, however, has the following definition, viz., "*Wealc*, a revolving, a revolution of heavenly bodies. Wealcan p. Wealc, (hence to walk.) To roll, turn, &c.; to return often. Wealcre, es. m., a fuller; in Lancashire, a Walker, s." A writer in the Edinburgh Review, in an essay on

English surnames, says, "Many of these names of employment survive, and remind us of crafts which have long ceased to exist," and he gives among his illustrations, "Le Waliker, (Waliker that is Fuller.")*

It will be seen that authorities differ as to the signification of the name, and leave it difficult to determine which theory is the more correct. Probably, however, both meanings are true, and the name had a double origin; in some parts of England, being derived from the occupation of a forest officer, and in the North of England and Scotland, originating from the employment of a fuller. This seems the more rational conclusion. The change in the ancient surname of the Walkers of Manor House, Bushey, Co. Hertfordshire, from Forestier to Walker, (see few pp. onward) favors this supposition. And may not some branch of the Fullers have adopted the name of Walker, and as a fulling mill was also a walking mill, may not some have chosen the former, while others selected the latter as their surname?

ANTIQUITY OF THE NAME.—The following in respect to persons bearing the name, in England, mostly persons of distinction, is introduced as part of its history. It is with no idea that these very ancient Walkers are in any way related to the Walkers who came to New England. The English origin and pedigree of the Families included in this work are entirely unknown, and it would be sheer presumption to infer that they were descended from any whose names are given in this introduction. The name even before the year 1600, was so common and extensive, and as a name of occupation had so many independent roots, or an origin in so many different places, as to give no justification to any theory of descent and relationship. So "mighty" or numerous was the name in England 250 years ago, that the compiler came at length to entertain no hope of ascertaining the pedigree of his ancestor, or of other Walkers contemporaneous, in the Old Colony, having no other fact to guide his researches, than that James and William sailed from London in 1635. He has found no coats of arms nor tradition of any, in these Families, and if their ancestors were entitled to any, which is not probable, all memory of them is lost.

As most of the English surnames took root between the Norman Conquest of 1066 and the Revolution of 1688, the historical notices which follow, are embraced within this period. These are selected from a great number, as there is no end to the use of the name in numerous English works.

---

*This interesting essay is re-published in Littell's Living Age, No. 574.

HISTORICAL NOTICES OF THE NAME.—St. Michael's Mount in Cornwall, was surrendered in 1194, to Hubert Walker, Archbishop of Canterbury.—(Lyson's Brittannia, Cornwall.)

There was Walcre or Walkern, in 1215, also Willi Waliker.—(Rotuli Litterarum, vol. I.)

Walke and Walkern, probably meant for Walker, are found in the Taxatio Ecclesiastica.

There was a William Walkere in the reign of Henry III., (1216—1272).—(Placitorum Abbreviatio.)

Nichs Walk lived in the time of Edward I., who began his reign, 1272.—(Rotuli, vol. II.)

Sir Roger Walker was parish priest of Hockwold in Suffolk, about 1349.

John Walker, L.L. B., Archdeacon of the East Riding of Yorkshire, d. about Dec. 1475.

Mr. Miles Walker was Rector of St. Lawrence Ch. in South Walsham, in 1478.

There were two chantries founded at Lewsham, about 1490, one by Richard Walker, for the priest to celebrate mass at the altar of the Trinity, for the founder's soul.

Jacobz Walker F. civis Lond. ob. 4 Nov. 1491.

John Walker was Vicar of the Ch. of Boughton Monchensie, in 1492.

Hugh Walker was Rector of Mereworth, Nov. 20, 1497.

Richard Walker, Provost and Master of Wye Coll. in 1518, d. Oct. 20, 1543.

Sir Thomas Kylson, Knt., made a lease "for terme of certeyn yers of Parcel of Premysses, in citie of London, to oon Thomas Walker." Date, 4th June, 1533.—(Rhymer's Foedera.)

William Walker of Bury fletcher, 1539, directed "all his peyntyd clothgs to be gevyn vnto fore yong copylls yt be newly maryed."—(Bury Wills and Inventories.)

Jane, dau. of Thomas Walker of London, S. P., m. as 2d wife, about 1550, the 5th son of Sir John Boys of St. Gregory's, Knt.

The following are the names of Walkers who were Vicars and Rectors in the time of Henry VIII., (1509—1547,) viz., Dr. William, John, James, George, Thomas, Hugo, David, Henry, John, Rector of Tackley, and John, Rector of Wotton.

Christopher Walker was Vicar, 1540, also Nicholaus Walker.

Edmund Walker was presented to the vicarage of Wensbury, 1550.

Peter Walker became Rector of Colcester, 1556.

Roger Walker, M. A., became Dean of Chester, 1558 or '59.

Henry Walker had a position in the Academy of Canterbury, 1564.

Queen Elizabeth granted the rectory of Collumpton to John Walker, in 1565.

There were Walkers in Exeter, Devonshire Co., from middle of 16th century. Rev. Rob't Walker, Vicar of St. Winnow in Cornwall, was the representative of the family.

William Walker, Rector of Charing, in diocese of Canterbury, resigned, 1586.

Anthony Walker of St. Andrew's Wardrobe, Lond., d. 1590.

Dr. Thomas Walker, Master of Univ. Coll., was elected 1632, dispossessed 1648, restored 1660, and d. 1665. He was related to Archbishop Laud, and was a deserving and modest man.—(Neal's Puritans.)

William Walker was one of the assistants of Burrough of St. Albans, in 1634.

Peter Walker. His father sacrificed his property in the cause of the royal house of Stuarts, and fled from Cheshire into Ireland. He m. Mary Walker, of Yorkshire Walkers.

William Walker, b. in 1650, resided in the parish of Ecclesfield, Co. York, and d. 1708. He left Joseph, who had 2 sons by 1st wife, and 3 sons by 2d wife. The last 3 were the celebrated brothers at Masborough, Samuel, Aaron, and Jonathan, called the "Great Iron Founders." Samuel was a man of remarkable ability, and excellence. For an interesting sketch, see County Hist. of York, 5th vol.

Richard Walker, was Rector of Boughton Aluph, Aug. 6. 1644.

Henry Walker was presented to be minister of Knightsbridge Chapel, 1655.

Dr. Walt. Walker, Knt. Doctor of Civil Law, formerly of Staffordshire, was one of the Judges of Court of Admiralty and Court of Prob. of Wills, 1659. He was also Advocate General to His Royal Highness, James, Duke of York.

Sir Geo. Walker, Knt. Dr. of Civil Law, d. 1679.

Henry Walker, Rector of Church of Kensington, 1677, resigned 1681.

Henry Walker, Rector of Church of Willesborough, 1681, d. 1695.

John Walker, Rector of Church of Kensington, 1681, till 1683.

John Walker, was Rector of Church of Halden, 1683.

The ancient surname of the Walkers of Manor House, Bushey, Co. Hertfordshire, was Forestier or De Forestier, derived, at a remote period from their occupations, in the royal forests, as forestiers, walkers, verderers, &c.; but subsequently, in order to distinguish a numerous progeny, certain branches, those of Sir Hovenden Walker, Knt., Sir Walter Walker of Bushey Hall, &c., assumed the name of Walker only.

Extent of the Name.—From the preceding notices of persons of eminence, it may be inferred that Walker was also a common name, among the humbler ranks of society through all the periods of

English history. It is not only English, but prevails extensively in Scotland,* and to some extent in Ireland. There are many of the name now in this country, who are of Scotch birth.

With "the list of the Pedigrees contained in Wm. Paver's consolidated Visitations of Yorkshire," being those taken in 1584, 1612 and 1665, there is also a list of allied families, with the number of times each name appears. There are 1352 names. Walker appears 11 times, and is exceeded by only 9 names in the list.

At one time, a list of 60 of the most common surnames, in England and Wales, was made, and a register was kept of the number of births, marriages and deaths, in one year, with this result: Of the strictly English family names, Smiths were most numerous, Jones next in order, and Taylors, third. Of the names derived from employments, whether official or manual, Wright, Walker, Turner, Cooper, Clark, Baker, occupy next to Smith & Taylor, the highest place. The names in this list are called "the mighty sixty." Walker is the 17th in rank, and of names of occupation holds the 4th place.

"The Encyclopedia of Heraldry" gives 52 different families of Walkers, with their arms. Of these, 5 were in Scotland, 1 in Ireland, and 1 in Barbadoes. The others were distributed in almost every county of England.

"Burke's Landed Gentry," published 1853, gives 11 families of Walkers, (with their arms,) to be found in different counties.

Seventeen persons named Walker, had been graduated at Oxford University, previous to 1828.

The London Directory for year 1855, gives 234 names of Walkers, business and professional.—(See Appendix, pp. 407, 8, for the commonness of the name in the cities of this country.†)

---

*The original of Jeanie Deans, in the "Heart of Mid-Lothian" by Sir Walter Scott, was Helen Walker, who d. 1791. He erected a monument to her memory, in the church-yard of Irongrey, Edinburgh, inscribing it with a just and beautiful tribute to her worth. It closes thus, "Respect the Grave of Poverty, when combined with love of truth and dear affection."

†In the year 1858, there were 55 Postmasters in the U. S., named Walker, and only 4 of them belonging to the families included in this work—a fact that shows how widely and numerously the name has spread over this country.

NOTE.—The following items have come to the compiler's notice since the Appendix was printed.

Jo. Walker, ae. 16, imbarqued for Virginia, Aug. 1, 1635.
Walter Walker, ae. 23, " " " " 21, 1635.
Margaret Walker, ae. 20, " " " 1635, in another ship.

There are numerous Walkers in the Southern States, and several have risen to distinction.

1. "WIDOW WALKER," (2)

Of Rehoboth, Mass.

She was one of the first purchasers and proprietors of the town of Rehoboth or Seacunk, now Seekonk, and one of the company who first settled there. Her name is in the list of those who in 1643 gave in the value of their estates, for a pro rata division of the lands. Hers was £50. In the division made June 31, 1644, she had a share, and lots were assigned her in several divisions afterward, as in drawing for the Great Plain, and on the 18th of 12 mo. (Feb.) 1646, for the new Meadow.

Her name then disappears. When and from whence she came to New England, and where she died, are not known. There is no record to tell us her age or her character. No trace of her biography is found, save the already noticed facts of her being associated with an adventurous company, most of whom went out from Weymouth into the wilderness,—a company marked for its religious character, (being a majority of the church at W.,) the highly educated and scholarly Rev. Samuel Newman being in some respects the Leader of the enterprise.—Her christian name and that of her husband, are never given. In the early records of the town, she has invariably the touching, sorrowful title of Widow, suggesting the history of blighted hopes, and a grief-stricken heart. Perhaps she had one to protect and cherish her when she left her native land,—and burying him in the sea came here alone,—or perhaps together, they had reached these shores, and were struggling in mutual help and loyalty to bear the toils, trials and perils incident to the settlement of a new country,—when death snatched him from her fellowship. But the more probable supposition is, that becoming a widow in England, she emigrated, perhaps with her younger son Philip, after the coming of James and Sarah. Bereft of counsellor and helper, she would naturally follow her children, and seek the sympathy and aid of her brother, or possibly only her brother-in-law, Mr. John Browne. That she did not come with them in 1635, and did not appear till 8 years afterward, favors this theory. James and Sarah, as favorites of their uncle Mr. Browne, and bereft of a father's counsel and support, may have been induced by his encouragements, to try their fortunes in the New World, leaving the mother behind with their younger brother, till they should learn how the experiment would issue.—Old enough to be of service, perhaps they were really indentured as "servants to Jo. Browne," and not merely, as a device to escape the pursuivants of the King in their attempt to get out of England. But these are conjectures merely. The interest of Mr. Browne in his nephew and niece, the two young emigrants of 1635, and the fact of their mother the "widow" being associated with Mr. B. in the settlement of Rehoboth, favors the belief that she was his sister, though he might have manifested the same regard, had she been only the sister of his wife. We may however see among the group of pious and brave settlers, not only the godly man who is their religious teacher, but also the form of one, whose sable garments tell us, she is a "Widow." The vision passes quickly before us, and is lost to our sight, awakening sympathy and interest for the woman, who, bereft of the companion of her youth, became a pioneer in founding the church and colony at Rehoboth. She was buried no doubt, in the ancient place of graves in Seekonk, where many of the fathers repose, but no stone marks the spot.

Philip Walker, afterward Deacon, and whose name first appears in 1653, to whom lands were assigned in 1658, and of whom the record commences, soon after her's ceases, was her son. In the description of his lands in the Proprietors' Records, 48th p., he says, "100 pound commons that was Thos. Pitts', 100 that was the Governor's, half a hundred that was *my mother's*." It is evident therefore that he was the son of "Widow Walker," for had his "mother" not been a widow, the lands would have been described as those of his father, and furthermore, there was no other person of the name in the Rehoboth Company, who could sustain this relation to him.

James Walker appears in the list of those in 1643 giving in the value of their estates. His name is next to that of the "Widow," and the amount is £50, but it is subjoined that his share is "now John ffitches." He however forfeited his lots to the town in 1644, in accordance with an order enacted by the proprietors in 1643, that those who did not fence their lands, or remove there with their families, should forfeit their lots. His name however, is mentioned in one division of lands afterward, viz., that of 1645. It is probable however, that he never removed to Rehoboth, but concluded to remain in Taunton. Mr. John Browne, whose lots were forfeited at the same date with James Walker's, lived in Taunton at the time, and was his "cousin," (uncle.) Thus connected with the "Widow" and Mr. Browne, who was also one of the original Proprietors of Rehoboth, having been the agent of the company, while in Weymouth, and appointed by the Court at Plymouth, to make the purchase of Asameeum the Indian Chief, James Walker very naturally became associated with the settlement. Accordingly neither their names nor that of Mr. Browne is found in the list of the company that went from Weymouth. The strongest reason, however, for concluding he was of "Widow Walker's" family, is found in the fact that when Deacon Philip died in 1679, James was one of the appraisers of his estate. When it is remembered that there was no James Walker in R., at that time, that Rehoboth and Taunton townships were contiguous, and moreover, that James was about 60 years of age, it is beyond a reasonable doubt that he was not only nearly related to Philip, but was his brother, and accordingly was the son of "Widow Walker."

If we may judge of her worth from the virtues of her sons, and infer that they inherited the spirit and piety of their Pilgrim mother, and that her fidelity entitled her to use the language of the Roman matron respecting the Gracchi, "These are my jewels," then was she a compeer worthy to be associated with the pious and distinguished Mr. Newman and the useful Mr. Browne, leaders in the Rehoboth settlement.

And as "the glory of the fathers is their children," her name is not unhonored, and her character and worth not without their monument.

It is upon this evidence, which, though fragmentary and circumstantial, is nevertheless conclusive, that

"WIDOW WALKER"

is placed at the head of the Taunton Family, and in respect to them, as well as the more numerous and widely scattered family of Rehoboth, must be honored as

"THE MOTHER OF US ALL."

CHILDREN OF WIDOW WALKER[1] [1] of Rehoboth.

2. JAMES WALKER,[2] (5)

OF TAUNTON, MASS.

SON of —— Walker and his wife, —— afterward called "Widow Walker" of Rehoboth, was born in England in 1619 or '20. All efforts to discover his birthplace, and learn from which branch of the numerous race of Walkers he sprung, have proved fruitless. Nor can the time of his emigration to this country, be determined with *absolute* certainty. The following fact from "Gleanings for New England History by Hon. James Savage, from a Manuscript vol. at the Augmentation office," England, which are published in the Collections of the Mass. Historical Society, 8th vol., 3d series, will at least furnish ground for a conjecture, if not, in connection with contemporaneous facts, for a conclusion, which leaves no room for a reasonable doubt. The record is thus:

Imbarqud Apr. 15. In Elizabeth, de London,
Master Wm. Stagg versus New England,
Richard Walker, 24
William Walker, 15

and 3 others of different names; these persons having taken the oath of allegiance and supremacy before Sir Wm. Whitmore and Sir Nicholas Ranton.

In another paragraph on the same page, it is added:

15 Apr. In the Elizabeth, de London,
Master Wm. Stagg vs. New England,
James Walker, 15 yrs.
Sarra Walker, 17 yrs. servants* to
Jo. Browne, a Baker and to 1 Wm. Brasey,
linen draper in Cheapside, London, per
certificate of their conformity.

*Mr. Savage says it is probable that some of those persons who entered as servants assumed this title to escape the vigilance of the pursuivants.

On a following page is added:

17th Apr. for New England in Elizabeth,
Wm. Stagg, master, 28 more, among whom
Jo. Browne, 40 yrs.

That this was the James Walker who settled at Taunton is confirmed by the following facts:

In all the town histories of the Plymouth and Massachusetts Colonies, and the Probate Records, which have been thoroughly examined, there is no trace of any other James Walker, previous to the year 1655.† It is the single instance of the name. And in respect to his birth and age, there is only a variation of one year, between the statement just given, and the age and date upon the grave stone still standing in the Walker Burial Place in South Taunton. And this is a slight discrepancy, and may have arisen from a mistake in the original English record, or in Mr. Savage's transcription of it, or which is more probable still, from an error in the inscription upon the grave stone, either by the failure in memory of those who reared it, (perhaps at some considerable time after his death) or by the mistake of the stone cutter in putting 73 for his age instead of 72. Grave stones are proverbially uncertain in respect to dates. It is no infrequent thing to find such variations.

Besides this, William was in Hingham in 1636, the year after their embarkation from London, and had a lot assigned him, and his name is in the list of the inhabitants and proprietors of that year. And it is a well known fact, that many of the first settlers of Taunton were from Hingham and Scituate. And it is not improbable, that the ship Elizabeth landed her passengers at H. or somewhere on the South Shore.

Richard Walker was the son of Richard of Lynn or Saugus, who came before him. His age at his death, concurs with his age given in Mr. Savage's Gleanings, and with his birth in 1611, as given by Lewis in Hist. of Lynn, published before Mr. Savage made his researches in England. But another fact, which contributes to change what otherwise might be a conjecture, into a firm conviction, is, that James Walker was the brother-in-law* of John Tisdill, and

* Mr. John Browne of Rehoboth Nov. 23d, 1655 gave to "his cousin (nephew ?) John Tisdill, dwelling house bought of Goodman, &c., &c. and house he lived in at Taunton, to John Tisdill and his cousin (nephew) James Walker, John Tisdill's brother-in-law." Plym. Reg. Deeds, 3d vol., 181 p.

† A James Walker appeared in Chelmsford in 1659.

as it is known that James Walker married Elizabeth Philips, this relationship could have been, only by John Tisdill's marriage with James Walker's sister. And as John Tisdill's wife was named Sarah, and James Walker, his brother-in-law, had a sister Sarah Walker, it is unquestionable, that Mrs. Tisdill was the "Sarra Walker 17 yrs. of the Elizabeth from London," and that we have in Mr. Savage's Gleanings an account of the Embarkation of the Taunton and Hingham (afterward Eastham) Walkers.

If it be said that there is nothing about Widow and Philip Walker in these Gleanings, it may be answered, that possibly she and the younger son, as Philip was, may have come afterward, for it was not unusual then, any more than now, for members of the same family to come at different times, and the fact of Richard of Lynn, though only a young man, coming several years after his father, corroborates the theory. The obvious conclusion then, in respect to the relationship existing between the four is, that James and Sarra were brother and sister, and that they were all near kindred; perhaps the two mentioned first, Richard and William, were cousins of the others, and also of each other. Emigrants at the same time and in the same ship, it is probable that they came from the same district in England. Richard went to Lynn where his father had settled, William to Eastham, and James and Sarra to Taunton, with Mr. John Browne, their guardian and uncle.

James first appears in Taunton in 1643; his name being included in the list of those in T. between the age of 16 and 60 able to bear arms.* He also gave in the value of his estate with the first settlers of Rehoboth in 1643, for a share in the division of lands. But the fact that the next year, his lands were forfeited to the town, together with Mr. John Browne's, then of Taunton, his cousin, (or if as used anciently his uncle,) either because he did not according to a previous order fence them, or did not remove there, (the latter probably,) will account for his early disappearance from the list of the inhabitants and proprietors of Rehoboth. Only one other notice of the said James of Rehoboth is found, viz: in the division of land, made in the year 1645. The absence of his name, therefore, is explained most naturally by the supposition, that he never became a settler there, and not that there was a different James from the one in Taunton, who may have died in 1645 or just after.

---

*The list commences thus, Mr. John Browne, Mr. Willm Poole, John Browne, James Browne, James Walker.

And as James Walker was one of the appraisers of the estate of Philip Walker of Rehoboth, in 1679, and there was no James at that period in R., it is reasonable to infer that James of Taunton, was the James mentioned in the first Rehoboth divisions of land, and surviving Philip, helped appraise his estate. His mother and Mr. John Browne his uncle being interested in the enterprise, he doubtless contemplated settling there, yet concluded to remain in T. where he became very useful and highly honored. (See sketch of Widow Walker.) As he was married just at this time, to Miss Philips of T., we may guess that love had stronger influence than lands, and over-ruled his purpose to settle in Rehoboth, securing his active services and wise counsels through a long life, to the town of Taunton. It deserves to be noticed in this connection, as showing the intercourse between the families of the two towns, that James Walker Jr., married Bathsheba, daughter of Gilbert Brooks of Rehoboth, a pious, worthy and somewhat prominent man.

There is also another fact to corroborate this theory. In Dec. 1644, "It was ordered (in Rehoboth) that no man's lands be recorded till he be an inhabitant among us," or receive a certificate, that lands are butted and bounded, and in the allotments ordered to be recorded in March 28, 1645, his name does not appear with Widow Walker's. Though it is true that in April following, he is mentioned as one of those who drew lots for lands on the Great Plain, there is not a single record of his lands in the Proprietors' Books, and hence it is an inevitable conclusion, that he did not become an inhabitant of Rehoboth. Had he done so, there would have been a record of the boundaries of the lands which fell to him in the division, and then the record of the transfer. There was a James Walker who drew lots in the divisions of 1643 and 5, and who yet had no lands recorded and described. There was, at that time, a James Walker in Taunton, the adjoining town, at that time, and there is no trace of another any where in New England.

It would be a remarkable coincidence, were there another James so nearly of the same age, who had a sister Sarah, a guardian or patron, John Browne, (that was his uncle also,) and until such a James has been found, with whose life these circumstances will concur, it may be claimed, that we have the record of the English origin and advent to this country, of the first male ancestor of the Taunton Walkers.*

---

* This proof has been given in detail because of an effort to make another use of this portion of Mr. Savage's Gleanings. See Gen. Reg. vol. 9, p. 219.

James Walker was propounded to take up his freedom 6th June, 1649, and admitted a freeman 4th June, 1650. He married Elizabeth Philips, daughter of William Philips and wife Elizabeth (Parker,) sister of William and John Parker, ancient and leading men of Taunton. She died Aug. 14th, 1678, aged 59, (according to grave stone,) July 8th, (Prop. Rec.) and July 30th, (Plymouth Rec.)* They had five children who survived them, viz: James, Peter, Eleazer, Hester, and Deborah. Probably there were others who died early, as, in 1659, before the birth of Deborah, he had "eight heads" in his family. He married 2d, Sarah Rew, Nov. 4th, 1678, widow of Edward Rew, one of the ancient settlers and proprietors of T., who died July 16th, 1678. She was a daughter of John Richmond of Taunton. James Walker died Feb. 15th, 1691, aged 73, which date regarded as 1691–2, makes his age in 1635, 16 instead of 15, as given in Savage's Gleanings.† He and his w. Elizabeth were buried in the Walker grave yard on the bank of the Taunton River, in the South part of the town. Her grave stone has an earlier date by 8 years than any in the town. He lived near the ancient meeting house and on the "highway that goeth from James Walker Sen., to the Great Plain on the northerly end." He was an extensive landholder and a partner in the Iron Works and the Saw Mill.‡

The following are the notices of him in the ancient records. In Oct. 4th, 1648, Jas. Walker of Taunton, informing against William

* This is a striking illustration of conflict in authorities in respect to a single date.

† This, however, is a slight discrepancy and does not invalidate the conclusion that he was the same who came in the Elizabeth in 1635.

‡ There is an ancient deed by James Walker Sen., that has been thought worthy of being framed and preserved in the Bristol Reg. of Deeds, Taunton. By whom and when this distinction was given is unknown. It is dated Sept. 11th, 1688, and the following is a copy of all that is essential.

"To all Christian People, before whom these presents shall come, James Walker Senior of Taunton, sendeth Greeting. Know ye that the said James Walker for and in consideration of the loue he beareth unto his son, Petter Walker of Taunton, abouesaid, doeth by this deed of guift vnto his said son, Petter Walker, freely and fully guie, make over from me, the said James Walker, my heirs and executors and assignes, to him, my abouesaid son, Petter Walker, and to his heirs, successors and assignes for euer, these particular parcels of Land following, lying, scittuate and being within the Townshipt of Taunton aforesaid.

Imprimis, a lott of land lying on the Westerly side of Taunton, Great River, (soe called,) at a place called the pond, which was formerly Thomas Gilbert's, containing by estimation twenty acres, be it more or less, to which joins two lotts more of fourteen acres or thereabouts, all footing on the said great Riuer and headed by the highway, and bounded on the Northerly side by the land of Nathaniel French, and on the Southerly side by the land of Samuel Sheepard, alsoe more ninety and nine acres of land joyning to the Lower fales of the three mile riuer, (soe called,) and soe extending to the highway that lyeth on the heads of the Lott above mentioned, &c."

Hedggis for yt the sd Hedggis, knowing of one yt that had traded shote vnto the Indians, and refusing to declare who it is, by sommons sent vnto him is required to apeer at the next General Court; acordingly hee did and was cleared. (Plym. Court Orders, 2d vol. 135th p.)

In reference vnto a controuersy betwixt Willam Hailstone and James Walker, which hath bine of long standing, relateing to an award made by Mr. John Wiswall, Mr. Richard Callicott and Capt. James Johnson, concerning and for the issueing of some difference betwixt the said pties., they, the said Willam Hailstone and James Walker, refering the case for a finall issue to the determination of the Court, having heard their please on both sydes, and pused all such writings that were produced relateing thervnto, doe determine and conclude as followeth, viz.: that forasmuch as that it appeers vpon examination that the said James Walker hath not pformed the latter pte of the said arbetration, viz.: to repaire the said Hailstone, his reputation in the church, and to make a returne therof vnto the said arbetrators, which hee neglected to doe, the Court doe therfore order that hee shall pay or cause to be payed vnto the said Hailstone, the sume of fiue pounds, in either good merchantable porke or good barr iron, betwixt this date and the fifteenth day of October next, att prise then currant; and wheras the said James Walker did openly and vnaduisedly, on a Lord's day, accuse the said Willam Hailstone of telling seueral palpable lyes, and founded vpon a lye, whereby the said Hailstone was much scandalised. This Court doth hereby aduise the said James Walker, publickly to acknowlidge the wronge hee hath done him, in the meeting, on the Lord's day, in the congregation; and this our award and joynt determination to be a full and finall issue of all such differences and controuersyes as relate vnto the pmises. July 1st, 1672.

Homer seems to have nodded here. The good man fell into sin if we may judge from the record, and like Moses, "spake unadvisedly with his lips!"*

This "son Petter Walker," thus owned lands and lived in that section of the town lying in the angle formed by the Taunton Great and the Three Mile rivers. There his descendants have lived till the present time.

* Perhaps, however, judgment was rendered against him in this instance on the principle that "the greater the truth, the greater the libel." This William Hailstone was far from blameless He was fined £15 for breach of contract with Jonathan Briggs, and 20 shillings for telling 2 lyes in a petition to General Court in 1656.

Apr. 7th, 1664. Willam Witherell acknowlidyeth to owe to our sou lord the Kinge, the sume of £20; Hezekiah Hore £10; Gyles Gilbert, £20; Gorg Watson, £10.

The cause of the bonds aboue written is, that wheras James Walker, being a p'tnor in the saw mill att Taunton, complained of great hurt done to the said saw mill, by som psons that came in the night in a fellonious manor and stole away seueral things, and did great spoile, and left a libellous paper behind them; and it being suspected that the aboue bounden Willam Witherell and Gyles Gilbert, were the psons, or some of them, that haue done the said mischiffe, they, the said Willam Witherell and Gyles Gilbert, being sumoned, appeered att Plymouth, before the Gou. and Captaine Southworth, on the day and yeare first aboue written, and being examined, it appeered that they were guilty in the aforesaid pticulars, and therfore the said majestrates saw cause to take the said bonds of them for their good behauior, &c.,, Court Orders, vol. 4th, 5, 6, & 7, pp.

May 3, 1664. Josepth Gray and Samuell Linkorn were arraigned for being ptenors in doeing great hurt to the saw mill att Taunton, &c., "and being examined about the pmises, owned that they were guilty therin" and were put under bonds, together with Gorg Watson and Thomas Leanard. Then follows this order of the Court.

Wheras, att this Court, the aboue bounden Josepth Gray and Samuell Linkorne, together with Georg Watson, complained of great wrong, sustained, not onely by them, but by the whole towne of Taunton, by James Walker, his neglecting, according to engagement, to leaue a sufficient passage for the herrings or alewiues to goe up in the river on which the saw mill standeth, the Court directeth an order to the constable of Taunton, to require him to signify vnto the said James Walker, that hee speedily take course, that a free passage bee left for the goeing up of the alewiues in the said river, whiles yett some pte of the season remaines of their goeing vpp.

8th June, 1664, Court ordered.

In reference to the complaint of sundry of the inhabitants of the towne of Taunton against James Walker and others, for the restraining of the alewiues from goeing vp according to there vsual manor, by reason of a saw mill on thire herring riuer, by which obstruction of the said fish, the said towne hath, and is in danger to suffer much damage, this Court hath ordered, that betwixt this date and the next season of the fishes goeing vp, they, the said owners of the mill, shall make or cause to ^ made, a free, full and sufficient passage for the goeing vp of the said fish, or otherwise vpon the further complaint of the towne, the Court will take an effectuall course that the same shall bee done.

Att this Court, Willam Witherell, Mr. Gyles Gilbert, Josephth Gray and Samuell Linkhorne were sentanced by the Court to pay each a fine of twenty shillings for an abuse done to a Saw Mill at Taunton, belonging to James Walker and others, by coming in the night and breaking downe some pte of the said mill, and found takeing away seuerall thinges from the same.

George Watson, Gyles Gilbert and William Witherley complained against James Walker, Robert Crossman, John Maycomber and Nicholas White, in an action of tresspass on the case, to the damage of an hundred pounds, for hindering the fish for haueing a convenient passage vp and downe the Mill River, att Taunton, by the worke about the saw mill, contrary to the inhabitants of the towne of Taunton, and contrary to the promise of the said James Walker, all of which hath bine great damage to the complainants and others.

Tried att Generall Court held att Plymouth, 31 Oct., 1666.

The jury find for the plaintiffes, that a sufficient passage be made by the defendants att the Mill River, att Taunton, for the fish where they vsually goe vp and downe, where the saw mill or dam now erected is an anoyance to the said fish, the expence of time, and the cost of the suite.*

In 1671 James Walker was fined £1 for breaking an order about a stray horse.

We pass now to more honorable notices.

In 1651, he was on the inquest respecting the death of William England, aged 10 years, seruant to Joseph Wilbor of Taunton. The next morning being the Lord's Day, hee with diuers others, sought on the river for him and found him not; but James Walker and Richard Burt passing vp the river, towards meeting, found the said William floating on the water, who made it known, and caused him to be taken vp. Col. Rec. vol. 2.

In 1663, Richard Williams, Walter Dean, James Wyatt and James Walker, made over land to Rev. Geo. Shove, minister of Taunton, house and land 10 acres, bounded &c.,——which they bought of Elizabeth Philips. This was given "for the use of the ministry."

* The people of Taunton have ever since been very ready to complain of any damage to "thire herring riuer," but in 200 years, manufacturing enterprise has conquered, and mill owners now, have less trouble than James Walker.

The Court alloweth vnto James Walker, towards his paines, the charge and trouble hee hath been att about Jonathan Briggs, in the controuersye betwixt Willam Hailstone and the said Briggs, the summe of twenty shillings, conceiueing that the said Briggs ought to satisfy the said James Walker further, what is meet in the above said respect, att least to make it vp forty shillings. March 2, 1657–8.

June 1, 1658. This is to certify all whom it may concerne, that all that was required vpon the arbetration betwixt James Walker and Willam Hailstone is pformed by the said James Walker.

"The countrye's stocke of powder and shott was distributed in different towns for safety and use." Taunton's portion.

"It. to James Walker, att Taunton, one barrell of powder and the other halfe of the cake of lead." 1658, 2 Oct. "James Walker and William Harvey, were appointed by the Court, to review, in the countrys behalf, the public whipping of William Paule, Katheren Aines and her husband." 1656–7.

The several towns were required to send each, one man as deputy to the Court, and to envest them with full power in their behalfe, to treat and conclude about leting of the trad, att Kennebecke; James Walker was chosen the deputy of Taunton, Oct. 1659.

March 4, 1661–2, James Walker was authorised by the Court to adminnister an oth, as occation shall require, att Taunton, as alsoe, to marry psons, as occation shall require, vntil the next June Court. This order was c x. att June 9th, 1662, soe that the said James Walker is to giue oath and marry, as above said. On the margin opposite the above order, it is stated. "The Court doeth order, James Walker, to sellebrate marriage in the towne of Taunton, vntell June, 1684."

Oct. 3, 1662. The oath of Jonathan Briggs, taken before this Court, is as followeth;—I, Jonathan Briggs, aged twenty-fiue years, or therabouts, doe testify, that about 6 yeares agone, as I was in the house of James Walker, of Taunton, I heard James Walker aske Willam Browne, what hee would doe with his land, if hee should not returne from England againe. Willam Browne answared, that if hee did not returne againe, then hee would giue all his land to his little cousen, which was Peter Walker, whoe then stood before him.

8 June, 1664. James Walker and Frances Smith were "the psons, (in Taunton,) nominated to take vp the excise—whoe are likewise to take notice of what liquors, &c., are brought into the Gou'ment."

July 2, 1667. The Court haue graunted vnto some ancient freemen liueing in Taunton, viz., James Walker, (and 7 others,) some supplyes of land, vpon the west syde of Taunton Riuer—or some other place, if it may be obtained."

1668. He was one of the six original proprietors of Assonet Neck.

1670. He and William Harvey were appointed to "look after the minister's rate," also, "to examine Jane Holloway, in regard to Samuel Holloway's appeal for a divorce, from his said wife, Jane."

1671. He was one of the Committee "to have inspection of the ordinary, or in any other places suspected; to take notice of such abuses as may arise, in reference to the pmises, or otherwise, and to make oath therof to the Court." This was an order "for prevention of great abuse by excessive drinking of liquors in ordinaries."

1671, 23 August.

1. The councell of warr, haueing seriously considered of the case, in reference to the Phillipe, the cheife sachem of Pacanacutt, hee having neglected, to answare his engagement, to bringe in his armes att the day appointed, and alsoe in his not coming in to giue the reason thereof, being required thervnto, and his vnkind carriages towards vs, as otherwise, &c., &c., &c.

2. It is unanimously agreed and concluded by the said councell, that wee are nessesarily called to cause the said sachem, to make his psonall appeerance, to make his purgation in reference to the pmises; &c., &c.

Accordingly pers were despatched and sent from the councell, one vnto the said Phillip, the said sachem to require his psonall appeerance att Plymouth, in the 13th day of September next, in reference to the pticulares aboue mencioned against him; this letter was sent by Mr. James Walker, one of the councell, and hee was ordered to request the companie of Mr. Roger Williams and Mr. James Browne, to goe with him att the deliuery of the said letter. (Plym. Col. Rec. vol. 5th.) (See 16th p.)

1671–2, 5 March.

James Walker and John Richmond are authorised by the Court to purchase the land of the Indians, in the behalfe of the towne of Taunton, lying on the west syde of Taunton Riuer, from the Three Mile Riuer, downe to a place called the Store House. (vol. 5, 88th p.)

They were the Com. of town of Taunton, to settle the disputed boundary between Swansey and T.

1675–6, March 10.

Wheras, the Court for the incurragement of the souldiers, sent forth on the first expedition against the Indians, did order and engage, according to theire desire, that they should haue theire pay in money or lands, and noe way att psent appeering to raise monyes, doe therfore, for theire satisfaction order, that certaine tracts of land be assigned, to the vallue of about one thousand pounds, to be deuided amongst them, for the payment of theire respectiue ptes due vnto them;—and for the better effecting thereof, the Treasurer, Major Cudworth, Cornett Studson and James Walker are desired and appointed to take view therof, and make reporte therof, to the Court or Councell, for the settleing of the same, at such reasonable rates, as to them shall seeme meet, to be deuided to the said souldiers, or sold for theire pay, or discharge of other nessarie dues, occationed by this warr. Col. Rec. vol. 5, 191st p.

The order and distribution of this collonies pte of the contribution, made by diuers Christians, in Ireland, for the relieffe of such as are impouerished, destressed, and in nessestie by the late Indian warr, was as it respects this collonie, proportioned as followeth:

William Harvey,
James Walker,
John Richmond. } appointed to distribute the portion allotted to Taunton.

March 6, 1656–7. Col. Rec. vol. 5, 222d p.

James Walker,
James Wilbore and
Encrease Robinson, } are appointed and established by the Court to take notice of such liquors as are brought in disorderly unto the toune of Taunton, and to make seisure theroffe, according to order.

1678, Oct. 30. Col. Rec. vol. 5, 271st p.

James Walker was one of a Com. "to lease out some of the lands of Leiftenant Wyatt, for the relieffe of Mistris Mary Wyatt, of Taunton, his widdow, and in great necessitie." 1678, 30 Oct.

In 1683–4, James Walker and John Richmond were the Com. in behalf of inhabitants of Taunton, to purchase a tract of land of the Indians.

He served as juryman, and on the Grand Inquest repeatedly. He was constable in 1652; surveyor, 1672; one of the "Celect men," 1666, 7, 8, 9, 70, 8, 9 and 80,—8 years.

He was elected deputy to the Plymouth Court, 16 years, viz.: 1654, 7, 8, 9, 60, 1, 3, 6, 7, 8, 9, 70, 1, 6, 7, 9.

He was a member of the Com. (composed of 10 of the leading citizens in the Colony,) to take the Treasurer's account in 1664, 7, 8 and 70.

He was a Member and Chairman of the Town "Councell of Warr," 1667, 75 & 8. These Councils were elected in time of war, and the most efficient men of the towns were appointed, as in Plymouth, the Gov. Capt. Bradford, in Rehoboth, Capt. Willett. He was also one of the "Councell of Warr," for Plymouth Colony, in 1658, 61, 71, 81, and associated with its most energetic and sagacious men. In 1681, the Council consisted of Capt. Nathaniel Thomas, Capt. Josiah Standish, Capt. Jonathan Sparrow, Lieut. Joseph Laythorpe, Lieut. Eph'm Morton, Lieut. John Thacher, Ensign Mark Eames, Cornet Rob't Studson, Sec'y Nath'l Morton, Mr. James Walker.

In the division of lands in 1659, his rate is £1, 5s., 7d., and 8 heads. Ninety six acres were assigned him.

He was also one of the committee of five, to revise town records of lands.

"In 1669, 51 acres over the great river, at head of the great Meadows, also 3 acres on this side, (that is West,) of river, little beyond Edward Rew's Saw pit," were assigned him. (Prop. Rec.)

In the Proprietor's Records, there is also a record of the names of the persons who gave lands to Capt. Batholomew Tipping, as remuneration in full, for the house and land he sold to Rev. Mr. Danforth, in 1687. It is as follows:

James Walker,	10 acres.
Peter Walker, (son of James,)	10 acres.

Then follow the names of 19 others, 15 of whom gave 5 acres each, one 6 acres, one 4, and two, 10 each.

In vol. 6th, 1st series of the Collections of the Mass. Historical Society, there is allusion to a letter of James Walker, of Taunton, dated Jan. 1676, written to Gov. Winslow, (in reply to one of his,) giving an account of the suffering and the loss of life by Indian depredations, in Philip's War, and also the names of the sufferers.

This letter is lost; and it is a loss greatly to be deplored, as such a letter from an intelligent observer, would give us a vivid conception of those perilous and barbarous times, when our ancestors, few, and grouped in small and scattered settlements in the wilderness, had to struggle with the banded natives, bent on the extermination of the pale faces from the land, they thought their own heritage, guided and inspired too, by the patriotism and bravery of the able and renowned chieftain, King Philip.

Even the list of those who fell or suffered, would be invaluable now, and furnish a thrilling chapter in the domestic and social history of the early colonists—a tearful record of graves and griefs, of fortitude and faith, of terror and triumph.*

We are more fortunate however, in respect to a letter he wrote to Gov. Prince, for though the original may be lost, we have its contents published, in the 6th vol. of Mass. Hist. Col. 197th p. The letter is as follows:

Much Honored Sir:

After my humble respects presented to you, these are to acquaint you with Philip's answer to your letter. My sons being visited with the ague, forced me to procure brother Harvey† to go over to cousin James Browne with the letter, who sent for Mr. Williams to interpret. Mr. Williams, not being well, came not till afterward; yet cousin James and brother Harvey went down to Mount Hope; and the dance being broken up, Philip, and the most of his chief men, were much in drink; only Acumponin and Tom Sancsink were sober; so that Philip could not give them any answer. Only there passed some words betwixt Philip and cousin James, and Philip struck off cousin James Browne's hat. The day following, they went again to Philip, and Mr. Williams with them. The letter being read, and Philip caused fully to understand it, they could get no positive answer about Philip's coming to Plymouth, because Mr. Eliot had sent for him to Boston, and he looked for another messenger that day; which messenger they met about 2 miles from Philip's house; which messenger told them that his message was to desire Philip to be at Punkapoge, the last day of this week, and at Boston, the Tuesday following. Philip and Tom exclaimed much against Sawsiman, for reporting that any of the Narragansett sachems were there; Not further to trouble you, but rest, desiring the good Lord to be with you, and guide you, in all your weighty affairs.

Yours to serve,

JAMES WALKER.

Taunton, Sept. 1, 1671.

---

* King Philip's summer residence was in Taunton, (now Raynham,) near the Iron Works.

† Was he a "brother" by marriage, or only a "brother" in the church? Perhaps there was another and younger sister, than Sarah, who came with the "Widow" and Philip. The mention of "cousin James Browne," in connection with "brother Harvey," favors this supposition, but Mr. John Browne's remembrance of James and Sarah only, in the gift of his house in Taunton, suggests a doubt, which is strengthened by the record, "Wm. Harvey m. Joane Hucker of Taunton, April 2, 1639." May not "Hucker" be a clerical error for Walker?

"Yours to serve," the unique form with which he concludes his letter to Gov. Prince, is singularly appropriate and in keeping with his life. When a youth of 15 years, he was "servant to John Browne." In mature manhood, he was the "servant" of the Colony, employed in various civil offices and trusts, through a long series of years.

He had no military title, no hereditary arms, but the numerous services assigned him, and the positions of responsibility and confidence which he filled, justify us in awarding him the title of "servant of the church" and the State.

From the records now given, we conceive of him as a man of more than ordinary intelligence, judicious in counsel, energetic in action, steadfast in integrity, sagacious, public spirited, benevolent and alive to the secular and religious prosperity of the Colony. Surpassed by none of the town in his contributions for the ministry, and in the number and continuance of civil trusts, he needed no heraldic distinctions, and he transmitted none. Worthy of remembrance and honor by those of his name and lineage, yet he is an honor to them, only as they strive to emulate his usefulness, and reproduce his virtues and his piety.

Fac-simile of his autograph written in 1676.

3. SARAH WALKER,[2]

OF TAUNTON, MASS.

Born in England in 1618, died Dec. 1676. She married John Tisdall, of Duxbury.

It is recorded that John Tisdall entered against Stephen Hopkins, Assistant of the Gov't, an action for Battery, by which he was dangerously wounded. 1636. S. H. was fined £5 and costs. Also, "John Tisdall, upon the good report of him and of his good carryage, is allowed to keepe house and plant for himself, provided he so continue his carryage still. 1638." Is it not probable that he had been recently married?

He did not altogether "continue his carryage," for Dec. 6, 1653, he was fined 20 shil., for "unfaithfulness in prizing and exchanging a cow," of Mrs. Bryant's. (Plym. Col. Rec. vol. 3, 42d p.)

He settled first in Duxbury, about 1636, and removed to Taunton, before Dec. 6, 1653. He was constable in T. 1659, one of the proprietors of Taunton No. Purchase 1668, Selectman and Deputy to Plym. Court 1774. Besides lands in Taunton, he owned a farm near Assonet. He took an active part in the. affairs of the town, and was murdered by the Indians, June 27, 1675. In'y, £150. Nothing is known of his origin, nor of the date of his arrival in the Old Colony. He has not had very numerous descendants, yet all the Tisdalls, of American birth, are of his lineage. The professional men among his descendants have been Elkanah, a lawyer, and Nathan, 1732—1787, called "Old Master Tisdale," the eminent classical teacher of the time, by whom, during about 40 years, a large number of the distinguished men of the country were instructed. (See his Epitaph, Gen. Reg. 1858, 62d p.) Both of Lebanon, Ct. Dr. Tisdall, of Norwich, Ct., and Rev. James, lately of Shutesbury, (son of James, of West Taunton.) Samuel T., Esq., an intelligent and successful merchant in N. Y. City, 7th generation from John, has a genealogy of the Tisdalls in manuscript.

JOHN TISDALL and wife SARAH WALKER had 8 chil., viz.,

(1) JOHN, b. in Duxbury, d. about last of Dec. 1677.

He m. Nov. 23, 1664, Anna dau. of John Rogers of Duxbury. He was in list of freemen 1670. His 4 chil. were—

1 *Abigail*, b. July 15, '67, m. Dec. 2, 1685, Wm. Makepeace.

2 *John*, b. Aug. 10, '69, and d. Jan. 26, 1728. He m. 1700 Deborah Dean, dau. of Thomas. She was born about 1675, and d. 1703–4. He m. 2dly, Abigail. His chil. were John, 1702. Of 2d wife, Abraham, 1704, Israel, 1706, Ephraim, 1708, Jedediah, 1710, Deborah, 1712, Abigail, 1714, Anna, 1716.

3 *Anna*, b. Jan. 27, 1672, m. July 4, 1695, Hon. George Leonard, 3d son of Thomas, b. April 18, 1671, and d. Sept. 5, 1716. He settled in Norton, where he became possessed of very large tracts of land, and was progenitor of the N. family of Leonards. His family became very wealthy, and owners of the largest landed estate probably in New England.

4 *Remember*, b. July 8, '75.

(2) JAMES, b. 1644 in Duxbury, d. Jan. 15, 1715, ae. 71.

He m. Nov. 5, 1666, Mary Avery, who d. Sept. 9, 1713, ae. 66. Res. Berkley He was freeman as early as May, 1670, and one of the original proprietors of Assonet Neck, when the purchase was made in 1680. His 6 chil. were—

1 *James*, b. about 1670, m. 1700, Abigail Coleman, dau. of John, of Nantucket. Res. Lebanon, Ct., where he d. May 3, 1727, ae. 48 yrs. She d. Nov. 18, 1726, in 45th yr. (See Gen. Reg. 1858, 58th p. for their epitaphs.) He m. 2dly Mindwell. 2 *Mary*, b. about 1672. m. Richard Haskins of Taunton. 3 *Martha*, b. 1674, m. John Hodges, of Norton. 4 *Margaret*, b. 1675, m. Josiah Winslow, of Taunton. 5 *Sarah*, b. 1677, m. John Johnson, Lebanon, Ct. 6 *Ebenezer*, b. 1682, d. Nov. 11, 1705, ae. 22.

(3) JOSHUA, b. in Duxbury, 1646, d. ae. 72 yrs. in Freetown.

He m. July 5, 1688, Abigail Andrews, dau. of Henry. She d. 1741. He was sometime of Taunton, but dwelling on Assonet River, 1682. His 3 chil. were—

1 *Joshua*, b. April 1, 1689, 2 *Samuel*, b. March 3, 1691, m. Mary Church of Little Compton, Jan. 30, 1724–5 and d. 1769, having 6 chil. viz., Samuel, June 22, 1727, Mary, Jan. 7, 1729, Deborah, Feb. 16, 1730, Sarah, Feb. 22, 1732, Abigail, Dec. 19, 1738, Rebecca, Nov. 24, 1742, 3 *Elizabeth*, June 2, 1693, 4 *Hepsibeth*, March 19, 1695, 5 *Abigail*, April 11, 1697, 6 *Henry*, May 17, 1699, m. Oct. 24, 1728, Elizabeth Billings of Little Compton, R.I., 7 *Mary*, 1701, 8 *Barnabas*, 1703, 9 *Ephraim*, 1707.

(4) JOSEPH, b. in Duxbury, 1656, d. 1721–2 in 65th yr. in Taunton. He m. Aug. 1681, Mary Leonard, dau. of Major Thomas, and b. Aug. 2, 1663. Res. Taunton. He inherited a large estate from his father. His 7 chil. were.

1 *Joseph*, b. 1682, m. March 13, 1706–7, Ruth Reed, 2 *Elkanah*, b. 1684, 3 *Mary*, b. 1686, m. Joseph Winslow, of Swansey and d. March 28, 1719, 4 *Hannah*, b. 1688, m. Feb. 8, 1710–11, Wm. Hodges, of Norton, and d. March 7, 1715, 5 *Sarah*, b. 1690, m. Thos. Reed of Dighton, 6 *Abigail*, b. 1692, m. Ephraim Hayward, of Bridgwater, 7 *Elizabeth*, b. 1694, m. Elkanah Leonard, of Middleboro'.

The 1st son, Capt. *Joseph*, b. 1682—1739, had Simeon, and he had James the merchant, and he, James, of Taunton and Barney of Elizabeth City, N. C., and this James, of T., had Samuel T., of N. Y. City. All were b. in T. He also had Job, who d. May 19, 1755, ae. 47, father of James, 1740,—1811, who m. Abigail (Freeman) of Norton, and had Rev. James, b. in West Taunton, Nov. 7, 1799, grad. B. U. 1821, studied Theology with Rev. A. Cobb, West Taunton, ord. Sept. 29, 1830, over the churches in Guildhall and Granby, Vt., dismissed May 4, 1836, preached 4 years in Dublin and 7 years in Gilsum, N. H., and after Oct. 1851, in Shutesbury, Mass. He m. Oct. 5, 1831, Margaretta C. Tubbs of W. T.

(5) ELIZABETH.
She m. John Smith.

(6) SARAH.
She m. James Dean.

(7) MARY, b. in T., d. May 18th, 1731, in 73d yr.
She m. Jan. 9th, 1676, Nathaniel French, who d. June 14th, 1711, ae. 73. Both were buried in the Walker grave yard.

(8) ABIGAIL, b. in T.
She m. Feb. 1st, 1683, Edward Bobit, (Babbitt,) who was son of Edward, and b. July 15th, 1655. They had Edward, b. Feb. 14th, 1684, and perhaps others.

4. III. PHILLIP WALKER,[2]

OF REHOBOTH, MASS.

His biography may be found in connection with the Genealogy of his descendants, immediately following that of the Taunton Family.

THIRD GENERATION.

CHILDREN OF JAMES WALKER,[2] [2] OF TAUNTON.

5. I. JAMES,[3] (10) b. 1645–6, d. June 22, 1718, ae. 72 yrs.

He m. Dec. 23, 1673, Bathsheba Brooks, dau. of Gilbert, of Rehoboth. She was b. 1655, and d. Feb. 24, 1738, in 85th yr. (Ins.) Will was proved, April, 17, 1739. He was constable in T. in 1689, and admitted to freedom in 1689. He had 50 acres of land laid out for him, near Wm. Hacks' line. The lot began at So. Purchase line, and run north, 2 points. (Prop. Rec.)

In 1697, there was a graunt to him of "50 acres on the west syde of Three Mile river, below the brook that runs into it, below John Hodges' lot."

He lived at the Weir, in Taunton, where Col. Israel Dean, late of T., lived, and where the road from the Weir, to Dighton, leaves the river and turns west, towards the Presbrey brook.

It is conjectured, that the following graunt refers to this James, because the father would have been called Mr. James Walker.

"Libertie is graunted by the Court, vnto James Walker, of Taunton, to keep an ordinary att Taunton, and for that end, that hee be prouided of all necessaries for that purpose, and that he keep good order in his house, that, soe no damage may acrew vnto any, respecting the pmises." 1679, Plym. Col. Rec. vol. 6, 15th p.

In his will, proved Sept. 1, 1718, bequests are made to wife, 6 sons and 5 daus. These indicate the places where the sons lived, viz.: "To James, eldest son, 50 acres, where he lives. To 2d son, Nathan, land in Taunton, So. Purchase. To 3d son, David, 2 lower lotts, in Dighton, where he now dwells. To 4th son, Nehemiah, my new dwelling house, in T., and my home lott, and barn thereon, and my lott lying by Jas. Burt's, in T., and my land over the Creek,—and 50 acres lying on the three mile river, at a place called the narrow passage. To 5th son, Josiah, 3 upper lotts, in Dighton."

Fac-simile of his autograph of 1690.

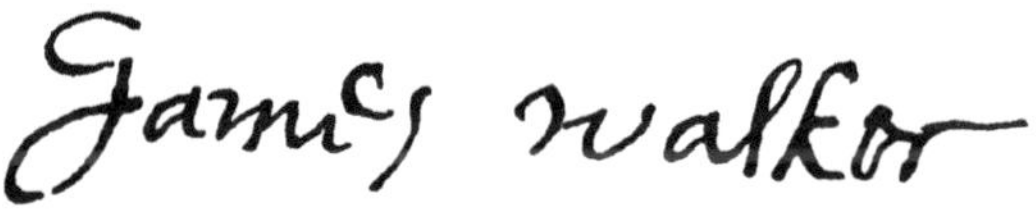

6. II. PETER,[3] (21) b. 1649, d. April 4, 1711, ae. 60. (Ins.) [62 ?]

He m. Hannah, who d. Jan. 15, 1704, ae. 44 yrs. (Ins.) Nothing more is known of her. He was an iron dealer, in company with Hon. James Philips. He was appointed with Joseph and Samuel Richmond, to lay out "the highway from Bayting Brook, to Assonet."

His will proved July 2, 1711, gives names of 3 sons and 3 daus. He made a bequest, also, "to Thomas Elyot, who did live with me 6 yrs.," viz.: "6 acres joining the land of my brother James, where said Elyot now dwelleth," (See No. 16.) His Inventory £751, includes "homestead, with housing, orchard, with little island joining, to Nicholas Stephen's, his mill, with all the land belonging to the farm, being 400 acres." This "little island" is in the centre of No. Dighton village, and is now the site of an old foundry. There were his Iron Works, which in later years went by the name of Baylies' Forge, and were on the site of the present Paper mill. By a "deed of guift," in 1688, from James Walker, Sen., "to his son Petter Walker," and other grants, he became an extensive land holder, in the Southern part of Taunton, between and on the Taunton Great and Three Mile rivers, and especially on the latter, at what is now the North Dighton village. In the Proprietors' Rec. we find that Peter Walker had "84 acres laid out near James Walker and Wm. Hack, near the lower powers on the country road to Three Mile river." There was also a grant in 1697, to Peter, of "40 acres, in the low country, between his lands and Jas. Walker's." He also owned land near the meeting house, and on the Mill river, near where his father lived. But his homestead was in the South part of the town, and his dwelling, remodelled 60 yrs. ago, is the 1st house north of Three Mile River, on the road from Taunton to Dighton Four Corners. A portion of his estate, half a mile north has been held by him, and his descendants 175 yrs., and is now owned and occupied by Edward Walker, [See No. 233,] and there is scarcely room for a doubt, that this is a part of the grants, to James, Sen., which, in this section of the town, became almost wholly, the portion of his "son Petter." We are sure, that it was Peter's, either by grant to him, or by inheritance, and as it included when it was bequeathed to his sons, in 1711, the ancient cemetery of the Walker Family and kindred, where his mother and father were buried, in 1678 & 91, we feel confident, it was a part of the lands of James Walker, Sen., and by transmission in the name over 200 years, is the ancestral Farm of the family.

Fac simile of his signature, 1676.

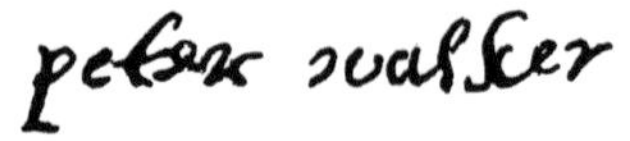

7. III. HESTER,[3] b. 1650, d. April, ye 8th, 1696, ae. 46. (Ins.) ancestor of the Atwoods, of T. and Dighton, who d. Feb. 12, 1696–7,

She m. Jan. 1, 1679, Joseph Woode,* (Atwood now,) of Taunton, ae. 47. (Ins.) Will made, Feb. 12, 1696–7, proved, May 19, 1698. He m. 2d, Abigail Paul, Oct. 18, 1697. [1696 ?] Chil. were—

(1) *Joseph*, b. Aug. 4, 1681, d, Sept. 26, 1724, in 43d yr. He m. Mary Reed, Jan. 11, 1702–3, who d. April 23, 1748, ae. 66 yrs. 7 mos. and 8 days. He represented Dighton in the General Court, in 1729. They had, 1 Joseph, b. Aug. 1, 1704, d. June 1, 1780. His dau. Hannah, m. Thomas Rose, of Dighton, 2 Benj., b. March 17, 1707, d. Feb. 3, 1713–14, 3 Esther, b. Feb. 19, 1710–11, m. Jotham Burt, 4 John, b. Feb. 7, 1712–13, d. May, 1749, In'y £458, 5 Benj., b. July 3, 1715, d. July 28, 1753, 6 Mary, b. March 16, 1718–19, m. Eben'r Winslow, of Berkley.

(2) *John*, b. Feb. 28, 1683, d. 1764, (See No. 26)

(3) *Ephraim*, b. about 1639, d. Aug. 14, 1776, in 87th yr. (Ins.) He m. Aug. 27, 1724, Ruth Richmond, dau. of Sylvester. She d. Nov. 13, 1776. Rep. from Dighton to General Court, 1718. Chil. 1 Sylvester, b. Sept. 4, 1725, (See No. 56,) 2 Ruth, b. May 4, 1727, 3 Ephraim, b. June 16, 1737, 4 Son, b. Aug. 23——d. Oct. 31.

(4) *Joanna*, b. after death of father. She m. Wm. Nichols, about 1726, and had 10 chil.

8. IV. ELEAZER,[3] b. 1662, d. Dec. 15, 1724, ae. 62. (Ins.)

His will indicates that he never married, or if so, left no children. Inventory, £1100. He owned a large tract of land in Dighton, but lived in Taunton.

9. V. DEBORAH,[3] d. about May 1726.

She m. Feb. 9, 1685–6, in Dighton, George Goodwin, of Somersetshire, England. He settled in Taunton, South Purchase, afterward, D. in 1677–8, and is the father of the Gooding Family. The record of his birth has been found in the Parish of North Petherton, Somersetshire, by Alanson Gooding, Esq., of New Bedford. He was 3d son of Matthew, who was yeoman, and who had 4 sons and 1 dau. viz.: Thomas, Matthew, George, Richard, and Johannah. He d. in D. 1712, ae. 79 yrs. Tradition says she was about 18 yrs. of age at her marriage, and he was over 50 yrs. Her name is not mentioned in her father's will, but the following leaves no doubt that there was such a dau. It is a copy of a note, at the foot of a very old deed in parchment, in possession of A. Gooding, Esq., of New Bedford. "This is to declare, that my father-in-law, James Walker, gave me the money, that bought the land mentioned in the deed, for which I humbly thank him," Geo. Gooding.

---

* The compiler has a genealogy in manuscript of a large number of his descendants.

This gift of money will account for the omission of her name, in her father's will. Her will was proved, May 16, 1726. Tradition gives names of 4 chil., the same as those in her will, viz.:

(1) *Johanna*. b. March 13, 1687, m. Feb. 2. 1716, John Godfrey, who d. Nov. 4, 1758, ae. 67. She d. March 9, 1765, ae. 78 yrs. less 16 days. Chil., 1 George, b. March 19, 1720–1, who was Brigadier General, and a man of great influence, 2 John, b. Dec. 24, 1723, d. Oct. 29, 1725, 3 John, b. Nov. 25, 1728, d. Nov. 26, 1749.

(2) *Mary*, m. Josiah Walker, (?) (See No. 18.)

(4) *Sarah*, m. April 25, 1732, Josiah Talbot, of D.

(4) *Matthew*. b. June 12, 1695, m. 1723, Abigail Richmond? dau. of Lieut. Joseph, of Middleboro. He d. March 15, 1756, Res. Dighton. Had 5 sons and 2 daus. (See No. 73,) viz.: 1 Geo. m. Sarah Reed, of D., and had 4 sons and 4 daus., 2 Deborah, m. Jacob Packard, of Bridgwater, 3 Joseph, b. 1730, m. 1755, Rebecca Macomber, of Taunton, and had 5 sons and 3 daus., 4 Matthew, m. Mercy Crane, of Berkley, 5 William, m. Bathsheba Walker, (See No. 71,) 6 Mary, m. Wm. Nichols, of Berkley, 7 Job, m. Polly Claket or Clagit, of Newport, R. I.

FOURTH GENERATION.

CHILDREN OF JAMES WALKER[3] [5] OF TAUNTON.

10. I. JAMES,[4] (27) b. Dec. 1674, d. Sept. 12, 1749, ae. 74 yrs. 8 mos. and 19 days. (Ins.)

He m. Oct. 6, 1699, Sarah, dau. of John Richmond[2] of Taunton. She was b. Feb. 26, 1670, and d. Nov. 27, 1727, in 57th yr. (Ins.) He m. 2dly, Mrs. Sarah ———, who survived him, and d. 1759, ae. about 75 years. He was styled Lieut. in 1744, and upon his grave stone is called Ensign. He and his 1st wife were buried in the Walker Cemetery.

His will gives the names of 4 sons and 1 dau. His homestead, in Taunton, west of Three mile river, south of Westville, and on the west side of the road to Dighton Factories, was given to his eldest son, James. It has passed from the possession of his descendants, and is the farm now owned and occupied by Geo. T. Lee.

11. II. ELIZABETH,[4] d. before 1762.

She m. Jan. 7, 1695–6, Ephraim Emerson, who d. April 8, 1706, ae. 34 yrs. In'y £376. They had—

(1) *Theodotia* alias Ephraim, b. Dec. 24, 1696, who m. Elizabeth. He was a cooper in Rehoboth, and had 7 chil. viz, 1 Mary, 1727, 2 Ephraim, 1730 who was in Continental army, 1780, 3 Joseph, 1732, 4 Benjamin, 1735, 5 Elizabeth, 1739, 6 Stephen, 1739–40, 7 Mehetable, 1743.

(2) *Elizabeth*, m. Samuel Andrews.

She[4] m. 2dly, Deacon Elisha May of Atttleboro'. He was Deacon of the ch. at Palmer's river. She united with the ch. in 1714. She had, by 2d marriage—

(3) *Benjamin*, m. March 3, 1736, Susanna Clark, who d. March 11, 1743. He had 4 chil. viz., 1 Susanna, b. Dec. 3, 1737, 2 Elisha, b. March 25, 1739, m. Sept. 22, 1763, Ruth Metcalf, who d. May 11, 1815, ae. 72. He d. Nov. 15, 1811, ae. 73, and had 11 chil. He was Major, and member of the Legislature 27 years in succession, with one exception. Res. Attleboro'.—(See Daggett's Hist. of A.) 3 Elizabeth, b. Dec. 18, 1741, 4 Benjamin, b. Feb. 23, 1743, m. Hopestill Dexter, and had 7 chil.

12. III. NATHAN,[4] (32) b. about 1677, d. Dec. 23, 1747, ae. 70 yrs. (Ins.) He m. July 29, 1708, Abigail Richmond, dau. of John of Taunton. She was b. Feb. 26, 1678, and d. Feb. 28, 1763, in 84th yr. (Ins.) Res. Dighton. Had 6 chil.

13. IV. DAVID,[4] (38) d. 1765.

He m. Oct. 18, 1703, Mary, who d. May 19, 1750, in 69th yr. She was of Scituate, probably, as marriage is recorded in S. He m. 2dly, Mrs. Esther (Paul) Dillingham, dau. of Edward Paul of Berkley. Res. Dighton, on the farm next south of the late John Walker's homestead.

He was a member of the Legislature in 1721 and '45; one of the Selectmen of D., 1732, and held a Captain's Commission. His will was proved, Sept. 11, 1765. Had 9 chil.

14. V. BATHSHEBA,[4] d. 1756.

She m. Dec. 15, 1709, Richard Godfrey, Jr., who was son of R. G. and Mary Richmond, b. March 1, 1681, and d. 1753. Her will proved, Feb. 3, 1756, mentions 4 chil., viz.:

(1) *Richard*, b. March 23, 1711, m. Theodorah Dean, and had Richard, John, father of Geo., Brig. Gen., Joseph, d. childless, Ezra, Seth, Koz and Theodorah.

(2) *Bathsheba*, b. May 24, 1713, m. Samuel Williams, of Taunton.

(3) *Mary*, m. Thomas Gilbert, Esq., of Freetown.

(4) *James*, Res. Norton.

15. VI. MEHETABLE,[4] b. 1685 or 6, d. April 13, 1759, in 74th yr. (Ins.) She m. about 1713, Cornelius White, who d. April 18, 1754, in 79th yr. (Ins.) They had—

(1) *Content*, m. June 5, 1735, Thomas Shepard, of Norton, who was b. March 24, 1706, son of Jacob, of Foxboro', and d. Oct. 19, 1774. Res. Norton. (See his ancestry Gen. Reg. 1856, 101 p.) She d. April 7. 1790, ae. "75 yrs. on ye day of her death." (Ins.) Chil. 1 Sarah, b. May 5, 1736, m. Jan. 25, 1757, John Bassett, d. Dec. 1815, in Bedford, N. H., 2 Jacob, b.

4

Sept. 7, 1737, d. Nov. 3, 1737, 3 Phebe, b. April 4, 1739, d. Sept. 15, 1755, 4 Jacob, b. Nov. 30, 1741, m. Jan. 4, 1781, Mrs. Lydia Clapp, d. Sept. 18, 1816, ae. 74, in Norton. He was father of Rev. Thomas Shepard, D.D., of Bristol, R. I., a grad. of B. U., in 1813, and an able and highly estimable Cong. minister, 5 Thomas, b. Nov. 29, 1743, d. Dec. 29, 1743, 6 Jemima, b. Dec. 23, 1744, d. unm. Nov. 27, 1793, ae. 49, 7 Rachel, b. Jan. 18, 1746, d. unm. Oct. 25, 1823, ae. 76, in Amherst, 8 Thomas, b Feb. 1748, d. Feb. or March 1748, 9 Seth, b. Jan 21, 1750, m. May 28, 1776, Rachel Dunham, m. 2dly, June 3, 1795, Esther Carroll, and d. Nov. 5, 1812, ae. 62, in Mansfield, 10 Olive, b. March 10, 1752, d. April 7, 1752, 11 Olive, b. June 3, 1754, m. April 16, 1776, Noah Clapp, d. Feb. 13, 1845, ae. 90, in Canton, 12 George, b. Jan. 2, 1757, m. Sept. 6, 1781, Eunice Makepeace, and d. July 13, 1819, ae. 62, in Bedford, N. H., 13 Mace, b. May 28. 1759, in N., m. July 6, 1788, Deborah Haskins, dau. of Capt. John, of Boston. She was b. Nov. 5, 1765, and d. in Amherst, Feb. 11, 1841, ae. 75. He was a grad. of Dart. Coll., in 1785, ord. in Little Compton, R. I., Sept. 19, 1787, and d. there Feb. 14, 1821, after a long and honored ministry. His chil. were, 1 John Haskins, b. Sept. 3, 1789, d. Sept. 16, 1807, 2 Thomas, b. Jan. 26, 1793, d. Jan. 29, 1814, 3 Hannah, b. June 2, 1795, m. June 7, 1837, Hon. Seth Terry, of Hartford, Ct., Res. H., 4 Mary, b. May 2, 1797, unm. Res. Amherst and H., 5 Ralph, b. May 24, 1799, grad. of B. U., 1821, and d. at Amherst, June 20, 1824, during the Senior Year, in Andover Theol. Sem'y, 6 George Champlin, b. Sept. 7, 1802, m. May 24, 1827, Sally J. Kastman, grad. at Amherst Coll. 1824, settled as an Episcopal clergyman, in Hebron and Stratford, Ct., and received Doctorate of Divinity, from Am. Coll., 1843, 7 Charles Upham, b. June, 29, 1804, grad. at A. C. 1824, m. Sept. 1831, Harriet Taylor. He is Prof. of Natural Hist. in A. C. and Prof. of Chemistry in Med. Coll.. of S. C. at Charleston, 8 Ann Elizabeth, b. June 24, 1810, m. Hon. Edward Southworth, of West Springfield, and d. Aug. 1855, ae. 45, 9 Fanny Haskins, b. March 23, 1807, m. Aug. 30, 1824, Lucius Boltwood, Esq., of Amherst. Their son, Lucius M., is Cong. Clergyman and Librarian of Am. Coll. He m. June 6, 1860, Clara B. dau. of Hinckley Williams, of Goshen.

(2) *Priscilla*, m. Jacob Newland, of Norton. Living 1748.

(3) *Mehetable*, m. Nov. 18, 1733, Paul Pratt.

(4) *Cornelius*, b. about 1721, m. Susannah Haskell, who d. April 29, 1768, in 43d yr. He d. Nov. 18, 1787, in 66th yr. Had 2 chil. who d. young, perhaps others.

(5) *Job*, m. Susan Staples, of Mansfield. Res. Norton.

(6) *Keziah*, m. May 7, 1742, Benj. Bird, of Stoughton.

(7) *Mary*, m. Benj. Pratt, d. about 1748.

(8) *Jemima*, m. Seth White, and d. about 1748.

16. VII. Mercy,[4] b. 1686 or 7, d. Aug. 28, 1758, in 72d yr. She m. about 1713, Thomas Elyot, eldest son of Thomas of Rehoboth. He d. May 25, 1752, in 71st yr., and she removed to Norton. This is probably the T. E. "who lived 6 yrs." with Peter Walker,[3] (See No. 6,) and was mentioned in his will. His farm was next North

of Peter's, was inherited by his son-in-law, Joseph Read and grandson, the late Uriah Read. Chil. were—

(1) *Thomas*, d. Sept. 21, 1742, in 24th yr.

(2) *Noah*, m. Phebe Richmond, dau. of Edward, and she d. March 9, 1741–2, in 30th yr.

(3) *Mary*, m. Josiah Andrews, of T.

(4) *Jane*, m. Gershom Makepeace, of Weston, Worcester Co.

(5) *Abiah*, m. Dec. 9, 1736, Sylvester Richmond, of Middleboro', who settled in New Braintree, (See Richmond Genealogy.)

(6) *Elizabeth*, m. Joseph Read of Taunton, who d. 1801, and was buried in Walker Cemetery. They had, 1 Thomas, 2 Joseph, 3 Uriah, 4 Elizabeth, m. William Walker, (See No. 79,) and she had Elizabeth, who m. Matthew Briggs, and her son Charles H. m. Mary A. F. Walker, (See No. 397,) 5 Ebenezer, 6 Job, 7 Rhoda, 8 Solomon, d. Oct. 24, 1767, in 2d yr.

17. VIII. NEHEMIAH,[4] (47) b. 1689, d. Oct. 4, 1760, in 71st yr. (Ins.) He m. Mehetable Dean, dau. of Israel, of Taunton, who m. 2dly, Stephen Smith, of T. He inherited his father's "new dwelling house in T., and his home lot, and barn thereon," &c., &c. He was one of the selectmen in T., in 1743. None of his chil. survived him. His In'y was £2049.

18. IX. JOSIAH,[4] (49) d. 1748 or 9.

He m. Mary [Gooding, ?] dau. of George and Deborah Walker, (See No. 9.) She d. before 1780. Letter of administration was issued, March, 1749. In'y £1036. He lived in Dighton, and inherited by father's will, 3 upper lots in Dighton. Had 4 chil.

19. X. REBECCA.[4]

She m. between 1713 and 22, Wm. Lincoln, of Taunton. Res. Taunton.

20. XI. MARY.[4]

She m. between 1713 and 22, John Gilbert, of Taunton, app'd adm'x, March, 7, 1748. In'y £240, besides her thirds. In 1766, she was a widow and "Lace Maker," in Norton. Chil—

(1) *John*, d. about 1750.
(2) *Seth*.
(3) *Ebenezer*.
(4) *Benjamin*.
(5) *James*.
(6) *Bathsheba*, m. Tewell, and d. before 1750.
(7) *Elizabeth*.
(8) *Abigail*.

CHILDREN OF PETER WALKER,[3] [6] OF TAUNTON.

21. I. PETER,[4] (53) b. 1690, d. Jan. 7, 1770, in 81st year.

He m. Sarah* who d. Nov. 22, 1760, in 72d yr. His will, made 1767, gives names of 6 chil. He lived till 1747, at the Mansion House, called the Holloway Place afterward, the last house in Taunton, on the Bristol road, and first north of the Three Mile river, and now owned by Stephen Pierce.

22. II. EDWARD,[4] b. 1692, d. Dec. 9, 1752, in 60th yr. (Ins.)

He m. Mercy Richmond, dau. of Edward,[3] of Taunton. She d. Jan. 27, 1760, in 67yr. (Ins.) His will shows that he was childless, and its bequests are principally, "to wife Mercy, to Josiah Richmond, my kinsman, who lives with me, my homestead, farm, buildings, &c., where I now dwell, in Taunton, to possess the same after marriage or death of my wife. To my kinsman, Elisha Walker, son of my brother James, deceased, and to Eleazer Walker, grandson of my brother Peter, all the lands in Dighton, excepting 20 acres, given to Josiah Richmond,——and if either Elisha or Eleazer die, without issue, then to Nathan Walker, son of Nathan, and if he die without issue, then to the next of my kin, in the name of the Walkers, and not to go out of the name of the Walkers, to all generations. Will proved, Feb. 6, 1753. His homestead was in the South part of Taunton, East of the Bristol road, ¼ of a mile, and near the Burial Place, which he gave for the use of his kindred, and which has the oldest inscription in the town. It long since passed from the possession of the Richmonds, by their removal to Vermont. He was one of the Select men of Dighton, in 1726. The following is his deed of land for a burial place, copied from Folio 33, 288 p. of. Bristol Deeds.

"Edward Walker, of Taunton, to my kinsman, Joseph Atwood, of Dighton, land on Taunton Great river, running north in the range of Mr. Edward Blake's land, and so to said Blake's fence, and is that piece of land, and is at that place, where Joseph Atwood, and many others lie buried, it being about one acre, to have, and to hold, to Joseph Atwood and all relations, that I have, or shall have, to lye forever for a burying place, where I or any of my relations, that shall see cause, may bury their dead, with full power, leave and liberty to pass and repass through any other part of my land, to carry their

* Sarah Godfrey, dau. of Richard, Jr. and Mary (Richmond,) b. May 15, 1689, m. Walker, probably, this Peter, as his wife's age and name, correspond with her birth, and name.

dead to said burying place, provided they go where it is most convenient, and least prejudicial to me, or my heirs or assigns, without any molestation from me or my heirs, executors, administrators, forever, reserving wood on it to my heirs, &c.

In witness whereof, I give, and bequeath, said piece of land for a burying place, April 23, 1750. Bounded W. corner, heap of stones, Easterly, to river, to a small black oak with stones about it, then, Northerly, to a white oak tree, in range of Mr. Edward Blake's land, and from W. corner, by a rock N. to said Blake's fence, a rock with stones upon it."

Signed, EDWARD WALKER.

Witnesses, { EBENEZER RICHMOND, JOSIAH RICHMOND.

23. III. JAMES,[4] (58) d. 1726.

He m. Nov. 25, 1725, Mary, dau. of David[4] and Mary (Walker,) of Dighton, (See No. 38,) who was b. Aug. 16, 1704, and d. April 21, 1782, ae. 77 yrs. and 9 mos. In'y £537, Sept. 20, 1726. Division of his estate in 1743, was as follows: "To widow, land from Great river, up over county road, and ½ of cellar and ½ of chamber. To Elisha, only child and son of the deceased, north ½ of cellar, north ½ of chamber, and north room in house and rest of land, about 67 acres."

He was a Brewer in Boston, 1720, but d. in Taunton. His homestead is now in possession of his descendants. She m. 2dly, April 23, 1730, Eben'r Richmond, of Middleboro, afterward, of Taunton, and had large family. (See No. 38.)

24. IV. ABIGAIL.[4]

25. V. CATHARINE,[4] not of age in 1711.

She and her sister, Abigail, d. before 1753, and without heirs.

26. VI. HANNAH,[4] not of age in 1711.

She m. —— Place, and had 3 chil, viz.: Elizabeth, Hannah, and Mary.

She m. 2dly, and was 2d wife, John Atwood, son of Joseph and Esther (Walker.) (See No. 7.) He was b. Feb. 28, 1683, and d. 1764, In'y £134. Owner in Forge and Iron Works. She survived him. Res. Dighton. Chil.—

(1) *John*, b. May 9, 1735, d. June 27, 1755, in 21st yr. (Ins.) "John Atwood, son of John and Hannah, departed this life in a very surprising manner, being killed by a cart wheel, ae. 20 yrs. 1 mo. 18 days." He was drawing pig iron, and the wheel went over his head.

(2) *Susannah*, b. April 19, 1737, and d. Oct. 4, 1753, in 17th yr.

FIFTH GENERATION.

CHILDREN OF LIEUT. JAMES WALKER,[4] [10] OF TAUNTON.

27. I. JAMES,[5] (59) b. about 1703, d. Aug. 11, 1761, in 59th yr.

He m. July 21, 1761, Mary Pitts, who m. 2dly, Abner Thayer, and living, 1783. His In'y included Mansion House, &c., £2200, (it was west of Three Mile River, and where Geo T. Lee, now lives,) ½ Saw Mill, at Jos. Stephens, in Dighton, 11¼ little lots, in D., 4 yoke of oxen, 7 cows, and negro man, Cambridge. Amount £3517. He was a man of affluence for the time, and prominent in the affairs of the town. His death was sad and untimely. In digging a well he came to a rock. Thinking that heat would break it, he built a fire upon the rock. Leaving this to burn while he was taking dinner, he returned, and descended the well to see the condition and effect of the fire. But a little before reaching the bottom, he fell, and two others following to rescue him, fell upon him. Water was then poured into the well, and a fourth descended with a rope fastened to him. This he then fastened to the last who fell, and he was taken out, and in this way all were taken from the well. Mr. Walker being the first who fell, was the last taken out, and was then found to be dead. This occurred about a month after his marriage. After his death a son was born, who was named James, in honor of his father, and removed to New York City.

28. II. PETER,[5] b. 1704, d. Aug. 6, 1762, in 58th yr.

He m. Helen Baylies, sister of Nicholas. Will approved, Aug. 18, 1767, indicates that he had no children. He bequeathed his farm to nephew, Peter, £3 yearly to Rev. John Lyon, for 10 yrs., if he remains minister of St. Thomas' Church,—to his wife, the negro woman Peggy, and her 2 children, and man Cambridge. In'y £300. He lived ½ a mile south of Westville, Taunton, on the road to Mt. Hope Factory, where the late Ebenezer Walker lived. The farm was north of, and adjoined that of his brother James. His widow m. 2dly, Rev. John Lyon.

29. III. ELIAKIM,[5] (60) b. 1704 or 5, d. Feb. 21, 1785, in 81st yr.

He m. Mary, who d. Dec. 1785, in 79th yr. Had 6 chil. Res. Taunton. Had a farm of 300 acres, bounded W. by Rehoboth, and S. by Dighton. His valuation was £1555, and his tax on the minister's rate, 1756, was the largest in the town, excepting James Walker's. He was Ensign.

30. IV. ELNATHAN,[5] (66) d. June 6, 1775, in 69th yr.

He m. Hannah Crossman, (dau. of Robert,) who d. April 4, 1728, in 23d yr. He m. 2dly, Bethiah Tisdale, (dau. of Joseph,) who d. May 11, 1759, in 49th yr. (Ins.) He m. 3dly, Nov. 6, 1760, Mrs. Phebe King, dau. of Dea. Sam'l Leonard, of Raynham. After his death she removed to Middleboro' and lived with her daughter, Phebe King, (who married the Rev. Caleb Turner, Feb. 11, 1763,) where she died, April 3, 1803, in 89th yr.

Col. Walker lived on a farm in the N. W. part of Dighton, adjoining his brother Elakim's, in Taunton. His will was proved, Aug. 5, 1775. In'y, £437. Had 10 chil. He was a Member and a Deacon of the 1st Cong'l Church, in Dighton, and contributed more for the building of the Meeting House, at Buck-plain, than any other person. He was one of the Com. to plan and build it, with David Walker and Geo. Ware. He was moderator of Town Meeting, 1756, '66, '69 to '75, and Selectman, 1764, 5, 6, 8, 9 to '76. He was Representative of the town of Dighton, in the General Court, in the years 1748 and 9, '69, '70, '71, '72, '73 and '74, and probably other yrs. of which there is no record of those who served as representatives, viz.: 1738, 9 '40, 2, 3, 4, and 6. He held a commission of Justice of the Peace, and was Colonel of a Regiment of Militia. He exerted a large influence in public affairs, and was distinguished for high moral worth and exemplary piety.

The following is the epitaph on his grave stone, in the Burial Place, in West Taunton.

Beneath the sacred honors of the tomb,
In awful silence, and majestic gloom,
The man of mercy, here conceals his head,
Amidst the awful mansions of the dead;
No more his liberal hand shall help the poor,
Relieve the distrest, nor scatter joys no more.

31. V. SARAH.[5]

She m. June 23, 1726, Thos. Leonard, Jr., of Raynham. His In'y, Aug. 24, 1774, intestate. Children—

(1) *Mary*, b. Oct. 5, 1727.

(2) *Sarah*, b. June 26, 1729, m. Rev. Eliab Byram, of Mendham, N. J. and was the mother of the wife of the late Hon. Josiah Dean, who was owner of the old Raynham Forge.

(3) *Hannah*, b. July 18. 1731.

(4) *Gamaliel*, b. April 30th, 1733, d. March 12, 1809. Had 10 chil.

(5) *Paul*, b. Nov. 17, 1735, d. Jan. 5, 1799. Res. in E. Raynham. Numerous descendants.

(6) *Caroline*, b. July 3, 1738.

(7) *Phebe*, b. July 20, 1740.

CHILDREN OF NATHAN WALKER,[4] [12] OF DIGHTON.

32. I. NATHAN,[5] (77) b. Oct. 27, 1709, d. Sept. 30, 1771, in 62d yr. (Ins.) He m. Nov. 20, 1737, Dorothy, dau. of John Burt, of Berkley. She d. March 22, 1790, in 83d yr. (Ins.) Both were buried in the Walker Cemetery. Had 2 chil. He was Town Clerk, 1755, and also Deacon of the church in Dighton. The latter is his title on the Grave Stone. He lived just South of the late Thomas Rose, half a mile from Three Mile River, on the Bristol road.

33. II. ABIGAIL,[5] b. Dec. 3, 1711, d. Aug. 13, 1749, ae. 37 yrs. 7 mos. and 21 days. (Ins.) She m. Jacob Austin, of Dighton. Their chil. were—

(1) *Benj'n*, b. 1733, (2) *Phebe*, b. Aug. 3. 1735, (3) *Abiathar*, b. Dec. 23, 1738, (4) *John*, b. July 13, 1741, (5) *Seth*, b. Feb. 9, 1743, d. March 18, 1826, in 83d yr. m. Elizabeth, and had 5 chil., (6) *Jacob*. b. May 17, 1747.

34. III. PHEBE,[5] b. Sept. 29, 1713.

She m. Dec. 17, 1741, Seth French, of Berkley. She petitioned for Administration, Sept. 15, 1756. His In'y £370. Their chil. were—

(1) *Joseph*, b. March 6, 1743, (2) *Abigail*, b. Oct. 11, '44, (3) *Thomas*, b. July 5, '45, (4) *Phebe*. b. Oct. 18, '46, (5) *Nathan*, b. May 23, '48, (6) *Sarah*, b. Feb. 5, '49, (7) *Seth*, b. April 26, '52, (8) *John*, b. Feb. 13, '54, (9) *Silence*, b. April 22, '56.

35. IV. WILLIAM,[5] (79) b. Aug. 17, 1715, d. Aug. 3, 1749. (Ins.) He m. May, 31, 1743, Hannah Shaw, dau. of Dea. Abraham, of Dighton, She survived him. In'y £2844. He was a "Boatman" in 1743. Had 3 chil. She m. 2dly, Ephraim Hathaway, Jr., pub. Feb. 1, 1752, and d. Feb. 12, 1761.

36. V. LYDIA,[5] b. Aug. 31, 1717.

She m. Doct. Wm. Ware, (his 4th wife,) pub. Sept. 6, 1755. He d. June 11, 1764, ae. 67 yrs. (Ins.) A successful Physician and Surgeon, in Dighton. Chil—

(1) *Joseph*, May 5, 1756, m. Hannah Richmond, of Taunton. 2 chil. Abigail and Joseph.

(2) *Lydia*, June 6, 1758, d. unm.

(3) *Abigail*, June 8, 1760, d. unm.

37. VI. DEBORAH,[5] b. Aug. 13, 172–.

She is called "spinster," in 1762. Wm. Ashmand was pub. to Deborah Walker, Jan. 9, 1763. It was probably to the "spinster," as there was no other Deborah for Ashmand to marry.

CHILDREN OF DAVID WALKER,[4] [13] OF DIGHTON.

38. I. MARY,[5] b. Aug. 16, 1704, d. April 21, 1782, ae. 77 yrs. and 9 mos. She m. Nov. 25, 1725, James Walker, (See No. 23.) and had Elisha.

She m. 2dly, April 23, 1730, Ebenezer Richmond, formerly of Middlebury, who d. March 6, 1793, ae. 91 yrs. and 11 mos. (Res. Taunton.) Had 3 sons and 6 daus., viz.:

(1) *Ebenezer*, b. 1732, d. young.

(2) *Molly*, m. Lincoln, and then Lemuel Richmond, d. April 9, 1820, ae. 89.

(3) *Anna*, m. Luther Stetson.

(4) *Ebenezer*, b. 1738, m. Mercy Paul. (See 150.)

(5) *Sally*, m. Obed Randall, of Woodstock, Vt.

(6) *Rachel*, d. unm.

(7) *Patience*, d. unm.

(8) *Content*, m. Vickery.

(9) *Amaziah*, m. Abigail Burt, (See No. 54.) dau. of John and Hannah (Walker,) Burt. Had 11 chil. These emigrated early to Vermont.

39. II. HANNAH,[5] b. Sept. 26, 1707, d. before 1765.

She m. Daniel Gachet, son of Henri Gachet, Gassett or Gushee, who m. Sept. 12, 1697, Sarah Haskins, of Taunton. About year 1700, 2 bros. Frenchmen and Huguenots, Henri and David Gachet, emigrated to this country, from Rochelle, France. Their descendants have Anglicised the name in different ways. Those of the elder, writing Gassett, those of the younger, Gushee. Most of them reside in Bristol Co., Mass., and are numerous, but most are females and do not retain the name. Daniel's chil. were—Isaac, Hannah, Henry, Seth, Sarah, Mary, Levi, John, Phebe, Simeon, Benj'n, and Reuben. He removed with his family to Hopkinton, Oct. 26, 1746. (Gen. Reg. 1847, 344 p.)

40. III. ELIZABETH,[5] b. April 1, 1712, d. before 1765.

She m. Wm. Austin.

41. IV. BATHSHEBA,[5] b. March 8, 1714, d. Sept. 15, 1763, in 49th yr. She m. Robert Luscombe, and had no chil. He was Deacon. Res. Taunton.

42. V. DAVID,[5] (82) b. May 24, 1717. In'y, 1781, £1262.

He m. pub. April 5, 1755, Mary or Molly Wilmarth, of Taunton, who d. June 9, 1756. She had 1 child.

He m. 2dly, March 25, 1758, Sarah Richmond, of Little Compton, R. I., dau. of William and Anna (Gray,) sister of Col. William of L. C., and b. Jan. 8, 1738. Res. Dighton. He lived where the late Seth Austin lived, next South of the late John Walker, ¾ of a mile from Three mile river, on Bristol road. He was a farmer and had 12 child.

43. VI. JONATHAN,[5] (93) b. July 19, 1719, d. 1808.

He m. Jan. 6, 1742–3, Elizabeth Hathaway, dau. of Ephraim, Jr., and Ann, and grand dau. of Ephraim and Elizabeth. One child.

He m. 2dly, pub. Feb. 17, 1748–9, Deborah Burrell, of Weymouth, and had 5 chil. He was in Capt. Elijah Walker's Co., and went to R. I., Dec. 1, 1776, also to Tiverton, July 27, 1780. Will proved, 1808. Res. Dighton. Farmer.

44. VII. NATHANIEL,[5] (99) b. April 27, 1721, d. 1753.

He m. pub. June 8, 1745, Lydia Hathaway, and had 2 chil. Res. Dighton.

45. VIII. MARCY,[5] b. Macrh 8, 1722.

She m. Oct. 10, 1739, Silas Lincoln, of Taunton.

46. IX. ESTHER,[5] b. May 21, 1724, d. May or June 1805, in Oxford, N. Y. She m. July 13, 1745, Seth Richmond, of Taunton, son of Joseph and Abigail (French.) He removed to Gloucester, R. I., where he d. 1790 or 91. He was a farmer, of large stature, and possessed great muscular strength. His character was good, yet he was not a professor of religion. She was m. ch., Bap. After his death she removed with her son to Oxford, now Guilford, N. Y., where she d. Had chil—

(1) *David*, b. 1748, m. Nancy Davis. Res. Oxford, N. Y. Was Major in Revolutionary Army, and d. 1818. Has numerous descendants in N. Y.

(2) *Mary*, b. about 1750, m. Wm. Howland.

(3) Child d. in infancy.

CHILDREN OF NEHEMIAH WALKER,[4] [17] OF TAUNTON.

47. I. CATHARINE,[5] d. July 27, 1761 in 14th yr. (Ins.)

48. II. NEHEMIAH,[5] d. March 10, 1755, ae. 4 yrs. 6 mos. and 12 days.

CHILDREN OF JOSIAH WALKER,[4] [18] OF DIGHTON.

49. I. JOSIAH,[5] b. Nov. 29, 1720, d. before 1787, and after 1780, unm. He had a double portion in the estate of his father, being the oldest son. But of weak mind, he was swindled out of his property. He was left destitute, and suffered much from neglect.

50. II. ABIJAH,[5] b. Oct. 20, 1722, d. Nov. 28, 1806, in 84th yr. unm. In'y $4694. He was in Capt. Elijah W.'s Co., and went to R. I., Dec. 1, 1776. In the latter part of his life he was unable to walk. Res. Dighton.

51. III. NEHEMIAH,[5] b. Nov. 2, 1726, d. unm. March 1, 1769, in 44th yr.

52. IV. ELIJAH,[5] (101) b. Nov. 15, 1730, d. Aug. 31, 1804, in 74th yr. He m. Dec. 2, 1749, Hannah Piggsley, dau. of Robert and Hannah, and b. April 10, 1727, and d. Oct. 30, 1809, in 84th yr. They had 14 chil. 2 or 3 of whom were drowned, in the well which was left without any curb. He commanded the 9th company, 46 men, of the 2d Regiment of Bristol Co. militia, in the Revolutionary War. They marched to Roxbury once, went to R. I., Dec. 8, 1776, to Tiverton, Aug. 2, 1780, and to Dorchester Heights, Sept. 30, 1778. He was select man, 1779–80. Res. Dighton. Farmer.

CHILDREN OF PETER WALKER,[4] [21] OF TAUNTON.

53. I. PETER,[5] (115) d. between 1740 and '47.

He m. Sarah Sampson, of Middleboro', pub. Nov. 11, 1742. Res. Taunton. He was a farmer, and had 2 chil.

54. II. HANNAH.[5]

She m. (pub. Dec. 1742,) John Burt, Jr., of Berkley, who d. Dec. 19, 1749. In'y £1781, 14s. 6d. old tenor. Chil—

(1) *Charity*, b. Feb 23, 1743, m. pub. April 20, 1761, John Dillingham.

(2) *Abigail*, b. Jan. 19, '45, m. pub. Dec. 3 '64, Amaziah Richmond.

(3) *John*, b. Feb. 19, '49 or '50, d. ae. 1 yr. 7 mos.

A widow Hannah Burt, of B., m. (pub. Dec. 21, 1754,) Melatiah Hathaway.

55. III. SARAH.[5]

She m. May 12, 1737, William Holloway, of Middleboro', who d. Oct. 7, 1778, in 72d yr. (Ins.) He removed from M. to Taunton, in 1747, having bought the homestead of his father-in-law. Chil. were—

(1) *William*, b. Feb. 16, 1738.

(2) *Josiah*, b. Nov. 9, '39, d. Dec. 23, ae. 1 mo. and 14 d.

(3) *George*, b. Sept. 26, '40.

(4) *Elizabeth*, b. Dec. 23, '42.

(5) *Sarah*. b. Feb. 1, '44.

(6) *Josiah*, d. Oct. 9, 1771, in 15th yr. This is doubtful.

56. IV. DOROTHY,[5] d. March 4, 1808, in 83d yr.

She m. Feb. 16, 1748–9, Sylvester Atwood, of Dighton, who was b. Sept. 4, 1725, and d. April 19, 1815, in 90th yr. He was son of Ephraim and Ruth (Richmond,) (See No. 7,) and grand son of Hester Walker. Chil—

(1) *Ruth*, b. Nov. 30, 1749–50.

(2) *Sary*, b. Jan. 10, '53.

(3) *Mary*, b. Oct. '54.

(4) *Esther*, b. May 1, '59.

(5) *Doritha*, b. Aug. 14, '62.

(6) *Sylvester*, b. July 1, '65, d. Dec. 20, 1840. Res. Dighton. He had 8 chil., of whom Wm. R. was the only son who lived to be married.

57. V. MARY,[5] d. before 1767.

She m. out pub. March 25, 1747, John Sampson, of Middleboro'. She left 1 son, Peter.

CHILDREN OF JAMES WALKER,[4] [23] OF TAUNTON.

58. I. ELISHA,[5] (117) b. Nov. 5, 1726, d. 1761.

He m. Miriam Richmond, dau. of Josiah and Mehetable (Dean,) of Taunton, and then of Middleboro'. He was an only child, and of him, little is known, as he died in early manhood, 2½ yrs. after the birth of his son, the late Capt. James Walker. Had 4 chil. His In'y £518, was taken 26 May, 1761. His widow m. Sam'l Ray, and then lived in Wrentham. After Mr. Ray's decease, and about 1790, she returned to her early home, in T., to live and die with her son. Richmond Walker, a grand son, remembers her well. He used to walk to church with her, when a boy, a distance of more than 3 miles, she being 70 yrs. old, and it is to her counsels, he ascribes his first productive religious impressions. She lives in his memory a venerable and saintly woman. She d. in the summer of 1813, ae. over 80 yrs.

SIXTH GENERATION.

CHILDREN OF JAMES WALKER,[5] [27] OF TAUNTON.

59. JAMES,[6] b. 1761.

He bought house and land of Levi Whipple, in Providence, 1782, and was a merchant in P., 1783. In 1784 he was in N. Y. city. Nothing more is known of him, and all efforts to discover his descendants, have proved fruitless.

CHILDREN OF ELIAKIM WALKER,[5] [29] OF TAUNTON.

60. 1. MARY,[6] d. before 1784.

She m. William Ware, of Dighton. Chil., James, Perez, who both d. young, and William, who m. ——— Williams, sister of Hon. John M. Williams, of Boston, and d. before 1784, having 1 child, whose mother, after Ware's death, m. Robert Crossman, and had James W. Crossman, now of Taunton.

61. II. ELIAKIM,[6] (121) b. 1734 or 5, d. March 9, 1801, in 66th yr., (Ins.) ae. 66 yrs. 2 mos. and 19 days. (Fam. Rec.) He m. Jan. 21, 1758, Hannah Waldron, of Dighton, dau. of Benj'n and Hannah. She was b. 1734, and d. Dec. 24, 1824, ae. 89 yrs. 1 mo. 27 days. He with Benj'n and Peter Walker, and Edward Richmond, were petitioners to the General Court, for a new religious society, in 1790. He was a Lieutenant in the 3d Regiment, of the County of Bristol, 1772, was in Capt. Blake's Co., to Bristol, Dec. 8, 1776, on secret expedition, Sept. 28, 1777, ☞ Oct. 29; in Fish —— service, May, 1778, and to Howland's Ferry, July 1778. His valuation, £1555, was among the largest in the town. Res. Taunton. He was a farmer and had 2 sons.

62. III. PEREZ,[6] (123) b. 1737 or 8, d. Feb. 3, 1801, in 63d yr. He m. June 30, 1768, Elizabeth Tisdale, dau. of Ephraim, of Dighton. She d. ae. about 80. Res. D. His In'y $5857. His farm is now owned by the heirs of Gilbert Walker. He had 3 sons, was in Capt. Elijah Walker's Co., and Col. Hathaway's Reg., and marched to R. I. Dec. 1, 1776, and to Tiverton, Aug. 1780.

63. IV. JAMES,[6] d. April 14, 1761, ae. 17 yrs. and 14 days. (Ins.)

64. V. SARAH,[6] d. May, '59, ae. 10 yrs. and 8 mos. (Ins.)

65. VI. SARAH, d. very aged.

She m. March 17, 1774, David Whitmarsh, of Dighton, son of David and Susanna, and b. Jan. 24, 1731. She was his 2d wife, and had—

(1) *Walker*, b. July, 1776. who m. pub. Aug. 16, 1800, Charlotte Pierce, and had 6 chil., from 1801 to 1813 He d. June 3, 1854, (2) *Eliakim*, b. Nov. 1, 1778, (3) *Benj'n*, b. March 5, 1782, unm.

CHIL. OF COL. ELNATHAN WALKER,[5] [30] OF DIGHTON.

66. I. ELNATHAN,[6] (126) b. Feb. 9, 1727–8. (Dighton Rec.) 1727, (Fam. Rec,) d. Nov. 1815. He m. 1751, Hannah Works, of Woodstock, Ct., who d. 1754, m. of ch. Bap., and a woman of rare excellence.

He m. 2dly, 1756, Hannah Bugbee, of Woodstock, Ct., who d. May 8, 1810, in Hartland, Vt.

He removed to Woodstock, Ct., then to Sturbridge, Mass., and finally in 1778, to Hartland, where he died. He was a clothier. But possessing great mechanical ingenuity, he made spinning wheels for both wool and flax, was an excellent rake maker, and supplied the inhabitants in the new settlements, with various useful articles, such as rakes, chests, drawers, &c. There was scarcely an article that he could not make. He was also remarkably expert with a gun, seldom missing his mark, whether the distance were long or short, and so making havoc among the bears and wolves. He was of a bold, fearless spirit, of fine physical proportions, of noble appearance, and when 87 yrs. of age, walked as erect as men usually do at 30. "I remember" says a grand son, "seeing him run to overtake a team, and with considerable rapidity in his 88th yr." He had 4 chil. His descendants inherit his ingenuity, and many of them have quite a rich vein of wit and humor. As for the morals, character, and intelligence of the members of this branch, all stand fair in the world, not one of them having Walker blood, has ever disgraced the name.

67. II. EBENEZER,[6] (130) b. Nov. 2, 1732, d. Dec. 7, 1812, in 81st yr. He m. Sept. 4, 1770, Hannah Woodward, of Taunton. She d. Dec. 13, 1812, in 69th yr. He inherited land in Dighton from his father, and lived there. In'y $3830. Had 5 chil. He was in Capt. Elijah W.'s Co., and went to R. I., Dec. 1, '76, also to Tiverton, Aug. 2, 1780. He was very eccentric. If any one exhibited any awkwardness, they were said to resemble Uncle Eben. Many anecdotes respecting him have been handed down.

68. III. HANNAH,[6] b. April 4, 1734, d. June 9, 1750, ae. 16 yrs. and 2 mos.

69. IV. RUTH,[6] b. Aug. 30, 1736, d. before Aug. 1775.

She m. pub. Jan. 4, 1755, Jeremiah Fisher, son of Nath'l and Elizabeth, and b. Sept. 22, 1728. They had—

(1) *Nathaniel*, b. Oct. 25, 1756, who removed to Bristol. N. Y., was Deacon of the Cong'l ch., and d. about 1815. His 5 chil. were—1 Nathaniel, m. Lovisa, his 1st cousin, dau. of Dea. Abiezer and Bathsheba (Walker,) (Gooding) Philips. (See No. 71.) He was a man of some military distinction, d. 1855, 2 Jeremiah, 3 Ruth, m. Col. Charles Gooding, 4 Hannah, 5 Phebe.

70. V. EDWARD,[6] b. 1741 or 2, d. July 12, 1775, in 34th yr., unm. Res. Dighton.

71. VI. BATHSHEBA,[6] b. Oct. 12, 1743, d. Oct. 22, 1822, ae. 79.

She m. (pub. Sept. 11, 1760,) William Gooding, son of Matthew, of Dighton, and Abigail (Richmond.) (See No. 9.) Res. Dighton. He was Deacon of Cong'l ch. His death was caused by the small pox, given him by Doct. Wm. Baylies, about 1776 or '77. Had 5 sons and 3 daus. viz.:

(1) *William*, b. Jan. 18, 1761, m. Lydia Andrews, and had large family. He was Dea. in Pres. ch., in Bloomfield, N. Y.

(2) *Mary*, b. Aug. 17, 1762, m. Jonah Lincoln. Res. Vermont.

(3) *Bathsheba*, b. Jan. 24, '65, m. Seth Hathaway. Res. Bristol, N. Y., chil., in 1822, Seth, Abiel, Gooding, Elnathan, Chandler and others.

(4) *James*, b. March 10, 1767, m. Caroline Andrews, sister of Lydia. Had James, b. in B. and now of Gooding Grove, Ill. He m. 2dly, Phebe, (No. 136,) his cousin, and dau. of Peter Walker, of Taunton. He was Dea. of Cong'l ch. in Bristol, N. Y., d. in Gooding's Grove, about 1848, ae. 82 yrs.

(5) *Ruth*, b. Feb. 20, 1769, m. Jonathan, son of Abiel Simmons, (pub. Nov. 5, 1790.) He was a clothier. Res. B. Removed about 1830, to Ohio or Ill. Had chil.

(6) *Elnathan*, b. Oct. 15, 1771, m. sister of Jonathan Simmons. Res. B. Had large family.

(7) *George*, b. Dec. 14, 1773, m. Res. B. Was wealthy, and had large family.

(8) *Zephaniah*, b. Sept. 25, 1777, m. Res. B.

The descendants of Wm. G., writes a grand son, have been of the medium class, in wealth, capacity and enterprise.

Mrs. G. m. 2dly, Abiezer Philips. They removed to Genesee Co., N. Y. Had 1 dau. Lovisa, who m. Col. Nath'l Fisher. (See No. 69.) He d. Jan. 25, 1806, in 76th yr., and she went to live with her dau. Dea. P. was Representative from Dighton, 1780 and '83.

72. VII. Bethiah,[6] b. Aug. 20, 1745, d. Jan. 27, 1823, in 77th yr., in Rehoboth. She m. Sept. 26, 1769, Ebenezer Jones. Chil.—

(1) *Nancy*, m. John Simmons, and removed to Ontario Co., N. Y., 1. dau., Nancy. Mrs. S. m. 2dly, Dea. Nath'l Fisher, and 3dly, —— Beach. No chil.

(2) *Ebenezer*. Had chil. Res. Bristol, N. Y.

(3) *Seth*, m. —— Barrows, and 2dly, Betsey Simmons. Res. B.

(4) *Sally*, m. Lemuel Peck, of Rehoboth, and had 2 sons, Josephus and Philip, who are deceased. Res. R., where she d.

(5) *Ephraim*, m. —— Waldron, dau. of Joseph. He was a farmer and held a Colonel's Commission. Res. B.

(6) *Andros*, removed to far West, and his kindred know nothing of him.

(7) *Elnathan*, b. June 18, 1787. Res. Norton. He m. Betsey Dunham. No chil. He m. 2dly Amanda Peck. Had 3 chil., who died. He m. 3dly, Polly Dean, dau. of Abijah, by whom 3 chil., viz.: 4 Wm. D. who m. Betsey B., dau. of Abel and Betsey Crane, (See No. 148,) and 5 George W. now in Wis., and 6 Harriet.

Mrs. Jones m. James Codding, Jr., (out pub. Nov. 27 '92,) who d. in a fit. No chil.

73. VIII. Peter,[6] (135) b. Dec. 19, 1747, d. Sept. 26, 1824.

He m. Aug. 1, 1769, Deborah, dau. of George Gooding. (See No. 9,) of Dighton, who d. Feb. 15, 1823, in 74th yr. Had 9 chil.

He m. 2dly, Deborah Lincoln, (pub. Jan 4, 1824,) who d. May 8, 1851, ae. 83 yrs. Res. Taunton, near the Factory at Westville, on the farm given him by his uncle Peter, and now held by the heirs of the late Ebenezer Walker. He was Lieutenant in Capt. Edward Blake's Co., in the Revolutionary War.

He was one of the petitioners, to Gen. Court, for a new religious society, in 1790. He was m. ch. Cong., Rev. Alvan Cobb's, and contributed $300, towards building the 1st Cong'l church edifice, at West Taunton. A comparison of the greater part of the town, shows his valuation, which was £1800, about the year 1790, to have been larger than all, excepting two.

74. IX. Phebe,[6] b. 1748, d. Oct. 23, 1830, in 92d yr.

She m. Dec. 29, 1769, Alden Sears, of Rochester, Mass. who d. March 25, 1803, ae. 64. He held a Captain's commission. They removed to Bristol, N. Y., in 1792, and had 7 chil., most of whom resided in B.

(1) *Alden*, m. Delany Vincent, and d. Feb. 28, 1829, ae. 59, in B. Had 10 chil. who settled in Ill. and Mich.

(2) *Phebe*, m. Major Sylvanus Jones, of B.,—had 9 chil. and d. Oct. 22, 1841, ae. 71.

(3) *Hannah*, m. Sisson, of B., had 7 chil. and d. March 1849, ae. 76.

(4) *Abigail*, m. Kent, had 6 chil., and d. March, 1813.

(5) *Edward*, m. Root, in N. Y., and settled in Ohio. Nothing known of them.

(6) *Eleanor*, m. Simmons, has 8 chil. Living, ae. 75, (1856.)

(7) *John*, m. Betsey Low, 2dly, Jane Pendry, b. 1786, and 3dly, Rhoda Blount, b. Oct. 22, 1790. He had 8 chil., of whom is Rasselas L., b. May 25, 1811. (See No. 279.)

75. X. ZEPHANIAH,[6] b. July 14, 1754, d. July 14, 1775, unm. Res. Dighton. He enlisted in the army of the Revolution, April 30, 1775, and d. in Roxbury, the day he was 21 yrs. old. He was in Capt. Peter Pitts' Co., and Col. Timothy Walker's Regiment.

BY 3d MARRIAGE.

76. XI. GEORGE,[6] (144) b. Sept. 7, 1761, d. Oct. 13, 1844, ae. 83. He m. Nov. 21, 1791, Thankful Burt, dau. of David, who d. Dec. 13, 1837, ae. 72 yrs. She was blind several years. Her tombstone represents her,

A companion dear, a parent kind,
A heart to righteousness inclined.

After the death of his father, Mr. W., then about 14 yrs. of age, went to Middleboro', with his mother. He was there apprenticed to a wheelwright. Pursuing this occupation a while, the War commenced, and he was drafted for military service, and went in Sullivan's expedition, to R. I. He was in Capt. Edward Blake's Co., and marched to Tiverton, R. I., Aug. 2, 1780. Returning, he attended school, and studied medicine, with Pentacost Blackington. He then bought the homestead of his father, in Dighton, and removed there, April 4, 1792. He practised as a Physician, through life, or nearly 50 yrs.; frequently served the town as an Assessor and Select-man, and represented it in the General Court, in the years 1799, 1802, 3, 9, '10, '11, and '12. He received a pension for service in the Revolutionary War. He held a Justice's commission, nearly 40 yrs. Had 5 chil.

Dr. W., says Rev. A. Cobb, who knew him well, was a man of high moral worth, and of exemplary piety, though not a professor of religion; and as a physician, was skillful, and benevolent to the poor.

CHILDREN OF DEA. NATHAN WALKER,[5] [32] OF DIGHTON.

77. I. NATHAN,[6] (149) b. Sept. 6, 1739, d. May 17, 1775, in 36th yr. (Ins.) He m. March 3, 1768, Rebecca Paul, who d. May 13, 1786, in 41st yr. (Ins.) Both were buried in the Walker Cemetery. Res. Dighton. In'y £500. Had 5 chil.

78. II. JOHN,[6] b. Oct. 22, 1743, d. April 15, 1766, in 23d yr. unm.

CHILDREN OF WILLIAM WALKER,[5] [35] OF DIGHTON.

79. I. WILLIAM,[6] (154) b. Dec. 14, 1743, d. March 20, 1816.

He m. Sept. 3, 1767, Elizabeth, dau. of Joseph Read, and Elizabeth (Eliot,) of Taunton. (See No. 16.) She d. Feb. 28, 1832.

He was in Capt. Elijah W.'s Co., and went to R. I., Dec. 1, 1776, 16d, and in the same Co., to Tiverton, R. I., Aug. 2, 1780, 7 days. Res. Wellington, now Dighton. In'y $14029. Had 16 chil.

80. II. ABIATHAR,[6] b. March 17, 1745.

He m. Elizabeth Haskins, of Berkley, pub. Aug. 5, 1772. He was in Capt. Elijah Walker's Co., and went to R. I., Dec. 1, 1776. Res. Dighton. No chil.

81. III. GEORGE,[6] b. Dec. 19, 1749.

He m. but had no children.

CHILDREN OF DAVID WALKER[5], [42] OF DIGHTON.

82. I. DAVID,[6] b. March 5, 1756, d. before July 3, 1759.

BY 2d MARRIAGE.

82.[1] II. DAVID,[6] b. July 3, 1759, d. unm.

He was a seaman, and is supposed to have been lost at sea, or d. of yellow fever, at Phil'a. He was Fifer in the Revolutionary army, in 8 mos. service 1775.

83. III. WILLIAM RICHMOND,[6] (170) b. Feb. 9, 1760.

He was pub. Aug. 27, 1785, to Margaret Bowers, of Swansey, who d. Nov. 1822.. Res. Somerset, ½ m. from S. shore. He was master of a small vessel. Soon after his marriage, and about 1790 or '92, he sailed, and was never heard of. It is supposed the vessel foundered, and all on board perished. He enlisted in the Continental Army for 3 yrs., Sept 10, 1777. Was Sergeant in Capt. Henry Brightman's Co., and Fifer in Col. Carpenter's Reg. Had 1 son.

84. IV. GILBERT,[6] (171) b. April 30, 1763, d. May 30, 1825, in Providence, R. I. He m. 1793, Bridget Corey, of Tiverton, who d. Aug. 14, 1794, without issue.

He m. 1795, Mary Corey, (sister of Bridget,) who d. in Somerset, Oct. 18, 1808.

He m. Dec. 9, 1810, Sarah Swasey, dau. of Jerathamel, of Somerset, who d. Aug. 3, 1824, ae. 43 yrs. in S. She was m. ch. Bap. He was a trader, in Somerset, Bristol, R. I., at the South, and at the time of his death, residing in Providence. He was a very intelligent man, and possessed considerable literary taste. Had 10 chil.

85. V. POLLY,[6] b. Dec. 16, 1765, d. April 2, 1854, [in 89th yr.?] ae. 90 yrs. (Ins.) She was pub. July 4, 1789, to Nathaniel Rose, of Dighton, who d. Feb. 24, 1840, ae. 83 yrs. He was called Captain. Had—

(1) *Edward*, b. 1790, m. Oct. 27, 1816, Nancy Thayer, of Taunton. He d. March 19, 1840, ae. 50. His chil.—1, Angenette, b. July 20, 1817, and m. 1839, Eber C. Luther. 2, Wm. Throop, b. Oct. 24, 1820, pub. to Almira A. Lubeck, of Dighton, Nov. 25, '43, trader, d. May 9, 1853. 3, Mary Jane, b. Sept. 15, 1822, m. 1859, Dr. Talbot, of D. 4, Horace Richmond, b. Aug. 22, 1825, m. Elizabeth F. Marston, Furnaceman. 5, Nancy, unm. 6, Edward, in California. 7, Nathaniel, unm.

86. VI. ANNA,[6] b. Jan. 30, 1767.

She m. Capt. Noah Chase, of Somerset, by whom 2 sons—

(1) *Noah*, d. young.

(2) *Gilbert*, m Betsey Trafton.

Capt. Chase was lost at sea, with Wm. R. Walker, his brother-in-law.

She m. 2dly, Aug. 19, 1792, Francis Church, son of Col. Thomas. They removed from Dighton, to Bristol, N. Y., and then to Buffalo, where they died. Chil.—

(3) *Benj'n*, a merchant, in Ohio.

(4) *Charles*, d. in Buffalo.

87. VII. BATHSHEBA,[6] b. Jan. 30, 1767. Twin.

She m. Amos Wood, of Little Compton, R. I. and removed to Poughkeepsie, or to Genesee Co. N. Y. No chil.

88. VIII. SILVESTER,[6] (181) b. 1769, d. Feb. 28, 1836.

He was pub. May 19, 1792,* to Sally Burt, of Taunton, who d. of small pox, in Dighton, about 11 mos. previous to his 2d marriage.

He m. June 1, 1790, (Fam. Rec.) dau. of John and Ruth (Talman) Pullen, of Somerset, and b. 1774 or 5. In the Autumn of 1791, he, and a friend, went to Charleston, S. C., and engaged in the Boot and Shoe trade, and returned in the May following. In Dec. 1799, went to Havana, and spent 3 winters successfully, in the Stove

* Dighton records have it 1792, but there must be an error.

trade, returning each spring to R. I. In his last voyage to Cuba, he was taken by a French privateer, and after being rifled of all, was put on shore, at Matanzas. In June, 1802, he returned, and went to Brattleborough, Vt., where he bought a farm. In April, 1815, he removed with his family to Adams, Jefferson Co., N. Y., where he died. His widow survives, in Adams, in her 85th yr., (1859.) He was a religious man, and universally respected. Had 9 chil.

89. IX. HANNAH,[6] b. March 16, 1771, d. June 2, 1849.

She m. Oct. 20, 1795, (22 Bristol Rec.,) William Throop, of Bristol, R. I., who was b. Aug. 15, 1771, and d. May 30, 1850. Res. Bristol, R. I. She was "the neatest woman in R. I.," said Dr. J. W. Richmond. Both were m. ch. Cong., and very excellent people. Rev. Dr. Shepard, of B., says of Mr. T., that "he was one of his most respected friends, and as cordial and fine a man as he ever knew." He was stone cutter by trade. He held the office of Town Clerk, and Clerk of the Court of Probate, in B. Chil.—

(1) *Thomas*, b. Jan. 26, 1797, d. Oct. 26, 1797.

(2) *Juliana*, b. Sept. 9, 1798, m. May, 1820, James Eppinger, a planter, of Savannah, now resident in Zebulon, Pike Co., Georgia. He has held the office of alderman, in S., 3 years, member of Legislature, 2 yrs., and Judge of the Inferior Court, 16 yrs. His chil—1, James Throop, b. Aug. 1821. Res. Cherokee Co., Texas. 2, Juliana T., b. May 9, 1823, m. Nov. 2, 1843, W. W. Arnold, of Z., who d. Nov. 25, 1853, leaving 3 chil., Attorney at Law. 3, John, b. April 4, 1825, m. Dec. 17, 1844, Elizabeth S. Milnor, and d. Oct. 1, 1850, in Texas, leaving 2 chil., Attorney at Law. He was a man of extraordinary attainments, sufficient to distinguish him any where, and would have soon attained a high position. He was engaged upon a work on Texas, which was not completed. The map has since been published. 4, Annie E., b. May 29, 1827. 5, Wm. Throop, b. Feb. 21, 1829. 6, Augusta F., b. June 30, 1831, d. June 22, 1833. 7, Robert, b. Oct. 5, 1833. 8, Edward Montgomery, b. Dec. 1, '35. 9, J. Augusta, b. Dec. 7, 1838, 10, Alethea F., b. June 21, '41.

(3) *J. Augusta*, b. Feb. 1812. Res. Zebulon, Ga. She is m. ch. Epis.

The following Obituary, published in the Griffin papers, is no unmerited tribute:—

Departed this life, at her residence in Pike County, Georgia, June 18th, 1859, in the 61st year of her age, Mrs. Juliana Eppinger, wife of Hon. James Eppinger, and daughter of the late Col. Wm. Throop, of Bristol, R. I.

In the decease of Mrs. Eppinger, society has lost one of the brightest monitors, to an intellectual and spiritual life. Endowed with remarkable grasp of intellect, her early education was thorough in philological studies, and elegant female accomplishments, while her unceasing thirst for knowledge, added to her attainments, all modern progression in science and literature. Gifted with a retentive memory, and uncommon fluency of diction, it was ever a pleasure to her, to communicate to others, from her ample intellectual stores, in language, unstudied, elegant and appropriate.

Noble and pure minded, her thoughts dwelt only on such subjects as refined human nature. Possessed of warm social instincts, her ready sympathy extended to all with whom she held intercourse, while her society and conversation elevated all around her.

Equally remarkable with her extensive mental attainments, was the extraordinary zeal with which she performed all domestic duties. Energetic and untiring, a faithful wife, a devoted mother, a warm friend, to her servants indulgent and affectionate to an extreme degree, none save those within her immediate circle, could realize her diligence in all that could contribute to the comfort and happiness of those around her, while her unselfish nature ever led her to assume every burden, to relieve others.

Unbounded in her benevolence of heart, she ever considered herself as but a stewardess of the gifts of fortune. Self-denying, in all personal gratification, her ready aid through life was ever extended to the poor and needy. None, save the almoners and recipients of her bounty knew of the countless benefits her charity ever extended; her heart responded to the claim of those less favored to a share of all that she possessed.

Comparing her attainments with the vast field of knowledge in Science and Art, and her spiritual life with the one model, she judged herself with a humility of self appreciation, few could comprehend. who knew her many and diverse gifts.

In her intense love of Nature, her heart breathed forth a constant hymn of gratitude to the Great Author of the Universe. Her appreciation of all that was beautiful, was one of her highest sources of enjoyment, and brightened each moment of her life, departing only with her last breath.

In early life, she dedicated herself to God's service, and having thus diligently walked in His commandments, her last moments were unobscured by a single shadow; no fear, no doubt, or regret visited her beatified soul. Joy and Love and Peace ineffable, filled her heart to overflowing. In the promises of Holy Writ, in the eloquent language of all her familiar poets, and in her own flowing diction, her lips breathed unceasingly, comfort to those to be soon bereaved; and without pain or struggle, her soul passed from peace on earth, to "life in Christ unchangeable."

"No strength of our own,
Or goodness we claim,
But since we have known
The Savior's great name,
In this our strong tower,
For safety we hide,
The Lord is our power,
The Lord will provide.

90. X. BETSEY,[6] b. 1773, d. March 9, 1827, ae. 54.

She m. pub. April 15, 1791, Benjamin Waldron, of Dighton, who d. 1836, over 60 yrs. of age. They removed to Bristol, N. Y., where they died. He was farmer and hotel keeper. Chil.—

(1) *William Richmond*, b. Aug. 24, 1792, d. Sept. 7, 1849. He m. and had 7 chil. Merchant in Ypsilanti, Mich., where his widow and chil. live. Chil.—1, Ann Elizabeth, b. Sept. 29, 1826, d. Aug. 26, '43. 2, Maria Louisa, b. Nov. 9, '28, d. April 21, '32. 3, Wm. Manson, b. March 30, '31. Res. Detroit. 4, Maria Louisa, b. Jan. 26, '33. 5, Thomas Barzillai, b. Nov. 29, '34. 6, Mary Esther, b. March 20, '37, d. Dec. 6, '39. 7, James Frederic, b. July 21, '40.

(2) *Eliza*,, b. May 13, 1794, m. Oct. 4, 1814. Horace Richmond, of Canandaigua. They removed to C. in 1814, and thence to Fremont, Ill., 1835, where he d. Sept. 1855. Jeweller and farmer. His chil.—1, Wm. H. b. July 5, 1815, m. Feb. 20, 1845, Dorcas E. Stoddard, m. 2dly, Oct. 1. 1848, Rosanna Quackenbush. Jeweller, in Peoria, Ill., 2 chil. 2, Arouet, b. Dec. 11, 1817, m. Oct. 9, 1845, Winifred Windate, 2dly, March 20, 1854, Caroline Locy. Bookseller in Detroit, Mich. 3, Emily M. b. April 11, 1820, m. Dec. 16, 1841, Seth Talbot, son of Seth, of Dighton. Res. Tremont, Ill. He is a

farmer, and has 2 chil. 4, Laura S. b. April 24, 1822, m Dec. 16, 1841, Alfred Lowell, of Tremont, Ill., and d. 1853. Three chil. 5, Elizabeth, b. Dec. 6, 1824, m. Aug. 14, 1845, Clifton H. Moore, a lawyer, in Clinton, Dewitt Co., Ill., 4 chil. 6, Benj'n B., b. March 18, 1827. Bookseller in Detroit. 7, Charles W., b. April 19, 1830, m. Aug. 20, 1855, Nancy Ely. Farmer in Mt. Pleasant, Dewitt Co., Ill. 8, Caroline, b. Aug. 25, 1832. Res. Pooria, unm.

(3) *Barzillai*, b. 1799, d. Sept. 24, 1840, unm. Merchant in Ypsilanti, Mich.

(4) *Nancy*, b. May 30, 1805, unm., and resides in Y., Mich.

91. XI. Barzillai,[6] b. Nov. 9, 1775, d. unm. before 1817.

He was a trader, in Somerset, at one time, a school teacher, in Dartmouth, and became deranged. He had fair abilities, and education, and some poetical talent. He became pious at an early age.

92. XII. Sarah,[6] b. June 2, 1777, d. June, 1795, unm., in Little Compton, at Col. Wm. Richmond's, her uncle, with whom she lived.

Children of JONATHAN WALKER,[5] [43] of Dighton.

93. I. Elizabeth,[6] b. Sept. 29, 1743.

She m. May 1766, Thomas Knowles, of Swansey, a farmer, first in Dighton, then removed to Norton, and d. about 1838. Had 6 sons, and 3 daus.

(1) *David*, Res. Washington, D. C. (2) *Henry*, Res. W. (3) *Asa*, Res. Norton, and d. about 1821. Had 5 chil. (4) *Edward*, Res. Providence, d. about 1825. Had children. (5) *Jonathan*, m. Ruth Richmond, and Lydia Walker. (See No. 194.) Res. Norton, and d. 1855, ae. 84 yrs. (6) *William*, removed to W. (7) *Polly*, m. Edward Kingman. Res. Mansfield. She d. May, 1855, ae. 82. Had 6 sons and 5 daus. (8) *Betsey*, m. Richard Newcomb, of Norton, a farmer. Had 8 chil. (9) *Deborah*, m. Elijah Avery, farmer. Res. Vermont. 5 chil.

By 2d Marriage.

94. II. Deborah,[6] b. Sept. 19, 1749, d. in infancy.

95. III. Deborah,[6] b. Sept. 28, '52, d. unm.

96. IV. Mary.[6]

She m. 1766, Thomas Layton or Lawton, of Swansey, who d. before 1787.

She m. 2dly, Kingsley.

97. V. Abigail,[6] d. about 1834.

She m. Oct. 1777, Joseph Newcomb, of Norton, who d. about 1832. Res. Norton. Farmer. No chil.

98. VI. JONATHAN,[6] (190.)

He m. June 4, 1792, Hannah (Anna, Rehoboth Rec.) Pierce, of R. Had 3 chil. He was in Capt. Elijah W.'s Co., and went to R. I., Dec., 1, 1776, 16 days. He was corporal, and went to Tiverton, Aug. 2, 1780. Res. Dighton, next to Gideon Walker's, on the south and not far from the Brick Meeting House.

CHILDREN OF NATHANIEL WALKER,[5] [44] OF DIGHTON.

99. I. NATHANIEL,[6] b. Dec. 19, 1747, d. ae. about 4 yrs.

100. II. EPHRAIM,[6] (194) b. Dec. 19, 1748, d. March 16, 1834. His brother, Nathaniel, d. about 4 yrs. of age. His name was then changed to Nathaniel. He m. Dorothy Bailey, of Little Compton, who d. Jan. 17, 1833. Res. Wellington, now Dighton. He was in Capt. Elijah Walker's Co., and went to R. I., Dec. 1, 1776, and to Tiverton, Aug. 2, 1780. He was a farmer, and a worthy man. Had 11 chil.

CHILDREN OF ELIJAH WALKER,[5] [52] OF DIGHTON.

101. I. HANNAH,[6] b. Feb. 12, 1744–5, d. Nov. 24, 1793, in 44th yr. unm. A very intelligent woman.

102. II. SARAH[6], b. June 13, 1752, d. July 11, 1824, in 74th yr.

She m. Gen. Asaph Wheeler, son of Rev. Aaron. He d. May 25, 1823, in 65th yr. Res. Dighton. Had 1 child—

(1) *Walker*, who d. Nov. 26, 1846. He was a teacher, and quite well educated.

103. III. WEALTHY,[6] d. Nov. 25, 1842, unm.

104. IV. RUTH,[6] d. Jan. 13, 1819, in 54th yr.

She m. Nov. 24, 1798, Abijah Austin of Dighton, who d. Jan. 29, 1856, in 86th yr. Had 1 child—

(1) *Hannah*, who m. Capt. Nathan Goff, farmer in Rehoboth, and d. March 28, 1831, in 27th yr. Had 4 child.

105. V. DARIUS,[6] d. of dysentery, ae. about 11 yrs.

106. VI. JOSIAH,[6] d. at same time, of dysentery.

107. VII. ZEBEDEE,[6] d. " " ae. 6 or 7 yrs.

108. VIII. MERCY,[6] d. " " 4 or 5 "

109. IX. ELIJAH,[6] drowned in the well, ae. about 8 yrs.

110. X. ELIJAH,[6] d. June 18, 1825, " 63 "

He was pub. April 6, 1821, to Sarah Chase. No chil. Farmer in Dighton. He fell dead in the woods while driving his oxen. In'y $5388. He was a soldier in the Revolution.

111. XI. MARY,[6] b. Sept. 28, 1753, d. unm.

112. XII. —— b, —— d. in infancy.

113. XIII. —— b. —— d. in infancy.

114. NEHEMIAH,[6] (205) b. Oct. 6. 1769, d. May 7, 1856, ae. 87 yrs. 7 mos. and 1 d. He was pub. Oct. 29, 1796, to Elizabeth Francis, who d. Feb. 18, 1847, in 71st yr. Res. Dighton, Farmer. He was Selectman, several yrs, and Representative in the State Legislature, 8 yrs, 1829 to 1836, inclusive. He exerted a large influence in town affairs. Had 11 chil.

CHILDREN OF PETER WALKER,[5] [53] OF TAUNTON.

115. I. ELEAZER,[6] (216) b. June 22, 1745, d. Sept. 1817.

He m. April 13, 1768, Caty, dau. of Comfort Carpenter, of Rehoboth, (Attleboro',?) who was b. Dec. 28, 1751, and d. May 11, 1834, ae. 82 yrs. Had 11 chil. Res. Norton. He was one of the minute men from N. in the Lexington alarm.

116. II. HANNAH, b. —— d. about 1815.

She was pub. Mar. 23, 1771, to Zebedee Sproat, of Middleboro', from whom she was divorced. Chil.—

(1) *Samuel.* (2) *Peter.* (3) *Lucinda,* a deaf mute. (4) *Caty.*

She m. 2dly, —— Walcott, of Attleboro'. No chil.

CHILDREN OF ELISHA WALKER,[5] [58] OF TAUNTON.

117. I. MOLLY,[6] d. in middle life.

She was pub. Jan. 16, 1778, to Darius Briggs, of Dighton. He was a Ship-joiner. They removed to N. Y. State, and nothing is known of their descendants.

118. II. MIRIAM,[6] b. 1756, d. 1839, ae. 83 yrs.

She m. Jonathan Richmond, son of Dea. Seth, of Taunton. He was b. Aug. 9, 1749, and d. Jan. 17, 1822. Farmer in (Richmond

James Walker

town,) Taunton. He was in 8 mos. service, 1775; went to R. I. on alarm, Dec. 8, '76, 25 days; on secret expedition, Sept. 29, '77, 24 miles 32 days, to Marshfield; to R. I. Aug. 1780, 3 mos. 19 d., and to R. I. July 12, 1781, till Nov. 30. He was Corporal in Brig'r Godfrey's Reg. Chil.—

(1) *Lucy*, b. June 24, 1778, m. Samuel Cain, of T. Had 4 chil.

(2) *Lydia*, m. Elias Richmond, and d. ae. 64.

(3) *Polly*, b. Jan. 10, 1782, m. Silas Richmond, bro. of E. R. 3 chil. She m. 2dly, Capt. Linus Washburn, and had 2 chil. She d. 1845, ae. 63.

(4) *Hannah*, b. Dec. 20, 1784, d. Oct. 1826, unm.

(5) *Sally*, b. July 4, 1786. m. Zenas Knapp, of T. No. chil. Res. South Bridgewater.

(6) *Walker*, b. June 23, 1788, m. Chloe Padelford. Res. Taunton. 7 chil.

(7) *Elisha*, b. Nov. 8, '90, m. Susanna Tinkham, and d. Sept. 10, 1849. 2 chil.

(8) *Miriam*, b. Nov. 12, '92, m. James Padelford. Res. T. 5 chil.

119. III. HANNAH,[6] d. young and unmarried.

120. IV. JAMES,[6] (227) b. Nov. 23, 1759, d. June 29, 1849, ae. 89 yrs., 7 mos. He m. Deborah Holmes, dau. of Gershom, of Taunton, (originally of Plymouth,) b. May 19, 1766, and d. Feb. 20, 1833, in 67th yr. They had 7 chil., 7 sons in succession. He was a farmer. Res. Taunton. He enlisted in the Revolutionary struggle, at the age of 17—was in the service, from Aug. 1, to Nov. 1776; in Capt. Haskin's Co., to guard the shore of Freetown, 11 days. On the alarm, Dec. 8, 1776, he went to Slade's Ferry, and was on duty 31 days; to Providence, June 22, '78, 23ds; was on R. I., 1 mo., 13ds, from July 29, '78; to Tiverton, March, '79, 24 days, and was one of the 6 mos. men from July 25, 1780, to Jan 25, '81. He was in the service longer than any one of his company, 34 of whom were from Taunton, and was discharged 200 miles from home. Though serving at various times during the War, he was in no battle. From 1831, he received the pension of $56,66. He was appointed 1st sergeant of Infantry, in the 5th Division, Sept 15, 1798, and received a Captain's commission, April 20, 1801, which he resigned, April 17, 1805. Having participated in the scenes of the Revolution, he was an ardent patriot, and could not brook the thought of any danger, to the liberties of his country.

Physically, he possessed a remarkable activity and power of endurance, and in youth excelled as a racer, and wrestler. He was high spirited, and had a keen sense of honor and wrong. He could never stoop to a mean thing, nor suffer his rights to be invaded. He and his wife united with the Cong'l ch. about 1800. Few persons become so familiar with the Scriptures as he was. (The author has never known any one.) The Bible, was for years his library, his study, and the whole seemed to be treasured in his memory, so that in his old age, he was exceedingly entertaining and instructive, in his recital of the history of the Old, and his exposition of the doctrines of the New Testament. It was a beautiful sight, the venerable old man, with his long white locks, and his face glowing with the inspiration of his favorite Book and theme.

He d., not by disease, but of old age. Both he and wife are buried in the orchard, in the rear of his house, he having selected 20 yrs. ago, a family burial place on the ancestral homestead.*

His fitting epitaph is—

> The hoary head is a crown of glory,
> When found in the way of righteousness.

She was a very domestic and amiable woman, and though of slender constitution, was patient, and resolute. Her epitaph is a just estimate of her character—

> Behold the Christian's grave; she walked with God,
> In the same path the dear Redeemer trod;
> She loved the church, and prayed for its increase,
> Lived much beloved, and died in perfect peace.

SEVENTH GENERATION.

Chil. of Lieut. ELIAKIM WALKER,[6] [61] of Taunton.

121. I. James,[7] d. June 21, 1831, in 71st yr.

He m. Mary, dau. of Elkanah Tisdale. She d. April 30, 1851, in 89th yr. No chil. Res. Taunton, (Rocky Woods,) on the farm now owned by Geo. Walker, Esq. (See No. 144.) He gave $500 to the 1st Cong'l Ch., for the building of a new Meeting house, in 1825. His widow gave the organ to the society. Both m. ch. He possessed unusual intelligence, and vigor of mind, and was very orthodox in religious opinion. Says Rev. A. Cobb, his pastor many years, "he knew Jonathan Edwards from beginning to end."

* It was not then known, that the Cemetery on the bank of the Taunton river, is the Family Burial Place of the Walkers. The compiler has since discovered, that their oldest ancestor and his wife were buried there, (1678 and 1692,) and that it is almost wholly occupied by his descendants, and was deeded for that purpose, by Edward Walker, (See Nos. 2 and 22.) Had this been known, there would, undoubtedly, have been no departure from the custom of 150 yrs., nor from the purpose of their kinsman, the grantor, "to all relations that I have, or shall have, to lye for a burying place, forever," where they "may bury their dead."

122. II. BENJAMIN,[7] (238) b. July 30, 1763, d. Sept. 13, 1835, ae. 72 yrs. He m. Aug. 4, 1789, Hannah Crane, dau. of John, of Norton, and sister of Rev. Dr. Crane, of Northbridge, b. June 8, 1766, and d. Aug. 16, 1790, in 25th yr., leaving 1 child.

He m. 2dly, pub. Sept. 28, 1799, Hannah, dau. of Ebenezer Walker. (See No. 130.) She was m. ch. Cong'l. He gave $1000, in 1825, towards the erection of the church edifice of the 1st Society, in Taunton. He was a man of superior excellence of character, and of uncommon understanding. Res. T., (Rocky Woods,) on the homestead now occupied by his grandson, Mr. Gulliver. In'y $10,245. He was in Capt. Blake's Co., and went to Tiverton, Aug. 2, 1780, and also served in Capt. Haskin's Co., and Col. Dean's Regiment.

He was one of the petitioners to the Gen. Court, respecting the religious society, in T., in 1790. He was active in the movement in 1792, which separated the ancient church from the Town Parish, and organized a new society in the west part of the town. Their first meeting was held in Dea. Isaac Tubbs' barn. The cause of the separation was the attempt to settle Mr. John Foster, over the old Society. The love of sound doctrine lead these separatists, who comprised all the church excepting 4 persons, to make these sacrifices. Active in the movement, he was willing to devote his money to its maintenance. He is entitled to gratitude for his christian patriotism, on the principle, that "he loveth our nation, for he hath built us a synagogue."

CHILDREN OF PERES WALKER,[6] [62] OF TAUNTON.

123. I. PERES,[7] (239) b. Jan. 22, 1769, in Dighton, d. Jan. 11, 1807, in 38th yr. He m. Nov. 5, 1789, Chloe Wheeler, of Rehoboth, dau. of Capt. Aaron. She was b. April 26, 1773, and d. May 1, 1844, in Canandaigua, N. Y., having married twice since his death. He removed to Bloomfield, Ontario Co., N. Y., in Autumn of 1804, where he died. He was a Farmer, and m. ch. Bap.

124. II. ELIAKIM,[7] (244) b. April 30, 1776, d. Oct. 9, 1839.

He m. March 14, 1800, Rhoda Horton, of Swansey, who d. March 25, '58. He emigrated to Bristol, N. Y., about 1802, and in 1831, settled as a farmer, in Salem, Washtenau Co., Mich., where he died. Had 6 chil. His widow m. 2dly, and d. March 25, 1858.

125. III. TISDALE,[7] (250) b. Nov. 11, 1785, d. Oct. 24, 1816, in 31st yr. He m. Feb. 10, 1805, Mercy Lincoln, of Taunton, dau.

of Benj'n, b. March 5, 1785, and d. Aug. 26, 1844. He emigrated to Bristol, N. Y., in 1806, where he died, a farmer. She m. 2dly, 1817, Ephraim Hicks, and removed to Mich.

CHIL. OF ELNATHAN WALKER,[6] [66] OF HARTLAND, VT.

126. I. HANNAH,[7] b. 1753, d. quite aged.

She m. in 1773, Peter Saunders, of Woodstock, Ct., a nephew of Admiral Saunders, of the British Navy. He served in the War of the Revolution. Res W. Had 8 chil.

127. II. MATILDA,[7] b. Dec. 18, 1760, d. July 2, 1835.

She m. Dec. 9, 1779, Dr. Jacob Corey, of Sturbridge. Res. S. He was remarkable for his indefatigable industry, perseverance and uniform cheerfulness. He made the most of his mental and bodily capabilities, and became a skillful physician. Quite a number of young men pursued their professional studies under his direction. Chil.—

(1) *Betsey*, b. Feb. 26, 1781, d. March 13, 1826. She m. May 11, 1806, Doct. Justus Keyes, of Western, son of Edward, of Ashford, Ct. He was an eminent physician. Both Cong'ts. Res. Brimfield, and Western. Chil. —1, Mary Ann, b. March 4, 1808, m. Russell T. Wheelock, and d. in Amherst, Feb. 16, 1844. He is a farmer, in A., Chairman of Select-men in 1856. His 7 chil. are—Edward Keyes, b. April 4, 1827, d. April 14, 1857. George Vernon, b. Jan. 25, 1829. Res. Chicopee. One of the Proprietors and Editors of the Chicopee Journal. John Francis, b. Feb. 23, 1831. Elizabeth Ruth, b. June 12, 1834. Wm. Augustus, b. July 25, 1837. Arthur H., b Nov. 1839, d. May, 1842. Mary Annette, b. Nov. 1843, d. May, 1844. 2, Erasmus Darwin, b. May 19, 1810. He was educated at West Point, and is Capt. in U. S Army. He m. Miss Clark. 3, Elias, afterward Edward Lawrence, b. Aug 3, 1812, m. Lucy Brooks, grand dau. of Gov. Brooks, and had 5 chil. He was a merchant, but became Editor, Representative and Senator in the State Legislature, Member of the Governor's Council, Commissioner for building alms-houses, and was honored with other offices of trust and distinction. He posessed a high order of talents, and d. June 6, 1859, of softening of the brain. Res. Dedham.

(2) *Matilda*, b. Feb. 28, 1783, d. June 5, 1831. She m. June 30, 1805, Doct. Elijah Morse, of South Brimfield. He was a shrewd, grave and religious man. Both Bap. Chil.—1, Laura A. 2, Charlotte M. 3, Elijah C.

(3) *Enoch*, b. Jan. 23, 1785, d. July 19, 1827, in S. He m. April 29, 1810, Lydia, dau. of Richard Cole, of S.

(4) *Jacob Jr.*, b. June 13, 1788, d. Oct. 31, 1841. He m. Oct. 17, 1813, Mrs. Mary, relict of Capt. Benj'n Bullock, of S. Both Cong'ts. He was

a physician in S., and honored with several town offices. Chil.—1, Eliza, d. 2, Charlotte, d. 3, Jacob A.

(5) *Hannah*, d. in infancy.

(6) *Lucinda*, d. in infancy.

(7) *Fanny*, b. Dec. 12, 1793, d. June 29, 1839. She m. May 15, 1814, Col. Hiram Wheelock, of S., son of Eli, of Charlton. Both Cong'ts. Had 6 chil.

(8) *Charlotte*, b. Aug. 27, 1796, d. May 14, 1824. She m. Doct. Sylvanus Curtis, of S., Aug. 8, 1818, an amiable and talented man. Both Bap. Res. S. and Mt. Vernon, Me. Has dau. Mary.

(9) *George Vernon*, b. Oct. 8, 1800. He m. Nov. 28, 1828, Eliza Warren, of S. He m. 2dly, Oct. 1837, Martha M. Griggs, dau. of Orlando, of Brimfield. She is Cong'st. Res. S., on the old homestead. He has been Town Clerk, Representative to the Legislature, and held other town offices. He is a Printer and Farmer, and in religious opinions a Unitarian. His chil.—1, George Gordon, b. 1829. 2, Gilbert M., b. 1831. 3, Charles V., b. 1838. 4, Elizabeth M., b. 1841. 5, Charlotte L., b. 1844. 6, Francis E., b. 1856.

(10) *Francis E.*, b. Sept 25, 1804. He m. April 25, 1831, Vernera, dau. of Rev. Zenas L. Leonard, of S. She is m. ch. Bap. He is now a merchant, in Madison, Ind. Chil.—1, Helen. 2, Sally. 3, Josephine.

128. III. ELNATHAN,[7] (254) b. Dec. 12, 1765, in Woodstock, Ct., d. May 22, 1848. He m. 1794, Olive, dau. of Major Joseph Call. She d. July 28, 1797, ae. 28 yrs.

He m. 2dly, 1800, Olive, dau. of Lieut. John Burke. She d. Aug. 11, 1849. He was a farmer, in Hartland, Vt. It is said of him and his brother James, that when in their prime, there were few men who could outwork or outwit them. Had 7 chil.

129. IV. JAMES,[7] (261) b. Feb. 5, 1768, d. March 29, 1816.

He m. 1796, Jane, dau. of Robert Morrison, of Windsor, Vt. She d. Sept. 15, 1817, ae. 39 yrs. and 4 mos. He removed from Woodstock, Ct., with his parents to Hartland, Vt., about 1778. He was a farmer, and d. in H. Had 6 chil. See what is said of him under No. 128.

CHILDREN OF EBENEZER WALKER,[6] [67] OF DIGHTON.

130. I. HANNAH,[7] b. Feb. 26, 1772, d. July 27, 1833, ae. 61 yrs. and 5 mos. She m. Benj'n Walker. (See No. 122.)

The sermon preached by Rev. Mr. Cobb, Sept. 22, 1833, occasioned by her death, was published.

131. II. RUTH,[7] b. Nov. 3, 1773, d. Nov. 1850.

She was pub. Sept. 9, 1796, to Moses Lincoln, of Taunton. Res. Norton. Chil.—

(1) *Ruth*, b. 1797. (2) *Benj.* b. Aug. 5, 1800. (3) *Ginnason*, d. June 4, 1846. (4) *Silas*. (5) *Sumner*, b. April 1, 1810.

132. III. ELIZABETH,[7] b. March 15, 1780, d. Jan. 6, 1836, ae. 55 yrs. She m. April 15, 1802, Abijah Pratt, of Taunton, who d. July 1851, ae. 75 yrs., an intelligent and worthy man. She is m. ch. Cong'l. Chil.—

(1) *Ebenezer Walker*, b. Oct. 1802, m. Abigail, dau. of Gilbert Lincoln, of Taunton, b. May 1804. She is m. ch. Cong. He is mason and farmer, in Taunton. Have 2 chil.—1, Gilbert W., m. Sarah A. Lincoln, have Lizzie Florence, b. Jan. 17, 1856. 2, ———.

(2) *Almira*, b. Sept. 1804, m. ch. Cong., unm.

(3) *Lovina*, b. Nov. 1807, m. Calvin Hunt, of Norton. Chil.—1, Sarah, 17. 2, George, 15. 3, Laura Jane, (1855.)

(4) *Sidney Tisdale*, b. Sept. 1816. Res. Dartmouth, unm.

(5) *Hannah*, b. Aug. 1813, m. Jones Godfrey, of Norton, farmer. She is m. ch. Bap. Chil.—1, Hannah E., b. Aug. 1837, Teacher. 2, Lebe Ann, b. Dec. 1838. 3, Martha A., b. 1839 or 40. 4, Emily Judson, b. about 1842. 5, Jones W., b. 1844.

(6) *Eliza*, b. Sept. 1821, m. John Calvin Crane, of Norton. Res. in N. She is m. ch. Bap. Chil.—1, Henry Calvin, b. Nov. 30, 1845. 2, Chas. Newcomb, b. July 14, 1852. 3, Lillie Anna, b. March 19, 1858.

133. IV. POLLY,[7] b. May 10, 1784.

She m. June 18, 1809, Israel Pierce 3d, of Rehoboth. Had—

(1) *Walker*, b. 1810. (2) *Israel*.

134. V. LYDIA,[7] b. Jan. 4, 1786.

She m. Nov. 26, 1806, Peter Burt, son of Thomas and Zilpha (Haskins,) of Taunton. Res. T. Chil.—

(1) *Peter*, b. Dec. 7, 1807, m. April 4, 1837, Laura Taylor, of Ct., and has Lydia Ann, b. 1838.

(2) *Henry*, b. July 24, 1810, d. Dec. 23, 1830.

(3) *Leonard*, b. Feb. 15, 1814. Farmer in T., unm.

(4) *Benjamin*, b. June 20, 1816, m. Harriet F. Standish, and had 2 chil. m. 2dly, Elizabeth Warren, of N. H. Res. Nashua, N. H. A moulder.

(5) *John*, b. June 14, 1822. Farmer in T., unm.

CHILDREN OF LIEUT. PETER WALKER,[6] [73] OF TAUNTON.

135. I. HELEN,[7] b. about Feb. 1771, d. Feb. 23, 1811, in 41st yr.

She m. Leonard Hathaway of Dighton, who d. March 12, 1820, in 53d yr. He was Rep. to Legislature from D. 1813. She was m. ch. Cong'l. Chil.—

(1) *Leonard*, b. Dec. 17, 1792, was pub. Aug. 14, 1819, to Sally H. Lincoln, of Taunton, and have Helen, Allen, Leonard and Amelia W. (See No. 454.)

(2) *Sally*, b. Feb. 28, 1795, m. William Reed, of T. Four chil. She m. 2dly, —— Jones, son of Seth.

(3) *Allen*, b. Jan. 15, 1799, d. unm.

(4) *Bradford*, b. Oct. 19, 1801, d. Oct. 15, 1842, was pub. Aug. 6, 1825, to Mary Burt of T., who d. Dec. 4, 1837, in 33d yr. Was Lieut.

136. II. PHEBE,[7] b. June, 1773, d. about 1847, in Ill.

She m. Jan. 18, 1818, Dea. James Gooding, of Bristol, N. Y., her cousin, (See No. 71.) No chil. Res. Gooding's Grove, Ill., where he d. about 1849, ae. 82 yrs.

137. III. BETHIAH,[7] b. July, 1775, d. Sept. 1835.

She was pub. April 21, 1821, to Silas Lincoln, of Taunton, who d. Feb. 1, 1726, ae. 54. Farmer in T. She m. ch. Cong. No chil.

138. IV. PETER,[7] (267) b. Feb. 8, 1778, d. Aug. 9, 1800.

He m. Sept. 30, 1798, Rhoda Lincoln, dau. of Benj'n, 2d, of Taunton, b. 1781, d. Dec. 9, 1825. He held the office of Lieut., and was cut down in early manhood, from good health and high hope, by rapid consumption. Had 1 son.

139. V. ELNATHAN,[7] (268) b. Feb. 18, (Feb. 7, Fam. Rec.) 1780, in Taunton, d. June 4, 1820. He m. 1811, Aurelia King, of Sharon, Conn., who d. Nov. 26, 1821, ae. 40 yrs. He fitted for Coll. at Bristol Academy, in T.; grad. at Brown University, Sept. 7, 1803; united with the Ch. in Dighton, Jan. 31, 1805. He began the study of Theology, with Rev. Dr. Emmons, of Franklin. He was ord. Oct. 25, 1809, and at the same time installed Pastor of the Pres. Congregation in Homer. N. Y., which relation he sustained till his death.

The following is part of the sketch in the History of the Mendon Association, furnished by Rev. A. Cobb, of Taunton and Rev. S. Raymond, of Bridgwater. (See Hist., p. 282.*)

"Mr. W. was a slow, but patient and thorough scholar. In his youth, he was sedate, amiable, and beloved by all in his native place."

"It is related that several persons became at one time somewhat uneasy, under Mr. W.'s ministry, and agitated the subject of his dismission. He promptly responded to the suggestion, and a council was invited to consider the question. An anxious people assembled to await the result. The Moderator opened the Session with a prayer, of peculiar fervor and earnestness, especially praying for the movers of so responsible a step as severing the pastoral relation. The spirit of the prayer awakened new thoughts and feelings in the assembly. At its close, one of the chief agitators requested a delay of the proceedings, and moved before the church, are consideration of the matter

* The account of Mr. W.'s children in Hist. of M. Association is incorrect.

to be presented to the council: which motion was unanimously carried. The council, instead of dismissing the pastor, were invited to stay, and assist him in gathering in the fruits of a most extensive and precious revival, of which God's answer to that prayer was the beginning. The question of his dismission was never afterwards agitated."

In an Obituary in the "Cortland Repository," Homer, N. Y., June 9, 1820, his character, ministry and last days, received the following tribute:—

"In his removal, his bereaved family have lost an amiable and affectionate husband and father, the church and people of H. have lost a faithful and beloved pastor, and the public a real and worthy friend. Mr. W. possessed an assemblage of amiable qualities. He was a man of real politeness and good breeding, frank, mild, and hospitable. His affection for his family appeared sincere and ardent, and he participated largely in the pleasures of domestic life. His house was a habitation of friendship and peace, open to receive his friends and acquaintances with the greatest cordiality. His mind was formed for society, and he possessed a talent for rendering himself agreeable to those who were favored with his company.

As a Christian, he was diligent and exemplary. Though he was seldom carried out in high religious transports, yet he appeared to maintain a steady and solid hope in Christ, and an habitual peace in believing. He was a "lover of good men, sober, just, holy and temperate," in such a degree as rendered him a real ornament to the religion he professed. He was of a remarkably pacific disposition and excelled in the exercise of meekness, forbearance, and good will towards those who differed from him in religious opinion. Though his own sentiments were settled and firm, he was not forward to denounce those who thought differently from him. He evidently succeeded in an eminent degree in suppressing those envious and malignant feelings which are too apt to be indulged towards other denominations.

As a Minister, he set an example of prudence, patience and fidelity. He was a firm advocate for the doctrines of grace. He preached them plainly; and cheerfully and decidedly bore testimony in their favor on his dying bed. He was a friend to revivals of religion by the efficacious influences of the Holy Spirit, and with these the people of his charge have been peculiarly blessed. No less than three general revivals were experienced in the congregation during his pastoral connection with them. The following summary will exhibit the state of the church, at the commencement and close of his ministry:

The whole number of communicants in the Ch. at the time of his settlement, was 99. He received into membership during his pastorate of 10½ yrs., 468; dismissed, 88; lost by death, 48; excommunicated, 4; and left a membership of 427. He baptized 108 adults, 563 infants—whole number, 671.

We record this to the honor of Divine Grace; and also for the purpose of illustrating the ministerial character and usefulness of the deceased. These things appear to contain a Divine testimony in his favor, as an approved herald of Redeeming grace.

He was not so much a man of display as of real good sense and merit. His discourses were plain, instructive and practical, calculated to edify the pious mind, and to alarm the sinner. The spiritual interests of his congregation, appeared to lie near his heart, and he was ready to spend and be spent in their service.

During the revival, the winter past, he was exceedingly laborious, in preaching, attending conferences, and visiting from house to house. He appeared to spare no pains by day or night which were necessary for the good of his flock. His last public performance was at a conference meeting, in the centre of the parish. At the close of this meeting he informed individuals that he was much indisposed, and expressed his belief that he was going to be sick. He was seized with a violent fever, and a local affection in the left side of the chest, attended with a cough, which could not be removed by the most anxious and spirited efforts of physicians. His case soon became dangerous, and at length extinguished all hope of his recovery. The period from the commencement of his sickness to his decease, was about 7 weeks. The first part of this time, he manifested a considerable anxiety to recover, especially for the sake of his family. But for 3 or 4 weeks before his death he became much resigned to the thought of his departure, and spoke upon the subject with great freedom and composure. He was able to resign his wife and children into the hands of God, together with his congregation and friends, and to wait with cheerfulness and submission for his Master's call. His religious views and affections, though not of so ravishing a description as are sometimes manifested, were clear, rational and soul-satisfying. It is not saying too much, to affirm that he appeared and conversed like a christian. The hope which he had indulged for many years, now increased and brightened, and the grounds of this hope appeared to be truly scriptural. He had many happy hours, so that his "sick bed," to use his own words, "was like a bed of roses." He seemed evidently to enjoy a good degree of divine consolation and support. With solemn composure he arranged his temporal concerns, and set his house in order. He appeared confident that his time to die had come, and spoke freely to the numerous and anxious visitants, as one that was just about to appear in the presence of his Judge. He expressed great affection for his people, which was reciprocated by great numbers who came to his house. He was anxious to say something, either by way of instruction, counsel or warning, to every one who came in.

He exemplified the religion of his Savior in exercising a tender and forgiving spirit, towards such as had formerly been his opposers, and in expressing an anxious desire to see every one of them, and if possible, to have everything removed out of the way, so that he could die in peace with all men. No revenge, malice or envy, seemed to have a place in his heart. But on the contrary, his bosom glowed with forgiveness, kindness and love.

Near the last stage of his sickness, he was so much afflicted with an accumulation upon his lungs, that he was obviously in danger of suffocation. At one time, a few days previous to his death, he observed to his attendants, "It is best to call the people into the room, for I am so much distressed for breath that I can not live but a short time." He was asked if he could say, "Come, Lord Jesus, come quickly," "O, yes," he replied, "Lord Jesus, come quickly, thou Savior of sinners. Thou knowest that I have been a great sinner. My hope is in Thee. Thou Savior of sinners, take me to Thyself;" and folding his arms together he said, "Fold me in Thine arms, O, Divine Savior. I am about to leave my friends in this world, O, Savior of sinners, take me to Thyself. Thou knowest that I have given myself to Thee, time after time. Have not I done it without reserve? O, Lord, Thou knowest, Thou knowest, whether I have deceived myself." He was asked if he could not put his confidence in God. "O, yes," he said, "my confidence is strong in the Lord. Oh! my friends, I am just going into Eternity, how important to be always ready. I am going my friends, to sing the song of Moses, and the Lamb forever, and ever, and ever, and ever." He afterwards revived, and said it had been his earnest desire that he might not die by suffocation, but calm, composed and calling on God, as Stephen did, to receive his spirit. He was asked if he could not say "Father, not my will but thine be done." "O, yes," said he, "Father, not my will but Thine be done. If it be for Thy glory that I should die in this manner, Thy will be done. I go at Thy bidding." He did not finally suffocate. He lived about 3 days, and while his reason continued, made many interesting remarks, and the last words which he was heard to articulate, were, "Lord Jesus, receive my spirit."

In short, his whole conversation and deportment were such as to furnish the most satisfactory evidence, that he was what he professed, and that he was prepared for the exchange of wolrds. Some days previous to his decease he said that it would be very desirable to depart on the Lord's day. His desire in this respect was granted.

His funeral was attended on the 6th inst., by a concourse of more than 2000 people assembled to pay their last tribute of respect to departed worth.

Eleven of the neighboring clergy were present to participate in the affecting solemnities of the day. An interesting and instructive discourse was delivered by Rev. Dirck C. Lansing, from Heb. 11th, 27th, "For he endured as seeing Him who is invisible."

The conclusion of a sermon preached to his people in Groton, N. Y., by Rev. Joshua Dean, in reference to the death of Rev. Mr. W., his intimate friend, was published in the Cortland Repository, June 16, 1820, and contains an affectionate and deserved tribute.

The "Cortland Repository," of Dec. 4, 1821, contained an Obituary of Mrs. W., from which the following extracts are taken :—

Died, in this village on the 26th ult., after a very lingering and distressing illness, Mrs Aurelia Walker, aged 40 yrs. Mrs. W. was born and educated in Sharon, Conn. Possessing an unusual share of native politeness, a sound judgment, a mild and uniform temper, and a kind and generous disposition, accompanied with a modest and amiable deportment, excellent economy, a good

George Walker

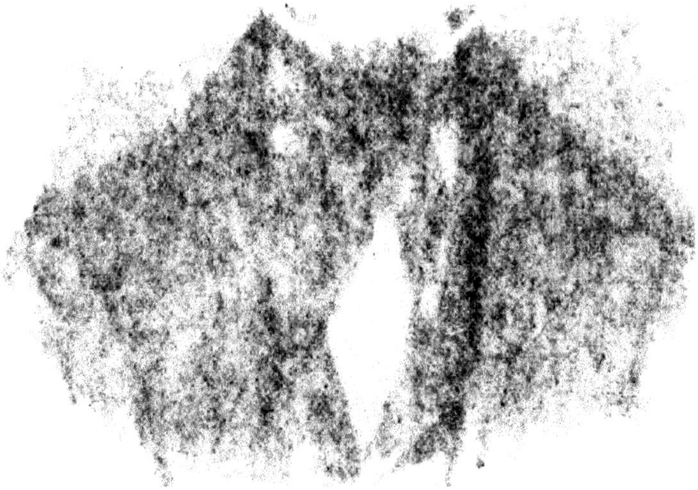

education, a knowledge of human nature, and a spirit of piety and christian benevolence, she was eminently qualified for the important and conspicuous station in which Providence had placed her. Always in possession of the ornament of a meek spirit, she exhibited an example, which not only gained the confidence and esteem of her other christian friends, but of all with whom she formed an acquaintance. Uncommon as it is in these degenerate times, we cannot learn that the tongue of slander ever assailed her. About six months after the death of Mr. W., she was attacked with hemorrhage from the lungs, and gradually declined. During the whole period, 11 mos. and a half, she had to pass through the most trying scenes of bodily pain and distress. But amidst all her sufferings and affliction, she was patient and submissive. Not a murmur escaped her lips, her soul was stayed on God. In this tranquil state of mind she continued with an unwavering faith anticipating her passport to Heaven, in the full exercise of her reason till she sunk into the arms of death. Near the closing scene, being asked the state of her mind she said, "All is well." The last words which she distinctly articulated, were, "God bless my children."

140. VI. GEORGE GOODING,[7] (271) b. Feb. 17, 1781, d. Feb. 16, 1831. He m. Sept. 22, 1803, Zilpha, dau. of Benj'n Lincoln, 2d, of Taunton. She d. Oct. 26, 1822, ae. 36 yrs. He commanded a company of Militia several years. In religious opinion a Universalist. Had 6 chil.

141. VII. DEBORAH,[7] b. Aug. 1785, d. Nov. 1850.

She m. Sept. 24, 1805, Henry Baylies, of Dighton, and had—

(1) *Henry*, deceased. (2) *Horatio*, nothing known of him.

She m. ch. Cong. She m. 2dly, James Wilbor, and had 6 chil.—

(3) *Elnathan W.*, b. 1812. (4) *James L.* (5) *George.* (6) *Perry A.* (7) *Deborah W.* (8) *Phebe.*

142. VIII. ZEPHANIAH,[7] b. 1787, d. ae. 28 yrs., at Alexandria, D. C., of consumption.

143. IX. EBENEZER,[7] (277) b. Feb. 25, 1789, d. March 3, 1857, in a fit. He m. Dec. 26, 1810, Betsey Lincoln, dau. of Benj'n, 2d, and Zilpha Lincoln, of West Taunton. Both m. ch. Cong. Res. West Taunton, on homestead that was his father's. Had 8 chil.

CHIL. OF DOCT. GEORGE WALKER[6], [76] OF DIGHTON.

144. I. GEORGE,[7] (285) b. Sept. 15, 1792.

He m. June 22, 1828, Eliza Briggs, dau. of Eliakim and Elizabeth, and b. Sept. 13, 1801. She is a pious woman, Cong. Have 10 chil. He lived in Dighton and served the town of D. and Wellington as an Assessor for a number of years, and did Military duty as Ensign and Lieut. about 7 yrs. In 1828, removed into Taunton, hired a house and performed farm labor for those who needed assistance, and represented the Town in the Legislature, in 1833, 4, 5, 6 and 7. He was one of the Select-men for several years, and received, the Commission of

Justice of the Peace in 1840. He has been a surveyor of land more than 40 yrs., and as such, been employed in most of the towns of Bristol Co., and somewhat in Plymouth Co.

He is theoretically and practically a strong opposer to the use of intoxicating liquors. From his youth to the present time, he has labored as hard in all weathers, with axe, hoe and scythe, as any person of his acquaintance, and from his earliest childhood, never drank one drop of intoxicating liquor of any kind. In the yr. 1822, in Western, N. Y., when mowers were pouring down the whiskey, he drank his milk and water, and on no day did he find a man who could do more work than himself. He writes, "I claim to be the oldest person in the state, who has totally abstained from all intoxicating drinks." It is his firm conviction that a condition of health, never needed spirituous liquors. Res. Taunton, (Rocky Woods.) He is a man of sound judgment, great energy, fearless and faithful to his convictions. No man is more respected for sterling integrity, and he has wielded no small influence in the affairs of the town. With a retentive memory he has preserved the traditions of the family, and by his unwearied interest has done much to aid the author of this Genealogy, gathering many facts which supplement the lost records of the town. The author is indebted to no man more than to him for appreciative sympathy, and industrious gleaning.

145. II. LEONARD,[7] b. Jan. 23, 1794, d. Sept. 18, 1795.

146. III. ABIGAIL,[7] b. June 8, 1796.

She m. Sept. 28, 1826, Lemuel Morse, of Rehoboth, son of Elijah. Farmer in R., possessing great mathematical talent. She and all her daus. are m. ch. Meth. Chil.—

(1) *Ruth Ann*, b. June 19, 1827, m. 1851, Artemas Briggs, of Rehoboth, and have, Elroy A., b. Feb. 14, 1856.

(2) *Abigail M.*, b. Oct. 18, 1828, d. Feb. 19, 1830.

(3) *Abigail M.*, b. March 29. 1830, m. Oct. 30, 1853, Othniel G. Stephens, of Rehoboth, and have—1, Abbie E. F., b. Sept. 24, 1854, d. July 30, 1857. 2, Frederick M., b. June 24, 1856. 3, Abby Maria, b. March 10, 1858.

(4) *Maria, P.* b. Dec. 22, 1831.

(5) *Lemuel*, b, March 24, 1834.

(6) *Eliza J.*, b. Feb. 28, 1836.

(7) *Lydia E.*, b. Feb. 24, 1838.

147. IV. PHEBE,[7] b. 1799, d. Oct. 8, 1844, ae. 45, unm. She was m. ch. Cong., and an excellent christian woman.

148. V. BETSEY,[7] b. May 13, 1801.

She m. July 4, 1822, Abel Crane, son of Luther and Sarah (Strobridge,) of Berkley. Res. West Taunton, a farmer. Both m. ch. Cong. Chil.—

(1) *Alvan S.*, b. Aug. 27, 1823, unm., farmer.

(2) *William S.*, b. March 4, 1825, d. April, 1832.

(3) *Sarah J.*, b. Aug. 18, 1827, d. April 10, 1832.

(4) *Abel*, b. Sept. 14, 1829, d. April 2, 1832.

(5) *Betsey B.*, b. Aug. 2, 1831, m. Wm. D. Jones, (See No. 72,) of Norton, June, 1854. 1 son, b. 1855.

(6) *Sarah J.*, b. Sept. 8, 1833, d. April 18, 1833.

(7) *Sophia A.*, b. June, 1835, m. Francis Stephens, of Rehoboth, Jan. 1855.

(8) *Abel*, b. June 4, 1837.

(9) *Caroline F.*, b. June 18, 1839.

(10) *Emily Josephine*, b. Oct. 9, 1842.

CHILDREN OF NATHAN WALKER,[6] [77] OF DIGHTON.

149. I. JOHN,[7] (295) b. 1769, d. Feb. 14, (15, Ins.) 1850, in 81st yr. (Ins.) He m. Feb. 26, 1791, Rebekah Williams, dau. of Simeon Williams, of Dighton, who d. Oct. 18, 1848, ae. 81. (Ins.) (Fam. Rec., in 81st yr.) He was a private in the Continental Army. Res. Dighton. Farmer, and had 4 chil.

150. II. ABIGAIL,[7] b. March 31, 1770, d. July 20, 1854.

She m. Sept. 9, 1799, Ebenezer Richmond, of Barnard, Vt. He was son of Ebenezer and Mercy, and b. in Taunton, (See No. 38,) June 10, 1770, d. June 6, 1840. He early emigrated to Vermont, and settled in B. as a farmer. Chil.—

(1) *Dorothy.* (2) *Laurinda.* (3) *William.* (4) *Lorenzo.* (5) *Charles.*

151. III. DOROTHY or DOLLY.[7]

She m. Jan. 1793, Wm. Pitts, and d. one yr. after. No chil. He m. 2dly, and left a large estate. Res. Pittstown, Genesee Co., N. Y., which was named from him.

152. IV. CATHARINE,[7] b. March 20, 1776, d. Sept. 2, 1827, in Hanover, N.Y. She m. May 3, 1796, Billings Throop, of Bristol, R.I. who was b. in B., Aug. 26, 1771, and d. July 21, 1856. Removed to Barnard, Vt., soon after his marriage, and bought a farm, which with his trade of cooper, occupied him several years. He then engaged in the business of driving cattle and horses to Boston and Providence. In 1822, he removed to Middlebury, N. Y., and in a year and a half, to Hanover, N. Y., and then his wife dying, he went to Toronto, C. W. and finally to Algonquin, Ill., and died. He was not educated

but had a strong mind. She was a sprightly, interesting, and pious woman. Their chil.—

(1) *Billings*, b. March 23, 1796, in Barnard, d. unm. in Hanover, N. Y., Aug. 1, 1829. Farmer, and Universalist.

(2) *Nathan*, b. July 1, 1798, m. Jan. 20, 1830, Mary E. Munshaw, in Canada West, and d. Aug. 23, 1850. He was carpenter and machinist, removed to C. W. Remaining only 4 yrs., he went to Marshall, Mich., thence in a year, to Gull Prairie, thence a year after, to Grand Haven, Mich., and then in 1838, took charge of a Public House, and in 1840, bought a steam saw mill, and engaged in the lumber trade, till his death. He left a wife and daughter, bequeathing a large property to them, in equal division.

(3) *Rebecca W.*, b. Aug. 8, 1801. She m. Feb., 1819, in Rochester, N. Y., Muston C. Luce, who was b. in Stow, Vt., and was the adopted son of his uncle, Judge Elihu Luce. He was b. 1800, and was a carpenter, but took charge of a Public House, and then engaged in the grocery trade, at Grand Rapids, Mich., June, 1846. He left $ 75,000 to a wife and son. She is m. Bap. ch.

(4) *Susan*, b. Aug. 16, 1804, m. in Hanover, N. Y., Aug. 10, 1829, Rufus W. Nevins, who was b. in Hadley, C. E., Aug. 24, 1802. A farmer in Hanover, N. Y. Have 5 ch. Both are m. Meth. ch.

(5) *Hosea B.*, b. July 24· 1806. He m. in Perrysburg, N. Y., Zilpha Prentiss, and is a farmer in Algonquin, Ill., where he settled in 1839. He has been County Commissioner of McHenry County, for 6 yrs. In 1851, he removed to Woodstock, Ill., where his wife died, Dec. 17, 1853, ae. 48, m. Meth. ch. He m. 2dly, May 10, 1854, Lizzie Shafer, in A. who was b. in Dundaff, Pa., Jan. 27, 1829. She is m. Meth. ch, and he is a Universalist. Has 3 chil.

(6) *Abigail S.*, b. July 26, 1809, d. Oct. 9. 1843. She m. Stephen M. Ball, March 6. 1831, in Hanover, and had 4 chil. She was a Universalist, and d. in her faith. He was b. in Pompey, N. Y., Dec. 4, 1804, and m. 2dly, ————. Is m. Meth. ch. and independent farmer, in H.

(7) *Barzillai*, b May 22, 1811, remained with his father till 18 yrs. of age, and then was sick 4 yrs. He went to Detroit, in 1836, and to improve his health, commenced peddling dry goods, and then hats, caps and furs, in which business he was quite successful. In 1845, he began the wholesale and retail trade in hats, caps and furs, in Milwaukie. He is now doing a large business. He m. Sept. 6, 1846, in Buffalo, N. Y., Charlotte Morrison, who was b. in Wales, N. Y. Has one son. She is m. of Bap. ch. He is Universalist.

(8) *Adelia*, b. Dec. 31, 1813, m. in Hanover, N. Y., Dec. 8, 1835, Martin Thrall, of H., who was b. in Vernon, N. Y., Jan. 3, 1813. He was a carpenter. In 1840, he removed to Illinois, McHenry Co., and in 1842, bought a public house in Woodstock, (county seat.) He was Postmaster 4 yrs. in W. In 1848, he sold his hotel, was Recorder of the County, a short time, commenced trade in dry goods, and continued it till 1852. In 1856, he left Woodstock, and removed to Algonquin, Ill., Cary Station on Chicago, St. Paul and Fon du Lac R. R. Is now a dealer in produce. Both Universalists. Have 2 boys.

(9) *Catharine A.*, b. June 26, 1817, m. March 5, 1840, at Grand Haven, Mich., John Brink, who was b. in Phelps, N. Y., Jan. 12, 1811. In 1831, he went to Detroit, and contracted with John Mullet, as a surveyor. They went from Detroit to Galena, wading through water a great part of the way, as the country is marshy; and had to sleep on the prairie without tent or fire, in month of Nov. At night, their legs resembled a dipt candle, largest at the bottom, from the quantity of ice on them. They would get into their blankets, lay there till their boots thawed, pull them off and lay them under their heads for a pillow. At this time, 1831, there was nothing but the military post, and the settler to the United States Army, and one Indian trader, at Chicago. He commenced surveying in Spring of 1832, was interrupted by the Indian War breaking out in May of same year. He returned home, but in Oct. 1832, started for Galena, on foot, with only one young man. As the War had driven the inhabitants from the country, they had to go from 24 to 36 hours without eating. He got through in season, and took charge of Mr. Mullet's party, and continued with him from Oct. 1832 till June, 1833.

In Aug. 1833, he received an appointment as United States Deputy Surveyor of the public lands. At the same time, he received a contract for running Township lines in Wisconsin, in company with Mr. M., and together, they ran all the Township lines from Range No. 3, through to Lake Michigan, and finished the contract in Dec. 1836. During this service, in 1833 and '34, there were eleven months in which he did not sleep in a house, and lived on fresh fish, there being no inhabitants in the territory.

He then contracted with the Government for a large job in Mich., and commenced in Feb. 1838. This was the hardest trip. In this expedition, he came near starving twice. Once he was caught in a snow storm, in which the snow fell 4 ft. deep, and he was 175 miles from any inhabitants.

At another time, his horses all died but one, and there was a swamp 42 miles wide, to travel through. He got his party through to the mouth of the Manistee river, where he had stored his provisions, a distance of 140 miles from where he came near starving. On the way, he found a beech ridge of timber, and gathered beech nuts, which gave him and his party strength to get through. He finished the contract in 1840, and settled in Algonquin, Ill., in July, 1841. He has had two contracts since from the Government, one in 1843 and one in 1844. Has been Surveyor of McHenry Co. 8 yrs. and Sheriff of the County 2 yrs. He commenced the world in limited circumstances, and has been successful. He and w. are both Universalists. Have 2 daus.

153. V. Nathan, d. under 8 yrs. of age.

Children of WILLIAM WALKER,[6] [79] of Dighton.

154. I. William,[7] b. Nov. 16, 1768, d. Sept. 29, 1769.

155. II. William,[7] (299) b. March 24 1770, d. May 25, 1834. He m. Oct. 1, 1797, Sally, dau. of Simeon Williams, who d. Sept. 7, 1853, ae. 79. Lieutenant and school teacher several years. Farmer in Dighton. Had 10 chil.

156. III. HANNAH,[7] b. Nov. 20, 1771, d. May 24, 1778.

157. IV. JOSEPH[7], } b. Jan. 14, '74, d. Oct. 2, 1797, in Providence.
158. V. ELIZABETH,[7] } b. Jan. 14, '74, d. May 21, 1778.

159. VI. NATHAN,[7] b. Sept. 14, 1775, d. Feb. 10, 1791.

160. VII. DEBORAH,[7] b. June 14, 1777, d. May 24, 1778.

161. VIII. GEORGE,[7] (309) b. Aug. 1, 1779, in Dighton, d. Feb. 20, 1839, ae. 59 yrs., 5 mos., 20 days. He m. Mary Taft, dau. of Grindall and Elizabeth, of Pittstown, Rensellaer Co., N. Y., and b. in P., Feb. 26, 1786, and d. July, 1855, ae. 69 yrs., 4 mos., 25 days. He removed to P., N. Y., where he d. He was for many years an exemplary member and officer, and at the time of his death an Elder in the Dutch Ref. Ch., at Fiashoke.

Mrs. W. having been feeble was taken daily to ride. On the day of her death, a boy living with the family, although told to harness the family horse, harnessed one that was young and skittish. She had gone only half a mile, when the horse, becoming frightened, turned round, and Mrs. W. was thrown out upon a board fence, breaking her ribs. Her lungs were perforated. She was taken up in an unconscious state, and d. in the evening. She was an exemplary christian, m. of Dutch Reformed Ch. They had 11 chil., all b. in P.

162. IX. ABIATHAR,[7] (320) b. May 4, 1781, d. Aug. 3, 1809.

He m. Oct. 26, 1804, Amy Francis, dau. of Peleg. He went West and d. in Pittstown, N. Y., leaving 2 chil., who returned to Dighton. She resides in Taunton.

163. X. HANNAH,[7] b. Sept. 5, 1782, d. Oct. 3, 1782.

164. XI. HANNAH,[7] b. Sept. 5, 1783.

She m. Oct. 4, 1804, Capt. Joseph Pierce, of Dighton. Both deceased. Chil.—

(1) *William.* (2) *Joseph.* (3) *Susan.* (4) *Mary.*

165. XII. HENRY,[7] (322) b. May 28, 1785, d. May 17, 1849, ae. 63 yrs., 11 mos., 19 days. He m. June 7, 1807, Polly Gardner, of Rehoboth, dau. of Stephen. She d. 1820, ae. 31.

He m. 2dly, May 8, 1821, Mary Simmons, dau. of Brown Simmons, of Somerset. She d. 1855, ae. 70. He was a Farmer in Dighton, and had 7 chil. He bore the reputation of a man of honest purpose, was upright as a citizen, and consistent as a christian.

166. XIII. SAMUEL,[7] (327) b. Jan. 15, 1787, d. Sept. 26, 1844, ae. 57 yrs., 8 mos., 11 days. He m. Dec. 19, 1816, Nancy Hale, of Swansey, who was b. Nov. 23, 1796, and d. Jan. 25, 1821, ae. 24 yrs., 2 mos., 2 days.

He m. 2d, July 3, 1823, Fanny Nichols, who was b. Aug. 26, 1799. He was a farmer, in Dighton, and also a Deacon of the Orthodox Cong'l church. The typhus fever entered his home and swept him, a son and a daughter, irresistibly into the grave, in the short period of a month, leaving the family to lament the bereavement of a kind husband and father, the town to deplore the departure of a highly worthy citizen, and the Church of Christ, to mourn the loss of one of its most excellent and generous helpers. He had 6 chil.

167. XIV. NICODEMUS,[7] (333) b. Dec. 20, 1788.

He m. Nov. 22, 1814, Betsey E. Whitman, of No. Providence, who was b. in Smithfield, R. I. He removed from Dighton, the same Autumn, and having bought a farm, settled in Sherburne, N. Y., in the Spring of 1815. Both are now living in S., and have had 6 chil. They lost their house by fire on the night of April 18, 1850, the family barely saving their lives.

168. XV. ELIZABETH,[7] b. April 29, 1791.

She m. Aug. 30, 1817, Matthew Briggs, son of James, of Dighton, b. Sept. 21, 1782, and d. June 12, 1857, ae. 75 yrs. Farmer in D. Chil.—

(1) *Matthew*, b. 1819. (2) *Elizabeth*, b. 1820. (3) *Abraham*, b. 1823. (4) *Amelia*, b. 1826. (5) *Chas. H.*, b. 1829, (See No. 397.) (6) *Wm. J.*, b. 1834.

169. XVI. NATHAN,[7] (339) b. Jan. 13, 1795, d. March 4, 1846.

He m. Oct. 18, 1818, Sally, dau. of Josiah, and sister of Dea. Seth Talbot, of Dighton. Removed from D., Sept. 1, 1837, to Huntersville, Hardin Co., Ohio. Both m. ch. He held the office of Deacon. Had 6 chil. She resides in H.

CHILDREN OF WILLIAM R. WALKER,[6] [83] OF SOMERSET.

170. I. WILLIAM RICHMOND,[7] (345) b. Dec. 5, 1788.

He m. 1808, Keziah Baker, of Swansey, dau. of Sam'l and Patience. She was b. April 3, 1789, and res. in Swansey. He left home, and the last that is known of him, with absolute certainty, is that he was working at his trade, as shoemaker, in Pittstown, N. Y., about 1825. Had 5 chil.

Children of GILBERT WALKER,[6] [84] of Somerset.

171. I. Bridget,[7] b. Nov. 7, 1796, in Tiverton, R. I. Res. Bristol, R. I. unm., and m. ch. Epis'l.

172. II. Sarah,[7] b. May 20, 1798, in Tiverton, R. I.

She m. Feb. 14, 1827, Abraham B. Lawton, of Providence. He was Captain of a Whaler, out of New London, Ct., and is supposed to have been lost at sea, in 1849, as nothing has been heard of him since. No chil. She resides in New London and is m. ch., Cong.

173. III. Mary,[7] b. May 27, 1800, in Somerset, Mass.

She m. April 19, 1822, Nathan Simmons, of Bristol, R. I. Chil.—

(1) *Mary Almy*, b. April 2, 1823, m. Allen S. Simmons, of Bristol, March, 1847.

(2) *Elizabeth S.*, b. March 5, 1826, m. Geo. H. Farrington, Jan. 1854.

(3) *Gilbert Walker*, b. July 16, 1828, unm.

(4) *Horace Richmond*, b. April 23, 1831, d. 1851, at sea.

Res. Bristol, R. I. She is m. of Meth. ch.

174. IV. Eliza,[7] b. March 9, 1803, in S. Res. New London, Ct. She is unm., and m. ch. Cong.

175. V. Gilbert,[7] (350) b. May 9, 1805, in S., d. March 16, 1852, in Peoria, Ill. He m. 1831, Hope P. Munro, dau. of Major Hezekiah, of Bristol, R. I. He was clerk for Messrs. Crocker & Richmond, Taunton, several years, afterward a Cashier of the Cabot Bank, in Chicopee, 10 yrs. Had 2 chil.

176. VI. David,[7] (352) b. July 16, 1807, in Somerset.

He m. May 15, 1842, Laura A. Slocum, of Newport, and she d. Feb. 16, 1852, in Newport, ae. 29. He is Captain of a Whaler from New London. Res. N. L. He m. 2dly, July 9, 1857, Mary Fitch, and has 3 chil.

By 2d Marriage.

177. VII. Ann Richmond,[7] b. Feb. 22, 1812, in Bristol.

She m. Nov. 14, 1840, Sanford B. Smith, of Ledyard, Ct., son of

Jesse, and b. in Groton, Ct. He was a Teacher, in L., 1835—1838, and since in New London. She is m. Cong'l ch. Have—

(1) *Mary Helen*, b. Oct. 9, 1843, in L.

178. VIII. JANE H.,[7] b. Sept. 9, 1814, and m. ch. Meth. Res. Somerset, unm.

179. IX. IZANNAH FRANKFORD,[7] b. Sept. 25, 1817, and m. ch. Meth. Res. Central Falls, R. I., unm.

180. X. SON,[7] b. 1824, d. ae. 11 days.

CHILDREN OF SILVESTER WALKER,[6] [88] OF ADAMS, N. Y.

181. I. SALLY,[7] b. April 22, 1791, in Swansey, now Somerset.

She m. David Cudworth. It was an unhappy marriage. They rem. to "the West," where she d. Chil.—

(1) *Silvester*. (2) *Henry*. (3) *Eliza Ann*.

182. II. NANCY,[7] b. May, 1793, in Swansey.

She m. James Neeland, who d. 1858. Res. Port Dalhousie, C. W. Chil.—

(1) *Silvester*, Res. St. Catharine, C. W. (2) *Sophronia*, m. Norris. Res. St. C. (3) *Edward*. (4) *Harvey*. (5) *Mary*. Res. Port D. The sons are extensively engaged in commerce. The daus. m. extensive ship owners.

183. III. DAVID,[7] (355) b. Oct. 28, 1799, in Swansey, now Somerset. He m. March, 1820, Eunice Thomas, dau. of Ira and Lucy, of Adams, N. Y., who d. Aug. 3, 1824, leaving 2 daus.

He m. Sept. 19, 1826, Lucy Thomas, sister of first w., by whom he has 2 chil. He is a local preacher, of the Meth. Epis. ch. He was educated to some extent in Academic halls, but more extensively in the chimney corner, in the fields and the woods. He is also a successful farmer and surveyor.

184. IV. MARY[7], b. April, 1803.

She m. Feb. 9, 1825, Daniel Cole. Res. Adams, N. Y., and a farmer. Chil.—

(1) *Charles H.*, b. Dec. 12, 1826, m. June, 1851, Hannah L. Blood. Res. Rutland, N.Y. Farmer. Chil.—1, Charles Webster, b. Jan. 30, 1854. 2, Elgin, b. Sept. 26, 1856.

(2) *Egbert*, b. June 23, 1828, m. March, 1852, Amanda E. Stuyvesant. Res. Ellisburgh, N. Y. Chil.—1, Homer A. b. March 1, 1853. 2, Ellen A., b. March 25, 1855.

(3) *David Milo*, b. March 27, 1831, m. Feb. 16, 1854, Hannah Fassett. No chil.

(4) *Mary A.*, b. June 30, 1833, m. March 29, 1851, John D. Clark, who d. Jan. 3, 1853, 1 child. She m. 2dly, Jan. 26, 1854, Zebulon Burdick. Res. Wis. Four chil.

185. V. RICHMOND,[7] (359) b. March, 1805, in Brattleboro', Vt. He m. Spring of 1829, Mary A. Wallace. Res. Cape Vincent, N. Y. Has 8 chil.

186. VI. ELIZA,[7] b. Dec. 1807, in B.

She m. Wm. Jones, by whom 1 child, Sarah, b. Sept. 21, 1830.

She m. 2dly, —— Hull, by whom Alonzo, b. Feb. 16, 1837, and Silvester, b. Dec. 22, 1839.

She m. 3dly, July 10, 1847, Stephen Merrill. Res. Adams, N. Y.

187. VII. JOHN,[7] (362) b. March, 1809. At the age of 9 yrs. he lost one of his legs. He is a machinist, and an esteemed m. ch. Bap. Res. in vicinity of Green Bay, Wis. Has 2d wife, and chil. probably.

188. VIII. HANNAH,[7] b. 1811.

She m. —— Brown, in Oneida Co., and rem. to the "far West." Their res. is near Green Bay, Wis. Chil.—

(1) *Mary*. (2) *Silvester*. (3) *George*.

189. IX. JANE,[7] b. May 26, 1818, in Adams, N.Y., d. Oct. 15, 1845.

She m. Abram Gregory, lived and d. a christian. Chil.—

(1) *Celistia*. (2) *George*. (3) *Elnathan*. (4) *Maryette*. (5) *Wm. Franklin*, b. about June, 1845.

CHILDREN OF JONATHAN WALKER,[6] [98] OF DIGHTON.

190. I. ROBERT,[7] (367) b. Dec. 10, 1792, d. Dec. 16, 1850, in Placer Co., California. He m. Oct. 6, 1816, Lydia, dau. of Elder Sylvester Rounds, of Rehoboth. She res. in Marion Grant Co., Wis. He rem. to Allen, near Angelica, N. Y., in 1820, and was one of the first settlers of A. He left his family about 1842, and went West, near Galena, Wis. Had 10 chil.

191. II. POLLY,[7] b. Sept. 21, 1794, d. Sept. 1849, in Marion, Mich. She m. May 6, 1811, Sylvester Rounds, of Rehoboth, (son of Elder S. R.,) b. Jan. 9, 1788, and d. April, 1849, in Mich. He removed to Angelica, N. Y., June 25, 1820, and then to Mich. Chil.—

(1) *Sylvester*, b. Jan. 13, 1812.

(2) *Jonathan W.*, b. Sept. 23, 1813, m. July 15, 1838, Matilda F. Hicks. 9 chil.

(3) *Asahel*, b. Aug. 27, 1815, d. March 11, 1839.

(4) *Roxana*, b. Jan. 3, 1817, m. Oct. 11, 1835, Robert Munns. 11 chil.

(5) *Jabez C.*, b. Aug. 29, 1818. (See No. 377.) Res. Marion, Clayton Co., Iowa. Justice of the Peace.

(6) *Polly*, b. Oct. 27, 1820, m. Oct. 10, 1841, Edward Ellsworth. 6 chil. Res. Marion, Mich.

(7) *David P.*, b. May 29, 1822, d. ae. 1 week.

(8) *Joseph W.*, b May 2, 1823, m. March 8, 1848, Lucinda. 6 chil.

(9) *Mahitta*, b. Feb. 12, 1826, m. Nov. 21, 1847, George Baker. 3 chil. Res. Marion, Mich.

(10) *Betsey*, b. April 7, 1828, d. May 5, 1828.

(11) *Betsey E.*, b. May 3, 1829.

(12) *Andrew J.*, b. March 4, 1832, m. Jan. 22, 1860, Caroline J. Pardee. Res. Marion, Livingston Co., Mich.

(13) *Prudence*, b. Aug. 27, 1834.

192. III. JOSEPH,[7] (377) b. Jan. 2, 1800, in Dighton.

He m. Aug. 9, 1823, (Aug. 5, 1822, Rehoboth Rec.,) Emerancy, dau. of Elder Sylvester Rounds, of Rehoboth, and b. Aug. 28, 1803. Res. Hickory Grove, Grant Co., Wis. Had 7 chil.

193. IV. ABIGAIL,[7] d. 1856, in Grant Co., Wis.

She m. Jacob Ostrander, in N. Y. Chil.—

(1) *Jacob*, b. Oct. 12, 1825, m. Oct. 12, 1845, Betsey. Had 6 chil.
(2) *Horace L.*, b. April 6, 1834, m. May 8, 1855, Mary. Had 3 chil.

CHILDREN OF NATHANIEL WALKER,[6] [102] OF DIGHTON.

194. I. LYDIA,[7] b. April 6, 1775, d. 1840.

She m. May 6, 1802, Jonathan Knowles, of Norton, son of Thomas. (See No. 93.) He d. 1855, ae. 84. Chil.—

(1) *David*, b. 1803, m. Fidelia Dauforth. A carpenter, in Boston. Chil.—1, Eliza. 2, Lydia. 3, Andrew.

(2) *William*, b. about 1804, m. Almira Griffin. A shoemaker, in Norton. Chil.—1, Charles. 2, Theodore. 3, Edward. 4, George. 5, Eunice.

(3) *Wesley*, b. 1806, m. Lydia Totman, of Scituate. Res. Canton. He is a carpenter. Has chil.

(4) *Elbridge*, b. 1812, m. Elizabeth Drake. Res. Lowell, Manufacturer.

(5) *Lydia*, b. 1808, m. Hiram Kingman. Res. Mansfield, has William.

(6) *Eliza*, youngest, d. ae. 13.

Jonathan, father of aforementioned, m. first, Nov. 7, 1793, Ruth Richmond, of D., who d. March 30, 1801, in 30th yr. Had 4 chil.

195. II. ELIZABETH,[7] b. Feb. 18, 1777, d. about 1846.

She was pub. July 5, 1800, to Baylies Philips. Res. Bloomfield, N. Y., where he died. She then rem. to Mich., and died. Chil.—

(1) *Samuel*, b. July 29, 1802. Res. Chili, N. Y. (2) *Eliza*, b. April 10, 1804, d. unm., in C., Oct. 26, 1839, m. ch. Bap. (3) *Baylies*.

196. III. COMFORT,[7] b. Feb. 14, 1779, d. April 17, 1843, unm.

197. IV. NATHANIEL,[7] b. Feb. 9, 1781, d. unm. He had a face singularly marked from birth, and was blind many years. He was, however, a very intelligent, pious and worthy man, and having a retentive memory, was remarkably familiar with the Scriptures. A m. ch. Cong.

198. V. DOLLY,[7] b. March 23, 1783, d. June 20, 1847, ae. 63. (Ins.) She was pub. Sept. 12, 1807, to Matthew Briggs, who d. July 19, 1845, ae. 62. Res. Dighton, Lower Four Corners. Blacksmith. Chil.—

(1) *Harriet*, b. 1809. (2) *Geo. W.*, b. 1811. (3) *Alson*, b. 1812. (4) *Chas. W.*, b. 1813. (5) *Matthew*, b. 1815. (6) *Andrew J.* b. 1817. (7) *Hodijah B.*, b. 1819. (8) *Horatio L.*, b. 1826. All m. but 7th.

199. VI. JOHN BAYLEY,[7] b. March 7, 1785, d. Jan. 11, 1808, unm., in Windsor, N. C. A shoemaker.

200. VII. SETH,[7] b. June 11, 1787, d. March, 1808, unm. A shoemaker.

201. VIII. CHARLES,[7] (384) b. Feb. 9, 1790.

He m. 1826, Lovina Merlin, in Bloomfield, N. Y., where he had settled. She was b. in Riga, N. Y. Res. Michigan. He is m. Bap. Ch. and Farmer. Has 2 chil.

202. IX. DAVID,[7] (386) b. May 14, 1792.

He m. Jan. 1835, Mary Ann Sheldon, who was b. in Conway, Oct. 6, 1806. Res. Chili, N. Y. Both m. ch. Bap. He holds the office of Deacon. Has 2 sons.

203. X. SARAH,[7] b. May 14, 1792, d. Feb. 5, 1843.

She m. Oct. 18, 1816, James Crane of Berkley. He was a master mariner, sailed from Charleston, S. C., about 1825, and was never heard of. She d. in Dighton, m. ch. Cong. Chil.—

(1) *James W.*, b. 1817. Res. Springfield. (2) *Sarah*, b. 1819.

204. XI. Gideon,[7] b. Sept. 21, 1793, d. May 12, 1848, ae. 54 yrs., 7 mos. He m. Aug. 5, 1817, Lucy Wheeler, dau. of John, of Dighton. Res. D. Farmer. A man of intelligence, and great moral worth, and for many yrs. Deacon of Cong'l ch. No chil. She lives in D., (1855.)

Children of NEHEMIAH WALKER,[6] [114] of Dighton.

205. I. Gilbert,[7] (390) b. 1797, d. April 9, 1845, ae. 47 yrs., 10 mos. He m. Sept. 30, 1825, Abby Wheeler, dau. of John and Deborah (Gough,) of Dighton. Res. Dighton. Farmer.

206. II. Jasper,[7] b. about 1799, d. ae. 23 yrs., unm.

207. III. Betsey,[7] b. 1801, d. 1823 or first part of 1824.

She was pub. June 29, 1822, to Otis Nichols, of Rehoboth, and d. soon after her brother Jasper's death, (taking the fever from him.) Res. R. Had—

(1) *Betsey*, who m. Albert Cole.

208. IV. Hannah,[7] b. 1803.

She was pub. March 12, 1825, to Otis Nichols, who m. 1st, her sister. Res. Rehoboth. Chil.—

(1) *Hannah*, b. about 1830, m. John Warren Briggs. Res. Providence.
(2) *Child*, b. about 1834, d. 1854.

209. V. Peleg Francis,[7] (397) b. Dec. 1805.

He m. Oct. 30, 1830, Mary Ann Pierce, dau. of Joseph, of Rehoboth. Farmer in Dighton. Has 4 chil.

210. VI. Nancy H.[7]

She m. Nov. 7, 1831, William Stearns, of Mansfield. Chil.—

(1) *William Lowell*, b. about 1832. (2) *Leroy*. (3) *Elijah Walker*. (4) *Wilhelmine*.

211. VII. Wealthy,[7] b. June, 1810. Res. Taunton, unm.

212. VIII. James Madison,[7] (401) b. March 21, 1812.

He m. Nov. 11, 1848, Louisa J., dau. of Josiah Read, of Dighton. Res. Mount Hope Factory, North Dighton. Has 3 chil.

213. IX. Nehemiah,[7] (404) b. April, 1814.

He m. Jan. 20, 1844, Emily Ann Bliss, of Rehoboth. Res. Dighton, on the homestead of Col. Elnathan (See No. 30,) and his son Dr. George Walker. Had 4 chil.

214. X. RUTH ANN,[7] b. Aug. 1816.

She m. April 23, 1838, Capt. George B. Simmons, of Dighton. He is a Housewright and Farmer in Dighton, on the homestead of the late Wm. Walker. (See No. 155.) Chil.—

(1) *Ruth Ann*, b. about 1839. (2) *Georgianna*, b. about 1851.

215. XI. ELIJAH,[7] b. 1818 or '19, d. June 24, 1841, in 23d yr.

He m. April 11, 1841, Hannah W. Dean, of Taunton. Res. Dighton. No chil.

CHILDREN OF ELEAZER WALKER,[6] [115] OF NORTON.

216. I. SARAH,[7] b. March 22, 1771, d. June 27, 1822.

She m. June 29, 1790, Samuel Hunt, of Norton, who d. Oct. 18, 1830. Chil.—

(1) *Content*, b Jan. 17, 1791, m. Lemuel Perry, of N., and had—1, Cordelia E, m. Horatio Gilbert. 2, Caroline E. and 3, Lemuel. She died in N. after giving birth to triplets, all of whom d. soon after. (2) *Samuel*, 1792. (3) *John*, 1794. (4) *Lawrence*, 1796. (5) *Elbridge G.*, 1798. (6) *Jonathan*, 1800. (7) *Catharine*, 1803. (8) *Nancy T.*, 1806. (9) *Adaline Eliza*, 1809.

217. II. GEORGE,[7] (408) b. in Norton, April 9, 1773, d. April, 1855, ae. 82 yrs.

He m. Jan. 20, 1803, Nancy Titus, who d. Jan. 5 or 7, 1805, leaving 2 chil.

He m. 2dly, June 22, 1806, Polly Titus, who d. March 10, 1846, by whom he had 8 chil.

He was for many years a leading man in Norton, and for a considerable period commander of the Norton Artillery, one of the finest companies of the State. He was twice called out during the last War, once to New Bedford when the British attempted a landing there, and once to Boston, after the destruction of the Capitol at Washington, as it was feared the enemy designed a similar act at B. He was for 7 consecutive yrs. Town Clerk and Treasurer. In 1820, he represented N. in the State Legislature, and in the same year, was a member of the Convention for the revision of the State Constitution.

In 1826, he removed to Petersham, where he remained 28 yrs., engaged in farming, universally respected by his fellow townsmen. Thence he removed to Worcester, in 1854, where he died.

218. III. CATY,[7] b. Aug. 1, 1775, d. Dec. 9, 1778.

219. IV. PETER,[7] b. Nov. 13, 1777, d. June 16, 1779.

220. V. CONTENT,[7] b. July 22, 1780.

She m. about 1801, Joseph Titus. Chil.—

(1) *Mary Ann*, b. 1802. (2) *Oliver*, b. 1804. (3) *Harrison Gray*, b. 1806 (4) *Harriet*, b. 1812. (5) *Cordelia*, b. 1819.

221. VI. JOHN STARKWEATHER,[7] b. March 9, 1783, d. June 7, 1787.

222. VII. HANNAH,[7] b. June 12, 1785, d. June 23, 1822.

She m. Asa Danforth, of Norton, who d. July 21, 1830, having m. 2dly, Phebe Sweet, of N., about 1828. Res. Norton. Both m. ch. Unitarian. His chil. are Unitarians. Chil.—

(1) *George W.*, b. Sept. 5, 1807. Res. Washington, Ill., unm. Banker

(2) *Content W.*, b. June 6, 1811, m. about 1830, Walter Haines, of Winthrop, Me., who d. May 15, 1840, ae. 37 yrs. Farmer. Had 4 chil. She m. 2dly, July 15, 1843, John May, Esq., of W., a Lawyer, and had 3 chil. She d. July, 1857.

(3) *Asa H.*, b. June 4, 1813, m. Feb. 25, 1839, Catharine A. Rupert, dau. of Henry S., of Point Pleasant, Va. Res. Washington, Ill. Banker, (Prairie State Bank,) with his brother Geo. and son. A. G. His chil. are— 1, Almon G., b. Dec. 8, 1840. 2, Henry R., b. Nov. 3, 1842. 3, Lemuel E., b. Aug. 9, 1845. 4, Harriet C., b. Dec. 9, 1848. 5, Caroline H., b. June 5, 1853. He went to Fall River, at age of 17, 4 yrs. after to Milford, Pa., and 1 yr. after to Coshocton, O., and 1 yr. after, in 1836, to Washington, Ill. He has been engaged in cabinet making, building store houses and dwellings, then steam, flouring and saw mills, and running them, operating in land, and now in Banking business.

(4) *Emily S.*, b. about 1815, d. ae. 21 yrs., in Winthrop, Me., unm.

(5) *Hannah I.*, b. 1817. Res. Dorchester, unm., at John J. May's.

(6) *Cordelia E.*, b. July 1, 1822, m. Jan. 13, 1845, R. J. Weeks, at Wayne, Me. Res. Santa Cruz, California.

(7) *Sarah H.*, b. about 1824, m. Charles Elmes, in Taunton. In 1851, they removed to Washington, Ill. Had 6 chil. She d. Autumn of 1852. with cholera, and also 4 of her chil. He returned to T. and d.

223. VIII. ELEAZER,[7] (418) b. Oct. 15, 1787.

He was pub. June 17, 1815, to Abigail N. Horton, of Norton, who d. in Kaskaskia, Ill., Aug. 1833, leaving 5 chil.

He m. 2dly, about 1836, Mrs. Frances Widen, widow of Raphael, by whom 1 child. Res. Rensellaer Co., N. Y., Kaskaskia, Ill., and now in Chester, Randolph Co., where he was Postmaster.

224. IX. SAMUEL,[7] b. April 17, 1791, d. Dec. 25, 1796.

225. X. CLARISSA,[7] b. July 25, 1793.

She m. Feb. 1817, Newton Sweet, who d. Sept. 5, 1855, ae. 62 yrs. Soap Manufacturer in So. Lancaster. Had 6 chil.

(1) *Eleazer*, b. Feb. 8, 1818, d. young.

(2) *Clarissa*, b. July 4, 1821, d. young.

(3) *Horatio N.*, b. Sept. 29, 1823, m. Feb. 16, 1848, Frances M. McQuesten. Soap Manufacturer in So. Lancaster. Has 2 ch.—1, Geo. N., b. Nov. 28, 1849. 2, Emma F., b. April 16, 1853.

(4) *Nancy W.*, b. Feb. 21, 1826, unm., in Worcester.

(5) *Thomas*, b. Aug. 11, 1830, m. 1855, Candia Brigham.

(6) *Geo. Walker*, b. June 21, 1833.

226. XI. Chloe Nelson,[7] b. March 26, 1796.

She m. Oct. 11, 1818, Daniel Morey. Res. Taunton. Chil.—

(1) *Sophia*, b. Oct. 22, 1819, m. Dr. Benj'n Rounds, of Norton.

(2) *Samuel*, b. Dec. 10, 1823.

(3) *Daniel Emory*, b. Jan. 22, 1829.

(4) *Charles*, b. Sept. 6, 1834.

Children of Capt. JAMES WALKER,[6] [120] of Taunton.

227. I. James,[7] (424) b. June 18, 1789.

He m. May 22, 1815, Lucinda Townsend, dau. of George and Polly (Richmond,) who was b. Feb. 12, 1790, and d. March 15, 1836. "She was the greatest worker in Barnard, Vt., and could do more work in a day or yr., than any woman I ever saw." Had 7 chil.

He m. 2dly, Feb. 22, 1837, Roxana Townsend, sister of Lucinda, first w., and she b. March 8, 1797, d. July 25, 1837. She was the counsellor in her father's family, ever peaceful, amiable, and an excellent nurse in sickness.

He m. 3dly, Sept. 5, 1838, Permelia Thomas, who was b. June 14, ——, and d. Aug. 23, 1842.

He m. 4thly, March 18, 1845, Martha Perry, who was b. April 20, 1800. The first w. only had chil. He removed to Barnard, Vt., in Autumn of 1815, and in March, 1853, to Royalton, Vt., and in March, 1860, to East Barnard village. Farmer.

228. II. Elisha,[7] (433) b. April 30, 1791, d. April 2, 1853, ae. 62 yrs. He m. June 17, 1821, Narcissa, dau. of Capt. Uriah and Polly (Pratt) Reed, of Taunton, who was b. July 26, 1798, and d. May 4, 1846, having 5 chil.

He m. 2dly, (pub. June 5, 1847,) Mrs. Jane (Butler) Stone, of Martha's Vineyard, who was b. April 1, 1798, d. Jan 8, 1855. He d. April 2, 1853, of congestion of the lungs, having never been sick a day for more than 40 yrs. He was a Farmer, also a Representative

Richmond Walker

Richmond Walker

to the Legislature one yr. He was a good neighbor, a useful citizen, and esteemed for his upright character and generous nature. His death was the first breach in the circle of children for one-half a century. A Universalist in religious opinion. Res. Westville, Taunton.

229. III. RICHMOND,[7] (436) b. June 19, 1793.

He m. Dec. 2, 1819, Abigail Presbrey,* dau. of Simeon and Anne, of Taunton. She was b. in Norton, June 23, 1794, d. Oct. 17, 1825, in her 32d yr., leaving one son.

Taking a sudden and severe cold she was reduced from perfect health. An internal abscess was formed, (as it appeared after her decease,) which baffled all medical skill, and bore her irresistibly to the grave. Stricken in the prime of womanhood, "her sun went down while it was yet day." During a sickness of a year she calmly set her house in order, and then with meek, placid resignation of the hopes and loves of earth, though fraught with peculiar promise, and with a cheerful religious faith, she fell asleep in Jesus.

She was endowed with great energy, decision and fortitude of character. Her piety was unostentatious, but steadfast and fruitful, ripening into a growth of sweet submission to the will of the Father, and of undoubting, joyful trust in the Savior. She possessed an amiable and equable temper. There were blended in her nature, warm sympathies, generous impulses, moral sensitiveness, and steadfast principle, forming a character of admirable harmony and worth. And this well proportioned and graceful column which Nature reared, Religion strengthened and adorned with the "beauty of holiness." Loving peace, she was devoted to the interests of her household, and it is no extravagance to give her the eulogy—of the faithful wife and mother, "The heart of her husband doth safely trust in her," and "to know her was to love her."

Her epitaph is as follows:—

This is the sweet repose,
  Where lies the slumbering saint;
When God appeared to call her home,
  She uttered no complaint.

He m. 2dly, Dec. 13, 1826, Mary Seabury, dau. of John W. Seabury, Esq., and Hannah (Church,) of Taunton. She was b. April 16, 1797, and has one dau. She early united with the Cong. ch., and for 40 yrs. has been an exemplary member. An invalid over 30 yrs., she has been patient and resolute, evincing a rare conbination

* The compiler has the Presbrey Genealogy in manuscript.

of energy and loveliness of character, serene, amiable and cheerful through all the discipline of impaired health and uncertain life. He has been a Shoe Manufacturer in T., 40 yrs. He was Representative to the Legislature, in the session of 1851 and 2, a session memorable for its enactment of the Prohibitory Liquor Law, and was "one of the two men," Hon. Mr. Keyes, of Dedham, remarked, "who pursued a straight forward, uncompromising, and perfectly consistent course," in pressing the Bill to its enactment. As a member of the Com. who reported the Bill, he offered a speech in favor of it, which was solicited for the press and published in the Boston Atlas, and several of the Temperance Journals. He has been an earnest advocate of Temperance from the inception of the Reform; united with the Cong. ch. in 1815, and was elected Deacon, in 1837, and the interests of the church have had his unceasing sympathies and efforts. Though living nearly all this period 3 miles from the place of worship, no one has been less frequently absent from the social and Sabbath services.

He was a Director of the Cohannet Bank, is now a Trustee of the Bristol Co. Saving's Bank, and one of its Com. of investments. With few opportunities for early education, spending his youth on the farm, and in the brick yard, instead of the school house, he is, however, a man of much more than ordinary intelligence. He is highly esteemed for sound judgment, clear and fearless convictions, unimpeachable business integrity, and active, consistent piety.

230. IV. OTIS,[7] (438) b. July 14, 1795.

He m. Dec. 8, 1817, Nabby, dau. of John Brown, of Taunton, and b. March 29, 1796. Res. Taunton. Both m. ch. Cong. He is a contractor in stone work and in moving buildings. Has 4 chil.

231. V. BARZILLAI,[7] (442) b. Oct. 18, 1797.

He m. July 5, 1821, Nancy F. Hinds, dau. of John and Elizabeth, of Boston, and b. June 5, 1798. Res. Taunton, (Weir Village.) He is house joiner, and contractor. Both m. ch. Cong. Had 8 chil.

232. VI. SON,[7] d. in infancy.

233. VII. EDWARD,[7] (451) b. March 4, 1800.

He m. June 6, 1824, Harriet Walker, (See No. 271,) dau. of Geo. Gooding Walker, of West Taunton, and b. Jan. 26, 1804. Had 4 chil. He is a shoe maker and farmer, and lives on the homestead of his father and ancestors, in T. The farm he occupies has been in possession of the Walkers 175 yrs., and is probably a part of the grants which were made to the first James Walker, 200 yrs. since. (See 22d p.)

234. VIII. MARY,[7] b. April 27, 1802, unm., and m. ch. Bap.

235. IX. SON,[7] }
236. X. DAU.[7] } Twins, and d. in a few hours.

237. XI. HANNAH,[7] b. Sept. 24, 1805.

She m. Dec. 2, 1828, George Luther, son of Ebenezer, of Warren, R. I., and b. Nov. 18, 1800. Res. Warren. She is m. ch. Epis. Chil.—

(1) *Hannah Walker*, b. Nov. 29, 1830, m. Sept. 1858, Dr. Francis I. Parker, who was born in Newport, N. Scotia, about 1828. He was educated at Wilbraham, and grad. of Med. school, Harv. Coll. Res. Windsor, N. S.

(2) *Joanna B.*, b. June 28, 1833, d. Nov. 23, 1844.

EIGHTH GENERATION.

CHIL. OF BENJAMIN WALKER,[7] [122] OF WEST TAUNTON.

238. I. SALLY,[8] b. May 30, 1790, d. March 20, 1836, in 46th yr.

She m. March, 1810, Samuel Gulliver, son of Gershom, of Taunton. Both were m. ch. Cong. Res. Westville, Taunton. He was b. in T., Aug. 27, 1787, and d. Nov. 30, 1844, ae. 57. Had 6 chil.—

(1) *Sally Walker*, b. July 15, 1811, d. Jan. 6, 1833.

(2) *Samuel Walker*, b. July 13, 1815. Res. West Taunton, on the homestead of his grandfather Benjamin. He m. Mary A. Leonard, dau. of Wm. of T. She d. April 18, 1838, in 23d yr. He m. 2dly, June 3, 1840, Ruth A. Lincoln, dau. of Calvin Lincoln of Norton, and b. Aug. 22. 1820. His chil.—1, Martha Ann, b. Jan. 18, 1837. 2, Emily A., b. Aug. 17, 1841. 3, Jas. Walker, b. Jan. 24, 1844. 4, Calvin Newton, b. June 8, 1846. 5, Sarah J., b. May 11, 1850.

(3) *Phebe H.*, b. June 17, 1820, d. Nov. 11, 1845, m. March 4, 1844, Rufus M. Bullock, of Richmond, N. Y. Farmer. No chil.

(4) *Hannah Crane*, b. Feb. 11, 1826, d. July 25, 1851, m. Dec. 2, 1845, Zeba F. Bliss, son of Zeba, of Attleboro', 1 child. (See No. 447.)

(5) *Mary Jane*, b. Oct. 6, 1829, d. Feb. 27, 1832.

(6) *Zilpha J.*, b. Feb. 2, 1832, d. July 26, 1853, m. Sept. 1, 1852, Wm. W. Rowe, of Lewiston, Me. Res. Portland, 1 child.

CHILDREN OF PEREZ WALKER,[7] [123] OF DIGHTON.

239. I. JAMES,[8] b. in Dighton, July 24, 1790, d. Oct. 5, 1844, of consumption, in Bloomfield, N. Y., where he lived, a farmer, and unm. He was an invalid 35 yrs.

240. II. BRADFORD,[8] (455) b. Oct. 17, 1792, in Dighton.

He m. March 2, 1815, Eliza Holcomb. She d. March 4, 1847, ae. 48, and was m. ch. Meth. From the early age of 14 yrs., she was an exemplary and devoted Christian.

He m. Dec. 22, 1852, Lois T. Peck, ae. 36, dau. of Nathaniel and Mary, of Seekonk. He removed from Dighton to Bloomfield, N. Y. with his father in 1804, settled in Canandaigua, before 1815, where he still resides. He is a successful Farmer, and engaged principally in Hop growing. Had 12 chil. He has been m. Cong. ch. since 1841, and is highly esteemed for integrity and christian worth.

241. III. POLLY,[8] b. in Dighton, Sept. 21, 1795, d. May 14, 1830. She m. in Bloomfield, Nov. 31, 1813, Mason Lee, formerly of Taunton, and b. March 18, 1790. He was a Farmer in Bloomfield, N.Y. She was a m. ch. Bap. Had 6 chil.—

(1) *James M.*, b. Oct. 15, 1814, m. Sept. 1847, Melissa C. Gunn, of Ohio.

(2) *Mary W.*, b. May 9, 1816, m. Josiah Mayes, June 2, 1835. Res. Cohoes, N. Y.

(3) *Eliza I.*, b. April 29, 1818, d. March 25, 1839.

(4) *Nathan B.*, b. May 20, 1820, m. 1851, Eliza Smith, and d. June 27, 1854.

(5) *Perez A.*, b. March 2, 1822, m. Mary W. Mead, April 22, 1847. Had 2 chil. He m. 2dly, Elizabeth Ellsworth, Sept. 12, 1852. Had 2 chil.

(6) *George H.*, b. Sept. 2, 1829, d. May 6, 1848.

242. IV. BETSEY,[8] b. in Dighton, Nov. 10, 1797, d. 1847.

She m. 1814, Micah Wilder, who d. since 1856. They removed to Clinton, Vermillion Co., Ind. Both m. ch. Had 12 chil., and all deceased but two, Eliza and Mary. Chil.—

(1) *Eliza*, m. Matthew Basinger, 3 chil. (2) *Lucinda*, m. Wm. Nichols, 5 chil. (3) *Marilla*. (4) *Marilla*. (5) *Joshua*. (6) *George W.* (7) *Alvira*. (8) *Priscilla*. (9) *Mary*, m. Alexander Johnson. Res. Peoria, Iowa. (10) *Dorcas*, m. Henry Sumpter, 4 chil. (11) *Andrew J.* (12) *Ingerbo B.*

243. V. SALLY,[8] b. in Bloomfield, N.Y., Nov. 10, 1805, d. 1829. She m. 1824, Samuel Marble, a farmer. Had—

(1) *Walker S.*, b. in B., Oct. 16, 1827, who m. Laura M. Walker, (See No. 463.)

CHILDREN OF ELIAKIM WALKER,[7] [124] OF SALEM, MICH.

244. I. ELIAKIM J.,[8] (467) b. Feb. 6, 1801, in Dighton.

He m. Sept. 18, 1823, Nancy Wheeler, dau. of Aaron, of Bristol, N. Y., b. June 14, 1802, and is m. ch. Bap. He is a substantial

78

240.

Bradford Walker

farmer in Salem, Mich., and a man of exemplary moral character. Nine chil.

245. II. PEREZ,[8] (476) b. Nov. 12, 1805.

He m. April 10, 1831, Hannah A. Sage, in Bristol, N. Y. She is m. ch. Bap. He is a Farmer, Surveyor, and Teacher of Music. Has been Highway Commissioner and Town Treasurer, and is held in high esteem. Res. Salem, Mich. Nine chil.

246. III. AMY H.,[8] b. Dec. 15, 1807, deceased.

She m. June 10, 1827, Osmon Smith, of Bristol, N. Y., son of Daniel, formerly from Mass. He was b. Nov. 17, 1805, d. Sept. 4, 1850, in San Francisco. Chil.—

(1) *Mary J.*, b. Feb. 15, 1829, d. April 14, 1843.
(2) *Daniel W.*, b. May 9, 1833.

247. IV. OTIS H.,[8] (485) b. Oct. 29, 1809, d. March 12, 1844.

He m. March 8, 1832, Sarah Wheeler, dau. of Aaron, of Bristol, N.Y. She d. Aug. 18, 1841. Both m. ch. Pres.

He m. 2dly, Sarah Dower, Aug. 21, 1842. Farmer in Salem, Mich. Has 4 chil.

248. V. RHODA ANN,[8] b. Oct. 11, 1815, m. Jan. 24, 1833, Almon Isham, who was b. in Kingsbury, N. Y. He is a mason by trade, and is now farmer in Salem, Mich. Has—

(1) *Almon H.*, b. May 23, 1841.

249. VI. BETSEY J.,[8] b. Jan. 20, 1821, m. April 8, 1838, Lawrence Noble, who was b. in East Bloomfield, N. Y., March 23, 1812. He was several yrs. in mercantile life, removed to Michigan, and became a farmer. Has been Supervisor, School and Highway Commissioner, School Inspector, &c. Res. Salem, Mich. Both m. ch. Bap. No chil.

CHILDREN OF TISDALE WALKER,[7] [125] OF BRISTOL, N.Y.

250. I. HENRY T.,[8] (489) b. April 29, 1808, m. Oct. 31, 1827, Leonora Abbey, of Bristol, N. Y., daughter of Joshua, and b. Sept. 13, 1808. He removed to Lenawee Co., Mich., in 1836, and in 1837, to Washtenaw Co., and was farmer and merchant. He was a member of the State Legislature in 1842, '45 and '49. In 1849, he began the study of medicine, (in which he had been interested somewhat from his youth,) with Dr. Cushman, of Ohio. Two yrs. later, he removed to Detroit, Mich., and was associated with Drs. Olds and

Hastings one yr. each, and then began his professional practice alone, which he has pursued successfully to the present time, (1860.) Res. D. Has 4 chil.

251. II. ELIZABETH,[8] b. Dec. 23, 1810, m. Dec. 31, 1829, Alanson Philips, of Bristol, N.Y. They removed to West Ogden, Lenawee Co., Mich., in 1835, where they now live, (1860.) He is a wealthy farmer, and worthy man. Chil.—

(1) *George C.*, b. Jan. 4, 1831, m. Dec. 30, 1857, Mary I. Aldrich. Has Edwin F., b. Nov. 25, 1858.

(2) *Elizabeth C.*, b. Feb. 5, 1834, m. Dec. 12, 1855, Ira Goodsell, a farmer. Have Arthur A., b. July 7, 1858.

(3) *Mary M.*, b. Aug. 14, 1836, d. March 30, 1854.

(4) *Henry W.*, b. July 10, 1842.

(5) *Franklin S.*, b. June 28, 1852.

252. III. MERCY G.,[8] b. Sept. 23, 1812, d. Sept. 11, 1847. She m. Jan. 9, 1831, Seymour West, of Richmond, N.Y. They emigrated to Lenawee Co., Mich., in 1835. In 1848, he began the study of Medicine, grad. at Philadelphia Med. Coll., and was a successful practitioner in Canandaigua, N. Y., till his death, Dec. 24, 1855. They had—

(1) *Nathan T.*, b. Sept. 20, 1846, d. Aug. 20, 1847.

253. IV. LYDIA D.,[8] b. Dec. 6, 1814, d. Sept. 8, 1838. She m. Sept. 20, 1832, Wm. Paul, of Bloomfield, N. Y., removed to Lenawee Co., Mich., in 1835. No chil. He was a farmer, m. 2dly, and d. Dec. 3, 1848.

CHIL. OF ELNATHAN WALKER,[7] [128] OF HARTLAND, VT.

254. I. ABEL B.,[8] (495) b. Jan. 26, 1797, in Hartland, Vt. He m. Dec. 17, 1826, Martha, dau. of John Phipps, of Sherborn. He has resided in Taunton and Hopkinton, and is now a farmer in West Andover. Has 4 chil., and is Cong'st.

BY 2d MARRIAGE.

255. II. WEALTHY W.,[8] b. Oct. 17, 1806, m. Dec. 3, 1826, Charles G. Steele, who d. March 24, 1860. He was a farmer in Windsor, Vt. Chil.—

(1) *Mary Jane*, b. Dec. 1, 1827, in W., m. Ellis Dunklee, of Claremont, N.H. Res. Springfield, Vt. He is a machinist.

(2) *Julia A.*, b. July 3, 1830, unm.

(3) *Charles H.*, b. May 1, 1836. Now in California, (1860,) unm.

256. III. ELNATHAN[8] (499) b. Dec. 1, 1808, d. Nov. 18, 1859. He m. 1831, Minerva Boltwood, who d. March 18, 1856. He was a farmer, in Windsor, Vt. Had 3 chil.

257. IV. JAMES,[8] (502) b. July 1, 1810, m. 1837, Sarah Saunders, of Weathersfield, Vt. He is a farmer in W., and Baptist. Has 5 chil.

258. V. JANE C.,[8] b. March 3, 1812, m. Dec. 1, 1835, Carlos Smith, of Windsor, Vt., who d. in W., June 3, 1843. He was a Miller. Have—.

(1) *Justin C.*, b. Oct. 15, 1842, in W.

259. VI. LUCINDA M.,[8] b. Dec. 7, 1814, m. Sept.. 28, 1833, Samuel I. Russell, of Windsor, Vt., who d. Aug. 9, 1857. He was one of the officers in the Vermont State Prison, in W. 14 yrs., first as guard, then overseer of the workshop, and also warden, 3 yrs. Rem. to Nashua, N. H., 1842, and afterward to Boston. Chil. reside in N., unm.

(1) *Caroline*, b. July 9, 1834. (2) *William E.*, b. March 26, 1836. (3) *Albert M.*, b. Feb. 29, 1838. (4) *Angeline E.*, b. July 9, 1841. (5) *Martha L.*, b. March 14, 1843. (6) *Eudora F.*, b. Jan. 14, 1845. (7) *Ada J.*, b. Nov. 8, 1851.

260. VII. GEORGE W.,[8] b. Feb. 14, 1816, d. in Providence, R. I., 1844, unm. He was a saddle and harness maker, and an excellent workman. He was ingenious, and noted for his prompt and keen wit.

CHILDREN OF JAMES WALKER,[7] [129] OF HARTLAND, VT.

261. I. MATILDA,[8] b. Feb. 13, 1798, d. Nov. 30, [29?] 1856. She m. March 1821, Gardner Marcy Jr., of Hartland, Vt., who d. Dec. 22, 1848. He was a farmer. She was a m. ch. Bap. Chil.—

(1) *Laurette L.*, b. July 25, 1822, d. Aug. 14, 1845, m. Nov. 1838, Joseph F. Temple, of Windsor, Vt., and had—1, Martha A., b. Jan. 25, 1840. 2, Orman F., b. Oct., 1841, d. Sept. 9, 1853.

(2) *Orman D.*, b. April 2, 1825, d. Aug. 1827.

(3) *Lucia A.*, b. Dec., 10, 1826, m. May 8, 1848, Joel Burnham, of Windsor, Vt. Res. W. Had 5 ch.—1, Electa A., b. April 4, 1849. 2, Celia M., b. Aug. 8, 1852, d. April 10, 1853. 3, Clarence, b. May 26, 1854. 4, George, b. Feb. 10, 1856. 5, Flora, b. May 3, 1858.

(4) *Jacob G.*, b. April 2, 1828, m. May 5, 1854, Charlotte C., dau. of —— Wheeler, of Haverhill, N. H. Res. H. He is a farmer, also a Baptist. Has—

1, Julius G., b. April 10, 1856. 2, Emma, b. Nov. 25, 1857. 3, Alice J., b. Oct. 28, 1859.

(5) *Caroline*, b. Oct. 12, 1833, d. Aug. 1834.

(6) *Julius C.*, b. June 3, 1837, d. Oct. 15, 1855. A Printer.

(7) *Celia A.*, b. June 25, 1840, m. Feb. 2, 1859, Edward J. Sylver, of Windsor, Vt. Res. in W. Carpenter.

262. II. William,[8] (507) b. April 7, 1800. He m. Feb. 7, 1822, Rachel Stevens, dau. of Daniel, of Hartland, Vt. She was b. July 1, 1800. He is a farmer in H., lives on the old homestead, and is an energetic business man. Has 8 chil.

263. III. Mary,[8] b. Feb. 19, 1805, m. Dec. 2, 1824, Sebastian Cabot, of Hartland Vt., who was b. June, 1799, and d. Nov. 26, 1833.

She m. 2dly. Foster F. Alexander, of H., Nov. 27, 1834. Both m. ch. Meth. Chil.—

(1) *Jane M.*, b. Jan. 21, 1826, m. Feb. 12, 1845, Newton A. Chandler, of Westford, Vt. He is a stone cutter. Chil.—1, Francelia M., b. Dec. 2, 1845, d. Sept. 9, 1848. 2, Willie N., b. Oct. 10, 1847. 3, Clara, b. May 30, 1850. d. Sept. 15, 1850. 4, Mary E., b. Nov. 29, 1852, d. May 19, 1860. They live in H.

(2) *Lucian S.*, b. May 22, 1827, m. Jan. 26, 1852, Charlotte J., dau. of Jonathan Bagley, of H., a farmer. Has—1, Willie L., b. Feb. 10, 1854. 2, Clarence L., b. Oct. 28, 1855.

(3) *Loring B.*, b. July 2, 1832, m. May 20, 1856, Isabel J., dau. of Jefferson T. Crosby, of H. Farmer in H. Has—1, Asa A., b. Sept. 30, 1857.

By 2d Marriage.

(4) *Asa B.*, b. Sept. 19, 1836, d. Nov. 20, 1854. Farmer.

264. IV. Jacob C.,[8] b. June, 1809, d. Dec. 31, 1811.

265. V. Harriet,[8] b. Feb. 24, 1812, d. April 10, 1852. She m. April 28, 1833, Dr. J. S. Miller, of Hartland, Vt. They removed from H., to Flushing, Genesee Co., Mich., in 1836. She was m. of ch. Meth. Res. 1860, Springfield, Oakland Co., Mich. Chil.—

(1) *Albert W.*, b. March 15, 1834. Farmer, and m. ch. Meth. (2) *Elvira*, b. Feb. 21, 1836, m. Jan. 6, 1856, Chas. D. Fisher, of Ovid, N. Y. Has—Albert Walker, b. Oct. 1857. She is m. ch. Meth. Res. Portsmouth, Mich. (3) *Caroline A.*, b. Oct. 13, 1839. Teacher. (4) *Azro*, b. April 27, 1842. (5) *Lucian C.*, b. Oct. 21, 1847. (6) *Harriet*, b. April 4, 1852.

266. VI. Caroline F.,[8] b. Dec. 19, 1814, m. May 5, 1833, Capt. Wells G. Hadley, of Hartland, Vt. He is a farmer. His chil. are unm., and the sons are farmers. Chil.—

(1) *James W.*, b. April 11, 1834. (2) *Abby*, b. May 26, 1836. (3) *Wells*, b. Aug. 13, 1838. (4) *George L.*, b. April 11, 1842. (5) *William W.*, b. Feb 14, 1855.

CHILDREN OF LIEUT. PETER WALKER,[7] [138] OF TAUNTON.

267. I. EDWARD,[8] (515) b. June 3, 1799, m. Feb. 14, 1822, Elizabeth Blake, dau. of Capt. Edward, of Taunton, and b. Oct. 13, 1801. They lived in Wareham, removed to Fairhaven, in 1854, and have had 7 chil.

CHIL. OF REV. ELNATHAN WALKER,[7] [139] OF HOMER, N.Y.

268. I. TRYPHENA,[8] b. in Homer, N. Y., Dec. 3, 1813, m. July 3, 1834, Charles H. Read, of Sharon, Ct. He was b. in Reading, Ct., Nov. 12, 1811; began a course of education for the ministry, but his health failing, he engaged in mercantile pursuits. After his marriage and having been in business 8 yrs., in Troy, N. Y., his health was restored, and with the advice of Drs. Miller and Alexander, of Princeton Seminary, (where he had formerly commenced his Theological course,) he resumed his studies in private, and was licensed by the Presbytery of Troy, in 1843. In Dec. 1843, he was ordained and installed pastor of the Pearl St. Pres. Ch., in N. Y. City. In 1849, he was installed, and is now, (1860,) pastor of the United Pres. Ch., in Richmond, Va., which has 350 members, and a large and influential congregation. He possesses superior talents, and especially oratorical gifts, of a high order. She "is one of the best of wives and mothers." Chil.—

(1) *Emma*. (2) *One*, deceased. (3) *Charles Lansing*.

269. II. JAMES,[8] (522) b. June 9, 1816, in Homer, N. Y., d. latter part of 1857. He m. May 23, 1839, Sarah Amanda King, in Darien, Ga. He possessed superior intelligence and culture, and d. of consumption. Had 5 chil.

270. III. ELNATHAN GEO.,[8] (527) b. June 1, 1819, d. May 31, 1855, in Lafayette, Ala. He m. Nov. 1, 1849, Nannie Alzie Wilson, dau. of Sam'l S., and b. in Rutherford Co., N. C., May 28, 1826. They had 3 chil. Nothing has been learned respecting his youth and early manhood. He concluded his Theological studies, at Princeton Seminary, N. J. He was licensed to preach, by the Charleston Presbytery, Oct. 9, 1848, at Columbia, S. C.; ordained and installed pastor of Little Britain ch., Rutherford Co., N. C., Dec.

1, 1849. He afterward took charge of the Pres. churches in Fort Gains, Ga., and Eufala, Ala., which he was soon compelled to relinquish on account of failing health. As a man, he was social and hopeful, fluent in conversation and agreeable in manners. In his habits he was methodical and industrious. He was a great tourist, frequently on foot, as well as on horseback. As a minister, he was always at his post, and discharged his duties faithfully. In the pulpit he was doctrinal and scholarly, which was sometimes urged as an objection, as the illiterate did not comprehend him. His discourses evinced the Theologian more than the Revivalist. Mrs. W. m. Oct. 29, 1858, W. R. Coleman, and resides in Ellijay, Gilmer Co., Ga.

CHIL. OF GEO. GOODING WALKER,[7] [140] OF TAUNTON.

271. I. HARRIET,[8] b. Jan. 26, 1804, m. Edward Walker. (See No. 233.)

272. II. PETER,[8] (529) b. July, 1806, d. Oct. 1, 1844, ae. 38. He m. Dec. 24, 1830, Rebecca C. Bryant. Res. Westville, Taunton. Had 7 chil.

273. III. ELIZA,[8] b. Jan 3, 1809. She m. March, 1838, Leonard Harvey. Res. Taunton. Chil.—

(1) *Eliza.* (2) *John.*

274. IV. DEBORAH,[8] b. Jan. 10, 1811, m. March, 1840, Seba C. Perry. Res. Rehoboth. Chil.—

(1) *Granville*, b. about 1841. (2) *Sarah*, b. about 1847.

275. V. GEO. GOODING,[8] (536) b. May 14, 1813, was pub. to Rebecca H. Leonard, April 1, 1837. He is house joiner, in Westville, Taunton. Has had 4 chil.

276. VI. CYRUS,[8] b. Nov. 5, 1815, d. unm. April, 1848.

CHILDREN OF EBENEZER WALKER,[7] [143] OF TAUNTON.

277. I. EBENEZER,[8] b. Aug. 10, 1812, d. July 9, 1816.

278. II. HELEN,[8] b. Oct. 2, 1815, m. July 4, 1853, Marcus Read, son of Elder John, of Middleboro' and Cranston, R. I., and b. about 1813. Res. Dighton. Carpenter.

279. III. REBECCA,[8] b. Oct. 4, 1818, m. Sept. 11, 1842, Rev. Rasselas L. Sears, of Marshall, Mich., son of John, of Bristol, N. Y.,

(See No. 74,) b. in B., May 25, 1811, and d. May 11, 1844, in Lima, Ind. He graduated at Union Coll., in 1838, and at Andover Theo'l Seminary, 1841. Soon after his marriage he became pastor of the Pres. ch. in Lima, Ind. His memory is still cherished there with devoted affection. In all respects, intellectually, socially, religiously, he was a superior man.

The following Obituary was published in the Boston Recorder, June 13, 1844:—

Rev. Rasselas L. Sears, became hopefully pious at the age of 17, at which time, he solemnly consecrated himself to the work of the Gospel ministry, if God should spare his life. After encountering various pecuniary embarrassments, in obtaining an education, in the Autumn of 1838, he was graduated at Union College with high honor. During his College course, he ever maintained a consistent christian character. Though ardent in pursuit of knowledge, he neglected not the cultivation of his heart. Upon leaving college, he engaged in teaching, at Utica, New York, where he soon secured the warm attachment of his pupils, and numerous friends, with whom he became acquainted. After pursuing with great industry and success, the prescribed course in the Theo'l Institution, at Andover, he was licensed to preach the Gospel, and soon after came to Mich., where he engaged for a year, as principal of Marshall Academy. While there, he received a pressing invitation from the churches at Lima, and Greenfield, Ind., to become their pastor, and acting upon the advice of his friends, he consented to accept the charge. His labors were highly acceptable, and abundantly blessed. Eminently qualified as he was, in mind and heart for his work, the recollection of his many virtues will live long in the hearts of his people. Of a naturally feeble constitution, and deeply devoted to his studies, the seeds of an insidious and fatal disease had taken deep root before he was aware of its approach. But so ardently desirous was he to lead sinners to the Cross, and to build up the walls of Zion, that he yielded with the greatest reluctance to the entreaties of his friends to suspend his labors in the ministry. Though the spiritual wants of this new country, his love for his people, the recollections of the years spent in preparation for the ministry, and his tender affection for his beloved companion, all contributed to render life dear to him, yet his wish to be restored to health, if such were the will of God, seemed to arise mainly from his desire to preach the Gospel. But when he became fully aware that his work on earth was done, he desired to be absent from the body, that he might be present with the Lord. Though for him to live was Christ, yet to die was evidently gain. At times, in the early part of his sickness, more particularly, he complained of a want of faith, but usually, all was bright, and cloudless, and oftentimes he was favored with enrapturing views of the Saviour. While conversing with a brother in the ministry, a few days before his death, he pleasantly remarked, "How blessed it is, that God takes his own way in removing the timbers, one after another, that sustain this frail tabernacle." When he became conscious that his last hour was come, like the great Apostle, when about to leave forever his beloved church of Ephesus, he sent for the Elders of the church, and in a most solemn and affecting manner exhorted them to discharge their duties and weigh well their responsibilities. He told them of his love for them and the church, over which they were placed, and expressed his satisfation that he had remained to die with them, instead of returning to the East. His reason continued to the last. The dying scene was bright and glorious. He gently faded away, like a summer cloud, and fell asleep in Jesus, without a struggle or a groan. As a man he was a gentleman, a *Christian gentleman*, and a thorough scholar. As a christian he was a humble and eminently devoted servant of the Cross and an able and faithful minister of the Gospel. The day following his death, which was the Sabbath, attended by his brethren in the ministry, slowly and sadly, his smitten flock bore the remains of their beloved pastor to the grave.

Mrs. Sears m. Dec. 24, 1855, Rev. O. P. Hoyt, D.D., of Kalamazoo, Mich. He was b. in Vt., grad. at Middlebury Coll., 1821, Andover Theo. Seminary, 1824. He has resided as Pastor or Agent of the A. B. C. F. M. & A. H. M. Society, at Potsdam, Utica and Cambridge, N. Y., at Cleveland, O. and Kalamazoo, Mich., and was editor of the Western Recorder. He was for 12 yrs. pastor in K., and then became District Secretary of the Am. Board of Foreign Missions. Res. Elkhart, Ind.

280. IV. EBENEZER,[8] (540) b. Oct. 28, 1820, d. Oct. 17, 1852. He m. Feb. 6, 1849, Abby L. Paul, dau. of Benjamin, of Dighton. He d. in Jamestown, California.

281. V. ELNATHAN,[8] b. April 18, 1823.

282. VI. CATHARINE L.,[8] b. March 8, 1826, m. Jan. 1, 1855, John B. Jackson, of Taunton, who was b. about 1820. Res. Westville, Taunton.

283. VII. BETSEY L.,[8] b. Dec. 6, 1831, m. July 4, 1852, Benj'n A. Wheeler, son of Cromwell, of Rehoboth, and b. 1827 or '28. He shot himself by accident in the summer of 1855, and d. in two weeks. Mason. She m. Oct. 24, 1858, Geo. L. Wheeler of Mansfield.

284. VIII. SARAH,[8] b. July 31, 1828, d. Dec. 18, 1846.

CHILDREN OF GEORGE WALKER,[7] [144] OF TAUNTON.

285. I. MARY,[8] b. June 16, 1829, d. March 24, 1835, of scarlet fever.

286. II. ELIZA,[8] b. Sept. 20, 1830, d. March 31, 1835, of scarlet fever.

287. III. GEORGE,[8] b. Aug. 11, 1832.

288. IV. CLARISSA ELMINA,[8] b. Aug. 10, 1833, m. Jan. 1, 1854, Wm. E. Manchester, of New Bedford, son of Wm., of Taunton. Res. N. B. Chil.—

(1) *William Arthur*, b. Jan. 3, 1855. (2) *Ida Frances*, b. Sept. 10, 1856. (3) *Charles Henry*, b. Sept. 1, 1858.

289. V. ELNATHAN,[8] b. April 22, 1835.

290. VI. MARY E..[8] b. Feb. 11, 1837. A successful teacher in Taunton.

291. VII. DANIEL B.,[8] b. Sept. 21, 1838, Res. Taunton.

292. VIII. WILLIAM L.,[8] b. Sept. 18, 1841, Res. Taunton.

293. IX. LAVIRA,[8] b. Dec. 22, 1842, Res. Taunton.

294. X. BENJAMIN FRANKLIN,[8] b. June 4, 1846, Res. T.

CHILDREN OF JOHN WALKER,[7] [149] OF DIGHTON.

295. I. CLARISSA,[8] b. Dec. 16, 1793, m. Oct. 16, 1817, Casina Shaw, of Raynham, a farmer, of irreproachable character, and one of the wealthiest men in R. Chil.—

(1) *Rebecca W.*, b. 1818, m. A. P. Slade, of Somerset, in 1844. Chil.—1, Edward Slade, b. 1848. 2, Nathan R., b. 1850. 3, Casina S., b. 1854.

(2) *Nathan W.*, b. 1823. Farmer in R.

296. II. JOHN,[8] b. Aug. 27, 1795, d. July 31, 1824, ae. 28 yrs., 11 mos., 4 days. Was Captain of a Military Company.

297. III. NATHAN,[8] b. Feb. 15, 1798, d. Nov. 5, 1823, ae. 25 yrs., 8 mos., 12 days.

298. IV. MARY,[8] b. Nov. 5, 1799, m. Sept. 28, 1829, Charles H. Greene, of Westmoreland, N. H., who d. 1859. Mr. Greene was formerly a successful school teacher. Res. Dighton, on the homestead of the late John Walker. Their chil.—

(1) *Mary Walker*, b. Aug. 26, 1830. (2) *Charles H.*, b. Oct. 17, 1832, d Feb. 3, 1834. (3) *John Walker*, b. July 30, 1835.

CHILDREN OF WILLIAM WALKER,[7] [154] OF DIGHTON.

299. I. NANCY,[8] b. Jan. 3, 1798, unm.

300. II. DEBORAH TALBOT,[8] b. Jan. 4, 1800, unm.

301. III. WILLIAM,[8] (541) b. Aug. 29, 1801, d. July 31, 1834. He m. Nov. 24, 1825, Lydia Hathaway, of Berkley. He was a Captain of a Company of Infantry. Res. Dighton. Three chil.

302. IV. SALLY WILLIAMS,[8] b. March 9, 1803, m. Oct. 30, 1823, Wm. H. Harnden, who sailed from port about 1835, and has not been heard from since. She m. 2dly, 1848, Sylvanus Jones. Chil.—

(1) *Wm. W.*, b. about 1825. Res. N. Y. City. (2) *Benj. F.* Res. Malden.

303. V. AMANDA,[8] b. July 28, 1805, pub. July 5, 1835, to Tamerlane Horton, of Dighton. Res. Rehoboth. Chil.—

(1) *Dexter Wheeler*, b. Dec., 1837. (2) *Amanda Maria*, b. 1839. (3) *Harriet Amelia*, b. Dec., 1840. (4) *Wm. Walker*. (5) *Jeremiah Wheeler*. (6) *Henry T.*

304. VI. MARY,[8] b. Nov. 12, 1807, m. Aug. 14, 1835, Abijah Babbitt, of Berkley. Res. B. Chil.—

(1) *Henry Lincoln*, b. 1836. (2) *Mary Adelaide*, b. 1838.

305. VII. JOSEPH,[8] (544) b. Nov. 8, 1809, m. Jan. 17, 1832, Laura Ann Austin, dau. of Jonathan, of Dighton. He was a Master Builder and Contractor, in Taunton, and a man of high moral worth. Rem. to Dighton, March, 1860. Has had 6 chil.

306. VIII. ELIZABETH ALICE,[8] b. Feb. 25, 1812, d. Sept. 16, 1813.

307. IX. AMELIA,[8] b. Sept. 22, 1814, m. May 10, 1840, John P. Wade, of Freetown, a Tack manufacturer. Res. Dighton. Chil.—

(1) *Edward Emmons*, b. 1842. (2) *Irene Amelia*, b. March, 1847. (3) *Lyman*, b. 1850. (4) *George*, b. 1855.

308. X. GEORGE E.[8] (550) b. March 18, 1817, m. Nov. 19, 1841, Lucinda D. Paine, of Dighton, dau. of Benj. Res. D. Four chil.

CHIL. OF GEORGE WALKER,[7] [161] OF PITTSTOWN, N. Y.

309. I. ELIZABETH,[8] b. Jan. 17, 1808, m. March 10, 1829, Harvey A. Orcutt, of Pittstown, N. Y., who d. 1858, in Cambridge, N. Y. He was a carpenter. She m. 2dly, Geo. Spreene, of N. Y. City. Res. cor. 37th St., 6th Avenue. Her chil.—

(1) *George W.*, b. Dec. 27, 1829, m. Oct. 15, 1853, Lucy A. Sterry. Res. Ann Arbor, Mich. Carpenter. 3 chil.

(2) *Mary Ann.*, b. April 28, 1831, d. April 25, 1847.

(3) *Ann M.*, b. Jan. 17, 1834, m. Sept. 9, 1851, Geo. H. Welling, of Bethlehem, N. Y. A farmer. Chil.—1, Adolphus E. 2, Adella N. 3, Laura E. 4, Kate A.

(4) *Sarah E.*, b. Aug. 12, 1836, m. Feb. 9, 1859, Lawrence Keyhoe, of N. Y. City.

(5) *Chauncey G.*, b. Dec. 25, 1838, m. 1857, Susan Bailey. Res. Ann Arbor, Mich.

(6) *Electa Jane*, b. Dec. 17, 1842, d. Nov. 25, 1846.

310. II. WILLIAM,[8] (554) b. May 27, 1809, in Pittstown, N. Y. He m. Jan. 29, 1832, Cyllania Taylor, dau. of Wills, of Ann Arbor, Mich., and b. Sept. 27, 1809, in Mt. Holly, N. J. Res. Ann Arbor. Hotel Keeper. Has had 6 chil.

311. III. ANNE M.,[8] b. April 3, 1811, m. Feb, 29, 1834, Wm. Austin, son of Isaiah, of Pittstown, N. Y. Farmer. Res. Greenbush, N. Y. Chil.—

Joseph Walker

(1) *Mary E.*, b. May 8, 1835, d. July 14, 1849, of consumption.

(2) *Elijah*, b. Sept. 18, 1837.

(3) *Edwin I.*, b. Oct. 12, 1842.

(4) *Emma E.*, b. Nov. 10, 1846.

312. IV. WARREN,[8] (560) b. Feb. 10, 1813, m. Sept. 3, 1856, Prudence Lee, dau. of Charles, of Pittstown, N. Y. Rem. to Mich., 1840. Res. Battle Creek. Farmer, and has one son.

313. V. WATIE S.,[8] b. June 16, 1815, m. May 7, 1835, Nicholas T. B. Shepard, son of Giles, of Pittstown, N. Y., and b. Nov. 25, 1806. Shortly after marriage they settled upon a farm in Dryden, N. Y., and in the Autumn of 1859, removed to Birmingham, Oakland Co., Mich. He is a farmer. Chil.—

(1) *Sarah Augusta*, b. April 18, 1836, and is a Teacher in the Wing Lake school, Bloomfield, Oakland Co., Mich.

(2) *Caroline Ellen*, b. Aug. 22, 1837. Res. Sherburne, N. Y.

(3) *Giles Warren*, b. Nov. 22, 1843. Farmer in B.

(4) *George Walker*, b. Nov. 1, 1845.

314. VI. CAROLINE,[8] b. May 8, 1817, m. Jan. 12, 1839, Wait Doolittle, son of David, of Pittstown, N. Y. Farmer in West Hoosic, N. Y. Chil.—

(1) *Ellen M.*, b. Oct. 28, 1841. (2) *Lucy C.*, b. Feb 8, 1844. (3) *Harriet R.*, b. Feb. 27, 1847. (4) *Annette*, b. May 26, 1850. (5) *David*, b. Sept. 21, 1853. (6) *Caroline*, b. Sept. 8, 1855. (7) *John W.*, b. Sept. 1, 1857.

315. VII. MARY,[8] b. March 20, 1821, m. Feb. 22, 1858, Amos Bloomingdale, of Greenbush, N. Y., son of Geo. I. Carpenter in G. Have—

(1) *Warren C.*, b. Nov. 28, 1858.

316. VIII. GEORGE L.,[8] (561) b. Nov. 16, 1822, m. June 14, 1855, Maria Prindle, dau. of George, of Bethlehem, N. Y. He is a Dairy Farmer, in B., 2 m. from Albany. Has one child.

317. IX. NAHUM T.,[8] (562) b. March 23, 1825, m. April 24, 1857, Nanny M. Arbuckle, dau. of Wm., of Taylor's Grove, Benton Co., Iowa. Farmer in Taylor's Grove. Has one child.

318. X. EMILY,[8] b. Sept. 30, 1828, m. March 21, 1855, Charles A. Denison, son of Charles G., of Chatauqua Co., N. Y. Farmer. Res. 23 Canal St., Albany, N. Y. Chil.—

(1) *Cortland*, b. Feb. 2, 1856. (2) *Edwin W.*, b. Sept. 7, 1857. (3) *George C.*, b. July 24, 1859.

319. XI. HARRIET A.,[9] b. July 20, 1832, d. March 30, 1833.

CHIL. OF ABIATHAR WALKER,[7] [162] OF PITTSTOWN, N.Y.

320. I. ABIATHAR[8] (563) b. 1804, m. Feb. 19, 1829, Bathsheba Babbitt, dau. of Sam'l, of Dighton, and b. 1807. He is a carpenter and farmer, and was Select-man, 1860. Res. D. Has 5 chil.

321. II. ELIZA,[8] b. May 11, 1807, d. May 17, 1848. She m. May 24, 1826, Silas Dean, of Taunton, son of Abiathar, of Berkley, and b. Dec. 16, 1794. He m. 2d, Nov. 1852, Mrs. Emily W. Walker, relict of Rev. Wm. (See No. 327.) He is a farmer in Taunton. Chil.—

(1) *Ann Eliza*, b. April 18, 1827. (2) *Augustina Frances*, b. March 12, 1829. (3) *Elizabeth Amy*, b. May 12, 1831. (4) *Wealthy Nichols*, b. Aug. 1, 1834. (5) *Myra Luther*, b. Jan. 30, 1837. (6) *Fanny*, b. Oct. 21, 1839, d. Oct. 17, 1844.

CHILDREN OF HENRY WALKER,[7] [165] OF DIGHTON.

322. I. HENRY,[8] (568) b. Jan. 28, 1808, m. Sept. 16, 1830, Nancy, dau. of Timothy Perry, of Rehoboth, b. Feb. 10, 1803, and d. June 30, 1858. He m. 2dly, March 5, 1860, Alma M., dau. of Capt. Seth and Lydia Pratt, of Taunton, and b. 1814. Res. New Bedford, since 1829. Housewright. He was a member of the City Council, in 1854. Has had 6 chil.

323. II. NATHAN,[8] (574) b. Jan. 1810, m. June, 1833, Rebekah Thrasher, dau. of Noah, of Taunton. She d. Oct. 2, 1842. He m. 2dly, 1843, Sarah Thrasher, sister of first wife. He is a farmer in Dighton, on the homestead of his father, and has 5 chil.

324. III. MARY GARDNER,[8] b. Jan., 1812, d. June, 1845.

325. IV. WILLIAM,[8] (579) b. Sept. 21, 1817, m. Sept. 20, 1840, Esther C. Brown, dau. of Robert, of R. I. Res. New Bedford, since 1840. A Housewright. Has had 3 chil.

326. V. JOSEPH BROWN,[8] (582) b. Feb. 23, 1822, m. June 16, 1844, Elizabeth Wheeler Baker, dau. of Nath'l, Esq., late of Rehoboth. She was b. June 8, 1820.

His early education was in the district school, with one year divided between Bristol Academy, in Taunton, and a classical school, in Rehoboth. The last three years of his minority were spent, chiefly in teaching, the remainder in study and upon the farm. Having by personal effort, and entirely unaided, become qualified to commence the study of a profession, he entered the office of Dr. Nathan Jones, of Wenham, in the spring of 1843, where he remained two years, including time spent in attending Medical lectures. The third year was spent in the office of Dr. Henry H. Childs, of Pittsfield. He grad. at the Medical school of Harvard University, in March 1846, and began professional practice, in East Stoughton. He spent 8 yrs., in S., with a large and increasing business, until his health failing, having had several attacks of hemorrhage from the lungs, he retired from professional service, purchased a farm, in Warren, R. I., where he lived till 1857, and then removed to Bloomington, Ind. He has held several municipal offices, and has had 7 chil.

CHILDREN OF DEA. SAMUEL WALKER,[7] [166] OF DIGHTON.

327. I. WILLIAM,[8] (589) b. Sept. 19, 1817, d. Oct. 26, 1846. He m. Nov. 28, 1844, Emily W. Savery, of Middleboro', dau. of Lemuel and Rispah (Thomas) Savery, of Plymouth, and b. 1819. They had one dau. (She m. 2dly, Silas Dean, of Taunton. See No. 321.) He learnt the trade of shipwright, in New Bedford. While there his attention was given to the subject of religion, and he became a christian. He was prepared for College at the Middleboro' Academy, graduated at Brown University, in 1842, and studied at Newton Theo'l Seminary, six mos. After a limited course of professional study, he entered the ministry. The claims of the West affected his warm and pious heart, and determined him to choose a field of labor there. But his career was destined to be brief. After preaching at Dixon, Ill., a year and a half, he was assailed by disease while attending a meeting of the Association, at Peoria, Ill., where he had gone to be ordained. He was attacked the day of his arrival, and his constitution not naturally very robust, soon gave way. He d. in nine days after, of congestive fever, at the Planter's House. His wife arrived three days before his death. He was perfectly sensible of his approaching end, and with his eye and hope on that Jesus, whom he had preached to others, with composure, he closed his eyes on all around. His funeral sermon, Text, Rev. 14, 3, was preached by Rev. H. G. Weston, a college acquaintance.

328. II. SAMUEL,[8] b. Jan. 15, 1819, d. Sept. 14, 1844, ae. 25 yrs., 7 mos., 29 days. He was one of the victims of the typhus fever which ravaged his father's family. Farmer in Dighton.

329. III. JOHN H.,[8] b. Oct. 14, 1820, d. May 6, 1821, ae. 6 mos., 24 days.

330. IV. FANNY,[8] b. Aug 26, 1824, m. Jan. 1, 1843, Geo. B. Townsend, son of Job, of Taunton. He is a farmer, and resides in Dighton, upon the homestead of his father-in-law. Chil.—

(1) *Samuel Bradford*, b. Sept. 24, 1844, d. Nov 26, 1844. (2) *Mary Elizabeth*, b. Sept. 17, 1846. (3) *Emma Jane*, b. April 20, 1849. (4) *Geo. Herbert*, b. Feb. 7, 1853.

331. V. NANCY H.,[8] b. Dec. 9, 1826.

332. VI. ELIZABETH,[8] b. Dec. 26, 1830, d. Sept. 2, 1844, ae. 13 yrs., 8 mos., 5 days, of typhus fever, which cut down her father and her brother, all in the same month.

CHIL. OF NICODEMUS WALKER,[7] [167] OF SHERBURNE, N.Y.

333. I. WILLIAM H.,[8] (590) b. Oct. 10, 1815, m. July 4, 1842, Sarah M. Fisher, of Plymouth, N. Y., who was b. Jan. 13, 1814, and is m. ch Bap. He is a farmer in Columbus, Chenango Co., N. Y., and has 4 sons.

334. II. FANNY M.,[8] b. Oct. 22, 1817. She m. James W. Greene. He has been Principal of the High School, in Camden, N. Y. She is m. ch. Bap., and has 1 son and 2 daus. Res. Rome, N. Y., (1860.)

335. III. ELHANAN W.,[8] (594) b. May 27, 1820, m. Oct. 18, 1841, Harriet Byington, of Utica, N. Y., who is m. ch. Meth. He is a carriage maker, in Sherburne, N. Y., and has 5 chil.

336. IV. ANNA ELIZA,[8] b. June 11, 1825, m. Edwin P. Shepard, of Cooperstown, N. Y. He is a carpenter, in Camden, N. Y. Has 2 daus. and 1 son.

337. V. CATHARINE E.,[8] b. May 6, 1827, d. June 13, 1828.

338. VI. CAROLINE ELIZABETH,[8] b. March 29, 1830, d. Sept. 27, 1847, in Quincy, Mass.

CHIL. OF DEA. NATHAN WALKER,[7] [169] OF HUNTERSVILLE, O.

339. I. NATHAN,[8] b. Nov., 1819, d. Dec., 1820.

340. II. NATHAN H.,[8] b. Sept. 13, 1821, m. Feb., 1844, N. S. Emerson. He is a Builder and Draughtsman in Urbana, Champagne Co., Ohio. No chil.

341. III. SARAH J.,[8] b. July 3, 1823, d. unm., April 3, 1840.

342. IV. JOSIAH T.,[8] (599) b. Nov. 1, 1831, d. Oct. 5, 1858. He m. Dec. 24, 1857, Micha E. Ford. He was a Surveyor in Huntersville, O., and had 1 dau.

343. V. MARY A.,[8] b. March 30, 1835, m. Jan. 1, 1860, S. C. Wilson. Res. Huntersville, O. He is Book-keeper and farmer.

344. VI. SARAH J.,[8] b. Sept. 20, 1843. Res. Huntersville, O.

CHIL. OF WM. RICHMOND WALKER,[7] [170] OF SOMERSET.

345. I. RICHMOND,[8] (600) b. Sept. 5, 1809, m. 1828, Mary Ann Church, of Exeter, R. I. Res. E. Has 1 dau.

346. II. ANN MARIA,[8] b. April 15, 1811, m. Sept. 18, 1828, George E. Bliss, of Rehoboth, son of Ezra, Esq. He was b. in R., Feb. 27, 1807, and is a farmer and mechanic, in R. Chil.—

(1) *Ann Maria*, b. Sept. 17, 1829, m. C. F. B. Smith, Feb. 3, 1847. Have Ida, b April 24, 1849. He is a mechanic.

(2) *Geo. E. W.*, b. Dec. 24, 1831, m. Phebe Marvel. Oct. 30, 1855. Mechanic. Res. Somerset.

(3) *Keziah Walker*, b. June 5, 1834, d. March 17, 1850.

(4) *Elizabeth Bowers*, b. Sept. 23, 1836, m. Henry C. Peckham, Oct. 15, 1855. Have Percival H., b. Sept. 19, 1856, and child, b. Feb. 1859.

(5) *Juliana P.*, b. July 26, 1838, d. Dec. 21, 1845.

(6) *Mary M.*, b. May 4, 1842.

(7) *Angeline S.*, b. Oct. 30, 1843.

(8) *Sarah Richmond*, b. April 22, 1849, d. Dec. 5, 1850.

(9) *William Richmond*, b. March 31, 1852.

347. III. DAVID BOWERS,[8] (601) b. Jan. 2, 1814, d. March 2, 1854. He m. Jan. 28, 1840, Harriet E. Webber, who was b. Columbia, Ct., Nov. 15, 1817. Had 5 chil.

He was a blacksmith, resided in Hartford, Ct., and was killed by the explosion of a steam boiler in the Car Factory where he was at work. A heavy beam was thrown upon him, and he died a few hours after. He was an industrious and good citizen.

348. IV. ELIZABETH BOWERS,[8] b. Oct. 15, 1816, m. Oct. 8, 1834, Alvah Slade, of Swansey. He is a Shoemaker. Res. in S. No chil.

349. V. SARAH CHASE,[8] b. Feb. 19, 1819, m. May 3, 1840, Zebulon P. White, of Norton. He is son of Zebulon, and b. in N., July 26, 1810. Res. Pawtucket, R. I.

He is a Book-keeper in an Iron foundry. Chil.—

(1) *Zebulon L.*, b. in N., July 23, 1842.
(2) *Wm. P.*, b. in Attleboro', Dec. 21, 1844.
(3) *Frederic H.*, b. in N., Feb. 20, 1848.
(4) *Sarah J.*, b. in North Providence, R. I., July 1, 1852.

CHILDREN OF GILBERT WALKER,[7] [175] OF CHICOPEE.

350. I. EDWARD SPALDING,[8] b. May 3, 1837, in Bristol, R. I. He was a student of engineering in Harv. Coll., (1854) and d. in Honolulu, Sandwich Islands, Jan. 27, 1859. He was a young man of much promise.

351. II. ISABELLA,[8] b. Aug. 25, 1843.

CHIL. OF CAPT. DAVID WALKER,[7] [176] OF NEW LONDON, CT.

352. I. CHARLES W.,[8] b. Feb. 5, 1849.

353. II. DAVID HENRY,[8] b. Jan. 25, 1852, in Newport, R. I.

354. III. LAURA A.,[8] b. May 17, 1858.

CHIL. OF REV. DAVID WALKER,[7] [183] OF ADAMS, N. Y.

355. I. LUCY ELMIRA,[8] b. April 15, 1821, d. Aug. 1, 1837, very suddenly, in consequence of a fall a short time previous. She was a very lovely and promising girl.

356. II. EUNICE,[8] b. July 13, 1824, d. a little over 1 yr. old.

BY 2d MARRIAGE.

357. III. SARAH JENNETTE,[8] b. July 5, 1827, m. Dec. 31, 1850, Jonathan Hall, of Smithfield, Bradford Co., Pa., who d. June 8, 1854. He was a farmer, and a worthy and influential m. of Bap. ch. Had *Brayton J.*, b. in S., Jan. 28, 1852. She resides in Adams, N. Y.

358. IV. GEORGE SUMMERFIELD,[8] b. Nov. 27, 1830. He is a Farmer and Teacher, unm., in Adams, N. Y.

CHIL. OF RICHMOND WALKER,[7] [185] OF CAPE VINCENT, N.Y.

359. I. ADALINE,[8] m. Orville Curtis, and has 1 son.

360. II. EMELINE,[8] m. Seneca Rogers, and has 1 dau.

361. III. VIOLA,[8] m. Peter Coselman, and has 1 son.

362. IV. JOHN,[8] unm.

363. V. ERSKINE,[8] "

364. VI. DELIA ANN,[8]

365. VII. HARRIET,[8]

366. VIII. GEORGE KENDRICK,[8] "

CHILDREN OF ROBERT WALKER,[7] [190] OF ALLEN, N.Y.

367. I. GEORGE B.,[8] (605) b. April 1, 1816, (1817,) in Dighton, m. March 10, 1839, Julia A., dau. of Mark and Abigail Dempsey, b. 1817, in Sempronia, Cayuga Co., and d. March 7, 1858. He is a farmer in Allen, N.Y., where he removed in 1820. Both m. ch. Meth. Epis. He is an active church member and a Class Leader. Has 8 chil.

368. II. LYDIA,[8] b. about 1819, m. Philo Dempsey. Res. Fennimore, Grant Co., Wis. Farmer, and a Class Leader in Meth. ch. Chil.—

(1) *George P.* (2) *Silas H.* (3) *Charles S.* (4) *Robert W.*

369. III. SILAS,[8] (613) b. Feb. 11, 1823, m. April 22, 1847, Sarah M. Noel, who was b. July 1, 1825. He is a farmer in Plattville, Grant Co., Wis., and has 5 chil.

370. IV. JOHN C.,[8] (618) b. about 1823, m. Clarinda Samnion. Res. Boscobel, Grant Co., Wis. Farmer, and m. ch. Meth. Has 4 chil.

371. V. ISAAC W.,[8] (622) b. April 13, 1828, m. July 1, 1849, Mary N. Long, who was b. July 14, 1833. Res. Boscobel, Grant Co., Wis. Farmer, and m. ch. Meth. Has 3 chil.

372. VI. ELIZA,[8] d., ae. 5 yrs., in Allen, N.Y.

373. VII. CLARISSA,[8] b. Sept. 12, 1834, m. April 5, 1849, David Blanchard, who was b. Oct., 1822. Res. Boscobel, Grant Co., Wis. He is a Farmer. Chil.—

(1) *Charles D.*, b. April 15, 1850. (2) *Geo. W.*, b. Jan. 28, 1855. (3) *Lydia A.*, b. Dec. 2, 1858.

374. VIII. MARY E.,[8] b. Feb. 27, 1836, m. Sept. 12, 1852, Thomas L. McReynolds, who was b. March 12, 1832. Res. Boscobel, Grant Co., Wis. He is a farmer. Chil.—

(1) *Henry Manning*, b. July 11, 1853. (2) *Thomas W.*, b. Nov. 14, 1856.

375. IX. CHARLES R.,[8] b. Sept. 5, 1838. Res. Marion, Wis.

376. X. MANNING H.,[8] b. April 20, 1841. Res. Marion, Wis. Farmer.

CHIL. OF JOSEPH WALKER,[7] [192] OF MARION, WIS.

377. I. MAHITTA,[8] b. April 24, 1824, m. Feb. 7, 1841, Jabez C. Rounds, who was b. Aug. 29, 1818. Res. Marion, Clayton Co., Iowa. He is a farmer and Justice of the Peace. (See No. 191.) Chil.—

(1) *Rosaltha M*, b. Jan. 2, 1842. (2) *Ashley J.*, b. Dec. 18, 1843. (3) *Priscilla M.*, b. Feb. 5, 1845. (4) *Clarillar*, b. March 11, 1847. (5) *Montville A.*, b. April 25, 1850. (6) *Joseph S.*, b. Sept. 29, 1854. (7) *Marion M.*, b. Feb. 6, 1857.

378. II. JOSEPH NEWCOMB,[8] (625) b. Dec. 17, 1825, m. Oct. 1, 1848, Isabella Horne, who was b. April 1, 1832. Res. Boscobel, Wis. Has 5 chil.

379. III. HANNAH,[8] b. May 8, 1827, m. Sept. 29, 1846, Charles D. Smith, who was b. Sept. 22, 1825. Res. Grant Co., Wis. He is a Hotel Proprietor. Chil.—

(1) *Emerancy R.*, b. Oct. 6, 1847 (2) *Alvah S.*, b. Jan. 5, 1850. (3) *Charles M.*, b. March 11, 1852. (4) *Ann A.*, b. Oct. 3, 1854. (5) *David F.*, b. Jan. 3, 1857. (6) *Franklin*, b. June 11, 1859.

380. IV. DAVID R.,[8] (630) b. April 17, 1830, m. Sept. 25, 1853, Sylvia E. Hough, who was b. Sept. 7, 1833. Res. Boscobel, Grant Co., Wis. Merchant. Has had 3 chil.

381. V. JONATHAN,[8] (633) b. Aug. 28, 1833, m. Sept. 25, 1853, Louisa Eldred, who was b. May 27, 1836. Res. Boscobel, Wis. Merchant. Has had 3 chil.

382. VI. CHARLES,[8] b. Oct. 18, 1840. Res. Boscobel, Wis.

383. VII. SYLVESTER R.,[8] b. Oct. 17, 1843.

CHILDREN OF CHARLES WALKER,[7] [201] OF MICHIGAN.

384. I. CALISTA.[8]

385. II. POLLY.[8]

CHIL. OF DEA. DAVID WALKER,[7] [202] OF CHILI, N. Y.

386. I. HENRY S.,[8] b. Dec. 16, 1836. Farmer in C.

387. II. CHARLES N.,[8] b. May 27, 1838, m. ch. Bap. Farmer.

388. III. ADALINE E.,[8] b. Jan. 24, 1842. Member of ch. Bap.

389. IV. MARY ANN,[8] b. Feb. 21, 1850.

CHILDREN OF GILBERT WALKER,[7] [205] OF DIGHTON.

390. I. ELIZABETH A.,[8] b. July 4, 1826, d. July 22, 1854. She m. Jan. 13, 1848, Henry A. Williams. Chil.—

(1) *Henry E.* (2) *Sarah E.* (3) *George.*

391. II. JOHN GILBERT,[8] b. April 25, 1828, d. July 20, 1831.

392. III. GEORGE A.,[8] b. May 1, 1830. In California, (1854.)

393. IV. GILBERT,[8] b. Aug. 14, 1832. Wheelwright, and lives in Dighton, (1854.)

394. V. ENOCH,[8] b. June 19, 1834, d. Sept. 2, 1834.

395. VI. LUCY,[8] b. Oct. 19, 1835. Res. Dighton, (1854.)

396. VII. GIDEON B.,[8] b. March 6, 1838.

CHILDREN OF PELEG F. WALKER,[7] [209] OF DIGHTON.

397. I. MARY ANN F.,[8] b. Oct. 27, 1831, m. Nov. 27, 1850, Charles H. Briggs, (See Nos. 168 and 16,) son of Matthew and Elizabeth (Walker) Briggs, of Dighton. He was b. April 15, 1829. Housewright in D.

398. II. SAMANTHA JANE,[8] b. April 1, 1838.

399. III. LYDIA BLISS,[8] b. March 3, 1840.

400. IV. BETSEY JOSEPHINE,[8] b. July 14, 1843.

CHIL. OF JAMES MADISON WALKER,[7] [212] OF DIGHTON.

401. I. JAMES ORIN, b. Aug. 4, 1851, in Dighton.

402. II. JOSIAH REED, b. Jan. 2, 1853, in Dighton.

403. III. OTIS NELSON, b. Oct. 1, 1854, in Dighton.

403.[1] IV. ELIJAH EMMONS, b. Aug. 4, 1856, in Dighton.

403.[2] V. ELLA JANE, b. March 22, 1858, in Dighton.

CHIL. OF NEHEMIAH WALKER, JR.,[7] [213] OF DIGHTON.

404. I. CHARLOTTE A.,[8] b. Oct. 20, 1844.

405. II. NEHEMIAH A.,[8] b. Jan. 8, 1847.

406. III. ALONZO,[8] } b. Aug. 24, 1849. d. ae. 1½ yrs.

407. IV. ELIJAH,[8] }

CHIL. OF CAPT. GEORGE WALKER,[7] [217] OF NORTON.

408. I. JOHN STARKWEATHER,[8] (636) b. Oct. 16, 1803, m. Dec. 24, 1830, Catharine Eliza Dean, of Taunton. He has been solicited to hold offices, but declined them. Res. Raynham. A shovel maker.

409. II. NANCY TITUS,[8] b. Dec. 31, 1804, m. April 19, 1831, John Willard. Have one child by adoption, Julia Ann, who is a young lady of talent and enterprise. She has been a successful Teacher in several select schools, and is now in Northumberland, Pa., Principal of a school which she originated. Mr. Willard is a Rail Road Car Builder in Philadelphia.

By 2d MARRIAGE.

410. III. HARRIET,[8] b. April 8, 1807, d. May, 1807.

411. IV. SARAH JANE,[8] b. July 19, 1809, d. Jan. 16, 1834.

412. V. GEORGE CLINTON,[8] (639) b. April 14, 1812, m. April 25, 1839, Eliza Hovey, of Whitestown, Oneida Co., N. Y. Has 3 chil. He became religious in 1830, and united with the Baptist Church in Athol, Mass. He commenced his academical course at Amherst, in Autumn of 1832, and grad. at Hamilton Theo'l and Literary Institute, N. Y., Aug. 1838. He was ord. at Gilbertsville,

Otsego Co., N. Y.. Jan. 1, 1839, and preached there 9 mos., and at Kendall, Orleans Co., about the same length of time. He then became Pastor of the Ch. in Wilson, Niagara Co., N. Y., where he remained 5 years, thence to Somerset, same Co., where he was settled 6½ years, thence to Hartland, (Johnson's Creek,) same Co., about 1852, where he resides, (1860.) Previous to 1855, there had been admitted to the ch., under his ministry, by baptism, and a profession of faith, 224 members.

413. VI. CATY CARPENTER,[8] b. March 15, 1815, m. Nov. 2, 1840, Benj. Meacham. Res. Worcester. He is a Boot and Shoe Manufacturer. Both m. ch. Cong'l. Chil.—

(1) *Sarah Jane*, b. March 25, 1844. (2) *Charles Benj'n*, b. June 9, 1850.

414. VII. SAMUEL PALMER,[8] (642) b. April 22, 1818, m. April 21, 1847, Hannah Jane Holmes. Has 2 chil. Res. Worcester. Wholesale and retail Flour and Grain merchant.

415. VIII. HANNAH DANFORTH,[8] b. Feb. 21, 1821, m. July 28, 1846, Chauncey Gale. Res. Shelburne Falls. A mechanic. Child—

(1) *Charles Sumner*, b. Sept. 21, 1854.

416. IX. LEWIS EMORY,[8] b. Dec. 13, 1823, m. Dec. 19, 1848, Clara B. Hammond. Res. Washington, D. C. Photographer to U. S., Treasury Extension.

417. X. HENRY JUDSON,[8] (644) b. July 7, 1828, m. June 7, 1854, Elizabeth Gregg. He is a Mechanic. Res. Philadelphia.

CHIL. OF ELEAZER WALKER, JR.[7] [223] OF CHESTER, ILL.

418. I. CONTENT R.,[8] b. Aug. 27, 1818, m. Feb. 4, 1834, Amzi Andrews. He was b. in Hartford, Ct., Dec. 15, 1800, and is a Ruling Elder in the Pres. Ch., Chester, Ill. Have an adopted dau.

419. II. MARY JANE,[8] b. Nov. 22, 1819, m. April 17, 1836, Thomas Segur, son of John and Mary, and b. in King William's Co., Va. Res. Chester, Ill. Chil.—

(1) *Frances A.*, b. April 30, 1840, d. May 19. (2) *Thomas Walker*, b. May 10, 1842. (3) *Elsey C.*, b. 1844. (4) *Richard S.*, b. July 27, 1847, d. Aug. 19, 1848. (5) *Amzi A.*, b. Oct. 6, 1850. (6) *Josiah Walker*, b. July 12, 1853.

420. III. WILLIAM,[8] b. in Lansingburgh, N. Y., and d. in Chester, Ill., 1843, ae. about 20.

421. IV. SARAH E.,[8] b. Nov. 11, 1826, in N. Y., m. Nov. 24, 1842, James Prine, who was b. in Va. about 1819. Cabinet maker. Now in California, mining. Res. Chester, Ill. Chil. b. in C.—

(1) *Mary C.* b. Nov. 6, 1843. (2) *William Walker*, b. April 12, 1846. (3) *Abigail F.*, b. Oct. 11, 1847.

422. V. JOSIAH T.,[8] b. in Kaskaskia, Ill., 1832. He emigrated to California, in 1852, to engage in mining.

BY 2d MARRIAGE.

423. VI. THOMAS,[8] b. ———, d. 1847.

CHIL. OF JAMES WALKER,[7] [227] OF BARNARD, VT.

424. I. JAMES RICHMOND,[8] b. Jan. 31, 1816, d. Aug. 13, 1816.

425. II. OTIS,[8] b. July 14, 1817, d. Sept. 4, 1817.

426. III. GEORGE WILLARD,[8] (646) b. Dec. 24, 1818, m. Feb. 26, 1844, Susan Chapman, dau. of William, of Barnard, Vt., and b. Aug. 17, 1817. Res. Barnard. Farmer, and has 3 chil.

427. IV. LEONARD,[8] b. March 1, 1820, m. March 30, 1858, Augusta Maria Crowell, of Barnard, Vt., who was b. May 1, 1858. Res. B. Carpenter.

428. V. DEBORAH DILLINS,[8] b. Nov. 16, 1821, m. March 20, 1845, Simeon Gates, who was b. Nov. 9, 1817. "She is a woman of remarkable energy." Res. Barnard, Vt. Chil.—

(1) *Theron*, b. Dec. 20, 1845, d. Nov. 18, 1846. (2) *Twin boys*, b. Jan. 20, 1847, both died. (3) *Martha*, b. Nov. 7, 1847. (4) *Maria*, b. Nov. 7, 1847, d. May 1, 1852. (5) *Mary*, b. March 13, 1849. (6) *Ednah*, b. Dec. 16, 1853. (7) *Harriet Augusta*, b. Jan. 6, 1857. (8) *Simeon*, b. July 13, 1859.

429. VI. HANNAH MARIA,[8] b. Feb. 19, 1824, d. Aug. 14, 1825.

430. VII. DEXTER DANA,[8] b. June 28, 1826, m. Jan. 6, 1856, Harriet E. Palmer, of Woodstock, Vt. Res. W. 1 mile from the Centre. Machinist. No chil.

CHILDREN OF ELISHA WALKER,[7] [228] OF TAUNTON.

431. I. ELISHA W.,[8] b. June 17, 1823, d. Oct. 3, 1823.

432. II. ADALINE NARCISSA,[8] b. Aug. 3, 1826, m. June 2, 1846, Zenas F. Bliss, son of Zeba and Lepha (Peck) of Attleboro', and b. April 2, 1824. He is a machinist and farmer, in Taunton. Chil.—

J. B. R. Walker

J H Daniels Lith

(1) *Narcissa F.*, b. March 8, 1847. d. Oct. 26, 1847. (2) *Ellen Everett*, b. Aug. 5, 1848. (3) *Mary Emma*, b. March 30, 1851. (4) *Elizabeth Reed*, b. Sept. 26, 1855. (5) *Francis Walker*, b. May 6, 1860.

433. III. WILLIAM JASON,[8] b. May 20, 1830, m. June 3, 1860, Maria G. dau. of John Earl, of Rehoboth, and b. April 10, 1837. Res. Taunton. Farmer.

434. IV. MARY ELLEN,[8] b. Nov. 4, 1832, m. Dec. 23, 1853, Charles J. King, of Penn. He was b. April, 1832. Res. Taunton. Child—

(1) *Anna*, b. Jan. 8, 1856.

435. V. IRVIN F.,[8] b. June 28, 1837, d. Sept. 18, 1837.

CHIL. OF DEA. RICHMOND WALKER,[7] [229] OF TAUNTON.

436. I. JAMES BRADFORD RICHMOND,[8] (649) b. April 15, 1821, in Taunton. He m. May 2, 1850, Mary Adams, of Roxbury, dau. of the late Dea. Thos. Adams, of Pembroke, N. H., by birth, an intelligent and successful merchant of Castine, Me., afterward of Boston, a man of large benevolence, fervent piety, and remarkable loveliness of character. She was b. in C. April 1, 1824, and is descended from Henry Adams, who came from England to Braintree, and whose descent has been traced from Ap. Adams, of England, in the 13th century. He was educated at Bristol Academy, Taunton, from the age of 8 to 17th yr.; entered Brown University, Sept. 1837, grad. Sept. 1841, and entered the Theological Seminary, at Andover, Oct. 1841. Studying 1 yr. in A. he was then employed in teaching, 2 yrs. as Assistant in the Friends' Academy, New Bedford, and as Principal of Bristol Academy, in T. Returning to Andover, in 1844, he completed the Theological course, Sept. 1846. Another year having been spent mostly in A. as a Licentiate, he was invited in June, 1847, to preach as a candidate, at Bucksport, Me. He received a unanimous call to become Pastor of the Elm St. Cong. Church, in B. and was ordained Oct. 27, 1847, Rev. E. Maltby, of T. preaching the ordination sermon. By his own request, he was dismissed, July 11, 1853, after a pastorate of 5½ yrs. He then removed to Roxbury, Mass. In this respite from pastoral labor, he commenced the genealogical researches, a part of which are embodied in this volume. He received several invitations to settle as pastor, none of which seemed to indicate the path of duty, till in Aug. 1855, he accepted the call of the 2d Cong. Ch. in Holyoke, and was installed Nov. 8, 1855. Res. H. Has 1 dau.

By 2d Marriage.

437. II. Hannah Church,[8] b. Dec. 9, 1827. She m. Sept. 11, 1850, William Rufus Davenport, of Taunton, son of Francis and Abigail, of Milton, and b. April 6, 1825, in M. He is descended from Rev. John Davenport, who was b. in Coventry, Warwick Co., England, and arrived in Boston, in 1637, and was 17th generation from Ormus de Dauneporte, of Co. Chester, Eng., b. 1086.

He is of the firm of Davenport & Mason, Express Agents, between Taunton and New Bedford, Taunton and Boston, and New York City. He is a Director of Taunton Bank, a man of enterprise and stainless integrity. Both are m. Cong Ch. Res. Taunton. Chil.—

(1) *Charles Francis*, b. June 24, 1851. d. in Taunton, Aug 10, 1851.
(2) *Mary Walker*, b. May 6, 1853, d. in Taunton, Sept. 4, 1853.
(3) *William Church*, b. July 18, 1854.
(4) *Helen Walker*, b. Oct. 19, 1855.
(5) *Frances Whiting*, b. May 29, 1859, d. Aug. 23, 1860, in Barrington, R.I.

Children of OTIS WALKER,[7] [230] of Taunton.

438. I. Abigail Amelia,[8] b. Nov. 10, 1818. Res. Taunton, unm. and is m. ch. Cong.

439. II. James Otis,[8] b. Oct. 19, 1820. Res. Taunton, unm.

440. III. Catharine Melinda,[8] b. Oct. 28, 1826, m. April 5, 1848, Geo. Washington Dean, of Taunton, son of Leander B Dean, of T. He was b. May 2, 1824. Res. T. Both m. ch. Cong. Chil.—

(1) *Edwin Lawrence*, b. April 12, 1849.
(2) *Charles Franklin*, b. Aug. 7, 1851.
(3) *Irving Brown*, b. Aug. 10, 1853, d. March 25, 1860.
(4) *Francis Dean*, b. May 2, 1855.
(5) *Helen Louisa*, b. July 27, 1856.
(6) *Emily Richmond*, b. Dec. 8, 1859.

441. IV. Nathan Franklin,[8] b. March 11, 1830. Res. Pawtucket, R. I., till lately, now in Taunton. A merchant and unm.

Children of BARZILLAI WALKER,[7] [231] of Taunton.

442. I. Elizabeth T.,[8] b. July 29, 1822, d. Oct. 29, 1824.

443. II. SARAH H.,[8] b. Jan. 10, 1824, m. 1856, Franklin Warner, who was b. in N. H. She was educated at Warren Seminary, R. I., went to California in 1852, and was a Teacher in Oakland and other towns, till her marriage. He is Professor of Mathematics in the College school at Oakland, Cal. No chil.

444. III. ELIZABETH TYLER,[8] b. May 30, 1826, d. Oct. 1855. She m. Sept. 30, 1849, Jacob Burt, of Taunton, son of Jacob and Priscilla, and b. 1822. She was m. ch. Meth. No chil. Res. T.

445. IV. BARZILLAI HENRY,[8] (650) b. Oct. 20, 1827, m. Sept. 8, 1848, Lydia M. Sandford, dau. of John and Sarah (Borden,) of Swansey, and b. April, 1832. Res. Taunton. A Carpenter. Has two chil.

446. V. MARY H.,[8] b. July 7, 1829, d. April 1, 1833.

447. VI. DEBORAH HOLMES,[8] b. Aug. 23, 1831, m. July 20, 1859, Zeba F. Bliss, of Taunton. (See No. 238.) Res. T.

448. VII. JAMES RICHMOND,[8] b. Dec. 29, 1833, went to California in 1849, and is a cattle trader. Res. Los Angelos, Lower Cal.

449. VIII. JOHN HINDS,[8] b. April 10, 1835. Res. T. A Carpenter.

450. IX. GEORGE EDGAR,[8] b. April 19, 1838. Res. T. A Carpenter.

CHILDREN OF EDWARD WALKER,[7] [233] OF TAUNTON.

451. I. GEO. EDWARD,[8] (652) b. April 27, 1829, m. March 13, 1849, Ruth Ann Pearl, dau. of Josiah, and b. Aug. 22, 1828. Res. Taunton. Has 4 chil.

452. II. DEBORAH ELIZA,[8] b. Aug. 4, 1831, d. June 21, 1854, of consumption, ae. 22 yrs., 10 mos., 17 days.

453. III. HARRIET ELVIRA,[8] b. April 16, 1834, m. Nov. 29, 1855, Alfred W. Balkam, of Taunton, a Moulder, son of Ansel and b. in Dighton, 1830. Has—

(1) *Edward Ansel*, b. about May, 1859.

454. IV. JAMES GOODING,[8] (656) b. Aug. 29, 1836, m. Nov., 1858, Amelia W., dau. of Leonard Hathaway, of Taunton. (See No. 135.)

NINTH GENERATION.

CHIL. OF BRADFORD WALKER,[8] [240] OF CANANDAIGUA, N.Y.

455. I. PEREZ H.,[9] b. Feb. 4, 1816. Res. Canandaigua, unm.

456. II. MARY A.,[9] b. Jan. 26, 1818, d. Dec. 28, 1839.

457. III. ELIZA C.,[9] b. June 16, 1820, in Canandaigua, N. Y., d. July 6, 1841. Both she and her sister Mary were superior scholars, and successful teachers. Their mental and moral attainments gave promise of uncommon worth and usefulness. Both m. ch. Cong.

458. IV. SALLY M.,[9] b. Oct. 21, 1822, d. June 9, 1825.

459. V. SETH T.,[9] b. Nov. 7, 1824. He was trained a farmer, and was robust and energetic. As one of the first emigrants to California, (at the age of 24 yrs.) he was highly successful, but his plans and "hopes were broken off" by death, at Sacramento City, Sept. 28, 1850.

460. VI. HARRIET,[9] b. Sept. 21, 1837, d. Nov. 25, 1840.

461. VII. TISDALE B.,[9] b. Nov. 19, 1826, d. Nov. 10, 1839.

462. VIII. SARAH P.,[9] b. June 13, 1829, m. Aug. 2, 1855, Ansel Spencer Wolcott, of East Bloomfield, N. Y., son of Anson and Lorinda, and b. April 21, 1827. He is a Rectifier of Liquors and Pure Native Wines. He is m. Bap. ch. and an active Christian. She united with Cong. ch. at the age of 19. Chil.—

(1) *Charles Spencer*, b. May 13, 1856.

(2) *Eliza Lorinda*, b. Aug. 4, 1859.

463. IX. LAURA M.,[9] b. Nov. 13, 1831, m. Jan. 1, 1857, Walker S. Marble, her cousin. (See No. 243) He is a farmer, in Canandaigua, N. Y. At the age of 16, he united with the Bap. ch. and has been a steadfast example of a consistent christian. He sustains a character upon which the world cannot find a blemish. Child—

(1) *Eliza Alzina*, b. Nov. 19, 1859.

464. X. LOUISA A.,[9] b. May 6, 1834.

465. XI. BRADFORD T.,[9] b. Oct. 5, 1843.

BY 2d MARRIAGE.

466. XII. MARY ALICE,[9] b. June 20, 1855.

CHIL. OF ELIAKIM WALKER,[8] [244] OF SALEM, MICH.

467. I. NANCY J.,[9] b. Aug. 22, 1824, d. April 18, 1847. She m. Nov. 12, 1844, Benjamin Hicks, who was b. June 14, 1820, in Bristol, N. Y. Settled in Ogden, Mich., 1834. He is a farmer, and has been School Inspector, Town Treasurer, &c.

468. II. CHLOE E.,[9] b. April 22, 1826, m. Nov. 11, 1845, Martin Vansickle, and had—

(1) *Agnes M.*, b. Aug. 4, 1849.

She m. 2dly, Jan. 27, 1854, Wm. Thurbur. Res. St. Louis, Mo. Both m. ch. Bap. He is a Carpenter and holds the office of Deacon.

469. III. EMILY C. F.,[9] b. Dec. 29, 1827, m. Sept. 27, 1849, Geo. Renwick, a farmer. Res. Ada, Kent Co., Mich. Both m. ch. Chil.—

(1) *Geo. Walker*, b. Aug. 19, 1850. (2) *Eliza Jennette*, b. July 22, 1852, d. Feb. 9, 1853. (3) *Maria A.*, b. Nov. 29, 1855.

470. IV. ELIAKIM T.,[9] b. Aug. 13, 1829. He m. Oct. 27, 1853, Isadore Ham. Res. Salem, Mich.

471. V. AMY ANN,[9] b. Oct. 17, 1831, d. Oct. 7, 1856. She m. Nov. 3, 1852, James Haman, and had *Ella A.*, b. June 30, 1856, Farmer in South Lyon, Mich. By her death, the popular vocalists, known extensively in the North and West, as the "Walker Family," were compelled to suspend their concerts, after travelling together 5 yrs. The family consisted of Dr. Harvey, Mrs. Haman, her brother, Geo. W., and sister, Mary J.

472. VI. GEORGE W.,[9] b. Feb. 2, 1834. He is pursuing a Medical course at Mich. University, Ann Arbor, and gives promise, by good habits and studiousness, of usefulness and success.

473. VII. MARY J. N.,[9] b. May 10, 1837.

474. VIII. ALBERT L.,[9] b. Aug. 6, 1839.

475. IX. MARIA A.,[9] b. Sept. 7, 1842, and is m. ch. Bap.

CHILDREN OF PEREZ WALKER,[8] [245] OF SALEM, MICH.

476. I. MERCY A.,[9] b. April 10, 1834, m. July 4, 1852, John Bogert, who was b. in Patterson, N.J., July 4, 1829, emigrated to

California, in 1854, and is Proprietor of a Public House at Michigan Bar, Sacramento City. Have—

(1) *Henry P.*, b. June 5, 1857.

477. II. MARY J.,[9] b. Sept. 7, 1836, m. May 28, 1857, Wm. Cordley, who was b. in England, and is a farmer. She is m. ch. Cong.

478. III. EUGENE,[9] (657) b. March 5, 1839, m. Feb. 1, 1858, Anna J. Van Buren, and has 1 son.

479. IV. JAMES,[9] b. June 26, 1841.

480. V. CHESTER,[9] b. Nov. 12, 1843, and m. ch. Bap.

481. VI. JOSEPHINE,[9] b. Jan. 27, 1846.

482. VII. GEORGE O.,[9] b. Nov. 7, 1848.

483. VIII. MATILDA A.,[9] b. Jan. 6, 1852.

484. IX. HORTENSIA,[9] b. Aug. 5, 1854.

CHILDREN OF OTIS H. WALKER,[8] [247] OF SALEM, MICH.

485. I. WELLINGTON J.,[9] b. April 26, 1835. Teacher in Texas, (1860.)

486. II. OTIS M.,[9] b. Oct. 11, 1837. Teacher in Missouri, (1860,) and is m. ch. Bap.

487. III. MORRIS G.,[9] b. May 7, 1839, and m. ch Bap.

BY 2d MARRIAGE.

488. IV. JANE ANN,[9] b. July 29, 1844.

CHILDREN OF DR. HENRY T. WALKER,[8] [250] OF DETROIT.

489. I. HENRY A.,[9] (658) b. Aug. 3, 1830, m. Feb. 22, 1854, Cynthia Smith, and has 2 chil. He is a farmer in Salem, Washtenaw Co., Mich.

490. II. BENJAMIN,[9] b. June 17, 1832. Res. Salem, Mich., unm. He owns a farm in Gratiot Co.

491. III. ELIAKIM,[9] b. Jan. 20, 1834, d. Aug. 21, 1834.

492. IV. CHARLES,[9] b. June 6, 1835, m. Nov. 19, 1857, Hester Ann Soler, and is a farmer in Salem, Mich.

493. V. LYDIA L.,[9] b. Oct. 24, 1838.

494. VI. ANN ELIZA,[9] b. July 20, 1842, d. Aug. 18, 1842.

CHILDREN OF ABEL B. WALKER,[8] [254] OF ANDOVER.

495. I. CHARLES ELNATHAN,[9] b. Dec. 24, 1827, d. Oct. 13, 1831.

496. II. CAROLINE AUGUSTA,[9] b. Dec. 21, 1829, in Hopkinton. She m. Aug. 23, 1852, Perry M. Jefferson, of Washington, Vt. He is Soap Manufacturer, in Andover, Mass. Chil.—

(1) *Herbert*, b. Feb. 13, 1856. (2) *Sarah Alice*, b May 30, 1859.

497. III. GEORGE PHIPPS,[9] b. Aug. 2, 1833, is a mechanic and unm.

498. IV. HARRIET COOLEDGE,[9] b. Oct. 5, 1835, is unm. Res. Andover.

CHIL. OF ELNATHAN WALKER,[8] [256] OF WINDSOR, VT.

499. I. GEORGE,[9] b. about 1838. Res. South Oregon, (1860.)

500. II. MARTHA,[9] b. about 1840, m. Oct. 30, 1859, Sylvanus Small, of West Windsor, Vt. He is proprietor of a Saw and Grist Mill, in W.

501. III. JANE,[9] b. about 1842, d. March 24, 1828.

CHIL. OF JAMES WALKER,[8] [257] OF WEATHERSFIELD, VT.

502. I. CAROLINE,[9] b. Dec. 13, 1838, in W.

503. II. MARY,[9] b. Jan. 1, 1841.

504. III. WESLEY,[9] b. Feb. 28, 1842.

505. IV. CHARLES,[9] b. March 14, 1844.

506. V. GEORGE,[9] b. Feb. 18, 1846.

CHILDREN OF WILLIAM WALKER,[8] [262] OF HARTLAND, VT.

507. I. WILLIAM,[9] b. Nov. 30, 1822, d. March 11, 1826.

508. II. JAMES,[9] b. May 4, 1824.

509. III. SIMON S.,[9] b. June 14, 1826.

510. IV. FRANCES M.,[9] b. July 18, 1828.

511. V. SUSAN M.,[9] b. Sept. 20, 1830, m. July 5, 1859, Geo. A. Morse, of Medfield. He is a Blacksmith in M.

512. VI. MARY A.,[9] b. April 2, 1835, m. June 13, 1858, Franklin F. Hodgman, of Hartland, Vt., a farmer. She was a Teacher and is m. ch. Dutch Ref. Has—

(1) *Frank A.*, b. May 24, 1859.

513. VII. WM. H. H.,[9] b. March 21, 1837.

514. VIII. JOANNA S.,[9] b. May 7, 1840.

CHILDREN OF EDWARD WALKER,[8] [267] OF FAIRHAVEN.

515. I. EDWARD B.,[9] b. Jan. 13, 1823, was killed by a whale near St. Paul's Island in the Indian Ocean, Dec. 15, 1844.

516. II. ELIZABETH J.,[9] b. Jan. 13, 1825, m. Oct. 1843, Sam'l N. Gurney, of Rochester, who was b. Sept. 1819. Res. R. Chil.—

(1) *Mary A.*, b. Oct., 1844. (2) *Elizabeth B.*, b. Dec. 26, 1846. (3) *Geo. N.*, b. Dec. 28, 1848. (4) *Sarah A.*, b. March 10, 1850. (5) *Abbie A.*, b. Sept., 1854. (6) *Martha W.*, b. Dec. 4, 1856.

517. III. AMASA E.,[9] b. Sept. 2, 1826, in Taunton, d. Nov. 20, 1858. He was Master of the Whaling Barque, Samuel and Thomas, of Mattapoisett.

518. IV. MARTHA A.,[9] b. Jan. 9, 1835, in Wareham.

519. V. MERCY M.,[9] b. April 10, 1839, in Wareham.

520. VI. WM. HENRY,[9] b. June 21, 1842, d. Oct. 19, 1843.

521. VII. RHODA L.,[9] b. Jan. 11, 1846, d. Jan. 12, 1846.

CHILDREN OF JAMES WALKER,[8] [269] OF DARIEN, GA.

522. I. CHARLES READ,[9] b. July 26, 1840.

523. II. REUBEN KING,[9] b. March 17, 1842.

524. III. JAMES,[9] b. Feb. 11, 1845.

525. IV. LILLIE ISABEL,[9] b. Feb. 1, 1850.

526. V. JOSEPH AUSTIN,[9] b. Sept. 23, 1852.

CHIL. OF REV. E. G. WALKER,[8] [270] OF LAFAYETTE, ALA.

527. I. AURORA AURELIA, b. Aug. 6, 1850.

528. II. AMELIA SARAH, b. Sept. 27, 1852, d. Nov. 30, 1853.

528.[1] III. Io. TRYPHENE, b. Jan., 1855, d. Oct. 31, 1856.

CHILDREN OF PETER WALKER,[8] [272] OF TAUNTON.

529. I. ZILPHA L.,[9] b. Sept. 18, 1831, m. June 21, 1853, Geo. M. Rounds, son of Marcus, and b. about 1829. Res. Taunton. Machinist.

530. II. ANN,[9] b. Jan. 16, 1834.

531. III. SUSAN C.,[9] b. Sept. 3, 1836, m. June, 1859, Charles Morey. Res. West Taunton.

532. IV. LOUISA M.,[9] b. Sept. 2, 1838.

533. V. BENJ'N L.,[9] b. May 29, 1841.

534. VI. REBECCA A.,[9] } b. Jan. 11, 1845, d. Nov. 17, 1847.

535. VII. CHILD,[9] } b. Jan. 11, 1845, d. at birth.

CHIL. OF GEORGE GOODING WALKER,[8] [275] OF TAUNTON.

536. I. GEO. LLOYD,[9] b. May, 1838.

537. II. MARY T.,[9] b. Nov. 7, 1840.

538. III. REBECCA AUGUSTA,[9] b. Jan. 19, 1844.

539. IV. WM. HERBERT,[9] b. Nov. 3, 1846, d. Sept. 19, 1855.

CHILD OF EBENEZER WALKER,[8] [280] OF TAUNTON.

540. I. CHARLES E.,[9] b. Aug. 21, 1850.

CHILDREN OF WILLIAM WALKER,[8] [301] OF DIGHTON.

541 I. ELIZABETH ALICE,[9] m. Wm. Polsey.

542. II. WILLIAM HENRY.[9] Lost at sea, about 1845.

543. III. OREN EMMONS,[9] (660) m. March 12, 1856, Charlotte A. Codding, dau. of Wm. and Abby, of Mansfield. He is a farmer, in Norton. Has 2 chil.

CHILDREN OF JOSEPH WALKER,[8] [305] OF DIGHTON.

544. I. LAURA AUGUSTA,[9] b. Aug. 17, 1834, m. Dec. 5, 1855,

Caleb C. Collins, of Taunton, who was b. 1830, of Sam'l and Laura. He is a Machinist in T. Child—

(1) *Laura Geraldine*, b. Sept. 1856.

545. II. JOHN COLLINS,[9] b. Nov. 10, 1835, m. Feb. 7, 1860, Laura L. Austin, of Howell, Mich. Res. Taunton.

546. III. ERASTUS MALTBY,[9] b. Oct. 28, 1840.

547. IV. LUCINDA AUSTIN,[9] b. July 23, 1847.

548. V. SARAH WILLIAMS,[9] b. July 27, 1849, d. Nov. 16, 1849.

549. VI. CHARLES,[9] b. March 29, 1860.

CHILDREN OF GEORGE E. WALKER[8] [308] OF DIGHTON.

550. I. WILLIAM E.,[9] b. Sept. 11, 1844, (Dighton Rec.,) Sept. 15, 1843, (Fam. Rec.)

551. II. GEORGE LEONARD,[9] b. July 29, (9?) 1847.

552. III. LUCINDA ISABELLA,[9] b. May 13, 1849.

553. IV. SARAH WILLIAMS,[9] b. May 20, 1851.

CHIL. OF WILLIAM WALKER,[8] [310] OF ANN ARBOR, MICH.

554. I. MARY E.,[9] b. July 12, 1833, in Brockport, N.Y. She m. April 19, 1852, John Brinknel, of C. W., who was b. July 8, 1829. Has—

(1) *Wm. Walker*, b. Feb. 16, 1854.

555. II. CHARLES,[9] b. Dec. 1, 1836, d. Sept. 1, 1838.

556. III. JOHN JAY,[9] b. Oct. 19, 1839, in Northfield, Mich.

557. IV. WARREN E.,[9] b. Feb. 11, 1842, in Johnsonville, Rensselaer Co., N.Y.

558. V. ANN E.,[9] b. Sept. 13, 1846, in Northfield, Mich.

559. VI. GEORGE W.,[9] b. Jan. 25, 1849, " "

CHILD OF WARREN WALKER,[8] [312] OF BATTLE CREEK, MICH.

560. I. WARREN,[9] b. May 22, 1858.

Child of GEO. L. WALKER,[8] [316] of Bethlehem, N. Y.

561. I. Charles,[9] b. June 2, 1856.

Child of N. T. WALKER,[8] [317] of Taylor's Grove, Ia.

562. I. Annette Jane,[9] b. Jan. 15, 1859.

Chil. of ABIATHAR WALKER,[8] [320] of Dighton.

563. I. Abiathar Francis,[9] (662) b. 1830, m. Oct. 23, 1851, Emily F. Westcott, dau. of John, and b. 1829. Res. Taunton. Machinist, and has one child.

564. II. Edwin Augustus,[9] b. 1832. Machinist.

565. III. Sally.[9]

566. IV. Sam'l Horace,[9] b. May, 1840, m. Sept. 8, 1859, Mary F. Newell, of Taunton.

567. V. Bathsheba A.,[9] b. 1846.

Children of HENRY WALKER,[8] [322] of New Bedford.

568. I. Henry Gardner,[9] b. June 26, 1831, d. Aug. 1, 1831.

569. II. Geo. W.,[9] b. July 18, 1832, d. Aug. 2, 1832.

570. III. Nancy Perry,[9] b. Dec. 19, 1833, d. Jan. 12, 1834.

571. IV. John Wesley,[9] (663) b. Sept. 14, 1837, m. April 1, 1858, Catharine A. Cannon, of Fairhaven, has one son, and is a Carpenter in New Bedford.

572. V. Mary Fletcher,[9] b. Dec. 31, 1839.

573. VI. Nancy Brown,[9] b. June 8, 1843, d. Oct. 2, 1843.

Children of NATHAN WALKER,[8] [323] of Dighton.

574. I. Mary Elizabeth,[9] b. Jan. 1835, d. Oct. 1, 1855, ae. 20 yrs. She m. May, 1855, Leprilete (?) Smith, of Dighton.

575. II. WM. HENRY,[9] b. Jan. 1836. He m. July, 1857, Lydia A. Brown. Res. Dighton.

576. III. NATHAN OTIS,[9] b. Jan. 1839.

577. IV. JOHN GARDNER,[9] b. July, 1845.

578. V. SARAH REBECCA,[9] b. Sept. 1850. (Nov. 8, D'n. Rec.)

CHIL. OF WILLIAM WALKER,[8] [325] OF NEW BEDFORD.

579. I. LYDIA GARDNER,[9] b. June 20, 1841, d. April 28, 1845.

580. II. WM. HENRY,[9] b. Aug. 4, 1843.

581. III. AMELIA AUGUSTA,[9] b. April 20, 1846.

CHIL. OF DR. JOS. B. WALKER,[8] [326] OF BLOOMINGTON, ILL.

582. I. JOSEPH WARREN,[9] b. April 18, 1845.

583. II. GEORGE HENRY,[9] b. April 29, 1848, d. Oct. 16, 1849.

584. III. HORACE EVERETT,[9] b. April 15, 1850.

585. IV. MARY FRANCES,[9] b. Nov. 23, 1852.

586. V. CHARLES FOREST,[9] b. Dec. 16, 1854.

587. VI. WILLIAM CLIFTON, b. July 20, 1858.

588. VII. WALTER F. B.,[9] b. March 20, 1860.

CHILD OF REV. WILLIAM WALKER,[8] [327,] OF DIXON, ILL.

589. I. DAU.,[9] b. and died same day, without name.

CHIL. OF WILLIAM WALKER,[8] [333] OF COLUMBUS, N. Y.

590. I. JAMES H.,[9] b. Jan. 5, 1844.

591. II. CHARLES L.,[9] b. Dec. 20, 1845.

592. III. WILLIAM R.[9] b. Jan. 13, 1848.

593. IV. LANDING S.,[9] b. July 3, 1850.

CHIL. OF ELHANAN WALKER,[8] [335] OF SHERBURNE, N. Y.

594. I. KATE E.,[9] b. July 27, 1842.

595. II. WILLIAM H.,[9] b. Oct. 20, 1843.

596. III. HELEN E.,[9] b. April 28, 1845.

597. IV. CARRIE E. S.,[9] b. May 20, 1850.

598. V. HATTIE E.,[9] b. Jan. 1, 1860.

CHILD OF JOSIAH WALKER,[8] [342] OF HUNTERSVILLE, O.

599. I. MARY ALICE,[9] b. Nov. 8, 1858.

CHILD OF RICHMOND WALKER,[8] [345] OF EXETER, R. I.

600. I. ANN MARIA,[9] m. Feb. 3, 1851, Sam'l Snow, Jr., of Taunton, son of Sam'l and Philindia (Walker) Snow, (See Eastham Branch,) and b. March 26, 1828. Res. Exeter, R. I. Chil.—

(1) *Paulina E.*, b. March, 1854. (2) *Willard Richmond*, b. June, 1856.

CHIL. OF DAVID B. WALKER,[8] [347] OF HARTFORD, CT.

601. I. JULIA MARIA,[9] b. Dec. 21, 1840. She m. Nov. 9, 1859, Horace B. Steele, son of Mason, of West Hartford, Ct. He was b. Aug. 6, 1837, and is a Book-binder, in H.

601[1]. II. SARAH JANE,[9] b. Sept. 25, 1842.

602. III. CHARLES HENRY,[9] b. May 23, 1846.

603. IV. WILLIE ORIMEL,[9] b. Dec. 12, 1848.

604. V. HARRIET J.,[9] b. April 27, 1851.

CHILDREN OF GEORGE B. WALKER,[8] [367] OF ALLEN, N. Y.

605. I. ELIZA ANN,[9] b. Jan. 13, 1840.

606. II. GEORGE L.,[9] b. Sept. 21, 1841.

607. III. THEODORE McH.,[9] b. Dec. 30, 1843.

608. IV. DAVID T.,[9] b. Dec. 14, 1846.

609. V. JAMES M.,[9] b. Sept. 24, 1848.

610. VI. LUCY J.,[9] b. Nov. 16, 1850.

611. VII. JOHN A.,[9] b. Dec. 31, 1852.

612. VIII. CHARLES L,[9] b. Dec. 2, 1855.

CHILDREN OF SILAS WALKER,[8] [369] OF PLATTVILLE, WIS.

613. I. LYDIA FRANCES,[9] b. March 30, 1848.
614. II. CECELIA PHILENA,[9] b. May 26, 1850.
615. III. TELORA ELIZA,[9] b. April 12, 1854.
616. IV. VIOLIA,[9] b. Aug. 26, 1856.
617. V. JOHN SOLOMON,[9] b. Feb. 4, 1859.

CHILDREN OF JOHN C. WALKER,[8] [370] OF BOSCOBEL, WIS.

618. I. GEO. LEANDER.[9]
619. II. JOHN MANSFIELD.[9]
620. III. LYDIA MARIA.[9]
621. IV. ALMIRA ELIZA,[9] b. Jan. 14, 1857.

CHILDREN OF ISAAC W. WALKER,[8] [371] OF BOSCOBEL, WIS.

622. I. CHARLES A.,[9] b. July 17, 1851.
623. II. MARY M.,[9] b. May 24, 1853.
624. III. LUCY A.,[9] b. Feb. 29, 1856.

CHILDREN OF JOSEPH N. WALKER,[8] [378] OF BOSCOBEL, WIS.

625. I. SARAH ELIZA,[9] b. Aug. 17, 1850.
626. II. JUSTUS,[9] b. July 14, 1852.
627. III. JEROME,[9] b. April 14, 1854.
628. IV. CORNELIUS,[9] b. May 14, 1856.
629. V. EDGAR EUGENE,[9] b. Feb. 13, 1858.

CHILDREN OF DAVID R. WALKER,[8] [380] OF BOSCOBEL, WIS.

630. I. PERRY JUDSON,[9] b. Dec. 23, 1854.
631. II. GEORGE DAVID,[9] b. May 19, 1857.
632. III. ROSA LUELLA,[9] b. Aug. 14, 1859.

Chil. of JONATHAN WALKER,[8] [381] of Boscobel, Wis.

633. I. Luthura Olive,[9] b. Aug. 30, 1854, d. Sept. 4, 1859.

634. II. Dora Ellen,[9] b. Feb. 21, 1856.

635. III. Joseph J.,[9] b. March 20, 1858.

Children of JOHN S. WALKER,[8] [408] of Raynham.

636. I. Nancy Titus,[9] b. March 21, 1831, m. Nov. 6, 1851, Philander Williams, son of Simeon and Eliza, of Raynham.

637. II. John Edward,[9] b. Sept. 12, 1833.

638. III. Ellen Frances,[9] b. June 25, 1835.

Chil. of Rev. G. C. WALKER,[8] [412] of Johnson's Creek, N.Y.

639. I. Wm. Gage,[9] b. July 3, 1842. He is preparing for College.

640. II. Henry Augustus,[9] b. Aug. 23, 1845.

641. III. Lewis W.,[9] b. May 19, 1857.

Chil. of SAMUEL P. WALKER,[8] [414] of Worcester.

642. I. Ella Jane,[9] b. June 7, 1849.

643. II. Sarah Elizabeth,[9] b. Feb. 24, 1853.

Chil. of HENRY J. WALKER,[8] [417] of Philadelphia.

644. I. Henry,[9] b. March 17, 1859, d. April 12, 1859.

645. II. Helen Frances,[9] b. Feb. 28, 1860.

Children of GEO. W. WALKER,[8] [426] of Barnard, Vt.

646. I. Laura Susan,[9] b. July 16, 1845.

647. II. Sarah Frances,[9] b. Nov. 12, 1849.

648. III. Jason Willard,[9] b. May 8, 1858.

Child of Rev J. B. R. WALKER,[8] [436] of Holyoke.

649. I. Mary Adams,[9] b. March 19, 1851, in Bucksport, Me.

Children of B. HENRY WALKER,[8] [445] of Taunton.

650. I. Henry Arnold,[9] b. Jan. 8, 1850.
651. II. Sarah Florence,[9] b. April 5, 1855.

Children of GEORGE E. WALKER[8] [451] of Taunton.

652. I. Estella Church,[9] b. Oct. 31, 1851.
653. II. Ruth Annie,[9] b. Dec. 28, 1852, d. Sept. 1, 1853.
654. III. Francis Irving,[9] b. March 23, 1856.
655. IV. Lizzie Ann,[9] b. Nov. 9, 1859.

Child of JAMES G. WALKER,[8] [454] of Taunton.

656. I. Fred Alton,[9] b. Sept. 14, 1859.

TENTH GENERATION.

Child of EUGENE WALKER,[9] [478] of Salem, Mich.

657. I. Wm. Perez,[10] b. April 21, 1859.

Children of HENRY A. WALKER,[9] [489] of Salem, Mich.

658. I. Mercy Ann,[10] b. Nov. 23, 1854.
659. II. Charles H.,[10] b. June 8, 1857.

Children of OREN E. WALKER,[9] [543] of Norton.

660. I. Ida Augusta,[10] b. Feb. 8, 1857.
661. II. Lydia A.,[10] b. Nov. 23, 1858.

Child of ABIATHAR F. WALKER,[9] [563] of Taunton.

662. I. Cora Frances,[10] b. Jan. 11, 1854.

Child of JOHN W. WALKER,[9] [571] of New Bedford.

663. I. Henry E. P.,[10] b. 1859, in N. B.

PHILIP WALKER,[2]

OF REHOBOTH,

AND HIS DESCENDANTS.

I. PHILIP WALKER,[2] (2) was the son of "Widow Walker,[1]" of Rehoboth, and brother of James Walker, of Taunton. (See 1st p.) The earliest record of him is a deed bearing his signature dated at Rehoboth, 1653. He was one of the Grand Jury, May 17, 1655, propounded for freedom, June 8, 1655, and took the oath of fidelity, June 1, 1658. In June 22, 1658, his name appears in the first division of Rehoboth No. Purchase, (now Attleboro',) when lots were drawn for "the meadow, on the North side of the Town," and again, May 26, 1668, in the division of lands, in the North Purchase.

His birth-place, and age, and date of his arrival in this country, are not known. He married, about 1654, Jane, dau. of —— Butterworth, of Rehoboth, or Michael Metcalf, of Dedham.*

She survived him, and afterward m. June 2, 1684, John Polley, of Roxbury, and lived there till her death, in 1702. Dea. Walker was buried Aug. 21, 1679, and his dust, reposes, no doubt, in the ancient grave-yard, at Seekonk. His estate was appraised, Oct., 1679, on oaths of James Walker,† and Samuel Walker. In'y £681.

His home and farm were on Watchemoket Neck, south of the Great Plain, at what is now the Kinnicut Place, on the road from

---

* The compiler had supposed, till lately, that Philip's wife was a Butterworth, as his son, Samuel, had an "Uncle Samuel Butterworth." It is, of course, possible, that a Butterworth married a sister of Philip, but it is not known that he had any sister, except Sarah, w. of John Tisdale. What is more probable is, that Butterworth was the uncle of Samuel's wife. Late investigation respecting "Joane Walker," dau. of Michael Metcalf, of Dedham, who, it is stated, in Metcalf's Genealogy, married Samuel (?) Walker, of Rehoboth, has led to the opinion that it was Philip, and not Samuel Walker, whom she married. For reasons, see Samuel Walker, immediately following the descendants of Philip.

† There is no record of any James Walker, in R., in the town register, nor in the Probate Rec. of the County, excepting as far back as 1643 and 45, which have been alluded to, in the sketch of James Walker, of Taunton. (See 6 and 7 pp.) He was about 60 yrs. of age at the time of Philip's death, and was, undoubtedly, the James, who helped appraise his estate.

Providence, R. I., to Barrington, about 1 mile from India Bridge, and in Rehoboth, now Seekonk, an attractive and fertile spot, overlooking the Providence river.*

He left a house unfinished, which the Court ordered to be completed at the expense of the estate. The estate was to be divided as follows :—

"In reference vnto the disposall of the estate of Phillip Walker, late of Reboboth, deceased, the Court ordered, that the now house in building shall be finished out of the whole intire estate, and that those that shall injoy it, shall make some proportionable abatement, of what shall be theire pticular interest, in the said estate, and that the widdow shall have a comfortable, and convenient being therein, during her widdowhood, and that the said widdow shall have her third of the said estate, and the sume of twenty pound, for and towards the bringing vp of the youngest child, and that the remainder of the said estate be deuided into seauen equall ptes, whereof the eldest, to have a double pte, and the rest to be deuided vnto the other children, in equall and alike proportions."

She gave bond of administration, Oct. 29, 1679,

"June 7, 1681, This Court graunts libertie vnto Jane Walker, widdow of Rehoboth, to make sale of a small psell of meddow ground, with the advice and approbation of Mr. Daniell Smith and Ensigne Pecke.

Philip Walker's occupation in 1659, was that of weaver. He became at length one of the wealthiest men of Rehoboth. In the allotments in 1671, his estate was estimated at £387, and was exceeded by only two in the town, the whole number being 78. In 1678, it was exceeded by only one, in a valuation of 83 estates. He held various positions of trust and honor. He was surveyor, 1657, constable, 1658, on the Grand Inquest, 1668 and '78, one of the Select men, several yrs. between 1666 and '75, and was deputy to Plymouth, 1669. May 14, 1669, he was chosen one of a Committee, to meet a Committee of the new town of Swansey, to settle a controversy, (probably about boundaries.) He also held the office of Deacon, in the Church. Nov. 2, 1663, Goodman Walker was appointed one of a Committee, to buy or build a parsonage,

* The first permanent settlement in Rehoboth, was around the "Great Plain," in that part of the township called Seekonk, meaning, "the abode of the wild goose." It is supposed that Rev. Mr. Newman, and his society, selected this spot because it was an extensive plain, already cleared of forest trees, and favorable for the cultivation of Indian corn. It is not far from the Pawtucket and Providence rivers, and had abundant facilities for obtaining fish and fowl.

or "house for the ministry." This "Goodman,"* was undoubtedly Philip, as there is no trace of any other Walker in R. at that time. June 20, 1678, the town having unanimously called Rev. Mr. Angier, to settle amongst them, "the townsmen and Deacon Walker, were chosen to treat with Mr. A. about it." It was also agreed upon by the town, that the sums to be raised, be freely subscribed, "if it may be," but if the subscriptions fell short, "Deacon Walker, Gilbert Brooks, and 3 others, should devise the mode to raise said sums."

In one period, the towns were obliged to sustain the war against Philip. Many who served as private soldiers, advanced money. The list of those in R. is preserved, and shows that the amount furnished by Deacon Walker, was £26, the largest sum, with two exceptions, and about double what was advanced by any of the 77 others in the catalogue.

Thus, like his elder brother, James, of Taunton, he was prominent in efforts and sacrifices for the maintenance and usefulness of the ministry, and the protection of the settlement from Indian ravages; sustaining at least, one kind of relationship and resemblance to him, and one which is certainly no dishonor. While James in Taunton, was distinguished and useful as one of the Council of War, for Plymouth Colony, Philip, in Rehoboth, was among the foremost in furnishing the "sinews of war." Rehoboth, an isolated plantation, was especially exposed to the incursions of the savages. The first and last blood of that fierce struggle, in which Metacomet or Philip, the powerful and subtle Indian chieftain, fought for the destruction of all the colonists in New England, was shed in Rehoboth. Here the conflict opened in 1675, here it closed by the fall of Philip, in 1676.

Deacon Walker, it is probable, was in that gallant fight of the people of Rehoboth, with Philip, and his best warriors. Driven to desperation, and fearing if he remained at Mt. Hope, he would be taken captive, the sachem fled into the interior, about the 1st of Aug. 1675. Encouraged by the strong appeals of Mr. Newman, their minister, and though not a part of the military force of the Colony, under his leadership, they pursued Philip, with great courage and activity. So rapid was their movement, that they overtook the rear of his forces at night, and with the aid of a party of friendly Moheagan Indians, who had joined them, attacked him and killed 30 of his men, and carried away much booty, without any loss. When the minister led the way in so noble an enterprise, it is no

* It was anciently the custom, to use this prefix, "Goodman," in place of Mr.

groundless conjecture, that his Deacon was with him, especially one who had advanced money so generously for the defense of the settlement.

March 28, 1776, just after "Pierce's Fight," the Indians fell upon that part of Rehoboth, called Seekonk, and burnt 40 houses and 30 barns. As Dea. Walker, at the time of his decease, 3 yrs. later, left a house unfinished, it may have been, that his was one of those burnt by the Indians. Philip designed an assault upon Taunton, but apprised of it, the town was prepared for defense, and when he approached, July 11,'76, he was met with such determined resistance, that he was compelled to fly, after burning two houses.*

Apprehensive of their destruction, the Cape towns sent a Com. to Bridgwater, Taunton, and Rehoboth, to invite the inhabitants to take up their residence with them during the war, but the invitation was declined. The answer of Rehoboth, by their Com. indicates an unflinching bravery, and a sublime, though submissive faith. The heroic independence, the undaunted fortitude of those isolated settlers, in the face of the appalling perils which threatened their extinction, prove that they were worthy to be among the founders of civilization, and the defenders of religion, in the New World, and are entitled to the grateful remembrance and honor of their descendants and beneficiaries.

"Though no tablets cast their shadows,
Where they slumber from their toil,
Blood of theirs is on our meadows,
Dust of theirs is in our soil."

All the notices of the position and character of Dea., Philip Walker, though few in number, are highly honorable. There is not a single spot on his escutcheon. He was prosperous, accumulating a property that was large for that period. He was entrusted with the most responsible office in the church, save that of the minister. It is indeed a grateful record, his generous contribution for his country and for Christ. His office and his services are a proof of superior excellence in character and usefulness, and leave no doubt that he was eminently a Patriot and a Christian. Cut down in the vigor of his manhood, his death must have been a sore calamity to the colony and the church, "as when an armor bearer falleth."

* When Philip escaped from Mt. Hope, in '75, a part of his warriors scattered in the wilderness, about Taunton, and burnt the houses of James Walker, and John Tisdill, his brother-in-law. John Tisdill, was killed, and 2 other soldiers, who were from Eastham. Though Baylies states this as in 1675, may not the "two houses" burnt July 11th, '76, have been those of J. W. and J. T. It is known that John Tisdill was killed June 27, '76.

"Buried Aug. 21, 1679," as the brief, sad record is, it is no groundless conjecture, that the members of the church, and the inhabitants of Rehoboth, gathered on this early autumnal day, to recognize the services, and honor the memory of the departed Deacon. The thought and utterance of their hearts, interpreting their great loss, may naturally have been, "How is the strong staff broken, and the beautiful rod."

His moral worth and piety have been inherited in a remarkable degree by his numerous descendants, unto the 8th and 9th generations. They furnish proof that the moral character, is an inheritance more surely entailed than any other. They illustrate the law that, "if the root be holy, so are the branches." They teach that, if it be a great privilege, it is also a great responsibility, to "partake of the root and fatness of the olive tree," in a godly ancestry.

For their virtues and piety are to be remembered, not for the fostering of family pride, but as an example and incentive to a worthy life.

It is an idle and self condemnatory boast to say, "we have Abraham to our father," unless we "do the works of Abraham." But a multitude sleep in the old grave yard, at Seekonk, who proved their legitimacy from Deacon Philip Walker, by their christian worth, and many others have gone forth into other wildernesses, to help establish, and sustain the institutions, connected with religion and the public weal, and are now laboring, or resting from their labors, in many sections of the country. Not many illustrious names are found among his numerous, and widely scattered descendants. They have swelled the ranks of the honest, and faithful yeomanry of the land. They have cherished and transmitted the doctrinal faith, and reproduced the piety and usefulness of their ancestor. Of a great number of them it is true.

"They were never squires and teachers,
They were never wise and great,
But they listened to their preachers,
Worshipped God, and loved the State.

"They were men of humble station,
They were women pure and true,
And they served their generation,
Worked, and fought, and lived for you."

CHILDREN OF PHILIP WALKER,[2] [1] OF REHOBOTH.

2. I. SAMUEL,[3] (12) b. Feb., 1655, d. Aug. 12, 1712. He m. Nov. 11, 1681, Martha Ide, dau. of Nicholas, b. Oct. 6, 1654, and d. Aug. 1700. He then m. Elizabeth. After his death she m. John Smith, of Roxbury, pub. March 17, 1714, and d. March 13, 1718, in 42d yr.

He was admitted freeman, in 1682, and was constable the same year. He served under Major Bradford in King Philip's War, and is variously styled, Cornet, Lieut., Capt. and Gent. His In'y was £1586, 18s., 3d., a large estate for the time, including about 700 acres besides personal property. In the appraisal there is mention of "his Trooping Horse and furniture belonging to him." He was Rep. to the General Court in 1705, lived on Watchemoket Neck, in R., now Seekonk, and had 8 chil.

3. II. SARAH,[3] b. Feb. 16, 1657, buried Aug. 2, 1693. She m. Dec. 27, 1677, Abraham Perrin, son of John, b. March, 1, 1647. He was buried May 15, 1694. In'y £230. Chil. 1679—1692—

(1) *Sarah.* (2) *Rebekah.* (3) *Elizabeth.* (4) *Abraham*, d. y. (5) *Anne.* (6) *Ruth.* (7) *Isaac*, m. Susanna, and had 2 sons and 4 daus. (See No. 86.) (8) *Jacob*, d. y.

4. III. PHILIP,[3] (20) b. March, 1661, (1661–2?) d. Feb. 17, 1739–40, in 78th yr. (Ins.) He m. —ember, 1689, Mary Bowen, dau. of Richard probably. She was buried May 22, 1694. He m. 2dly, Sarah, who d. Feb. 6, 1739, in 68th yr. (Ins.) He united with the Ch. April, 25, 1697. Inv'y £1750. He had 10 chil. On his grave stone in Seekonk Cemetery, is the epitaph, "Blessed are the dead which die in the Lord."

5. IV. ELIZABETH,[3] b. in 1662. Twin with Philip. According to the inquest, she "was accedentally drowned; shee, being sent to scoole, was found alsoe accedentally in the river first by two youthes; and they makeing known the same to two wemen, the wife of Nicholas Jyde and the wife of Roger Annadoune, and then to William Sabine, whoe forthwith came and drew her out of the water, as hee saith. From the testimony of the afor specified psons with other concurring cercomstances, wee, the subscribers, conceive that the child, which was two yeares and a halfe old, before specifyed, came accedentally to her end. Seauenth of Aug. 1664." Plym. Col. Rec. 4th vol. 83, 84 pp.

6. V. MARY,[3] b. May, 1663, d. May 8, 1694. In'y £44. Her Will, proved May 28, 1694, contains bequests "To cousin (niece) Ann Perron, the book 'Cordial Comfort.' To cousin (niece) Abraham Perron, 'Secret thoughts in dying times.' To cousin (niece) Sarah Perron, my Bible."

7. VI. EXPERIENCE,[3] birth unknown, buried Nov. 10, 1674.

8. VII. ELIZABETH,[3] b. April 1, 1666, m. March 31, 1687, Henry Sweet, of Swanzey, who d. Dec. 8, 1704. In'y £100. Chil.—

(1) *John*, b. 1695, m. 1719, Hannah Peck, and 1730, Sarah Claflen. 13 chil. (2) *Philip*, d. y. (3) *Thomas*, b. 1701, m. 1728, Rebecca Peck. 11 chil. (4) *Michael*, d. y. (5) *Dorothy*.

9. VIII. MICHAEL,[3] b. March 1, 1667, buried Feb., 1677.

February the 16th, 1677.

"Wee, whose names are vnderwritten, being called together on a corroners inquest, vpon that sad accedent, which befell Micaell Walker, about ten yeers of age, wee doe find, that hee came accedentally to his end by his falling through the flore of the saw mill vpon the water wheel, or just by it when it was goeing, and was carried away with the streame vnder the iyce."

STEUEN PAINE, Sen'r and 11 others.

10. IX. EBENEZER,[3] (30) b. "Mid Nov." 1676, d. March 13, 1717–18. He m. Nov. 19, 1700, Mehetable Willmarth, who d. Oct. 27, 1702. He m. 2dly, Oct. 11, 1703, Dorethy Abell, dau. of Lieut. Preserved, and b. Nov. 18, 1677. He and w. renewed covenant, 1709. He had 11 children. In'y £1575. Res. Rehoboth, now Seekonk. She m. 2dly, 1724, John Reed and d. Aug. 1, 1741, in 64th yr. (Ins.)

11. X. MARTHA.[3] Not of age in 1680.

FOURTH GENERATION.

CHILDREN OF SAMUEL WALKER,[3] [2] OF REHOBOTH.

12. I. SAMUEL,[4] (41) b. Nov. 11, 1682, d. Aug. 23, 1712. He m. Feb. 9, 1705–6, Bethya Read, who d. Oct. 18, 1708. He then m. Nov. 10, 1709, Ruth Bliss, dau. of Sam'l and Mary, and b. Nov. 11, 1687. In'y £129. Had 3 chil. His widow m. Jan., 1713–14, Noah Saben.

13. II. PATIENCE,[4] b. March 30, 1685, d. Nov. 28, 1730. She m. June 14, 1705, Noah Perrin, of Roxbury. He was a tailor. They were admitted to the ch., April, 1724, and had 7 chil. from Jan. 18, 1708, to Dec. 22, 1729—

(1) *Noah.* (2) *Mary.* (3) *Samuel.* (4) *Elizabeth.* (5) *Patience.* (6) *Thankful.* (7) *John.*

14. III. TIMOTHY,[4] (44) b. Sept. 14, 1687, d. Nov. 17, 1745, in 59th yr. He m. May 14, 1713, Grace Child, dau. of Edward, [was it not Benjamin? See No. 15.] and b. about 1678, in Rehoboth. She was admitted to the ch., June 14, 1724, and d. Oct. 30, 1729. He m. 2dly, Jan. 15, 1729–30, Rachel Beverly. He exerted a great influence in the affairs of Rehoboth. In'y £2743, old tenor. Had 7 chil. His widow m. Daniel Greenwood, of Sutton, Nov. 15, 1748.

15. IV. PETER,[4] (51) b. Sept. 18, 1689, d. March 24, 1760. He m. June 9, 1715, Mary Child, of Roxbury, dau. of Benj'n and Grace (Morris.) She d. between 1730 and 32. They were admitted to Communion, Oct. 10, 1724. He m. 2d, Jan. 18, 1732–3, Mrs. Martha Read, who d. Jan. 16, 1747–8, in 58th yr. (Ins.) He m. 3d, Bethiah, who was a widow in 1760, and in Woodstock, Ct. His In'y was £238. Res. Rehoboth. Had 13 chil.

16. V. EPHRAIM,[4] (64) b. Sept. 4, 1692, d. March 2, 1731–2, in 40th yr. (Ins.) He m. Mary, dau. of Lieut. Preserved Abell. She d. July, 1747. In her will she bequeathed £10, to the 1st Church in Rehoboth, for the purchase of a cup for the communion service,—to Jas. Clay, her negro boy Cæsar, and provided for his liberty. They had 8 chil.

17. VI. MARTHA,[4] b. Sept. 8, 1696. She m. Oct. 5, 1721, Ichabod Bowen, who d. March 20, 1760. Chil.—

(1) *Eleazer*, b. 1722, m. Dorothy, d. before 1760. (2) *Samuel*, b. 1724. (3) *Alse*, d. Feb. 25, 1791. (4) *Simeon*. b. 1730. (5) *Ichabod*, b. 1735. (6) *Martha*, b. 1737.

BY 2d MARRIAGE.

18. VII. ELIZABETH,[4] b. Aug. 10, 1702, d. Dec. 28, 1702.

19. VIII. BENJAMIN, (72) b. Aug. 12, 1703, d. 1787. He m. —— Bicknell, then Elizabeth Childs, and 3dly, —— Cadwell, of Hartford, Ct. He was in Rehoboth 1725, but settled in Ashford, Ct. Had 8 chil. all by 1st wife. Tradition says he had 5 chil. born in 5 successive yrs. in the month of July, that the first 3 sons were Benj., Eben'r and Eph'm, and the 3d, went alone first. Benj'n 1st born, was 5 yrs. of age when he walked, yet he became robust and athletic, as have been all the W's of his branch.

CHILDREN OF PHILIP WALKER,[3] [4] OF REHOBOTH.

20. I. EBENEZER,[4] b. Oct. 21, 1688. He probably d. unm. or without issue, as there is no mention of him or heirs, in his father's will.

21. II. JAMES,[4] (80) b. Sept. 3, 1690, d. Nov. 28, 1747. He m. Elizabeth, who d. Dec. 29, 1747-8. They renewed covenant Oct. 3, 1735. Res. Rehoboth. In'y £818. Had 6 chil.

22. III. PHILIP,[4] (86) b. Aug. 13, 1693, d. Nov. 5, 1742. He m. Dec. 7, 1721, Mary Chard, who d. Sept. 3, 1737. He then m. March 4, 1737–8, Ann Martin, of Bristol, R. I., dau. of Melatiah, and b. Sept. 9, 1699. He was Captain. Inv'y, £1429. Res. Rehoboth. Had 8 chil. His widow m. 2dly, July 27, 1743, Jeremiah Allen, and d. July 7, 1747.

BY 2d MARRIAGE.

23. IV. SARAH,[4] b. Jan. 8, 1695–6. It is inferred that she first m. Thomas Kilton, Feb. 3, 1724, as there was no other Sarah, born early enough for this marriage. Had—

(1) *Amey*, b. Oct. 9, 1726.

Sarah[4] was w. of ——— Holdridge, in 1739. (Will of father.)

24. V. ESTHER,[4] b. ———, baptized July 4, 1697. She m. ——— Avery, (father's will) and had—

(1) *Esther*, living in 1749.

Esther Walker m. May 16, 1709, Isaac Averill. (Re'th Rec.) Was it Esther[4]? If so, she must have been oldest child. There is no other E.

25. VI. MARY,[4] b. March 19, 1699–1700. It is supposed she m. 1st, Josiah Ide, June 18, 1724, who d. Nov. 30, 1731. She was w. of ——— Robinson, in 1739. (Father's will.) Chil.—

(1) *Elizabeth*, b. March 19, 1725. (2) *Daniel*, b. June 13, 1726. (3) *Josiah*, b. Oct. 16, 1728. (4) *Mary*, b. Jan. 1, 1730–1.

26. VII. JANE,[4] b. March 21, 1702. She m. Dec. 23, 1724, Samuel Newman, Jr., of Rehoboth. They had chil. baptized in Seekonk. (Ch. Rec.) Chil.—

(1) *David*, b. April 20, 1727. (2) *Jesse*, b. Aug. 2, 1730, (3) *Sarah*, b. July 3, 1733. (4) *Nathan*, b. Dec. 25, 1735. (5) *Samuel*, b. March 22, 1738–9.

27. VIII. NATHANIEL,[4] (94) b. Jan. 31, 1703–4, d. April 20, 1783. He m. May 11, 1727, Anna Sweeting, dau. of Henry, b. May 1, 1707, and d. March 23, 1772. He is called "best beloved

son," in his father's will. He united with the ch. March 25, 1738, held the office of Deacon, and was also Rep. to General Court, 1750 and '51. Res. R. Had 9 chil.

28. IX. Daniel,[4] (103) b. Oct. 10, 1706. He m. Jan. 1, 1729–30, Mary Perry, dau. of Jasiel and Rebecca, and bro. of Jasiel, Jr. (See No. 44.) She d. in Rutland, Vt. Both m. ch. He joined the expedition to Quebec, and was there at the taking of the city in 1759. On his return, when between Clarendon (then Socialboro',) and No. 4, New Hampshire, (now Charleston,) he froze his feet badly. Attracted by the appearance of the country on his way home, he travelled up the Otter Creek, as far as Clarendon. On the 1st of April, 1768, removed with his family to C., where he died. He early settled in Coventry, R. I., and built him a house, which was situated a little East of South, from the Summit Station, on Providence and Hartford R. R. All that now remains is the chimney, still standing, (1857,) the house having been taken down in 1853. He left also, other traces of his sojourn in C. South of his dwelling on the hill are two little graves, always said by oldest inhabitants to be graves of Walker children. They are still visible, and the present owner of the farm has lately enclosed the place for a grave yard. It is a tradition there, that Mr. W. one evening saw a strange light on the hill. Losing his 2 chil. soon after, he had them buried where he saw the singular light. These two graves on the hill, alone, and yet guarded for more than half a century, and remembered as Mr. W.'s children, confirm the record in Attleboro', which gives names and births of his chil. He was living in A. in 1750, where he owned lands inherited by will, from his father's estate. It is no wonder that in view of the lands on the Otter Creek, he should abandon the rough soil of Coventry, R. I. Had 12 chil.

29. X. Stephen,[4] (115) b. Aug. 7, 1709. He m. Jan. 3, 1733-4, Rebekah Millerd, dau. of Solomon and Elizabeth, b. Sept. 2, 1706, and d. Sept. 17, 1837, ae. 31 yrs. and 15 days. They had 2 chil. He m. 2dly, July 20, 1738, Mehetable Harris of Roxbury, and had 2 chil. He was a Weaver; removed to Pomfret, Ct., and was recommended to the ch. in P., 1739. He probably left P., as search has been fruitless, to learn more of him or his chil.

Children of EBENEZER WALKER,[3] [10] of Rehoboth.

30. I. Ebenezer,[4] b. June 30, 1701, d. May 26, 1702,

31. II. Mehetable,[4] b. Dec. 18, 1702, d. May 5, 1705.

BY 2d MARRIAGE.

32. III. JOHANNA,[4] b. July 18, 1704, d. Jan. 22, 1786, ae 81. She m. Nov. 12, 1724, David Carpenter, son of David, b. June 1, 1701, and d. July 11, 1787. A farmer in Rehoboth. Chil.—

> (1) *Thomas*, b. July 15, 1725, m. Dorothy Bosworth. (2) *David*, b. Oct. 1, 1727, d. unm. (3) *Elizabeth*, b. March 15, 1730. (4) *John*, b. April 6, 1733, m. 3dly, Mary Ide, (See No. 35.) (5) *Nathaniel*, b. Jan. 13. 1743–44, m. Elizabeth Carpenter.

33. IV. MARY,[4] d. Jan. 12, 1708–9.

34. V. CALEB, (119) b. Oct. 30, 1706, d. April 3, 1768, in 62d yr. He m. Abigail Dean, of Taunton, dau. of Doct. Ezra, b. Dec. 10, 1704. She united with the ch. in R. April 12, 1730, and d. Jan. 1, 1795, in 91st yr. (Ins.) They had 5 chil.

35. VI. DOROTHY,[4] b. Jan. 11, 1708–9, d. April 22, 1796, ae. 87. She m. as 2d wife, Dec. 2, 1743, Edward Carpenter, son of Obadiah ? b. Oct. 5, 1705, and d. Feb. 24, 1771, in 66th yr. He was a Farmer and Ensign. Chil.—

> (1) *Mary*, b. Nov. 13, 1744. (2) *Edward*, b. Dec. 6, 1746 (3) *Dorothy*, b. Jan. 26, (June ?) 1749. (4) *Mary*, b. Nov. 18, 1752, m. 1st, Edward Ide, then John Carpenter, (No. 32.)

36. VII. JOHN, } b. Feb. 18, 1710–11, d. Feb. 27, 1710–11.
37. VIII. SARAH, } b. Feb. 18, 1710–11, d. March 2, 1710–11.

38. IX. ELIZABETH,[4] b. March 24, 1711–12, d. March 18, 1753, in 42d yr. (Ins.) She m. Oct. 28, 1731, Miles Shorey, who d. May 31, 1752, in 42d yr. Chil.—

> (1) *Sarah*, b. May 1, 1732, (2) *Elizabeth*, b. Jan. 31, 1733–34. (3) *John*, b. March 30, 1736, m. Patience, and had 6 chil. (4) *Jacob*, b. July 24, 1738, m Kezia, and had 7 chil. (5) *Sarah*, b. Aug. 1, 1740. (6) *Molle*, b. Sept. 24, 1743. (7) *Miles*, b. Jan. 22, 1745–6. (8) *David*, b. March 16, 1747–8, m. Alathea. (9) *Hannah*, b. April 1, 1750.

39. X. MARTHA,[4] b. July 20, 1714. She m. April 4, 1733–4, David Chaffee. Res. Attleboro. Chil.—

> (1) *David*, bapt. 1733. (2) *Martha*, bapt. 1735. (3) *Martha*, bapt. 1737. (4) *Dorothy*, bapt. 1739. (5) *Patience*, bapt. 1742. (6) *Abner*, bapt. 1746.

40. XI. EBENEZER,[4] (124) b. Dec. 9, 1716, d. Sept., 1799. He m. Jan. 26, 1737, Bethiah Brown, dau. of Wm. and Elizabeth, of Rehoboth, and b. July 8, 1718. They united with the Ch. in R., Jan. 6, 1739, and were dismissed to the 2d Ch. in Ashford, (West-

ford Parish,) Ct., Jan. 8, 1769. They had 4 chil. He was a blacksmith, and was called Capt. Res. Ashford. He m. 2d, Mrs. ——, in R., who after his death returned to R., where she died.

In a letter to Judge Walker, of Lenox, in 1798, he "conjectures his ancestors were of Scotch origin, but does not *know* at what time they came, nor from what country. He reproaches himself that he had not obtained an account of his ancestry, when it was possible, and writes that he has made great inquiries, but could not obtain any sufficient information."

FIFTH GENERATION.

CHILDREN OF SAMUEL WALKER,[4] [12] OF REHOBOTH.

41. I. OLIVER,[5] b. March 12, 1706–7, had a guardian in 1763.

42. II. MOSES,[5] b. Oct. 11, 1708; d. Sept. 10, 1724.

43. III. RUTH, b. Dec. 2, 1710, d. March 6, 1790, in 80th yr. (Ins.) She m. Oct. 10, 1728, William Brown, son of Samuel. Both m. Cong. ch. Chil.—

(1) *Ruth*, m. Thos. Williams, and 2d, Col. Hawes, of Franklin, and 3d, Wm. Dryer, of Rehoboth.

(2) *Ann*, bapt. April 16, 1732.

(3) *William*, bapt. Nov. 23, 1735. Res. Dighton, rem. to R., d. over 80 yrs.

(4) *Sarah*, bapt. Dec. 11, 1837, m. Eben'r Peck, of Rehoboth.

(5) *Samuel*, bapt. March 30, 1740, m. Esther Bucklin, and had 6 chil.; m. 2d, Huldah Hunt, and had 3 chil. 1, Lucy, d. y. 2, Samuel, m. Adah. (See No. 222.) 3, Josiah, had 8 chil. 4, Esther, m. Crosby. Res. Shrewsbury. 5, Molly, m. Capt. Eben'r Dean, and then Elisha Angell. No chil. 6, Theophilus, a physician, d. unm. 7, Joseph, d. unm. 8, Ira, d. unm. 9, Peter H. (See No. 388.)

(6) *Molle*, bapt. April 25, 1749. (7) *Deborah*. (8) *John*. (9) *Chloe*. (10) *Huldah*.

CHILDREN OF TIMOTHY WALKER,[4] [14] OF REHOBOTH.

44. I. ELIZABETH,[5] b. April 26, 1714. She m. March 12, 1740, Jasiel Perry, Jr., of Rehoboth. (See No. 28.) Both m. ch. Cong. Chil.—

(1) *Rebecca*, b. Sept. 4, 1742. (2) *Timothy*, b. Aug. 3, 1744, m. 1769, Huldah Hill, of Attleboro', and had Timothy, 1770, and 2 daus. (3) *Rebecca*, b. Aug. 5, 1746, bapt. as Mehetable. (4) *Stephen*, b May 4, 1751. (5) *Jasiel*, b. June 15, 1753, m. Betsey, and had Jasiel, 1777, and 7 others. (6) *Elizabeth*, b. Dec. 16, 1755. (7) *Grace*, b. April 7, 1758.

45. II. MARTHA,[5] b. April 22, 1716, d. May 1, 1733.

46. III. TIMOTHY,[5] (128) b. July 26, (Fam. Rec.) 18, (Ins.) 1718, d. Dec. 26, 1796, in 79th yr. He m. Dec. 10, 1741, Elizabeth Carpenter, dau. of Eben'r of Attleboro', b. April 21, 1720, and d. July 2, 1780, in 61st yr. (Ins.) She was admitted to ch., July 27, 1760. He m. 2dly, Mrs. Patience. Res. Rehoboth, and had 7 chil. He was Colonel in the alarm of April 19, 1775, and in 3 mos. service in 1776. He was Colonel, and on duty at Tiverton, from May 9, to July 5, 1779. This, however, was but a small part of his service in the Revolution. He was one of the Selectmen of R., 1760, Rep. to Gen. Court in 1756, 7 and 8, and Delegate to the Provincial Congress 2 yrs., 1774–5, holding its sessions at Concord.

His religious opinions were evangelical and he was a mem. of the Cong. society in Seekonk. He was greatly esteemed for his uprightness, benevolence, hospitality and public spirit. It was his custom to go on horseback every year, and invite personally all his children and grand children, to the "Thanksgiving Festival," in the old Mansion.

47. IV. HULDAH,[5] b. Jan. 19, 1720–1. She m. Oct. 25, 1742, Josiah Carpenter, son of Obadiah, b. Oct. 8, 1719, d. 1747. Res. Cumberland, R. I. Chil.—

(1) *Cyril*, b. Aug. 27, 1743, d. Nov. 23, 1811, m. Lucy Lang or Lane, Nov. 28, 1765, who d. April 10, 1793. Res. Attleboro'. 11 chil. (2) *Josiah*, b. Jan. 5, 1747–8, d. Jan. 19, 1821, m. Hepsibeth Willmarth, Sept. 21, 1769, who d. Nov. 23, 1832, ae. 84. Res. A. 5 chil.

48. V. ALATHEA,[5] b. Dec., 1724. She m. Aug. 14, 1746, James Dexter, of Attleboro'. Res. Cumberland, R. I. Chil. 1747–1768—

(1) *Hopestill*. (See No. 11 Taunton Branch.) (2) *James* m. Rebecca Wheeler. (3) *Huldith*, m. Stephen Brown and Follet. (4) *Oliver*. (5) *Mercy*, m. Benj. Wolcott. (6) *Simeon*, d. unm. (7) *Esek*, m. Margaret Coleman. (8) *Benj.*, m. Mary Dexter. (9) *Nancy*, m. Jeremiah Whipple. (10) *Alathea*, d. unm. (11) *Lucina*, m. Dea. John Dexter. (12) *Timothy*, m. Sarah Messenger. See Chart of Rev. Gregory Dexter's descendants.

49. VI. EUNICE,[5] b. Sept. 4, 1728, d. Dec. 31, 1772, in 45th yr. She m. May 11' 1749, James Hill. He was a blacksmith, noted for his strict honesty and punctuality. He united with the Cong. ch. when young, but in after life, his sympathies were with the Baptists and most of his descendants are such. Res. Rehoboth. Chil.—

(1) *Barbara*, d. unm. (2) *Phebe*, d. unm. (3) *Eunice*, d. unm.
(4) *James Jr.*, m. Freelove Andrews. Res. Johnston, R. I. 6 chil.
(5) *Hannah*, m. Jonathan Hayes. Res. Seekonk. 9 chil., viz.:—1, d. y. 2, d. y.

3, Eunice H. Hayes, m. 1804, David Brown, Dea. of Bap. ch. in S., over 30 yrs., rem. to Fisherville, N. H., 1844; and d. 1847. Had 10 chil., viz.:—[1, Henry H., Cotton Manufacturer. 2, Mary A. 3, John S. 4, Esther C., d. ae. 5 yrs. 5, Eunice A., d. 1844. 6, Hannah M. 7, David A. 8, Esther C., d. 1838. 9, Sam'l F. 10, Jonathan E., d. 1850. All the living reside in F., and are Baptists.] 4, Henry B. 5, James H. 6, Barbara H. 7, Jonathan R. 8, Joseph A. 9, Benj'n E.

(6) *John*, m. Mehetable Walker. (See No. 244.) Res. Clarendon, Vt.

(7) *Cynthia*, m. Asa Angell, and had several chil. Res. New Berlin, N. Y.

(8) *Sarah*, m. John Larned. Res. Clarendon. Has 1 son, John.

(9) *Daniel*, m. Sarah Hutchins. Res. N. Y. Had several chil.

(10) *Lucy*, m. David Hill, of S. Had 2 chil., who have died.

BY 2d MARRIAGE.

50. VII. MARTHA,[5] b. Feb. 17, (April 11, Fam. Rec. N. S.) 1738–9, d. Jan. 11, 1835, ae. 95 yrs., 10 mos. and 11 days. She m. Stephen Hastings, who d. about 1792. Res. Boylston. Chil.—

(1) *Rachel*, b. 1764, m. Oliver Glazier. (2) *Sarah*, b. 1775, m. Elias Bennett. (3) *Martha*, b. 1778, m. John Smith.

CHILDREN OF PETER WALKER,[4] [15] OF REHOBOTH.

51. I. MARY,[5] b. Aug., 1716, m. March 9, 1737, Daniel Perry, of Rehoboth. Chil.—

(1) *Daniel*, b. Jan. 15, 1738–9. (2) *Ezra*, b. May 22, 1741. (3) *Noah*, b. Oct. 3, 1743. (4) *Mary*, b. Aug. 5, 1745. (5) *Daniel*, b. April 3, 1748. (6) *Lydia*, b. April 30, 1750. (7) *Elijah*, b. Nov. 19, 1752.

52. II. SAMUEL,[5] (135) b. July 14, 1718, d. in or before 1746. He m. and had 1 son. Res. Rehoboth.

53. III. PETER,[5] (136) b. July 14, 1718, date of death unknown. He m. Hannah Fuller, of Willington, Ct. He settled in Ashford, (Westford Parish,) Ct., as early as 1760. Both m. Cong. ch. He was a farmer and had 6 chil. (Martha, w. of Peter, d. Aug. 22, 1756. Probably 2d w. of this Peter.)

54. IV. PATIENCE,[5] b. April 27, 1720, was m. ch., and d. July 19, 1744.

55. V. JOHN,[5] (142) b. Oct. 3, 1721. Will proved, 1809. He m. Molly, and had 13 chil. He was a glacier, in 1759, "Capt. and Gent." in 1788, and was a noted man in Rehoboth. He was m. ch. 1763, sergeant in Co. of minute men from R., in Lexington alarm, and was in service during the War of the Revolution.

56. VI. HANNAH,[5] b. March 6, 1722–3, m. John Peck. Res. Sutton. Chil.—

(1) *John.* (2) *Hannah.* (3) *Deborah.*

57. VII. GRACE,[5] } b. Dec. 14, 1724, d. Dec. 14, 1724.
58. VIII. ESTHER,[5] } d. Dec. 14, 1724.

59. IX. MOSES,[5] b. Nov. 2, 1725, d. Nov. 21, 1725.

60. X. MOSES,[5] (155) b. Oct. 5, 1726, d. 1806. He m. March 15, 1753, Sarah Bowen, dau. of Peter and Susanna, b. Jan. 2, 1735–6, and d. March or May 3, 1768. He m. 2dly, March 2, 1769, Deliverance (Carpenter) Read, dau. of Obadiah, b. Feb. 27, 1737–8, and d. March 20, 1789. He m. 3dly, Mrs. Jemima (Walker) Bishop. (See No. 120.) Res. Rehoboth. He was m. ch. Cong. 1763, Lieut. in one of the companies of minute men from R., in Lexington Alarm, and served at various times during the War. Had 11 chil.

61. XI. AARON,[5] (166) b. Oct. 19, 1728, d. Oct. 19, 1775. He m. Jan. 30, 1755, Esther Carpenter, of Rehoboth, dau. of Abiah and Experience, b. Dec. 27, 1735, and d. June 16, 1763, in 28th yr. He m. 2dly, Huldah Whittaker, of R., Dec. 22, 1763, dau. of Israel and Margaret, b. March 24, 1737–8, and d. in Attleboro', 1822. He was in Capt. Sam'l Bliss' Co. of minute men from R., and was Lieut. under Col. Timothy Walker. He d. in Roxbury, at the siege of Boston, of camp fever. In'y £1004. Had 9 chil.

62. XII. GRACE,[5] b. Dec. 28, 1730.

BY 2d MARRIAGE.

63. XIII. EPHRAIM,[5] (175) b. Dec. 1, 1736, d. June 20, 1812, in 76th yr. (Ins.) He m. Dec. 26, 1771, Leaffe Ide, of Rehoboth, who d. March 3, 1829, in 79th yr. (Ins.) Res. R. Had 10 chil.

CHILDREN OF EPHRAIM WALKER,[4] [16] OF REHOBOTH.

64. I. SARAH,[5] b. June 30, 1718, d. before 1733 or 5.

65. II. MARY,[5] b. Sept. 11, 1721. She m. April 22, 1743, Timothy Willmarth, and had 1 dau.—

(1) *Sarah.*

66. III. ANNE,[5] b. Dec. 5, 1722, d. April 4, 1722–3.

67. IV. LYDIA,[5] b. May, 172–, bapt. June 7, 1724. She m. Feb. 9, 1743, James Clay. Both m. ch. Cong., 1747. Chil.—

(1) *Ephraim*, b. April, 1747, m. Ephah Houghton, a farmer, of Putney, Vt., and had 12 chil. Res. P.

(2) *Sarah*, b. Oct. 2, 1749, m. Col. Eliphalet Slack, of Pawtucket. No chil.

(3) *James*, b. Oct. 29, 1751, m. Nov. 1779, Elizabeth Warner, of Westmoreland, N. H. Res. Putney. He was a Capt. in the Revolution. 11 chil.

(4) *Lydia*, b. Jan. 27, 1754, m. James Fitch, of P., Vt. 2 chil.

(5) *Amy*, b. Aug. 8, 1756, d. 1774, in Seekonk, unm.

(6) *Melicent*, b. June 21, 1759, d. 1816, m. Cyril Peck, of Pawtucket, and had 1 son and 3 daus. (See No. 322.) Res. P.

(7) *Mary*, b. June 21, 1759, twin, d. ae. 10 mos.

(8) *Mary*, b. June 7, 1761, d. young in Seekonk, and unm.

(9) *Miriam*, b. Nov. 3, 1764, m. Oliver Starkweather, a cotton manufacturer in Pawtucket. Chil.—1, John, b. 1786, Grad. B. U., 1805. Eminent Physician in Upton, m. a Carpenter. 2, Sarah, m. Wm. Allen, of Rehoboth. 3, James C., b. July 4, 1797, m. Almira C. Underwood, of P., d. July 26, 1856. Manufacturer in P., 7 chil. 4, Samuel C., b. Dec. 27, 1799, Grad. B. U., 1822, settled in Cleveland, O., 1826, as Attorney at Law, where he still resides. Mayor of C., 2 yrs. 1844 and '45, and in 1852, elected Judge of the Court of Common Pleas. 5, Rebecca, m. Lyman Claflen, of P., a Manufacturer. 3 chil.

(10) *Martha*, b. April 2, 1768, m. Dr. Joseph Goodhue, of Putney, Vt., son of Rev. Mr. G., 1st minister of P. He was a Surgeon in the Navy, during the last War, and connected with the Navy Yard in Portsmouth, N. H. He settled in Deerfield, and attained eminence as a physician. Had 3 chil.—1, Clarissa, m. David Chandler, of So. Hadley, and then Jesse Aiken, of Chester, Vt. 2, Mark, d. at the South, leaving w. and chil. 3, Martha, m. Lyman Kendall, of Cleveland, Ohio, a Banker, and dec'd. She resides in Grand Rapids, Mich. Nine chil., 1 of whom is George, in the firm of H. D. Kendall & Co., Wholesale Dry Goods Dealers, Cleveland, Ohio.

68. V. AMY,[5] b. March 4, 1727, m. Oct. 29, 1747, Eleazer Harding, of Providence, R. I.

69. VI. EPHRAIM,[5] b. Sept. 28, d. Oct. 19, 1728.

70. VII. MARTHA,[5] b. Dec. 22, 1729, m. Dec. 24, 1747, John Humphrey, Jr., of Rehoboth, who was b. Aug. 9, 1727. Had 10 chil., 1748—1767.

71. VIII. FREELOVE,[5] b. Aug. 14, 1731, d. April 2, 1732. (Ins.)

CHILDREN OF BENJAMIN WALKER,[4] [19] OF ASHFORD, CT.

72. I. BENJAMIN,[5] (185) b. 1737, d. 1793. He m. Molly Johnson, of Mansfield, Ct., was a farmer in Ashford, a Cong., and had 4 chil.

73. II. Ebenezer,[5] (189) b. 1738, d. 1801. He m. Hannah. Farmer in Ashford, Ct. He was m. ch. Cong. Most of his descendants are Baptists. Had 6 chil.

74. III. Ephraim,[5] b. 1739, d. 1808. He m. Abigail Yeomans, who d. 1803. He was a farmer in Ashford, Ct., and Cong. Had no chil., but adopted Timothy, his nephew, and made him his heir. He gave a part of his property to the Cong. Society, in Westford.

75. IV. Samuel,[5] (196) b. 1740. He m. Bethiah Crary, who d. 1804, ae. 52 yrs. Farmer in Ashford, Ct., and Cong. Had 3 chil.

76. V. John,[5] (199) b. 1741. He m. Mary Cadwell. He was a farmer and Cong. in Ashford, Ct. Had 4 chil.

77. VI. Joseph,[5] d. young.

78. VII. Mary,[5] m. Avery, of Ashford, Ct. A farmer, in Ashford, Ct.

79. VIII. Ruth,[5] m. —— Post, of Boston, and had 3 chil.

Children of JAMES WALKER,[4] [21] of Rehoboth.

80. I. Elizabeth,[5] b. April 24, 1718, d. Feb. 15, 1736–7, m. ch. Cong.

81. II. James,[5] b. Dec. 12, 1719, d. March 3, 1742–3.

82. III. Nathan,[5] b. Dec. 24, 1721, d. Feb. 18, 1742–3.

83. IV. Esther,[5] b. May 1, 1724, d. April 13, 1743–4.

84. V. Daniel,[5] (203) b. June 12, 1726. He m. Aug. 1, 1745, Hannah Bairstow, who d. Feb. 8, 1747–8. He m. 2d, Feb. 23, 1748, (1748–9 ?) Sible Smith, dau. of Daniel and Ruth Ormsbee. Res. Cumberland, R. I., 1767. He had 6 chil. His father gave him in will, 200 acres of land in Ashford and Willington, Ct.

85. VI. Rachel,[5] b. Oct. 16, 1730, d. Dec. 26, 1747–8.

Children of PHILIP WALKER,[4] [22] of Rehoboth.

86. I. Oliver,[5] b. April 19, 1723, d. April 6, 1778. He m. March 2, 1757, Elizabeth Perrin, dau. of Isaac and Susanna, of Rehoboth. (See No. 3.) Her will was proved Jan. 1, 1782. He was a farmer in R. No chil.

87. II. PHILIP,[5] b. Feb. 15, 1724–5, d. 1725.

88. III. PHILIP,[5] (209) b. Oct. 27, 1726, d. July 5, 1761, in 35th yr. He m. March 21, 1748, Hannah Baker, of Rehoboth. He was a blacksmith, and resided in R. Had 6 chil. In'y £485. His grave stone is "In memory of the valient Capt. Philip Walker, who departed this life, July 5, 1761, in 35th yr. of his age." His widow m. Dec. 18, 1764, Eben'r Medbury.

89. IV. ELIJAH,[5] b. Jan. 11, 1730–1, was a Distiller in Providence, R. I., in 1756, '62, '78. All efforts to learn more of him, have been fruitless.

90. V. EZRA,[5] d. Aug. 12, 1736.

91. VI. PETER,[5] d. Aug. 3, 1737.

BY 2d MARRIAGE.

92. VII. JOSEPH, (215) b. Jan. 5, 1738–9, d. Jan. 1789. He m. Mary, and had 1 dau. He m. 2d, before 1767, Lydia, dau. of Stephen Shippey, of East Greenwich, R. I., who had 4 chil., and d. 1779 or '80. He m. 3d, Hannah Case, dau. of Benjamin. She had 2 chil., and d. Jan. 2, 1790. He was in the French War, and was wounded several times; had his leg broken and three of his fingers shot off, and travelled three days before they were dressed.—He was in the Revolutionary War, and had his leg broken at Newport, R. I. He settled first at West Greenwich, R. I., but sold his farm in 1767, and settled in Coventry, near what is now the Summit Station on the Hartford & Providence R. R.

93. VIII. MUNRO,[5] d. 1764 or 5, unm.

CHILDREN OF NATHANIEL WALKER,[4] [27] OF REHOBOTH.

94. I. NATHANIEL,[5] (222) b. Sept. 5, 1728, d. March 24, 1814. He m. Nabby Smith, of Rehoboth, who was b. May 8, 1731, and d. Sept. 24, 1822. He resided in No. Providence or Pawtucket, R. I., and was a Blacksmith. Had 9 chil. He was admitted to the ch. Sept. 9, 1764, but he never spoke the name of God in the presence of others. He thought it should never be uttered.

95. II. ENOS,[5] (231) b. Dec. 9, 1730, d. May 3, 1782. He m. Jan. 17, 1750, Patience Peck. He was one of the minute men in Capt. John Perry's Company, in the Revolutionary War. Surviving the perils of the War, he met with an untimely death. Finding some

difficulty with the wheel in his sawmill, he attempted to rectify it. His son Charles came in, and not knowing that his father was in the wheel-pit, started the wheel, and killed him. He had 7 chil.

96. III. SUSANNA,[5] } Twins, b. March 3, 1732–3. d. Nov. 19, 1744.
97. III. ANNA,[5] } She was m. Cong. ch., rem. to Clarendon, Vt., and d. unm., about 40 yrs. of age.

98. IV. EPHRAIM,[5] (238) b. March 8, 1735–6, d. March 29, 1815, in 80th yr. He m. Priscilla Rawson, dau. of Thomas and Anne (Waldron,) of Mendon, afterward of Milford, b. May 22, 1740, and d. Aug. 22, 1813, in 74th yr. She was descended from a family of great reputation, eminent for public services and piety. A brother was Deacon, 2 uncles, Stephen and Edward, were Deacons, 1 in Providence, R. I., the other in Mendon, honored and influential in their respective towns; another possessed great mechanical genius. Her grand father, Wilson Rawson, was 5th child of Rev. Grindal Rawson, (of whom a long account in Rawson Genealogy,) and grand son of Edward, the Secretary Rawson. (See Gen. Reg., 1849.)

Both Mr. W. and wife were exemplary and devoted christians, members of Cong. ch. They had 7 chil., all of whom were professedly and actively religious. Their descendants constitute a worthy and highly respectable branch of the Rehoboth Family. He removed to Providence as early as 1755, and was a housewright. Walker St., in Providence, took its name from him. He built and lived in the house on the corner of Westminster and Walker streets.

99. V. AMOS,[5] b. May 9, 1740, d. about 1780, unm. His mind was ruined by epilepsy.

100. VI. ESTHER,[5] b. Oct. 6, 1743, d. 1816, ae. 73 yrs., m. ch. Cong. She was "a weaver," in 1785, and rem. to Clarendon, Vt., where she d. unm.

101. VII. LEWIS,[5] (244) b. Dec. 13, 1745, d. May 21, 1813. He m. Sept. 11, 1770, Hannah, dau. of Dea. Cooper, of Rehoboth. She d. 1821. He removed from R. to New Providence, (now Cheshire,) where he married. In 1779, they settled in Clarendon, Vt., where they lived till their death. He was m. Bap. ch., and highly esteemed. Had 5 chil.

102. VIII. BENJAMIN,[5] b. April 1, 1747, d. March 17, 1748.

CHILDREN OF DANIEL WALKER,[4] [28] OF CLARENDON, VT.

103. I. MARY,[5] bapt. Sept. 6, 1730, d. Aug. 19, 1777. She m. Ebenezer Bates. They removed to Shaftesbury, Vt., in 1768. He d. in Autumn of 1816, ae. 92, having m. 2dly, Mrs. Elizabeth Buck, who d. Oct. 1812, ae. 80. He was an honest and estimable farmer. She had 8 chil., who married, and 3 or 4 more d. in infancy. Three of her sons were in the Battle of Bennington, and she d. 3 days after.

(1) *Rufus*, m. Polly Goff, of S. He was a Bapt. Clergyman. Rev. Merrit Bates, an eminent Meth. Clergyman, is his grand son. (2) *Mary*, m. Geo. Walton. Res. Dorset, Vt. (3) *James*, m. —— Corey. Res. Queensboro'. (4) *Walter*, m. —— Corey. Res. Queensboro'. (5) *Sarah*, m. John Egbert. (6) *Ebenezer*, b. Dec. 15, 1768, d. Dec. 9, 1837, m. Elizabeth Wiltze, of Pownal. Res. S., 9 chil. (7) *Nathan*, m. Ophelia Innis. Res. S. (8) *Jerusha*, m. Johnstone.

104. II. MEHITABLE,[5] b. Jan. 6, 1731–2, d. in Rehoboth.

105. III. MEHETABLE.[5] b. Sept. 22, 1733, m. Capt. Pierce, and settled in Providence, R. I.

106. IV. SARAH,[5] b. Sept. 2, 1735, d. at advanced age. She m. Elisha Willmot, and rem. to N. Y. Had 2 daus.

107. V. DANIEL,[5] (249) b. March 11, 1736, d. 1777. He m. Jerusha Bates, and then Mary Young, an English woman, by whose influence, he espoused the side of the British in the Revolution. The Committee of Safety, of which his brother Gideon was a member, notified him, that if he was found off his farm, he would be declared an outlaw. He, at once, with five other tories, started for Canada, and d. the same year. His property in Clarendon was confiscated, and his family soon after went to Canada. He was a very eccentric man, and said his children's names should all begin with W. He had several chil.

108. VI. GIDEON,[5] (256) b. in Attleboro', Nov. 20, 1738, (Att. Rec.) and d. Nov. 2, 1793. He m. about 1764 or 5, Rachel Foster, of A., dau. of Benj'n and Rachel (Day,) b. April 21, 1743, and d. in Whiting, Vt., March 31, 1815, ae. 72. They first settled in Coventry, R. I., but in 1768, removed to Clarendon, Vt., and a year or two later, to Rutland. In 1784, they removed to Whiting, Vt., where they died. He served in the War of the Revolution. At the time of the retreat from Ticonderoga, in 1777, his wife, with 4 children, went on horseback from Rutland to New Providence, now Cheshire, Mass., and remained with Lewis Walker, (See. No. 101.)

cousin of her husband, who afterward removed to Clarendon, Vt. He was a staunch Whig, and was one of the Committee of Safety for Vermont. In 1777, Col. Baum on his way to Bennington, with his forces passed through Clarendon. Mr. W. had a team of 4 very large and fine oxen. Col. B. pressed him, to help convey the ordnance of his army. Having crossed the Butten-kill river, and encamped for the night on the south bank, Mr. W. watched his opportunity, and before morning, eluded the guard, made his escape, and returned home. Both were m. ch. Bap., and had 8 chil. The 6 sons were all farmers in Whiting, Vt., and their farms were adjoining, and formed one of the best tracts of land in Addison Co., embracing about 1200 acres on the Otter Creek. His descendants have been distinguished for their industry and integrity, their pure and exemplary character. And those who have made a profession of religion have adorned it, by deep and heart-felt piety.

109. VII. REBECCA,[5] b. June 14, 1740. She m. Elijah Oshurn and they settled in Clarendon, Vt. An incident is told of 3 of their children who were lost in the woods, 4 days, lived on snails, and when found, were 3 or 4 miles from home and nearly famished. The neighbors and the people of Rutland went out in search of them. The oldest, a boy of 7 yrs., said, "they ate but little themselves, and saved the snails for the baby, and that a great black dog pawed leaves over them in the night." At that time, such dogs were numerous in Vt. Chil.—

(1) *Mehetable*, m. Chas. Seamans or Simmons. Res. C., and 12 chil.

110. VIII. ESTHER,[5] b. June 9, 1742, d. about 1773, in Coventry, R. I. She m. William Roy. They settled in C., and had no chil. She was m. Bap. ch. and a very excellent woman. He afterward rem. to Pownal, Vt., where he m. Mrs. Hunt, and d. Jan. 7, 1822, ae. 83. He was in the French War, having enlisted at the age of 19, and was also a Captain in the War of the Revolution. Though not religiously connected, he was a man of good morals, upright character, and highly respected as a citizen.

111. IX. NATHAN,[5] (264) b. May 4, 1744, (Attleboro' Rec.) Oct. 19, about 1736, (Fam. Rec.,) and d. in Ferrisburgh, Vt., Oct. 19, 1823, ae. 87. (?) He m. Catharine Johnson, who d. Aug. 28, 1820, ae. 82, and was a woman of unusual energy and perseverance. They settled in Shaftesbury, Vt., but in 1790, rem. to Ferrisburgh, Vt. He was a farmer, and m. Bap. ch. in Pownal. Had 9 chil.

112. X. KEZIAH,[5] b. Jan. 6, 1745–6, d. Nov. 1, 1747, in Coventry, R. I.

113. XI. JOHN,[5] b. Sept. 1, 1748, d. Oct. 15, 1748, in Coventry, R. I.

114. XII. ICHABOD,[5] (273) b. Dec. 23, 1749, d. March 21, 1832. He m. 1769, Abigail Logia, who d. April 4, 1798. He m. 2dly, Feb. 20, 1799, Mrs. Penelope Ring, of Worthington, (relict of Joseph,) who d. Dec., 1836, in Lancaster, Ohio. He settled in Rutland, Vt., about 1770, and lived where the Court house now stands. In the commencement of the Revolutionary War, he was driven from his home, and afterward settled in Clarendon, Vt. In 1831, he rem. to Potsdam, N. Y., where he soon after died. He was a farmer, m. Bap. ch. and "a good man:" had 14 chil., and all b. in C., except the 1st two.

CHILDREN OF STEPHEN WALKER,[4] [29] OF POMFRET, CT.

115. I. STEPHEN,[5] b. Feb. 22, 1734–5.

116. II. LEVI,[5] b. April 3, 1736.

BY 2d MARRIAGE.

117. III. SARAH,[5] b. May 7, 1739.

118. IV. MEHETABLE,[5] b. Jan. 9, 1740–1.

Every endeavor to learn more of these and their descendants, has been without avail. Whither they went from P., is unknown.

CHILDREN OF CALEB WALKER,[4] [34] OF REHOBOTH.

119. I. CALEB,[5] (288) b. Feb. 14, 1728–9, d. March 4, 1753, ae. 25. He m. Oct. 16, 1750, Elizabeth Perrin, dau. of John and Rachel, b. Nov. 17, 1728. She survived him, and June 10, 1756, m. Joshua Smith. She possessed uncommon excellence as a christian, resided in Rehoboth, and d. Aug. 6, 1820. He was m. ch. 1763. His son Wm., afterward Judge Walker, of Lenox, when visiting Rehoboth, nearly half a century after the death of his father, reared a monument, "in token of that filial respect for the memory of a deceased Parent, which he never had opportunity personally, to pay, Sept., 1797."

120. II. ABRAHAM,[5] (290) b. Nov. 1, 1731–2, d. Nov. 17, 1774. He m. Nov. 12, 1761, Jemima Bishop. Res. Rehoboth. Both were m. ch. They had 6 chil. She m. 2dly, Moses Walker. (See No. 60.)

121. III. Abigail,[5] b. Feb. 11, 1733–4, d. Feb. 2, 1817, ae. 83 yrs. She m. Sept. 27, 1753, Jonathan Carpenter, son of Ephraim, b. April 25, 1732, and d. May 17, 1810. Res. Rehoboth. Chil., 1755—1772.

(1) *Hannah*, m. Amaziah Peck. Res Barre, Vt. (2) *Jonathan*, m. Olive Sessions. Res. Randolph, Vt. (3) *Jacob*, m. Huldah Drier, and Polly Carpenter. Res. R. (4) *Abigail*, m. Jacob Hoar, 1787. Res. Rehoboth. (5) *Ephraim*, m. Betsey French, 1797. Res R. (6) *Zeruiah*, m. Benj· Carpenter, 1791. Res. R. (7) *Orinda*, d. Oct. 16, 1775.

122. IV. Abel,[5] (296) b. May 11, 1736, d. Feb. 17, 1819. He m. April 14, 1763, Lois Read, dau. of Thomas, Jr., and Bathsheba, of Rehoboth, b. May 27, 1741, d. March 24, 1801. They had 7 chil. He served in the Continental Army, removed to Hardwick in 1779, and bought a farm in the westerly part of the town, to which additions were made as money was acquired. The tillage and improvement of this, almost exclusively occupied him for the remainder of his life. Happy in all his domestic relations, he very seldom went from home, to any considerable distance. True to his Puritan origin, he was scrupulously exact in the performance of every duty devolving on him, and few men enjoyed in a higher degree, the confidence and esteem of the community in which he lived. He and his wife were m. of Cong. ch., in Greenwich, and although the house of worship was about 3 miles from his dwelling, for a long series of years, his seat in the sanctuary was rarely vacant on the Sabbath.

Dr. Abel Baker, of Owasco, N. Y., who lived with his grand father during his youth and early manhood, writes, "I doubt whether there has been a man, among those with whom I have since become fully acquainted, that has more uniformly exemplified the precepts of the Gospel than he did." He m. 2dly, Nov. 25, 1801, Bathsheba Read, sister of 1st wife, and b. Sept. 7, 1745.

123. V. Comfort,[5] (303) b. May 26, 1739, d. April 14, 1818. He m. Nov. 24, 1762, Mehetable Robinson, of Attleboro', who d. May 21, 1814, ae. 75. They had 9 chil. He m. 2dly, Lucy Cooper, of Attleboro', Oct. 23, 1815. He sold land and homestead in Rehoboth, in 1773, for £330, and removed to Killingly, Ct. He was m. Cong. ch. in 1763. His descendants form a highly intelligent, and worthy branch of the family. An unusually large number have been or are religious.

Children of EBENEZER WALKER,[4] [40] of Rehoboth.

124. I. Ebenezer,[5] (312) b. Jan. 27, 1738–9, d. about 1825. He m. Sept. 13, 1765, Sabrina Whittaker, dau. of Joseph and

Rachel, and b. Feb. 1, 1744–5. He was in Capt. Baker's Co., in the Revolutionary service, removed to Ashford, Ct., before 1782, and had 2 chil.

125. II. BETHIAH,[5] b. July 3, 1745. She m. Nov. 11, 1762, James French, of Rehoboth. Chil.—

(1) *Hannah*, b. April 3, 1763, d. unm.

(2) *James*, b. Dec. 31, 1764, was Capt., and d. Feb. 21, 1846, in 83d yr. He m. Abigail, daughter of Daniel Carpenter, Esq. She d. Sept. 1807, in 41st or 47th yr. Had 6 chil. He m. 2d, Betsey Peck, and had James, now in Seekonk.

(3) *Ebenezer*, b. April, 1767, m. Sarah Walker. (See No. 158.)

(4) *Bethiah*, b. Feb. 13, 1769, m. Abel Shorey, of R., and d. Sept. 20, 1798. Chil., 1, Bethiah. 2, Abigail. 3, David. 4, Miles.

(5) *Dorothy*, b. July 8, 1771, m. Jonathan Brown, of Seekonk, d. July 9, 1856. Chil., 1, Ephraim. 2, George, was a Cong. clergyman in Me.. and resides in Pawtucket. 3, Herman, m. and dec'd. 4, Lovina, m. Capt. Wooster Carpenter, of S., who d. March 1, 1858. They had 8 chil., viz., [Wm., b. Sept. 8, 1822, now in California. Maria, b. Dec. 21, 1823, m. Erastus Woodward, a farmer in S., and has had 4 chil. Martha, b. March 25, 1825, d. May 25, 1832. Solon, b. Jan. 21, 1827, d. June 27, 1832. Eliza Jane, b. June 23, 1829. George, b. July 17, 1831, engraver in N. Y. city. Horatio, b. Sept. 11, 1833, farmer in S. Solon, Oct. 23, 1839, farmer in S.] 5, Miranda. 6, Eliza. 7, Amy F.

(6) *Huldah*, b. March 15, 1774, m. Asher Ellis, of R., and had 4 chil. 1, James, in N. H. 2, Wm., a Dea. of Cong ch. in S. 3, Asher, dec'd. 4, dau., d. y.

(7) *William*, b. July 17, 1776, d. Sept. 12, 1778, ae. 2 yrs. and 2 mos.

(8) *William*, b. Dec. 31, 1778, dec'd.

(9) *Ephraim*, b. April 1, 1781. Res. Warren, R. I., and m. ch. 2 chil.

(10) *Ezra*, b. April 10, 1783, m. 1815, Nancy Smith, of S., dau. of Joshua and Huldah. Res. S. He is m. Cong. ch., and has had 10 chil., 1, Asher Ellis, b. May 24, 1816, m. 1850, Eliza McBlain, of No. Providence, who d. Nov. 1856. 2 chil., both dec'd. He m. 2d, Dec. 25, 1857, Kate (McBlain) Perry. 2, Horatio N., b. Feb. 8, 1818, d. Nov. 29, 1842. 3, Henrietta Smith, b Feb. 3, 1820. (See No. 388.) 4, Nancy M., b. April 14, 1822, d. Jan. 14, 1823. 5, Jas. Austin, b. Jan. 14, 1824, m. Nancy F. Capron, of Attleboro.' Res. No. Prov. 1 child. 6, Sam'l Egbert, b. Sept. 24, 1826, m. Jane Fuller, of Central Falls, R. I., who d. soon; m. 2d, Harriet Fuller, a sister. 1 dau. 7, Eph'm Walker, b. April 14, 1829, m. Susan Martin, dau. of Doct. Calvin, of S. Res. Pawtucket. 8, Wm. Carpenter, b. June 30, 1831, m. Esther C. Perrin, of S. Res. Providence. 9, Ezra Granville, b. June 23, 1833, m. Ann J. Daggett, of Pawtucket. Res. S. 1 dau. 10, Warren E., b. Feb. 18, 1836, d. Aug. 23, 1836.

(11) *Polly*, b. July 24, 1785, was m. ch., and d. Aug. 23, 1839.

(12) *Lucy*, b. July 30, 1787, m. Henry Maxcy, of Wrentham. Large family.

126. III. WILLIAM,[5] (314) b. March 25, 1747, d. Sept. 1826, ae. 79. He m. Hannah Smith, who d. Nov. 1841. They rem. from Rehoboth to Ashford, Ct., about 20 yrs. of age. Had 6 chil. He was a farmer, held several town offices, was a Select-man, a Justice of the Peace, 30 yrs., and several yrs. a member of the Legislature. He was also Deacon of the Cong. ch.

127. IV. DOROTHY,[5] b. Sept. 21, 1749. She m. Squier Hill, of Ashford, Ct. They removed to Wales, Mass., and thence to Canajoharie, N. Y., about 1790, where they d. about 1830. He held a Captain's commission in the Militia and commanded a company in the Revolutionary army. Chil.—

(1) *Bethiah*, b. 1772, m. Darius Rogers, of Wales. (2) *Zaccheus*. Res. Canajoharie, N. Y. (3) *Ebenezer*. Res. Canajoharie, N. Y. (5) *William*. Res. Canajoharie, N. Y. (6) *Squier*. Res. Canajoharie, N. Y. (7) *Pliny*, d. ae. 10 or 12 yrs. (8) *Mary*, m. Asel Utley. (9) *Elizabeth*, m. Noah Durren, a Meth. Clergyman. Res. Lowville, N. Y. (10) *Dorothy*, b. about 1793, m. —— Tracy.

SIXTH GENERATION.

CHIL. OF COL. TIMOTHY WALKER,[5] [46] OF REHOBOTH.

128. I. LEPHA,[6] b. Aug. 4, 1742, d. March 10, 1814, in 73d yr. She m. April 16, 1761, John Perry, of Rehoboth, who was b. Aug. 21, 1735, and d. March 5, 1814, in 79th yr.; son of John and grandson of Nath'l. He settled in Sterling, Ct., where they both died. Both religious, and Bapt. He united with the ch. at the age of 45. He was Capt. of a company of minute men in the Revolution, and was in active service during most of the War. Chil.—

(1) *Samuel*, d. young. (2) *Isabel*, m. Daniel Hunt, and had chil. (3) *John*, b. Dec. 3, 1772, m. Jan. 14, 1802, Jane Stanwood, of Brunswick, Me., dau. of Col. Wm. Res. B., and Orono, Me. He was Town Clerk and Select-man of B., and Deacon many yrs. of Cong. ch., and d. suddenly in the street, in Bangor, of disease of the heart, March 18, 1846. Had 7 chil. The eldest, John A., b. 1803, grad. at Bowdoin Coll., 1840, and is Cong. Minister in Guilford Village, Me. (4) *Lepha*, m. Phineas Howe, and had 4 chil. (5) *Lydia*, m —— Bennett. Had 2 chil. (6) *Betsey*, m. Col. Abraham Ormsbee, and d. Feb. 1817.

129. II. SARAH,[6] b. July, (Fam. Rec.) Aug. (Town Rec.) 14, 1745, d. Oct. 26, 1779. She m. May 21, 1766, John Bishop, who d. before 1788. Chil.—1766—1775.

(1) *Sarah*, d. unm. (2) *Molly*, m. Jabez Bucklin. (3) *Newman*, d. unm. (4) *John*, was lost at sea. (5) *Warren*. No chil.

130. III. Betty,[6] b. April 8, 1747, d. 1793, unm. and insane.

131. IV. Lydia,[6] b. May 1, 1749, d. about 1800. She m. Amos Read, Nov. 16, 1767. No chil. He was in Capt. John Perry's Co. of minute men. Res. Rehoboth.

132. V. Timothy,[6] (320) b. May 22, 1751, d. April 2, 1814, in 63d yr. (Ins.) He m. June 2, 1774, Molly Willmarth, dau. of Eph'm and Molly, b. Feb. 10, 1758, and d. Sept. 7, 1791, ae. 33. She had 7 chil. He m. 2dly, July 11, 1793, Lucy Redway, who d. Nov. 18, 1813, (Ins.) in 50th yr. She had 7 chil. He was a farmer, inheriting the homestead of his father, Col. Timothy, and was an industrious, honest, and benevolent man. In religious opinions he was a Baptist. He d. on a visit to his sister, in Sterling, Ct., and she d. soon after of the same fever. He served in the War of the Revolution, and held a Captain's commission and represented the town of Rehoboth in the Legislature in 1810 and 11.

133. VI. Huldah,[6] b. April 29, (F. Rec.) May 22, (Town Rec.) 1755. She m. 1791, Joseph Chaffee, of Seekonk. Res. Rehoboth, now Seekonk. Chil.—

(1) *Walker*, b. about 1800, m. —— Bowen, and has a large family. Res. S. (2) *Wilder*. Res. Pennsylvania. Has chil. (3) *Charlotte*, m. John Arnold. (4) *Huldah*, m. Benj. Peck.

134. VII. Martha,[6] b. June 12, (Fam. Rec.) 1758. She m. Feb. 3, (Ch. Rec.) May 3, (Town Rec.) 1780, John Davis of Kingston, Mass. He removed to Concord, N. H., thence to Norway, Maine, where both died. Had 9 chil.—

(1) *John*, d. unm. (2) *Huldah*, d. unm. (3) *William*, m. Sophia Paine, and was a merchant in Portland, Me. (4) *Martha*, m. Dan'l Mitchell as 3d wife. (5) *Stephen*, was lost at sea, unm. (6) *Joseph*, d. unm. in New Orleans. (7) *Sarah*, m. Capt. Reuben King, of Me., then Capt. Loring. Res. Yarmouth, Me. (8) *Sophronia*, m. John Young. Res. Y. (9) *Samuel*, m. Lucy Ann Walker, his cousin. (See No. 329.)

Children of SAMUEL WALKER,[5] [52] of Rehoboth.

135. I. Peter,[6] b. about 1740 to 46, probably d. young, or without issue. The kindred can tell nothing about him.

Children of PETER WALKER,[5] [53] of Ashford, Ct.

136. I. Samuel,[6] (334) b. Sept. 2, 1748, d. Nov. 21, 1804. He

m. Alice Case, who d. Jan. 3, 1827. Farmer in Ashford, Ct. Both m. Cong. ch. They had 11 chil., all b. in A.

137. II. PETER,[6] (345) b. 1760, d. 1834, ae. 74 yrs., in Willington, Ct. He m. Sally Carpenter. He was a farmer, and lame for many years. Res. Ashford Ct., m. Cong. ch., and had 3 chil.

138. III. MARY,[6] m. David Tuttle. Res. Albany, N. Y. Chil.—

(1) *Leonard.* (2) *Polly.* (3) *Sally.* (4) *David.* (5) *Merritt.* (6) *Wealthy.*

139. IV. SARAH,[6] m. Jonathan Peek. Res. Randolph, Vt. Chil.

140. V. HANNAH,[6] m. Ebenezer Cross. Res. Canada.

141. VI. GRACE,[6] m. Levi Wakefield, and was m. Bap. ch. Res. Stafford, Ct. 6 chil.

(1) *Polly.* (2) *Sally.* (3) *Levi.* (4) *Eli.* (5) *Clarissa.* (6) *Huldah.*

CHILDREN OF JOHN WALKER,[5] [55] OF REHOBOTH.

142. I. JOHN,[6] b. Nov. 1, 1752, d. about 1832. He was in Capt. James Hill's Co. in the Revolution. He went to Richmond, Va., when a young man, resided there till his death, and accumulated a large property. He had no intercourse with his relatives at the North, and nothing has ever been obtained by them from his estate, though he d. unm. and intestate.

143. II. CALVIN,[6] (348) b. Jan. 5, 1754, d. March 25, 1835. He m. Phebe Cole, of Warren, R. I., Feb. 30, (Town. Rec.) Dec. 7, (Ch. Rec.) 1780, and had 8 chil. He served in the Revolutionary War, and was a pensioner. Res. Providence, R. I. A Housewright.

144. III. MOLLY,[6] b. Dec. 6, 1756, d. July 30, 1796. (Ins.) She m. Sept. 22, 17—, Caleb Ormsbee, of Providence, who d. 1807, ae. 55 yrs. Chil.—

(1) *John*, d. y. (2) *Mary*, m. Daggett. No chil. (3) *Elizabeth*, m. Wing. (4) *Geo. W.*, m. in Portland, and d. many yrs. ago. (5) *Wm. Walker*, Physician in Newbern, N. C.

145. IV. PETER,[6] b. March 29, 1759. He sailed out of Providence, R. I., and was never heard of after.

146. V. JOSEPH,[6] (356) b. Feb. 24, 1761, d. Feb. 2, 1838. He m. Dec. 3, 1784, Sarah Lane, who was b. May 26, 1764, and d. June 17, 1831. Res. Nelson, N. Y. Had 8 chil.

147. VI. AMY,[6] b. Feb. 24, 1762, d. in childhood.

148. VII. ELIZABETH,[6] b. Feb. 27, 1763, d. in early womanhood.

149. VIII. LUTHER,[6] (364) b. Jan. 7, 1767, (Fam. Rec.) 1766, (Town Rec.) d. Dec. 5, 1832. He m. Mary Weaver, of Lansingburg, N. Y., dau. of Capt. Lewis, b. June 4, 1770, and d. April 19, 1810. Both m. ch. He 1st learned the Baker's trade and disliked it, afterward the Tailor's. When 21 yrs. old he left Providence for N. Y. City, remained a few yrs., went to Troy, bought 7 acres of land which is now in the centre of the city. Here he built the 1st 2 story house in T. He at length became involved, and removed to Middletown, Vt.,—a comparatively unbroken forest—where he was subjected to all the toils and hardships of a settlement in a new country. He was Commissioner of highways, a Constable, and Deputy Sheriff. Had 5 chil.

150. IX. LYDIA,[6] b. Feb. 10, 1768, (Fam. Rec. 1769,) d. May 3, 1852. She m. Aug. 30, 1796, Nath'l Croade, of North Providence. Chil.—

(1) *Nathaniel*, b. Feb. 23, 1799, d. Sept. 26, 1800.

(2) *Edmund R.*, b. Feb. 3, 1798. Res. Pawtucket, unm. Book-keeper.

(3) *Elizabeth B.*, b. Aug. 19, 1800, m. Oliver E. Williams, of Hartford, April, 1818. He is a grad. of Yale Coll. in the class of 1816; is a lawyer, but has retired from the practice of his profession. Res. H. They have 4 chil., viz., 1, Ellen, who m. Cornelius Vanderbilt, Jr., of New York city, Nov. 26, 1856. Res. H. 2, Elizabeth. 3, Mary. 4, Augusta.

(4) *Adelia*, b. June 24, 1804, m. John A. Taintor, Esq., of Hartford, Ct., May 11, 1831. He is a retired wool merchant in H. She is a woman of great refinement and excellence. They have 2 daus. 1, Louisa, b. July 28, 1832, m. May, 1854. Charles Kneeland, Jr., of N. Y. city, who is Sec'y and Treas., of the Jersey City Locomotive Works, and has Adele, b. May, 1856. George, b. May, 1859. 2, Alice, b. Dec. 29, 1836.

(5) *Nathaniel T.*, b. Aug. 28, 1802, d. Sept. 12, 1803.

151. X. GEORGE WHITEFIELD,[6] (369) b. Feb. 7, 1770, d. Oct. 13, 1838. He m. April 14, 1796, Mehetable Bucklin, who d. Feb. 26, 1847. He was at one time a farmer in Seekonk; afterward of Pawtucket, where he d. He was Select-man in S., 1819, '20 and 21, and represented the town in the General Court in 1819. Had 8 chil.

152. XI. BOSWORTH,[6] (378) b. March 1, 1773, d. Oct. 11, 1846. He m. Feb. 9, 1802, Elizabeth Weaver, dau. of Capt. Lewis, of Lansingburg, N. Y., and b. March 4, 1778. Both m. ch. He was a Thread Manufacturer in Pawtucket, R. I., and a man of uncommon excellence and piety. In'y $20,590. Had 7 chil.

153. XII. William,[6] b. March 27, 1775, d. in infancy.

154. XIII. Elijah,[6] b. Feb. 10, 1777, d. in youth.

Chil. of Lieut. MOSES WALKER,[5] [60] of Rehoboth.

155. I. Susannah,[6] b. July 1, 1754, d. about 1840. She m. David Bliss, and removed to Savoy. Chil.—

(1) *Warren.* (2) *Walker.* (3) *Moses.* (4) ——

156. II. Huldah,[6] b. Sept. 20, 1756. She m. Feb. 15, 1785, Isaac Brown, of Rehoboth, and rem. to Barnet, Vt. She was m. Cong. ch. Chil.—

(1) *Leah.* (2) *Huldah.* (3) *Ann.* (4) *Isaac,* m. in Fleming, N. Y., and is a Physician in Mich. (5) *Moses.* (6) *Preston.* (7) *Betsey.*

157. III. Moses,[6] (385) b. Dec. 16, 1760, d. Jan. 23, 1849, ae. 87? yrs. He m. Anna Brown, of Seekonk, April 10, (7, Ch. Rec.) 1783, who d. Feb. 4, 1786. He m. 2dly, Aug. 14, 1787, Mary Whittaker, dau. of John and Mary, b. Feb. 28, 1768. He m. 3dly, 1790, Hannah Carpenter, dau. of Zechariah, b. Nov. 10, 1767, and d. Jan. 22, 1838. He was in the Revolutionary service, and was Lieut. in the Militia after the War. Res. Seekonk. He had 12 chil.

158. IV. Sarah,[6] b. June 13, 1763, d. about 1852. She m. Eben'r French, of Rehoboth, son of James and Bethiah. (See No. 125.) He d. about 1850. Res. Halifax, Vt. Chil.—

(1) *Eben'r.* (2) *Lepha.* (3) *Lucy.* (4) *Bethiah F.* (5) *Leonard* and 2 daus.

159. V. Ethel,[6] (398) b. Aug. 28, 1769, d. Sept. 27, 1844. He m. Nov. 25, 1795, Susannah Carpenter, youngest dau. of Col. Nath'l of Seekonk, and b. Aug. 16, 1778, and d. April 14, 1857. He rem. to Savoy, and when quite aged, went to Mich., and d. in Webster, "not of age, but of medicine," says a son, who is an M. D. He was Select-man in S., a Deacon in the Bap. ch. over 20 yrs., and a man of consistent and devoted piety. Both were m. ch. from early life. Two sons have succeeded him in the same office and same ch. He had 11 chil.

By 2d Marriage.

160. VI. Benjamin,[6] (409) b. Oct. 19, 1770, d. Sept. 10, 1847, ae. 77 yrs. He m. Nov. 22, 1801, Susannah Bullock, of Rehoboth, who was b. in R., May 9, 1769, and d. in Burke, Vt., May 14, 1859,

ae. 90 yrs. He removed to Lyndon, Vt., in 1797, and was a farmer, Select-man, Lister, Justice of the Peace, and Rep. to State Legislature. He was m. ch and had 4 chil.

161. VII. AARON,[6] (413) b. Jan. 9, 1776, d. Dec. 15, 1845. He m. 1800, Betsey Hoffman of Lyndon, Vt., who d. Oct. 18, 1826. They removed from L. to Indiana. He m. 2dly, Feb. 25, 1827, Mrs. Sally (Gould) Leman. He was 1st, a Methodist, 2d, of United Brethren, 3d, a Cumberland Pres., 4th, a Dunkard and 5th, a Baptist. At his death he was Deacon of Bap. ch. Had 12 chil.

162. VIII. DILLE now DELIA,[6] b. Aug. 21, 1772, d. Aug. 31, 1845. She m. April 7, 1803, Henry Hoffman, of Lyndon, Vt., who was b. in Providence, R. I., Aug. 18, 1777, and d. in Burke, Vt., Aug. 27, 1847. She was m. ch. He was a farmer in L. Chil.—

(1) *Ezra W.*, b. June 24, 1806, in L., m. Dec. 13, 1837, Arabella Doyle, of Burke. Res. Brighton, Vt. He has been Deputy Sheriff and Lister.

(2) *Frederick H.*, b. Oct. 2, 1808, m. Dec. 1832, Fanny Hubbard, of L., who d. May 5, 1848. He m. 2d, Oct. 23, 1849, Betsey C. Jones, of Burke, Vt. Farmer and has 3 chil.

(3) *George W.*, b. July 20, 1815, m. 1848, Eliza Way, of Barton, Vt., and d. May 1850.

163. IX. LUCY,[6] b. April 3, 1774. She m. Feb. 27, 1794, (T. Rec.) Feb. 26, 1793, (Fam. Rec.) Abel Wilmarth, of Rehoboth, who was b. June 30, 1772, and d. Aug. 14, 1821. They settled in Lyndon, Vt., about 1800. She is living, (1855,) and is m. ch. Chil.—

(1) *Geo. W.*, b. April 26, 1794, d. in R., June 16, 1815. A saddler.

(2) *Ira*, b. Dec. 16, 1795, m. Samantha Tolman, of Greenboro', Vt., Dec. 25, 1819, and d. in L., March 3, 1843. He was farmer, Select-man, Lister and Justice of the Peace. She d. 1852.

(3) *Susan*, b. Aug. 7, 1798, m. July 20, 1824, Hiram Bemis of L.

(4) *Asaph*, b. Aug. 27, 1800, m. Jan. 1824, Florina Meigs, of L. He was a farmer, Justice of the Peace, Rep. to Legislature, and d. Sept. 26, 1849.

(5) *Nancy W.*, b. May 4, 1810, m. March 27, 1836, John F. G. Cunningham, Esq., of L., a farmer, Lister and Justice of the Peace.

164. X. HANNAH,[6] b. Dec. 23, 1777, d. before 1806.

165. XI. EZRA,[6] (425) b. Oct. 28, 1780. He m. Martha Blanding, dau. of Col. Christopher and Martha, who d. Sept. 21, 1816, in 29th yr. (Ins.) She was m. Cong. ch. He m. 2d, Dec. 1, 1819, Mary Robinson, dau. of Capt. Joel, of Attleboro', b. Dec. 3, 1794, and d. April 23, 1855, a woman of acknowledged piety, though not m. ch. He is a housewright and farmer, of sound judgment, and strict integrity. Res. Attleboro'. He has had 11 chil.

CHIL. OF LIEUT. AARON WALKER,[5] [61] OF REHOBOTH.

166. I. PATIENCE,[6] b. March 21, 1756, d. Jan. 12, 1834. She m. July 30, 1778, (1777, Ch. Rec.) Ezra Reed, who d. Oct. 30, 1834. He was a soldier in the Revolution, removed to Charlestown, now Langdon, N. H., and was Selectman. Chil.—

(1) *Leonard*, b. April 17, 1781, m. July 29, 1804, Cynthia Goodenow, and had 6 chil. He is deceased.

(2) *Ezra*, d. ae. 4 yrs.

(3) *Esther C.*, b. Feb. 14, 1788, d. Sept. 13, 1859, in Abington, Mass., ae. 71 yrs. She m. Isaiah Durant, of Charlestown, N. H., who d. in C., about 1847. Had 8 chil. of whom 3 d. in infancy, viz.:—1, Henry. Res. Lynn. Leather Dealer, in Boston. 2, Harriet, dec'd. 3. Martha, m. Baxter Cobb. Res. Abington. Leather Dealer, in B. 4, Gardner, b. Sept. 11, 1824, m. 1849, Permelia Silsby, of Acworth, and d. June 28, 1855. She was b. Sept. 15, 1826, had 1 ch. who d. in infancy. 5, Esther Amanda, b. Dec. 16, 1829, m. Feb. 7, 1854, Abiathar Richards, Merchant, who was b. Oct. 8, 1825. Have chil.—1, Hallett C., b. Dec. 4, 1854, d. Sept. 3, 1855. 2, Fred. W., b. Jan. 30, 1856. 3, Emma F., b. July 6, 1857. Res. Newport, N. H.

(4) *Permelia A.*, b. Aug. 23, 1790, d. Oct. 24, 1834, m. John Brooks, of Langdon, Jan. 16, 1810. Had 5 chil.

(5) *Arnold*, b. July 24, 1792, d. Dec. 8, 1830, m. Dec. 19, 1813, Theda Perrin. Had 4 chil.

167. II. HANNAH,[6] b. March 7, 1758, d. July 13, 1801. She m. May 29, 1777, Elkanah French, of Rehoboth, where they d. Chil.—

(1) *Esther*, b. Aug. 30, 1777, m. Joseph Wilmarth, and d. 1813. Res. Lyndon, Vt.

(2) *Aaron W.*, b. April 16, 1779, d. July 2, 1779.

(3) *Lucy*, b. June 8, 1780, m. Capt. Loring Cushing, of Rehoboth, and d. Jan. 18, 1850. She has 1 son, Loring, a farmer of respectability in Seekonk, who has been Select-man.

(4) *Elkanah*, b. June 19, 1782, d. Sept. 23, 1856. Yeoman.

(5) *Aaron*, b. July 31, 1784, d. Oct., 1850. Housewright.

(6) *Zechariah*, b. Sept. 18, 1786, d. March 25, 1822. Sea Captain.

(7) *Ezra*, b. Feb. 2, 1789, d. Sept. 2, 1840. Butcher.

(8) *Calvin*, b. Aug. 15, 1791, d. Aug. 25, 1829. Trader.

(9) *Milton*, b. July 25, 1793, d. 1831.

(10) *Hannah*, b. Sept. 24, 1795, d. March 18, 1837.

(11) *Elpha*, b. Oct. 7, 1797, m. Nov. 25, '21, Capt. Davis Carpenter, of Seekonk. Chil.—1, Davis, b. Sept. 26, 1822, m. Eliza J. Putman, of Schenectady, N. Y. Res. Missouri. 2, Charlotte A., m. Jonathan Chaffee, of S. Res. S. 2 chil. 3, Elpha, d. y. 4, Elpha F. 5. Harrison G. O., m. Fanny Barclay, of N. Y. City, and res. there. 6, Alice Howland. 7, Sarah Frances. 8, Sophia Amelia. 9, Lucy Emily. 10, Mary Eliza, dec'd.

168. III. ABIAH,[6] b. March 2, 1760, d. about 1830, unm. in Langdon, N. H. He served in the War for Independence.

169. IV. SAMUEL,[6] (436) b. Feb. 4, 1762, d. Feb. 19, 1831. He m. 1784, Anna, dau. of Oliver and Sarah Carpenter, who d. April 9, 1815. He enlisted in the Continental army, and served several yrs. He early removed to Charlestown now Langdon, N. H. Had 5 chil.

170. V. ESTHER,[6] b. Oct. 27, 1764, d. Aug. 24, 1807. She m. July 1, 1790, John White, who was b. Aug. 13, 1760, and d. Jan. 13, 1804. Res. N. H. Chil.—1792—1801.

(1) *Lucy*, m. Aaron G. Holden. (2) *Nancy*, m. Wm. Jones. (3) *Esther*, m. Sam'l Mann. (4) *Aaron*, m. Mildred Woodbury. (5) *John*, m. Maria Baker. (6) *Lawson*, d. y.

171. VI. WALTER,[6] (441) b. Nov. 16, (17?) 1766, d. July 25, 1846, ae. 80. He m. June 11, 1801, Grace Loomis in Alstead, N. H., who was b. Oct. 17, 1777, in Tolland Ct., and d. Aug 3, 1844, in Maidstone, Vt. He was a shoemaker and a farmer; removed to Charlestown, N. H., and then to Clarendon, Vt. Both Meth. Had 7 chil.

172. VII. RELIEF,[6] b June 25, 1769, (Town Rec.) (Jan. 25, 1773, Fam. Rec.) d. Nov. 18, 1848, in Central Village, Ct, She m. March 9, 1793, Otis Walcott, of Cumberland, R. I., who was b. Nov. 11, 1768, and d. July 4, 1833, in Pawtucket, R. I. Res. P. Both m. Bap. ch. Chil.—

(1) *Perley*, b. Feb. 12, 1794, in Cumberland, R. I., d. Feb. 16, 1826.

(2) *William Augustus*, b. Sept. 20, 1795, in Providence, d. Sept. 20, 1796.

(3) *Sarah Ann*, b. July, 1797, m. as 2d wife, Jan. 24, 1833, Uriah Benedict. Both m. Bap. ch. He was a wealthy manufacturer at Central Falls, Smithfield, R. I., and d. in Plainfield, Ct., Feb. 23, 1858, ae. 74 yrs.

(4) *Susan*, b. Feb. 16, 1800, in C., m. July 10, 1829, Dr. John S. Gallup, of Woodstock, Vt. Res. Medfield. No chil.

(5) *Marietta*, b. 1803, in C., d. 1812.

(6) *Adeline*, b. April 10, 1806, in Attleborough, m. Arnold Fenner, of Johnston, R. I., April 15, 1833. He is a Cotton Manufacturer in Central Village, Ct. Both m. Cong. ch. Chil.—1, Helen W., b. April 14, 1835, m. March 1, 1855, Philip Mathewson, of Lisbon, a farmer. 2, Adeline, b. Sept. 9, 1836. 3, Sarah W., b. Nov. 3, 1837, d. Aug. 9, 1839. 4, Susan B., b. Jan. 17, 1840. 5, Arnold B., b. June 21, 1843.

(7) *Cornelia*, b. April 21, 1813, in Smithfield, R. I., m. Jas. M. Kimball, of Chepachet, R. I., Feb. 10, 1846. Res. Sterling, Ct. Both m. Cong ch.

173. VIII. NANCY,[6] b. July 19, 1771, d. about 1850. She m. Dec. 30, 1794, George Sweetland, of Attleboro'. Had 2 chil.

174. IX. PAMELIA A.,[6] b. Nov. 22, 1773, d. March 1, 1844. She m. Sept. 27, 1796, Joseph Baker, of Warwick, R. I. Res. Providence, R. I., where he d. Oct. 1, 1842. He was a Machinist. Chil.—1797 to 1812.

(1) *Lucy*. (2) *Sally*, m. Daniel Armington. (3) *Maria*, m. Geo. Lawton, and 2dly, (See No. 170.) (4) *Joseph*, m. Cynthia Hardel. (5) *Almira*, m. Henry T. Dunham. (6) *Pamelia*, d. in 20th yr. (7) *William A.*, m. Susan Ellis of Seekonk.

CHILDREN OF EPHRAIM WALKER,[5] [63] OF REHOBOTH.

175. I. CHARLOTTE,[6] b. Oct. 18, 1772, d. about 1840. She m. Dec. 26, 1805, Capt. Jesse Drown. Res. Seekonk. Chil.—

(1) *Simeon*. (2) *Charlotte*, d. y. (3) *Lepha*, d. y. (4) *Anna*, dec'd.

176. II. EPHRAIM,[6] b. Jan. 24, 1774, was drowned in crossing the river at Marietta, Ohio, when about 25 yrs. old, unm.

177. III. ORINDA,[6] b. Sept. 24, 1775, d. July 24, 1831. She m. Feb. 13, 1800, Samuel Perrin. Res. West Randolph, Vt. Both m. Cong. ch., and had 10 chil.—1802—1821.

178. IV. SIMEON,[6] (448) b. Feb. 13, 1777, d. Oct. 29, 1857, in 81st yr. He m. Dec. 18, 1810, Nancy Whittaker. (See No. 179,) of Seekonk. Res. Seekonk. He was a Sea Captain, and Select-man 11 yrs., viz.: 1824, 5, 6, 7, 8, 9, '30, 1, 3, 4, 5. Had 10 chil.

179. V. JOEL,[6] (458) b. Nov. 19, 1778. He m. March 13, 1810, Sarah Whittaker, sister of Nancy. (See No. 178.) His In'y was taken, 1825. He had 7 chil. Res. Seekonk.

180. VI. STEPHEN,[6] (465) b. Sept. 28, 1781, d. Oct. 25, 1813, ae. 32 yrs. He m. April 20, 1809, Rebecca Talbert Pearce, who d. Oct. 1, 1820, in 37th yr. (Ins.) Res. Seekonk. Had 3 chil.

181. VII. HANNAH,[6] b. April 15, 1783, m. Nov. 29, 1810, David Bucklin; m. 2d, John Perrin. Res. Seekonk, and has no chil.

182. VIII. EBENEZER,[6] b. March 30, 1786, d. Feb. 10, 1860, in 74th yr. He m. Nov. 20, 1825, Abigail Carpenter, of Seekonk, dau. of Thomas, and b. Feb. 12, 1797. Both m. Cong. ch. He was a machinist and highly esteemed for moral worth. Res. Pawtucket, R. I. Had 3 chil.

183. IX. LEPHA,[6] b. Jan. 17, 1789, d. April 23, 1844. She m. Oct. 1832, Samuel Perrin, who m. 1st her sister Orinda. She was m. Cong. ch. Res. Randolph, Vt.

184. X. PETER,[6] b. Jan. 15, 1795, d. Oct. 12, 1823, unm.

CHILDREN OF BENJAMIN WALKER,[5] [72] OF ASHFORD, CT.

185. I. HANNAH,[6] b. 1759, d. June 16, 1813. She m. 1778, Jedediah Amidon, of Willington, Ct., who was b. 1759. He was a farmer, 1st in W., then in Ashford. Both m. Cong. ch. Chil.—1779—1800.

(1) *Experience J.* (See No. 198.) (2) *Abigail.* (3) *Jedediah.* (4) *Ebenezer.* (5) *Hannah.* (6) *Henry.* (7) *Wealthy.* (8) *Horace*, b. July 27, 1793, Twin. (9) *Horatio*, Twin, m. Maria Strong, of Stafford, Ct. (10) *Sally*, Twin. (11) *Polly*, Twin. (12) *Jedediah*, a physician in Paxton, and d. July 5, 1837.

186. II. POLLY,[6] b. Aug. 14, 1763, d. Sept. 2, 1844, ae. about 80 yrs. She m. Aug. 14, 1781, Elijah Hanks, who was b. in Mansfield, Ct., Aug. 5, 1761, and d. Feb. 11, 1839, ae. 77 yrs. He was a blacksmith, and Dea. of Bap. ch. many yrs., and an exemplary christian. He removed to Rootstown, Ohio, about 1807. Mrs. H. was a worthy help-meet of her husband in his early struggles with poverty, and the hardships of a new country. She was m. Bap. ch. and a consistent christian. Chil.—

(1) *Joseph*, b. Dec. 1, 1782, d. March 29, 1796. (2) *Elijah*, b. April 10, 1784, m. Oct. 4, 1807, Betsey Tisdale, and d. May 20, 1835, m. Bap. ch. 8 chil. (3) *Chlorinda*, b. Dec. 24, 1785, m. March 12, 1814, Mark Young. Res. R., d. June 6, 1852. 7 chil., m. of Bap. ch. (4) *John*, b. June 12, 1788, m. Jan. 10, 1844, Rosanna Haile, and d. Sept. 17, 1837. 8 chil. Twin. (5) *Benjamin*, b. June 12, 1788, m. Sept. 1, 1811, Martha Knowlton, and d. 1843. 12 chil., m. ch., Twin. (6) *Lucinda*, b. June 14, 1790, d. April 9, 1796. (7) *Martha*, b. April 29, 1792, m. May 20, 1813, Artemas Cunningham, and d. 1849. 13 chil., m. Bap. ch. (8) *Esther*, b. Oct. 13, 1794, m. Jan. 3, 1813, John Young, and d. Aug. 16, 1853. 13 chil., m. Bap. ch.

187. III. BENJAMIN,[6] (471) m. March 29, 1787, Rhoda Nott, dau. of Samuel? and sister of President Nott of Union College, N. Y. She d. Nov. 20, 1791. Had 3 chil. He was Lieutenant in the Militia.

A year or two after the death of his wife, Mr. W., by the dishonesty of others, became involved in his business, not only losing his valuable farm, but was burdened with a heavy debt. Fearing imprisonment, he fled from his home, leaving his young children, and his native State. His calamity and separation proved to be one for life. He was unable to rise above and conquer his misfortunes, wandered from place to place, engaging in any business which promised present success, and failing in all endeavors, he at length died in Chenango Co., Penn.

His wife possessed many of the qualities that distinguish the family to which she belonged, such as talent, sound judgment, kindness and piety. In her early death, her husband lost a wise counsellor and a devoted wife; her children an affectionate and faithful mother; and the world a bright christian example. Love inspired her heart, kind words were the fruit of her lips, and benevolent acts the cheerful offering of her hands.

188. IV. Esther,[6] m. Israel D. Chaffee, and d. in Ashford, Ct., 1806. No chil.

Children of EBENEZER WALKER,[5] [73] of Ashford, Ct.

189. I. Ebenezer,[6] (474) b. 1761, d. Oct. 8, 1841, ae. 80 yrs. He m. Oct. between 1780 and '90, Elizabeth Hanks, of Ashford, Ct., dau. of Dea. John She d. March 15, 1844, ae. 78. He removed to West Becket, and thence in 1840, to N. Y., where they died. Had 9 chil.

190. II. James,[6] (483) b. July 8, 1762, d. Dec. 25, 1849, ae. 87. He m. 1787, Sarah Flint, dau. of Aaron, Esq., of Windham, Ct., b. Oct. 15, 1761, and d. Feb. 16, 1845, ae. 84. Both m. ch. Bap. They removed to West Becket in 1795, where they lived till their decease. He was a farmer and had 7 chil.

191. III. Amasa,[6] (490) b. 1767, d. 1828, ae. 61 yrs. He m. Martha Smith, dau. of Ebenezer, of Ashford, Ct., b. 1767, and d. Nov. 7, 1851, aged 84 yrs. He soon after his marriage removed to Becket, and in 1811 to Byron, N. Y. He had 12 chil.

192. IV. Amy,[6] m. Burchard, had 1 son; m. 2d, ——, and d. about 1830, in Lee.

(1) *Harvey.*

193. V. Hannah,[6] m. Ezekiel Gleason. Res. Tyringham. No chil.

194. VI. Sarah,[6] d. in Lee, unm., about 1830.

195. VII. JERUSAH,[6] d. about 1835, ae. 80, in Genesee Co., N.Y. She m. Oct. between 1780 and '90, Charles Kimball. Res. Becket. Had 7 chil.—

(1) *Alvin.* (2) *Betsey.* (3) *Lucinda.* (4) *Amy.* (5) *Ann.* (6) *Roza.* (7) *Charlotte,* m. and res. in West Stockbridge.

CHILDREN OF SAMUEL WALKER,[5] [75] OF ASHFORD, CT.

196. I. SAMUEL,[6] (501) b. Nov. 8, 1776. He m. Nov. 25, 1803, Lovina Robinson, who d. Sept. 27, 1815. He m. 2d, April 15, 1825, Mrs. Ruth (Brownson) Ransom, who was b. June 4, 1794. He rem. to Jessup, Penn., where he lives, (1860) venerable and beloved, though helpless with the infirmities of age. He has had 11 chil.

197. II. TIMOTHY,[6] (512) b. May 17, 1781, in Ashford, Ct., d. Sept. 15, 1855. He m. Joanna Whiton, who was b. in A., May 10, 1784. His father died when he was young, and he lived with, and was adopted by his uncle Ephraim, and inherited his homestead in A. Both m. Cong. ch., and had 10 chil. b. in A.

198. III. ELIZABETH,[6] b. Nov. 8, 1786, m. Jan. 5, 1809, Experience J. Amidon, her cousin, (see No. 185) a farmer in Westford, Ct. Chil.—

(1) *Louisa.* (2) *Wealthy M.* (3) *Experience J.* (4) *Hannah.* (5) *John.* (6) *Dan.*

CHILDREN OF JOHN WALKER,[5] [76] OF ASHFORD, CT.

199. I. JOSEPH.[6]
200. II. JOHN.[6]
201. III. ABIGAIL.[6]
202. IV. REBECCA.[6]

The compiler has been unable to find any trace of these, save that the daus. m. (whom is unknown) and lived in Hartford, Ct.

CHIL. OF DANIEL WALKER,[5] [85] OF CUMBERLAND, R. I.

203. I. ESTHER,[6] b. Nov. 20, 1745.

204. II. NATHAN,[6] b. Aug. 2, 1747, d. July 12, 1752.

BY 2d MARRIAGE.

205. III. JAMES,[6] b. Dec. 19, 1749, d. July 15.

206. IV. HANNAH,[6] b. May 1, 1751.
207. V. JAMES,[6] b. Dec. 1752.
208. VI. ELIZABETH,[6] b. July 3, 1756.

} Diligent search has been made for these and No. 203, but without success.

CHILDREN OF CAPT. PHILIP WALKER,[5] [88] OF REHOBOTH.

209. I. AMY,[6] b. June 27, 1748. She m. Jan. 2, 1772, William Jennings, and had 5 chil.—1772—1780.

(1) *Sylvester.* (2) *Lucy.* (3) *Hannah.* (4) *Oliver.* (5) *William.*

210. II. SON,[6] } Twins probably. Bapt. Aug. 1749, d. y.
211. III. BETTE,[6] } d. Sept. 20, 1750.

212. IV. LYDIA,[6] b. Aug. 25, 1750.

213. V. PHILIP,[6] (522) b. Aug. 3, 1751. He m. Abigail Knapp, of Rehoboth, who d. April 17, 1775. He m. 2d, Hannah Hall, Nov. 8, 1775, and 3d, Mrs. Mott. He was a soldier in the War of the Revolution, and Town Clerk of Rehoboth from 1787 to 1801 inclusive. He removed about 1802 to Roxbury, Delaware Co., N. Y., thence to Tompkins Co., N. Y., where he died. Had 7 chil.

214. VI. HANNAH,[6] b. Aug. 5, 1753, m. Aug. 31, 1775, John Caswell.

CHIL. OF JOSEPH WALKER,[5] [92] OF WEST GREENWICH, R.I.

215. I. MARY,[6] b. March 10, 1762, (1760, Fam. Rec.) in Coventry, R. I. She m. May 18, 1780, Benjamin Jordan, who was b. in Rehoboth, and d. in Columbia, N. H., July 18, 1846, ae. 84 yrs., and 4 mos. He was a soldier in the Revolution and his widow draws a pension. About 5 mos. after their marriage, they removed to Plainfield, N. H., and in July, 1816, to Columbia. He was a m. Bap. ch. in R. I. She has had uncommon strength and health, and is an intelligent and pious woman, living (1860,) at the great age of 100, (98?) retaining her strength and memory remarkably. She has had 14 chil., about 200 descendants and 3 or 4 of 5th generation. Chil.—

(1) *Joseph.* Res. C., 6 chil. (2) *Lydia,* m. Benj. Sweet. Res. Plainfield, N. H. 6 chil. and 40 descendants. (3) *Mercy,* m. John Thomas. No chil. (4) *Ruth,* m. Joseph Sims. Res. Leamington, Vt., then in C. Both dead. (5) *Charles,* m. Olive Jordan, and d. May, 1835, ae. 44 yrs. 5 chil. (6) *Hannah,* m. James Boutwell. Res. Lancaster, N. H. 10 chil. (7)

Johnson, m. Minerva Buell and Mrs. Martha F. Dinsmore. 5 chil. He is m. Cong. ch. Res. Colebrook, N. H. (8) *Lyman*, m. Fanny Dearth. Res. C. 8 chil.—[1, Rosanna B. 2, Lyman L. 3, Wm. R. 4. Fanny G. 5, Emily C. 6, Susannah B. 7, Royal W. 8, John H.] (9) *Polly*, unm. (10) *Benjamin*, d. ae. 8 yrs. Four other chil. d. in infancy.

By 2d Marriage.

216. II. Stephen,[6] (529) b. May 1767, d. May 10, 1833, ae. 66 yrs. He m. Mary Bennett, dau. of Capt. Ezekiel, of Coventry, R. I., b. May, 1770, d. Sept. 14, 1849. Both m. ch. They removed to C., 1797, where they died. Had 11 chil.

217. III. Anna,[6] b. Nov. 1, 1768, d. Nov. 1808. She m. about 1788, Zorobabel or Zerry Potter, who was b. Sept. 14, 1764, and d. by a cancer, Aug. 3, 1834, ae. 71. Both were consistent m. Bap. ch. Res. Pownal, Vt. Had 10 chil. He was a quiet and retiring man, and held no offices. He m. 2d, Mrs. Bayley, Jan. 5, 1810, and 3d, Lois Knight, who is living, (1860.) Chil.—

(1) *Lydia*, b. Oct. 29, 1789, m. Joseph Millard, of Savoy, where she lived till his death. Res. Pownal. (2) *Catharine*, b. June 12, 1791, d. ae. 19 yrs. (3) *Amy*, b. Jan. 14, 1794, d. ae. 18 mos. (4) *Joseph*, b. Nov. 24, 1795, m. Sally Gardner. Res. P. (5) *Stukeley*, b. Jan. 13, 1797, unm. (6) *Almon*, b. Nov. 21, 1798, d. y. (7) *Hannah*, b. July 8, 1801, m. John Grinold. Res. P. (8) *Susan*, b. July 12, 1803, m. Samuel Proud. Res. P. (9) *John*, b. Oct. 8, 1806, m. Mrs. Sally Potter, widow of his brother Joseph. Res. P. (10) *Anna*, b. Oct. 17, 1808, m. John Crandall, and d. in Grafton, N. Y.

218. IV. Ruth,[6] m. David Cahoon, d. before 1833. Res. Pownal, Vt. Chil.—

(1) *Polly*. (2) *Lydia*. (3) *William*. (4) *Walker*. (5) *Almon*.

219. V. Stukely,[6] (540) b. June 26, 1776, d. Nov. 8, 1851. He m. Jan. 1801, Alice Bennett, dau. of Capt. Ezekiel, of Coventry, R. I., b. Feb. 13, 1778, and d. July 6, 1842. He lived in C., till 1815, and they rem. to N. Y. He was a carpenter, and 1st corporal in a cavalry company. Both m. ch. They had 12 chil.

220. VI. Joseph,[6] b. July 15, 1782, joined the Shakers, somewhere in N. Y., but did not remain with them long. He never married says one, but his half sister, (No. 215,) thinks he m. and with his brother Caleb, lived near Saratoga Springs—a locality so indefinite, that the compiler can find no trace of him.

221. VII. Caleb,[6] (551) b. Aug. 18, 1784, removed when young to Shaftesbury, Vt. He left S., and all trace of him has been lost, save that he m. and had 2 sons.

CHIL. OF NATHANIEL WALKER,[5] [94] OF NO. PROVIDENCE.

222. I. BETSEY,[6] b. May 18, 1753, d. about 86 yrs. of ae., in Watervliet, N. Y., and was m. Bap. ch. She m. Samuel Healy, a ship builder, and had—

(1) *Adah*, who m. Samuel Brown, of Seekonk, (See No. 43,) and d. about 1847.

223. II. SAMUEL,[6] b. March 7, 1755, d. about 1775. He is supposed to have been lost at sea when about 20 yrs. old.

224. III. SUSAN,[6] b. Feb. 28, 1757, d. less than 2 yrs. old.

225. IV. MARY,[6] b. April 29, 1759, d. ae. 13 yrs.

226. V. NATHANIEL,[6] (553) b. July 21, 1761, d. March 11, 1826. He m. Sarah Whitford, of Rehoboth, dau. of John, an Englishman, b. March 12, 1758, and d. Dec. 15, 1815. She was m. ch. He was a blacksmith, and resided in Pawtucket, R. I., and had 7 chil. He was an Ensign and Lieutenant in the Rhode Island Regiment, and was taken prisoner and chained with a negro, in the old Jersey Prison Ship, undergoing the severest sufferings. His back was covered with scars, where the vermin had eaten.

227. VI. ABIGAIL,[6] b. April 3, 1764, d. Oct. 1852. She m. Thomas Shrimpton, a paper mould maker. Both were exemplary members of the Bap. Ch. in Troy, N. Y., of which he was a Deacon. They lived to a good old age and were greatly esteemed. Had 3 daus.

228. VII. SALLY,[6] b. Feb. 28, 1766, d. Nov. 1843. She m. June 10, 1789, James Durfee, of Freetown, 10th child and 6th son of Thomas and Patience, (Borden,) b. March 28, 1768, and d. March, 1850. Both m. Free Will Bap. ch. They had 9 chil.—

(1) *Susannah*, b. March 6, 1790, d. 1815, ae. 25 yrs.

(2) *Nathan*, b. Sept. 19, 1791, m. June 2, 1816, Hetty Delany, of New Bedford. Res. N. B. till a few yrs. since, and now in Rochester. Blacksmith and farmer. Chil.—1, Lucy, b. April 17, 1817, d. April 20, 1821. 2, Harriet Harrison, b. May 25, 1818, m. July 5, 1853, Capt. John S. Dorman, of Geneva, N. Y. 3, James, b. July 30, 1820, d. May 14, 1822. 4, Lucy, b. Feb. 13, 1822, d. Sept. 23, 1822. 5, Lucy, b. April 28, 1824, m. 1845, Lorenzo Dillingham, of N. B.

(3) *Cynthia*, b. Nov. 26, 1793, d. May, 1837, ae. 44 yrs.

(4) *Thomas*, b. Feb. 21, 1795, m. Dec. 14, 1818, Elizabeth Maxfield, of Dartmouth, who was b. June 10, 1790, and d. Oct. 18, 1829. He m. 2dly, May 22, 1830, Delight Sherman, of Dartmouth, who was b. June 1, 1796. Chil.—1, Abby Elizabeth, b. June 25, 1822, m. May 4, 1841, Abner Sherman, of Westport, who was b. Dec. 19, 1816, and has James Leonard, b. Feb. 11

1842, and Wm. Bradford, b. Sept. 7, 1848. Res. N. B. Free Will Bap. 2, Judith Maxfield, b. May 22, 1824. 3, Zoheth Sherman, b. April 22, 1831, 4, Child, d., ae. 1 hour. 5, Child, d., ae. 11 days. 6, Thomas James, b. Oct. 1, 1837, in N. B., and d. Aug. 4, 1855, ae. 18. All the others were b. in Fall River. Res. N. B. Blacksmith, and Free Will Bap.

(5) *Abby Walker*, b. March 22, 1798, m. Feb. 21, 1828, Col. Richard Borden, of Fall River, son of Thomas and Mary, and b. April 12, 1795. She united with Cong. ch. in 1816. His occupation till 1814, was farming and lumbering. Upon the death of an elder brother, he took charge of the saw and grist mill of his father, and soon commenced trading in grain and flour. About 1818, he, with the late Bradford Durfee, built the sloop "Golden Age," the timber having been cut and drawn from the forest by themselves. In 1821, they bought the land which is now the site of the Iron Works, extending from the F. R. Cotton Mill to the Taunton river. The same year, a company was organized, Mr. Durfee chosen Agent, and Mr. B. an Assistant, and in 1829, Mr. B. was elected Agent, Clerk and Treasurer of the Iron Works, which position he has held to the present time. He has been Agent of the Annawan Manufacturing Company—Agent of the Metacomet Co.—was the originator of the Bay State Steamboat enterprise, (a line of Steamers between Fall River and N. Y. City,)—Agent for the building the boats—and from the first, has been President of the Company. As to Military distinction, he was chosen Ensign in 1814, and successively, Lieut., Capt. of a Militia Co., then Capt. of a Light Infantry, Lieut. Col., and Col. He has been Constable, Assessor, Selectman, Rep. and State Senator. In 1826, he united with the Cong. ch.—soon became interested in the Sabbath School, and for a series of years, sustained a Sabbath Mission School, 7 miles from F. R., engaging also in the Sabbath School at home. Having accumulated large wealth, not exceeded by any in F. R., and maintaining, withal, a character marked by probity and christian excellence, no man in F. R. has more influence, or is more relied upon, for sound judgment, and sagacity in financial and religious enterprises, than he. His chil. are—1, Caroline, b. Sept. 20, 1829. 2, Thomas James, b. March 1, 1832, m. Feb. 20, 1855, Mary E. Hill, who was b. Aug. 5, 1834. He is agent of the Troy Cotton and Woolen Manufactory, in F. R., and has—Harriet Minerva, b. June 15, 1856. Anna Howland, b. April, 1858. Richard, b. 1860. 3, Richard Baxter, b. Feb. 21, 1834, is Superintendent of 3 Cotton Mills in F. R. 4, Edward Payson, b. Feb. 12, 1836, is Book-keeper of the Am. Print Works in F. R. 5, Wm. Henry Harrison, b. Sept. 30, 1840. 6, Matthew Chaloner Durfee, b. July 18, 1842, entered Yale College, Sept. 1860. 7, Sarah Walker, b. May 13, 1844.

(6) *Sally Durfee*, b. June 14, 1801, d. Nov., 1839, m. Samuel Wood, of New Bedford, who is deceased. Res. N. B. Chil.—1, Mary Hill, b. April 14, 1823, m. Nathan Brightman, and d. Dec. 5, 1843. 2, Sally, b. Nov. 6, 1825, d. June 19, 1827. 3, Samuel, b. Oct. 2, 1826, d. July 7, 1843. 4, James, b. August 10, 1828.

(7) *James*, b. Aug. 3, 1803, m. June 3, 1824, Mary Allen, of New Bedford, who d. Oct. 4, 1842. Free Will Bap. He m. 2dly, March 23, 1843, Julia Vinal, of Scituate, who d. Oct. 26, 1855. He m. 3dly, April 24, 1856, Clarissa (Chase) Hendrickson, who is m. Bap. ch. Res. N. B. Chil.—1, Susan, b. Dec. 27, 1827, and d. Oct. 6, 1855. She m. March 11, 1851, Charles M.

Pierce, of N. B., and has—Francis Chaloner, b. Jan. 10, 1852. Res. N. B. Free Will Bap. 2, Francis Allen, b. April 17, 1829. 3, Charles, b. Jan. 8, 1832, m. Abby Batty, of Providence, R. I., and d. 1853. Res. P. 4, James, b. May 22, 1834. 5, Horatio Nelson, b. Feb. 5, 1837. 6, Wm. Henry, b. July 22, 1840, d. June 22, 1842. By 2d marriage.—7, Mary Walker, b. 1847. 8, Ellen Wade, b. April 28, 1849.

(8) *Judith Russell*, b. Feb. 22, 1805, d. Sept. 27, 1832. She m. March, 1829, Jethro Hillman, of N. B., who was b. 1789, and d. Oct. 12, 1854. Res. N. B. Chil.—1, Sarah Durfee, b. May 24, 1830, m. Dec. 4, 1854, Wm. Shockley, of N. B., who was b. 1817, and has—1, Wm. Hillman, b. Sept. 18, 1855. 2, Zechariah, b. May 18, 1832, d. Sept. 28, 1832.

(9) *William*, b. Dec. 20, 1807, m. Aug. 23, 1830, Alice Sherman Talbot, of Dighton, who was b. Oct. 11, 1802. Res. N. B. and Fall River. Chil.—1, Wm. Franklin, b. Nov. 15, 1833. 2, Elizabeth Alice, b. Jan. 1, 1831. 3, Mary Judson, b. Jan. 15, 1840, d. Nov. 9, 1841. All b. in N. B. He is a Carpenter.

229. VIII. DAVID,[6] (560) b. April 16, 1768, d. July 25, (26 Prov. Rec.) 1854, ae. 86 yrs. He m. Aug. 17, 1791, Mrs. Mary (Shepardson) Sweetland, of Attleboro', who d. May 17, 1832, ae. 72 yrs. Res. Providence, R. I., upon Constitution Hill. Blacksmith. He and all his family were m. Bap. ch. He was subject to melancholy and sometimes insane, yet an excellent man when free from depression. Had 5 chil.

230. IX. CYNTHIA,[6] b. June 10, 1771, (1770, Fam. Rec.) d. Dec., 1848. She m. Cromwell Hill, of Rehoboth, who was a blacksmith, and d. Dec., 1822. Both m. Cong. ch. Chil.—

(1) *Asa*, b. Aug. 1801, m. Jerusha Miller. Merchant in Providence, R.I.

(2) *Mary*, b. May, 1803, m. 1849, Ray Potter, of Pawtucket.

(3) *Thomas J.*, b. 1805, m. Betsey Brown. Manuf'r in Providence.

(4) *Abby Smith*, b. 1814, d. 1816.

CHILDREN OF ENOS WALKER,[5] [95] OF REHOBOTH.

231. I. BENJAMIN,[6] (565) b. Aug. 14, 1751, d. May 14, 1822, in 73d yr. He m. Nov. 15, 1773, Margaret Rawson, of Mendon, who d. in Barre, Vt., Aug. 14, 1793, in 41st yr. She was dau. of Wm. and Margaret (Cook,) "a lawyer and considered a man of learning in his day," and grand dau. of Capt. Wm., a farmer in M., and probably grad of H. C., 1703. (See Rawson Gen.) He m. 2d, June, 1794, Mrs. Eunice (Willard,) widow of Doct. John Caryl, of Chester, Vt. He lived in Grafton till March, 1793, and then removed to Barre, Vt., where he d. Had 10 chil. He joined the army at the commencement of the Revolution, and attained the rank of Colonel. He was at the capture of Burgoyne, and commanded a company of

brave fellows of the Massachusetts Line, although he was then only 1st Lieutenant, (the Captain being sick.) He was also in the battle on Long Island, and became a pensioner under the 1st Pension Act, but his name was stricken off, because it was said he had a little property. He was a Universalist, all his descendants in B., without a single exception, hold the same religious belief.

232. II. CHARLES PHILIP,[6] (575) b. March 3, 1754. He m. Elizabeth Aldrich, and had 2 chil. He removed from Smithfield, R. I., to Ballston, N. Y. One of his legs was broken by the fall of a tree upon him. He lay all day without help, and when he was found, it was set wrong, and he became a cripple for life. Not able to work, he obtained a livelihood by travelling with exhibitions. He went into Vermont about 1810, and descending a steep hill, was thrown out of the carriage, and his leg was broken again in 2 places. It being a hot day, and he very fleshy and heavy, it was found necessary to amputate the leg, and he d. in, or soon after the operation, in Newbury, Vt. He was accidentally the cause of his father's death, and his son Nathan was killed in a sand pit, in Ohio.

233. III. ENOS,[6] b. March 14, 1756. He was taken prisoner in the Revolutionary War, and d. in the Jersey Prison Ship, unm.

234. IV. RICHARD,[6] (577) b. March 10, 1758, d. Feb. 24, 1838. He m. June 26, 1783, Abigail Estabrooks, of Bristol, R. I., who d. in her 53d yr. A woman of great excellence. He m. 2d, Oct. 29, 1787, Sarah Ormsbee, dau. of Abraham, of Rehoboth. He was Captain in the Revolutionary service, and aided in bearing Col. afterward President Munroe from the field, at the battle of Trenton, after he was wounded. And when the President made his visit to New England, Capt. Walker was introduced to him, and received the warm expressions of the President's gratitude. Res. (Seekonk) Rehoboth. He had 4 chil.

235. V. NATHAN,[6] b. July 21, 1760, d. unm.? He enlisted in the Continental Army for 3 yrs., May 28, 1777, and served the whole period. He afterward went to sea, was taken by the British, and having the yellow fever, he with others was put on shore, on one of the Capes of Virginia. The others recovered and returned, but nothing was ever heard of him afterward. He is supposed to have died there.

236. VI. JEDEDIAH,[6] (581) b. Aug. 25, (21, Fam. Rec.) 1762, d. Jan. 19, 1841, in Covington, N. Y. He m. 1783, Polly Goss, of Mendon, who was b. in M., Feb. 20, 1766, and d. Oct. 20, 1794, in Rutland, Vt. He m. 2d, March 8, 1795, Olive Squire, who was b.

in Woodbury, Ct., Nov. 18, 1766, and d. Oct. 8, 1855, in C. He enlisted in the army of the Revolution, and was in Capt. Amadowne's Co., of Rehoboth. He was a carpenter, and removed to Clarendon, Vt. Remaining a short time, he went to Rutland, and thence in 1817, to Hamilton, N.Y. He was a m. Bap. ch., and had 12 chil.

237. VII. Lewis,[6] (593) b. Nov. 18, 1765, (Fam. Rec.) Dec. 17, 1763, (Rehoboth Rec.*) d. Dec. 31, 1841, ae. 76. He m. Nov. 27, 1788, Mary, dau. of Capt. Oliver Potter, of Clarendon, Vt., b. July 5, 1772, and d. Sept. 5, 1854. He removed about 1786, to C., where he learned the carpenter's trade. In 1793, he settled as a farmer in St. Albans, Vt., where he died. He was overseer of the Poor 7 yrs., and also represented the town in the Legislature. He had 11 chil.

Chil. of EPHRAIM WALKER,[5] [98] of Providence, R.I.

238. I. William,[6] (604) b. Jan. 11, 1759, d. Dec. 13, 1843. He m. Oct. 20, (19, Prov. Rec.) 1782, Cynthia, dau. of John Hoppin, Esq. of Providence, b. July 18, 1758, d. Oct. 21, 1839. Res. Thompson, Ct., from 1788 till their death. He was a carpenter, a man of sound judgment, and of considerable influence in the town. He was one of the founders and pillars of the Meth. ch. in T. Had 8 chil.

239. II. Sarah,[6] b. Dec. 17, 1761, d. Aug. 16, 1837. She m. Feb. 21, 1779, Col. Thomas Coles, of Providence, R. I., who was b. in England, Dec. 4, 1752, and when a boy, ran away from family persecutions. He d. Oct. 13, 1844. In'y, $26,038,64. No chil. He was a Col. in the Revolution, Aid de-camp to LaFayette, and afterwards a naval commander. He was at Valley Forge all winter, and came near perishing with hunger and cold, and was saved only by the care of a farmer's daughter, for whom he searched, years after the Peace, but in vain. He was Collector of the Port of Providence many years, till removed by President Jackson. He always kept as cherished mementoes, a sash and sword given him by Gen. LaFayette. He was a splendid specimen of an old soldier, and had the gait and air of the soldier, as long as he could walk. He retained his physical and mental vigor to a great age. When at length his strength began to fail, his spirits sank at once, and mortified by his growing infirmities and stooping form, he shut himself in his room, and staid there till he was carried out.

* It is possible that there was a Lewis b. 1763, who d. in infancy.

240. III. STEPHEN,[6] (612) b. Jan. 2, 1765, d. Jan. 16, 1845, ae. 80 yrs., and 14 days. He m. Jan. 28, 1790, Polly Campbell, of Becket, Mass., who d. Oct. 5, 1795, leaving 2 sons. He m. 2d, Dec. 25, 1796, Lydia Gardner, of Hudson, N. Y., who was b. in Nantucket, Oct. 9, 1775, and d. Oct. 23, 1838, ae. 63 yrs., and 14 days, having 11 chil. He was a housewright, emigrated to Johnstown, Saratoga Co., N. Y., and about 1812, removed to Butternutts, N. Y. He was a man of fair abilities, sterling good sense, honest, temperate and remarkably industrious. He was in youth a Congregationalist. His wife was a Friend, and her stronger intellect carried him with her. He ever afterward, worshipped "in the Meeting," and his house was the "home" for all the Ministers of the persuasion. Two only of his children continued their connection with the Friends. He labored for the education of his family, and his ambition was to train them up in honor, usefulness and piety. In 1831, most of the children being settled in life, the old homestead was deserted, and they passed the pleasant sunset of their lives in the home of their dau., Mrs. Munson. Mrs. W., was strong in character, and in person. Of inexhaustible energy and resources, the care of 13 children sat lightly upon her. She d. soon after leaving her home, at Camillus, and both are buried in C.

Says one who knew him well—"He was one of the lights of the earth. A plain, simple mechanic, he brought up 13 children in the fear of God, and in the strictest honesty, and stranger still, in the strictest temperance."

It is the family pride of his descendants, that not one has ever dishonored the life and virtues of the Father, or the sterling goodness of the Quaker Mother.

Of his 7 sons, 4 are mechanics, one a merchant, and 2 are lawyers. All but one of his 13 children are professedly religious.

241. IV. NANCY,[6] b. in Providence, d. May 17, 1807. She m. Jan. 24, 1798, Charles Hartshorne, of Providence, (his 2d wife.) Chil.—

(1) *John Thomas*, b. Nov. 4, 1798; has been a Cotton and Wool Broker, in Boston. He m. Feb., 1822, Mary Ann, dau. of Richard Harding, of Providence, R. I. She had 5 chil. and d. 1846. He m. 2dly, Louisa F. Pickens, of Boston, and had 2 chil.

(2) *Thomas Coles*, b. March 27, 1800, d. Feb. 1, 1854, m. and had 5 chil. He was for many yrs. a successful Teacher in Providence—a man of considerable scientific attainments.

(3) *Samuel Weld*, b. Jan. 6, 1802, m. and had no chil.; m. 2dly, ——, dau. of Peyton Dana, of Providence, and has one son.

(4) *Jacob*, b. Feb. 6, 1807, m. Nov. 4, 1827, Jane Dixon Fisher, dau. of Capt. John, of Edgartown. Res. Danvers, Mass. Had 10 chil.

242. V. SUSANNAH,[6] m. Samuel Weld and d. 1845. He was an officer in some low rank in the Revolutionary War, and died at its close. Mrs. W. received a pension till her death. A few yrs. ago in endeavors to get this pension, his diary was found, kept during his term of service. Her father bequeathed to her for life, certain rooms in his homestead, on the corner of Westminster and Walker Sts., and a share of the rent, and there she lived alone for half a century, on a mere pittance, the hoarding of which, as was natural, became at last, the great object of her life. She however, maintained a devout christian character, and was m. of Richmond St. Cong. ch., to which she made a bequest, the interest to be expended in behalf of the poor of said church.

242[1]. VI. BETSEY,[6] b. in Providence, d. May, 1817. She m. Oct. 7, 1785, Barnard Eddy, of P., a carpenter, who was b. Feb. 12, 1762, and d. July 3, 1848. Both m. Bap. ch. Chil.—

(1) *Ruth*, m. Dea. Benj. Gardner. Both m. Bap. ch. (2) *Stephen*, d. 1816, ae. 28, unm. (3) *Patience*, b. 1791, unm. m. Bap. ch. (4) *Betsey*, b. Feb., 1795, m. Nehemiah Williams. Res. Vernon, Ct. Both m. Cong. ch. (5) *Jeremiah*, d. ae. 2 yrs. (6) *Maria*, b. Sept. 10, 1797, m. Feb. 11, 1821, Dea. Daniel R. Clark. He d. April 9, 1860. Res. Pawtucket. Both m. Cong. ch.

243. VII. NATHANIEL,[6] (625) b. Feb. 28, 1774, d. Oct. 16, 1823, in Monticello, Ga. He m. Dec. 15, 1794, Mary, dau. of Amos Horton. Had 8 chil. She resides in Providence. R. I.

CHIL. OF LEWIS WALKER,[5] [101] OF CLARENDON, VT.

244. I. MEHETABEL,[6] b. May 17, 1771, d. Nov. 7, 1847. She m. May 5, 1793, John Hill, (See No. 49,) who d. before his wife. He was a blacksmith and a farmer. She was m. Bap. ch. Chil.—

(1) *Eunice*, b. Jan. 24, 1794. (2) *Hannah*, b. July 13, 1795, d. Oct. 26. (3) *Hiram*, b. Aug. 21, 1796, d. Oct. 26, 1826. (4) *Lydia*, b. Nov. 6, 1798, d. Nov. 3, 1821. (5) *Henry*, b. Nov. 2, 1801. (6) *Lucy*, b. April 29, 1803, d. Oct. 31, 1856. (7) *Mehetabel*, b. July 1, 1805. (8) *Emily*, b. Aug. 2, 1807. (9) *Sarah Ann*, b. Feb. 26, 1811.

245. II. SIMEON,[6] (632) b. April 4, 1773, in New Providence, now Cheshire, d. Dec. 13, 1857. He m. Jan. 13, 1793, Ruth Gough, of Hebron, N. Y., who d. March 11, 1797, about 30 yrs. old. He m. 2d, July 20, 1797, Mary Liscomb, of Southboro', b. Sept. 1763, and

d. May 2, 1836. He went with his parents to Clarendon, Vt., in 1779, where he married. In 1803, removed to Pittsfield, Vt., in 1819, to Fort Ann, N. Y., in 1833, to Weathersfield, Genesee Co., and thence to Little Valley, Cataraugus Co., N. Y., where he d. He served on the School Committee, and was m. Bap. ch.

246. III. SUSANNAH,[6] b. Nov. 28, 1774, d. Jan. 30, 1858. She m. Feb. 19, 1795, Josiah Dwight Dean, who d. about 1825. Res. St. Albans, Vt. Chil.—

(1) *Julia*, b. Feb., 1796. (2) *Daniel*, b. Sept., 1798. (3) *Hannah*, b. April, 1801, d. June, 1825. (4) *Susan*, b. Sept. 1803, m. March 8, 1858, Asaph Wheeler, of Enosburg, Vt. (5) *Josiah*, b. March, 1806. (6) *John*, b. Sept., 1808. (7) *Lewis*, b. March, 1811. (8) *Nathan*, b. 1814. He was a physician in Georgia, Vt., and d. March 15, 1848. (9) *Sarah*, b. Aug., 1817.

247. IV. HANNAH,[6] b. April 17, 1779, d. March, 1857. She m. Dec. 17, 1815, Preston Southworth, a shoemaker, who d. 1825. She is a m. Bap. ch. Res. Clarendon, Vt., till 1855, and then in Middletown, Vt. She possessed a remarkable memory, and was a repository of family history. Child—

(1) *Seymour Walker*, b. March 11, 1817.

248. V. LEWIS,[6] (636) b. Jan. 24, 1781. He m. Feb. 25, 1802, Sarah Gates, of Rutland, Vt., who was b. June 2, 1780, and d. 1841. He is a farmer in Clarendon, Vt., on the homestead of his father, and is m. Bap. ch. He has been Select-man, several years, Town Treasurer 20 yrs. or more, Justice of the Peace as long, and has represented the town in the State Legislature, 2 yrs. As a citizen he has been useful, public spirited, and as a man, highly esteemed for moral worth. He has 5 chil.

CHILDREN OF DANIEL WALKER, [107] OF CANADA.

249. WILLIAM,
250. WHEADON,
251. WALTER,
252. WORDEN,
Three daus.

} Res. Canada. All efforts to learn of these and their descendants, have proved fruitless.

CHIL. OF GIDEON WALKER,[5] [108] OF WHITING, VT.

256. I. JESSE,[6] (641) b. July 21, 1767, (1766?) in Coventry, R. I., d. Feb. 17, 1822, ae. 55 yrs. He m. Prudence Sawyer, of

Leicester, Vt., dau of Col. Thomas, who was a Capt. in the Revolution. She was b. in Templeton, Jan. 14, 1767, and d. Aug. 13, 1856, in 90th yr. Blind for the last 20 years of her life, gifted with invincible will and unusual abilities, she sank at last beneath the weight of years, to rest, loved and lamented by all. He was a systematic farmer, and devoted much attention to the grafting and improvement of fruit trees, and Addison Co. is greatly indebted to him. He had 10 chil. Res. Whiting, Vt.

257. II. RACHEL,[6] b. in Coventry, R. I., Aug. 4, 1769, (1768, Fam. Rec.) d. March 13, 1849. She m. 1783, Aaron Beach, who was b. in Va., June 10, 1761, and d. June 17, 1846. He was a farmer, settled in Whiting, Vt., rem. in 1791, to Scottsville, N.Y. In 1794, compelled by the Indian wars to return to Vt., he settled in W., and represented the town in the Assembly in 1801 and 5. He also held various town offices. In 1811, he rem. to Cambria, Niagara Co., N.Y. War with Great Britain having been declared, in 1813 the enemy crossed at Niagara, and his family were again driven in terror from their home, taking nothing with them, but a few articles, which were stolen the following night. They carried with them upon a bed, a son sick through exposure and privations. Their privations and sufferings during the War were extreme, and a vivid and sad remembrance of its scenes of terror and disaster, is preserved by their children. They returned to Vt., and again in the Fall of 1815, went to Cambria, where they lived until their death. Mrs. B. was a woman of great excellence and moral worth. Few persons are called upon to pass through the trying scenes that fell to her lot. But her fortitude and patient resignation under all her trials, her firm religious trust, through all her sufferings, taught a lesson worthy to be engraven upon every heart.

(1) *Noah*, b. Sept. 14, 1784, d. Oct. 1788.

(2) *Olive*, b. May 17, 1788. Res. Cambria, N. Y., unm.

(3) *Phebe*, b. Dec. 12, 1789, m. Jan. 1, 1807, Joel Luce. He was murdered by a band of smugglers in Hubbardton, Vt., in 1812. His wife, who beheld the dreadful tragedy, was so shocked and grief stricken, that she lost her reason for the remainder, (over 30 yrs.) of her life. She was a woman of uncommon mental endowments. A little vol. of 100 pages, entitled, "Maternal Admonition or the Orphan's Manual, by Mrs. Phebe Luce to her children," was published at Cooperstown, N. Y., 1819. She prepared an autobiography entitled, "Vicissitudes of Life," containing about 300 pp. This was never published.

(4) *Child*, b. in Scottsville, N. Y., 1791, d. in infancy.

(5) *Aaron*, b. April 11, 1793. He was left by his parents at school in Hanover, N. H., in 1811. In 1812 he left to take charge of a school, and

since then, nothing has ever been learned in respect to him. It is supposed he entered the U. S. Naval service.

(6) *John H.*, b. Jan., 1795, m. Dec. 1, 1815, Fanny, dau. of James Higgins, of Mass., and d. in Buffalo, Feb. 1, 1824.

(7) *Arunia*, b. 1797, d. March 21, 1815.

(8) *Moses*, b. May 19, 1799, m. April, 1823, Mary, dau. of Benj. Foster. She d. in Cambria, N. Y., Aug., 1824. He m. 2d, 1825 or 6, Ann M. Sherman, formerly of Washington, Duchess Co., N. Y. Res. Newfane, Niagara Co., N. Y. Chil.—1, Mary, b. Aug. 29, 1824, and m. Jan. 16, 1850, Alfred Doty, son of Harvey, and a farmer in Davison's Centre, Genesee Co., Mich. Has 2 chil. 2, Charles, b. Dec. 20, 1826, is in Australia. 3, Sherman, b. July, 1828, m. Jan., 1853, H. J. Mandeville, and is a farmer in Newfane. Has 1 ch.

(9) *Sophronia*, b. Oct. 26, 1801, m. Jan. 23, 1824, Harvey Beach, son of Philip, of Cambria, N. Y. Reside in C., and have 4 chil.—1, Fanny, b. Dec. 20, 1824, d. Sept. 23, 1825. 2, Arunia, b. July 23, 1828, d. Sept. 8, 1828. 3, Fanny, b. Dec. 10, 1829. She is a Teacher. 4, Maria, b. Oct. 23, 1838.

(10) *Rachel*, b. July 8, 1804, d. in Cambria, N. Y., Nov. 8, 1851.

(11) *Maria*, b. July 2, 1806, m. July, 1828, Samuel Scott, who d. April 20, 1842. Res. Cambria. She had 6 chil., and d. Aug. 8, 1858. "A devoted follower of Christ many yrs."—1, Sam'l Jr., b. Nov. 3, 1829, and m. Sept. 20, 1854, Ann Rogers. He is a farmer, in C. 2, Arunia, b. March 21, 1831, m. Martha, dau. of Harvey Doty, May, 1853, and is a farmer in Davison's Centre, Mich. Has one child, Martha Maria, b. May, 1854. 3, Harvey, b. May 23, 1823, d. May 6, 1845. 4, Aaron, b. Oct. 18, 1834. Daguerrean Artist, in C. 5, Henry T., b. March 9, 1838, d. June 16, 1859. A pious and promising young man. 6, Erastus, b. Jan. 23, 1840.

(12) *Walker*, b. July 6, 1808, d. in Whiting, Vt., 1824.

(13) *Cooley*, b. April 6, 1810, in Hubbardton, Vt., m. July, 1831, Nancy Durant. He went to Adrian, Mich., in 1837, thence, after several yrs. to Peoria, Ill. He left P., in 1845, since which time nothing is known of him.

258. III. LUCY,[6] d. ae. about 1 yr.

259. IV. LEVI,[6] (651) b. May 22, 1772, in Rutland, Vt., d. July 27, 1822. He m. 1793, Lovina Branch, of Whiting, Vt., dau. of John and Priscilla, b. in Preston, Ct., Aug. 8, 1767, and d. Feb. 2, 1839. She possessed a retiring disposition, yet, had qualities withal, which gained her friends wherever she was known. She will long be remembered for her amiable and excellent character, and her uniform and exemplary life. He is said to have been the first white male child born in Rutland. He was a farmer, lived in Whiting, after 1784, and had 9 chil. He was m. Bap. ch. Under Pres't Madison's Administration, he was appointed the Assessor for the towns of Whiting and Leicester, for the purpose of raising the Direct Tax. He was first Constable of W. for several years,—also,

J H Daniels Boston

a Selectman, a series of years. He was proverbial for his generosity and his public spirit. If there was a house of worship to be built, a minister of religion to be obtained and supported, any benevolent object to be aided, or public improvement to be accomplished, his purse and influence were generously offered, and to these, was owing the success of many a benevolent and useful enterprise. His benevolence was expended particularly in behalf of the poor. In 1812, he bequeathed to the town of Whiting, 20 acres of land at Whiting Centre, (then valued at $500,) one acre to be used for a Cemetery, and the yearly income of 10 acres to be appropriated to the support of common schools, and the income of the remaining 9 acres, to maintain the preaching of the Gospel. The following tribute is inscribed on his grave-stone :—"The memory of his public spirit will outlast this monument, which marks the humble spot where he lies."

260. V. AMOS ELMORE,[6] (660) b. May 25, 1775, (1774?) in Rutland, Vt., d. Jan. 19, 1850, ae. 75. He m. May 24, 1798, Sally Miller, dau. of Timothy, of Sudbury, Vt., and d. in Hubbardton, Aug. 28, 1849. He was a farmer, lived in Whiting, and after 1838, rem. to H. where they both died. They had 6 chil. He gave the land in the centre of the town of Whiting, as a site for the church edifice.

261. VI. JAMES OTIS,[6] (667) b. Aug. 6, 1778, d. Nov. 27, 1857, ae. 79 yrs. He m. Oct. 12, 1798, Mary Olin, dau. of Justin and Sarah, of Shaftesbury, Vt., and sis. of the late Gov. Henry Olin, b. Sept. 25, 1779, and d. Feb. 28, 1806, in Whiting, ae. 26. He m. 2dly, Dec. 4, 1806, Eunice Marsh, of Clarendon, Vt., dau. of Daniel and Phebe, b. in New Milford, Ct., Dec. 25, 1779, and d. Dec. 22, 1858. His early opportunities for education were very limited. The first school in W. was one of 4 weeks, taught by a woman, in 1789, when he was 11 yrs. old. After this, he used to lie in the corner in the evenings, and read, having only pine knots for a light, occasionally going to school a few weeks. At the age of 15, he taught school in Shoreham, for $4 per month, giving instruction only in reading and writing. In 1800, he built and opened a Public House in W., which he and his sons continued with the intermission of 3 yrs. till 1839. His house was one of great celebrity, in that region. He became a magistrate, Dec. 1809, and held the office till he rem. from W. in 1839. During this period, he transacted a large portion of the public business of the town, and often served as administrator, arbitrator, and in similar public and private trusts. As a proof of the high estimation in which he was held, it is a noteworthy fact,

J. O. Walker

that while he was an elevated member of the Masonic Fraternity, and W. was a strongly Anti-Masonic town, he held his office through the entire struggle in respect to Masonry, and such was the confidence reposed in his integrity, that none of his most bitter opponents, questioned the propriety of his retaining his office. His decisions as a Magistrate, were seldom overruled, and his honesty was never questioned by friend or foe. He was, pre-eminently, a peacemaker, and his advice was frequently sought by contending parties. He was an ardent patriot of Whig politics, and till the close of life, watched the course of public affairs with deep and intelligent interest. He represented the town in the State Legislature, 5 yrs., in 1821, '22, '23—and '26. He was the travelling Agent of the Vermont Mutual Fire Ins. Co., 8 years, and no man rendered it more important service, or was more successful in disseminating a knowledge of its principles through the State. His public spirit was proverbial. If a house of worship was to be erected or repaired, a minister to be sustained, any educational or benevolent object to be effected, his purse and his influence were liberally furnished. In 1839, he rem. to St. Albans, Vt., and thence in '47, to Swanton, the adjoining town. Says Rev. J. W. Sawyer, who knew him well,—"He was a friend to education, and gave of his means liberally, to promote it. In all his social relations, he was amiable and generous, active and ever ready to spend, and be spent in the service of his friends, meeting all who approached him, with frankness, courtesy and kindness." His domestic and social virtues shone forth with increased brightness in his later years. He was beloved by all, and especially by children. He delighted more in making a sacrifice to please a child, and receive his happy look and "thank you," in return, than to gain the friendship of the great or affluent. His large and generous heart never grew old. Cheerful and lively, he never became imbittered by misfortune, age or infirmities. Affluent in humor and anecdote, as a companion, he was unusually entertaining. His mind was comprehensive and practical, rather than speculative. A sound judgment, and integrity above impeachment, secured for him confidence in the public and private relations of life. Though without early advantages, yet possessing good natural endowments, his information became extensive by reading, and a wide intercourse with men. Having a retentive memory, he became a living encyclopedia of the age in which he lived. His pen was often employed by public request, in the preparation of temperance addresses, in which reform he took a deep interest, and in poems and other contributions to the newspaper press. In manhood, he was energetic and indefatigable—

in old age, genial and busy, even after the 2d shock of paralysis, which rendered him almost helpless. The last two years of his life, he could not walk a step, and his hand was unnerved, yet he maintained an extensive correspondence with a wide circle of friends, and wrote his "Early Reminiscences," as a pastime. He had long been interested in the genealogy of his ancestors and kindred, but had been unable to trace his pedigree beyond his grandfather, (No. 28.) Accordingly, he entered most enthusiastically into the plan of the compiler of this work, and pledged his generous and cheerful co-operation. Becoming religious in early life, he united with the Bap. ch., and his hope in Christ enabled him, in old age, to contemplate his departure with serene and cheerful composure. His end was peace. He was buried in Whiting. The simple epitaph which he left for his tombstone, reads thus,—"He strove to be useful, and to make others happy."

262. VII. GIDEON,[6] (671) b. June, 1782, in Rutland, Vt. He m. Jan. 16, 1803, Barbara Olin, of Shaftsbury, Vt., dau. of Hon. Gideon, b. 1786, d. March 7, 1859, in Ellicottville, N.Y. He was a non-commissioned officer, in Harrison's army, in the war of 1812. Dr. Lanier, a surgeon in the army, wrote to the family, that he was bayoneted by a British officer, after he had surrendered, in the Massacre at Youngstown or Fort Niagara, in 1813, in his 32d year. Res. Whiting, Vt. Had 3 chil.

263. VIII. SAMUEL BEACH,[6] (674) b. in Whiting, Vt., Dec. 17, 1784, d. Oct. 16, 1842, in Chicago, Ill., ae. 57. He m. Nov. 17, 1805, Patty Bent, of Mt. Holly, Vt., who was b. Aug. 19, 1784. They had 8 chil. He held the office of Town Clerk, and was Justice of the Peace, several years, in Hubbardton, Vt. He was a merchant, and engaged in farming, lumbering and milling.—"One of the excellent of the earth."

CHIL. OF NATHAN WALKER,[5] [111] OF FERRISBURGH, VT.

264. I. PHILIP,[6] (684) b. in Attleboro', April 28, 1766, Fam. Rec., (Feb. 1764,?) d. March 31, 1840. He m. Jan., 1796, Hannah Field, dau. of Anthony, in Ferrisburgh, Vt., b. March 20, 1778, and d. March, 1853, ae. 75. She was m. Meth. ch. They settled in Williston, Vt. In his youth he was a fur hunter. At one time he had as companions, his younger brother Johnson, and Capt. Jas. Powers. In attempting to traverse the wilderness from Lake Champlain to the St. Lawrence river, they lost their way and were 8 days without food

or sustenance of any kind. And the preservation of the party was owing to the muscular energy, and dauntless fortitude of Philip Walker. Johnson's strength became entirely exhausted, and Philip had to make continual exertions to rouse him from stupor, and help him on the journey. Their dogs died of starvation. On the 9th day, they fell in with a party of Indians, who had just killed a bear, the intestines of which, after being slightly rinsed in a brook near by, were their first harmless repast, and relief from the pangs of starvation. Remaining a few days to recruit their exhausted strength, an Indian guide directed them to their hunting ground. He was a man of indomitable energy and perseverance, and left at his decease a large landed property.

265. II. JOHNSON,[6] (694) b, Sept. 15, 1768, d. April 17, 1826, ae. 57. He m. 1799, Elizabeth, dau. of George Gaige, of Ferrisburgh, Vt., b. Nov. 18, 1780, d. Dec. 31, 1855. Both m. Bap. ch. They removed to Panton, Vt., and had 12 chil. He was a man of good character, and had the esteem of his townsmen.

266. III. OBADIAH,[6] (706) b. Nov. 1770, d. Jan. 13, 1813, ae. 42. He m. Jan. 17, 1795, Betsey, dau. of Zuriel Tupper, of Ferrisburgh, Vt., b. 1778, and is a m. Meth. ch. He was a man of great industry and ability in business, and possessed high moral worth, both in the private and public relations of life. He was a zealous politician, a Democrat of the Jeffersonian school; a member of the State Legislature 8 yrs.. and enjoyed the unbounded confidence and esteem of his fellow citizens. Res. Ferrisburgh. Had 7 chil.

267. IV. DANIEL,[6] (713) b. 1771 or 2, d. Aug. 1851. He m. 1793, Electa Newton, dau. of Jason. He removed to Canton, St. Lawrence Co., in 1800, and was one of the pioneers in the settlement of the town. The farm he bought on going to C., distant about a mile from Canton village, he lived on till his death. He had a strong constitution, though predisposed to apoplexy and a species of paralysis, of which, combined, he died. His wife being a Universalist, he became one, and all his chil. He was a man of strong practical sense, of great moral excellence, and was honored with the most important offices of the town and county in which he resided. He was Supervisor 10 yrs. in succession. Had 6 chil.

268. V. WILLIAM, (719) b. Feb. 23, 1775, d. Feb. 5, 1852. ae. 77 yrs., less 18 days. He m. Oct. 10, 1798, Betsey, dau. of James Burroughs, formerly of Ct. She was b. Jan. 3, 1783, d. Oct.

29, 1820. He m. 2d, Dec. 1, 1821, Mrs. Fanny Shumway, who was b. April 8, 1781, d. May 3, 1852, ae. 71 yrs., 21 (25?) days. Both m. Bapt. ch. They resided in Ferrisburgh, Vt., till 1829, when he rem. to Ohio, where he d. He had 13 chil.

269. VI. NATHAN,[6] (732) b. 1777, d. May, 1853. He m. Wealthy Tupper, dau. of Zuriel, of Ferrisburgh, Vt., and sis. of his brother Obadiah's w. They settled in Canton, N. Y.; rem. in 1823, or 4, to Smith's Creek, Canada West, and from thence to Waupun, Fon du Lac Co., Wis., where he died. His 8 chil. were b. in Canton.

270. VII. SOLOMON,[6] (740) b. 1779, d. Dec. 3, 1810, ae. 31. He m. Polly Tupper, dau. of Absalom, and gd. dau. of Zuriel. She was "one of the best of women," possessing a strong mind and devoted piety; m. Meth. ch., and d. March 7, 1818. He was one of the 1st settlers in Canton, N. Y., a man of fine personal appearance, affectionate as a husband and parent, and possessed of great energy and excellence of character. He had 4 chil.

271. VIII. CATHARINE,[6] b. 1780, d. 1844 or 5. She m. 1804, Wm. M. Saxton, son of Jonathan, of Ferrisburgh, Vt. They lived in F. till 1818, then rem. to Smith's Creek, C. W., where she d. Had 7 chil.—

(1) *Levi*, fell from the barn loft and was killed. (2) *William*, &c.

272. IX. EBENEZER,[6] (744) b. about 1784 or 5, d. Feb. 10, 1844. He m. in Spring of 1806, Electa, dau. of Thomas Hill, Esq., of Charlotte, Chittenden Co., Vt., gd. dau. of Gov. Chittenden, of Vt., b. March 4, 1786, and d. Sept. 2, 1820. He resided in Ferrisburgh till 1816, and then rem. to Eddyville, Kentucky. He had 8 chil.

CHIL. OF ICHABOD WALKER,[5] [114] OF POTSDAM, N. Y.

273. I. OLIVE,[6] b. March 1, 1770, d. Sept., ae. 6 mos.

274. II. ASA,[6] (751) b. March 1, 1772, d. Sept. 3, 1845, in Lenox, N. Y. He m. 1794, Sibilla Cushman, in Clarendon, Vt., who was b. Feb. 26, 1776, and d. in C., Oct., 1811. Both m. Bap. ch. In 1812, he m. 2d, Mrs. Rebecca (Trask) Brink, of C., who d. in Lenox, N. Y., Aug. 6, 1851, ae. 79 yrs. He was a carpenter and rem. from C., to Lenox, N. Y., Oct., 1814. There were only 3 families in the town, at the time. He had 12 chil.

275. III. HANNAH,[6] b. May 9, 1774, d. Feb. 26, 1860, in 86th yr. She m. Jan. 14, 1796, Asa Moon, in Clarendon, Vt., who was b. Nov. 17, 1772, and d. Oct. 15, 1842. He was a farmer in Hopkinton, N. Y., also a pious and devout man. For over 40 yrs. he endeavored to walk with God, and for many yrs. was Deacon of the Bap. ch. She was m. Bap. ch. Chil.—

(1) *Benjamin*, b. July 30, 1797, d. Feb. 28, 1799.

(2) *Isabel*, b. Feb. 21, 1802, unm. Res. H.

(3) *Jesse*, b. April 28, 1803, m. Sophia Baker. Res. H., and is a farmer. Chil.—1, Hannah W. 2, Rhoda Ann, d. Jan. 16, 1858. 3, Maryette. 4, Priscilla. 5, Sophia M. 6, Amanda M. 7, Jesse W. S. 8, Asa. 9, Millard F.

(4) *Levina*, b. Sept. 5, 1804, m. 1831, John P. Roberts, a farmer. Res. Forestville, Iowa. Chil.—1, Martha J. 2, Abigail. 3, Martin L. 4, Myron L. 5, Elisha R. 6, Anna L.

(5) *Orange B.*, b. Dec. 20, 1805, in Hinesburgh, Vt., m. Nov. 17, 1831, Margaret Wing. He is a farmer in Forestville, Iowa. Chil—1, Zelia, b. Nov. 11, 1832, d. April 10, 1836. 2, Asa, b. Jan. 15, 1834. 3, Walter, b. Jan. 25, 1835, m. Mary C. Harrass, Dec. 20, 1855, who d. Sept. 17, 1856. Res. Iowa. He m. 2d, Aug. 21, 1859, Sarah A. Gilbert. 4, Phebe, b. May 7, 1836, m. Jan. 12, 1857, John Nimmo. 5, Abigail, b. July 29, 1837, m. July 4, 1859, John A. Gilbert. 6, Ellen, b. Sept. 10, 1838, m. March 4, 1856, Micajah Lane. 7, Delorme Lorenda, b Sept. 15, 1839. 8, Zelma Lisette, b. May 28, 1844, d. Dec. 4, 1847. 9, Giles Wing, b. Sept. 17, 1845, d. Jan. 15, 1846. 10, Lucy Maria, b. March 15, 1847. 11, Celia Celinda, b. June 30, 1849, d. March 26, 1853. 12, Eoline Effa, b. June 1, 1853. 13, Hannah Levina, b. Aug. 22, 1855.

(6) *Abigail*, b. Feb. 14, 1809, m. Stephen R. Witherell, a farmer. Res, Hopkinton, N. Y. Chil.—1, Clarissa C., m. Aaron L. Warner, and has 1 ch., Clarissa E. 2, Charlotte C. 3, Henry E. 4, George R. 5, Ellen E.

(7) *Rhoda S.*, b. Nov. 1, 1812, m. Orange Wing, who was a farmer in H., and d. Feb. 13, 1834, leaving 3 chil.—1, Charles M. 2, Annis P., m. June 15, 1858, Fullom M. Corwin, a farmer in H., who was b. Oct. 16, 1834. 3, Delia A., d. Nov. 4, 1859. Mrs. W. m. 2d, May, 1845, Jacob R. Norris, who d. July 14, 1848. He was a farmer. Res. H.

(8) *Henry G.*, b. June 15, 1815, m. Lydia A. Jenks. Farmer in Ticonderoga, N. Y. Chil.—Isabel and Minor.

276. IV. ABRAHAM,[6] b. May 1, 1776, d. ae. 3 yrs.

278. V. BENJAMIN,[6] (763) b. June 26, 1778, in Clarendon, Vt., d. April 3, 1856, in 78th yr. He m. Susan Green, in C., who was b. in Rehoboth, Jan. 22, 1779, and d. Aug. 27, 1844. They settled in Canton, N. Y., and in 1839, rem. to Campton, Ill., where he died. He was a man of influence, wealthy, m. Bap. ch. and had 7 chil., all b. in Canton except the eldest.

William Walker

279. VI. SARAH,[6] b. June 26, 1780, m. True Evans, in Canton, N. Y., a farmer. Res. Potsdam, N. Y. She is m. Bap. ch. No chil.

280. VII. ICHABOD,[6] b. July 6, 1782, d. Sept. 10, 1838, ae. 52.

281. VIII. ABIGAIL,[6] b. Dec. 10, 1784, d. Sept. or Dec. 16, 1786, ae. 2 yrs.

282. IX. ABEL,[6] b. March 6, 1786, d. April 2, 1792, ae. 6 yrs.

283. X. SYLVANUS,[6] b. Nov. 1, 1787, d. 1790, ae. 3 yrs.

284. XI. ABRAHAM,[6] b. Dec. 1, 1788, d. 1815, ae. 26 yrs.

285. XII. ABEL,[6] (771) b. April 26, 1790, d. 1839, ae 49. He m. Sept., 1811, Ruby Davis, in Clarendon, Vt., who d. 1853, (1854?) They rem. to Bloomingdale, Ill., where they died. He was a carpenter, m. Meth. ch., and had 15 chil., of whom 12 d. under 4 yrs. of age.

286. XIII. POLLY,[6] b. July 3, 1793, d. Sept. 1, 1816, ae. 23 yrs.

287. XIV. ABIGAIL,[6] b. May 12, 1796. She m. Dec. 8, 1812, Elias Crary, who was b. in Wallingford, Vt., Feb. 13, 1795. From Clarendon, Vt., they rem. to Potsdam, N. Y., in 1814, where he cleared a farm from the forest, and from thence to Kane Co., Ill., in Sept., 1835, and in 1854 to Geneva, Ill., where they reside. For the 1st 18 yrs. after his marriage, he was a farmer and kept a public house. He is Justice of the Peace, and both are m. Meth. ch. Chil.—

(1) *Son*, d. ae. 23 hours.

(2) *Mary L.*, b. Sept. 14, 1817, in Canton, N. Y. She is an adopted dau.

(3) *Cushman Walker*, b. Aug. 12, 1822, in P. He m. July 8, 1846, in Campton, Ill., Hannah R. Nichols, who was b. Feb. 12, 1824. They have—1, Lewis J., b. Dec. 3, 1847, in C. 2, Marietta E. L., b. Jan. 18, 1851. 3, Hamilton, b. Oct. 28, 1853.

CHILDREN OF CALEB WALKER,[5] [119] OF REHOBOTH.

288. I. WILLIAM,[6] (786) b. June 22, 1751, (R. Rec. O. S.) July 3, (Fam. Rec. and Ins.) d. Oct. 31, 1831. He m. Dec. 31, 1777, Sarah Woodruff, of Farmington, Ct., who was b. 1749, in F., and d. Sept. 1, 1789, in her 40th yr., having 3 chil. He m. 2d, March 24, 1790, Mrs. Mary (Hutchinson) Parmelee, of Goshen, Ct., who was b. in Salisbury, Ct., Oct. 14, 1760, and d. Dec. 10, 1838, having 4 chil., who d. young. She was widow of Rev. Elisha Par-

melee, of G., who was ord., July 3, 1783, 1st Pastor of Cong. ch. in Lee. In person, Mr. W. was over 6 ft. in height, and well proportioned. He was member of the Congress of Deputies of the several towns of Berkshire Co., convened at Stockbridge, July 6, 1774. This County Convention or Congress so called, of the inhabitants of Berkshire, partook largely of the feelings which pervaded the country, in respect to the Revolutionary crisis. The covenant signed in Lenox, July 14, 1774, in reference to the English Gov't, not to import, purchase, &c., was signed by over 100 persons. Among the names was that of Wm. Walker, who with one other only, survived in 1828. (Barber's Hist. Coll.) He was Associate Justice of the Court of Sessions, (a County Court,) 1809, and from 1811 to 1814. The following account of Judge Walker was written by his son, Judge Wm. P. Walker, on the day of his death, Oct. 31, 1831, addressed to Rev. Dr. Shepard, his pastor.

"He was born in Rehoboth, July 3, 1751, and came to this country when about 19 yrs. of age. He joined the army in May, 1775, at Cambridge. immediately after the battle of Lexington. He did not remain in the army till the close of the War. At what time he left, I cannot ascertain. I have heard him mention being with the army in Canada, and their great sufferings, especially from the small pox, which he had the natural way at Montrose. On the retreat of the army from Canada, which I think must have been in the Fall of 1776, he joined Washington's army in N. J., and was in the battles at Trenton and Princeton. He was also in the battle at Bennington, Vt. He was a member of the Convention which framed the Constitution of this Commonwealth, and was repeatedly a member of the General Court from this town. In 1781, soon after the adoption of the Constitution, he was appointed a Justice of the Peace in this county, and was in Commission till his death. In the same yr. he was appointed by Gov. Hancock, Register of Probate, which office he soon after resigned, (1785?) In 1783, he was appointed Senator from this county, but never took his seat at the Board. In Nov., 1795, he was appointed by Gov. Adams, Judge of Probate for this county, which office he resigned in Jan., 1824. In 1807, he was appointed by Gov. Sullivan, a Judge of the Court of Common Pleas in this county, which office he held till a new system for that Court was established. In 1824, he was chosen elector of President and Vice President of the U. States.

He expired this morning at 2 o'clock.

In haste yours, WM. P. WALKER."

The following tribute to Judge W.'s worth, in the Lenox newspaper, was written, it is supposed, by Jas. W. Robbins, Esq.

Died, in this town, on Monday morning last, the venerable Judge Walker, ae. 80 yrs. Gov. Lincoln says, he was the most venerable man he ever saw. All who were acquainted with him, will say the same. If locks whitened in the snows of 80 winters; if great personal dignity, connected with distinguished excellence of character; if the practice of the social virtues, together with a long life of public service; if exemplary morals and genuine piety give one the title of venerable, he was venerable. He was an officer in the American troops at Cambridge, in 1775, and from that period for more than ½ a century, he was a public man. Of the Convention that formed the Constitution of Mass., he was a member. For a long time he held the office of Judge of the County Court, and still longer that of Judge of Probate. He took a deep interest in the religious and charitable institutions of the last 25 yrs., and of the Bible Society, he was a President from its organization. He was extensively known in the Commonwealth, and as extensively respected. In the Co. of Berkshire, no man was better known or commanded more respect. Of the town of Lenox he was a father, and the inhabitants looked up to him with filial affection He was a companionable man. Persons of all ages, the young as well as the old, sought his society, and few enjoyed it without sensible benefit. From his general intelligence, they obtained valuable information; from his practical wisdom, they derived useful lessons, applicable to the various concerns of life; and by his bright example they were stimulated to improvement. In his last yrs., he partially withdrew from the bustle of politics, from the labors and honors of office, and from the attractions of the world, and looked forward as an old man should do, to another state of existence.

Faith helped his vision to reach beyond the grave, and the anchor of his hope was moored in Heaven. Towards the close of his life, his religious character brightened, and as worldly objects grew less in his esteem, the objects of faith grew more distinct and more glorious. In expectation of appearing before the Eternal, his many virtues, and the usefulness of his life vanished from his view, and for acceptance he relied entirely upon the atonement and righteousness of his Divine Master. During his last sickness, he was deprived of his speech, and the most of the time, of his reason, so that he was unable to say anything of his hopes and prospects, but he has left to his friends for their consolation and improvement, the history of his whole life.

Allen's Biographical Dictionary, has in addition to a brief outline of his public services, this tribute.

"In his politics he was a republican in the party times of 1801. He was tall, with white locks, and of great personal dignity, * * * He was, indeed, venerated by those who knew him, not only for a long life of faithful service, but for his social virtues, his pure morals, his disinterested benevolence and ardent piety. Of the church at Lenox, he was an exemplary member; of the Berkshire Bible Society, President. In one of the last yrs. of his life he travelled over the bleak hills of Berkshire, with the sole object of arousing his fellow citizens in different towns, to a sense of the value of some moral or charitable institution designed for their benefit.

His epitaph, written it is supposed by Rev. Dr. Shepard is as follows:—

THIS IS ERECTED TO THE MEMORY OF THE

HONORABLE WILLIAM WALKER.

He was born at Rehoboth, in the County
of Bristol, July 3, 1751, and died Oct. 31, 1831.
He removed to this town in 1773, was an
officer in the army of the Revolution in 1776,
a member of the convention which formed the Constitution of this Commonwealth
in 1780, a judge of the Court of Common pleas four,
and judge of probate twenty-eight years.
In all the relations of life he sustained a
character of unshaken integrity:—
He lived as a follower of Christ: was
an able advocate of his doctrines;
and died rejoicing in a Gospel hope.

289. II. CALEB,[6] (793) b. April 5, 1753, d. Aug. 10, 1790. He m. Mrs. Huldah, dau. of John Clarke, of Farmington, Ct. She d. Feb., 1778. He d. in Canandaigua, N. Y., of bilious colic, after a few days illness, and was buried in Lenox, Mass. He served in the Revolution under Col. Timothy Walker. Had 1 son.

CHILDREN OF ABRAHAM WALKER,[6] [120] OF REHOBOTH.

290. I. OLIVE,[6] b. Jan. 31, 1763, d. May 29, 1817, in 55th yr. She m. Dec. 2, 1798, John Grimes, now Graham, of Bourcliff, England, (Bristol Rec.) who d. March, 1833. They rem. about 1810, to Savoy, where they died. Chil.—

(1) *Son*, d. y. (2) *Almina*, m. John Hall, of Adams. Res. A.

291. II. LEWIS,[6] (794) b. March 17, 1765, d. April 3, 1805, in 41st yr. (Ins.) He m. Oct. 6, 1791, Bethiah Carpenter, dau. of Zechariah, b. May 12, 1762, and d. May 18, 1833, in 72d yr. (Ins.) (See No. 157.) They had 7 chil.

292. III. JESSE,[6] b. Jan. 11, 1767, d. young.

293. IV. OTIS,[6] (801) b. April 13, 1769, d. June 25, 1842. He m. April 13, 1797, Zerviah West, of Lenox or Litchfield, dau. of Daniel, b. April 4, 1777, and d. Aug. 25, 1844. They had 10 chil. He learned his trade, as shoemaker, in Lenox, and engaged in the business of tanning, currying and shoemaking, in L. He rem. to Brighton, N. Y., in Spring of 1802, was 1 of the 1st settlers, and a farmer. In 1829, he rem. to Alleghany Co., and in 1835, to Homer, Calhoun Co., Mich., where he died. He was Justice of the Peace

6 yrs. Though he became pious in early life, he did not unite with any church, but ever maintained a consistent christian character. He had as much influence, and as many freinds, as any man in the town where he spent most of his life.

294. V. WILKS,[6] (811) b. June 21, 1771, d. Nov. 22, 1835. He m. Nov. 10, 1796, Ruth Bliss, dau. of Ephraim, of Rehoboth, b. Nov. 24, 1773, and living, (1856) in Savoy. Res. S. He had 6 chil.

295. VI. DANIEL,[6] b. June 27, 1773, d. young.

CHILDREN OF ABEL WALKER,[5] [123] OF HARDWICK, MASS.

296. I. CYRILL,[6] b. Feb. 9, 1764, d. in Hardwick, unm. Dec. 30, 1849. He was a man of intelligence and excellent moral character.

297. II. LOIS,[6] b. Oct. 18, 1766, d. Aug. 12, 1853. She m. Feb. 8, 1787, Lewis Baker, of Pelham, now Prescott, who was b. in Barnstable, Dec. 28, 1761, of Isaac and Rebecca (Lewis) Baker, and rem. to Pelham with his parents. They lived in P., a few yrs., and then rem. to Orange. In 1808, they rem. to Marcellus, N. Y., where he d. Feb. 18, 1834. He was an industrious and worthy man. His widow in 1846, removed to Paris, Wis., where she died. She early became religious, and well exemplified the character of a christian. Having the examples and precepts of godly parents—possessing a good mind—a retentive memory, a heart to sympathize with, and a hand ever ready to relieve the distressed, she was well qualified for the various duties of life. In filial reverence a son writes, "Thanks to God that I had a praying Mother."

(1) *Anna*, b. Dec 5, 1787, m. Cephas Weed, Sept. 21, 1809, d. in Hannibal, Oswego Co., N. Y., Sept. 21, 1826, and had 8 chil.—1, Sarah. 2, Justin. 3, Huldah. 4, Attira. 5, Anna.

(2) *Abel*, b. June 17, 1789. He studied medicine in N. Y., attended Med. Lectures at the Coll. of Physicians and Surgeons in Fairfield, N. Y., was licensed by the Censors of the Med. Society of Onondago Co., May 19, 1815, went to Owasco, Cayuga, Co., N. Y.. Sept., 1816, where he has resided since. with the exception of an interval of 7 yrs., (from 1821 to '28,) at Kelloggsville, N. Y. He is a skillful physician in O.. and a man of high christian worth. He m. April 23, 1818, Aurora Price, who d. June 11, 1827, leaving 3 sons. He m. 2d, Oct. 25, 1831, Laura Bailey, who d. Oct. 19, 1836. He m. 3d, Sept. 28, 1841, Udolphia Osborn, who d. Nov. 25, 1843. His chil. are—1, Elijah P., b. June 12, 1819, m. Elizabeth Austin, of Skeneateles, who d. leaving, E. Aurora, and Henry Price. He m. 2d, 1859, Libbie Spengler, of Weedsport, and is a Physician in Fleming, N. Y. 2, Abel

W., b. May 12, 1821, m. Charity Brinkerhoff, and has—1, James Lewis, 2, Udolphia O., 3, Frank H. 3, Erasmus Darwin, b. June 17, 1823, grad. of Amherst Coll., teacher in Smithfield, N. C., and now, 1860, resides in Pecan Grove, Carroll Co., La.

(3) *James Lewis*, b. Aug. 5, 1791, d. Aug 9, 1802.

(4) *Read*, b. April 26. 1794. He m. Elizabeth Baker, who d. without issue. He m. 1854, Elizabeth Cooper. Res. during the last 20 yrs., in Waterdown, Gore District, Canada West. He is a manufacturer of farming utensils, and m. Bap. ch.

(5) *Lois*, b. Aug. 10, 1796, m. about 1828, Cephas Weed, (who m. her sister Anna 1st.) They rem. to Southport, now Kenosha, Wis., in 1835. He was a farmer, and d. 1858. She is m. Bap. ch. and now in K. Had 6 chil.—1, James. 2, Lewis. 3, John, &c.

(6) *William*, b. March 15, 1799, m. 1822, Roxana Baker. who d. 1854. He is a farmer in Paris, Racine Co., Wis., and m. Pres. ch. Chil.—1, Wm. W. 2, Lewis E. 3, Roxana. 4, Anna. 5, Sarah. 6, Martha. 7, Mary. 8, Jonathan. 9, Lois.

(7) *Erastus*, b. Feb. 1, 1802, d. Sept. 18, 1803.

(8) *Huldah*, b. July 22, 1804, m. 1823, Nath'l Clark, who d. leaving 2 daus. She m. 2d, Stephen Story, rem. to Wis., in 1847. Res. Waupacca Falls.

(9) *Thomas W.*, b. July 26, 1808, m. Mary Ellis, Oct., 1854. Res. Manitowoc, Wis. He is in Lumber trade, and manufacturing marble from a valuable quarry on his farm.

(10) *Elisha*, b. June 8, 1811, m. Adeline Bailey, Oct., 1832. Rem. to Wisconsin in 1840, is a farmer near Kenosha, and m. Bap. ch.

298. III. ABEL,[6] (817) b. Sept. 27, 1770, d. Nov. 15, 1811. He m. Jan. 27, 1797, Mary Snow, of Hardwick, who was b. March 7, 1775, and lives, (1855) in Greenwich, on the homestead. He was crushed to death by a rock which he was endeavoring to sink. Both m. Cong. ch. and also their 8 chil., all sustaining an unblemished christian character.

299. IV. WILLIAM,[6] (825) b. Oct. 29, 1772, d. Jan. 30, 1852. He m. Nov. 29, 1804, Eunice Powers, who was born in Greenwich, Aug. 10, 1781, and d. May 29, 1828. She was m. Cong. ch. He was a farmer, and had a physical constitution of uncommon strength and vitality. He held the office of Select-man, and was Unitarian in religious opinion. He m. 2d, Feb. 3, 1830, Mercy Brown, who was b. in G., Dec. 19, 1791, and now, (1855) resides in Mount Morris, N. Y. He had 6 chil. This is a family of much moral worth.

300. V. ABIGAIL,[6] b. Aug. 13, 1775, and d. unm. in Somers, Ct., March 16, 1853. She was m. Cong. ch. and a truly pious woman.

[illegible]

301. VI. THOMAS,[6] (831) b. in Rehoboth, Nov. 18, 1777. He m. 1800, Mary Eaton, of Worcester, who d. 1845. She was a godly woman. They had 7 chil. Most of his early youth was spent in Hardwick, until he began an apprenticeship in the Printing Office of Isaiah Thomas, of Worcester. In the year 1799, he went to Oneida Co., N. Y., and commenced the publication of a newspaper at Rome. In 1803, rem. to Utica, then a village, and was editor and publisher of the Utica Gazette, until 1825, when his health failed. He resides in U., (1860,) is President of the Bank of Utica, and Pres. also of the Savings Bank of Utica. He is peculiarly quiet, reserved, and unostentatious, but for good sense and sterling worth, he has few if any superiors. He is a most valuable citizen, and a perfect christian gentleman. He holds the office of Elder in the Pres. ch. Though in his 83d yr. he retains his mental faculties in an extraordinary degree. The eye of his mind is not dimmed, and he attends to his daily duties as Bank President.

302. VII. HULDAH,[6] b. Oct. 29, 1780, d. Nov. 19, 1858, ae. 78. She m. June 18, 1812, Daniel Sexton, of Somers, Ct. Res. in S. He is a farmer, and has held the offices of Select-man, Assessor, &c. Both m. Cong ch. Chil.—

(1) *Cyril Walker*, b. June 1, 1813, m. Sarah Baker, of Amherst, Sept. 15, 1847. She is m. Cong. ch. Res. S., a farmer. Chil.—1, Ellen Louise, b. Oct. 16, 1848. 2, Frances Augusta, b. May 13, 1850. 3, Clarence Enos, b. Oct. 6, 1853. 4, Leslie Cyril, b. April 19, 1856.

(2) *Anna Horton*, b. Nov. 30, 1814, d. Feb. 6, 1840.

(3) *Huldah Orinda*, b. March 15, 1818, d. June 1, 1841.

(4) *Florella*, b. April 19, 1820, d. July 10, 1840.

(5) *Emily*, b. May 11, 1822, d. April 18, 1840.

(6) *Eliza*, b. Sept. 4, 1825, m. —— Hunt. Res. Hardwick.

CHIL. OF COMFORT WALKER,[5] [123] OF KILLINGLY, CT.

303. I. SALLY,[6] b. July 5, 1763, d. April 24, 1853, in her 90th yr. She m. —— Bates, of R. I., who d. 1809. Chil.—

(1) *Lucy*, m. —— Freeman, and d. about 1826. (2) *Salluvia*, m. —— Potter, and d. about 1836. (3) *Caleb W.*, m. and d. about 1826. (4) *William*, b. 1800, m. and had 7 children, (1856.) Res. Scituate, R. I. (5) *Ezra D.*, b. 1802. (6) *Mehetable*, m. —— Hopkins, a teacher.

304. II. COMFORT,[6] (829) b. Jan. 18, 1765, d. July 31, 1840. He m. Tamar Clark, dau. of Timothy and Tamar (Plympton,) b. July 30, 1770, and d. May 28, 1813. He m. 2d, Dec. 2, 1813,

Peggy Whiting, who was b. Aug. 3, 1769, and d. Jan. 29, 1834. He m. 3d, Sept. 1834, Mary Harding. He went to Conn., with his father; rem. when a young man to Medway, Mass., and was a farmer and manufacturer. He had 9 chil. 8 of whom are m. ch.

305. III. EZRA,[6] b. Dec., 1766, d. Jan., 1852. He m. 1787, Abigail, dau. of Jacob and Phebe (Lilly) Manning, in Killingly, Ct., and had 9 chil. She d. ae. 76. He went to K., with his father at the age of 6 yrs., rem. to Ware, Mass., before 1790, thence to Greenwich, R. I. In 1798, he was in Poultney, Vt., and there as late as 1808. Thence he rem. to Ames, Ohio, where he remained till his death. As a physician he was successful, and maintained an irreproachable character through his long life. His descendants are no dishonor to his memory. Three were at one time officiating elders in the church. His life was eventful, and is an interesting and instructive biography, especially in regard to religious belief and experience.

The following account of his scepticism and subsequent conversion, is taken from the American Pastor's Journal and Home Missionary Magazine, vol. 5th, 201st p., 1832

Dr. W., was born in a New England village, in 1766. His parents were respectable and of reputed piety. He early gave indications of a vigorous mind, and of a susceptible heart. His religious education ended where it ought to have commenced—with a knowledge of the Shorter Catechism. At an academy, he distinguished himself as a scholar, and made considerable progress in the Latin language. At the age of 22, he commenced the practice of medicine. His profession, of necessity, brought him in contact with the world. And here commenced a series of associations, which threw a cloud over more than 40 yrs. of his life. He was first pressed with the doctrine of universal salvation. * * And as it required no sacrifices, no self denial, and no self abasement, it readily recommended itself to the unrenewed heart. He tried to believe it. But his discerning mind detected the sophistry of the system, and left him restless as the rolling billow. * * * * The next step was to destroy the veracity of the Bible. * * To aid him in this fearful work, he called in Paine, Voltaire and Rosseau. He went not to the Bible to contemplate the sublimity of its doctrines—the purity of its precepts, the harmony of the system of revealed truth, and its tendency, as illustrated by facts, to promote the happiness of man. Like other infidels, he cast off fear, and restrained prayer before the Almighty. Thus 12 yrs. passed away, all the while professedly seeking for light, and yet not once directing his eye to Heaven. Those who did pray, he thought infatuated; and though sometimes, he was compelled to think them sincere, yet in his view, they were *sincere hypocrites*. The next 12 yrs. he spent in the mercantile business. He read and *reasoned* much, but only on such subjects as were calculated to make his infidel fortress strong. At length, the embargo embarrassed his business, and he with his family removed to the State of Ohio. There he resumed his former profession, and after 12 yrs., declined practice, to spend the remainder of his days in the quiet of retirement on a farm. Three score winters had now whitened his head, and yet the old man bowed not his knee in prayer. He had been what the world would call a strict moralist. * * He gloried in his consistency, and in the pride of his heart, looked with contempt on those, whom he called *inconsistent christians*. Their irregularities, whether fancied or real, he readily seized, to confirm himself in infidelity. Although he was not forward to disseminate his principles, he occasionally sought an encounter, to try the temper of his weapons. Having been so long accustomed to them, he could use them with no ordinary skill. With the keenness of his satire, and the cunning of his sophistry, he almost invariably triumphed. Success inspired him with courage, and increased his intellectual pride.

In the winter of 1831, the debate between Campbell and Owen fell into his hands. His long cherished sentiments and feelings inclined him to espouse Owen's side in the argument. As he read, he was struck with the palpable weakness, and inconsistency of his reasoning. "What," said he, "if the Deist has no better arguments than these, to support his system, I am ashamed of it." For the first time in his life, he was now seriously alarmed at the thought, that possibiy, he had built his house upon the sand. Thought begat feeling and deep anxiety. In this state of mind, Providentially Wilson's "Evidences of the truth of Christianity" came within his reach. As he read, day began to dawn on a night of more than 40 years. The light of the truth rendered the darkness visible, and his danger apparent. * * * * He rose from the perusal of Wilson, convinced that the Bible is what it professes to be,—a Revelation from Heaven. This truth admitted, *conviction of sin* rushed upon his mind, and the old man bowed down his head in agony. He attended a meeting in the neighborhood, and heard two sermons by a passing preacher, from the following texts:—"Choose ye this day whom ye will serve:" and, "Now is the accepted time, behold! now is the day of salvation." The Holy Spirit made the word quick and powerful. He went home to read, and revere that volume, which for about half a century, he had neglected and despised. The man who had never prayed before, went home to cry—"God be merciful to me a sinner." His conscience was shaken, and he trembled under the mighty hand of God. After a short season of severe conflict, between the powers of light and darkness, the star of Bethlehem arose, and led him to Jesus. It was on a Sabbath morning. The night preceding had been dark to his soul. He arose from his pillow just as the day dawned, when the following train of thought passed through his mind. "This is the resurrection morning—on this morning Christ rose from the dead! But why did he die? To save sinners. Well, I am a sinner—a great sinner—and will he not save me?—Lord Jesus, save or I perish!" The storm was over, and the calmness of Heaven came over his spirit. He walked out. The winter was so far gone, that the birds were singing their morning anthems. The eastern sky appeared glowing in new and indescribable beauty. The fields and the forest seemed dressed in unwonted loveliness. Heaven and earth looked glad. He gazed and admired, and could no longer keep silent. Although unaccustomed to sing—

His tongue broke out in unknown strains,
And sung surprising grace.

The next day on meeting him, he readily gave vent to his new-born feelings and hopes. Said he, "I have lived 60 yrs. and am scarcely 2 days old. I am a miracle of the grace of God! O how could I support old age without the consolations of religion, and without the promises written in that blessed volume, which I have so long slighted and abused!" Soon after, he had the happiness to embrace a prodigal son, who had wandered in the same cheerless path of infidelity. On the same day they both entered into covenant with God, and with his people. * * * * After a life devoted to the cause of infidelity, he testified "I am led from a review of my past experience, to declare as my belief, that with all the infidel's boasted assurance, there never was a person brought up in a christian land, who could at all times, honestly and unhesitatingly say, I feel secure in a disbelief of the Bible."

306. IV. DEAN,[6] b. Jan. 1, 1769, d. 1787.

307. V. LUCY,[6] b. Feb. 13, 1771, d. 1814. She m. John Bassett, who was b. Aug. 16, 1769. Res. Killingly, Ct. A farmer and worthy man. Chil.—

(1) *Joseph*, b. March 7, 1796, m. Sally Vaughn, and d. Jan. 10, 1851.

(2) *Hannah*, b. 1798, m. 1823, Samuel Hutchins, and d. 1826.

(3) *John*, b. Dec. 1800, unm. Res. Killingly, Ct.

(4) *Almira*, b. 1805, m. Samuel Hutchins, (2d w.) Res. N. Y. City.

(5) *Roxana*, b. 1807, m. Lucius F. Bacon, who d. Dec. 18, 1840.

(6) *Lucy*, b. 1809, d. March, 1834. She m. Joseph Olverson, of R. I.

(7) *Samuel*, b. Aug. 1811, m. twice and both times Eliot, and is dec'd.

(8) *Elethea*, b. 1813, d. young.

308. VI. CALEB,[6] (856) b. April 20, 1773, d. July 7, 1819. He m. April 4, 1804, Mrs. Ann (Sybert) Brown, who d. July 10, 1851. He was a carpenter, went to Charleston, S.C., 1801 or 2, and resided there till the 4th of July, 1819, when he left home with the purpose of visiting his kindred in Mass. He left C. in full health, but d. suddenly 3 days after. He was generous, and truly the poor man's friend, his purse and time being always at their service. Had 7 chil.

309. VII. AARON,[6] (863) b. in Killingly, Ct., Jan. 14, 1776, d. Jan. 16, 1816. He m. Phebe Mowry, who was b. April 2, 1785, and d. May 28, 1847. He was a man of energetic character, and deemed no obstacle too great to be overcome, when it clashed with his purpose. He was elected to several town offices. Res. Killingly, Ct., and had 4 chil.

310. VIII. LETTICE,[6] b. Jan. 11, 1778, d. Oct. 3, 1836. She m. June 29, 1802, Joseph Clark, of Medway, who was b. July 9, 1771, d. July 31, 1826. Chil.—

(1) *Maria*, b. Jan. 1, 1804, d. Sept. 23, 1850.

(2) *Elijah*, twin, b. Jan. 28, 1806, m. Oct. 8, 1835, Mary Ann Kingsbury. He m. 2d, Elizabeth Adams, June 13, 1854. Res. M. His chil., 1, Mary Jane, b. Nov. 22, 1837, d. Aug. 21, 1843. 2, Ellen M., b. Sept. 9, 1840. 3, Sarah F., b. Jan. 20, 1845. 4, Lowell A., b. June 7, 1847, d. Sept. 6, 1847. 5, Willie E., b. April 22, 1850, d. Aug. 27, 1850.

(3) *Abijah*, twin. b. Jan. 28, 1806, m. April 13, 1834, Calista Sayles, who was b. March 10, 1810. Res. M. Chil., 1, Geo. E., b. Dec. 26, 1834. 2, Adelaide A., b. June 4, 1842. 3, Cha's F., b. Aug. 26, 1844, dec'd.

(4) *Sarah*, b. Jan. 31, 1809, m. April 15, 1840, Ferdinand Fiske, of Holliston, son of Dea. Timothy, and has chil.

(5) *Prudence*, b. July 6, 1811, m. William Fuller.

(6) *Caleb*, b. July 1, 1814, m. and lives in Carbondale, Ill.

(7) *Louisa*, b. July 7. 1816, unm.

(8) *Charles T.*, b. June 21, 1819, m. and has chil.

(9) *Amy W.*, b. Jan. 9, 1823, m. 1844, Cyrus Warren, who d. 1849; m. 2dly, Dea. Martin Fletcher, of Milford. Had 2 chil. dec'd.

311. IX. POLLY,[6] b. 1780, d. 1806. She m. John Lewis, who d. Jan. 9, 1816. No chil.

CHIL. OF EBENEZER WALKER,[5] [124] OF ASHFORD, CT.

312. I. RACHEL,[6] b. April 15, 1766, d. Aug. 19, 1804, in Sudbury, Vt. She m. about Sept. 1785, Aaron Parks, who was b. Oct. 5, 1764, and d. March 6, 1848, in Malone, N.Y. Both m. Cong. ch.

He was a farmer. They removed from Ashford about 1790 to Sudbury, Vt. Chil.—

(1) *Aurilla*, b. June 5, 1786, m. David Wood. Res. Batavia, N. Y.

(2) *Eben'r Walker*, b. June 3, 1788, d. in Blissfield, Mich.. about 1852, m. Meth. ch.

(3) *Sabrina*, b. May 18, 1792, m. Parmenter, d. in St. Joseph, Mich., about 1850, and was m. Bap. ch.

(4) *Polly*, b. May 11, 1794, m. David Livingston, who d., and she m. 2d, and lives in No. Ohio.

(5) *Aaron*, b. July 14, 1800, in S. Res. East Constable, N. Y., and active m. Cong. ch.

(6) *Alanson*, b. Jan. 3, 1798, in S. Res. Toronto, C. W.

(7) *Carlton*, b. Aug. 23, 1802, in S. Res. Mich. Shoemaker.

313. II. Dolly,[6] b. Oct. 15, 1770, d. Aug. 1858. She m. 1796, Nathan James, who was b. April, 1774, and d. Oct. 4, 1832. Res. Ashford, Ct. She rem. to Tolland after his death. She was m. Bap. ch. He was a farmer, and all his sons. Chil.—

(1) *Abigail*, b. Aug. 1797, m. David Jones, of Chaplin, Ct. She d. in C., May 5, 1856.

(2) *Ebenezer W.*, b. Jan. 17, 1796. Res. A.

(3) *Sabrina*, b. Jan, 25, 1802, m. Nov. 9, 1834, Hosea C. Robbins. Res. A. Chil., 1, James L., b. March 4, 1836. 2, Sabrina Jenette, b. Jan. 13, 1839. 3, Julia A., b. Jan. 22, 1842. 4, John H., b. Nov. 12, 1844, d. Sept. 2, 1853.

(4) *Nathan W.*, b. Jan. 22, 1804, d. Sept. 1, 1841. Res. Clarence, N. Y.

(5) *Jesse*. b. May 28, 1813, m. Feb. 15, 1842, Juliet Emeline Luce, of Tolland, who was b. April 22, 1812. Res. Tolland, Ct. till 1860. Chil., 1, Geo. Lyman, b. July 25, 1843, 2, Ellen Louisa, b. Jan. 12, 1846. 3, Harriet A. L., b. Nov. 3, 1847. 4, Mary L., b. Jan. 23, 1852. 5, Albert Elwyn, b. Jan. 17, 1855.

(6) *Lyman*, b. July 1, 1806, d. June, 1827.

Children of WILLIAM WALKER,[5] [126] of Ashford, Ct.

314. I. Judith,[6] b. May 17, 1769, d. July 5, 1854. She m. Nov. 9, 1790, Abner Chaffee, son of David. He d. Dec. 26, 1816. Chil.—

(1) *Amy*, b. Aug. 7, 1791, m. Abner Whiton, a farmer. Res. Willington, Ct. Both are dec'd, leaving 4 sons and 4 daus., one of whom is Geo., who m. (See No. 894.)

(2) *Hannah*, b. Nov. 30, 1792, m. Joseph Snell, of Union, Ct., a farmer, and Deacon of the ch. They rem. to Windham, Ct., and d., having 7 chil.

(3) *Anna*, b. Oct. 18, 1794, m. Reuben Robinson, and is dec'd. 5 chil.

(4) *Ebenezer*, b. Nov. 29, 1796, m. March 22, 1822, Hannah Smith, and has 1 son and dau., who are both married.

(5) *Lois*, b. Sept. 14, 1798, m. Philip Corbin, a farmer. Res. West Hartford, Ct. Has 8 sons and 2 daus.

(6) *William* b. April 20, 1801, m. Abigail Thayer, of Herkimer Co., N. Y. Res. Hartford City, Ind., and has 6 or 7 chil. He is a Baptist clergyman.

315. II. ELIZABETH,^{6} b. Jan. 1771, d. 1823 or 4, unm.

316. III. CALEB,^{6} (867) b. in Ashford, Ct., March 16, 1773, d. Dec. 13, 1853. He m. Oct. 22, 1795, Abigail Dimmock, of Ashford, Ct., who d. Dec. 31, 1848. About 1803, he removed to Willington, Ct., and April, 1826, to Belchertown, Mass. He taught school 23 winters, commencing at the age of 16; was Select-man of W. many yrs., Justice of the Peace, represented his town (W.) in State Legislature. He was an active business man, m. Cong. ch., and had 14 chil.

317. IV. CALVIN,^{6} }
318. V. LUTHER,^{6} } Twins, b. Jan. 1775. Both d. very young, and were buried together.

319. VI. WILLIAM,^{6} (881) b. 1781, d. Aug. 12, 1826, ae. 45 yrs. He m. April, 1804, Sylvia Corbin, of Dudley, dau. of Major Lemuel. She d. May 13, 1854, ae. 71, and m. ch. Res. Ashford, Ct. After his death, the family rem. to Dudley, Mass. He was an intelligent and active farmer, and held several offices. He was also a teacher, and had 5 chil.

SEVENTH GENERATION.

CHIL. OF CAPT. TIMOTHY WALKER,^{6} [132] OF REHOBOTH.

320. I. EUNICE,^{7} b. Nov. 25, 1774, d. 1805. She m. Dec. 25, 1796, Phanuel Bishop, son of Hon. Phanuel and Elizabeth, b. June 22, 1773, and d. 1831. Res. Seekonk. Chil.—

(1) *Eliza*, b. 1797, m. 1819, Job Carpenter, a farmer in S.

(2) *Amanda*, b. 1799, m. Wm. Ide, Esq. She has Catharine.

(3) *John Jefferson*, b. 1802, m. Sarah Walker, (See No. 580,) and d. 1850.

(4) *Eunice*, b. 1804, unm.

321. II. TIMOTHY,^{7} b. Oct. 28, 1776, d. Dec. 18, 1807, in 32d yr., unm. He was a farmer in Seekonk—held the title of Lieut., and was a man of excellent character.

322. III. EPHRAIM WILMARTH,^{7} b. Feb. 8, 1780, d. March 7, 1819. He m. Oct. 24, 1810, Zelinda Peck, dau. of Cyril. (See No. 67.) He was Lieut., and childless. Res. Seekonk.

"His life, tho' short, was virtuous and exemplary." (Part of epitaph.)

323. IV. SAMUEL,[7] (886) b. May 19, 1783, d. 1832. He m. Sept. 12, 1810, Hannah Cushing, dau. of Jacob and Elizabeth. She d. Oct. 22, 1852, ae. 64. Res. Seekonk. He had 7 chil.

324. V. JOHN,[7] b. March 1, 1786, d. March 8, 1786, ae. 8 days.

325. VI. GEORGE,[7] b. Feb. 10, 1788, d. May 22, 1818, unm. He was a trader in Seekonk, and had the military title of Lieut.

326. VII. BENJAMIN,[7] b. Oct. 10, 1790, d. Jan. 15, 1791, ae. 3 mos.

By 2d MARRIAGE.

327. VIII. MARY,[7] b. Feb. 13, 1794. Res. unm. in the old family mansion of Col. Timothy, which has been built 150 yrs., and is near the Cove Factory, Seekonk.

328. IX. SALLY,[7] b. May 22, 1796. Res. Seekonk, m. Bap. ch., and unm.

329. X. LUCY ANN,[7] b. Aug. 18, 1798, m. May 21, 1820, Capt. Samuel Davis, (See No. 134,) her cousin, of Portland, Me., who was b. in Seekonk, and d. at New Orleans, April 1, 1827, in 41st yr. He was Master of a ship in the European trade. She is m. Bap. ch. Res. S. Chil.

(1) *Lucy Ann*, b. 1824. Res. S., unm., and is a teacher.

(2) *Samuel F.*, d. Oct. 14, 1829, ae. 4 yrs. } Buried in one grave.

(3) *Timothy W.*, b. Dec. 23, 1829, ae. 9 yrs. }

330. XI. JOHN REDWAY,[7] b. June 20, 1800 ? (Seekonk Rec.) d. April 4, 1800, ae. 11 mos. (Ins.)

331. XII. ARVILLA,[7] b. Sept. 26, 1803, m. Feb. 5, 1825, Edward Dexter, Jr., who was b. 1797 or 8. She is m. Bap. ch. in Seekonk. Chil.—

(1) *Christopher*, b. 1826, m. Sarah Bishop, dau. of John J. (See No. 580.)

(2) *Edward Monford*, d. 1829, about 2 yrs. old.

332. XIII. EUNICE BISHOP,[7] b. Aug. 25, 1806. She m. Nov. 13, 1828, Henry H. Dexter, who was b. Oct. 10, 1801, and is a farmer in Seekonk. She is m. ch. Bap. Chil.

(1) *Sam'l F.*, b. Aug. 17, 1829, drowned while bathing, July 8, 1854. (2) *Sally S.*, b. Mar. 19, 1831, d. Oct. 11, 1832. (3) *John M.*, b. Jan. 1833. (4) *Joseph D.*, b. Dec. 28, 1834. (5) *Edward*, b. March 15, 1836. (6) *Timothy Walker*, b. Feb. 10, 1839. (7) *Abbie S.*, b. March 4, 1842. (8) *Charles H.*, b. July 21, 1843.

333. XIV. WILLIAM,[7] b. Nov. 27, (2, Fam. Rec.) 1810, d. Nov. 2, 1813, ae. 4 ? yrs. (Ins.)

CHIL. OF SAMUEL WALKER,[6] [136] OF ASHFORD, CT.

334. I. AARON,[7] (893) b. Jan. 21, 1776, d. Nov. 1, 1815. He m. Jan. 26, 1808, Lucy Holt, dau. of James and Lucy, of Willington, Ct. She d. Feb. 22, 1847, ae. 68 yrs. Res. Ashford, Ct. He was a farmer and had 2 chil.

335. II. HANNAH,[7] b. June 4, 1779, d. Nov. 23, 1824. She m. Elisha Barrows, who d. Nov. 2, 1824. Res. Mansfield, Ct. She was m. Cong. ch. Chil.—

(1) *Sherman A.*, b. Aug 15, 1810. Res. New Haven, Ct. (2) *Bushrod W.*, b. June 14, 1812. (3) *Mary H.*, b. April 16, 1814. (4) *Almira*, b. Nov. 12, 1816.

336. III. SAMUEL,[7] (895) b. May 24, 1781, d. Oct. 18, 1832. He m. 1802, Cynthia Brown, in Weathersfield, Ct., sister of Pliny, (No. 338.) He rem. in 1804, to Geneseo, N. Y., and in 1816, to Margaretta, Ohio, where he died. He was a farmer, and served in the army in 1812-13, as aid under Gen. Wadsworth, and had 10 chil. She lives in Iowa, (1859) ae. 76.

337. IV. PETER,[7] (906) b. Aug. 22, 1783, d. 1824. He m. 1812, Sally Allen, of New Haven, Ct., who d. 1833. He removed to Monson, and in a few years after to Margaretta, O., and d. in York, O. He was a shoemaker, and had 5 chil.

338. V. ASENATH,[7] b. Nov. 9, 1785. She m. 1810, Pliny Brown, who was b. in Wilbraham, Nov. 5, 1785, son of John and Savory (Colton.) The rem. to Margaretta, Ohio, in 1816. Both m. Cong ch. For several yrs. they endured great privations and hardships, but have lived to see the wilderness become a fruitful field. He is a farmer in M. Chil.—

(1) *William*, b. 1811, in Mansfield, Ct., d. 1814, in Ashford.

(2) *Phebe*, b. 1813, in A. and m. 1835, George Ward, in M. and d. 1837. He is a mechanic. She was m. Cong. ch.

(3) *Orlando*, b. 1815, m. 1839, Laura Boice. She is m. ch. Meth. He is a farmer in M. Has 7 chil., 1, Alice M. 2, Sophia L. 3, Cynthia L. 4, Frances I. 5, Millard F. 6, Lucy H. 7, Orlando P.

339. LEPHA,[7] b. July 1, 1788. Res. Ashford, Ct., unm., and m. Cong. ch.

340. LENDA,[7] b. July 1, 1788. Res. A., Ct., unm., and m. Cong. ch.

341. VIII. ABNER,[7] (911) b. March 7, 1791, d. 1825. He m. Hannah Allen, of New Haven, Ct., who d. in Sandusky City, O., 1847. He emigrated to Margaretta, O., in 1817, and soon after to York, O., where he died. He was a saddler, also m. Bap. ch. Had 3 chil.

342. IX. PHEBE,[7] b. July 22, 1793, d. ae. 5 mos.

343. X. ALICE,[7] b. Dec. 11, 1796, m. David Glacier. Res. Willington, Ct. No chil. He is a farmer, and both m. Bap. ch.

344. XI. JONATHAN C.,[7] (914) b. Jan. 5, 1799, m. Harriet Merrick. Res. Willington, Ct. Both are m. Cong. ch. He is a carpenter, and has had 2 chil.

CHILDREN OF PETER WALKER,[6] [137] OF ASHFORD, CT.

345. I. WEALTHY,[7] b. 1791, d. about 1828. She m. Joseph Turner, of Somers, Ct., a farmer. She was m. Cong. ch. Res. Ellington, Ct. They had 7 chil., all sons, who removed soon after her death, and their residence is unknown.

346. II. PHEBE,[7] d. quite young.

347. III. NATHAN,[7] d. quite young.

CHIL. OF CALVIN WALKER,[6] [143] OF PROVIDENCE, R. I.

348. I. JEMIMA,[7] b. May 21, 1781. She m. Gardner T. Levalley and had several chil. All d. in infancy, excepting one. He forsook his wife, taking this child with him. She being an heir to her gd. father's estate, has been advertised for, but in vain. Her name was—

Susan Ann, b. about 1823.

349. II. PETER,[7] d. in infancy.

350. III. WILLIAM,[7] d. in infancy.

351. IV. MARY,[7] b. Sept., 1789. She m. Daniel Russell, of Rindge, N. H., who was born 1787, and d. 1845. They removed from Providence, R. I. to Chilicothe, O., and then to P. again, where she resides. He was a shoe-maker. Chil.—

(1) *Mary*, b. in P., Oct. 10, 1812, m. 1846, Jas. A. C. Hathaway, of Fall River, who was b. in F. R., 1824. Chil.—1, Sarah Adeline, b. 1848. 2, Lizzie Ella, and 3, Willie Cleaveland, b. Dec. 19, 1849, twins, and d. March, 1850. He is a Delineator and Practical Worker in marble, in P.

(2) *Rachel Gould*, b. May, and d. Aug., 1814.

(3) *Herbert*, b. 1815, d. in infancy.

(4) *Eliza W.*, b. May 25, 1816, m. William Henry Quimby, of Haverhill; m. 2d, Dr. John Richards, who was b. in Newton. Res. Providence, Ill., and 3 children.

(5) *Sarah O.*, b. Oct. 3, 1818, in Ohio, m. 1841, Robert Almy, of Portsmouth, R. I. Res. Providence, Ill. Chil.—1, Robert Russell, b. Oct. 7, 1843, d. Jan. 29, 1850. 2, Edward Clarence, b. June 13, 1847. 3, Sarah Ella, b. Aug. 18, 1850. 4, Mary Adelaide Isabel, b. Sept. 17, 1853. 5, Robert Tillinghast, b. Feb. 14, 1858.

(6) *Phebe W.*, b. Aug. 17, 1820, in O., m. 1842, Thos. G. Howland, of R. I., and had 1 child who d. in infancy.

(7) *Rebecca H.*, d. in infancy.

(8) *Daniel*, b. July 16, 1824, m. Mary Lynde, of Melrose, Oct., 1850. No chil.

(9) *Wm. C. W.*, b. Aug. 9, 1828, and d. in Taunton, Dec. 26, 1854, ae. 27. A young man of considerable musical talent, and of very excellent character.

(10) *Emma W.*, b. June 24, 1830, m. in Taunton, Gordon Westcott Perkins, July 2, 1854. Has—1, Wm. Russell, b. Sept. 22, 1856. Res. Providence, R. I.

(11) *Albert Gould*, b. April 30, 1832, d. April 9, 1860. He m. June 24, 1857, Mary E. Irons, and had—1, Charles Albert, b. Oct. 24, 1859. Res. Buda, Bureau Co., Ill.

352. V. AMY,[7] b. in Providence, d. ae. 14 yrs.

353. VI. ELIZABETH,[7] b. in P., April, 1795, d. Aug. 26, 1854. She m. April 5, 1819, Capt. Wm. Martin, of Seekonk, who was b. Jan. 8, 1795, and resides in Providence, R. I. Chil.—

(1) *William W.*, b. March 30, 1820, d. Aug. 31, 1821. (2) *Mary R.*, b. Nov. 11, 1821, m. 1852, Alfred Higgins. (3) *Sarah P.*, b. Aug. 4, 1823, m. Jas. Greene, 1843. (4) *Charles B.*, b. March 27, 1826, d. July 31, 1828. (5) *Charles B.*, b. July 20, 1828. Lost at sea, 1842. (6) *James Wm.*, b. Sept. 18, 1831, m. Mary Maria D. Borden, of Fall River, 1851.

354. VII. LYDIA,[7] d. in infancy.

355. VIII. CALVIN,[7] (916) b. in Seekonk. He m. Isabel Jane Anderson, and has had 4 chil. He is a pencil maker. Res. Rock Island, Ill.

CHIL. OF JOSEPH WALKER,[6] [146] OF NELSON, N. Y.

356. I. GEO. A. F.,[7] b. Aug. 31, 1790, d. Jan. 13, 1791.

357. II. HENRIETTA,[7] b. Nov. 11, 1791. Res. Nelson, N.Y., unm.

358. III. LOUISA,[7] b. Oct. 24, 1793. Res. Nelson, N.Y., unm.

359. IV. AMANDA,[7] b. Feb. 29, 1796, d. Oct. 27, 1843, of cancer.

360. V. ALVAH A.,[7] b. Jan. 15, 1799, d. May 15, 1799.

361. VI. AUGUSTUS A.,[7] b. Nov. 19, 1800. Res. Nelson, N.Y., unm.

362. VII. LYDIA M.,[7] b. Oct. 21, 1802. She m. Jan. 7, 1830, Eli White, who was b. Dec. 20, 1803. Res. Nelson, Madison Co., N.Y. Farmer. She is m. Bap. ch. Chil.—

(1) *Lois M.*, b. Nov. 12, 1830, d. March 18, 1833. (2) *Sarah J.*, b. Aug. 17, 1834. (3) *Jason Judson*, b. Oct. 19, 1838, d. Nov. 22, 1838. (4) *Wells R. B.*, b. July 5, 1840, d. Nov. 10, 1843.

363. VIII. LOIS L.,[7] b. April 23, 1806, d. May 31, 1857. She m. Jan. 20, 1825, Ross Crandall. Res. Fayetteville, Onondago Co., N.Y. He is a mechanic. Chil.—

(1) *Sarah M.*, b. Jan. 28, 1827, m. Oct. 4, 1854, Harvey Morse, who was b. Oct., 1824. Res. F.

(2) *Warren D.*, b. Feb. 23, 1831, m. Lydia M. Wilbur, Oct. 4, 1854, who was b. June 30, 1833. Res. Nelson, N. Y., till 1856, and now in Palmyra, Marion Co., Mo. He is a contractor.

(3) *Eli J.*, b. Sept. 15, 1833. He m. Feb. 20, 1856, Polly H. Goodrich, who was b. April 19, 1838. He is a contractor. Res. P., Mo.

CHILDREN OF LUTHER WALKER,[6] [149] OF KEENE, N.Y.

364. I. JOHN,[7] b. Aug. 29, 1790, d. Dec. 14, 1815.

365. II. MARIA,[7] b. Dec. 14, 1792, in Troy, N.Y.

366. III. LYDIA,[7] b. Dec. 30, 1794, in Troy, N.Y.

367. IV. HORACE W.,[7] (921) b. July 9, 1798, in Middletown, Vt. He m. March 2, 1826, Mary S. Bartlett, who was b. Jan. 26, 1806. Both m. Meth ch. He is a farmer, and has 2 chil. Res. Keene, Essex Co., N.Y.

368. V. ALBERT L.,[7] b. May 20, 1803. He was in Canada when last heard from.

CHIL. OF GEO. WHITEFIELD WALKER,[6] [151] OF SEEKONK.

369. I. JOHN BUCKLIN,[7] (923) b. March 26, 1797. He m. Anna Sweet, of Pawtucket. Res. Woonsocket, R. I. He is a Clerk in Burnon Mills. Both m. Epis. ch., and have had 1 child.

370. II. ALFRED,[7] (924) b. Feb. 8, 1799. He m. Dec. 8, 1825, Huldah B. Perry, dau. of Zephaniah, of Seekonk. Res. Pawtucket, a farmer and worthy man. Has 3 chil.

371. III. LYDIA,[7] b. Dec. 22, 1800. She m. May 23, 1822, Milton Ingraham, of Attleboro', who is dec'd. Chil.—

(1) *Lydia Maria*, b. Aug. 1823, d. Jan. 1824.

(2) *Ellen Amelia*, b. 1827, d. Aug. 1829.

372. IV. RUSSELL D.,[7] a machinist in Pawtucket, unm.

373. V. GEORGE W.,[7] b. July 28, 1806, d. Sept. 10, 1811.

374. VI. NATH'L C.,[7] b. Feb. 3, 1809, d. Dec. 22, 1810.

375. VII. AMY,[7] b. April 5, 1812, d. Sept., 1812.

376. VIII. WILLIAM ORMSBEE,[7] b. April 25, 1816, d. Sept. 25, 1819.

CHIL. OF BOSWORTH WALKER,[6] [152] OF PAWTUCKET.

378. I. DUDLEY,[7] (927) b. Feb. 22, 1803. He m. May 22, 1830, Jane P. Hill, dau. of Capt. Geo. Hill, of (Manville) Smithfield, R. I., who d. Oct. 24, 1854, ae. 45. He m. 2d, Eliza Woodward. He has had 7 chil., and is a merchant in Central Falls, R. I.

379. II. JULIA,[7] b. May 17, 1805, d. unm., Sept. 30, 1821.

380. III. MARY B.,[7] July 20, 1807, d. Oct. 15, 1813.

381. IV. EMELINE,[7] b. Sept. 12, 1810, d. Sept. 19, 1813.

382. V. GEO. WHITEFIELD,[7] b. Jan. 18, 1814, d. Oct. 2, 1819.

383. VI. FRANCIS,[7] (934) b. Sept. 11, 1816, m. Sept. 19, 1838, Abby Carpenter, of Central Falls, R. I., dau. of Luther, b. March 4, 1815, d. June 29, 1851. He m. 2d, Louisa Borden, of Smithfield, R. I., Aug. 3, 1852. He is a thread manufacturer in Central Falls, and has had 5 chil.

384. VII. WM. BOSWORTH,[7] (939) b. Dec. 3, 1822. He m. March 29, 1848, Abby A. Brown, dau. of Nathan, of Pawtucket, b. Feb. 19, 1827. Res. P. He is a painter, m. Bap. ch., and has 1 child.

CHILDREN OF LIEUT. MOSES WALKER,[6] [157] OF SEEKONK.

385. I. HENRIETTA,[7] b. March 15, 1784, m. Nov. 23, 1831, Dea. Abner Lewis, of Ware, who d. 1853. She is m. Cong. ch.

386. II. ANNA,[7] b. Jan. 31, 1786, d. Sept., 1835. She m. April, 1814, Horace Evans, of St. Johnsbury, Vt., son of Zerah and Lucy (Savage,) and b. 1790, in Hartland, Vt. He has been Deputy Sheriff 7 yrs., and was High Sheriff of Caledonia Co., 1855. She was m. Meth. ch. They had 7 chil., and all but 2 d. in infancy—

(1) *Ferdinand*, b. Sept. 13, 1821. Res. Danville, Vt. Chil.—1, Frederika, b. June 22, 1850. 2, Eveline, b. April 22, 1852. 3, Georgianna, b. Dec. 1854, &c.

(2) *Ann E.*, b. 1827, m. Salomon Stevens, Jr., of Barnet, Vt. 1 dau.

BY 2d MARRIAGE.

387. III. MARY,[7] b. Nov. 5, 1787, d. before 1830. She m. April 19, 1810, Simeon Makker, of Seekonk. Chil.—

(1) *Simeon*, d. before 1849. (2) *Mary Ann*, dec'd. (3) *Caroline*. Res. Scituate, R. I. (4) *George*. (5) *Fanny*. Res Ill. (6) *Emeline*. (7) *Susan*.

BY 3d MARRIAGE.

388. IV. SALLY,[7] b. April 17, 1791, m. 1815, Dea. Peter H. Brown, of Seekonk. (See No. 43.) He is an intelligent farmer, in S., has been Select-man, and is highly esteemed for probity and christian worth. She is an active and exemplary christian. Chil.—

(1) *Joseph*, b. Aug. 7, 1816, m. Jan. 11, 1844, Henrietta Smith French, dau. of Ezra. (See No. 125.) Both m. Cong. ch. He has been one of the Town School Com. several yrs., was elected Deacon in 1858, and has the confidence of the community as an intelligent, faithful and upright citizen. Chil.—1, Helen Augusta, b. June 17, 1845, d. Sept. 15, 1848. 2, Herbert Edwards, b. Feb. 5, 1847. 3, Helen Augusta, b. Nov. 24, 1851. 4, Henry William, b. Oct. 14, 1856.

(2) *Huldah Hunt*, b. June 22, 1819, is m. Cong. ch., and unm.

389. V. BETSEY,[7] b. July 28, 1792. She m. June 10, 1819, James Bowen, of Rehoboth, a farmer. Res. in R., till recently, now in Pawtucket, R. I. Chil.—

(1) *Celia*, b. April 7, 1820. (2) *Betsey*, b. Sept. 8, 1821, d. July, 1833. (3) *George*, b. April 24, 1823. (4) *Mary*, b. Sept., 1825, d. Aug., 1833. (5) *Emily*, b. April 2, 1829. (6) *Alvah*, b. April 12, 1832. (7) *Lyman*, b. Feb. 9, 1834. (8) *Mary*, b. May 18, 1836.

390. VI. FANNY,[7] b. Jan. 24, 1794, d. unm., Aug. 23, 1852.

391. VII. SAMUEL,[7] (940) b. Jan. 9, 1796. He m. 1824, Polly Bowen, of Rehoboth. He is a farmer in Seekonk, and has 2 chil.

392. VIII. LEONARD,[7] b. Dec. 20, 1797, d. June, 1850, unm. He was a housewright; represented Seekonk in State Legislature, 2 yrs., and d. in Maysville, Cal.

393. IX. GEO. WASHINGTON,[7] (942) b. March 30, 1800, m. May 9, 1830, Esther Smith, of Smithfield, R. I. He is a housewright. Res. Seekonk. Has 3 chil.

394. X. AMANDA,[7] b. 1802, d. before 1808.

395. XI. LYMAN,[7] b. Nov. 15, 1805, is a mason. Res. Seekonk, unm.

397. XII. AMANDA CARPENTER,[7] b. Feb. 1, 1808. Res. Seekonk, unm.

CHILDREN OF ETHEL WALKER,[6] [159] OF WEBSTER, MICH.

398. I. EZRA,[7] (945) b. Feb. 20, 1797, in Savoy, d. Jan. 27, 1850. He m. 1821, Harriet Stewart, who was b. Dec. 11, 1797, and a m. Bap. ch., in N. Y. He was a farmer, rem. to Springwater, N. Y. in 1822, became a m. Bap. ch. in 1827, was elected Deacon in 1830, and was an exemplary and efficient officer till his death. Had 8 chil.

399. II. GEORGE,[7] (953) b. Dec. 29, 1798. He m. June 1, 1820, Rebecca Bliss, of Savoy, youngest dau. of Ephraim, and b. Jan. 5, 1802. His education was acquired in the Winter terms of a District school. His father being one of the 1st settlers in the town of Savoy, he as one of the oldest of the children, aided in the support of the family, by working in the summer. His theological education was obtained after he was 30 yrs. of age. Spending a part of a year at the Theological Institution in Hamilton, N. Y., he was ord. and became Pastor of the Bap. ch. in Windsor, Mass. His ministry in W. was successful. The ch. was doubled in its membership and strength. In Sept. 1835, he rem. to Dexter, Mich., and has labored rather as a Missionary, than as a Pastor, preaching for 2 churches in Pinkney and Genoa alternately, a soldier of Christ going to war upon his own charge, as the churches to whom he preaches are feeble. He has had 9 chil.

A. Walker.

400. III. WILLIAM,[7] (962) b. June 22, 1801, in Savoy, Mass. He m. Nov. 1826, Susan Macomber, of Savoy, who d. March 12, 1845, in Webster, Mich., leaving 4 daughters. He m. 2d, June 1, 1846, Eleanor Poyer, of Tuscala, Livingston Co., Mich., who d. at Warrenville, Ill., May 14, 1854, leaving 4 sons. He is a farmer in W., has been Justice of the Peace 4 yrs. and School Inspector 1 yr. He rem. to Mich. in 1835, and April 6, 1854, to Warrenville, Ill. He is m. Bap. ch. and has had 8 chil.

401. IV. MARTHA,[7] b. April 2, 1803, m. May 11, 1843, Daniel Hunt. Res. Dexter, Mich. He is a farmer. Both m. Bap. ch., and have no chil.

402. V. NANCY,[7] b. Sept. 21, 1805, d. Oct. 7, 1849. She m. 1835, Edward Johnson, of Fleming, Cayuga Co., N. Y., and removed to Dexter, Mich., in 1836. He d. in the winter of 1838–9. Both m. Bap. ch. Chil.—

(1) *William E.* (2) *Abel W.*

403. VI. HENRY,[7] (970) b. Feb. 28, 1808, in Savoy, Mass. He m. July 4, 1832, Louisa Hemmenway, of Florida, Mass., dau. of Daniel, and b. Oct. 23, 1810. Res. Ingham, Ingham Co., Mich. He rem. to York, Mich. in 1833, in 1835 to Dexter, in 1837 to Ingham. A farmer. Both m. Bap. ch. He is Deacon, and has 5 chil.

404. VII. AMOS,[7] (975) b. March 6, 1811. He m. Aug. 27, 1834, Mary Bliss, of North Adams. Both m. Bap. ch. He is a skillful physician in Pontiac, Oakland Co., Mich., and has achieved his eminence by self-reliance and persevering effort. He has had 9 chil.

405. VIII. ABEL WILMARTH,[7] b. May 20, 1814, d. Aug. 31, 1837, in Manchester, Washtenaw Co., Mich. A merchant.

406. IX. LELAND,[7] (984) b. July 15, 1816. He m. March 17, 1838, Nancy Winans, dau. of John and Ruth, of Genesee Co., N. Y., b. Aug. 31, 1818. He rem. to Hamburgh, Livingston Co., Mich., in 1838; has been Town Clerk 2 yrs., School Inspector 10 yrs., Justice 7 yrs., and Supervisor 7 yrs. Under the system of County Courts, he was second Judge. He has charge of a flouring mill, 2 saw mills, a farm of his own and the agency of another, is Postmaster, and practices medicine. He has had 5 chil.

407. X. NATHANIEL CARPENTER,[7] b. Nov. 14, 1818, m. 1856, Mrs. Ellen Danforth, of Ottawa, Ill. He was a teacher several yrs., then a merchant, and resides in O.

408. XI. Harriet,[7] b. April 30, 1821, was m. ch., and d. in Webster, Mich., Sept. 28, 1844.

Chil. of BENJAMIN WALKER,[6] [160] of Lyndon, Vt.

409. I. Ferdinand L.,[7] (999) b. in Lyndon, Aug. 24, 1805, d. Feb. 20, 1858, ae. 52 yrs., 5 m., 26 d. He m. Sarah Randall, March 3, 1831, who was b. in L., April 27, 1808. He was a farmer, m. ch. and honored with the offices of Select-man, Lister, and Justice of the Peace. Res. L. He had 2 chil.

410. II. Nancy B.,[7] b. in Lyndon, March 29, 1807. She m. Jan. 10, 1830, Abel Brown, M.D., son of Josiah, (See No. 43,) and Susanna (Wilmarth.) He was b. in L., March 1, 1804, and is now a merchant in Burke, Vt. She is m. ch. Chil.—

(1) *Adolphus W.*, b. March 18, 1831, merchant, m. June 22, 1858, Avaline Harvey.

(2) *Halsey R.*, b. Feb. 25, 1834, m. Nov. 13, 1856, Zilpha S. Smith. A merchant in B., in partnership with his brother.

(3) *Alson A.*, b. Nov. 30, 1838.

411. III. Adeline R.,[7] b. Feb. 20, 1809, m. Harris Smith, of Sheffield, Vt., Feb. 16, 1835, who was b. in Lyndon Vt., Aug. 20, 1802. He rem. to Barton, Vt., about 1838, and is now a farmer in Burke, Vt., and has been a Select-man, Deputy Sheriff, Justice of the Peace, and Representative to the Legislature. She is m. ch. Chil.—

(1) *Oliver H.*, b. Dec. 28, 1835, merchant in E. Burke. (2) *Isaac E.*, b. March 5, 1837, student in Wesleyan Univ., 1859. (3) *Benjamin W.*, b. May 29, 1839. (4) *Ashley W.*, b. Sept. 10, 1843. (5) *Susan R.*, b. Sept. 16, 1848.

412. IV. Rodolphus W.,[7] b. in Lyndon, Nov. 30, 1811. He is a farmer, unm.; has been Select-man and Justice of the Peace, and is now in the lumber trade in East Burke, Vt.

Children of AARON WALKER,[6] [161] of Lyndon, Vt.

413. I. Henry H.,[7] b. May 21, 1801, d. July 31, 1824.

414. II. Elizabeth,[7] b. July 25, 1803. She m. Jan. 9, 1823, John H. Wilfong. Res. Saltilloville, Ind. He is a farmer. Chil.—

(1) *Henry W.*, b. Aug. 8, 1824, m. Nov. 14, 1849, Nancy Stewart, who d. June 8, 1855, leaving 2 chil., viz.: Marquis S., b. June 5, 1853, and Orange

L., b. July 8, '54, d. Sept. 23, '55. He m. 2d, March 22, '59, Nancy C. Pierson, and has, Elizabeth Jane, b. Dec. 27, '59. (2) *Sarah Ann*, b. March 2, 1826. (3) *Mary E.*, b. June 12, 1828, m. July 4, '53, John W. Leach, and has—1, Sarah E., b. May 24, '54. 2, Althea J., b. April 28, '56. 3, Henry F., b. June 5, '58. (4) *Margaret*, b. Feb. 26, '31, m. Nov. 18, '58, Harvey Carr, and have Sayles E., b. Nov. '59. (5) *Nancy Elon*, b. Jan. 2, '33. (6) *John H.*, b. Oct. 8, '34. (7) *David H.*, b. Feb. 24, '37. (8) *Rebecca*, b. Feb. 17, '40, d. Sept. 27, '41. (9) *Eliza J.*, b. March 28, '42. (10) *Michael Aaron*, b. June 12, '44.

415. III. Almira,[7] b. March 5, 1806, m. Jan. 25, 1824, Daniel D. Jackman, who was b. Oct. 12, 1794, in Corinth, Vt. Res. Martin, Martin Co., Ind. Chil.—

(1) *Mary C.*, b. Feb. 19, 1826, m. May 8, '45, Leonard Marley, and d. Dec. 12, '48. She had—1, Almira A., b. March 18, '46. 2, Dau, b. and d. same day. (2) *Abel A.*, b. May 31, '28, m. Jan. 29, '44, Hannah Marley, who was b. Nov. 27, 1828. He is a farmer, and has—1, John, b. Nov. '46. 2, Mary C., b. Oct. '48, d. Sept. '51. 3, Almira A., b. Nov. '50, d. Sept. '51. 4, Ellen, b. Aug. '52. 5, Wm. D., b. Jan. '55. 6, Albert S., b. May, '58. 7, Martha E., b. March, '60. (3) *Geo. Winthrop*, b. Dec. 12, '31, m. Aug. 31, '54, Cynthia A. Wolfton, who was b. Aug. 9, 1836. They have 4 chil,—1, Wm. Adolphus, b. March. '56. 2, Sarah E., b. Feb. '58. 3, Albert G., b. April, '59, d. Sept. 4, Almira, b. Aug. '60. (4) *Dau*, b. Dec. 30, '32, d. Jan. 15, '33. (5) *Wm. Brown*, b. Sept. 25, '34, d. March 16, '54. (6) *Son*, b. Nov. 18, '36, d. same day. (7) *Son*, still-born, Oct. 5, '37. (8) *Sarah E.*, b. Sept. 30, '40, d. Oct. 12, '56. (9) *Aaron Walker*, b. Nov. 18, '43.

416. IV. Nancy,[7] b. July 6, 1817, m. at age of 15 yrs., John H. Bartlett, who d. 1839, having 2 chil. She m. 2d, Ephraim Doane and had 4 chil. Res. Seymour, Jackson Co., Ind. Chil.—

(1) *Lyndon D.*, m. Clemence Magoon. (2) *Leonard W.*, m. Amanda More, who is dec'd. (3) *Mary E.* (4) *Ephraim E.* (5) *Nancy*. (6) *Frances B.*

417. V. George W., (1001) b. Sept. 13, 1808, d. July 25, 1843. He m. Feb. 23, 1832, Mariette Hammersley, who d. He m. 2d, Mary Ann Stewart. He had 6 chil.

418. VI. Lyndon,[7] b. May 24, 1811, d. July 29, 1826.

419. VII. Albert,[7] b. Nov. 25, 1813, d. July 30, 1826, 5 hours after Lyndon, and both buried in same grave at one time.

420. VIII. Adaline,[7] b. Feb. 15, 1820, m. 1837, Oliver P. Pierce, who was b. March 2, 1817. Res. Martin Co., Ind. Chil.—

(1) *Mary E.*, b. Sept. 21, 1838, m. March 26, '57, Philip C. Hawkins, who was b. Jan. 27, 1825. They have 2 chil.—1, James P., b. Jan. 5, '58. 2, Philip C., b. Aug. 15, '59. (2) *Eliza J.*, b. March 11, '40. m. John Hawkins, who was b. Jan. 19, '35, and has, Sarah E., b. Sept. 6, '59. (3) *Nancy*

A., b. Jan. 31, '42. (4) *Caroline D.*, b. Feb. 12, '44. (5) *Oliver P.*, b. Jan. 16, '46. (6) *Laura A.*, b. Feb. 25, '48. (7) *Mahala E.*, b. Feb. 16, '50. (8) *Geo. W.*, b. Aug. 21, '52. (9) *Wm. T.*, b. July 22, '54. (10) *Harvey A.*, b. Sept. 17, '56. (11) *Sarah E.*, b. April 15, '59.

421. IX. ELIZA ANN,[7] b. Aug. 8, 1825, m. July, 1844, Jeremiah Claxton. Res. Paoli, Orange Co., Ind. Chil. (1860.)—

(1) *Wm. A.*, ae. 14 yrs. (2) *Eleanor S.*, ae. 11 yrs. (3) *George L.*, ae. 7 yrs. (4) *Jeremiah*, ae. 4 yrs.

BY 2d MARRIAGE.

422. X. HARRY,[7] (1007) b. April 6, 1830. He m. 1849, Mary Hayes, who was b. Dec. 1830. Res. Washington Co., Ind., P. O. Saltilloville.

423. XI. SALLY,[7] b. May 17, 1833, m. 1853, —— Moneyhan, a merchant. Res. Washington Co., Ind., Saltilloville P. O. Chil.—

(1) *Sarah E.* (2) *Nancy J.* (3) *T. I.* (4) *John R.*

424. XII. WILLIAM,[7] b. Aug. 28, 1836, d. 1838, ae. 2 yrs.

CHILDREN OF EZRA WALKER,[6] [165] OF ATTLEBORO'.

425. I. MARTHA BLANDING,[7] b. Oct. 4, 1807, d. March 30, 1854. She m. Oct. 24, 1831, Joshua H. Work, of Providence, R. I., son of John and Elizabeth, b. Jan. 17, 1809, in Newburyport. He is a merchant tailor, in P. She was m. Cong. ch. in Attleboro', at the time of her marriage, after which, he became interested in the subject of religion, through her faithfulness, in a great degree. He was one of the founders, and is Deacon of the 4th Cong. ch. in P.

(1) *Ezra Walker*, b. Sept. 4, 1832. (2) *Elizabeth H.*, b. Aug. 24, '35, d. July 8, 1838. (3) *Wm. Chas.*, b. May 7, '37, still-born. (4) *Joshua H.*, b. March 16, '38, d. June 29. (5) *Caroline E.*, b. Feb. 1, '41, is m. Cong. ch. (6) *Harriet F.*, b. Aug. 24, '42, d. Sept. 17. (7) *Martha B.*, b. Jan. 5, '44, d. Aug. 3. (8) *Willis W.*, b. Nov. 28, '47. (9) *Emma J. F.*, b. June 16, 1850.

426. II. EZRA C.,[7] b. Feb. 27, 1809, d. Aug. 21, 1810.

427. III. CAROLINE,[7] b. 1810 or '11. She m. Aug. 1836, John Work, brother of Joshua N., and d. very suddenly, and under very afflicting circumstances, March 24, 1837, in 27th yr. Her husband was in Mobile. The day before her death she did her usual work. At 5 o'clock she became ill, and in about 14 hours died, after premature child-birth, (not a living issue.) She had just taken a house in Prov., R. I., purchased furniture, and was expecting to enter it in a week. She was m. Cong. ch. in Attleboro', and a devoted christian.

428. IV. EUNICE CLINTON,[7] b. Feb. 25, 1813. Res. Attleboro', unm.

BY 2d MARRIAGE.

429. V. HARRIET,[7] b. May 6, 1821, m. Sept. 1844, Jas. Hodges, of Providence, R. I., a wholesale dealer in carpets. She is m. Cong. ch. Chil.—

(1) *Raymond Galen*, b. Jan. 5, 1847. (2) *Mary E.*, b. Jan. 29, '49. (3) *Wm. R.*, b. April 5, '52.

430. VI. MARIETTA BLACKINTON,[7] b. Nov. 27, 1824, m. Oct. 6, 1846, John Bayley of No. Providence. He is a painter and glacier. Chil.—

(1) *Clara Burt*, b. Feb. 21, 1849, d. 1857. (2) *Edward E.*, b. Feb. 2, 1851, d. July 8, 1852. (3) *Mary E.*, b. Jan. 24, '53.

431. VII. ANN EMELINE,[7] b. Jan. 1, 1826, m. May 10, 1848, Wm. Henry Robinson, of Attleboro'. She is m. ch. in West Attleboro'. He is a manufacturer of jewelry, in A., and has been very successful in business. Chil.—

(1) *Annie Eliza*, b. Aug. 13, 1850. (2) *Mary Emma*, b. June 10, 1854.

432. VIII. ARDELIA CEMANTHIA,[7] b. Nov. 2, 1828, unm.

433. IX. ELLEN MARIA,[7] b. Nov. 22, 1831, m. May 20, 1856, Chas. Philips, of Attleboro', a jeweler. Res. So. A.

434. X. WILLIAM HENRY,[7] b. Feb. 21, 1834, m. June 25, 1857, Fannie M. Blake, of Attleboro'. He is a jeweler in So. A.

435. XI. FRANK AUGUSTINE,[7] b. May, 1840.

CHIL. OF SAMUEL WALKER,[6] [169] OF LANGDON, N. H.

436. I. BETSEY,[7] b. Nov. 10, 1786, m. Randall Evans, and had 9 chil. May, 1811—Dec. 1823. Res. Rockingham, Vt. Chil.—

(1) *Jane*. (2) *Mary Ann*. (3) *Charles*. (4) *Martha*. (5) *Alden*. (6) *Betsey*. (7) *Mahala*. (8) *Randall*. (9) *Harvey*.

437. II. SARAH,[7] b. July 12, 1789, d. unm. Nov. 28, 1836.

438. III. SAMUEL,[7] (1010) b. Nov. 11, 1791. He m. March 26, 1815, Mercy, dau. of George Smith, b. June 22, 1791, and d. March 14, 1837. He has been a farmer in Grafton, Vt. since 1817: and has held the town offices of Constable, Select-man, Overseer of the

poor, Lister, and had 7 chil. He m. 2d, Nov. 1, 1837, Ulyssa Briggs, dau. of Allen, of Manchester, Vt.

439. IV. ALDEN,[7] (1017) b. Dec. 1, 1793, d. Jan. 1858. He m. Nov. 24, 1829, Susan, dau. of John Grimes, Esq., of Deering, N. H., b. March 4, 1803, in D., and d. Oct. 31, 1846. He served in the War of 1812, was a merchant and cotton manufacturer at Hillsboro' Bridge, N.H., and for several yrs. Deputy Sheriff. He m. 2d, Sept. 14, 1848, Elizabeth B., dau. of John Fisk, of New Hampton, N.H. She d. June 6, 1850. He m. 3d, May 4, 1852, Mrs. Abigail (Stevens) McKean, dau. of Wadleigh Stevens of Warner, N. H. They rem. to Grafton, Vt., May, 1855. He has 5 chil.

440. V. ANNA,[7] b. March 9, 1805, m. April 4, 1827, Capt. Russell King, of Charlestown, N.H., a farmer. Res. Haverhill, N.H. Chil. Jan. 1828—Feb. 1848.

(1) *Samuel R.*, d. y. (2) *Herbert D.*, d. y. (3) *Samuel D.* (4) *Hiram H.*, d. y. (5) *Henry F.* (6) *Alden Walker*, d. y. (7) *Sally Ann*, d. y. (8) *Charles R.* (9) *Ann Elizabeth.*

CHIL OF WALTER WALKER,[6] [171] OF LANGDON, N. H.

441. I. LEONARD,[7] (1022) b. Nov. 12, 1802, m. Feb. 1827, Cyrene Ames, of Orford, N. H., who d. Nov. 4, 1853, in Brunswick, Vt., a m. Meth. ch. He is a farmer, and was Representative to the State Legislature from Maidstone, Vt., in 1842–3. Res. Berlin, Wis., and has 4 chil.

442. II. JOHN,[7] b. June 27, 1804, d. in Langdon, N. H., Nov. 30, 1805.

443. III. JOHN CURTIS,[7] (1026) b. Sept. 27, 1806, m. Nov. 29, 1831, Mary M. Lovejoy, of Norway, Me., who was b. Dec. 3, 1810, and is m. Meth. ch. He was Select-man in Brunswick, Vt., 1832, afterward resided in Manchester, N. H., was engineer in steam saw mill, and rem. to Saxeville, Waushara Co., Wis., Oct. 1858. He has had 10 chil.

444. IV. ELIZA A.,[7] b. Aug. 19, 1808, d. March 12, 1812, in Langdon, N. H.

445. V. ESTHER L.,[7] b. Sept. 6, 1810, m. Feb. 11, 1836, in Maidstone, Vt., Thomas A. Twitchel, who was b. in Unity, N. H., April 13, 1810. He has been a woolen manufacturer, in Newport,

N. H., was Town Clerk, 1859, and is Justice of the Peace. Both are m. Meth. ch. He is class leader. Chil.—

(1) *Hamilton*, b. July 6, 1840, in Newport, N. H., d. Feb. 25, 1841.

(2) *Martha A.*, b. July 10, '42, in Newport, N. H., is m. of ch.

446. VI. ELEAZER L.[7] b. Dec. 23, 1812, d. July 6, 1815, in Langdon, N. H.

447. VII. URANIA E.,[7] b. Dec. 31, 1819. She m. in Maidstone, Vt., March 31, 1841, Andrew J. Peck, of Unity, N. H., b. Feb. 18, 1816, d. June 6, 1856. Farmer and m. Meth. ch. Res. Keene, N. H. She rem. to Newport, N. H., 1860. Chil.—

(1) *Philander H.*, b. Jan. 6, 1842, in Piermont, N. H. (2) *Mary L.*, b. Dec. 6, '43, in Maidstone, Vt. (3) *Horace F.*, b. Dec. 19, '47, in Newport, N. H.

CHILDREN OF CAPT. SIMEON WALKER,[6] [178] OF SEEKONK.

448. I. SIMEON IDE,[7] b. Sept. 13, 1811, d. Dec. 23, 1843, in Seekonk. A machinist, and unm.

449. II. CATHARINE,[7] b. Feb. 5, 1813. Res. Pawtucket, unm.

450. III. STEPHEN,[7] b. July, 1814, d. Oct. 10, 1844, unm.

451. IV. ANN ELIZA,[7] b. Oct. 16, 1815. Res. Seekonk, unm.

452. V. NANCY,[7] b. Oct. 16, 1815, m. Daniel Cole of Rehoboth, pub. July 3, 1848. Res. R., and have no chil.

453. VI. JOHN,[7] b. Sept. 22, 1817. Res. Seekonk, unm.

454. VII. EPHRAIM,[7] (1036) b. July 10, 1819, m. April 4, 1852, Susan Briggs, dau. of Geo. A. and Lydia. Res. Seekonk. A worthy man, and has 4 chil.

455. VIII. JAMES MUNROE,[7] b. Dec. 16, 1820. Res. Seekonk, unm.

456. IX. NELSON,[7] (1040) b. July 29, 1822, m. Ardelia Dean, of Taunton. Res. Providence, R.I. A moulder. He has 1 son.

457. X. GILBERT FRANCIS,[7] b. July 3, 1824. Res. Seekonk, unm.

CHILDREN OF JOEL WALKER,[6] [179] OF SEEKONK.

458. I. SARAH A.[7] b. Aug. 23, 1810, m. Harrison Wilmarth, pub. April 13, 1834. Res. Attleboro'. No chil. He was a trader, then an overseer, now a manufacturer.

459. II. ORINDA,[7] b. Feb. 5, 1813. Res. Pawtucket, unm.

460. III. JERUSHA,[7] b. Oct. 5, 1814. Res. Pawtucket, unm.

461. IV. HANNAH,[7] b. April 28, 1816, m. about 1844, Albert Coma. Res. Pawtucket. He is a cabinet maker, in California, (1854.) Chil.—

(1) *Charles*, b. about 1845. (2) *Frank*, b. about 1847.

462. V. SUSAN,[7] b. May 19, 1817, m. about 1840, Edward P. Davis. Res. Smithfield, R. I. Chil.—

(1) *Lamira*, b. about 1846. (2) *Herbert*.

463. VI. EUNICE,[7] b. Nov. 1, 1818, m. 1846, Arnold Moffat. Res. Smithfield, R. I.

464. VII. LEPHA,[7] b. March 5, 1821. Res. Pawtucket, unm.

CHILDREN OF STEPHEN WALKER,[6] [180] OF SEEKONK.

465. I. LUCY PIERCE,[7] b. Dec. 29, 1809. Res. Providence, and unm.

466. II. EMELINE REBECCA,[7] b. July 1, 1812. Res. Pawtucket, unm.

467. III. CHARLOTTE FRANCES,[7] b. June 28, 1814, d. April 20, 1828.

CHIL. OF EBENEZER WALKER,[6] [182] OF PAWTUCKET, R.I.

468. I. HENRY.[7] Res. Pawtucket, unm. He is a sash and blind manufacturer.

469. II. WILLIAM CARPENTER,[7] b. 1832, d. June 18, 1834.

470. III. FREDERICK CARPENTER,[7] b. 1837, d. Feb. 27, 1838, ae. 9 mos.

CHIL. OF BENJAMIN WALKER,[6] [187] OF ASHFORD CT.

471. I. DEBORAH,[7] b. Jan. 24, 1788, m. 1810, Alpheus Rogers, of Franklin (?) Res. Montville, Ct., (near Norwich.) They had—

(1) *Sarah*, b. Feb. 1. 1811, m. James Hoyt, of Norwich, Ct., and is dec'd.

472. II. BETSEY NOTT,[7] b. April 29, 1790, m. Jan. 1, 1813, Levi Bartram, who was b. in Reading, Ct., and d. May 12, 1857, in his 69th yr. Res. Unionville in Madison, Lake Co., O. He rem. to Madison, O., with his parents in 1810, and was farmer and shoemaker. She was truly a help-meet. Being a weaver, her industry united with his, raised them from poverty, to a condition of competence and comfort. "She looked well to the ways of her household," not only in regard to earthly comfort, but to the character, and religious training of her children. Both were active and exemplary members of the Meth. Epis. ch. and all their chil. except the youngest. Chil.—

(1) *Phebe Ann*, b. Feb. 19, 1814, m. Sept. 22, 1834, J. W. Shaw, both of Madison, O., now in Cal. (2) *Benj'n Walker*, b. Feb. 16, '16. d. July 20, 1817. (3) *Ulilly M.*, b. Feb. 17, '18, m. July 2, 1841, Eli, son of Rev. Jason Olds, both of M. (4) *Laura S.*, b. April 28, '20. Res. U., unm. (5) *Daniel C.*, b. Nov. 6, '22, m. Oct. 1, 1848, Irene Moulton, of Hartsgrove. (6) *Cortis Levi*, b. Jan. 22, 1828.

473. III. SON,[7] d. in a few days.

CHIL. OF EBENEZER WALKER,[6] [189] OF WEST BECKET.

474. I. ELIZABETH,[7] b. 1786 or 7, m. Joshua Wright, and d. ae. about 25 yrs.

475. II. NANCY,[7] d. Sept. 1833, ae. about 52; she m. Clemence Hart, who is dec'd. Res. Parma, N.Y. They had 10 chil.

476. III. LODICE,[7] b. 1791, m. Nathan Putnam. He was a cooper, rem. from Becket to Greece, N.Y., where he d. She res. in Monroe, Mich., and has 8 chil.

477. IV. EBENEZER,[7] (1041) b. Dec. 29, 1793, m. Betsey Bradley, dau. of Jesse, and b. Feb. 26, 1793. He is a farmer in Gates, N.Y., has 8 chil., and they are all m. ch.

478. V. JOHN,[7] (1049) b. Nov. 18, 1795, m. 1823, Betsey Sprague. He is a farmer, and has 4 chil. Res. Bergen, N.Y.

479. VI. ANNA,[7] m. Joshua Kibbe, of Otis. Res. Ohio.

480. VII. ELIJAH,[7] (1053) b. Oct. 17, 1800. He m. Ruth Putnam, who was b. 1791, and d. 1835. He m. 2d, March 4, 1837, Lucy ——, who was b. Dec. 9, 1797. He is a farmer in Orwell, Bradford Co., Pa., and has 3 chil. He and his wives are m. ch.

481. VIII. LORANIA,[7] or Lura, m. Otis Harris, of Becket. Res. Gates, N.Y. They had 2 chil. and d. about 1840.

482. IX. DIADAMA,[7] m. Allan Benton, of Otis, and d. Feb. 1, 1857. Res. Litchfield, Loraine Co., O. They have 6 chil.

CHILDREN OF JAMES WALKER,[6] [190] OF BECKET.

483. I. ALMIRA,[7] b. 1788, twin, m. Michael Paul. They settled in Volney, N.Y., and had chil.

484. II. PERSIS,[7] b. March 7, 1788, d. 1853, in Byron, N.Y. She m. Anson Norton, who d. about 1839, leaving a large estate. Res. B. They had 7 sons—

(1) *Alonzo.* (2) *Medad*, dec'd. (3) *Moses.* (4) *Daniel.* (5) *Benjamin.* (6) *Theoren*, dec'd. (7) *Franklin.*

These are farmers, and reside in Alabama, N.Y., except Alonzo, who has gone West.

485. III. JAMES HARVEY,[7] (1056) b. March 30, 1790, m. Feb. 14, 1816, Clara Norton, who was b. Jan. 1, 1787, and d. Feb. 19, 1828. He m. 2d, Elizabeth Kimber, March 14, 1828, (1829?) who was b. Dec. 1, 1802. She united with Bap. ch. in 14th yr. He enlisted in the War of 1812 for 1 yr., and was stationed on Staten Island. He held the rank of 2d and 1st orderly sergeant. Serving his time, he left Amenia in 1814, which was his residence then, and bought a tract of land in Byron, N.Y. He is Deacon of the Bap. ch. He has held the offices of sergeant, ensign and lieutenant in the militia. Res. Sweden, Monroe Co., N.Y. He has 8 chil.

486. IV. RUTH,[7] b. 1792, d. March, 1828. She m. in Byron, N.Y., Rufus King, a farmer, who is dec'd. Res. B. 2 chil.—

(1) *Albert*, b. about 1825. (2) *Dau.*, b. about May, 1827.

487. V. EPHRAIM,[7] d. ae. 2 yrs.

488. VI. MATILDA,[7] b. 1795, d. about 1845. She m. Josiah

Smith, in Volney, N.Y. Res. V. He is a farmer. She is m. Bap. ch., and left 3 chil.

489. VII. EPHRAIM,[7] (1064) b. July 25, 1798, d. April 10, 1859, ae. 61 yrs., m. June 3, 1828, Louisa Rice, of Conway, dau. of Dea. Benj., b. Nov. 23, 1806, and d. Nov. 10, 1844. She and 4 chil., d. with canker rash, in a period of 3 weeks. He m. 2d, Nov. 6, 1845, Emily Carter, dau. of Chandler, b. Nov. 23, 1812, and had 3 chil. He was a farmer in West Becket; m. Bap. ch. and esteemed for his probity and moral worth. He had 9 chil.

CHIL. OF AMASA WALKER,[6] [191] OF BECKET AND BYRON, N.Y.

490. I. ACHSAH,[7] b. April 7, 1789, m. 1804, Simeon Hosmer. He is a farmer in Byron, N. Y.

(1) *Lucretia*, b. 1816, m. Minor Bradley. No chil. (2) *Martha*, b. '18, m. —— Porter. No chil. (3) *Simeon*, b. '20, m. Porter. 2 sons and 2 daus. (4) *Rosina*, b. '24, unm. (5) *Cyrus*, b. '26, m. —— Edson. 2 ch.

491. II. AMASA,[7] (1072) b. April 14, 1791, m. March 11, 1813, Lydia Dwight, dau. of Samuel, of Belchertown. He m. 2d, Lydia, dau. of Elijah Nichols, of Belchertown. Res. Byron, N. Y. Farmer. Both m. Pres. ch. Has 7 chil.

492. III. JOSEPH,[7] (1079) b. 1793, d. Oct. 1821. He m. —— Fenn, of Byron, N. Y., and had 4 chil.

493. IV. CHLOE,[7] b. 1795, d. 1811.

494. V. MARTHA,[7] } b. Oct. 1797, d. ae. 4 yrs.

494.[1] VI. MARY,[7] } b. Oct. 1797, d. Oct. 16, 1849, ae. 52 yrs. She m. Samuel Hosmer, who d. March 28, 1845, ae. 57 yrs. Chil.—

(1) *Mary*, b. 1817, m. 1842, Wm. Chase. (2) *Louisa*, b. '19, m. 1840, Alpheus Godfrey. 5 chil. (3) *Dau.*, d. y. (4) *Son*, d. y.

495. VII. CYRUS,[7] (1083) b. 1799, m. Dec. 1822, Anna Hulett, of Byron, N. Y. He is a farmer in B. Both m. Pres. ch. and have had 5 chil.

496. VIII. SIDNEY,[7] (1088) b. 1801, m. Oct. 1823, Harriet Walton, of Byron, N. Y. Res. B.; a farmer and has 8 chil.

497. IX. CYRENIUS,[7] (1096) b. 1804, m. Dec. 20, 1832, Julia Chase, of Byron, N. Y. Res. in B. Farmer, and has had 5 chil.

498. X. SARDIS,[7] (1101) b. 1806, d. April 17, 1853, ae. 46. He m. Dec. 1830, Ostra Goodrich, of Byron, N. Y., and had 4 chil.

499. XI. HARRIET,[7] b. Dec. 1808, m. Oct. 1828, William Holt, of Byron, N. Y. He is a farmer in B. Both m. Bap. ch. and have 4 chil.

(1) *Walter*, b. 1830, m. Rebecca Benton. 2 chil. (2) *Louisa*, b. '32, m. —— Curtis. 1 child. (3) *Mary*, b. '33, m. Henry Cady. 3 chil. (4) *George*, b. '36.

500. XII. HANNAH,[7] b. Jan. 7, 1814, m. Nov. 1833, Charles Luce, of Byron, N. Y. Res. Sweden, Monroe Co. He is a farmer, and has 6 chil.

CHILDREN OF SAMUEL WALKER,[6] [196] OF JESSUP, PENN.

501. I. LYDIA,[7] b. Sept. 30, 1804, d. young.

502. II. LUCIUS,[7] b. May 10, 1806, d. Sept. 1850. Res. Jessup, Penn. When a boy, he was thrown from a horse and his skull was fractured. Several pieces were taken out and silver inserted. His mind was impaired. He roved about and d. away from home.

503. III. TRUMAN,[7] (1105) b. Nov. 18, 1807. He m. July 14, 1833, Diadamia Applebee. Res. Jessup, Penn. Meth. and farmer. Chil.—

504. IV. HARMONY,[7] b. Sept. 3, 1809. Res. Windsor, Broome Co., N. Y. Farmer.

505. V. EMILY L.,[7] b. July 31, 1811. She m. Dec. 31, 1837, Joseph Harris, who was b. in Colchester, Ct., March 15, 1806, and d. in Vestal, N. Y., Sept. 19, 1849. He was a farmer, and both m. Meth. ch. Res. Windsor, Broome Co., N. Y. Chil.—

(1) *Samuel W.*, b. March 8, 1839, in Rush Pa., a farmer. (2) *Mary L.*, b. Aug. 11, 1841, m. Aug. 11, 1858, Bennett L. Mayo, who was b. Feb. 5, 1837, in Windsor, Broome Co., N. Y. (3) *Daniel C.*, b. Feb. 1, 1844, in Vestal, N. Y., and d. July 9, 1851. (4) *Truman J.*, b. May 15, '46, in V. (5) *Maria Louisa*, b. Jan. 24, '49, in V., d. June 29, '51.

506. VI. ANNA,[7] b. June 7, 1813, m. April 5, 1838, James Young, who was b. Aug. 12, 1813. Res. Jessup, Penn., a farmer. Chil.—

(1) *Emeline Lovina*, b. Feb. 4, 1839.

(2) *Elijah W.*, b. Sept. 1, '40.

(3) *Ann Eliza*, b. May 16, '42.

By 2d Marriage.

507. VII. Willis M.,[7] (1107) b. June 16, 1826, m. March 11, 1851, Keziah Lyman. He is a farmer and has 2 chil. Res. Springville, Pa.

508. VIII. Ephraim,[7] b. July 5, 1827, d. Oct. 3, 1851.

509. IX. Sarah,[7] b. Jan. 8, 1830. Res. Jessup, Pa., unm.

510. X. Lydia B.,[7] b. Sept. 18, 1832. Res. Jessup, Penn., unm.

511. XI. Acklby,[7] b. Jan. 12, 1840. Res. Jessup, unm.

Children of TIMOTHY WALKER,[6] [197] of Ashford, Ct.

512. I. John Milton,[7] (1109) b. May 2, 1804, m. Caroline Ashley, of Hampton, Ct. He is a farmer in Westford, Ct., a Cong. and has 1 son.

513. II. Lyman,[7] b. Nov. 5, 1805, d. Sept. 30, 1828.

514. III. Harvey,[7] (1110) b. Feb. 2, 1808, d. Feb. or March, 1860. He m. May 16, 1833, Julia Ann White, who was b. April 16, 1816. He was engaged in an extensive shoe manufacturing and sale business, in Union, (Mashapang,) Ct., Fiskdale, Mass., Toronto, Canada, and Acton, C. W. He was a victim in the disease known as malignant pustule. On Saturday week, he cut from his face, while shaving, a small pimple; on Monday his face began to swell; and soon his head, neck and breast were swollen to an enormous size. No medical skill could give him relief, and he died on the Sunday following, or in less than a week. He was a Cong. and had 5 chil.

515. IV. Levi,[7] (1115) b. March 11, 1810, m. Laura Pearl, of Willington, Ct., who d. in Ill. He m. 2d, Ludocia Sebastian, is a blacksmith and has 3 chil. Res. Washington, Tazewell Co., Ill.

516. V. Minerva,[7] b. July 21, 1812, m. Willard Fuller, of Willington, Ct. He is a farmer in W. Both Bap. Chil.—

(1) *Janette*, m. Marvin K. Paul. Res. Geneseo, Ill. (2) *Harriet*. (3) *Edward E.*

517. VI. Hartley,[7] b. Dec. 22, 1814. Res. Union, Ct., unm.

518. VII. PAULINA,[7] b. Jan. 17, 1817, d. 1819.

519. VIII. TIMOTHY,[7] b. Sept. 25, 1819, is a farmer and unm.

520. IX. MILO,[7] b. Oct. 25, 1821, is a farmer, unm. He resides on the old homestead, in Ashford, Ct.

521. X. CELIA,[7] b. Sept. 15, 1823, d. June 2, 1856.

CHIL. OF PHILIP WALKER,[6] [213] OF ROXBURY, N. Y.

522. I. PHILIP,[7] (1118) b. March 1, 1776, m. Hannah Caswell, and had 5 chil. Res. Roxbury, N. Y. He was a lawyer many yrs., but has retired from active duties. Living 1854, with 2d wife.

523. II. SULLIVAN,[7] (1123) b. Sept. 20, 1777, (1778, Fam. Rec.) and d. 1824. He m. Feb. 23, 1800, Nabby Knapp, of Woodstock, Ct., who was b. —— 1, 1781, and d. Oct. 10, 1842. Both m. Meth. ch. He was a stone mason and carpenter. About 1821, he rem. from Roxbury, N. Y., to Westchester, Butler Co., Ohio, where he died. He had 6 chil.

524. III. HANNAH,[7] b. Aug. 13, 1779, d. July 10, 1831. She m. Nov. 10, 1801, Jacob Delong, a carpenter, who d. 1848. Res. Dryden, N. Y. They had 6 chil.

525. IV. AMY,[7] b. Oct. 2, 1781, m. Dec. 31, 1801, Daniel Voorhis, a farmer, who d. Nov. 18, 1846. They rem. to Caroline, (Motts Corner,) N. Y. Chil.—

(1) *Anna*, b. 1807, m. Peter Dennis, March, 1827. (2) *Julia A.*, b. 1817, m. Wm. Personius, 1835. (3) *Harriet*, b. 1821, m. Jacob D. Besemer, 1841. Four others d. y.

526. V. JOSEPH,[7] b. March 22, 1784, was a sailor, left home about 1815, and has not been heard from since.

527. VI. THOMPSON,[7] (1129) b. June 11, 1786, d. May 12. 1842, in Roxbury, N. Y. He m. 1806, Mary Lynch, dau. of Daniel, of Roxbury, N. Y., b. Sept. 10, 1785, and lives in Roxbury, (1856.) He was a carpenter, and had 4 chil.

528. VII. ABIGAIL,[7] b. Sept. 10, 1788, m. Simeon Dolph. They settled near Lake Champlain, and had 3 chil. She is dec'd.

CHIL. OF STEPHEN WALKER,[6] [215] OF COVENTRY, R. I.

529. I. LYDIA,[7] d. in infancy.

530. II. AMBROSE,[7] d. in infancy.

531. III. ANNA,[7] b. Dec. 27, 1792. She m. Dec. 24, 1812, Wm. Matthewson. Both m. Meth ch. Res. Foster, R. I., and had 11 chil., Dec. 1813—Sept. 2, 1830. These were b. in Foster, R. I. and are all married and all living.

532. IV. EZEKIEL,[7] (1133) b. Feb. 10, 1795, in West Greenwich, R. I. He m. Sept. 10, 1817, Lucy Scott, dau. of Joseph, b. Nov. 25, 1794, and d. Feb. 22, 1837, in Coventry, R. I. He m. 2d, Eunice Rouse, May 8, 1837, dau. of Jeremiah. He is a carpenter and farmer in Coventry, R. I., and has had 14 chil. He held the commission of Captain from the age of 23 to 28. He is m. ch. since 1838, and much esteemed for moral worth.

533. V. LYDIA,[7] b. March 5, 1797, d. Sept. 22, 1825. She m. Martin Kelley, a farmer in Coventry. No chil.

534. VI. DAUGHTER,[7] d. not named.

535. VII. STEPHEN,[7] (1147) b. Jan. 2, 1802, d. Feb. 16, 1836, (1837?) He m. Celinda Cornell, dau. of Capt. Benj'n. Res. in Phœnix Village, Warwick, R. I. He had 7 chil.

536. VIII. AMBROSE,[7] b. Jan. 4, 1804, is unm., in Coventry.

537. IX. DAUGHTER,[7] d. not named.

538. X. NATHAN,[7] (1154) b. Nov. 14, 1808, m. Polly Wells, b. Feb. 15, 1809, and d. July 19, 1847. Res. Coventry. He is a carpenter, and has 8 chil.

539. XI. SON,[7] d. not named.

CHIL. OF STUKELEY WALKER,[6] [219] OF COVENTRY, R. I.

540. I. ELECTA,[7] b. Oct. 19, 1801, d. Aug. 1828. She m. April, 1825, —— Wolverton, a carpenter, and had 1 child—

(1) *Jane*, b. March 15, 1826, m. —— Loveless, a farmer. Res. Penn.

541. II. PHEBE,[7] b. Jan. 12, 1803, d. April, 1856. She m. April, 1832, —— Emerson. He was an Ensign in the War of 1812,

under Gen. Scott, and since has held the commission of Colonel. He is a wealthy farmer in Conquest, Cayuga Co., N. Y. Child—

(1) *Lewis*, b. Dec. 28, 1832, m. Feb. 15, 1854, Jane Eliza Pratt, and has 2 chil.

542. III. ALMON,[7] (1162) b. Aug. 12, 1804, in Vt. He m. Dec. 17, 1828, Emeline Baylies, who was b. Aug. 14, 1810. He is a house painter, Deacon of Bap. ch., has held various town offices, and has 2 chil. Res. Weedsport, N. Y.

543. IV. SYDNEY S.,[7] (1164) b. March 22, 1806, d. Dec. 1846. He m. Sept. 10, 1835, Betsey Warren. He was a very industrious farmer, and "worked himself to death." He had 4 chil.

544. V. LYDIA S.,[7] b. March 24, 1808. She m. 1829, Daniel Rooker, a farmer. She is remarkable for patience, skill and success in training children. She has adopted 4, and never had occasion to use the rod in any case. Chil.—

(1) *Phebe P.*, b. 1830. (2) *Joseph L.*, b. '33. (3) *Sarah*, b. '38.

545. VI. JANE,[7] b. Feb. 15, 1810, d. April, 1823.

546. VII. JOSEPH,[7] (1168) b. Sept. 16, 1811. He m. Jan. 11, 1844, (Feb. 1836,) Abigail Witham, and has 4 chil. He is class leader in Meth. ch. and has held various town offices. Res. Penn.

547. VIII. SARAH,[7] b. Jan. 17, 1814, d. May, 1823.

547.[1] IX. ANNA,[7] b. Sept. 9, 1816, m. —— Ames, and has 6 chil. He is a miller. Res. Penn.

548. X. MARY ANN,[7] b. Nov. 24, 1819, m. Nathan Loveless. He is a farmer, and has 3 chil. Both m. ch. Res. Penn.

549. XI. CHILD,[7] d. young.

550. XII. CHILD,[7] d. young.

CHILDREN OF CALEB WALKER,[6] [221] OF ——.

551. I. CALEB,[7]
552. II. JOSEPH,[7]
} Res. Berlin, N. Y., writes a relative. But no trace of them has been found there.

CHIL. OF NATHANIEL WALKER,[6] [226] OF PAWTUCKET, R.I.

553. I. SUSAN,[7] b. March 21, 1784, m. Benj. Bentley Pierce, who was b. in East Greenwich, R.I., 1786, and d. 1839. He was a tan-

ner and currier, in Pawtucket, also a Deacon of the 1st Bap. ch. in P. She res. in Newark, N. J. Chil.—

(1) *Moses*, b. July 3, 1808, m. Nov. 24, '31, Harriet G. Hathaway, of Fall River, dau. of Simmons, and b. April 13, 1813. He is one of the Norwich Bleaching and Calendering Co., Norwich, Ct., has been Rep. from N. to the State Legislature 1 yr., and Trustee of the State Reform School 2 yrs. His chil. are—1, Edwin M., b. April 22, 1832. 2, Harriet A., b. April 10, '36. 3, Sarah Walker, b. Dec. 3, '38. 4, Geo. Lyndon, b. March 8, '41, d. Sept. 7, '52. 5, Henry A., b. July 2, '45. d. Jan. 1, '46. 6, Emily G., b. Dec. 4, '47.

(2) *George*, b. April 27, 1810, m. Harriet N. Brown, of Concord, dau. of Wm. and Beulah M. Both are m. Cong. ch. Res. Norwich, Ct. Chil.—1, George F., b. 1835, d. 1838. 2, Harriet A., b. 1837. 3, Wm. B., b. 1838.

(3) *Lyndon W.*, b. July 25, 1812, d. at Valparaiso, unm. 1840.

(4) *Sarah W.*, b. July 25, 1815, d. 1835.

(5) *William B.*, b. Aug. 12, 1818, m. Catharine Booth, of Norwich, and has 1 dau. Susan. Res. Greenfield, Ct.

(6) *Henry Niles*, b. Oct. 19, 1820, in Pawtucket, R. I., m. April 18, '54, Nannie Heywood Shepard, dau. of Abram and Eleanor, of Matagorda, Texas, and b. near Selma, Ala., March 6, '30. They have AbrahamW., b. May 28, '55. He was fitted for Coll. in P. High School, entered the Sophomore class of Brown University, in '39, and was graduated in '42. His Theological studies were chiefly under the direction of Dr. Francis Vinton, then of Newport, and Rev. Geo. W. Hathaway, then of Warren, R. I. In the Fall of '46, he went to Florida, thence to Texas in '48; was ord. Deacon of the Epis. church at Matagorda, April 23, '48, admitted to the priesthood Jan. 3, '49. He began his ministry in Washington Co., where he founded the churches of St. Peter, Brenham, and St. Paul, Washington. He became Rector of Christ church, Matagorda, in June, '52, and in June, '54, he took charge temporarily of the church of the Holy Trinity in New Orleans. He is now Rector of St. Paul's Parish, Rahway, N. J., 1855.

(7) *Susan E.*, b. Dec. 15, 1823, resides in Newark, N. J., unm.

(8) *Mary G.*, b. March 9, 1826, m. Wm. H. Pierce, of Pawtucket. Res. Newark. Chil.—1, Jennie Howitt, b. Jan. 7, '52. 2, Benj. B., b. Oct. 25, '53. 3, Mary Walker, b. June 9, '56, d. Aug. '56.

554. II. SAMUEL,[7] b. April 24, 1786, d. Feb. 9, 1825, m. Lucina Bump, of Pawtucket. No chil.

555. III. WILLIAM WHITFORD,[7] (1172) b. March 21, 1789. He m. Mrs. Sarah (Piper) Brown, in Waltham. He is a machinist, in Pawtucket, and has had 4 chil.

556. IV. NATHANIEL,[7] b. Nov. 29, 1791, d. Dec. 9, 1813, unm.

557. V. NICHOLAS,[7] d. in infancy.

558. VI. LYNDON,[7] b. Aug. 16, 1795, d. July 2, 1810.

559. VII. ELIZA[7] b. April 16, 1799. Res. Pawtucket, R. I., unm.

CHIL. OF DAVID WALKER,[6] [229] OF PROVIDENCE, R. I.

560. I. FRANCES,[7] d. 1½ yrs. old.

561. II. FRANCES,[7] d. 14 yrs. of age.

562. III. SARAH SHEPARDSON,[7] b. 1797 or 8. Res. Providence, unm.

563. IV. LUCINA,[7] d. before 1854, unm.

564. V. HARRIET,[7] m. March 25, 1824, Rev. Edward Seagrave, of Providence, R. I. He was settled in Scituate, R. I., a Baptist clergyman, then in Western, N. Y., and was in Kansas, in 1856. She is m. Bap. ch. Chil.—

(1) *Mary*, m. Thomas Carpenter, of Rehoboth. (2) *Harriet*, m. Osborn Perry, of Rehoboth. (3) *Edward*. (4) *Anna*. (5) *David*. (6) *Joseph*. (7) *Child*, d. y.

CHIL. OF COL. BENJAMIN WALKER,[6] [231] OF BARRE, VT.

565. I. NANCY,[7] b. April 29, 1775, d. Dec. 12, 1858. She m. April 28, 1799, Capt. Allen Cole, of Rehoboth, a farmer, who d. June 14, 1855. Res. Seekonk. Chil.—

(1) *Benjamin Walker*, b. Feb. 9, 1800, d. unm. Aug. 27, '33. (Fam. Rec.) July 2, '32. (Ins.) (2) *Celinda*, b. April 18, '04. m. Jonathan Ide. Res. S. 5 chil. (3) *Allen*, b. Oct. 9, '06. d. April 23, '10. (4) *Nancy*, b. Aug. 27, '08. Res. S., unm. (5) *Betsey*, b. Jan. 7, '12. d. Aug. 27, '46. unm.

566. II. BENJAMIN,[7] (1176) b. Oct. 26, 1777, in Mendon, d. May 30, 1856. He m. March 26, 1799, Jemima Farwell, of Barre, Vt., dau. of Rev. William Farwell, a Universalist clergyman, b. in Charlestown, N. H., May 7, 1781, and d. Dec. 29, 1809. He m. 2d, Feb. 1811, Mrs. Mary Bigelow, of Dummerston, Vt., who d. 1817. He m. 3d, at St. Charles, Mo., April, 1822, Mrs. Abigail Farwell, who was b. April 27, 1790. He had 11 chil. He was Major in the Vt. militia, Town Clerk and Select-man in several towns, Justice of the Peace in St. Charles, Mo., Trustee of Pres. ch. in Alton, Ill., and lived the latter part of his life in Macomb, Ill.

567. III. PATIENCE,[7] b. Dec. 21, 1779, m. March 1, 1798, Lemuel Farwell, and had 8 chil. Res. Barre, Vt. Chil.—

(1) *William*, b. Sept. 10, 1799, m. Rebecca Davis, Dec. 1820, and d. May 22, 1829. They had 3 sons. Res. B.

(2) *Enos W.*, b. Oct. 15, 1800, m. Catharine Davis, '29. Res. B.

(3) *Cynthia*, b. March 12, 1804, m. David D. Wing, Dec. 30, '23, and has 4 chil. He has been Constable, Lister, Select-man, 12 yrs. and Representative.

(4) *Nancy*, b. May 1, 1807, m. 1825, Arthur Daggett, and has had 3 chil. Res. East Montpelier, Vt.

(5) *Lemuel*, b. Dec. 28, 1808, d. Oct. 11, '11.

(6) *Lemuel*, b. Dec. 11, 1812, m. Mandana Goldsbury, Sept. '41. Chil.—1, John. 2, Arthur. 3, Carlos. 4, Isabella C. 5, Joel. Res. Barre.

(7) *Patience*, b. Feb. 24, 1815, unm.

(8) *Caroline*, b. Nov. 1819, m. Ebenezer D. Stevens, Jan. '42, and has 3 chil. Res. E. M.

568. IV. ENOS,[7] (1187) b. Nov. 5, 1781, m. May 12, 1804, Hannah Nichols, of Barre, Vt., and b. in Mass., Aug. 13, 1779. They have had 8 chil. He commanded a detachment in the War of 1812, and was stationed at Swanton, Vt., 6 mos. He was then appointed 1st Lieut. in the regular service under General Hampton, for 1 yr. He removed from Vt., between 1816 and '19, to North Bangor, N. Y., where he now lives.

569. V. BETSEY,[7] b. in Grafton, Dec. 25, 1783, and d. Aug. 1786.

570. VI. DANIEL,[7] (1195) b. Aug. 22, 1786, in G., d. March 10, 1839. He m. Sept. 22, 1814, Maria Abbott, dau. of Abijah, of Barre, Vt., and had 8 chil. She d. April 20, 1846, m. Meth. ch. He rem. from B. to Penn., in 1828, and thence to Mich., in 1831. Settling in a dense wilderness, he endured many hardships incident to pioneer life. He was a farmer and brick-maker; Town clerk several yrs., and Town treasurer nearly all the time from his going to Mich., till his death. His character was without blemish, and for several yrs., he was a Universalist preacher.

571. VII. JOHN,[7] (1203) b. in G., Sept. 17, 1788, m. Sept. 16, 1810, Mary French, of Barre, Vt., who was b. in B., March 3, 1792. He is a farmer, in B.; has held the offices of Jail Commissioner 2 yrs., Justice of the Peace, about 15 yrs., and Select-man 5 yrs. He lived in Morristown, Vt., from March, 1825 to March, 1840, when he returned to B. He has had 10 chil.

572. VIII. BETSEY,[7] b. in G., July 14, 1790, m. Nov. 28, 1813, Alvan Carter, who was b. in Dudley, Mass., Sept. 1, 1780. He was cloth manufacturer till 1820, then Deputy Sheriff 14 yrs., High Sheriff 6 yrs., Member of the Convention to revise the State Constitution, Representative in the State Legislature 3 yrs., has been

Justice of the Peace, Lister 10 yrs., Town Clerk since 1841 to the present time, (1855,) and has been Post-master at So. Barre, since July 1, 1839. Chil.—

(1) *Emily*, b. Aug. 9, 1818, m. Clark Day, of B., a farmer, June 2, '41. Chil.—1, Gertrude, b. April 3, '43. 2, Martha Peck, b. March 23, '48. 3, Alvan Carter, b. Feb. 22, '45. 4, Wm. Pierce, b. Sept. 18, '52.

(2) *William Davis*, b. in B., Sept. 8, 1828. He is in Portland, Oregon, and is publisher of the Oregon Weekly Times.

573. IX. NATHANIEL R.,[7] b. in G., Jan. 1792, and was drowned in Barre, the last of Aug. 1793.

BY 2d MARRIAGE.

574. X. LUCY,[7] b. May 2, 1806, m. Oct. 16, 1832, Dennis Britain, who was b. in Barre, Vt. He is a farmer and Justice of the Peace. Res. So. Barre, Vt. No chil.

CHIL. OF CHA'S P. WALKER,[6] [232] OF SMITHFIELD, R. I.

575. I. ANNA,[7] b. in S., March 17, 1780, m. in S. ———

576. II. NATHAN,[7] (1063) b. July 28, 1782, m. Mrs. ——, and had no chil. He rem. to N. Y. State. Getting into some trouble, he left his wife, and went to New Orleans; thence to St. Louis, where he was killed by the caving in of a sand pit, about 1835.

CHILDREN OF RICHARD WALKER,[6] [234] OF REHOBOTH.

577. I. ESTHER,[7] b. May 22, 1784, m. June 25, 1821, Nath'l Ide, Jr., who d. about 1835. Res. Seekonk. No chil.

578. II. ABIGAIL E.,[7] b. June 9, 1786, d. unm., Sept. 30, 1838.

579. III. LEWIS,[7] (1213) b. Sept. 7, 1788, m. Dec. 6, (16 Seekonk Rec.) 1832, Sarah Angell Comstock, who was b. Nov. 29, 1808. They have had 8 chil. He was a blacksmith, now a farmer; holds a Justice's Commission, was Select-man 6 yrs. in succession, 1833, &c., and Rep. to Legislature, 1836, 7 and 8. He was formerly active in town affairs and is highly respected. Res. Seekonk.

580. IV. SARAH,[7] b. March 30, 1800, m. March 30, 1824, John Jefferson Bishop, of Seekonk, (See No. 320,) who d. July, 1849. Chil.—

(1) *Richard*, d. 2 yrs. old. (2) *Sarah*, d. in infancy. (3) *Sarah*, b. Oct. 23, 1828, m. 1850, Christopher Dexter. (See No. 331.) (4) *Eunice*, b. Dec.

23, 1831, m. 1851, Wm. Carpenter, of Fall River. Res. S. (5) *Abby*, b. July 18, 1834, m. 1853, James, son of Gen. Barnes, of Providence, R. I.

Chil. of JEDEDIAH WALKER,[6] [236] of Clarendon, Vt.

581. I. Nathan,[7] b. and d. 1784.

582. II. Sylvia,[7] b. Sept. 15, 1785, d. Oct. 22, 1819, m. ch.

583. III. Polly,[7] b. April 28, 1788, d. Nov. 7, 1803.

584. IV. Henry Goss,[7] (1221) b. May 20, 1790, d. Aug. 23, 1856. He m. Sept. 14, 1814, Sarah Steele, dau. of Eithel and Anna (Cushman,) of Rutland, Vt., b. in R. July 24, 1793, and d. Oct. 4, 1850, in W. A m. Pres. ch. He m. 2d, 1851, Mrs. Aurelia Beebe, of Wyoming. He commenced business as a saddler in Middlebury, Vt., but in 1817, removed to Middlebury, N. Y., now W. and was a merchant. In 1835, he rem. to Conneaut, Ohio, in 1846, to Milan, O., and in 1848, returned to W., where he d. He was for many yrs. Postmaster and Supervisor of W., and elder in the Pres. ch., from its organization until his decease. He had 4 chil.

585. V. Enos,[7] b. and d. 1791.

586. VI. Clarissa,[7] b. May 8, 1793, m. June 20, 1819, James Burleigh, of Bethany, N. Y. He was b. in Stratham, N. H., Feb. 3, 1783. He is a farmer in Covington, N. Y. She is m. Pres. ch. Chil.—

(1) *Sylvia W.*, b. Dec. 1, 1822, m. Sept. 17, '46, Hezekiah S. Dolph, of Clyde, N. Y. They rem. to Mich., where he d. Aug. 25, '56.

(2) *James Edward*, b. June 25, 1829, m. Sept. 21, '53, Elvira Bradley, of Middlebury, N. Y. He is a farmer, in C.

By 2d Marriage.

587. VII. Daniel W.,[7] (1225) b. Nov. 29, 1795, m. Oct. 27, 1834, Elmira Rathbun, at Lawrence, Pa., and has had 2 chil. Res. L.

588. VIII. Patience P.,[7] b. Dec. 29, 1796, d. July 18, 1824.

589. IX. Anna M.,[7] b. Aug. 3, 1798, d. Aug. 23, 1838, in York, N. Y. She m. Oct. 30, 1820, Elijah S. Rust, of Lanesboro'. She was m. Pres. ch. Res. Oberlin, O. Chil.—

(1) *Elijah B.* (2) *Daniel W.* (3) *George.* (4) *Asahel.* (5) *Ada Ann.* (6) *Mary W.* (7) *Emily S.* (8) *Jedediah.*

590. X. Olive Emily,[7] b. Nov. 24, 1800, m. Jan. 11, 1827, John Doty, of Covington, N. Y., a farmer. Both m. Pres. ch. Chil.—

(1) *George W.*, b. Oct. 14, 1828, in C., d. Oct. 15, '28. (2) *Emily Elizabeth*, b. Sept. 13, '33, d. Jan. 19, '39, in C. (3) *Mary W.*, b. Nov. 28, '35, m. Sept. 15, '52, John R. Page, of Bethany, N. Y., a farmer. (4) *John C.*, b. Sept. 9, '41.

591. XI. MARY,[7] b. Aug. 15, 1806, d. March 21, 1856. She m. Nov. 29, 1832, Chauncey Sprague, who was b. in Conn., Dec. 13, 1797. He is a farmer in Covington, N. Y. Both are m. Bap. ch., and also their dau. He is Deacon, and has held various town offices. Chil.—

(1) *Helen M.*, b. Oct. 24, 1833. (2) *Dau.*, b. June 19, '36, d. Nov. 22, '39. (3) *Henry W.*, b. April 12, '39.

592. XII. JEDEDIAH S.[7] (1227) b. Jan. 9, 1809, m. Jan. 20, 1833, Sophia M. Tillotson, of Lanesboro', and has had 5 chil. He is a farmer in Covington, N. Y. Both m. Bap. ch. He has held the office of Highway Commissioner and Assessor of the town, and for the last 11 yrs., has been Superintendent of the Poor of Wyoming Co.

CHILDREN OF LEWIS WALKER,[6] [237] OF ST. ALBANS, VT.

593. I. AMANDA,[7] b. Feb. 6, 1791, d. March 8, 1825. She m. July 7, 1812, Jonathan R. Danforth, son of Jonathan of St. Albans, Vt. He was an architect and master builder, and d. Feb. 5, 1847, ae. 57. Res. St. A. Chil.—

(1) *Mary*, b. March 11, 1813, d. April, '14. (2) *Mary*, b. Jan. 17, '15, m. March 31, '39, Louis S. Judd, of Marine, Ill., formerly of Boston, who d. Dec. 28, '49, a merchant and farmer. She is m. Pres. N. S. ch. Chil.—1, Samuel, b. July 20, '40. 2, Henry Louis, b. Dec. 2, '42. 3, Mary Elizabeth, b. Oct. 27, '44. 4, dec'd.

(3) *Sarah Ann*, b. Aug. 26, 1817, m. Feb. '37, Rollin Howard, of Salisbury, Vt., and d. June, 1855. Chil.—1, Henry Danforth. Res. Galena, Ill. 2, Mary A. 3, dec'd.

(4) *Elizabeth*, b. April 6, 1820. m. July 7, '50, John Ellison, formerly of Hempstead, L. I., and has had 4 chil., 1 dec'd.

(5) *Henry*, b. Feb. 26, 1823, m. Jan. '45, Abbie Hathaway, of Swanton, Vt., and rem. to Washington, Ill., in '48. He is a farmer, has 4 boys, and he and wife are m. Meth. ch.

594. II. WILLIAM,[7] (1232) b. March 13, 1793, m. Dec. 24, 1823, Abigail Ensign, who was b. Jan. 27, 1795, and d. March 8, 1854, ae. 59 yrs., and was m. Meth. ch. He has had 8 chil., and all are m. Cong. ch. He rem. in 1815, from St. Albans, Vt. to Middlebury, N.Y., where he learned the trade of harness maker. Res. Warsaw, N. Y. since 1823.

595. III. SALLY,[7] b. July 16, 1795, m. March 31, 1827, Charles Caldwell, who d. July 21, 1856, and had 1 child, dec'd. Both m. Meth. ch. Res. Lebanon, St. Croix Co., Ill.

596. IV. HARVEY,[7] (1239) b. May 3, 1798, m. Feb. 4, 1830, Laura Hollis, of Madrid, St. Lawrence Co., N. Y., who is dec'd. He rem. from Mich. to Ill. in 1841, to Minnesota in 1842, and in 1854 to Marine Mills, Ill. He is a tanner, and has 1 dau.

597. V. NATHAN,[7] b. March 5, 1801, d. Nov. 23, 1801.

598. VI. ORANGE,[7] b. Sept. 4, 1802, m. 1848 or 9, Mrs. Georgiana (Barton) Lockwood, of Prescott, Wis., formerly of Wilkesbarre, Pa. Res. Marine Mills, Minn. He was a member of the State Legislature, (1860.) No chil.

599. VII. EDWARD G.,[7] (1240) b. March 28, 1805, m. Feb. 24, 1830, Roby C. Clark, of St. Albans, Vt. Res. St. A., on the homestead of his father. He is m. Cong. ch., and has 3 chil.

600. VIII. OLIVE E.,[7] b. May 13, 1808, d. Dec. 28, 1846, (29, 1847.) She m. Feb. 23, 1830, Hiram Ballard, a farmer. Res. Georgia, Vt. Chil.—

(1) ***Worthington***, b. March, 1830. Merchant in Marine. (2) ***Aldace***, b. April, '32. (3) ***Mary Asenath***, b. May, '34, m. '58 or 9, Draper. Res. Marine, Minn. (4) ***Adelia***, m. Caldwell. Res. G. (5) ***Harrison***. (6) ***Ann Eliza***. (7) ***Amanda***.

601. IX. LEWIS,[7] (1243) b. March 27, 1811, m. July 5, 1835, Calphurnia White. He is a farmer in Marine, Minn., and has 2 chil.

602. X. MARY MARIA,[7] b. July 12, 1813, m. May 7, 1835, Hiram Dee, who was b. Oct. 17, 1812. Res. near Highland, Madison Co., Ill. Both m. Meth. ch. Chil.—

(1) ***Edgar***, b. Jan. 20, 1836. (2) ***Charles Edson***, b. Dec. 12, '37. (3) ***Oscar Lewis***, b. Nov. 2, '39, d. Jan. 25, '44. (4) ***Lovina C.***, b. Sept. 17, '41. (5) ***Sarah***, b. April 15, '43, d. May 10, '43. (6) ***Henry Clay***, b. Sept. 26, '43? d. Sept. 30, '45. (7) ***Webster***, (twin.) (8) ***Frederick N.***, b. April 2, '47, d. April 8, '53. (9) ***Clara O.***, b. Jan. 13, '49. (10) ***James G.***, b. March 19, '51. (11) ***Lawrence W.***, b. Oct. 26, '54.

603. XI. PORTER,[7] (1245) b. Jan. 7, 1816, m. March 8, 1837, Sarah Ann Lewis, dau. of J. Lewis, of Fairfax, Vt., and b. April 6, 1816. Both m. Cong. ch. He was formerly a merchant, and for many yrs. a teacher. He rem. to Marine Mills, Minn., Oct. 6, 1858. He has had 5 chil.

CHIL. OF WILLIAM WALKER,[6] [238] OF THOMPSON, CT.

604. I. LEVI H.,[7] b. Sept. 1, 1783, d. in infancy.

605. II. SALLY,[7] b. July 15, 1785, d. 1822. She m. 1804, Isaac Barstow, of Providence, R. I. They rem. in 1806, to Marietta, O., where he d. 1824 or 5, leaving 6 chil. Chil. are all m. ch.

(1) *Albert.* (2) *Horace.* (3) *Adaline*, dec'd. (4) *Cynthia.* (5) *Henry.*

606. III. ELIZABETH,[7] b. Aug. 14, 1787, m. Oct. 25, 1807, Henry Eldred, of Providence, R. I. He is a mason, and both are m. ch. Res. Kingston, R. I. Chil., 1808—1825—

(1) *Henry.* (2) *James.* (3) *Maria.* (4) *William W.* (5) *Susan W.* (6) *John R.* (7) *Elizabeth.*

607. IV. WILLIAM,[7] b. July 27, 1789, in Thompson, Ct., was drowned when bathing, July 31, 1803.

608. V. CYNTHIA,[7] b. July 31, 1791, d. June 4, 1852. She m. May, 1812, Richard Carpenter, a farmer. Res. Thompson, Ct. Both m. ch. They had 6 sons and 4 daus. b. 1813—1839, of whom 7 are m. ch. Chil.—

(1) *Sally B.* (2) *Abby.* (3) *Wm. W.* (4) *Mary W.* (5) *Ephraim Walker.* (6) *John.* (7) *Adaline B.* (8) *Samuel.* (9) *Vernon E.* (10) *Edward S.*

609. VI. DAU.,[7] b. Aug. 21, 1793, d. in infancy.

610. VII. POLLY,[7] b. Dec. 6, 1795, m. Robert Wilson, a wealthy farmer in Boonville, N. Y. Both m. ch. and her 2 sons also, who are enterprising men. Chil.—

(1) *John.* (2) *Robert.*

611. VIII. SON,[7] b. Sept. 1, 1797, d. in infancy.

CHIL. OF STEPHEN WALKER,[6] [240] OF BUTTERNUTTS, N.Y.

612. I. WILLIAM,[7] (1250) b. in Johnston, N. Y., March 17, 1791, m. March 28, 1817, Olive Everett, in Brownville, Jefferson Co., N. Y. He was a tanner and early settled in Conhocton, Steuben Co., N. Y., where he spent most of his life, an honest and industrious man. In 1852, they went to Clarence, Wis. They have had 7 chil.

613. II. STEPHEN,[7] (1257) b. in J., Jan. 9, 1793, m. March 22, 1822, Mrs. Sally (Irish) Rudd, and has 2 chil. He rem. from Butternutts to Utica, N. Y., where he carried on a large business till 1832. He then, with his brother Samuel, rem. to Buffalo, N. Y., where they were extensively engaged as builders, in partnership till 1850, and since then, he has been in the same business alone. He is m. Epis. ch. has been Warden, Vestryman and Sabbath School Superintendent, both at U., and in St. Pauls ch., in B. He is a man of extensive reading and remarkable memory. Res. Buffalo.

614. III. POLLY,[7] b. in J., Nov. 5, 1797, m. Dec. 5, 1816, Geo. Andrews. He was a cotton manufacturer, at Whitestown, N. Y., many yrs. In 1840, he retired upon a farm in Camillus, N. Y. Not liking this, he engaged again in manufacturing, at New Hartford, N. Y., and in 1852, rented the Marshall Mills on Mt. Ida, Troy, N. Y., where he now lives, having been successful in business. Both are m. Meth ch. He is one of the Trustees of Wesleyan University, Ct., and has been an influential man in the Meth. denomination in Central N. Y. Chil.—

(1) *Frederick William*, b. Oct. 28, 1817, m. Susan C. Smith, Aug. 20, '40, and for several yrs. carried on the Factory in Brownsville, Jefferson Co., N. Y., and has rem. since '55 to Wabasha, Minn. He is an Elder in the Pres. ch., was member of the General Assembly that met at Buffalo '51, and a man of great worth. He has 1 son, Smith, b. '46.

(2) *Theodore F.*, b. May 9, 1819, m. Jane A. Hopkins, May 21, '43. He spent 2 yrs. in Wesleyan Univ., was a teacher, then a lawyer in Skaneateles and Syracuse, N. Y. He has since been one of the reporters for the Globe at Washington, and is m. Pres. ch. Res. Syracuse, in the summer.

(3) *Catharine Ann*, b. May 20, 1821, m. Sept. 18, '39, Dr. Hiram Baker, of Cazenovia, N. Y. They rem. about 1845 to Coldwater, Mich. She is m. Pres. ch., and has 4 chil.

(4) *Mary Gardner*, b. April 27, 1823, m. Sydney P. Gambia, of Hamilton, Steuben Co., Ind. He is a miller and merchant—a man of ability and intelligence. She is m. Pres. ch.

(5) *Edward G.*, b. Aug. 7, 1825, m. Aug. 7, '51, Susan M. Hotchkiss. He is a graduate of Wesleyan Univ., and a clergyman of the Meth. Epis. Ch. He has for several yrs. been Prof. and is now President of the Oneida Conference Seminary in Cazenovia, which position he fills with success and honor.

(6) *Charles*, b. May 27, 1827. He is a lawyer in Syracuse, and has been in practice since 1850. He was the Prosecuting Attorney of Onondago Co., N. Y., in '55.

(7) *Lydia*, b. Feb. 10, 1830, m. Rev. S. W. Robbins, of East Haddam, Ct., a Cong. minister. (8) *Clara*, b. April 23, '32. (9) *George*, b. July 8,

'34, d. Dec. 5, '36. (10) *Elizabeth*, b. Sept. 13, '36, m. Oct. 2, '60 O. W. Edson, of Troy, N. Y., a manufacturer. Res. Troy. (11) *George H.*, b. May 13, '39.

615. IV. SAMUEL GARDNER,[7] (1259) b. in J., Nov. 19, 1799, d. July 21, 1857, of paralysis. He m. Jan. 4, 1826, Waty Eldred, dau. of Thomas, and b. near Troy, March 9, 1799. She is m. Pres. ch. He lived in Utica, N. Y., till 1832, then rem. to Buffalo, where he died. He had 5 chil. He was contractor and builder with his brother till 1850, when he was elected Street Commissioner and Assessor. He was a "Friend" in heart and belief.

616. V. PHEBE ANN,[7] b. in Saratoga, Sept. 6, 1802, m. April 1, 1823, Samuel S. Munson. He is a farmer, 1st at Windsor, Broome Co., N. Y., then at Great Bend, Pa., and in 1837, rem. to Camillus, N. Y., and in 1858, to Fowlerville, Livingston Co., Mich. Both are active m. Meth. ch. Chil.—

(1) *Lydia Walker*, b. March 23, 1824, has been a teacher.

(2) *Amanda Munson*, b. Nov. 17, 1825, became a teacher of great excellence and promise, and d. Jan. 15, '47, while teaching in a Ladies' Seminary in Brooklyn, N. Y.

(3) *Charles Henry*, b. June 17, 1827, m. Jane West, Jan. 27, '49. Res. Tecumseh, Mich.

(4) *Susan Adelaide*, b. Aug. 4, 1829. Res. Detroit, Mich.

(5) *Ferdinand W.*, b. March 31, 1831, m. Frances R. Lake, dau. of Rial and Mary F., of Howell, Mich. He and w. are teaching in Hastings, Barry Co., Mich.

(6) *Albert Stephen*, b. March 13, 1833, d. April, '49.

(7) *Isabella*, b. March 9, 1835, m. Sept. 12, 1856, Levi A. Loveland. Res. Canistota. She was formerly a teacher in Maryland.

(8) *Benjamin Gardner*, b. Feb. 25, 1837.

(9) *Melvin Clinton*, b. May 23, 1840.

(10) *Clara Gertrude*, b. Feb. 17, 1842.

(11) *Edwin Walter*, b. July 25, 1844.

(12) *Ida Dayton*, b. Sept. 1, 1846, d. April, 1849.

617. VI. SARAH,[7] b. in Providence, N. Y., July 25, 1804, m. Edwin Walter, Jan. 4, 1827. He is a wheelwright, lived in Windsor, N. Y., rem. to Great Bend, Pa., and in 1837, to Litchfield, Hillsdale Co., Mich. Both m. Meth ch. Chil.—

(1) *Mary Matilda*, b. Nov. 28, 1827, d. May 20, '30. (5) *William Addison*, b. July 21, '29, a wheelwright in Cal., '55. (3) *Carrie E.*, b. June 28, '31, is a successful teacher in Coldwater, Mich. (4) *Harriet Maria*, b. July 9, '33, m. May 8, '60, Francis Sherman, of Chicago, Treasurer of a Rail

C. J. Walker

C. J. Walker

Road Co. Res. C. (5) *Frances Adelia*, b. Sept. 20, '35, is a teacher. (6) *Geo. Andrews*, b. Aug. 6, '37, is a clerk in a Shoe store, Detroit, (1855.) (7) *Eugene Erastus*, b. Nov. 9, '39. (8) *Sarah Matilda*, b. Jan. 16, '42. (9) *Edward*, b. Feb. 2, '45.

618. VII. FERDINAND,[7] (1264) b. in P., July 26, 1806, m. Jan. 15, 1829, Elmira Smith, and has had 12 chil. He commenced business in Hamilton, N. Y., thence he went to N. Y. City, and was in business till about 1845, when he became managing clerk in one of the largest Dry Goods houses in N. Y. He is now with Messrs. A. T. Stewart & Co., Broadway. He is m. Epis. ch.

619. VIII. CAROLINE,[7] b. in Providence, N. Y., May 30, 1808, m. Jan. 1, 1828, Isaac Caskey. He is a carpenter, has resided in Utica and Buffalo, N. Y., and in 1835 rem. to Pontiac, Mich., where they now live. Both m. Meth. ch. Chil.—

(1) *Samuel Gardner*, b. Oct. 30, 1828, is partner with Mr. McGraw, (See No. 623,) doing a large shoe business in Detroit. He is a young man of extensive reading, general information, and remarkable statistical memory.

(2) *Mary Jane*, b. Jan. 4, 1832, m. 1854, Jason Canfield, a lawyer in Cleveland, O.

(3) *Elmira Smith*, b. Feb. 25, 1834. (4) *Maria Louisa*, b. July 2, '36, d. Sept. 7, '40. (5) *Stephen Walker*, b. Aug. 26, '39, d. Jan. 30, '52. (6) *Geo. Andrews*, b. Sept. 23, '41, d. April 26, '42. (7) *Alexander Carey*, b. July 30, '44. Twin. (8) *Susannah Weld*, b. July 30, '44, d. Oct. 15, '46. Twin. (9) *Maria Louisa*, b. Sept. '46. (10) *Caroline Isadore*, b. Sept. '51, d. in infancy.

620. IX. MATILDA,[7] b. in P., Sept. 18, 1810, m. April 10, 1842, Sylvester Granger. He was a Lawyer in Grand Rapids, Mich., and d. July 7, 1845. She has 2 chil. and res. in Detroit, Mich.

(1) *Edward Gilbert*, b. April 10, 1843. (2) *Mary Luce*, b. Nov. 25, '45.

621. X. BENJAMIN GARDNER,[7] (1276) b. in Butternutts, Oct. 13, 1812, m. May 21, 1840, Mary A. West, and had 6 chil. He was a carpenter. Res. Tecumseh, Mich., where he was killed by the fall of a timber, while assisting a neighbor to raise a building, April 17, 1851. He was sincerely and thoroughly a Quaker.

622. XI. CHARLES IRISH,[7] (1282) b. in Butternutts, April 25, 1814, m. Mary A. Hinsdill, at Grand Rapids, Mich., April 12, 1838. He was trained for a merchant, at Cooperstown, N. Y., and commenced business there. In 1837, he went to Grand Rapids. After the bubble of land speculation had burst, he was editor 3 yrs., of

the Grand Rapids Enquirer, and a member of the Legislature of Mich. in the session of 1840 and '41. Commencing the study of Law in 1841, in the office of Hon. Henry Morris, Springfield, Mass., in a few mos. he went to Brattleboro', Vt., to read Law with Hon. J. D. Bradley, and soon became his partner. Remaining there 3 yrs., he rem. to Bellows Falls, Vt., to take the office of Judge Kellogg, promoted to the Supreme Bench, and was very successful. In 1851, he went to Detroit, Mich., and became law partner with his brother Edw. C. He has achieved an eminent position as an advocate and jurist, and has a large and lucrative practice. He is m. Cong. ch., and has 2 chil.

At the organization of the Law Department of the University of Michigan, at Ann Arbor, in 1859, he was elected by the Board of Regents, "Kent Professor of Law," which position he now holds, though still residing in Detroit, and continuing his professional business. He has for several yrs. been making researches into the early and romantic history of the North-West, and especially that of Mich. Through his instrumentality, principally, the Historical Society of Mich., founded by Gen. Cass and others in 1828, was re-organized in 1857, and he is its Corresponding Secretary. He delivered an address on "The Founding of Detroit," July 24, 1858, it being the 167th anniversary of its settlement; another on the "Early History of Mich.," March, 1859, which were published, and has read quite a number of papers upon similar subjects before the Hist. Society. Having collected a library of rare works, pertaining to the West, probably the best and most extensive of its kind, in that section of the country, he is gathering materials for a work on its early history. To him, though bringing no wealth, and exciting little attention, these studies have a special charm.

623. XII. Susannah Weld,[7] b. in B., July 7, 1817, d. June 6, 1842. She m. Oct. 31, 1836, Alexander McGraw, an extensive shoe merchant and man of wealth, in Detroit, Mich. She was a Teacher a year or two in one of the Public Schools in Providence, R. I., and was a woman of decided talent, strong character, and consistent piety. She was a m. Pres. ch. Chil.—

(1) *Edward Walker*, b. Sept. 4, 1837, was graduated at Mich. University, July, '59. He was admitted to the Bar in Detroit, Aug. '60, and Oct. 15, '60, left D., to establish himself in his profession in Portland, Oregon.

(2) *Theodore Andrews*, b. Nov. 11, 1839, was graduated at Mich. Univ., July '59, and now studying in Bonn Germany.

(3) *Lucius Miller*, b. April 5, 1842, d. Oct. '43, 1 yr. old.

624. XIII. EDWARD CAREY,[7] (1284) b. in B., July 4, 1820, m. June 16, 1852, Lucy Bryant, of Buffalo, N. Y. At the age of 11 yrs. he went to Hamilton, to prepare for Coll. When nearly fitted, he embraced an opportunity to become a civil engineer, and was for 2 yrs. in the employ of the State of N. Y. But a Sunday ride, a runaway horse, and a broken knee, put an end to his plans in that direction. He hobbled on crutches to visit his Western friends, and spent the winter of 1837, with Mr. McGraw, (See No. 623,) in Detroit. Mr. McG. with a father's interest, offered to aid him in his studies, and defray his expenses at Yale and Harvard Colleges. He accordingly entered the Junior Class, at Yale Coll., in 1840, was graduated in 1842; studied in the Law School of Harv. Coll., was graduated in 1844, and admitted to the Bar, in Oct. 1845. He has a large and remunerative practice in Detroit, Mich., where, till Feb. 15, 1858, he was in partnership with his brother, Prof. C. I. W., and now with Alfred Russell, Esq. He was the city orator on the 4th of July, 1859, and his oration was published. He is an Elder in the Fort St. Pres. ch., and Secretary of the Board of Education of Detroit. He has 2 chil., and has adopted *Lillie*, (*Lucy A.*,) (No. 1281,) youngest dau. of his brother Benj. G.

CHIL. OF NATHANIEL WALKER,[6] [243] OF PROVIDENCE, R.I.

625. I. MARY H.,[7] b. Dec. 26, 1796. She m. Jan. 26, 1818, Wm. P. Stanton, who was b. in Providence, R. I., June 1, 1794. He and his brother Henry, (See No. 629,) have been engaged in the wholesale and retail watch and jewelry trade, many yrs. in Rochester, N. Y. Chil.—

(1) *Thomas C.*, b. in P., Nov. 2, 1819, d. Dec. 11, '27.

(2) *Sarah C.*, b. Dec. 23, 1821, m. Henry M. True, July 8, '40, and has had 6 chil. Res. Memphis, Tenn.

(3) *Thomas C.*, b. in R., Jan. 10, '33, became successor of his father in business, Jan. 1, '56.

(4) *Mary E.*, b. in R., Aug. 18, '36.

625.[1] II. SARAH,[7] b. May 26, 1798, d. June 15, 1818.

626. III. ELIZABETH,[7] b. Oct. 8, 1800, m. Dec. 22, (27 White Memorials,) 1824, Normand Lyman, of Hartford, Ct., son of Elias and Anna, (White,) b. in Weathersfield, Vt., Feb. 23, 1795. He is a merchant, in H. Chil.—

(1) *Albert*, b. Nov. 16, 1825, m. June 19, '54, Eliza B. Fuller, who d. April 15, '55. He m. 2d, Feb. 12, '56. Res. Troy, N. Y. Hardware merchant. (2) *Normand*, b. July 31, '27, m. Louisa G. Wickham, April 24, '49. (3) *Frances E.*, b. Dec. 4, '28, d. Oct. 16, '29. (4) *Sarah Coles*, b. Aug. 1, '30. (5) *Thomas Coles*, b. June 15, '32. (6) *Anna*, b. Aug. 22, '34. (7) *Susan Walker*, b. Aug. 19, '36. (8) *Jane*, b. Jan. 17, '39. (9) *Elizabeth*, b. Jan. 5, '43.

627. IV. ANNE,[7] b. Sept. 2, 1803, d. Oct. 26, 1814.

628. V. SUSAN,[7] b. Aug. 23, 1806, d. Oct. 5, 1807.

629. IV. ALBERT,[7] (1286) b. May 22, 1809, m. Oct. 24, 1832, Marietta Forsyth, dau. of David and Betsey, b. in Clarkson, N. Y., Aug. 13, 1813, and d. Oct. 25, 1838. He m. 2d, Sept. 5, 1843, Frances Childs, at Buffalo, N. Y. He was in the watch and jewelry business about 20 yrs., in Brockport, N. Y., and rem. to Rochester, N. Y., about 1847. He has had 6 chil.

629.[1] VII. SUSAN W.,[7] b. Oct. 23, 1812, m. Aug. 9, 1838, Henry Stanton, of Rochester, N. Y., b. in Hudson N. Y., May 16, 1803, brother of Wm. P., (See No. 625,) and son of William. Res. R. Chil. b. in R.—

(1) *Elizabeth L.* b. May 25, 1839. (2) *Henry*, b. Jan. 6, '41. (3) *Sarah C.*, b. Nov. 11, '42. (4) *George W.*, b. Oct. 4, '45. (5) *William P.*, b. Dec. 26, '49.

630. VIII. EDWARD,[7] b. March 18, 1815. Res. Milan, O., unm. till 1859, and since, unknown.

631. IX. SARAH ANN,[7] b. Dec. 16, 1820, m. June 21, 1853, Jas. E. Cranston, of Providence, R. I., son of Bazzillai, and b. about 1823. He is a bookseller, in P.

CHIL. OF SIMEON WALKER,[6] [245] OF LITTLE VALLEY, N.Y.

632. I. HORATIO,[7] (1292) b. Sept. 21, 1794, m. Dec. 20, 1814, Sarah Pingrey, of Mt. Holly, Vt. He is m. Meth. ch., and has had 5 chil. Res. Neils Creek, Jefferson Co., Ind.

633. II. LEWIS,[7] b. March 4, 1797, d. March 6, 1797.

BY 2d MARRIAGE.

634. III. DAUGHTER,[7] still-born, April, 1799.

635. IV. ROXALANE,[7] b. Nov. 8, 1800, m. John Jarvis Keith, of Fort Ann, Washington Co., N. Y. Both m. Bap. ch. Res. Little Valley, N. Y, No chil.

D. C. Walker

CHIL. OF LEWIS WALKER,[6] [248] OF CLARENDON SPA, VT.

636. I. ELMINA CLARINDA,[7] b. Jan. 9, 1805, d. Jan. 28, 1836. She m. Aug. 24, 1826, Orrin Greene, of Rutland, Vt., who d. soon after. No chil.

637. II. LEWIS MERRITT,[7] (1297) b. Feb. 24, 1808, m. 1829, Adah Shepardson, and has 7 chil. He is a merchant and farmer in Clarendon, Vt. He has been Town Clerk 7 yrs., Select-man and 1st Assessor several yrs, Justice of the Peace about 20 yrs., and was Rep. in the State Legislature, 1857 and '58·

638. III. SARAH MARIA,[7] b. March 23, 1810, d. June 24, 1843. She m. July 23, 1835, George True, who d. early. He had one son who d. 2 yrs. and 2 mos. old. She m. 2d, July 30, 1839, Gershom Cheney, of Rutland. Vt. They had no chil.

639. IV. DE WITT CLINTON,[7] (1304) b. July 17, 1812, m. Aug. 31, 1837, Adeline Ketchum, of Sudbury, Vt., 2d dau. of Hon. Barnard Ketchum, and b. Oct. 15, 1811. They have 8 chil., all living.

The story of his youthful ambition and struggles for an education, and his subsequent honors and success is as follows :—

About the age of 16 years, he determined in his own mind, to obtain a liberal education; but his parents wishing to keep both their sons upon the old homestead, were much opposed to it, and would not accede to his wishes for several yrs. They however afforded him, as they did their other children, the opportunities of a good academic education. Unknown to his parents, he commenced the study of the Greek and Latin languages, while at the Castleton Academy, and made sufficient progress to enable him to pursue them without a teacher. On learning that he was engaged in such studies, his father took him home, and told him that he had better learn the art of farming. To this, he submitted cheerfully, and continued to labor on the farm for some time, but in the meanwhile pursued his studies, late every evening, and every rainy day. In the Winter, he taught school, and husbanded his money like a miser. In the month of Aug. 1829, the day when the haying was finished, his father gave his workmen an *extra treat,* as was then usual on such occasions. Calling them together, for this purpose, he found that this son was absent, and inquiring where he was, was told, that he was at his room studying Latin. The son was sent for, and asked what good he supposed his Latin would ever do him. He replied, "I thought I could prepare myself to enter Coll. by the time I should be 21 yrs. old. The father then asked, how he expected to defray the expenses of a Collegiate education. To this, he promptly answered, "by economy and industry," and then told him how much money he had laid up for the purpose, and that when this was exhausted, he could suspend his studies for a while, and obtain more by teaching. Musing a moment, his father said, "If you are resolved on obtaining an education, the quicker you are about it, the better," and, added, "Tell your mother to have your clothes ready, and I will take you to the Castleton Academy to-morrow morning." He did so, and the next morning, at 4 o'clock, was on his way to C. In Aug. 1830, he entered Coll. at Middlebury, Vt., and was graduated in Aug. 1834. He studied Law with John Pierpoint, Esq., at Vergennes, Vt., adapting his studies to the course pursued in the Law Department of Yale Coll. The next yr., he entered the Law School at New Haven, Ct., and by close application, was able to recite and keep up with both the Junior and Senior Classes, at the same time, and thus completed a two years' course in one year, and was examined and admitted as an Attorney and Counsellor at Law, in N. H., in July, 1836. Spending a few weeks with his parents at home, to recruit, and receiving and declining several very favorable overtures to go into partnership with old and established lawyers in his native State, he determined to seek his fortunes in the West; and after traveling in the Western States about 2 months, finally located in Romeo, Mich. In 1837, while on a visit to the East, the people of the County, unsolicited and unknown to him, petitioned the Governor, and obtained his his appointment as Prosecuting Attorney of Macomb Co., for the term of 2 yrs. In the Autumn of 1839, he was unanimously nominated by the County Convention, upon the 1st ballot, as candidate for Rep. to the State Legislature, and was triumphantly elected. He was then chosen Senator for 2 yrs., and in 1843 and '45, Representative again. In 1850, he was a member of the Convention to revise the State Constitution. He was appointed one of the Regents of the State University, in 1844, and succeeded in obtaining the establishment of a Branch of the University at Romeo, and was President of the Branch, until its discontinuance in 1853. The Dickenson Institute was then established in its place, and new buildings erected. He is one of the Trustees and its President.

Whitfield Walker

[illegible]

[illegible]

[illegible]

[illegible]

[illegible]

[illegible]

As an Attorney at Law, he never advises, nor engages in a suit, unless morally certain, that the cause is a just one. He has the reputation of being an honest lawyer, and has secured a large and lucrative practice, and is an extensive landholder.

March 4, 1857, he removed to a place in the woods, in St. Clair Co., on the Port Huron & Milwaukie R. R., and laid out a town, which he named "Capac," from Manco Capac, the first of the Peruvian Incas. He is now principally employed in extensive lumbering operations, and in developing the growth of his new town.

640. V. ANN MELISSA,[7] b. May 9, 1815, m. Oct. 31, 1834, Hiram Taylor, of Clarendon, Vt. He is an affluent farmer. Res. Armada, Mich. Chil.—

(1) *Melissa Ann*, b. 1835. (2) *Sarah*, b. '37.

CHILDREN OF JESSE WALKER,[6] [256] OF WHITING, VT.

641. I. WHITFIELD,[7] (1312) b. Jan. 5, 1794, in W., m. Sept. 20, 1820, Martha Hall, of Sudbury, Vt., dau. of Dea. Abner, of S., b. Dec. 17, 1795, and d. Dec. 1847. He m. 2d, Ap. 16, 1848, Hannah Brazee, of Whiting, dau. of Christopher and Hannah. In early life, he taught school considerably. He is a Surveyor, and has done the greater part of such business in his section of the County, for several yrs. He has held the offices of Constable, Captain, Superintendent of Schools, Lister, Town Clerk, Justice of the Peace, and was Delegate to the Convention for the revision of the State Constitution. He is the author of the "Life of Rev. Ephraim Sawyer;" has written the History of the town of Whiting, from the first charter to the present time,—and a vol. (8 vo., about 350 pp.) of poetry entitled "Progression and Poems on various subjects," the principal poem, giving the title, and comprising about 250 pages. The last two are not yet published. He is a farmer in W., and has had 8 chil.

642. II. HORATIO,[7] b. Oct. 5, 1795, d. March 18, 1812. From an early age, he was a remarkable scholar. Though of slender health, he devoted all his time to study. At the age of 15, he was fitted for College, but his health continuing to decline, he was unable to enter, and d., greatly lamented, at the age of 17 yrs.

643. III. PRUDENCE,[7] b. in W., Aug. 14, 1797, d. Oct. 2, 1851. She m. Feb. 22, 1824, Nathan Baker, of Lewiston, N. Y., (his 3d wife,) who was b. in L. I., April 9, 1787, and d. Sept. 10, 1851.

They rem. from L. to Plummer, Greene Co., Ind., in 1840, where they died. He was a cabinet maker. She was m. Epis. ch. Chil.—

(1) *Hiram Walker*, b. March 11, 1826, m. Nov. 11, '51, Amanda J. Osborne, b. Sept. 3, '27, in Linton, Greene, Co., Ind., and had—1, Wm. N., b. Aug. 1, '52, d. Oct. 9, '52. 2, Ira O., b. Sept. 23, '53. 3, Horatio Fellows, b. Jan. 8, '57. He is a carpenter, in L.

(2) *John*, b. June 24, 1828, m. Jan. 4, '53, Phebe Ingersoll, b. in L. Sept. 18, '34, and has—1, Walter E., b. March '55. 2, Tryphena P., b. Aug. '57, 3, Mary, b. Feb. '59. He is a carpenter.

(3) *George*, b. July 30, 1830, m. Margaret Hallsted, of Greene Co., Ind., June 8, '55. He is a carpenter in Greene Co.

(4) *Henry*, b. Aug. 24, 1832, m. Dec. 23, '58, Sarah Inman.

(5) *Horatio Walker*, b. Nov. 20, 1834.

(6) *Francis Carter*, b. Sept. 3, 1836, d. Aug. 11, '37.

(7) *Francis Carter*, b. Jan. 11, 1838.

644. IV. SAWYER,[7] (1320) b. in W., July 15, 1799, m. May 16, 1824, Melinda Guile, of Leicester, Vt., dau. of Moses and Elizabeth, b. in Mount Holly, Vt., April 29, 1799. They have had 7 chil. He is a farmer and housewright; has held the offices of Constable, Lister, Select-man and Justice of the Peace, and is a pious and exemplary man. He rem. from Whiting to Fairfax, Vt. in 1836, and in Nov. 1855 to St. Marie, Wis.

645. V. HIRAM,[7] b. in W., d. ae. 1 yr. and 6 mos.

646. VI. HIRAM,[7] (1327) b. in W., Feb. 9, 1804, m. June 8, 1829, Cynthia Skinner, dau. of Timothy, of Westmoreland, N.H. She is m. Pres. ch. They have had 2 chil. He is a farmer, and has held the offices of Overseer of the County Poor House 5 yrs., Treasurer of the County 3 yrs., and Town School Com. Res. Mexico, N.Y.

647. VII. LUCY,[7] b. in W. Jan 16, 1806, m. May 12, 1825, Dr. Nathaniel Hall, Jr., of Whitehall, N.Y., son of Judge Nath'l, and d. March, 1851. They rem. from W. in 1827, to Greece, (Handford's Landing,) N.Y. He was graduated at Castleton Medical Coll., Dec. 1823, and was a highly esteemed Physician in Greece, N.Y. She is m. Bap. ch. Chil.—

(1) *Esther Louisa*, b. Sept. 1827. Res. G., unm. (2) *Nathaniel*, b. May, '29, m. Sept, 15, '59, Ellen M. Medbury. He has been Deputy Comptroller of the City of Buffalo, N.Y., and now Insurance agent in B. (3) *Albert G.*, b. March, '31, m. April 23, '57, Mary E. Lyons, of Buffalo, N.Y. Res. B. (4) *Edwin*, b. Aug., 1833, is a housewright in Chicago, Ill. (5) *Charles N.*, b. April, 1835, d. May 14, 1855, Clerk in Rochester, N.Y., and a young man of sterling worth. (6) *Mason W.*, b. Feb. 1837, is a farmer in

Greece, N.Y. (7) *Cornelia A.*, b. Aug. 1839. Res. Greece. (8) *Augustus F.*, b. Dec. 1840, is a farmer in G. (9) Lucy R., b. June, 1844, d. 1845.

648. VIII. ELIZA,[7] b. March 3, 1808. Res. Rochester, N.Y.

649. IX. JESSE,[7] (1329) b. in W., Jan. 7, 1810, d. of cholera, Sept. 6, 1852. He m. Sept. 27, 1839, Betsey Ann Eldredge, adopted dau. of Bela D. Coe, Esq., of Buffalo, N.Y., and had 2 chil. He was graduated at Middlebury College in 1833, read Law in Rochester, N.Y., 1833–4, and in Buffalo, 1835–6, where he commenced his professional practice in 1836. After the alteration of the State Constitution, giving the election of Judges to the people, he was a Judge of Erie County Courts, until his death. He was also Clerk of the City of Buffalo several yrs. He was a close student, and a man of sound judgment and unblemished integrity. Since his decease, a small vol. of fugitive poems, which he wrote during the first yrs. of his professional life, has been published. For one of them, he received the prize of a silver cup, valued at $50, and no one can read them without conceiving a high respect for the poetic genius, and the nobility, both of heart and mind, which could dictate them.

The following resolutions of the Bar, testify to the ability and worth of the man, and the loss occasioned by his decease.

"Whereas, The Mysterious Providence of God has suddenly snatched from our midst, the Hon. Jesse Walker, Judge of Erie County, Therefore it is

Resolved by us, his surviving brethren of the Bar, that in the death of Judge Walker, Justice has lost from out her Temple, a pure and upright minister; the County of Erie, an able and valued Judge, and ourselves, a most worthy and deserving brother.

Resolved, that by this bereavement, so sudden, so unexpected, we are deeply and keenly afflicted. In the prime of life and health—in the maturity of ripened powers, cultured and enriched by much nice and varied learning—just entered upon the duties of an honorable and responsible official station, in which studious habits, patience of examination, solidity of judgment, integrity, courtesy and modesty, gave assured promise of excellence, and walking before men blameless in the purity of his private life and domestic relations, our friend has been cut down and removed. We mourn his loss, and will cherish his memory. How impressive the reiteration of that fearful truth, which we all so well know, yet so little heed, that 'in the midst of life we are in death.' * * *

Resolved, that the Court over which our deceased friend and brother so lately presided, in the flush and buoyancy of health, at its next session, be moved that these resolutions be entered in its minutes, as a permanent testimonial of our sorrow for his loss, and respect for his character." * *

"There is no allusion in the above proceedings, to the Christian calmness and resignation, which marked his last hours. He died in the full possession of his faculties, and in the peaceful trust of

'One who wraps the drapery of his couch
About him, and lies down to pleasant dreams.'

He received the Holy Sacrament of the Lord's Supper, and in peace with God and man, fell asleep, and 'was gathered to his fathers.'" (Preface to his Poems.)

650. X. EUNICE,[7] b. in W., Jan. 16, 1813, was a teacher in the Public Schools of Rochester several yrs., and is now Assistant in the Clover St. Female Seminary at Brighton, near R. She is m. Bap. ch.

CHILDREN OF LEVI WALKER,[6] [259] OF WHITING, VT.

651. I. SAMUEL T.,[7] (1331) b. March 4, 1794, in W., m. Sept. 7, 1815, Sally Swiss, of Medway, Mass., dau. of Samuel and Lydia. She d. Nov. 9, 1815. He m. 2d, Dec. 25, 1821, Fanny Ellis, of Whiting, Vt., dau. of Benj. and Chloe, and b. in Dummerston, N. H., Jan. 31, 1801. They have 1 son. He has been Selectman in W., several yrs., represented the Town in the Legislature 2 yrs., and was Delegate to the Convention for the revision of the State Constitution. Res. W.

652. II. LURA,[7] b. Sept. 20, 1795, in W., m. Feb. 7, 1819, Col. Benj. M. Barrow, of Woodstock, N. H., son of Benj. and Abigail (Varnum,) formerly of Dracut, Mass. He is a farmer and is also engaged in general business. He has been member of the Legislature 2 yrs., Col. of the Militia, and Justice of the Peace, and has held various minor town offices. She is m. Bap. ch. Chil.—

(1) *Lovina Walker*, b. Sept. 15, 1820, m. Nov. 3, '44, Lorenzo D. Glovier, son of Timothy, of W. He is a farmer, and has been Select-man. 3 chil. (2) *Benj. M.*, b. Aug. 5, '22, and m. May 13, '49, Clarissa E., dau. of Thomas Vincent, of W. He is a farmer, has been Select-man and Town Clerk, in W. 3 chil. (3) *Betsey*, b. June 29, '24, d. Sept. 5, '25. (4) *Hiram T.*, b. Feb. 15, '27, d. Feb. 3, '32. (5) *Abigail*, b. June 15, '30, d. Feb. 1, '32. (6) *Lura A.*, b. May 18, '34, m. Jan. 22, '54, Josiah, son of Stephen Tourtillot, of Maxfield, Me. Res. W (7) *Rachel W.*, b. Jan. 14, '39, d. Jan. 30, '52.

653. III. RACHEL,[7] b. in W., May 1, 1797, m. Oct. 13, 1822, Mark S. White, of Centreville, Alleghany Co., N. Y., son of Peter, of Leicester, Vt. He is a merchant, in Columbus, Warren Co., Pa. He has been Post-master 7 yrs., and Justice of the Peace about 15 yrs. Chil.—

(1) *Levi Jerome*, b. Aug. 12, 1824, m. Sept. 30, '47, Harriet N. Diboll, dau. of Dr. Virgil M., of Staunton, Ind. Res. Columbus. They have 4 chil. (3) *Lovina*, b. in C., Pa. June 21, '30, m. George, son of Edward Vermilye, of C., Oct. 8, '48. He is a mechanic in C. and has 2 chil. (4) *Lucius*, b. Aug. — (5) *Lyman*, b. May 29, '36. (6) *Lura Ann*, b. Aug. 29, '39. Two others d. in infancy, not named.

Abel Walker

V. LEVI,[7] (1332) b. March ... m. June 23, ...sey Pond, of Whiting, Vt., dau. of ... and has 4 chil. ...ed Hamilton Literary and Theological Institution in 1826, ...duated in 1828, and ord. over the Bap. ch. in Hubbardton, ...t. 24, 1829. He preached 3 yrs. in Hebron, N.Y., 4 yrs. in ...N.H., 2 yrs. in Hanover, N.H., 2 yrs. in ... N.H., ...Hebron, N.H., and since 1851, in Perkins' Grove, ...re he is farmer as well as preacher. He has been ... several yrs. Res. Clarion, Ill. He has ever sustained an ...and exemplary christian character, and been a laborious and ...minister.

VI. ABEL,[7] b. Oct. 17, 1804, resides in Whiting, Vt. ...He represented the town in the State Legislature ... and 1843, he was a Delegate to revise the Constitution of the ... He taught school 8 winters, has been Superintendent of ...several yrs., also Assessor, 1st Constable ... and Justice ...eace about 20 yrs. He has a fine farm ... and ...cipal business is farming. In 10 ... embra...ne of the wealthiest farming districts in the State, there is ...wyer. He is employed quite extensively in preparing legal ..., and occasionally appears as counsel. He writes for the ...elivers temperance lectures and is highly esteemed as a public speaker, and a man of high moral worth.

VII. GIDEON,[7] b. Dec. 23, 1806, d. unm. in Whiting, Vt., 1829. Taken away in the strength of his early manhood, ...he midst of his usefulness, his death was a great loss.

VIII. DANIEL,[7] b. Aug. 2, 1809, d. unm. in Whiting, Vt., 1848. The following is the substance of an appreciative ... published in the Boston Christian Reflector, Sept. 1848:—

...ecame the subject of religious impressions and hopes, when 11 yrs. ...th the Bap. ch. at the age of 18, and ... the day of his death adorned ...sion. He shunned all amusements and devoted every leisure hour to ...ition of knowledge. He worked with his brother as a farmer, for yrs., ... same time carried on his studies, preparatory to the mini... ...ving ...late. Such was the purity of his life that sin and ... ...n his presence. The church gave him a license to

653.[1] IV. JOHN B.,[7] b. Dec. 23, 1799. He is a farmer, has been Select-man several yrs., and Justice of the Peace. He is a man of extensive reading, and intelligence, especially in regard to political affairs. Res. Whiting, Vt., unm.

654. V. LEVI,[7] (1332) b. March 4, 1802, in W., m. June 29, 1828, Betsey Pond, of Whiting, Vt., dau. of Lewis, and has 4 chil. He entered Hamilton Literary and Theological Institution in 1826, was graduated in 1828, and ord. over the Bap. ch. in Hubbardton, Vt., Sept. 24, 1829. He preached 3 yrs. in Hebron, N. Y., 4 yrs. in Unity, N. H., 2 yrs. in Hanover, N. H., 2 yrs. in Campton, N. H., 4 yrs. in Hebron, N.H., and since 1851, in Perkins' Grove, Bureau Co., Ill., where he is farmer as well as preacher. He has been Town Clerk several yrs. Res. Clarion, Ill. He has ever sustained an upright and exemplary christian character, and been a laborious and faithful minister.

655. VI. ABEL,[7] b. Oct. 17, 1804, resides in Whiting, Vt., unm. He represented the town in the State Legislature 1839 and '40. In 1843, he was a Delegate to revise the Constitution of the State. He taught school 8 winters, has been Superintendent of Schools several yrs., also Assessor, 1st Constable 3 yrs., and Justice of the Peace about 20 yrs. He has a fine farm on Green Island, and his principal business is farming. In 10 contiguous towns, embracing some of the wealthiest farming districts in the State, there is not a lawyer. He is employed quite extensively in preparing legal writings, and occasionally appears as counsel. He writes for the press, delivers temperance lectures, and is highly estemed as an effective public speaker, and a man of high moral worth.

656. VII. GIDEON,[7] b. Dec. 23, 1806, d. unm. in Whiting, Vt., Oct. 5, 1829. Taken away in the strength of his early manhood, and in the midst of his usefulness, his death was a great loss.

657. VIII. DANIEL,[7] b. Aug. 2, 1809, d. unm. in Whiting, Vt., Sept. 4, 1848. The following is the substance of an appreciative obituary, published in the Boston Christian Reflector, Sept. 1848:—

"He became the subject of religious impressions and hopes, when 11 yrs old, united with the Bap. ch. at the age of 18, and to the day of his death, adorned his profession. He shunned all amusements, and devoted every leisure hour to the acquisition of knowledge. He worked with his brother as a farmer, for yrs., and at the same time carried on his studies, preparatory to the ministry, studying early and late. Such was the purity of his life, that sin and immorality stood abashed in his presence. The church gave him "a license to improve his gifts," but feeling the necessity of a well disciplined and well stored mind, he furnished himself with a large and valuable Theological library.—The most marked quality of his mind, was a sound and discriminating judgment. In all the relations he sustained, he was a peacemaker, and with unostentatious, but consistent piety, commended religion to others. He received a kick from one of the animals on the farm, which resulted in death about 4 mos. after."

658. IX. JEROME,[7] b. 1812, d. July 22, 1813, ae. 18 mos.

659. X. FRANKLIN,[7] (1336) b. Jan. 2, 1815, m. June 2, 1840, Murilla E. Haskins, of Wilmington, Vt., dau. of Jonathan and Susan, and b. March 11, 1820. He rem. to Perkins' Grove, Bureau Co., Ill. in 1838, is a Justice of the Peace, and Deacon of the Bap. ch. He is a farmer in Clarion, Ill., and has had 5 chil.

CHIL. OF AMOS E. WALKER,[6] [260] OF HUBBARDTON, VT.

660. I. GIDEON,[7] b. in W., 1799, d. July, 1803.

661. II. TIMOTHY MILLER,[7] (1341) b. in W., Feb. 24, 1801, d. Jan. 25, 1855. He m. Oct. 10, 1822, Nancy, dau. of Ephraim Moulton, of Whiting, and had 4 chil. He was a shoe-maker, m. Bap. ch. and much respected as a man and citizen. Res. Hubbardton, Vt.

662. III. AMOS E.,[7] (1345) b. in W., May 18, 1803, m. Betsey Branch, dau. of John, of W., and b. May 20, 1809. He is a farmer, in W., and has 6 chil.

663. IV. EMILY,[7] b. in W., 1805, m. Sept. 24, 1826, Rev. Albert G. Hall, D. D., son of Hon. Judge Nathaniel, of Whitehall, N. Y. He was 1st settled in Pennfield, N. Y., thence he rem. to Rochester, where for 20 yrs., he has been Pastor of the 3d Pres. (O. S.) ch. She is m. ch. Chil.—

(1) *Francis Theodore*, b. 1828, is a Physician, in R., and m. Pres. (O. S.) ch. (2) *Sarah E.*, b. about '31, m. —— Whiting, a Lawyer, of Buffalo. (3) *Eunice*, b. in R., '39.

665. V. SARAH,[7] b. Feb. 14, 1809, d. June 21, 1829.

666. VI. RICHARD HART,[7] (1351) b. in W., Aug. 11, 1811, m. Jan. 24, 1833, Caroline, dau. of Asahel Hubbard, of Whiting, b. Sept. 1, 1814, and d. Feb. 26, 1841. He m. 2d, Dec. 29, 1841, at Goshen, Vt., Eliza, dau. of Martin Allen, of G. She d. Oct. 1857. He m. 3d, March, 1858, Mrs. Angeletta Allen, of Kingston, Wis.,

who was b. March 19, 1832, in Sudbury, Vt. He is a farmer, and rem. from W. to Randolph, Wis., in 1855. He is m. ch., and has had 8 chil.

CHIL. OF JAMES OTIS WALKER,[6] [261] OF WHITING, VT.

667. I. BENJ. FOSTER,[7] b. June 14, 1800, d. Oct. 11, 1814.

668. II. HENRY OLIN,[7] b. Aug. 13, 1807, m. 1st, Nov. 18, 1832, Mary E., dau. of Ezra Smith, of Shoreham, Vt., b. 1807 or 8, and d. Jan. 22, 1835, ae. 26. He m. 2d, April 26, 1819, Julia, dau. of John Reynolds, of St. Amand, Canada East. She was b. April 24, 1810, and d. July 11, 1859, of erisypelas. He m. 3d, Spring of 1860, Cornelia White, of Whiting, Vt. He is a farmer, and rem. from Swanton Centre, Vt. to Fairfax, Vt., in 1857. No chil.

669. III. DANIEL MARSH,[7] (1359) b. Feb. 10, 1809, m. Nov. 11, 1830, Cornelia Austin Smith, dau. of Anthony, of Whiting, b. May 25, 1809, and d. Nov. 16, 1835. She had 3 chil., and was m. ch. He m. 2d, March 1, 1836, Marcia Polly, dau. of Moulton Needham, of W., b. March 13, 1815. She is m. ch. In Nov. 1838, he rem. to St. Albans, Vt., and in April, 1841, to Swanton Centre, Vt., and is a farmer. He is m. Bap. ch., and has the esteem of all who know him, for his integrity and high christian worth. He has had 5 chil., and all are m. ch.

670. IV. JULIETT,[7] b. Jan. 13, 1811, m. April 19, 1831, McKenzie W. Carpenter, of Whiting, and is m. Cong. ch. Res. Ferrisburgh, Vt. Chil.—

(1) *Juliett*, b. April 15, 1833, m. Charles Lyman, of F. Res. Vergennes, Vt. He is woolen manufacturer, and machinist. (2) *James O.*, b. Aug. 16, '36, d. in St. Albans, Feb. 12, '43. (3) *Cyrus*, b. Jan. 10, '37, d. Nov. 5, '42. (4) *Adelaide*, b. Feb. 20, '42. (5) *Otis*, b. March 15, '48. (6) *Henry*, b. April 10, '50. (7) *Eva*, b. Oct. 14, '52.

CHILDREN OF GIDEON WALKER,[6] [262] OF WHITING, VT.

671. I. BETSEY A.,[7] b. May, 1805, m. Sept. 1830, John Murdock, Jr., of Cazenovia, N. Y. He is a carpenter. She is m. Bap. ch. Res. C. Chil.—

(1) *Mary M.* (2) *Hattie L. D.* (3) *Alice A.* (4) *Henry Olin*, d. Sept. 25, 1858, ae. 18 yrs. (5) *Laura A.* (6) *John.* (7) *Katy.*

672. II. LAURA P.,[7] b. Aug. 1807, m. Jan. 1831, Hon. Horace C. Young, of Smithfield, now Fenner, N. Y., son of Henry, of

Geneva, N. Y. He was a member of the State Legislature in 1849 and '50, Supervisor of the town 6 yrs., Justice of the Peace, and has held various town and county offices. He is a farmer and contractor, resides in New Albion, N. Y., and has 6 chil. He is the author of a published Lecture, on the Obligations and Inducements to the practice of Virtue, delivered before Albion Lodge. Chil.—

(1) *Helen P.*, b. Dec. 1832. Teacher in one of the Public Schools of Chicago, Ill. (2) *Laura P.*, b. Aug. '34, m. April 12, '59, E. Young Arnold, of Ellicottville, N. Y. (3) *Carrie E.*, b. Jan. '38. Teacher in one of the Public Schools of C. (4) *Louise E.*, b. July, '40. (5) *Mary*, b. Dec. '44. (6) *Horace Olin*, b. May, '50.

673. III. Rachel Amanda,[7] b. April, 1810, m. June, 1826, Collins Batt. Res. Ellicottville, N. Y. Chil.—

(1) *Valney E.*, b. Sept. 1827. (2) *Eugene W.*, b. July, '34. (3) *Ellen A.*, b. Jan. '38, d. Dec. '42. (4) *Nancy L.*, b. July, '40. (5) *Charlotte E.*, b. Dec. '42. (6) *Alice L.*, b. '45. (7) *F. Malinda*, b. '49. (8) *Elmina*, b. Jan. '52.

Chil. of SAMUEL B. WALKER,[6] [263] of Hubbardton, Vt.

674. I. S. Bent,[7] (1364) b. in Whiting, Vt., Feb. 21, 1807, He m. March 5, 1828, Jennette Hamlin, of Hubbardton, Vt., who was b. in Rupert, Vt. He was a cloth-dresser by trade. He was also engaged in farming and lumbering in Vt., and was Town Clerk and Treasurer in H., 5 yrs. He removed to Chicago, Ill., and is now in partnership with his brother, M. O. W. (No. 675.) He has had 5 chil.

675. II. Martin O.,[7] (1369) b. in Whiting, June 9, 1809, m. April 18, 1850, Lurana T. Tiffany, of Oxford, Mass., and has had 3 chil. He was educated to a mercantile life in Castleton, Vt., and became stage proprietor in the firm of Baker & Walker, Albany, N. Y. In 1837 he went to Chicago, Ill., and started a similar business with John Frink. He is now in partnership with his brother, S. B., (No. 674,) running the most extensive line of stages in the State. He possesses superior enterprise and talent for business, and has accumulated a very large property.

676. III. Curran,[7] b. July 18, 1811, and is in the Recorder's office, Chicago, Ill., and unm.

677. IV. Livonia,[7] b. April 4, 1814, d. Sept. 22, 1815.

678. V. James Otis,[7] b. Oct. 8, 1816, d. Oct. 12, 1829.

679. VI. AMOS ELMORE,[7] b. April 19, 1819, is watchmaker and jeweler, in Chicago, Ill., unm.

680. VII. LOWELL GUERNSEY,[7] b. April 23, 1822, d. March 12, 1823.

681. VIII. MARYETTE,[7] b. Nov. 12, 1824, d. June 1, 1854, of cholera. She m. Aug. 7, 1847, Eleazer W. Dinsmore, who was b. in Paris, N. Y., June 11, 1820. He is a wholesale grocer in Chicago, Ill. Child—

(1) *Mary Catharine*, b. June 12, 1848.

CHIL. OF PHILIP WALKER,[6] [264] OF WILLISTON, VT.

682. I. JOHNSON,[7] (1372) b. May 30, 1797, m. April 4, 1822, Nancy Van Sicklen, who was b. May 23, 1798, and d. 1836. He m. 2d, 1836, Mary Field, who was b. March 8, 1809. Res. Williston, Vt. He is a man of wealth and influence, and has had 6 chil.

683. II. POLLY,[7] b. Nov. 28, 1799, d. May 26, 1851, ae. 51. She m. March 18, 1821, Alonzo F. Saxton, of Shelburne, Vt., b. Jan. 10, 1796. He settled in Williston, Vt., and rem. to S., Jan. 20, 1855. He is a gentleman of property and of more than ordinary abilities. He has served the town of W., as constable 6 yrs., as Lister 3 yrs., and Select-man 2 yrs. They had 9 chil. and 8 died young. Chil.—

(1) *Son*, b. April 17, 1822, d. April, '24. (2) *Mary Eliza*, b. July 5, '23, d. Jan. 22, '33. (3) *Edgar A.*, b. Feb. 11, '25, d. May 8, '32. (4) *Geo. F.* b. Nov. 10, '26. (5) *Sarah A.*, b. Feb. 3, '29, d. Jan. 25, '33. (6) *Arthur P.*, b. Jan. 9, '31, d. Jan. 25, '33. (7) *Martha*, b. July 27, '33, d. April 23, '51. (8) *Martin*, b. Sept. 24, '35, d. Dec. 15, '36. (9) *Hiram S.*, b. Feb. 20, '43, d. Nov. 8, '45.

684. III. CATHARINE,[7] b. Sept. 22, 1801, d. May 29, 1829. She m. Elihu Barber, and both d. early, leaving one dau., viz.,—

(1) *Helen*, m. Eleazer Taft. Res. Burlington, Vt.

685. IV. PHILIP FIELD,[7] (1378) b. July 16, 1803, d. Nov. 7, 1858. He m. Sarah Mason, of Kingsbury, N. Y., dau. of Andrew and Sally, and b. March 11, 1804. Res. Fayette, Missouri. He was a farmer, and had 6 chil.

687. V. SALLY,[7] b. June 12, 1805, m. Ephraim Griswold, of Williston, Vt. No chil.

688. VI. ANNA,[7] b. Aug. 9, 1808, d. Feb. 20, 1813.

689. VII. SOLOMON,[7] b. May 17, 1811, d. Oct. 27, 1829.

690. VIII. ANNA,[7] b. Feb. 8, 1813, d. June 9, 1831.

691. IX. GEORGE,[7] b. April 23, 1815, d. Nov. 23, 1830.

692. X. ELIZA,[7] b. Aug. 3, 1817, d. April 20, 1854. She m. Allen White, of Williston, Vt., a highly respectable farmer. Res. W. Chil.—

(1) *George Arthur*, b. April 20, 1835. (2) *Aurelia*, b. May 4, '39. (3) *Frederick P.*, b. May 30, '41. (4) *Eliza*, b. May 10, '43. (5) *Child*, d. ae. 2 weeks.

693. XI. LOUISA,[7] b. Feb. 16, 1821, m. Dec. 13, 1842, Doct. Hiram D. Smith, of Williston, Vt., son of Ira, and b. Nov. 2, 1818. He had a delicate child, and was thus led to the study of medicine. He had a tooth broken by a dentist, and he then studied dentistry. He was graduated at the Medical school of the Univ. of Vermont, 1856, and rem. from Painesville, Vt. to Lawrence, N. Y., Sept. 1856. Chil.—

(1) *Ira H.*, b. Oct. 15, 1843. (2) *Hiram A.*, b. Sept. 9, '46, d. Aug. 10, '48. (3) *Philip Walker*, b. Feb. 4, '49. (4) *Hannah A.*, b. Oct. 10, '51. (5) *Hiram E.*, b. June 3, '54.

CHILDREN OF JOHNSON WALKER,[6] [265] OF PANTON, VT.

694. I. CATHARINE,[7] b. Oct. 30, 1799, m. Oct. 30, 1829, Stephen Spencer, of Addison, Vt., who was b. Oct. 31, 1780, and d. Nov. 25, 1857. She is m. Meth. ch. They rem. to Bluffdale, Green Co., Ill., in 1833. He was a man of wealth and respectability. Chil.—

(1) *Catharine*, b. Feb. 3, 1831, m. April 27, '54, Vilray Robly. Chil.—(1, Edward, b. Jan. 23, '55. 2, Frederick A., b. Dec. 18, '57.) (2) *Henry R.*, b. May 8, '33, m. June 11, '56, Laura Smead. Chil.—(1, Mary, b. April 7, '57, d. March 11, '58. 2, Stephen, b. Feb. 5, '59.) (3) *Stephen*, d. ae. 19 yrs. (4) *Charles*, d. ae. 3 yrs. (5) *Johnson*, d. ae. 6 mos.

695. II. MARY,[7] b. April 6, 1802, m. May 30, 1822, Jonathan B. Spencer, son of Jonathan, of Panton, Vt., and b. Nov. 11, 1795. He is in the iron and ore business (Land Agency) in Port Henry, Essex Co., N. Y., and is an energetic and worthy man. Both m. Bap. ch. Chil.—

(1) *Semanthe*, b. June 20, '23, m. Sept. 2, '41, Ebenezer Collins, of Whitehall, N. Y., and b. 1810. He is a merchant in Port Henry, N. Y., and an active and exemplary m. Cong. ch. Chil.—1, Adelaide, b. June 28, '42. 2, Edward, b. Aug. 22, '45. 3, Le Roy, b. Sept. 14, '53. She was m. Bap. ch., and d. Nov. 9, '53. An obituary, published at the time of her death,

is condensed into the following testimony to her worth:—"In the Spring of 1837, and at the age of 13 yrs., she became the subject of a moral change, and soon after, made a public consecration of herself to the cause of Christ, of which, she was a cordial and devoted friend, till her death.—Few mothers, if any, have felt a greater solicitude for the moral, as well as intellectual training of their children.—But the interests of her own family were not allowed to keep her from efforts, to do good to others also. To assuage their pain, to relieve their distress and anguish, she seemed to be willing to imperil her own health, or endanger her life. The various causes of benevolence found in her a warm friend, a firm and effectual supporter. Possessing the means of aiding these objects, it was her pleasure to improve them; thus rendering herself one of our most generous, and useful members of society. Her departure was sudden and unexpected, but her hope, in the hour of extremity, did not fail her—her faith in her Savior remained unshaken."

(2) *Almary*, b. March 17, 1825, m. Solomon Walker. (See No. 711.)

(3) *Charlotte*, b. Feb. 15, 1827, m. May 13, '46, Jonathan G. Witherbee, of Crown Point, N. Y., son of Thomas and Milly, formerly of Bradford, Vt. He is engaged in the mining of ore and manufacture of iron. Res. Port Henry, N. Y. Chil.—1, Jennie, b. Sept. 21, '49. 2, Frank, b. May 12, '52.

(4) *Elizabeth*, b. Feb. 2, 1837. (5) *George*, b. Sept. 21, '40.

696. III. JOHNSON G.,[7] b. April 15, 1804, lives in Prophetstown, Whiteside Co., Ill., (1860.) He is a farmer and merchant, unm.

697. IV. GEORGE J.,[7] b. Sept. 15, 1805. He has held all the important town offices, has been 1st Constable, Select-man, and Justice of the Peace. He is a farmer, and lives in Panton, Vt., unm., on the homestead of his father.

698. V. ELIZABETH,[7] b. Aug. 28, 1807, m. Feb. 1830, Joseph Smith, of Addison, Vt. He is a highly respectable farmer, and a Deacon of the Bap. ch. She is a m. ch. also. Chil.—

(1) *Edward Walker*, b. Feb. 21, 1831, d. Nov. 12, '31. (2) *Helen Elizabeth*, b. Aug. 27, '33. (3) *George Walker*, b. Feb. 5, '35, d. Feb. 12, '36. (4) *Maria L.*, b. Aug. 4, '38, d. Feb. 22, '46. (5) *Therese A.*, b. July 23, '41 or 2.

699. VI. FREEBORN,[7] (1384) b. Jan. 22, 1809, m. March, 1836, Emily, dau. of George Gage, of Addison, Vt. He emigrated early to Ill., and resides in Prophetstown, Whiteside Co., Ill., (1860.) He has 7 chil.

700. VII. SAMANTHA,[7] b. Nov. 24, 1812. Res. Panton, Vt.

701. VIII. SEVIAH,[7] b. Aug. 16, 1814. Res. Panton, Vt.

702. IX. MATILDA.[7] She m. Jan. 1, 1829, George Spencer, brother of Jonathan B., and b. Oct. 12, 1800. Res. Panton, Vt. He has represented his town in the Legislature two yrs., been Town Clerk 11 yrs., Select-man 3 yrs., Trustee of U. S. surplus fund and Justice of the Peace 5 yrs. She is a m. Meth. ch. Chil.—

(1) *Harriet W.*, b. Jan. 23, 1830. (2) *Gideon*, b. Nov. 5, '31. (3) *Freeborn J.*, b. Oct. 1, '33, and d. June 19, '35. (4) *Jonathan*, b. Oct. 29, '35. (5) *Seviah W.*, b. May 23, '37. (6) *Clarissa G.*, b. July 17, '46. (7) *Lura J.*, b. Feb. 10, '50.

703. X. EDWARD,[7] b. Dec. 30, 1816, d. May 17, 1827.

704. XI. JULIA ANN,[7] b. Dec. 2, 1818, d. Aug. 28, 1819.

705. XII. CLARA L.,[7] b. Dec. 16, 1820, m. Sept. 11, 1853, Davis P. Cook. She res. in Panton, Vt., (1860,) and is a woman of more than ordinary excellence. They have—

(1) *Alice Gertrude*, b. Dec. 20, 1854.

CHIL. OF OBADIAH WALKER,[6] [266] OF FERRISBURGH, VT.

706. I. JERUSHA,[7] b. Oct. 22, 1799, m. June, 1815, Timothy Lovell. She m. 2d, June 26, 1825, Lanader Prindle, a farmer, who sometimes officiates as preacher of the Meth. ch. Both m. ch. Res. Prophetstown, Ill. Child,—

(1) *Timothy*, b. June 17, 1820, m. Sophia Fisk, of Burlington, Vt., April, '42, and has 5 chil.—1, Lucy, b. Dec. 1843. 2, Caroline, b. Oct. '45. 3, Helen, b. May, '47. 4, George, b. Oct. '52. 5, Eugene, b. May 1, '55. He is a merchant in B.

707. II. ZURIEL,[7] (1390) b. May 27, 1801. He m. Feb. 1827, Mary Johnson, dau. of William, of Cheshire, Ct., and has had 10 chil. At the age of 14, he was apprenticed to John H. Sherrill, Esq., of Vergennes, Vt., to learn the business of woolen manufacturing, where he remained till 21 yrs. of age. Pursuing this business 3 or 4 yrs., he bought the farm of his father and has since lived in Ferrisburgh, Vt. He was in the State Legislature, as Representative, 1832, 3 and 4, and in the Senate, 1848 and 9. He has been Justice of the Peace 25 yrs., Town Clerk 13 yrs., and at various periods Select-man, and Lister, and has been also Steward of the Meth. ch. for 15 yrs. He is an energetic, highly intelligent, and worthy man, and possesses in an unusual degree, the esteem and confidence of all who know him. He and w. and 2 oldest sons are m. Meth. ch.

708. III. Nathan,[7] b. Jan. 24, 1802. }
709. IV. Wealthy,[7] b. Jan. 30, 1804. } Died Dec. 13, 1815, and were buried in one grave.

710. V. Obadiah,[7] (1400) b. Nov. 17, 1808. He m. May, 1841, Lucina Parker, who d. 1844. He is a merchant in Vergennes, Vt., a Justice of the Peace, and has held most of the important offices of the city of Vergennes. He is m. Epis. ch., and has 1 son.

711. VI. Solomon,[7] (1401) b. Dec. 18, 1810, d. Aug. 24, 1849. He m. May, 1842, Almary Spencer, dau. of Jonathan B., his 2d cousin. (See No. 695.) She was a useful and exemplary m. of the Meth. ch., and d. Aug. 1843, leaving 1 child. He m. 2d, Helen E. Ensign, dau. of Dea. John, of Moriah, N. Y., by whom he had one son. She is an exemplary m. Bap. ch. He was a merchant, in Burlington, Vt., and having extraordinary industry and enterprise, and great business capability, accumulated a large property. Scarcely a man in Chittenden Co. had more friends.

712. VII. Amanda Melvina,[7] b. May 19, 1812, m. Nov. 1836, Levi Beach, son of Stephen, who emigrated from Ct. about 1800. Res. Ferrisburgh, Vt. till 1854, when they rem. to Prophetstown, Ill. Both m. Meth. ch. Chil.—

(1) *Elizabeth.* (2) *Ann.* (3) *Walker*, b. 1849 or '50.

Children of DANIEL WALKER,[6] [267] of Canton, N. Y.

713. I. Electa,[7] b. Feb. 8, 1794, in Ferrisburgh, Vt., d. 1852. She m. Sept. 17, 1840, Peter Pollard, a farmer and Universalist. No chil.

714. II. Harry,[7] (1403) b. Sept. 12, 1796. He m. Sept. 1817, Betsey Sturges. He m. 2d, Chloe Goodale, who d. March 6, 1857. He resides in Canton, N. Y., an honest, industrious farmer, and has had 6 chil.

715. III. Sally,[7] b. in Canton, N. Y., July 2, 1800, d. 1803.

716. IV. Ferdinand C.,[7] (1409) b. March 22, 1804. He m. Feb. 25, 1848, Zorilda (Turner) Bigwood, who was b. in Ky. He is a Universalist and mechanic. Res. Quincy, Ill., and has 3 chil.

717. V. Clarissa Jane,[7] b. May 17, 1808, in C., m. April 8, 1844, Benjamin Cox, of Potsdam, N. Y., as 2d w. He is a farmer

and was b. in Barnard, Vt., May 30, 1796, and resides in East Perriepoint, N. Y. Chil.—

(1) *Daniel Walker*, b. in E. P., July 29, 1848. (2) *Edna P.*, b. in E. P., Jan. 16, '51.

718. VI. LAURA E.,[7] b. Feb. 4, 1812, in Canton, m. Nov. 28, 1836, Cyrus F. Goodale, of C. He is a farmer. She is a Universalist. No chil.

CHIL. OF WILLIAM WALKER,[6] [268] OF FERRISBURGH, VT.

719. I. PATIENCE,[7] b. May 7, 1800, m. March 11, 1816, Lot Keeler, who d. March 28, 1820; m. 2d, April 27, 1827, Olmsted Keeler, of Panton, Addison Co., Vt., a wealthy farmer. She is m. Meth. ch. Chil.—

(1) *Orrin*, b. Oct. 18, 1818, m. Elvira E. Clark, March, '42; was a farmer and grocer, and d. Sept. 1, '54, in Clayton, Iowa. Chil.—1, Harriet, b. '47. 2, Mary Jane, b. '50. 3, Ella, b. '54.

(2) *Charlotte P.*, b. Sept. 1, 1820, m. Aaron Field, of Ferrisburgh, Vt., Feb. '41, a farmer. She is m. Meth. ch. Chil.—1, Orville, b. '43. 2, Theresa P., b. '45. 3, Marietta, b. '48. 4, Willard, b. '51.

(3) *Buren*, b. July 9, 1830, is a farmer.

720. II. BETSEY,[7] b. June 14, 1802, m. Jan. 1, 1822, Philo Fuller. Res. Centreville, Apanoos Co., Ia. Both are m. Bap. ch.

721. III. LYDIA,[7] b. May 9, 1804, m. Jan. 20, 1825, Carlos Sherman. Res. Jared, Erie Co., Penn.

722. IV. JOSEPH B.,[7] (1412) b. Feb. 15, 1806. He is m. and has chil. Res. Centerville, Ia.

723. V. WILLIAM,[7] (1413) b. May 9, 1808, d. March, 1853. He m. and had 6 chil. Res. West Canaan, O.

724. VI. SYLVENIA,[7] b. March 1, 1810, d. April 16, 1848. She m. March, 1835, Geo. Field, son of Benj., of Ferrisburgh, Vt., b. Aug. 26, 1802. He is a farmer, and one of the wealthiest citizens in F. Chil.—

(1) *Jane*, b. Aug. 2, 1836, m. Nathan Lee, 1858, and d. 1859. (2) *John*, b. Oct. 11, '37, d. Jan. 15, '49. (3) *Walker F.*, b. Feb. 26, '40. (4) *Benjamin F.*, b. June 22, '41, d. Sept. 8, '41. (5) *Martha*, b. Sept. 8, '42. (6) *Sylvenia*, b. Feb. 3, '48, d. April 16, '48.

725. VII. VELINA,[7] b. Jan. 23, 1812, m. Sept. 6, 1832, Hiram Keeler. Res. Jackson, Union Co., Ohio.

726. VIII. PERTHENA, b. June 22, 1814, d. Feb. 1, 1855. She m. Jan. 1, 1836, Hiram Field, son of Stephen, of Ferrisburgh, Vt. He was b. Feb. 12, 1807, is a farmer, and one of the wealthiest men of the town. She is m. of Meth. ch. Chil.—

(1) *Albert*, b. Oct. 14, 1837, d. April 5, '50. (2) *Carlinda*, b. Aug. 18, '39. (3) *Byron*, b. Dec. 17, '41. (4) *Carlton N.*, b. Dec. 7, '45, d. Feb. 3, '49. (5) *Carlton*, b. Sept. 24, '49. (6) *Lillie M.*, b. Oct. 25, '52. (7) *Emma*, b. Jan. 21, '55, d. Jan. 22.

727. IX. NATHAN,[7] b. June 13, 1816, is married and res. in West Canaan, Ohio.

728. X. DANIEL,[7] b. Aug. 3, 1818, m. and res. in W. C.

729. XI. EDELIA,[7] b. July 2, 1820, d. July 3, 1820.

BY 2d MARRIAGE.

730. XII. SOLOMON,[7] (1419) b. Oct. 25, 1822, twin. He m. May 20, 1845, Nancy Francis, who was b. Nov. 6, 1825, dau. of Wm. and Lucinda, in Co. of Botelourt, Va. He was a farmer in Ohio. In July, 1850, he rem. to Centreville, Iowa, and has since been a merchant, and a successful operator in real estate. He has 7 chil.

731. XIII. CATHARINE,[7] b. Oct. 25, 1822, m. Oct. 1, 1837, Elijah Ellis. Res. unknown.

CHILDREN OF NATHAN WALKER,[6] [269] OF CANTON, N. Y.

732. I. ALBERT,[7] (1426) b. Aug. 12, 1804. He m. Aug. 13, 1833, Mary McElroy, in Clarke, C. W., and has had 8 chil. From his boyhood he was highly esteemed. He left home when a young man, and was early brought into active business. Laboring under many disadvantages, and passing through many changes of fortune, he has, however, given evidence of good business talent, and energy of character, and always been esteemed an honest man. Through the treachery of others, he lost a handsome property in Canada. When he rem. to Waupun, Wis., he had only a few shillings in his pocket. He now owns and lives on a valuable farm of 400 acres. Both are m. Meth ch.

733. II. LEVI,[7] (1435) b. July 13, 1807, d. June 16, 1852. He m. March 30, 1837, Jane A. Powers, of Ferrisburgh, Vt., in Clarke, C. W., and had 6 chil. She is m. ch. and res. in Waupun, Wis. He was a strictly moral and estimable man, loved to hear his wife converse upon the subject of religion, but to the last, remained silent upon the subject. During the 15 mos. of extreme suffering, he uttered no murmur.

734. III. CHITTENDEN,[7] b. March 2, 1809, m. Feb. 1836, Caroline Decker, in Clarke, C. W. A respectable and industrious man, living in Canada.

735. IV. HIRAM,[7] b. April 11, 1812, spent 4 yrs. in California, and now res. in Waupun, Wis., unm.

736. V. LEVINA JANE,[7] b. Aug. 16, 1813, d. Aug. 30, 1838. She m. Jan. 1836, Joseph Powers, formerly of Ferrisburgh, Vt., and a farmer. He m. 2d, her sister. (See No. 738.) Res. Smith's Creek? C. W.

737. VI. SELINA JERUSHA,[7] b. June 25, 1815, m. Sept. 1836, Chili Averill, in Clarke, C. W., and has chil.

738. VII. CAROLINE AMELIA,[7] b. April 27, 1820, m. Autumn of 1839, Joseph Powers. (See No. 736.) He is a farmer.

739. VIII. GEORGE W.,[7] (1441) b. Sept. 24, 1821, m. Aug. 20, 1855, Mary Webster, of Baraboo, Wis., and has 2 chil. Res. Lyndon, Wis. He owns a farm on Wisconsin river, where he lives, but is principally, and successfully employed, as a pilot of lumber rafts.

CHIL. OF SOLOMON WALKER, [270] OF CANTON, N. Y.

740. I. ALBERT,[7] d. in childhood, before 1805.

741. II. SARAH,[7] b. 1805, m. Sept. 4, 1824, M. S. Prentise, son of Ezra, Esq. They lived in Canton, N. Y., and in Dec. 1856, rem. to Green Bay, Wis., where he d. Jan. 1857. She is m. Pres. ch. Chil.—

(1) *James Sartel*, b. June 8, 1831, d. Oct. 27, '53. He was first a student in the Franklin Academy, and afterwards a clerk for several years, in the Law office of Judge Flanders, of Malone, N. Y., where he pursued the whole term of his legal studies. In 1852, he went West to commence his professional career. Kind and genial in his disposition, generous and noble in his impulses, he was a young man of great promise.

(2) *Mary Candace*, b. July 23, 1833, m. May 25, '52, Geo. H. Wood, Esq. He is Land agent for Northern Wis. Res. Green Bay, Wis. They have Catharine, b. July 25, '55.

(3) *Ezra Parmele*, b. Dec. 17, 1838.

742. III. CLARISSA,[7] b. 1808, d. in childhood.

743. IV. MARY,[7] b. May 8, 1811, is a talented and accomplished woman, and m. Pres. ch.

CHIL. OF EBENEZER WALKER,[6] [272] OF EDDYVILLE, KY.

744. I. CHITTENDEN H.,[7] (1442) b. Feb. 1807, d. Jan. 30, 1845. He m. Aug. 5, 1840, Nancy Marshall, of Eddyville, Ky., who d. Aug. 9, 1846. He was farmer in E., and had 2 chil.

745. II. CAROLINE,[7] b. Sept. 24, 1809, d. Feb. 2, 1849. She m. Feb. 2, 1831, William Martin, of Yankeetown, Ky., who d. Aug. 9, 1848. Res. Ky. Chil.—

(1) *Jonas*, b. Jan. 5, 1833, d. Sept. 2, '58. (2) *Mary*, b. May 8, '36, d. Aug. 9, '57.

746. III. SAMUEL TUPPER,[7] (1444) b. July 9, 1811, m. Jan. 2, 1839, Elvira Grace, of Yankeetown, Ky., and has 2 chil. He is a farmer in Lyon Co., Ky.

747. IV. ELMEDA,[7] b. Nov. 18, 1813, d. Sept. 9, 1844. She m. Jan. 7, 1830, E. P. Ross. Chil.—

(1) *Mary Electa*, b. Nov. 6, 1834, m. March 8, 1843, (1853?) Franklin C. Grace, and has chil.—1, James Wm., b. Jan. 5, '54. 2, Mary S., b. Feb. 2, '56. 3, John E., b. Aug. 21, '57, and d. Nov. 17, '58. 4, Gideon, b. May 28, '59.

748. V. EMELINE,[7] b. Oct. 15, 1815, d. Feb. 6, 1853. She m. Nov. 10, 1842, John Peck. Chil.—

(1) *Francis*, b. April 6, 1847. (2) *Mary*, b. May 2, '49. (3) *Sarah*, b. June 4, '50. (4) *Emeline*, b. '52.

749. VI. MARY ANN,[7] b. Aug. 12, 1817, d. April 7, 1854. She m. Nov. 7, 1840, Thomas Coon. Chil.—

(1) *Sarah Ann*, b. Dec. 7, 1846. (2) *Mary E.*, b. Jan 9, '48. (3) *Electa*, b. May 4, '50. (4) *Caroline*, b. June 6, 52.

749.[1] VII. ANNIS,[7] b. May 6, 1819, d. Oct. 6, 1823.

750. VIII. TRUMAN C.,[7] (1446) b. Sept. 22, 1822, m. Aug. 19, 1847, Eliza Jane Winters, who d. Feb. 28, 1850. He m. 2d, Dec. 18, 1855, Hannah Doonos, of Eddyville, Ky. He is a farmer in Yankeetown, near E., Lyon Co., Ky., and has 2 chil.

CHILDREN OF ASA WALKER,[6] [274] OF LENOX, N. Y.

751. I. HANNAH,[7] b. Nov. 16, 1795? d. March 31, 1843. She m. Nov. 1814, Simon Cook, of Wallingford, Vt, who was b. in Swansey, N. H., March 26, 1791. He was Capt. in the War of 1812, and one of the most efficient and patriotic officers in the State. He is a farmer, and a hard working, honest, and worthy man. She was m. Bap. ch. and maintained an exemplary christian character. Chil.—

(1) *Lois*, b. Feb. 3, 1815, m. Nov. 26, '30, Amos Ripley, and d. Feb. 10, '38. (2) *Phebe*, b. Nov. 5, '16, d. Nov. '36. (3) *Charlotte*, b. Sept. 12, '18, m. June 17, '39, A. L. Hyde, who d. Sept. 18, '57. Res. Wallingford. Hotel proprietor. (4) *Jane*, b. May 12, '20, m. Nov. '37, J. D. Livingston, and d. Nov. '42. He m. 2d, and lives in W. (5) *James Alvin*, b. May 1, '24, d. '25. (6) *Sybil*, b. March 25, '26, d. Aug. 31, '47. (7) *Janette E.*, b. April 26, '27, m. July 7, '53, Hugh A. Frew, in Frewsburgh, N. Y. (8) *Herbert*, b. May 13, '29, d. June 30, '49. (9) *Laura Ann*, b. Nov. 5, '31, m. Nelson C. Hyde, Nov. 13, '50. Res. West Poultney, Vt. (10) *Helen*, b. March 13, '35. (11) *Hattie*, b. '38.

752. II. LAVINA,[7] b. March 19, 1798, d. Feb. 7, 1847. She m. Aug. 14, 1814, Harry Boardman, of Burlington, Vt. They emigrated to Medina, N. Y., and from thence in 1832, to Dupage, Will Co., Ill., (Barber's Corners.) She had 9 chil., 4 of whom survived her, viz.,—

(1) *Horace*, farmer. (2) *Adeline*, m. Wm. Freeman, of Dupage. (3) *Sabra*, d. since 1847. (4) *Rachel*, the youngest.

753. III. LAURA,[7] b. Sept. 5, 1799, d. Feb. 1852, in Plainfield, Ill. She m. Nathan Farr, of Oneida Co., N. Y. Res. Polk, Bremer Co., Iowa. Chil.—

(1) *Laura Amanda*, d. y. (2) *Nathan*, d. y. (3) *Silas*. (4) *William*. (5) *Lydia*. (6) *Asa*.

754. IV. LOIS,[7] b. Jan. 21, 1801, in Hindsburg, Vt. She m. Nov. 9, 1817, Noah Stevens of Lenox, N. Y., who was b. in Sangersfield, N. Y., Nov. 16, 1797. They lived in L. till 1835, then rem. to Ill., and now res. in Bloomingdale, Dupage Co. He is a farmer, and has been Deacon of the Bap. ch. 13 yrs. At the age of 17, she united with the ch., and all her chil. living, are m. ch. Chil.—

(1) *Sibbilla*, b. Feb. 11, 1820. (2) *Thomas Riley*, b. March 25, '22. (3) *Leonora*, b. April 3, '24. (4) *Lois*, b. May 19, '25. (5) *Lavina*, b. June 20, '28. (6) *Ethiel Henry*, b. March 28, '31, d. Sept. 7, '31. (7) *Josiah*, b. July 10, '32. (8) *Alvira Laura*, b. Dec. 31, '35, in Bloomingdale, Ill. (9) *Adaline D.*, b. June 28, '38. (10) *Mary Almeda*, b. Nov. 25, '40.

755. V. ALVIN,[7] (1448) b. Aug 31, 1802, m. about 1825, Lucy, dau. of Thomas Gray, and has 5 chil. He is a blacksmith, and res. in Sparta, Monroe Co., Wis.

756. VI. ASA,[7] b. Jan. 31, 1804, d. Jan. 1813.

757. VII. LUTHER BINGHAM,[7] (1453) b. April 10, 1806, in Clarendon, Vt. He m. Sept. 13, 1825, Joanna Francis, of Lenox, N. Y., dau. of Aaron, and b. Jan. 10, 1805. He is a farmer, and has had 4 chil. Res. Johnsonsburgh, Wyoming Co., N. Y.

758. VIII. SIBBILLA,[7] b. Feb. 26, 1808, d. Aug. 6, 1857. She m. 1829, or ae. 21, David W. Bangs, from Stamford, Vt. They rem. in 1833, to Elgin, Kane Co., Ill. He was a farmer, then a speculator: Chil.—

(1) ***Abigail Ann***, m. Washington J. Tillotson. Res. E. (2) ***Edward Cushman***, unm. (3) ***Marion***, dec'd. (4) ***Orville Wadsworth***, unm. (5) ***Henrietta***, unm. (6) ***Lucy Lydia***, unm.

759. IX. ETHIEL CUSHMAN,[7] (1456) b. Jan. 31, 1810, m. Nancy Rose, of Lenox, N. Y. Res. Jacksonville, Chickasaw Co., Iowa, and has had 9 chil.

BY 2d MARRIAGE.

760. X. MINERVA,[7] b. Dec. 1812, d. Feb. 1813.

761. XI. ASA L.,[7] (1465) b. May 4, 1814, d. Sept. 12, 1853. (Fam. Rec.) He m. Feb. 25, 1835, Nancy Jackson, who was b. Jan. 14, 1814. He was a farmer, and had 3 chil. Res. Lenox, N. Y., on the old homestead.

762. XII. URIAL,[7] (1468) b. April 23, 1818, m. Jan. 25, 1836, Mehitable Dessmore, of Lenox, N. Y., dau. of Capt. Abram, formerly of Boston, and has had 4 chil. He was a manufacturer of agricultural implements 9 yrs., and since 1853, has carried on an extensive grain and commission trade in Chicago, Ill., where he resides.

CHIL. OF BENJAMIN WALKER,[6] [278] OF CAMPTON, ILL.

763. I. OLIVE,[7] b. March 16, 1799, m. Daniel Reynolds. Res. King's Mills, Kane Co., Ill. Chil.—

(1) ***Morgan***. (2) ***Hiram***, dec'd. (3) ***Sophia***. (4) ***Daniel***. (5) ***Harry***, dec'd. (6) ***Sybil***. (7) ***Child***, d. at birth.

764. II. BENJAMIN CUSHMAN,[7] (1472) b. July 11, 1801, m. 1829, Joanna Southworth. He rem. to Louisiana, thence to Texas, in 1833, and had 1 dau. when last heard from.

31

765. III. WILLIAM GREEN,[7] (1473) b. Dec. 14, 1803, m. Persis Carver, and has had 6 chil. Both are m. Meth. ch. He is a farmer, and has held the offices of constable, and superintendent of the poor. Res. King's Mills, Ill.

767. IV. ANSON,[7] (1479) b. Sept. 7, 1806, m. March 22, 1829, Lois Ackley, who was b. June 1, 1811, in Canandaigua, N. Y. He has had 12 chil. He was a teacher several yrs., till the age of 25; in 1818, settled in Alabama, N. Y., and in 1829, rem. to Canandaigua, where he now lives, a farmer and a Baptist. He has held several town offices for 25 yrs., as Clerk and Assessor, and is an industrious, and influential man.

768. V. NELSON,[7] (1491) b. March 19, 1808, m. May 31, 1840, Louisa Woodruff, and has had 8 chil. He is a farmer and Post-master. Res. King's Mills, Kane Co., Ill.

769. VI. ABEL,[7] (1499) b. Feb. 12, 1810, m. March, 1831, Catharine Rogers, and has 7 chil. He is a carpenter and joiner, Post-master, and Justice of the Peace. Res. Pecatonia, Winnebago Co., Ill.

770. VII. HIRAM,[7] (1506) b. Feb. 19, 1812, m. Chastina Rogers, dau. of Josiah, of Windsor, Vt., and has 2 chil. He rem. to Mich. 1851; has been County Surveyor since 1855, Supervisor and Justice of the Peace 5 yrs., and was elected Prosecuting Attorney for Manistee Co., in 1857, for the term of 2 yrs. Res. Manistee, Mich.

CHIL. OF ABEL WALKER,[6] [285] OF BLOOMINGDALE, ILL.

771. I. SIBBEL,[7] b. 1814, d. 1846. She m. March 2, 1834, Alvin Smith, in Clarendon, Vt., who was b. 1814. Res. Bloomingdale, Ill. Chil.—

(1) *Josephine*, b. April 7, 1837. (2) *Harriet A.*, b. April 23, '39. (3) *Orick C.*, b. July 24, '41. (4) *Eveline M.*, b. April 25, '43. (5) *Henry A.*, b. Sept. 13, '46.

He m. 2dly, April, 1847, Margaret Sharp, and has 4 chil.

772. II. HARRY,[7] b. 1816, m. Ann Neller, in Bloomingdale, Ill., rem. to Mich. His relatives can give no clue to him, or his chil.

773. III. ABIGAIL,[7] b. 1818. Res. Bloomingdale, unm.

774. IV. TWELVE CHILDREN in this family died in infancy, or under 4 yrs. of age. Names not given.

William P Walker

CHIL. OF HON. WILLIAM WALKER,[6] [288] OF LENOX.

786. I. WILLIAM PERRIN,[7] (1508) b. Oct. 8, 1778, in Lenox, d. Nov. 11, 1858. He m. Jan. 29, 1807, Lucy Adam, dau. of John Adam, Esq,, of Canaan, Ct., and had 9 chil. He was graduated at Williams Coll. in 1798, was admitted to the Bar, and began the practice of Law in 1801, (1803 ?). He was proposed for admission to the Supreme Court in 1804, and the usual entry was made, "and the Court will advise." He was not actually admitted till 1810. He was Representative 1 yr., 1809, and Senator 1810, '11 and '15, in the State Legislature: was a candidate of the Republican party for Representative to Congress. He was Chief Justice of the Court of Sessions of the County, from 1819 to '28, a member of the Governor's Council in 1811 and '24, and in 1824, on the resignation of his father, he was appointed Judge of Probate, which office he held 24 yrs., till his resignation in 1848, when the infirmities of age compelled him to seek seclusion from public cares. He was also nominated by the Whig party, as a candidate for Lieut. Governor, with Gov. Everett, but declined the nomination. He was one of the most prominent of the old Jeffersonian party, in the Western part of the State; but he abjured politics, in the later years of his life. Over 6 ft. in height, and well proportioned, his personal appearance and manners, were uncommonly dignified and elegant, and could always command attention and deference. He possessed an unusual sensitiveness, which lent a refinement, delicacy and courtesy, to his character and deportment, and unfitted him for the strifes of political life. Shrinking from the vices, so common among men of his profession, always temperate, honorable and true, he was distinguished by remarkable purity of morals. He was fond of reading, exceedingly well informed, of quick discernment, and penetrating judgment. Hospitality and generosity, were prominent qualities in his character. Meanness, his soul never knew. His dispatch in business was remarkable. As a citizen he was mild, candid, and free from all partizan feeling and expression. His influence in the town, was very great, and all looked up to him for counsel, and paid him the highest respect. He was also very affectionate and amiable in temper, and in the relations of domestic and private life, he was exemplary and faithful. As a Judge he was courteous, patient, dispassionate, intelligent, and impartial. Honorable sentiments, unquestioned integrity, and genial and

pleasant manners, made him a popular citizen, and a highly satisfactory Judge; and during the active years of his life, he held an enviable position in the affections, respect and confidence of the people of Berkshire County. His father, the elder Judge, could control an audience wonderfully. The son was not so popular as a speaker. The two were very different men, yet alike in integrity, and strong sense of justice, and in the situations they occupied, these traits, peculiarly qualified them, to be the protectors of the widow and fatherless, and for the long period of more than half a century, they discharged the duties of the office, with signal ability and success. They are both remembered and spoken of to this day, as men of most excellent judgment, incorruptible honor, and spotless purity.

A Discourse in memory of Judge Walker, upon the text, Job, 19th chap., 21st v., was preached, Nov. 14, 1858, by Rev. E. K. Alden, pastor of the Cong. church in L. It is published and entitled, "The Lesson of Severe, Protracted Suffering." The following is an extract:—

"If what I have looked upon, was, as I have been told, but the wreck,—that silvered head, that brow, that front, were a noble ruin—it must once have been a princely crown. * * * * * The mere cold statement that, 'he moved into his sick room in Oct. 1851, and never left it without assistance; has continued almost perfectly helpless; for nearly four years has received his food from the hands of others; and for several months has been unable, but with extreme difficulty to converse even with his own family; how little such a brief summary tells us of what have constituted so many days and nights of continuous discomfort, often associated with excruciating pain. * * * * It is a grateful record to add, that on the Sabbath, the 7th of March, 1852, in the presence of a few friends—this venerable man was received in his sick room, to the fellowship of the visible church of Christ."

787. II. Richard Montgomery,[7] b. Sept. 18, 1780, d. March 12, 1784.

788. III. Sarah,[7] b. Aug. 1, 1783, d. Oct. 18, 1846, ae. 63. She m. Aug. 5, 1802, Dr. Charles Worthington, of Lenox, who was b. in Colchester, Ct., and d. May 23, 1840. She was a very superior woman, and m. Cong. ch. He pursued his professional studies under Dr. Hall, of Middletown, Ct., and was a highly respectable physician in L. He however, engaged early in manufacturing pursuits, which drew off his attention from his profession. He was a member of the Legislature about 1827, and was a sincere christian, honored and beloved. Chil.—

(1) *Mary*, b. Feb. 10, 1804, unm.

(2) *Sarah*, b. March 3, 1806, d. Dec. 23, '56. She m. April 19, '31, Hon. John Z. Goodrich, of Stockbridge, b. in Sheffield. He was a Lawyer in Lenox, also editor and proprietor 7 or 8 yrs. of the "Eagle," a newspaper published in L., Member of Congress in 1854, and now a successful manufacturer in Stockbridge. He is a gentleman of superior energy and ability, and uncommon rectitude in business. As an instance in point, as rare as it is commendable, it may be mentioned, that of a debt of $65,000, from which he was legally exonerated, considering himself morally liable, as he has recovered his prosperity, he has gradually paid off nearly the whole. He is Republican candidate for Lieut. Governor, 1860. Both are m. Cong. ch.

(3) *Elizabeth*, b. June 16, 1808, m. June 22, '37, John H. Strong, of Stockbridge, a merchant, and d. April 28, '52.

(4) *Harriet*, b. July 27, 1813, m. Oct. 12, '42, Henry W. Taft, Esq., of Lenox, and d. Oct. 17 '60. He was Register of Probate from '53 to '55, and has been Clerk of the Courts of Berkshire Co., since '56. He is a Lawyer in L.

(5) *Charles*, b. Feb. 23, 1822, d. May 28, '47, unm. He was graduated at Williams Coll., in '40, taking the 2d honor of his class. He was a lawyer of great promise. Res. Boston.

By 2d Marriage.

789. IV. Mary,[7] b. March 10, 1792, d. same day.

790. V. Alice,[7] b. June 16, 1795, d. same day.

791. VI. Caleb,[7] b. Dec. 30, 1796, d. same day.

792. VII. George,[7] b. April 6, 1801, d. May 18, 1801.

Children of CALEB WALKER,[6] [289] of Lenox.

793. I. Richard Montgomery,[7] (1517) b. Feb. 8, 1788, in Lee, (Lenox?) He is now known only as Caleb Richard, an is supposed to be living in Mich. He m. ———, who had 5 chil., and died in Lenox, and two daus. only survive, who are m. and living in West Mich.

Children of LEWIS WALKER,[6] [291] of Seekonk.

794. I. Caleb,[7] (1522) b. April 26, 1792, d. 1850. He m. Oct. 14, 1819, Kesiah Barney, of Rehoboth, who d. about 1837 or 8. He was a shoemaker. Res. Seekonk.

795. II. William,[7] (1525) b. March 9, 1794, d. Summer of 1859. He m. April 8, 1820, Patty Dean, of Attleboro', and had 5 chil. Res. A.

796. III. Esther,[7] is m. Cong. ch. Res. S., unm.

797. IV. ZECHARIAH,[7] (1530) m. May, 1826, Lydia Ide, of Seekonk, had 8 chil., and d. July, 1860. He was a cloth dresser. Res. Providence, R. I.

798. V. LOIS,[7] b. 1800, d. March 26, 1854, in S., unm.

799. VI. LEWIS,[7] d. 3 or 4 yrs. old.

800. VII. CHILD,[7] d. in infancy

CHIL. OF OTIS WALKER,[7] [293] OF BRIGHTON, N. Y.

801. I. . CHAUNCEY,[7] (1538) b. Jan. 17, 1798, d. Aug. 14, 1827. He m. Feb. 16, 1819, Clarissa Morse, who d. June 19, 1825. He m. 2dly, 1827, Sarah Bradford. He was a farmer, and had 4 chil. Res. Brighton, N. Y.

802. II. ANSEL W.,[7] (1542) b. Jan. 11, 1800, m. May 29, 1825, Naomi Jeffords, who d. 1828. He m. 2dly, Oct. 15, 1829, Mary D. Roberts. He is a carpenter, m. Meth. ch., and has 8 chil. Res. Detroit, Mich.

803. III. GEORGE,[7] (1550) b. Nov. 18, 1801, d. Sept. 14, 1836, in Rochester, N.Y. He m. Jan. 18, 1826, Hannah Benton. He was a tinner, and had 4 chil. Both m. Epis. ch.

804. IV. EMILY,[7] b. Jan. 31, 1804, d. June 19, 1811.

805. V. MELINDA,[7] b. March 23, 1806. Res. Detroit, Mich.

806. VI. THOMAS, J.,[7] (1554) b. Sept. 21, 1809, d. Aug. 6, 1851, in Detroit, Mich. He m. June 1, 1835, Sarah Bisbee, and had 5 chil. He was a farmer and Justice of the Peace. Both m. Pres. ch. She res. in Oivet, Eaton Co., Mich.

807. VII. EDWIN,[7] (1559) b. Nov. 9. 1811, d. Aug. 19, 1836. He m. 1832, Sabrina Ludden, in Rochester, N. Y., and had 1 dau. He was a tinner, and m. Bap. ch. He removed to Marshall, Mich., in 1836, where they died.

808. VIII. WILLIAM H.,[7] (1560) b. Sept. 20, 1813, d. March 4, 1843, in Marshall, Mich. He m. 1833, Eliza Lyport, in Rochester, N. Y., and had 2 chil. He rem. to Mich in 1837, was a tinner, and an active m. Meth. ch.

809. IX. CLARISSA,[7] b. Sept. 27, 1815, m. July 1, 1840, Benj. Scott. He is a joiner. Both m. Meth. ch. Res. Detroit, Mich. Chil.—

(1) *Henry Walker*, b. Jan. 15, '44.

(2) *Henrietta C.*, b. May 7, '48.

(3) *Charles Otis*, b. Aug. 19, '59.

810. X. ELIZA A.,[7] b. Dec. 17, 1817, m. Nov. 5, 1847, Henry Langley, a mason. She is m. Epis. ch. Res. Detroit, Mich. Child—

(1) *Harriet E.*, b. July 31, '49.

CHILDREN OF WILKS WALKER,[6] [294] OF SAVOY.

811. I. EPHRAIM,[7] (1562) b. April 10, 1800, m. Jan. 5, 1826, Esther dau. of Daniel Dunham, of Savoy, and had 5 chil. He is a farmer in S.

812. II. NANCY,[7] b. July 3, 1803, is m. Bap. ch. Res. S. unm.

813. III. LEWIS,[7] b. Oct. 11, 1806, m. Oct. 12, 1836, Chloe M., dau. of Elisha Brown, of Cheshire. He is a farmer and Bap. Res. Charlotte, Chautauque Co., N. Y. No chil.

814. IV. MARY,[7] b. Oct. 5, 1809, m. Jan. 16. 1842, Daniel, son of Isaac Brown, of Adams. He is a farmer and m. ch. Res. Ottowa, Lasalle Co., Ill. Child—

(1) *Ellen F.*, b. Dec. 4, 1846.

815. V. BETSEY,[7] b. Feb. 1, 1814, d. July 17, 1854. She m. April 15, 1841, Jacob Curtis, of Springwater, N. Y., a farmer. He d. March 27, 1854. Both m. ch. Chil.—

(1) *Ruth*, b. May 14, 1844.

(2) *Charles F.*, b. Feb. 28, '46.

(3) *Sarah P.*, b. July 9, '49.

(4) *Jacob W.*, b. April 17, '52.

816. VI. HULDAH S.,[7] b. May 27, 1816. She m. Feb. 2, 1851, Michael Barden, of Savoy. She is m. Meth. ch. Chil.—

(1) *Charles F.*, b. June 26, 1853.

(2) *Mary R.*, b. Aug. 11, '55.

CHILDREN OF ABEL WALKER,[6] [298] OF HARDWICK.

817. I. ALVAH,[7] (1567) b. April 9, 1798. He m. Sept. 8, 1821, Vesta Whitcomb, in Greenwich, who was b. April 5, 1801.

They are m. Meth. ch. He is a carpenter, and has had 7 chil., and all are m. ch. Res. Oswego, N. Y.

818. II. HORACE,[7] b. Oct. 12, 1799, d. Sept. 2, 1803.

819. III. OTIS,[7] b. Dec. 28, 1800, d. Aug. 26, 1803.

820, IV. CYRIL,[7] b. Dec. 6, 1802, d. Aug. 23, 1803.

821. V. MARY,[7] b. Aug. 27, 1804, is a m. of Cong. ch. and lives in Greenwich, unm.

822. VI. HARRIET,[7] b. Nov. 4, 1806, m. Sept. 15, 1830, John S. Hall, who was b. April 9, 1807. Both are m. of Cong. ch. He is a Deacon; has held a Captain's commission, and is a manufacturer of tools. Res. Columbus, O. Chil.—

(1) *Chester O.*, b. April 7, 1832, was Medical Student, and d. Jan. 31, '51, of inflammatory rheumatism. (2) *Abel W.*, b. Aug. 22, '34. (3) *John Q.*, b. June 10, '37, a grad. of Am. Coll., and now a student in the Theo'l Seminary, N.Y. City. (4) *Harriet A.*, b. Oct. 21, '40. (5) *Charles H.*, b. March 21, '44. (6) *Albert A.*, b. April 9, '47. (7) *George C.*, b. July 19, '50. The 4 oldest are m. ch.

823. VII. VASHTI,[7] b. Sept. 24, 1808, lives in Greenwich, Mass., is m. of the Cong. ch. unm.

824. VIII. ABEL,[7] (1572) b. Dec. 14, 1810, m. Oct. 14. 1835, Sarah S. Allen, of Brimfield, and had 4 chil. He is a carpenter. Both are m. of Cong. ch., and he holds the office of Deacon. Res. Elgin, Kane Co., Ill.

CHIL. OF WILLIAM WALKER,[6] [299] OF HARDWICK, MS.

825. I. LOIS READ,[7] b. Sept. 9, 1805, in H., m. Dec. 29, 1830, Joseph Cobb, who was b. in Deerfield, July 13, 1805. He is a farmer, resides in Athol, Mass., and has held the office of Colonel, in the State militia. Chil.—

(1) *William Walker*, b. Dec. 7, 1832, m. June 4, '56, L. R. Turner, and have—1, Wm. Herbert, b. July 24, '57. Res. Athol. (2) *Lois Josephine*, b. Sept. 24, '46, d. Oct. 15, '48. (3) *Joseph Henry*, b. July 25, '50.

826. II. THOMAS POWERS,[7] (1576) b. Jan. 20, 1807, m. April 13, 1836, Mary H. Gibbs, of Greenwich, and has 1 child. Res. G.

827. III. WILLIAM,[7] b. May 9, 1810, d. May 10, 1819.

828. IV. SUSAN,[7] b. Oct. 8, 1813, m. Hammond Hunt, April 30, 1839. He was b. in Hardwick, April 15, 1812, d. in H., Aug. 28,

1845. Both were m. Cong. ch. in H. He was a farmer. She m. 2d, Jan. 3, 1848, Joshua Conkey, of Rochester, N. Y., who was b. in Pelham, Mass., Feb. 26, 1804. He is a merchant, has been Alderman of the City, 5th ward, 5 yrs., and County Supervisor 3 yrs. Chil.—

(1) *Eunice Mercy Ann*, b. April 12, 1840, d. Nov. 15, '41. (2) *Mercy Ann*, b. Dec. 17, '41, d. Sept. 23, '42. (3) *Susan Elvira*, b. Jan. 28, '45. BY 2d MARRIAGE. (4) *Harriet Agnes*, b. Oct. 30, '48. (5) *Cornelia Almedia*, b. Sept. 20, '50. (6) *Frances Clara*, b. Jan. 30, '54.

829.* V. JAMES HERVY,[7] (1577) b. July 14, 1818, m. Nov. 9, 1852, Sarah McClintock, who was b. Aug. 31, 1825. They have 2 chil. He has been Select-man several yrs. Res. Hardwick.

830. VI. EUNICE ELVIRA,[7] b. Aug. 1, 1820, m. Oct. 30, 1838, John Allen. Res. Columbus, O. He keeps a Public House in C. Chil.—

(1) *John Hervy*, b. May 30, 1840, d. Sept. 8, '41. (2) *John Genery*, b. Nov. 12, '46.

CHILDREN OF THOMAS WALKER,[6] [301] OF UTICA, N. Y.

831. I. MARY ELVIRA,[7] b. Jan. 10, 1800, d. Sept. 5, 1859. She m. June 17, 1822, John Hancock Ostrom, son of Hon. David, of Paris, N. Y.

The following just estimate of Mrs. O.'s life and character, appeared in the Utica Morning Herald of Sept. 6, 1859:—

For her, few words of eulogy can be necessary, for the poor knew her liberal hand, the afflicted her sympathizing word, the church her ever active, ever disinterested energy, and the thousands of children now weekly gathered into the Sabbath schools of the city, enjoy the advantages of an institution of which she may fairly be recognized as here, the originator and graceful pillar. The qualities which, in her mature years, so endeared her to all, and brought forth such abundant fruit of usefulness, were early developed. Having been brought by her parents to this city, in childhood, nearly a half century of benevolent, religious labors, unremitting and humble, and therefore more than ordinarily efficacious, have secured for her a pre-eminent place, in the history of the charities and religious labors of our city. While with many who have grown up, meeting her weekly in the Sabbath school, her labors in that institution have chiefly commended her to their esteem and affection, it is but one of the many modes in which she exerted herself to do good. In tract distribution, in personal acts of benevolence, in zeal and energy, in

* The reference of No. 304 to 829 is an error, and should be 838.

all matters relative to the church, with which she was connected and the cause of religion generally, she had no peer in the system, constancy, and disinterested fidelity of her labors. Certainly not in the church of which she was a member, perhaps not in the whole community, is there a person whose religious influence has been so decided, and so pervading as hers. She had one master passion: to do good, to relieve suffering, and convert souls to CHRIST. Herein lay her ambition and her pleasure; the singleness of purpose with which she pursued this object, is the explanation of the degree of usefulness she achieved.

In 1816, the deceased, who had then recently (1814) made profession of religion during a revival, was one of four young ladies to originate Sabbath schools in this city, (the first West of Schenectady.)

For more than forty years Mrs. Ostrom continued her labors in the Sabbath school, and for months after she felt that the hand of death was upon her, she attended every Sunday, at a mission school, still prosecuting the self-denying labor, she had begun in the bright dawn of her maidenhood.

While Mrs. Ostrom chose the Sabbath school as the scene of active labor, she made it also the subject of careful study. As evidence of the well-digested opinions she had long ago formed concerning it, it may be mentioned that twenty years ago, or more, application having been made to her, with others, for hints towards a work on the "Sabbath School Teacher," by Rev. John Todd, she elaborated an essay on the question, "Ought unconverted persons to be employed as teachers in Sabbath Schools?" which is embodied in that work. She possessed a good degree of culture and accomplishments, which to another would have been conspicuous. With her, the depth of religious feeling, and the zeal of religious labor, rendered all other qualities subordinate.

Her practical liberality was commensurate with her theoretical benevolence, and her religion, while a light set upon a hill, yet irradiated, warmed, and blessed her home, and every private relation of life. While active beyond what is ordinary in either sex, in every good work, she never offended the nicest sense of female delicacy, never for an instant stepped beyond the strictest limits of woman's sphere.

For nearly three weeks she lay in almost hourly anticipation of death. She was peaceful, nay triumphant in her faith of a blissful immortality, and still exhibited that disinterested solicitude for the eternal welfare of her friends, which ever rested in her heart, and rose upon her lips.

A Discourse commemorative of Mrs. O., by Rev. P. H. Fowler, D. D., of Utica, upon the text, Rom. 16th chap., 3d and 4th verses, and entitled, "Woman's Sphere of Usefulness," has been published.

Mr. O. was a lawyer, and d. in Poughkeepsie, Aug. 10, 1845, ae. 51 yrs.

The following is condensed from the tributes to his memory, which appeared in the Utica papers:—

"He successively occupied the offices of Clerk, Trustee and Assessor of the then village, (Utica,) and after its incorporation as a city, those of a mem. of the Common Council and Mayor. He rose through the various Military grades, to that of Major General, and subsequently, for several yrs., discharged the duties of Chief Engineer of the City Fire Department.

His life was one of great activity and usefulness. Often called by his fellow citizens to occupy posts of honor, he discharged their duties with promptitude and fidelity. Never has our community been called to mourn the loss of a citizen more respected and beloved. The urbanity of his manners, the strength of his friendship, the tenderness and benevolence of his heart, had endeared him to a very large circle of acquaintance. Although overtaken by death, while absent from home, it found him not unprepared. For several yrs. he had been a m. of the ch. of Christ, and in his dying hour, his will was submissive, his faith was strong, and his soul was replete with love to God and man. So triumphant was his faith, that it robbed death of its sting, and communicated to surviving friends a comfort inestimable, in the sad hour of their bereavement."

832. II. WILLIAM,[7] (1579) b. in Rome, N.Y., May 24, 1802. He m. June 11, 1828, Caroline Lydia Steel, dau. of Robert Megget and Isabella (White) Steel, and b. in N. Y., Sept. 21, 1808. Mr. W. rem. to N. Y. in 1819,—engaged in the hardware trade in 1823, and since 1832, has been in the Banking business, and is of the firm of Messrs. Corning & Co., No. 63, Wall St., N. Y. City. He is an Elder in the Pres. ch. since 1845; a man of sterling integrity, superior business capabilities, and devoted piety. He has had 10 chil.

833. III. LOUISA,[7] b. March 9, 1804, in Utica. She m. Aug. 18, 1823, Charles E. Hardy, of U., b. in St. John's, New Brunswick, July 28, 1798, youngest son of Elias and Martha (Haggeford.) He was a hardware merchant, in U., rem. thence to Ithaca, N. Y., and has been for many yrs., Cashier of one of the Banks in I. Both are m. Pres. ch., with all their chil., and are widely esteemed for the highest qualities of personal excellence. Chil.—

(1) *Mary Haggeford*, b. in U., Dec. 2, 1824, m. Josiah Butler Williams, Sept. 6, '42, who was b. in Middletown, Ct., Dec. 16, '10, 4th son of Josiah and Charity. He is President of the Merchant's & Farmer's Bank of Ithaca. He is a farmer as well as a Banker, and has also been State Senator 3 yrs. in succession, and is m. Pres. ch.

(2) *Louisa Walker*, b. June 11, 1835. (3) *George Russell*, b. Sept. 19, '43. (3) *Charles*, b. July 4, '45, d. July 11, '46. (5) *Henry Shailer*, b. March 6, '47. (6) *Roger Butler*, b. May 8, '48. (7) *Mary Louisa*, b. March 13, '50. (8) *Augusta*, b. Jan. 15, '52. (9) *Charlotte Elizabeth*, b. March 6, '55. (10) *Jane Edwards*, b. Aug. 17, '57.

834. IV. THOMAS READ,[7] (1588) b. Jan. 24, 1806, m. May 9, 1829, Sarah Ann Breese, dau. of Arthur Breese, a man of note, who d. several yrs. since. They have had 4 chil. He was graduated at Hamilton Coll. 1824, and studied Law, with Gen. Ostrom, and began the practice of his profession in Utica. He is President of the "Utica Cemetery Association," and one of the Directors of the "Utica Gas Light Co.," and in 1859, was elected President of the N.Y. & Albany & Buffalo Electro Magnetic Telegraph Co., has been Mayor of the City two terms, and has had much to do as one of the Commissioners of Public Schools, in organizing a system of Common-School Education, and directing the erection of school houses. He is a gentleman of polished manners, variéd mental acquisitions, and high moral worth. In all the public enterprises of the city, he has taken a deep interest, and exerts a large and healthful influence.

835. V. GEORGE,[7] (1592) b. Oct. 7, 1809, m. Oct. 23, 1849, Anna Gird, a protege of Com. Mervine, of the U. S. Navy, and a relative of his wife. He is a merchant in Utica, m. Pres. ch., and has had 3 chil.

836. VI. JAMES,[7] b. June 13, 1812, d. Sept. 31, 1843. He was a Civil Engineer, and for several yrs. in the service of the State. He had for some time before his decease, charge of a portion of the Erie Canal, and his life was no doubt shortened by his excessive devotion to the duties of his office. He was grad. at Union College.

837. VII. SUSAN,[7] b. April 8, 1814, d. Dec. 6, 1833, ae. 19 yrs., 8 mos. She m. Sept. 4, 1833, Rev. A. M. Mann, D.D., of Ithaca, N.Y. He was born in Philadelphia, March 16, 1808, of Wm. Mann and Elizabeth (M'Calla.) His academical studies were prosecuted at Somerville, N.J., commencing Dec. 22, 1822. In Sept. 1825, he entered the Junior Class of Rutgers Coll., just then re-organized, and was grad. July, 1827. He immediately entered the Theo'l Seminary at New Brunswick, and having completed the regular course of study, was licensed to preach in April, 1830. He was ord. at Ithaca, May 1, 1830, where he remained seven yrs. In Aug. 1837, he received a call from West Troy, and although he did not accept it, labored there seven months. He was then invited to the pastorate of the 1st Ref. Dutch Church of Poughkeepsie, to which place he rem. in Feb. 1838, where he has remained ever since. He received the Doctorate of Divinity from Rochester University in 1856.

J. R. Walker.

The following is compiled from the several obituaries which appeared in the Ithaca, New Brunswick and Utica papers, after Mrs. Mann's decease :—

"She became pious, when very young, united with the Pres. ch. of Utica, and from that time evinced the genuineness of her conversion, by the interest she felt in the cause of her Redeemer. By her engaging deportment, she soon won the affection of all with whom she associated, and a very short acquaintance was sufficient to form the closest ties, and to excite the tenderest affection. Scarcely had she been united to him who had promised to nourish and protect her, and who fondly anticipated through a long series of yrs. to redeem his pledge, ere the dread foe to man, envious of mortal bliss, sent in advance his messenger of disease, and claimed her for his own. A fever of typhoid character, which baffled the skill of her physicians, and tantalized the vigilant watchings of her friends, at a period which promised recovery, proved treacherous and fatal. From the scene of nuptial festivity, from the bridal chamber to the grave, brief was the journey of this young and lovely victim.

She had before her, the fairest promise of happiness. Her intelligence, piety and gentleness of manners, admirably fitted her for the responsible station she had assumed as the wife of a clergyman; and during the few brief months of her married life, she had acquired the love and firm regard of her newly adopted friends. Death came upon her when the attachment to life is usually strongest, and the victim least prepared. But she was found confident in her faith, and resigned herself tranquilly to the summons above."

She was beautiful in person, more than ordinarily intellectual, of devoted piety, and the fragrance of her memory is still precious. The sermon preached by Rev. Dr. Bethune, in improvement of her early death, was subsequently published.

Children of COMFORT WALKER,[6] [304] of Medway.

838. I. Amey,[7] b. Oct. 9, 1790, m. Dea. Eben Eaton, of Framingham. Res. F. They have—

(1) *Edward*, b. Nov. 28, 1818, m. Nov. 25, '41, Sarah Ann Harding, who was b. Oct. 24, '15. Res. Medway.

839. II. Dean,[7] (1594) b. Feb. 25, 1793, in Medway. He m. Nov. 29, 1814, Rebecca Wright, who was b. in Boston, Oct. 10, 1793. He is a manufacturer, formerly in Baltimore, Md., but for many yrs. in Medway, (Rockville.) He combines superior moral worth, with enterprise and capability in business. Both m. Cong. ch. They have had 9 chil.

840. III. CLARKE,[7] (1602) b. March 11, 1795, m. Jan. 5, 1819, Sarah Lovering, dau. of Amos, and b. Dec. 3, 1799. He is a farmer, and has had 4 chil. Res. Medway.

841. IV. TAMAR,[7] b. Dec. 15, 1797, dec'd. She m. Orion Mason, son of Alpheus and Judith (Leland,) and b. June 17, 1799. He is a trader. Both m. Cong. ch. Res. Medway. Chil.—

(1) *Henry*, b. Aug. 27, 1829, d. Aug. 13, '31. (2) *Henry E.*, b. May 27, '33. (3) *William F.*, b. Aug. 1, '35, d. Dec. 17, '37. (4) *Elmira L.*, b. Jan. 26, '40. (5) *Maria J.*, b. Sept. 7, '41, d. Oct. 11, '41.

842. V. TIMOTHY,[7] (1606) b. April 26, 1801, m. April 29, 1824, Louisa Turner, dau. of Col. Amos, of Medway, and b. Aug. 26, 1801. Res. Medway, till Feb. 26, 1850, when he rem. to Holliston. He was formerly a thread manufacturer. He is Deacon in Cong. ch., and has been a Sabbath school superintendent 28 yrs. He has 2 chil.

843. VI. ELMIRA,[7] b. Oct. 27, 1803, d. Oct. 2, 1827. She m. Orion Mason, of Medway, his 2d wife. (See No. 841.) Chil.—

(1) *Orion A.*, b. April 5, 1825. Trader in M.

(2) *Olive*, b. June 1, 1827, d. Sept. 28, '27.

844. VII. CLARA,[7] b. Nov. 25, 1805, m. Sept. 11, 1831, Rev. Gilbert Fay, who was b. in Westboro', May 2, 1803, of Otis and Mary, (Morse,) and d. Oct. 27, 1835, in Wardsworth, O. Chil.—

(1) *Margaret*, b. June 24, 1832, d. Aug. 30, '32.

(2) *Gilbert Otis*, b. Nov. 8, 1834, took 1st rank as a scholar in Philips' Academy, Andover, was grad. at Yale Coll., '59, and is preparing for the ministry in Theo'l Sem., Andover.

"He was graduated at Brown University, 1826, and studied theology with Rev. Dr. Ide, of Medway. After two yrs. labor in various places, he was ord. at Westboro', Oct. 6, 1830, as Evangelist, and went under a commission of the Am. Home Miss. Society, into the Western Reserve. He preached as stated supply at Wardsworth, until his death, at the early age of 32 yrs. He was much loved and lamented by his church, and brethren in the ministry. Mr. Fay's labors were too brief to develop his full abilities. They were, however, signally blessed. The little church of 11 members at the commencement, numbered 70 at his death. (See Hist. of the Mendon Association, 311th p.) She res. in Medway village.

845. VIII. MARY,[7] b. Sept. 17, 1808, m. Charles Wheeler, son of Edmond and Catharine (Brown,) and b. April 4, 1811. He is a farmer. Res. Mexico, N. Y. Chil.—

(1) *George F.*, b. May 17, 1837. (2) *Charles*, b. June 14, '42.

846. IX. LOIS,[7] b. Aug. 6, 1810, m. June 17, 1833, Rev. Varnum Noyes, son of Josiah and Mehitable (White,) and b. in Acton, July 1, 1804. He made a profession of religion, in Nov. 1821, and commenced fitting for the ministry at the Academies of Chesterfield, N. H., and Amherst, Mass., and entered Dartmouth Coll., 1824. His studies were arrested in his 2d yr. by a severe and protracted illness. On his recovery he taught school a-while, and then studied theology with Rev. Dr. Ide, of Medway.

He was ord. as Evangelist for the West at Medway, Aug. 25, 1831, and commenced preaching at Guilford, O., Oct. 2, 1831. Half of the time for a few years was spent in other neighboring places. In Sept. 21, 1836, he was installed as pastor, in which relation he continued until May 8, 1849, when it was dissolved at his own request. The reason of this step was found in the prevalent impression among a portion of the people, that as he had been with them a long time, a change of laborers might be beneficial. The pastor was willing the experiment should be tried. But after a trial of about 3 yrs. he was invited to return, which he did, and accepted the invitation, March, 1852. In the interval he was the stated supply of the ch. in Wayne, O. (See Hist. of Mendon Association 313 p.) She is m. ch. and resides in Guilford, O. Chil.—

(1) *Edward Payson*, b. Sept. 30, 1834. (2) *Henry V.*, b. April 24, '36. (3) *Francis J.*, b. May 31, '38. (4) *Martha*, b. June 1, '40. (5) *Gilbert F.*, b. June 4, '42, d. Sept. 11, '50. (6) *Harriet*, b. March 5, '44. (7) *Emily*, b. May 4, '46. (8) *Sarah*, b. June 2, '48. (9) *Clarissa*, b. May 21, '50. (10) *Mary*, b. March 31, '53.

CHIL. OF DOCT. EZRA WALKER,[6] [305] OF AMES, O.

847. I. ARCHIBALD,[7] b. July 20, 1788, d. ae. 10 yrs.

848. II. ALFRED,[7] b. 1790, in Ware, d. ae. 17 yrs.

849. III. SOPHIA,[7] b. March 20, 1793, in West Greenwich, R. I., d. Sept. 25, 1853. She m. Oct. 24, 1811, Gen. John Brown, son of Capt. Benj., of Revolutionary memory. He was a Hotel proprietor till 1853. Res. Athens, O. Chil.—

(1) *Oscar Walker*, b. Aug. 5, 1812, is a graduate of the Ohio University. He m. Adeline Currier, dau. of Judge Currier, of Athens, O., in 1834, and practices Law in A. Chil.—1, Charles. 2, John. 3, Lawrence.

(2) *Charles Pitt*, b. June 23, 1814, was grad. at the Ohio Univ.; m. Angeline Crippen, of A., March 3, 1842. He was a merchant in A., and d. May 26, '46, at Pittsburgh, Pa., leaving 4 chil.

(3) *Edgar Thomas*, b. July 22, 1816, was grad. at the Ohio Univ., m. Maria Whipple, in Logan, O., about 1841. He was a Physician in L., till his death, June 1, '55, and was very highly esteemed.

(4) *William Loring*, b. Dec. 31, 1819, educated at Ohio Univ., m. Miss Sarah Weaver, of Lancaster, O., Feb. 1853. He is a merchant in Athens, and has 1 child, Charles E., b. June, '56.

(5) *John Alonzo*, b. Jan. 22, 1823, was grad. at Ohio Univ., m. 1849, Elizabeth Smith, at Logan, O., where he practices Law.

(6) *Hannah Maria*, b. Sept. 9, 1825, m. 1847, Robert Pratt, of Athens, a grad. of the Ohio Univ. They rem. to Salem, Ill., 1850, where he is a successful physician, a rising man, and active christian. They have 4 chil.

(7) *Lucy Ann*, b. May 7, 1828, m. Aug, 27, '51, James Hey, a merchant, in Cincinnati, O. They have 2 chil.

(8) *Archibald Douglas*, b. Aug. 2, 1831, was grad. at Ohio Univ., 1851, m. Eliza Clayton, in Athens, O., in 1855. He is teller in the Bank in A., and has 1 child.

850. IV. MARY,[7] m. July 27, 1815, James J. Fuller, who d. Sept. 29, 1853. He was a salt manufacturer in Ames, O. Chil.—

(1) *Louisa May*, b. Oct. 3, 1816, m. Rev. James B. Bane, Sept. 18, 1838, who was b. Aug. 18, 1815, in Washington Co., Pa., and educated at Washington Coll. He was ord. at the age of 19, and was pastor of the 1st Cumberland Pres. ch. in Alleghany City, Pa., till 1840, when his health failed, and he has since been in business. He is a most exemplary and amiable man, and of highly cultivated mind. Two chil. living, one dec'd.

(2) *Carlos Walker*, b. Oct. 9, 1818, went to California in 1849, and d. there the same year.

(3) *Lucy Matilda*, b. May 14, 1822, m. Ripley C. Hoffman, in 1842, who was educated at the Ohio Univ., and is a successful Lawyer in his native place, Jackson, O. He is one of the most prominent men in the County.

(4) *Charlotte M.*, b. July 20, 1826, m. Henry T. Brown, Dec. 16, 1847, a Lawyer in Athens, O.

(5) *Mary Jane*, b. Aug. 9, 1832, m. R. H. Stewart, of Athens, O., March, 1852, a merchant in Springfield, Ill.

(6) *Frances S.*, b. June 28, 1836. Res. Athens, unm.

851. V. WILLIAM ROBINSON,[7] (1608) b. May 23, 1798, in Poultney, Vt., d. June 17, 1855. He m. Nov. 13, 1825, Abigail Putnam Howe, of Belfre, O., who was b. Dec. 31, 1804, and d. Dec. 1835, having 5 chil. He m. 2d, April 16, 1837, Betsey Proctor, who was b. Nov. 12, 1798, and had 1 child. He rem. to Athens Co., Ohio, in 1810, then quite a wilderness. In 1817, he became a clerk in Lancaster, and remained there, and at Columbus about 6 yrs. But his preference for a rural life, induced him to return again to Ames in 1823, and settle on a farm, where he lived till his death. In 1833, he united with the Pres. ch., and for many yrs. held the office of ruling

Elder. He manifested at all times a deep, sincere, and heart-felt piety, and maintained a truly devotional spirit, while, by his uprightness, integrity and pious example, he secured the confidence and esteem of all who knew him, and his influence was widely felt for good, during many years, by the whole community in which he lived. The interests of religion ever found in him a steady friend, always ready to contribute to the extent of his ability, for the promotion of the Redeemer's Kingdom. In his death, the poor and needy sustained a great loss, as he never failed to administer comfort and relief to them, as he had opportunity.

852. VI. Archibald Bates,[7] (1613) b. Oct. 15, 1800, in Poultney, Vt., m. Oct. 2, 1825, Lucy Willis Ames, dau. of Judge Sylvanus Ames, formerly of Newburyport, and sister of Rev. E. R. Ames, Bishop of Meth. ch. They have had 8 chil. He is a salt manufacturer. Res. Athens, Ohio, about 30 yrs. He is energetic, highly intelligent, possessed of superior christian excellence, and an Elder in the Pres. ch.

853. VII. Ezra,[7] (1621) b. in Poultney, Sept. 23, 1802, d. March 31, 1853, m. Mary J. Smith, of Staunton, Va., who d. in 1847 or '48. He m. 2d, Julia M. Shepherd, niece of Rev. Dr. Plummer, of Baltimore, Md. He was grad. at Ohio Univ. with high honor in 1826;—went to the Kanawha Valley, Va., where he studied Law, and was a Lawyer and farmer in Charlestown, Va. He accepted a situation in the "James River and Kanawha Co.," which he held till his decease. He had 2 chil. Few men possess greater excellence of character. He was an Elder in the Pres. ch. Mrs. Robinson, wife of Rev. Solon Robinson, of Baltimore, who knew him intimately, says of him. "He was the best man I ever knew."

854. VIII. Lucy Phebe,[7] b. April 25, 1805, d. ae. 19 yrs.

855. IX. Ralph Manning,[7] (1623) b. Dec. 28, 1808, in Poultney, Vt., m. Jan. 2, 1836, Adeline Cornelia Griswold, of Gustavus, Trumbull Co., Ohio. They are both m. ch. and have had 5 chil. He rem. from P. with his father, to Amestown, Ohio, about 1810, received his collegiate education, except the last year, at the Ohio Univ., Athens, O., was graduated at Western Reserve Coll., Hudson, O., in 1832, and remained there 3 yrs. as Tutor. In Nov. 1835, he was appointed Principal of Grand River Institute, at Austinburg, O., where he remained 17 yrs., till Oct. 1852. In June, 1853, he was appointed Prof. of Languages, in Otterbein University,

Westerville, O., in 1857, elected President of the Univ., for the ensuing yr., and is now its Prof. of Latin Lang. and Literature. He is a man of culture and piety, and has been Elder in the ch.

CHIL. OF CALEB WALKER,[6] [308] OF CHARLESTON, S. C.

856. I. ELIZABETH MARTHA,[7] b. Nov. 3, 1805, d. March 17, 1806.

857. II. ADELINE,[7] b. April 13, 1807, d. March 27, 1808.

858. III. HENRY DEANE,[7] (1628) b. Aug. 9, 1808, d. Sept. 3, 1854. He m. March 9, 1836, Jane Ann Stewart, and had 6 chil. He was a carpenter and contractor, and much respected as a man and citizen. Res. Charleston, S. C.

859. IV. MARY MARIA,[7] b. May 17, 1811, m. July 31, 1839, E. W. Edgerton, who was b. in Bridgeport, Ct., Jan. 17, 1805. He is a merchant in Charleston, S. C. Chil.—

(1) *Henry Walker*, b. Jan. 14, 1841, d. Oct. 3, '41. (2) *Everett Cromwell*, b. Nov. 24, '42. (3) *Augustus Walker*, b. May 22, '45, twin, d. June 11, '45. (4) *Mary Maria*, b. May 22, '45, twin, d. June 6, '45. (5) *Joel Ives*, b. Jan. 7, '49.

860. V. EDWIN BLAIR,[7] b. Sept. 6, 1813, d. July, 1816.

861. VI. MARTHA CLEMENTINA,[7] b. Oct. 22, 1815, d. July, 1816.

862. VII. ANN ELIZA,[7] b. Dec. 18, 1817, m. July 3, 1839, Frederick Richards, who was b. in Hartford, Ct., March 31, 1817. Res. Charleston, S. C. He is a merchant. Chil.—

(1) *Caroline Sebring*, b. Feb. 3, 1841, d. July 26, '47. (2) *Anna Maria*, b. Aug. 29, '42. (3) *Frederick*, b. Nov. 19, '44. (4) *Frank*, b. July 18, '46. (5) *Caroline Sebring*, b. Sept. 12, '48. (6) *Herbert Walker*, b. Nov. 5, '50.

CHILDREN OF AARON WALKER,[6] [309] OF KILLINGLY, CT.

863. I. MARY,[7] b. Feb. 6, 1804, d. Nov. 24, 1822. She m. 1821, William Peck, of R. I., a farmer. No chil.

864. II. JULIETT,[7] b. Sept. 2, 1806, m. Feb. 1823, Elisha B. Vaughn, of Sterling, Ct., a farmer. Res. Killingly, Ct. Chil.—

(1) *Rhoda A.*, b. Sept. 14, 1824. (2) *Jared W.*, b. May 14, '27, is a mason. (3) *Mary*, b. April 8, '30. (4) *Aaron A.*, b. Sept. 3, '32, is a farmer. (5) *Lucy M.*, b. April 11, '38. (6) *Harriet M.*, b. Oct. 21, '40.

865. III. COMFORT,[7] (1634) b. Oct. 2, 1809, d. Sept. 2, 1852. He m. June 1? 1834, Betsey Bennett, dau. of Israel, and b. March 9, 1809. They had 5 chil. Res. Plainfield, (Central Village,) Ct.

866. IV. THOMAS MOWRY,[7] (1639) b. Dec. 14, 1812, m. Maria Carpenter. He is a farmer in Moravia, Cayuga Co., N. Y., and has 3 chil.

CHILDREN OF CALEB WALKER,[6] [316] OF BELCHERTOWN.

867. I. CALEB,[7] b. Jan. 26, 1796, d. ae. 4 days.

868. II. TIMOTHY,[7] b. May 18, 1797, d. July 24, 1800.

869. III. ELIZA,[7] b. Nov. 23, 1799, m. April 13, 1853, Daniel Poole, who was b. about 1780, and d. Jan. 4, 1858. He was a farmer. Res. South Belchertown. Both m. Bap. ch. She is an intelligent woman, and was a Teacher many yrs.

870. IV. NABBY,[7] b. Nov. 3, 1801, m. March 28, 1827, Daniel Rockwell, of Stafford, Ct., who was b. July 22, 1779. He was formerly a school teacher, farmer, and prominent in town affairs. Res. S. Chil.—

(1) *Lucy*, b. Feb. 19, 1828. Teacher. (2) *Samuel*, b. Dec. 21, '31. Farmer. (3) *John*, b. March 27, '37. Farmer. (4) *Huldah P.*, b. Dec. 5. (yr. not given.) Teacher.

871. V. CALEB,[7] (1642) b. Aug. 13, 1803, m. June 25, 1844, Rosetta Eaton, of Stafford, Ct., who was b. in S., July 7, 1814. He has had 7 chil. Res. Greenwich.

872. VI. EZRA S.,[7] (1649) b. March 8, 1805, m. March 26, 1829, Livonia Potter, of Willington, Ct., who is m. Bap. ch. They have had 7 chil. Res. Belchertown.

873. VII. EBENEZER,[7] (1656) b. Feb. 1, 1807, d. Jan. 27, 1846. He m. Hannah Fuller, of Belchertown, and had 1 dau. He was a farmer, and a worthy man. Res. B.

874. VIII. HORACE,[7] b. Nov. 12, 1808, d. Jan. 17, 1811.

875. IX. BETHIAH,[7] b. April 11, 1810, d. Feb. 12, 1811.

876. X. BETHIAH B.,[7] b. Dec. 5, 1811, m. May 24, 1836, Philip P. Potter, of Wilbraham, b. in Willington, Ct., July 6, 1811, son of Philip and Hannah (Preston,) both of Ashford, and grandson of Philip, who went from Rehoboth. He is a farmer, and lumber

merchant in Wilbraham. He held a Captain's commission in the State militia, and has been honored with various town offices, Assessor, 3 yrs., Select-man, 2 yrs., and in 1854, he was Representative to the General Court. He is m. Meth. ch. and Steward. Chil.—

(1) *Timothy D.*, b. April 12, 1840. (2) *William W.*, b. July 12, '42. (3) *Abigail B.*, b. Oct. 30, '44. (4) *Almenia M.*, b. Aug. 18, '46. (5) *Martha H.*, b. Oct. 18, '48, d. Aug. 25, '49. (6) *Philip H.*, b. Aug. 30, '51.

877. XI. DAU.,[7] still-born, Jan. 26, 1814.

878. XII. HULDAH D.,[7] b. March 1, 1815, d. Feb. 12, 1817.

879. XIII. HULDAH,[7] } b. Oct. 10, 1818, d. Nov. 1, 1818.

880. XIV. HORACE,[7] } b. Oct. 10, 1818, (1657) m. Oct. 11, 1842, Marilla N. Wariner of Monson, who had 3 chil. and d. June, 1854. He m. 2d, Harriet Babbitt, of Ware, who was b. 1818, and is m. Cong. ch. Res. Greenwich.

CHIL. OF WILLIAM WALKER,[6] [319] OF ASHFORD, CONN.

881. I. WILLIAM C.,[7] (1660) b. Sept. 11, 1810, m. Dec. 28, 1832, Eliza Quint, dau. of Wentworth, of Sanford, Me., and b. Sept. 29, 1808. Both m. Cong. ch. with several of their chil. He is a manufacturer, and has had 9 chil. Res. Sutton.

882. II. LEMUEL,[7] (1669) b. Aug. 12, 1812, m. April 2, 1835, Nabby D. Blanchard, dau. of John, of Vestal, Broome Co., N. Y. They are both m. Cong. ch., and have 2 chil. He has been engaged in cotton manufacturing 28 yrs. In 1835, he was overseer in Uxbridge, rem. to Southbridge, 1840, to Shirley, 1845, when he bought ½ of the Shirley Mill, which he managed 9 yrs., and then rem. to Shirbrook, Canada East, to take charge of a new enterprise for parties in Canada. They failed, and he hired the mill, which in 3 mos. after, was burned. He was Superintendent of the Sab. school, in Shirley. He is now a farmer, in Vestal.

883. III. SYLVIA H.,[7] b. Dec. 25, 1814, m. Aug. 1, 1838, Cyprian Whiting, of Douglas, now a farmer and shoe manufacturer, in Charlton. She is m. Cong. ch. and has had 4 chil. Chil.—

(1) *Edwin*, b. Sept. 6, 1839. (2) *Ellen*, b. March 20, '45, d. Aug. 3, '45. (3) *Andrew*, b. Feb. 27, '47. (4) *Ella Frances*, b. Oct. 14, '54.

884. IV. FRANCIS,[7] b. March 1, 1817, m. Jan. 1, 1839, Adeline Kelley, of Palmer, who was b. May 25, 1821, in Killingly, Ct., and is m. Bap. ch. No chil.

885. V. ABNER C.,[7] (1671) b. Oct. 13, 1819, m. April 12, 1846, Harriet M. Silsby, of Southbridge, who was b. Aug. 26, 1820. He is a farmer and m. Meth ch., and has 4 chil. Res. Dudley.

EIGHTH GENERATION.

CHILDREN OF SAMUEL WALKER,[7] [323] OF SEEKONK.

886. I. TIMOTHY,[8] (1675) b. July 29, 1811, m. May 5, 1836, Clarissa Wood, of Attleboro'. He is a housewright and has 1 child. Res. Newton Centre.

887. II. ELIZABETH CUSHMAN,[8] b. May 29, 1815, is unm.

888. III. BENJAMIN,[8] b. May 6, 1817, is a farmer and unm., in S.

889. IV. GEORGE,[8] b. May, 1819, d. Sept. 1820.

890. V. MARY WILMARTH,[8] b. June 8, 1821, is unm.

891. VI. GEORGE LAFAYETTE,[8] (1676) b. Sept. 23, 1824, m. 1846, Frances Read. He is a painter and has 1 child. Res. Pawtucket.

892. VII. JOHN PITMAN,[8] b. Jan. 9. 1829, is a marble worker. Res. Providence, R. I.

CHILDREN OF AARON WALKER,[7] [334] OF ASHFORD, CT.

893. I. MARIA,[8] b. July 11, 1810, d. May 18, 1812.

894. II. LUCY M.,[8] b. Nov. 12, 1813, m. April 8, 1840, Geo. Whiton, son of Abner, of Willington, Ct., (See No. 314,) and has 1 dau. He is a farmer. Res. W. Child—

(1) *Marietta A.*, b. Sept. 10, 1843.

CHIL. OF SAMUEL WALKER,[7] [336] OF MARGARETTA, O.

895. I. ELIZA,[8] b. 1803, d. ae. 9 mos.

896. II. ELIZA,[8] b. March, 1804, d. Oct. 10, 1855. She m. 1820, Elihu Parker, of Margaretta. Both m. ch. He served under Gen. Harrison in War of 1812. Chil.—

(1) ***Henry***, m. 1844, Polly Taylor. (2) ***Ruman***, m. 1846, Julia Ann Turner. (3) *Ira*, m. 1847, Elizabeth Thurston, who d. April, '56. 3 chil. He m. Oct. '57, Rachel Strong, of Hardin Co., O. (4) ***Levi***, m. 1852, Louisa Smith, and res. in M. 2 chil. (5) ***Cynthia***, res. in M., unm. (6) ***Malinda***, m. 1847, Ralph Magill. 2 chil. (7) ***Eliza Ann***, d. '34. (8) ***Elizabeth B.***, unm. (9) ***Lucy M.***, unm. (10) ***Phebe A.***, unm. (11) ***James***, unm. (12) ***Elihu***, unm.

897. III. Ruman,[8] b. in Geneseo, N. Y., d. ae. 9 mos.

898. IV. Samuel,[8] (1677) b. in Geneseo, N. Y., Dec. 25, 1807, d. Oct. 6, 1854. He m. April 5, 1835, Cynthia Mann, in Margaretta, O. Both m. Meth. ch. He was a farmer, and had 6 chil. Res. M.

899. V. John B.,[8] (1683) b. Nov. 11, 1810, in Geneseo, N.Y. He m. 1836, Anna Maria Hunt, of Lyme, Huron Co, O., and has had 7 chil. In 1840, he rem. to Marion, Linn Co., Iowa, where he resides, (1860.)

900. VI. Cynthia,[8] b. Jan. 25, 1813, m. April 5, 1835, Almon Hunt, of Lyme, O. He is a machinist. Res. Reedtown, Seneca Co., Ohio. Chil.—

(1) *Mary Ann*, b. May 22, 1837, d. ae. 8 yrs. (2) *James*, b. May 4, '40, d. ae. 6 yrs. (3) *Edward M.*, b. Dec. 6, '42. (4) *Wm. Henry*, b. July 19, '44, d. ae. 2 weeks. (5) *Laura Ann*, b. Nov. 1, '46, d. ae. 8 yrs. (6) *Frances M.*, b. March 7, '48. (7) *Rob't Emmet*, b. May 17, '50. (8) *Harriet Jane*, b. Sept. 16, '52. (9) *Lee*, b. Sept. 20, '57.

901. VII. Gamaliel,[8] (1690) b. May 7, 1815, in G. He m. May 8, 1843, Sarah Minton, who was b. Dec. 5, 1823, in Jennings Co., Ind., of William and Charlotte. He emigrated in 1838 to Ia. Res. Lyttleton, Buchanan Co., Ia. He is a farmer and has had 6 chil.

902. VIII. Aaron,[8] b. July 11, 1817, d. Sept. 1837, ae. 18 yrs.

903. IX. William C.,[8] b. Nov. 22, 1819, d. 1849, ae. 29, unm.

904. X. Nancy,[8] b. Feb. 28, 1822, d. Oct. 22, 1834, ae. 9 yrs.

905. XI. James,[8] b. July 6, 1824, d. Sept. 1837, ae. 12 yrs.

Children of PETER WALKER,[7] [337] of Margaretta, O.

906. I. Maria,[8] m. Green Parker, of Margaretta, O. They removed to Quasqueton, Buchanan Co., Ia. Chil.—

(1) *William*. Res. Texas. (2) *Sarah*. (3) *Elizabeth*. (4) *Esther*. Res. T. (5) *Nelson*. Res. T. (6) *Melissa*, dec'd. (7) *Nathaniel*. Res. T. (8) *Franklin*, dec'd. (9) *James*. Res. T. (10) *Francis*. Res. T.

907. II. Mary Ann,[8] m. Joseph Chapman, of York, Ohio, who d. 1844, in Buchanan Co., Iowa, where they lived. He was a farmer, and m. Bap. ch. Chil.—

(1) *William*. Res. Mechanicsville, Cedar Grove, Ia. (2) *Almon*, dec'd. (3) *Sarah Ann*. (4) *John*. (5) *Sylvester*. (6) *Elizabeth*.

She m. 2d, about 1850, Sam'l Solesby, res. in Pioneer Grove, Cedar Co., Iowa, and has had 3 or 4 chil. who all d. young.

908. III. HENRY,[8] went to Iowa, thence to California, and d. about 1853, unm.

909. IV. SALLY,[8] d. 1824, ae. 5 yrs. in York, Ohio.

910. V. ELIZA,[8] b. 1824, 3 weeks after the death of her father, d. 1824, in York, Ohio.

CHILDREN OF ABNER WALKER,[7] [341] OF YORK, OHIO.

911. I. CHARLES,[8] b. 1820, in Margaretta, O., is a farmer. In 1856 he started for the West, and has not been heard from since.

912. II. RHODA ANN,[8] b. 1823, in Y., d. 1841.

913. III. HARRIET,[8] b. 1825, in Y., d. 1846.

CHIL. OF JONATHAN C. WALKER,[7] [344] OF WILLINGTON, CT.

914. I. HARRIET J.[8] Res. Willington, Ct., unm., in 1858.

915. II. SAMUEL,[8] d. young.

CHIL. OF CALVIN WALKER,[7] [355] OF ROCK ISLAND, ILL.

916. I. CHILD,[8] d. in infancy.

917. II. HARRIET,[8] d. in infancy.

918. III. ELIZABETH A.,[8] b. March, 1834, m. Julius Lee, of Philadelphia, a music dealer.

920. IV. HARRIET,[8] b. 1838 or '39. Res. Philadelphia.

CHIL. OF HORACE W. WALKER,[7] [367] OF KEENE, N. Y.

921. I. JOSEPHINE RUTHA ARDELIA,[8] b. Jan. 17, 1836.

922. II. EUGENE NAPOLEON,[8] b. Nov. 27, 1848.

CHILD OF JOHN B. WALKER,[7] [369] OF WOONSOCKET, R.I.

923. I. GEORGE WHITFIELD,[8] d. ae. 4 mos.

Children of ALFRED WALKER,[7] [370] of Pawtucket.

924. I. Lucy B.,[8] b. Aug. 25, 1826.

925. II. Wm. Russell,[8] (1696) b. July 14, 1830, m. May 24, 1852, Eliza B. Hall, dau. of Nathan, of Providence, R. I., and b. in Fall River, about 1830. He is a housewright, and has 1 son. Res. Pawtucket.

926. III. Sarah Jane,[8] b. Sept. 21, 1835.

Chil. of DUDLEY WALKER,[7] [378] of Central Falls, R.I.

927. I. Elizabeth H.,[8] b. May 23, 1831, m. Sept. 20, 1852, Josiah K. Mallory. He is a superintendent of a cotton mill.

928. II. Horatio Nelson,[8] b. Aug. 8, 1833, d. Sept. 20, 1853.

929. III. George Bosworth,[8] b. Oct. 2, 1835, is a stone cutter.

930. IV. Albert,[8] b. Feb. 14, 1839.

931. V. Julia,[8] b. Oct. 20, 1842.

932. VI. Anna Sheldon,[8] b. May 29, 1844, d. Jan. 9, 1845.

933. VII. Alice,[8] b. July 8, 1851.

Chil. of FRANCIS WALKER,[7] [383] of Central Falls, R.I.

934. I. Charlotte Frances,[8] b. Sept. 1, 1839.

935. II. Edward Whitfield,[8] b. Oct. 1842, d. Aug. 1848.

936. III. Esther Jane,[8] b. Feb. 1844.

937. IV. Anna Ide,[8] b. Dec. 23, 1849.

938. V. Dau.,[8] d. 2½ yrs.

Chil. of WILLIAM B. WALKER,[7] [384] of Pawtucket.

939. I. Mary Frances,[8] b. March 29, 1852.

CHILDREN OF SAMUEL WALKER,[7] [391] OF SEEKONK.

940. I. LEONARD,[8] (1697) b. April 10, 1825, m. Oct. 10, 1849, Eliza L. Barney, dau. of Rev. James O., of Seekonk, and has 1 child. He entered Amherst Coll., but did not finish the course, on account of ill health. He has been teacher in Taunton, Principal of the High school in Walpole, and the High school in Somerville, and is now Principal of the Wrentham Academy.

941. II. SEBA,[8] b. Feb. 23, 1831, resides in S., unm.

CHIL. OF GEORGE WASH'N WALKER,[7] [393] OF SEEKONK.

942. I. ESTHER EMELINE,[8] b. April, 1832, is unm.

943. II. GEORGE HALSEY,[8] b. 1837, is unm.

944. III. MOSES,[8] b. 1839, is unm.

CHIL. OF EZRA WALKER,[7] [398] OF SPRINGWATER, N. Y.

945. I. MARY H.,[8] b. July 16, 1823. She m. June 1, 1847, Nelson P. Willis, who was b. 1817. He is a farmer, in Springwater, N. Y. She is m. Bap. ch. Chil.—

(1) *George M.*, b. June 14, 1848. (2) *Ezra W.*, b. April 9, '50. (3) *Mary E.*, b. March 10, '52. (4) *Cameron P.*, b. May 6, '54.

946. II. LUCY N.,[8] b. June 27, 1825, m. Jan. 1, 1845, Geo. C. Stratton, who was b. May 17, 1820. He is a farmer, in Springwater. She is m. Bap. ch. Chil.—

(1) *Rosalia J.*, b. Dec. 29, 1846. (2) *Charles N.*, b. May 29, '49.

947. III. JANE N.,[8] b. July 27, 1827, m. Jan. 1, 1850, Hiram W. Parshall, who was b. May 18, 1824. He is a farmer, in Springwater, N. Y. She is m. Bap. ch. and has—

(1) *Alice E.*, b. June 1, 1854.

948. IV. CHARLES H.,[8] b. May 17, 1830, emigrated to California, Feb. 19, 1853.

949. V. J. LELAND,[8] b. March 14, 1832, m. Lydia A. Grover, April 27, 1854. He is a farmer, in Springwater, N. Y.

950\. VI. Harriet S.,[8] b. Dec. 25, 1833, m. Erasmus D. Brown. (See No. 953.)

951\. VII. Lucinda C.,[8] b. May 14, 1840.

952\. VIII. Ellen A.,[8] b. Feb. 4, 1842, d. Feb. 9, 1851.

Chil. of Rev. GEORGE WALKER,[7] [399] of Dexter, Mich.

953\. I. Wealtha R.,[8] b. May 17, 1822, d. July 28, 1856. She m. E. D. Brown, April 6, 1842. He is a miller. Both m. Bap. ch. Child—

(1) *Herman E.*, b. June 24, 1845.

He m. 2d, Harriet S. Walker. (See No. 950.)

954\. II. George E.,[8] (1698) b. May 14, 1824, m. Feb. 8, 1855, Eliza Carpenter, and has 3 chil.

955\. III. Delsa S.,[8] b. Feb. 9, 1826. She m. Oct. 8, 1849, Rev. Edward Tenney, who was b. in Riga, N. Y., June 22, 1822. He was educated at Mich. Univ., ord. and settled as Pastor over the Bap. ch. at Stony Creek, Oakland Co., Mich. Res. Dansville, N. Y. Chil.—

(1) *Edward Locke*, b. Sept. 1850. (2) *Sarah L.*, b. Oct. '53, d. Sept. '54.

956\. IV. Martha Jane,[8] b. April 14, 1827, m. June 13, 1850, Augustus Case. He is a farmer. Res. Dexter Village, Mich. Child—

(1) *Geo. A.*, b. Nov. 29, 1856.

957\. V. Avera N.,[8] b. Feb. 29, 1829, d. June 11, 1831.

958\. VI. Francis L.,[8] b. April 25, 1838.

959\. VII. Roger W.,[8] b. Feb. 6, 1842.

960\. VIII. Ethel M.,[8] b. April 29, 1844.

961\. IX. Cynthia A.,[8] b. April 8, 1846, d. Sept. 6, 1846.

Chil. of WILLIAM WALKER,[7] [400] of Warrenville, Ill.

962\. I. Celia A.,[8] b. Oct. 6, 1828, m. Warren Halsey, Nov. 3, 1853, and has a son, b. Aug. 29, 1854.

963\. II. Marietta,[8] b. June 27, 1853.

963\. III. Lurana J.,[8] b. Sept. 3, 1839.

964\. IV. Cordelia S.,[8] b. June 18, 1843.

By 2d Marriage.

965. V. Almeron W.,[8] b. Feb. 19, 1847.

967. VI. Oliver E.,[8] b. Oct. 1, 1848.

968. VII. Amos B.,[8] } b. Sept. 22, 1850.

969. VIII. Abel P.,[8] }

Children of HENRY WALKER,[7] [403] of Ingham, Mich.

970. I. Manly H.,[8] b. April 26, 1835.

971. II. Electa L.,[8] b. Sept. 13, 1837.

972. III. Ezra C.,[8] b. Sept. 20, 1839.

973. IV. Eliza M.,[8] b. May 30, 1841.

974. V. William S.,[8] b. Dec. 6, 1842.

Chil. of Doct. AMOS WALKER,[7] [404] of Pontiac, Mich.

975. I. Son,[8] still-born, Oct. 29, 1835.

976. II. Mary Ellen,[8] b. Oct. 26, 1837.

977. III. Abel Willmarth,[8] b. April 5, 1839.

978. IV. Lawson Ethel,[8] b. March 6, 1842, d. Aug. 3, 1843.

979. V. Emory Judson,[8] b. Nov. 2, 1844.

980. VI. Dau.,[8] still-born, Aug. 10, 1846.

981. VII. George R.,[8] b. Nov. 2, 1845.

982. VIII. Frank,[8] b. Oct. 15, 1850.

983. IX. Wealthy Evelyn,[8] b. Aug. 9, 1854, d. Sept. 8.

Chil. of Hon. LELAND WALKER,[7] [406] of Hamburgh, Mich.

984. I. Augusta,[8] b. Dec. 14, 1842.

985. II. Susanna,[8] b. Aug. 3, 1844.

986. III. Harriet,[8] b. July 9, 1847, d. Sept. 19, 1847.

987. IV. Flora,[8] b. March 22, 1849, d. May 9, 1850.

988. V. Eva,[8] b. Sept. 26, 1852.

CHIL. OF FERDINAND L. WALKER,[7] [409] OF LYNDON, VT.

999. I. NANCY B.,[8] b. Jan. 27, 1832, d. Sept. 5, 1835.

1000. II. GEORGE B.,[8] (1701) b. April 21, 1835, m. Sept. 14, 1857, Mary Jane, dau. of Daniel Whipple, Esq., of Lyndon, Vt. He is an enterprising and intelligent farmer, in L., and has 2 chil.

CHILDREN OF GEORGE W. WALKER,[7] [417] OF ———

1001. I. HANNAH E.,[8] b. Aug 7, 1833, m. Francis Shaw, a house joiner. No chil.

1002. II. STEPHEN DANIELS,[8] b. Aug. 11, 1833, is a house carpenter, and unm. Res. Saltilloville, Ind.

1003. III. JAMES,[8] b. Feb. 1838, d. July, 1838.

BY 2d MARRIAGE.

1004. IV. CHARLES M,[8] d. before July, 1843.

1005. V. SARAH ELON,[8] d. soon after July, 1843.

1006. VI. GEO. WASHINGTON,[8] b. July 9, 1841.

CHIL. OF HARRY WALKER,[7] [422] OF SALTILLO, IND.

1007. I. JOHN CALVIN,[8] b. 1852, is dec'd.

1008. II. GEORGE,[8] b. Feb. 18, 1854.

1009. III. ALMIRA,[8] b. Sept. 2, 1854?

CHIL. OF SAMUEL WALKER,[7] [438] OF GRAFTON, VT.

1010. I. ROMANZO,[8] b. March 8, 1816, d. Nov. 8, 1850, unm. He studied law with Gen. Daniel Kellogg, and practiced his profession at Royalton, Vt., until 1849, with much more than ordinary ability. He possessed a memory of such remarkable retentiveness that he never took notes, and could repeat testimony, without the slightest error, in cases which had occupied several days. As an advocate, he had few equals. He represented the town of Royalton, in the Legislature, in 1847 and '48.

1011. II. LEWIS S.,[8] (1703) b. May 5, 1817, m. June 22, 1847, Cordelia E. Kidder, and has 2 chil. He is a woolen manufacturer, has been 1st Constable 9 yrs., Lister 3 yrs., and Representative in the State Legislature 1852 and '53. Res. Grafton, Vt.

1012. III. MINERVA V.,[8] b. July 13, 1819, d. Oct. 6, 1852. She m. Nov. 21, 1837, Joel Davis, of Grafton, Vt., a farmer. Res. G. Chil.—

(1) *Allen J.*, b. May 12, 1841. (2) *Norman*, b. May 7, '45.

1013. IV. SAMUEL M.,[8] (1705) b. Nov. 8, 1821, m. Nov. 1845, Mary Ann Ayres, and has 2 chil. He is a farmer, in Grafton, Vt.

1014. V. ORVAL CARPENTER,[8] (1707) b. Nov. 14, 1823, m. Jan. 1850, Frances A. Milliken, and has 3 chil. He is a farmer, in Wyoming, Ill.

1015. VI. ALDEN,[8] (1710) b. March 13, 1827, m. June 23, 1857, Mary Rugg, of Chester, Vt. He is a farmer, and has 1 son.

1016. VII. CORONA A.,[8] b. Oct. 17, 1827, d. unm., Feb. 15, 1852.

CHILDREN OF ALDEN WALKER,[7] [439] OF GRAFTON, VT.

1017. I. FRANCIS A.,[8] b. Feb. 6, 1831, is a farmer, in Huron, Ia.

1018. II. JOHN G.,[8] b. March 20, 1835, is midshipman, in U. S. Navy.

1019. III. BETSEY ANN,[8] b. April 2, 1840.

1020. IV. CHARLES E.,[8] } b. July 14, 1848.
1021. V. WILLIAM E.,[8] }

CHIL. OF LEONARD WALKER,[7] [441] OF BERLIN, WIS.

1022. I. JOHN C.,[8] (1711) b. Sept. 1, 1829, in Maidstone, Vt., m. Feb. 15, 1856, Rachel Morrill, of Brighton, Vt., and has 1 son. He is a carpenter, in North Stratford, N. H.

1023. II. MARGARET A.,[8] b. Oct. 8, 1832, m. April, 1851, Miron Carter, a farmer, Res. Berlin, Wis. Chil.—

(1) *Effie Laurette*, dec'd. (2) *Lillan May*, b. Aug. 12, 1853.

1024. III. NATHAN A.,[8] b. Feb. 1837.

1025. IV. ESTHER E.,[8] b. Oct. 17, 1839, is m. ch.

CHIL. OF JOHN C. WALKER,[7] [443] OF SAXEVILLE, WIS.

1026. I. ISAAC L.,[8] b. Oct. 24, 1832, d. Dec. 24, 1832.

1027. II. MARY ELLEN,[8] b. Nov. 2, 1833, m. March 5, 1857, Truman Martin Silsby, at Manchester, N. H., and rem. to Acworth, N. H. She is m. ch. and has—

(1) *Geo. Addison*, b. Dec. 27, 1857.

1028. III. AARON H.,[8] b. March 25, 1836.

1029. IV. WILLIAM W.,[8] b. Jan. 27, 1838.

1030. V. ELIZA A.,[8] b. June 30, 1839.

1031. VI. ISAAC M.,[8] b. Aug. 5, 1841.

1032. VII. CALISTA G.,[8] b. May 30, 1843, d. May 23, 1849.

1033. VIII. JAMES K. POLK,[8] b. Feb. 28, 1845.

1034. IX. HENRY C.,[8] b. Sept. 7, 1852.

1035. X. CHARLES A.,[8] b. June 2, 1854.

CHILDREN OF EPHRAIM WALKER,[7] [454] OF SEEKONK.

1036. I. FRANK P.,[8] b. Feb. 1853.

1037. II. HENRY R.,[8] } b. 1854.
1038. III. ANNA R.,[8] }

1039. IV. EDWARD,[8] b. Aug. 1859.

CHIL. OF NELSON WALKER,[7] [456] OF PROVIDENCE, R. I.

1040. I. CHARLES H.,[8] b. June 25, 1855.

CHIL. OF EBENEZER WALKER,[7] [477] OF GATES, N. Y.

1041. I. JESSE B.,[8] (1712) b. Oct. 21, 1817, m. Nov. 9, 1837, Fanny Bronson, who was b. Jan. 17, 1817, and d. March 24, 1858. They had 3 chil. He m. 2d, Sept. 11, 1858, Vesta Stevens, and is a farmer, in Gates, N. Y., and m. ch.

1042. II. LUCY,[8] b. Dec. 19, 1819, d. April 14, 1834.

1043. III. LYDIA,[8] b. Aug. 13, 1822, m. Oct. 18, 1842, Sheffield Lillibridge, and is m. ch. Chil.—

(1) *Bradley M.*, b. Nov. 8, 1843. (2) *Augustus H.*, b. Nov. 12, '45.

1044. IV. EMELINE,[8] b. Jan. 25, 1826, d. June 4, 1843. She m. Jan. 5, 1843, John Stevens.

1045. V. MAMRE,[8] b. April 14, 1828. She m. March 31, 1847, Nelson Green, and is m. ch. Chil.—

(1) *Frances E.*, b. June 2, 1848. (2) *Sarah A.*, b. Feb. 9, '50. (3) *Lucy A.*, b. Oct. 8, '52. (4) *Cynthia V.*, b. Nov. 24, '54. (5) *Augusta G.*, b. Feb. 9, '56. (6) *Jesse M.*, b. Nov. 9, '57.

1046. VI. AMANDA,[8] b. June 22, 1831.

1047. VII. BETSEY,[8] b. Sept. 30, 1833.

1048. VIII. CYNTHIA,[8] b. April 25, 1837, m. Aug. 25, 1859, Michael Coffey.

CHILDREN OF JOHN WALKER,[7] [478] OF BERGEN, N. Y.

1049. I. ABBY JANE,[8] b. April 30, 1828, m. Oct. 9, 1849, Dudley D. Palmer, a speculator, and has—

(1) *Eldura E.*, b. June 4, 1852. (2) *Cara* or *Cora S.*, b. April 12, '57.

1050. II. HARVEY I.,[8] (1715) b. 1830, m. Hannah J. Hill. He is a farmer, and has 1 son.

1051. III. WILLIAM C.,[8] b. April 30, 1832, m. April 4, 1857, Candace Gooding. He is a farmer.

1052. IV. IRENE F.,[8] b. May 12, 1834, m. Oct. 1, (7?) 1852, Truman A. Proctor, a dentist.

CHILDREN OF ELIJAH WALKER,[7] [480] OF ORWELL, PA.

1053. I. STEPHEN HARRIS,[8] (1716) b. Nov. 12, 1820, m. Jan. 1, 1847, Hannah Owens, of Orwell, Pa., and has 3 chil.

1054. II. ELIZA LORANIA,[8] b. Oct. 26, 1823, m. 1840, Isaac Glead, of West Becket, and has 1 son, b. 1843. Res. W. B.

1055. III. HANNAH AMANDA,[8] b. April 15, 1838, m. Oct. 28 or 29, 1854, Peter Hendershot, of Standingstone, Pa., a farmer. Res. Orwell, Pa. Chil.—

(1) *Sarah*, b. June 26, 1856. (2) *Chauncey*, b. March 14, '58.

Chil. of Dea. JAMES H. WALKER,[7] [485] of Sweden, N.Y.

1056. I. William N.,[8] (1719) b. April 5, 1817, in Byron, N. Y., m. March 12, 1843, Mary Ingolsby, who was b. in B., Aug. 23, 1823. He is m. Bap. ch. and has 4 chil.

1057. II. Uri,[8] (1723) b. Jan. 8, 1819, in B., m. Jan. 1, 1843, Eliza A. Munger, who was b. June 6, 1824. He is a farmer, in Bergen, N. Y., and has 1 dau.

1058. III. Aura,[8] b. Nov. 20, 1821, is m. Bap. ch., unm. Res. S., N. Y.

1059. IV. Clara.[8] } b. Feb. 4, 1828. d. March 4, 1828.

1060. V. Clarissa,[8] } b. Feb. 4, 1828. m. July 25, 1848, David E. Wakeman, who d. Oct. 20, 1851. She m. 2d, June 6, 1854, Lovinus Dibble, of Byron, N. Y., a farmer. She has—

(1) *James D.*, b. Sept. 8, 1850.

By 2d Marriage.

1061. VI. Alfred,[8] b. Oct. 30, 1830, d. Jan. 26, 1857.

1062. VII. Judson,[8] b. Oct. 14, 1834, m. May 14, 1857, Mary King, of Sweden, N. Y., who was b. about 1837. He is a Rail Road conductor.

1063. VIII. Martha,[8] b. Jan. 1, 1839, m. Oct. 14, 1854, Dennis Sprague, of Riga, N. Y., a farmer.

Chil. of EPHRAIM WALKER,[7] [489] of West Becket.

1064. I. Son,[8] b. Feb. 5, 1829, d. Feb. 16.

1065. II. Ephraim A.,[8] b. Jan. 2, 1830.

1066. III. Louisa M.,[8] b. Aug. 19, 1832.

1067. IV. Martha Ann,[8] b. Aug. 1, 1833, d. Oct. 29, 1844.

1068. V. Wayland,[8] b. Dec. 25, 1835.

1069. VI. Apollos,[8] b. April 9, 1839, d. Nov. 4, 1844.

1070. VII. Theodore,[8] b. Oct. 11, 1841, d. Nov. 8, 1844.

1071. VIII. Philemon,[8] b. Feb. 6, 1842.

1071.[1] IX. Son,[8] b. Nov. 5, 1844, d. Nov. 23, 1844.

Children of AMASA WALKER,[7] [491] of Byron, N. Y.

1072. I. Amasa,[8] (1724) b. 1814, m. Lucretia Bridgman, dau. of Guy. He is a farmer in Union, Monroe Co., N. Y., and has 5 chil.

1073. II. Emily,[8] b. 1816, is unm.

1074. III. Mary,[8] b. June, 1818, d. Dec. 6, 1843, unm.

1075. IV. George,[8] b. May 14, 1820, d. Feb. 14, 1843, unm.

1076. V. Asahel,[8] b. March 8, 1823, m. 1856, Sarah Ford, dau. of William. He is a farmer, in Byron, N. Y.

1077. VI. Joseph,[8] b. 1826, d. June 20, 1843.

1078. VII. Corydon,[8] b. May 13, ——, m. 1856, Harriet Clark, dau. of William. He is a farmer, in Byron, N. Y.

Children of JOSEPH WALKER,[7] [492] of Byron, N. Y.

1079. I. Sally,[8] b. 1815, m. —— Ingersol, a farmer. Res. Clarendon, N. Y. Chil.—

(1) *Lucy.* (2) *Julia.* (3) *Clamer.* (4) *Orton.* (5) *Clemantine.* (6) *Walker.*

1080. II. Chloe,[8] b. 1817, m. —— Hill. She m. 2d, —— Pratt, a farmer. No chil. Res. Clarendon, N. Y.

1081. III. Joseph,[8] b. 1819, is unm.

1082. IV. Ruth,[8] b. 1821, m. —— Coy, a farmer, and has 1 son. Res. Clarendon, N. Y.

Children of CYRUS WALKER,[7] [495] of Byron, N. Y.

1083. I. Julia,[8] b. 1824, d. 1842.

1084. II. Fidelia,[8] b. 1826, d. 1833.

1085. III. Emerette,[8] b. 1832, m. Dec. 1856, Geo. Bowen, a lawyer.

1086. IV. Sarah,[8] b. 1835, m. Charles Morrill, a merchant, and has 1 child.

1087. V. Edward,[8] b. 1837.

Children of SIDNEY WALKER,[7] [496] of Byron, N. Y.

1088. I. Harriet,[8] b. 1825, m. Heman Lewis, has 1 child.

1089. II. Julia,[8] b. 1827, m. —— Cook, and has 1 child.

1090. III. Mary Ann,[8] b. 1829, m. Elias Richardson. 2 chil.

1091. IV. Martha,[8] b. 1831, m. —— Cook. No chil.

1092. V. Clarissa,[8] b. 1836, m. —— Dodge.

1093. VI. Cyrenius.[8]

1094. VII. Emma.[8]

1095. VIII. Chales.[8]

Children of CYRENIUS WALKER,[7] [497] of Byron, N. Y.

1096. I. Franklin,[8] b. 1833.

1097. II. Jane,[8] b. 1836.

1098. III. Jeannette,[8] b. 1838.

1099. IV. Mariette[8], b. 1844.

1100. V. Charles,[8] b. 1845, d. May 14, 1847.

Children of SARDIS WALKER,[7] [498] of Byron, N. Y.

1101. I. Almeda,[8] b. 1831, (1832?)

1102. II. Almira,[8] b. 1837.

1103. III. Orlando,[8] b. 1840.

1104. IV. Giles,[8] b. 1844.

Children of TRUMAN WALKER,[7] [503] of Jessup, Pa.

1105. I. Wm. R.,[8] b. May 26, 1834, m. Feb. 6, 1856, Agnes Blaisdell. No chil. Res. Jessup, Pa.

1106. II. James R.,[8] b. Oct. 24, 1847.

CHIL. OF WILLIS M. WALKER,[7] [507] OF SPRINGVILLE, PA.

1107. I. EMMA J.,[8] b. April 22, 1852.

1108. II. ———, name not given.

CHILD OF JOHN M. WALKER,[7] [512] OF WESTFORD, CT.

1109. I. PHILO,[8] b. about 1834, is boot and shoe cutter, unm. Res. Union, Ct.

CHILDREN OF HARVEY WALKER,[7] [514] OF UNION, CT.

1110. I. ANDREW W.,[8] b. April 17, 1836, d. Oct. 23, 1838.

1111. II. LAURA W.,[8] b. July 14, 1839.

1112. III. JOSEPHINE,[8] b. March 30, 1841.

1113. IV. ANDREW W.,[8] b. Jan. 29, 1843, d. Nov. 9, 1849.

1114. V. MERRITT H.,[8] b. March 28, 1850.

CHIL. OF LEVI WALKER,[7] [515] OF WASHINGTON, ILL.

1115. I. HARVEY S.[8]

1116. II. MARY BELL.[8]

1117. III. FRANK.[8]

CHILDREN OF PHILIP WALKER,[7] [522] OF ROXBURY, N. Y.

1118. I. PHILIP HALL,[8] (1729) b. Aug. 23, 1798, m. Sarah Bartram, dau. of Ezekiel, and has 3 chil. He is a carpenter. Res. R.

1119. II. IRA CASWELL,[8] (1732) b. March 11, 1800, m. Paulina Jump, dau. of Edward, of Roxbury, N. Y., and has 4 chil. He is m. Meth. ch. Res. Campville, Tioga Co., N. Y.

1120. III. EZRA,[8] (1736) b. Feb. 4, 1804, m. April 5, 1827, Amanda Carroll, dau. of John, and had 5 chil. She d. May 20, 1840. He m. 2d, Jan. 22, 1847, Mary, dau. of Adam Schneider, and has had 6 chil. He is a carpenter, in North Branch, Sullivan Co., N. Y.

1121. IV. HANNAH,[8] d. July, 1829, ae. 23 yrs. She m. Stephen Brown, and had 1 son. Res. Penn.

1122. V. JOHN S.,[8] (1747) b. March 17, 1809, d. ——. He m. Olive, dau. of Eli Davis, and had 1 dau. Res. Chemung Co., N.Y.

CHIL. OF SULLIVAN WALKER,[7] [523] OF ROXBURY, N.Y.

1123. I. NANCY,[8] b. Dec. 20, 1801, m. Sept. 27, 1827, John Stinespring, a brewer and farmer, who was b. in Fairfield Co., O., May 30, 1806. They rem. from O., to Clinton Co., Ind., in 1853. She is m. Meth. ch. Chil.—

(1) *Leander Walker*, b. March 16, 1829, d. Nov. 4, '32. (2) *Jeremiah P.*, b. Aug. 30, '30. (3) *Sarah Ann*, b. Dec. 21, '33. (4) *Liberty S.*, b. April 15, '37. (5) *Zadok J.*, b. Sept. 31, '40. (6) *John B.*, b. April 4, '45.

1124. II. SON,[8] d. in infancy.

1125. III. OTIS,[8] b. 1804, d. 1811.

1126. IV. RUTH,[8] b. 1806, d. 1815.

1127. V. ZILPHA,[8] b. Nov. 11, 1809, m. Dec. 29, 1829, Zadok Wharton, a merchant, in West Chester, O., who was b. in Sussex Co., Del., April 1, 1799. She is m. Meth. ch. Chil.—

(1) *Caroline*, b. Nov. 14, 1830, m. Benj. F. Evans, Nov. 14, '54. Both m. ch. Res. W. C. (2) *DeKalb*, b. Jan. 26, '33, d. March 9, '34. (3) *Benj'n*, b. July 30, '34, is a book-keeper, in W. C. (4) *Eveline*, b. Aug. 27, '37, m. Nov. 15, '54, William Williams.

1128. VI. LIBERTY SULLIVAN,[8] (1748) b. Nov. 11, 1815, m. Nov. 15, 1838, Sarah Bone, who was b. in Warren Co., O., March 16, 1823. He is a farmer, and has had 10 chil. Res. Shelby Co., Ind.

CHIL. OF THOMPSON WALKER,[7] [527] OF ROXBURY, N.Y.

1129. I. DANIEL L.,[8] (1758) b. March 14, 1807, m. Feb. 26, 1829, Eliza S. Burhans, who was b. Dec. 17, 1810, and d. Oct. 29, 1851. They had 9 chil. He m. 2d, Aug. 20, 1854, Mrs. Gitty (Jerman) Lynch, widow of Patrick, and b. March 17, 1823. They have 1 dau. Res. Margarettville, Delaware Co., N. Y.

1130. II. GEORGE W.,[8] b. March 24, 1809. He m. June 7, 1838, Eunice Judson, of Otego, N. Y., dau. of Anson, of O., and b. Aug. 5, 1820. They have no chil. He learned the trade of a clothier, and superintended the business 5 yrs. His education was obtained

Geo.

Geo. W. Walker

at the Academy, in Delhi, N.Y. After teaching a few years, having made a profession of religion at the age of 19, he entered the ministry, in 1834, preaching 1st in Kortright, N.Y. In 1835, he was invited to Summit, Schoharie Co., N.Y., was ord., Aug. 16, 1835, an Evangelist in connection with the Christian Denomination, and extensive revivals accompanied his labors in these places. He then spent 2 yrs., in Monroe, Onondaga, Cayuga and Wayne Cos., as an Evangelist, and witnessed great displays of the power of the Gospel. Preaching a while in Otego, and vicinity, in 1840, he was settled in Roxbury, N.Y., his native town, and delivered the annual address before the N.Y. Eastern Conference, May, 1845. In 1846, he became pastor in Otego; in 1850, in South Valley; in 1853, of the 2d ch. in Lawrens; in 1855, of the 1st ch. in L. In 1857, he went West, preaching in Iowa, and Ill., several mos., and Nov. 1, 1858, became pastor in La Porte, Ind. His ministry has been attended with numerous tokens of Divine appoval. Mrs. W., has been a judicious and efficient helper. Res. La Porte.

1131. III. Delia C.,[8] b. 1814, m. Nov. 20, 1856, Jesse Blake, of La Porte, Ind., who was b. Feb. 2, 1856, in Livingston Co., N.Y. Both m. ch. Res. L. P.

1132. IV. Henry L.,[8] (1768) b. Sept. 6, 1818, m. Dec. 27, 1846, Alice Griffin, of Dutchess Co., N.Y., and has 2 chil. Res. Roxbury, N.Y.

Chil. of Capt. EZEKIEL WALKER,[7] [532] of Coventry, R.I.

1133. I. Erie,[8] (1770) b. June 14, 1818, m. May 9, 1843, Sally Stone, of Coventry. He is a farmer, in Webster, Mass., m. ch. and has 4 chil.

1134. II. Israel,[8] (1774) b. May 24, 1819, in Coventry, R.I., m. May 15, 1842, Clarissa A. Jenks, who was b. Oct. 9, 1819, in Foster, R.I. He is a carpenter, in Providence, R.I., is m. ch. and has had 5 chil.

1135. III. Mason,[8] (1779) b. Nov. 29, 1820, m. June 29, 1853, Almira Rice, who was b. in Coventry, March 13, 1827. He is a farmer, in Sterling, Ct., and has 1 son.

1136. IV. Sarah,[8] b. May 29, 1822, d. Jan. 14, 1837.

1137. V. Charles,[8] (1780) b. Nov. 5, 1823, m. March 4, 1855, Emeline Fisk, who was b. in Coventry, Feb. 19, 1827. He is m. ch. and has 1 dau. Res. Providence, R.I.

1138. VI. HANNAH,[8] b. May 28, 1825, d. Jan. 6, 1827.

1139. VII. ALMIRA,[8] b. Feb. 13, 1827, is unm.

1140. VIII. ISAAC,[8] (1781) b. Aug. 26, 1828, m. Maria Matteson, Aug. 25, 1853, who d. April 23, 1857. He is a mason, in Coventry, R. I., m. ch., and has 2 chil.

1141. IX. GEORGE,[8] b. July 22, 1830, m. June 5, 1853, Mary J. Babson, who was b. Dec. 12, 1831. No chil. He is a cloth dresser, in Webster, Mass, and m. ch.

1142. X. DANIEL,[8] b. May 5, 1832, m. Nov. 23, 1853, Sarah E. Calvert. He is a cloth dresser, in Clinton, Mass., and m. ch.

1143. XI. CYNTHIA,[8] b. March 18, 1834, m. Moses W. Collins, Oct. 9, 1853, in (Natick) Warwick, R. I., a printer. She is m. ch. Res. Pawtucket, R. I.

1144. XII. CLARK,[8] b. Jan. 8, 1836, is a farmer, in Coventry.

1145. XIII. LEWIS,[8] b. Jan. 14, 1838, is a farmer, in Coventry.

1146. XIV. WILLIAM H.,[8] b. June 6, 1840, d. Feb. 2, 1849.

CHIL. OF STEPHEN WALKER,[7] [535] OF WARWICK, R. I.

1147. I. ELIPHA,[8] b. June 23, 1822, m. Oct. 30, 1837, Stephen Andrew, and has 3 chil. He is a farmer. Res. Coventry.

1148. II. HENRY,[8] (1783) b. March 17, 1824, m. Oct. 28, 1845, Susan Ann Hutchins, and has 5 chil. Res. Warwick, R. I.

1149. III. SALLY,[8] b. July 16, 1826, m. Dec. 12, 1843, Joseph Myrick, Jr., a baker, in Phœnix Village, R. I. Chil.—

(1) *William Henry*, b. Sept. 1, 1846.
(2) *Abby Ann*, b. June 19, 1850.
(3) *Julia Alice*, b. Feb. 4, 1853.
(4) *Eunice Jennette*, b. April 18, 1854.
(5) *Fanny Elizabeth*, b. Sept. 29, 1856.

1150. IV. CLARISSA,[8] b. Aug. 19, 1828, m. Sept. 13, 1847, Martin Bradford, a tinman, in Phœnix Village, R. I. Chil.—

(1) *Amy Frances*, b. Aug. 7, 1848.
(2) *Caroline Frances*, b. April 15, 1850.
(3) *George Byron*, b. Oct. 11, 1852.
(4) *Emma*, b. April 11, 1854.

1151. V. FANNY,[8] b. May 1, 1830, m. Gustavus A. Snell, a carpenter. Res. Iowa.

1152. VI. ANGENETTE,[8] b. Nov. 1, 1832, m. Henry S. Hall, a carpenter. Res. Providence, R. I.

1153. VII. LYDIA,[8] b. June 6, 1835, m. July 22, 1855, James Johnson. Res. Coventry, R. I.

CHIL. OF NATHAN WALKER,[7] [538] OF COVENTRY, R. I.

1154. I. SUSAN,[8] b. April 14, 1828, m. Adam Tew, a blacksmith. Res. Coventry, R. I.

1155. II. DAU.,[8] b. July 20, 1830, d. July 22, 1830.

1156. III. MARY,[8] b. Feb. 13, 1832, d. Nov. 19, 1846.

1157. IV. STEPHEN,[8] b. Nov. 15, 1835.

1158. V. BENJAMIN W.,[8] b. Aug. 25, 1838, is a farmer in C.

1159. VI. ARNOLD,[8] b. Nov. 24, 1841, is a farmer.

1160. VII. SON,[8] b. Sept. 16, 1844, d. without age.

1161. VIII. JOSEPH,[8] b. Nov. 15, 1846.

CHIL OF DEA. ALMON WALKER,[7] [542] OF WEEDSPORT, N.Y.

1162. I. WILLIAM,[8] b. Oct. 27, 1829, d. May 11, 1851.

1163. II. PHEBE BELINDA,[8] b. Feb. 22, 1835, m. July 7, 1853, Jerome B. Williams, a miller. Chil.—

(1) *Emma*. (2) *Mary*, twins, b. May 7, 1854.

CHILDREN OF SYDNEY S. WALKER,[7] [543] OF ——.

1164. I. FRANCIS,[8] b. Nov. 12, 1836.

1165. II. ALFRED,[8] b. Jan. 3, 1838.

1166. III. ISABEL,[8] b. April 17, 1840.

1167. IV. THOMAS,[8] b. Dec. 18, 1844.

CHILDREN OF JOSEPH WALKER,[7] [546] OF PENN.

1168. I. FOUR CHIL.,[8] names not reported.

CHIL. OF WM. WHITFORD WALKER,[7] [555] OF PAWTUCKET.

1172. I. WILLIAM F.,[8] b. Sept. 24, 1818, d. Aug. 27, 1820.

1173. II. NATHANIEL L.,[8] (1788) b. Sept. 13, 1824, m. 1852, Margaret McDonald. He is a machinist, and has had 2 chil. Res. Pawtucket.

1174. III. WILLIAM F.,[8] d. ae. 4 yrs., about 1835.

1175. IV. ELLEN M.,[8] d. ae. 2 yrs., about 1837.

CHIL. OF BENJAMIN WALKER,[7] [566] OF MACOMB, ILL.

1176. I. ORSAMUS,[8] (1790) b. in Barre, Vt., June 15, 1801, m. Feb. 26, 1825, Adeline Waters, of B., who was b. Nov. 1808. They have had 6 chil. He held the office of Captain in the Vermont militia, is now a carpenter, in Macomb, and Deacon of the Universalist ch.

1177. II. PHEBE,[8] b. in Barre, Aug 15, 1804, (Aug. 24, 1805?) m. April 17, 1825, Robert Morse, of B., a farmer, b. Jan. 1793, and d. June 3, (2?) 1842. She m. 2d, May 12, 1850, Cyrus Bemis, who was b. March 9, 1799, in Baltimore, Vt. Res. Barton, Vt. Chil.—

(1) *Andrew J.*, b. April 4, 1826, m. June, '56, — Peck, of Barre, a farmer. Res. Ella, Wis. (2) *Elvira J.*, b. Oct. 9, '27, m. June 18, 1849, Lindall French, of Glover, Vt., a farmer. (3) *Martha G.*, b. Nov. 12, '29, m. March 4, '49, Wm. Farwell, of B., and d. Aug. 1, '49. (4) *Benj. F.*, b. Dec. 31, '31, m. Jan. 15, '52, Mary Goodwin, is a printer in Chicago, Ill. (5) *Robert*, b. Feb. 16, '34, is a shoemaker in Lynn. (6) *Eleanor*, b. Feb. 18, '36, d. Nov. 12, '46.

1178. III. ELVIRA,[8] b. April 24, 1807, d. 1845. She m. Brigham Gates, of Morristown, Vt., and has 1 son.

1179. IV. BENJAMIN F.,[8] (1796) b. in Irasburg, Dec. 25, 1809, m. Dec. 25, 1832, Diana Howard, of Montpelier, Vt., who was b. in M., Feb. 18, 1810. They have 3 chil. He was a Select-man in M., a Major in the Vermont militia, and is now Superintendent of the Water Works, Chicago, Ill. He is also Trustee of the 2d Universalist ch. in C.

1180. V. MARY B.,[8] b. in B., Aug. 24, 1813, m. Liberty Bacon, of New Worcester, Mass. He is a manufacturer. Res. Leicester. Chil.—

(1) *Addie A.*, b. April 24, 1839, m. Oct. '20, '60, Ira S. Morey, of Leicester. (2) *James*, b. May 2, '41. (3) *Clara M.*, b. May 22, '43. (4) *Eudora F.*, b. July 17, '46. (5) *Charles H.*, b. Jan. 29, '54.

1181. VI. EDWIN R.,[8] (1799) b. 1815, m. Emily Gleason, pub. April 9, 1843. He is a jeweler, and has 2 chil. Res. Providence, R. I.

1182. VII. DANIEL H.,[8] (1801) b. in St. Louis, Mo., Aug. 1, 1823, d. Aug. 1, 1851. He m. 1845, Margaret Jones, in Alton, Ill., and had 2 chil. He was a brick maker, in A.

1183. VIII. HARRIET A.,[8] b. in St. L., July 31, 1825, m. Dec. 1, 1845, James Phelps, of Macomb, Ill. He is a blacksmith, in M. No chil.

1184. IX. JOHN S.,[8] b. in St. L., Oct. 9, 1827, m. Dec. 1855, Elizabeth Hutchinson, in St. L. He is a carpenter, in Macomb, Ill.

1185. X. WILLIAM P.,[8] b. in St. L., July 13, 1829, is a R. R. engineer, in Macomb, Ill., and unm.

1186. XI. EMILY S.,[8] b. in St. L., Nov. 19, 1831, m. March 22, 1849, Rob't H. Broaddus, a blacksmith, of Macomb, Ill., who was b. in M. Chil.—

(1) *Henry A.*, b. Oct. 27, 1849.
(2) *Harriet A.*, b. Sept. 7, 1851, d. Nov. 1, '52.
(3) *John B.*, b. Sept. 17, 1853.
(4) *Charles W.*, b. Nov. 13, 1855.

CHIL. OF ENOS WALKER,[7] [568] OF NORTH BANGOR, N. Y.

1187. I. LEMUEL F.,[8] (1803) b. in Barre, Vt., 1804, m. 1825, Polly Delong, in N. Y., who was b. 1805, and has 4 chil. He is a carpenter, and has held the military office of Capt. Res. Plattsburgh, N. Y.

1188. II. JOHN B.,[8] b. in B., Jan 9, 1806, d. June 26, 1832, in N. Y. He was a farmer, in N. Y., and Captain.

1189. III. BENJAMIN R.,[8] (1807) b. in B., in 1808. He m. 1837, Vitera Warren, who was b. in Vt., 1814. He is a cabinet maker, has held the office of Capt., and has 3 chil. Res. Keeseville, N. Y.

1190. IV. Nancy N.,[8] b. in B., 1810, m. Henry O. Tilden, in N. Y., 1840, who was b. in 1809, in N. Y. He is Methodist Clergyman in the Black River Conference. They have—

(1) *Henry A.*, b. 1851.

1191. V. Hannah E.,[8] b. in B., 1812, m. 1840, Samuel Huntington, in N. Y., who was b. in Vt., 1811. He is a bookseller, and a class leader, in the Meth. ch. Chil.—

(1) *Samuel*, b. 1844, is an adopted son. (2) *Sarah A.*, b. '46. (3) *Lucy A.*, b. '50.

1192. VI. Samuel N.,[8] (1810) b. in B., 1816, m. 1840, Catharine Harrigan, in N. Y., who was b. in Canada, 1823. He is a carpenter, and has 1 son. Res. Watertown, Wis.

1193. VII. Clark E.,[8] (1811) b. in N. Y., in 1819, m. 1845, Nancy M. Towsley, in Vt., who was b. in Vt., 1825. He is a cabinet and piano manufacturer, in North Bangor, N. Y., and has 2 chil.

1194. VIII. Rebecca Ann,[8] b. in N. Y., in 1824. She m. Edgar J. Hull, in Vt., 1854, who was b. in Vt., 1820. He is a farmer, in Orwell, Vt.

Chil. of Rev. DANIEL WALKER,[7] [570] of Grass Lake, Mich.

1195. I. Margaret R.,[8] b. in Barre, Vt., May 29, 1815, m. Nov. 30, 1834, Eleazer W. Clark, of Grass Lake, Mich., a farmer. Both m. Meth. ch. Res. Grass Lake. Chil.—

(1) *Alson S.*, b. in Grass Lake, March 6, 1836, m. Dec. 12, '57, Lottie A. Luce, dau. of Gen. C. F. E. Luce, of Grass Lake, and b. Nov. 1, '35. (2) *John W.*, b. in Grass Lake, Sept. 29, '37. (3) *Daniel W.*, b. in Grass Lake, Oct. 24, '39. (4) *Mary M.*, b. in Grass Lake, Sept. 2, '41. (5) *George*, b. in Grass Lake, Dec. 5, '43. (6) *William*, b. in Grass Lake July 20, '46. (7) *Benj'n F.*, b. in Grass Lake, March 18, '53.

1196. II. Harriet A.,[8] b. Nov. 30, 1818, d. Sept. 10, 1844.

1197. III. Eliza,[8] b. in B., March 24, 1817, m. May 1, 1836, Eli Douglas, a farmer. He has been Supervisor 5 yrs., and is Justice of the Peace. She is m. Meth. ch. Res. Texas, Kalamazoo Co., Mich. Chil.—

(1) *Maria M.*, b. Jan. 28, 1837. (2) *Daniel*, b. May 24, '39. (3) *Emily*, b. Oct. 20, '42. (4) *George*, b. Feb. 1, '48.

1198. IV. William H.,[8] (1813) b. in B., Nov. 17, 1823. He m. Jan. 7, 1836, Mary Jane Burtch, dau. of William, of Grass Lake,

Mich., and has 2 chil. He is a farmer, brick manufacturer, and boot and shoe manufacturer. Both m. Meth. ch. He is a class leader.

1199. V. RICHARD A.,[8] b. in B., Feb. 7, 1827, d. 1848, in Cal.

1200. VI. BENJAMIN,[8] b. Dec. 22, 1828, d. April 19, 1846.

1201. VII. JOHN Q.,[8] b. Aug. 9, 1831, d. Jan 10, 1835.

1202. VIII. ASAHEL P.,[8] b. in Grass Lake, Nov. 8, 1838.

CHILDREN OF JOHN WALKER,[7] [571] OF BARRE, VT.

1203. I. ALLEN C.,[8] (1815) b. in Barre, Aug. 13, 1811, m. Emma Spalding, of Morristown, Vt., who was b. Aug. 23, 1818, and d. July 30, 1843. He m. 2d, Nov. 2, 1846, Bethiah K. Staples, of Taunton, who was b. March 1, 1822. He is a farmer, and has had 2 chil.

1204. II. LONDUS B.,[8] (1817) b. in B., Sept. 12, 1813, m. Jan. 2, 1842, Celia Harrington, of St. Johnsbury, Vt. She d. April 23, 1843, ae. 20 yrs., 2 mos., 18 days. He m. 2d, Jan. 7, 1847, Myra Morrison, of Barre, Vt. She was b. March 2, 1824. He is a millwright, and has 2 chil. Res. Chicago, Ill.

1205. III. OTIS F.,[8] (1819) b. in B., April 2, 1816, m. Jan. 27, 1846, Jane Brown, of B., who was b. in Orange, Vt. They have 2 chil. He is a farmer, and has been Justice of the Peace.

1206. IV. JOHN N.,[8] (1821) b. in B., Oct. 5, 1819, m. Oct. 23, 1843, Elizabeth Pratt, of Bakersfield, Vt., who was b. May, 1825. He is a merchant, in Montpelier, Vt., and has had 3 chil.

1207. V. MARIETTA,[8] b. in B., Sept. 20, 1820, m. Jan. 1845, Enos T. Fuller, of B., who was b. in B., Oct. 20, 1816. He is Superintendent of an Iron Foundry. Res. Mechanicsville, N. Y. Chil.—

(1) *John W.*, b. Nov. 4, 1846.
(2) *Martha*, b. July 27, 1848.
(3) *Aurora W.*, b. May 2, 1850.
(4) *Ida Elnora*, b. Aug. 7, 1852, d. Jan 15, '53.

1208. VI. BENJ. H.,[8] b. in B., Oct. 9, 1823, m. Phebe Williams, of Taunton, pub. Jan. 6, 1847. He is a millwright. Res. Taunton.

1209. VII. ALVAN C.,[8] b. in Morristown, Vt., Jan. 17, 1826. He entered Middlebury Coll., but sickness compelled him to leave.

When sufficiently recovered, he went to Illinois, and was a Teacher, and R. R. surveyor. Returning to Barre, he entered a Law-office, in B., as student. He is now a Lawyer, in Chicago, Ill.

1210. VIII. Martha Ann,[8] b. in M., Feb. 5, 1828, m. March 7, 1849, Geo. W. Harrington, of Barre, Vt., who was b. in B., Jan. 31, 1827. He is a farmer. Res. B. Chil.—

(1) *Davis Dean*, b. May 17, 1850. (2) *Frank E.*, b. Sept. 12, '53.

1211. IX. Susan Aurora,[8] b. June 5, 1832, in M., m. Jan. 29, 1855, Thomas B. Nichols, who was b. Feb. 25, 1830.

1212. X. Celinda E.,[8] b. Nov. 11, 1836, in M.

Chil. of Capt. LEWIS WALKER,[7] [579] of Seekonk.

1213. I. Richard,[8] b. Sept. 3, 1833, d. May 30, 1836.

1214. II. Mary Smith,[8] b. Jan. 23, 1836, is m. Cong. ch.

1215. III. Louis Ormsbee,[8] b. May 23, 1837.

1216. IV. William Henry,[8] b. Dec. 8, 1838.

1217. V. Sarah Maria,[8] b. March 24, 1841, is m. Cong. ch.

1218. VI. Josephine,[8] b. July 26, 1843, d. May 14, 1844.

1219. VII. Charles Frederick,[8] b. Jan. 17, 1846.

1220. VIII. Son,[8] b. June 2, 1854.

Chil. of HENRY G. WALKER,[7] [584] of Wyoming, N.Y.

1221. I. Henry C.,[8] (1824) b. May 3, 1815, in Middlebury, Vt., m. Phebe Sherman, of Lanesboro', dau. of Job, and b. May 27, 1812. They are connected with the Pres. ch., and have had 5 chil. He is President of the "Lake Navigation Co.," a Joint Stock Association, with a capital of $1,000,000. He possesses uncommon capabilities for business, and sustains an honorable position in respect to integrity and moral worth. Res. Buffalo, N. Y.

1222. II. Sarah Ann,[8] b. Nov. 19, 1816, in Rutland, Vt., m. 1837, John P. Skinner, Esq., son of Benj., of Williamstown, and b. in W., July 24, 1799. He was graduated at Williams Coll., in 1818, studied Law in Litchfield, Ct., and also with Judge Buel, of Troy, N. Y. He settled in Wyoming, N.Y., in 1821, where he still resides.

He has been a member of the State Legislature, First Judge of the Court of Common Pleas, several yrs., and in 1838, was appointed Judge of the Eighth Judicial Circuit, of New York. He is an Elder in the Pres. ch., of which his wife and dau. are also members. Child—

(1) *Mary Rachael*, b. Sept. 6, 1839.

1223. III. JENNETTE S.,[8] d. Sept. 1846. She m. May, 1840, Woodruff L. Barnes, of Conneaut, O. He was Cashier of the Bank in C., and is now a Banker in Buffalo, N.Y. She had 1 dau.—

(1) *Harriet Newell*, b. May 16, 1841.

1224. IV. ISAAC C.,[8] b. Dec. 10, 1823, in Wyoming, N.Y., d. May, 1858. He m. July, 1846, Harriet L. Saunders, of Milan, O., dau. of Rev. Stephen, and b. June 21, 1824, in South Salem, N.Y. They had 4 chil. He was a shipping merchant, and General Agent of the "Lake Navigation Co." at Chicago. Both m. Pres. ch. Res. Buffalo, N.Y.

CHIL. OF DANIEL W. WALKER,[7] [587] OF LAWRENCE, PA.

1225. I. DANIEL,[8] is dec'd.

1226. II. MARY EMILY.[8]

CHIL. OF JEDEDIAH WALKER,[7] [592] OF COVINGTON, N.Y.

1227. I. CHARLES H.,[8] b. Aug. 23, 1834.

1228. II. SARAH,[8] b. June 2, 1837, d. Jan. 1, 1860, m. Cong.ch.

1229. III. GEORGE W.,[8] b. Feb. 22, 1840.

1230. IV. HELEN G.,[8] b. Aug. 14, 1845.

1231. V. EUNICE S.,[8] b. June 1, 1847.

CHIL. OF WILLIAM WALKER,[7] [594] OF WARSAW, N.Y.

1232. I. SON,[8] b. Dec. 21, 1824, d. y.

1233. II. LEWIS ENSIGN,[8] (1834) b. May 15, 1826, m. Dec. 27, 1853, in Perrysburg, O., Susan A. Brown, who was b. Feb. 2, 1830, in Canandaigua, N.Y. She was a Teacher 5 yrs. They have 2 chil. He learned the harness maker's trade. Having a fair academical education, at the age of 21 he went to St. Albans, Vt., where he taught school 2 yrs.; thence to Milan, O., where he was Principal of Milan Public Schools 4 yrs., and also served as County Inspector of Public Schools. In 1853, he went to Sandusky, O., and was a Teacher, and in 1854, returned to Warsaw, and commenced business as a bookseller. He is also Town Superintendent of the Common Schools in W.

1234. III. Mary A.,[8] b. July 16, 1827, m. Aug. 15, 1855, Wm. M. Cowgill, who was b. May 18, 1811. She was grad. at Mt. Holyoke Seminary, in 1852, was a Teacher in Rockford and Petersburg, Ill., and is m. Cong. ch. He is a merchant. Res. P.

1235. IV. Charles,[8] b. April 19, 1829, went to California in 1849, and finally settled in Seattle, Kings Co., Washington Territory, and was shot by the Indians, Sept. 15, 1855, while employed as one of a party of exploration in search of gold. He was. m. Cong. ch.

1236. V. Adelia C.,[8] b. Oct. 21, 1830, was grad. at Mt. Holyoke Seminary, in 1853, was a teacher there, also in Detroit, Mich., and is now in the Western Female Seminary, Oxford, Butler Co., Ohio. She is m. Cong. ch.

1237. VI. Albert,[8] b. May 9, 1833, m. ——. He is a hardware merchant in Petersburg, Ill., and is m. Cong. ch.

1238. VII. George W.,[8] b. Aug. 11, 1835, m. Sept. 8, 1859, Emily E. Gilman, dau. of Calvin, of Ogden, N. Y. He was a student in Oberlin Coll., O., preparing for the ministry, but is now on a farm near Rochester, N. Y.

1238.[1] VIII. William H.,[8] b. July 18, 1838, is a clerk, unm.

Child of HARVEY WALKER,[7] [596] of Marine Mills, Minn.

1239. I. Mary Amanda,[8] m. April, 1849, Jacob Ellison, a farmer, and has had 6 chil., 3 dec'd. Res. Marine, Ill.

Chil. of EDWARD G. WALKER,[7] [599] of St. Albans, Vt.

1240. I. Leonora Maria, b. April 16, 1835, m. Jan. 25, 1854, Horace Jennison, a trader, and has 1 child. Res. St. Albans, Vt.

1241. II. William P.,[8] b. Dec. 10, 1837, is unm.

1242. III. David C.,[8] b. June 27, 1844, d. Sept. 24, 1849.

CHIL. OF LEWIS WALKER,[7] [601] OF MARINE MILLS, MINN.

1243. I. ELLA,[8] b. June, 1841.

1244. II. EMMA T.,[8] b. Oct. 1844.

CHIL. OF PORTER E. WALKER,[7] [603] OF MILAN, O.

1245. I. ELLEN L.,[8] b. May 2, 1838, m. May 31, 1859, H. A. Metcalf, of Cherry Valley, N. Y. Res. Warsaw, N. Y. Both m. Cong. ch.

1246. II. EDWARD H.,[8] b. June 25, 1840.

1247. III. EMMA L.,[8] b. Dec. 10, 1844.

1248. IV. LEWIS,[8] b. March 13, 1848.

1249. V. CHILD,[8] b. about Dec. 1, 1859.

CHIL. OF WILLIAM WALKER,[7] [612] OF CLARENCE, WIS.

1250. I. NANCY,[8] b. Oct. 5, 1808, m. April 15, 1844, Myron Halsted, of Dansville, Steuben Co., N. Y., a merchant. In 1852, he rem. to Clarence, Wis., and is a farmer. Chil., (April, 1856)—

(1) *Juan*, ae. about 11. (2) *Scott*, ae. about 9. (3) *Lee*, ae. about 5. (4) *Mary*, ae. about 2.

1251. II. FRANCIS GEORGE,[8] b. Nov. 2, 1820, d. unm. Jan. 3, 1844.

1252. III. POLLY,[8] b. Jan. 7, 1823, d. in childhood.

1253. IV. LYDIA,[8] b. March, 1825, d. in childhood.

1254. V. ELECTA JANE,[8] b. Sept. 1827, is a Teacher, in Dansville, N. Y.

1255. VI. MARY ARETHUSA,[8] b. Feb. 1830, d. Jan. 8, 1844.

1256. VII. SARAH MATILDA,[8] b. April 7, 1833, m. Nov. 11, 1852, Dr. John Mason, son of Paschal, Esq., and b. in Orleans Co., N. Y., Jan. 6, 1829. He began the practice of medicine May 20, 1852, and has been very successful. His preparatory studies were at

Louisville, and Univ. of Mich., Ann Arbor. Res. Dundee, Mich. They have—

(1) *Edward Walker*, b. Aug. 30, 1853.

CHIL. OF STEPHEN WALKER,[7] [613] OF BUFFALO, N. Y.

1257. I. CHARLES RUDD,[8] (1836) b. Jan. 22, 1823, m. Nov. 4, 1846, Angeline Lake, and has had 3 chil. He is a Druggist, in Buffalo, N. Y., and m. Epis. ch.

1258. II. WILLIAM HENRY,[8] b. Aug. 20, 1825. He was educated a shoe merchant, and was successful enough at the age of 26, to relinquish his business, and follow the bent of his mind, for the Bar. He studied in the Law School, at Albany, N. Y., and led his class, taking the gold medal for the best Law treatise. Intense study ruined his health, and he was constrained to give up his profession, and resume his old business. He is m. Epis. ch.

CHIL. OF SAMUEL G. WALKER,[7] [615] OF BUFFALO, N. Y.

1259. I. HELEN M.,[8] b. Oct. 4, 1826, m. Dec. 10, 1851, John Q. Dudley, a merchant in Detroit, Mich., and now in N. Y. city. They have—

(1) *Edward G.*, b. June 14, 1853.

1260. II. CAROLINE M.,[8] b. Aug. 8, 1828, m. June 10, 1844, Samuel P. Beecher. He is an extensive Horticulturist and Fruit Grower, in Erie, Pa. Chil.—

(1) *Helen*, b. July 28, 1845. (2) *Elihu B.*, b. May 24, '47. (3) *Fanny*, b. May 11, '49. (4) *Mary*, twin, b. Dec. 21, '51. (5) *Abby*, twin, b. Dec. 21, '51. (6) *Caroline Walker*, b. March 18, '58.

1261. III. DEWITT CLINTON,[8] b. Aug. 9, 1830, d. May 22, 1832.

1262. IV. FRANCES ELIZABETH,[8] b. Aug. 29, 1832, d. Sept. 19, 1836.

1263. V. SARAH GARDNER,[8] b. April 24, 1835, d. March 8, 1860, of consumption. She m. Sept. 4, 1856, Charles Gay Root, a merchant, son of Henry and Mary (Gay) and b. July 20, 1833, in B. They removed to Louisville, Ky., in 1859. Her short but painful illness was borne patiently, and she sweetly fell "asleep in Jesus." Chil.—

(1) *Henry Walker*, b. in B., Aug. 24, 1857. (2) *Sarah*, b. Feb. 10, '60. After the death of her mother, she was adopted by Mrs. Dudley, No. 1259.

CHILDREN OF FERDINAND WALKER,[7] [618] OF N. Y. CITY.

1264. I. MELVIN MORDAUNT,[8] b. Nov. 24, 1829, d. Jan. 28, 1830.

1265. II. ELIZA MELVINA,[8] b. Jan. 23, 1831, d. Feb. 25, 1831.

1266. III. FRANCES MELVINA,[8] b. May 17, 1833, d. March 23, 1845.

1267. IV. JANE AVERILL,[8] b. Aug. 23, 1835, d. Feb. 13, 1837.

1268. V. AMELIA MATILDA,[8] b. May 27, 1837, d. Oct. 29, 1838.

1269. VI. ADA,[8] b. Nov. 8, 1839.

1270. VII. HOBART,[8] b. June 9, 1842.

1271. VIII. MELVIN,[8] b. June 2, 1844, d. July 3, 1844.

1272. IX. JEROME,[8] b. Aug. 5, 1845.

1273. X. GEORGE DONALDSON,[8] b. Oct. 2, 1847.

1274. XI. ELIZA MARIA,[8] b. March 12, 1850, d. Dec. 29, 1850.

1275. XII. EMMA,[8] b. Nov. 5, 1851.

CHIL. OF BENJ. G. WALKER,[7] [621] OF TECUMSEH, MICH.

1276. I. SAMUEL GARDNER,[8] b. June 14, 1841. Res. Litchfield, Mich., with No. 617.

1277. II. MARY ELIZABETH,[8] b. July 21, 1842. Res. Buffalo, N.Y.

1278. III. STEPHEN,[8] b. March 30, 1844, d. Nov. 2, 1845.

1279. IV. CAROLINE AMELIA,[8] b. Sept. 2, 1845, is adopted by Mrs. Munson, Fowlerville, Mich. No. 616.

1280. V. EDWARD CAREY,[8] b. July 30, 1847, is adopted by Sam'l G. Walker, of Buffalo, N. Y. No. 615.

1281. VI. LUCY A.,[8] b. Nov. 28, 1849, is adopted by Edward C. Walker, Esq., Detroit, Mich. No. 624.

CHIL. OF PROF. CHA'S I. WALKER,[7] [622] OF DETROIT, MICH.

1282. I. THEODORE HINSDILL,[8] b. Feb. 15, 1850, d. June, 1850.

1283. II. CHARLES HINSDILL,[8] b. July 3, 1854.

CHIL. OF EDWARD C. WALKER,[7] [624] OF DETROIT, MICH.

1284. I. BRYANT,[8] b. July 3, 1856.

1285. II. JESSIE RAWSON,[8] b. Aug. 1, 1859.

CHIL. OF ALBERT WALKER,[7] [629] OF ROCHESTER, N. Y.

1286. I. DAVID F.,[8] b. March 13, 1834, in Clarkson, N. Y. He is a Physician, having studied medicine at the Medical Coll., Ann Arbor, Mich.

1287. II. ALBERT C.,[8] b. Jan. 15, 1845, in C.

1288. III. FRANCES E.,[8] b. July, 1846, d. March 20, 1848.

1289. IV. CLARA J.,[8] b. March 25, 1848, in Rochester, N. Y.

1290. V. MARY C.,[8] b. Jan. 27, 1850, in R., N. Y.

1291. VI. SON,[8] b. May 13, 1856, in R., N. Y.

CHIL. OF HORATIO WALKER,[7] [632] OF NEIL'S CREEK, IND.

1292. I. SARAH ANN,[8] b. May 16, 1816, m. 1832, John Strong.

1293. II. SON,[8] b. 1819, d. without name.

1294. III. MARY ANN,[8] b. Nov. 1820, d. ae. 18 yrs.

1295. IV. LEWIS,[8] b. Sept. 18, 1823, d. ae. 18 yrs.

1296. V. DEWITT C.,[8] b. July 9, 1832. Res. N. C., Ind.

CHIL. OF LEWIS M. WALKER,[7] [637] OF CLARENDON, VT.

1297. I. LOUIS MERRITT,[8] (1839) b. May 9, 1830, m. Feb. 17, 1852, Hannah P. Arnold. He is a farmer, in Clarendon, Vt., and has had 3 chil.

1298. II. ADAH ANN,[8] b. Oct. 13, 1831, d. March 30, 1835.

1299. III. SARAH J.,[8] b. April 20, 1833, d. July 10, 1852.

1300. IV. DEWITT C.,[8] b. March 14, 1837, d. April 28, 1842.

1301. V. WILLIAM WIRT,[8] b. April 27, 1839.

1302. VI. NOAH SHEPARDSON,[8] b. May 29, 1842.

1303. VII. DEWITT C.,[8] b. Oct. 19, 1843, d. April 10, 1846.

CHIL. OF HON. DEWITT C. WALKER,[7] [639] OF CAPAC, MICH.

1304. I. ADELAIDE,[8] b. June 3, 1839.

1305. II. BARNARD,[8] b. March 27, 1841.

1306. III. DEWITT,[8] b. Feb. 18, 1843.

1307. IV. LEWIS,[8] b. June 18, 1846.

1308. V. BYRON,[8] b. June 7, 1848.

1309. VI. CAROLINE,[8] b. April 1, 1851.

1310. VII. FRANK,[8] b. Dec. 15, 1853.

1311. VIII. JAMES BUCHANAN,[8] b. Nov. 4, 1856.

CHIL. OF WHITFIELD WALKER,[7] [641] OF WHITING, VT.

1312. I. ELMORE H.,[8] b. June 17, 1821. He is head clerk in Messrs. Niles & Wheeler's forwarding House, Buffalo, N. Y.

1313. II. ELLEN CELIA,[8] b. Aug. 30, 1822. Res. W., unm.

1314. III. LUCIUS WHITFIELD,[8] (1842) b. Sept. 4, 1823, m. Sept. 16, 1845, Ellen G. Herbert, of Orwell, Vt., and has 1 dau. He is architect and General Agent for the Ill. Central Rail Road. Res. Urbana, Ill.

1315. IV. MARY,[8] b. Oct. 1, 1825, m. Jan. 1, 1845, Alonzo A. Russigue, a merchant. Res. Franklin, Mass. Chil.—

(1) *Francis A.*, b. Jan. 24, 1847. (2) *Henry*, b. Aug. 11, '50.

1316. V. RUBY,[8] b. Oct. 1, 1825, m. March 23, 1850, Dan Russigue, of Whitehall, N. Y., a merchant, in W.

1317. VI. FRANCIS THEODORE,[8] b. Sept. 3, 1827. He is a Stage Agent. Res. Peoria, Ill.

1318. VII. GEO. MARTIN,[8] b. Nov. 27, 1829, d. May, 1859. He m. Feb. 1854, Martha, dau. of Capt. DeWitt. He was engaged at the time of his death, in a very large trade, as purchaser and forwarder of grain. Res. Chicago, Ill. Few equalled him in capability for business.

1319. VIII. JOHN HENRY,[8] b. Sept. 18, 1839, is a clerk, in Franklin.

CHIL. OF SAWYER WALKER,[7] [644] OF ST. MARIE, WIS.

1320. I. MARION B.,[8] b. Sept. 16, 1825, m. Oct. 21, 1852, Thomas A. Sayles, son of Doct. Welcome, of Vernon, Oneida Co., N. Y. She was educated at Rochester, N. Y.; and was a Teacher in one of the Public Schools of R. 3 yrs. He was educated at Vernon Academy; was a Teacher at the South, and is now a Lawyer in Ripon, Wis. Chil.—

(1) *Clara*, b. March 4, 1854, d. Sept. 24, '55, in St. Marie, Wis. (2) *Bertha*, b. Sept. 22, '56. (3) *Dau.*, b. Oct. 22, '59.

1321. II. DORWIN G.,[8] b. Dec. 17, 1826, is unm. Most of his youth till 1852, was spent in farming. After finishing his academical course, he taught school 12 Winters in Vt. and N.Y., and was at one time, Principal of an Academy. From April, 1855, he had charge of the store of the N. E. Protective Union in Whiting, Vt. 1 yr.; in May, 1856, rem. to Burlington, Vt., and is now an enterprising and prosperous merchant in B. Endowed with superior abilities, ardent, self-reliant and ambitious, he gives promise of achieving a marked and enviable position in society.

1322. III. EDWIN SAWYER,[8] b. Aug. 11, 1828, m. Aug. 11, 1858, Emily M. Hunt, dau. of Ira, of Fairfax, and b. in F., Jan. 7, 1835. She was educated at the New Hampton Lit. and Theol. Institution. Spending his youth on a farm, in 1847, he entered the Bakersfield Academy, Vt.; in May, 1848, rem. to Worcester, and was engaged in business two Summers, teaching in Vt., during the Winter. While in W., he became hopefully pious, and Aug. 20, 1849, united with the 2d Bap ch.; in Sept. 1850, he went to Rochester, N. Y., to pursue a course of study. After a preparatory training 2 yrs., he entered the Rochester Univ., July, 1852, and was at the same time licensed by the 2d Bap. ch. in R., to preach. He was grad. July 9, 1856; in Sept. entered the Roch. Theo. Sem., was grad. July, 1858, and Sept. 16, 1858, ord. Pastor of the 1st Bap. ch. in Dansville, Livingston Co., N. Y. He resigned his charge, March, 1860. Res. Rochester, N. Y.

1323. IV. ALMIRA,[8] b. Oct. 23, 1832, was graduated at the Clover St. Sem., Rochester, N. Y., April 10, 1857, and is now Teacher in a High School, in R.

1324. V. LUCY HALL,[8] b. Jan. 4, 1835, m. July 14, 1859, in Rochester, N. Y., Rev. Shadrach Washington, who was b. in Penn., 1832, and at 10 yrs. of age, rem. to Dayton O., with his father;

J H Daniels Lith Boston

[illegible] N. Y. [illegible]

[illegible] was graduated [illegible] N. Y., April [illegible] 18[illegible] [illegible]

[illegible] V. [illegible] Lucy H[illegible], b. Jan. [illegible] 1, 18[illegible]; m. July [illegible] [illegible] N. Y., Rev. [illegible] Washington, who was b. [illegible] [illegible] to [illegible] age, rem. to Dayton, O., with [illegible]

J H Daniels Lith Boston.

entered the Univ. of Rochester, 1852, and was grad. 1856. He was grad. at Roch. Theol. Sem., July, 1858, and Dec. 2, 1858, became pastor of the Bap. ch. in Woodstock, Ill. She was grad. at Clover St. Sem., in R., April 6, 1856, and until her marriage, was Preceptress of the Coll. Institute, Brockport, N. Y.

1325. VI. Fanny Melinda,[8] b. in Vt., Aug. 14, 1837, was educated at Lawrence University, Appleton, Wis., and is unm.

1326. VII. Albert Henry,[8] b. Nov. 25, 1844.

Children of HIRAM WALKER,[7] [646] of Mexico, N. Y.

1327. I. Avery S.,[8] (1843) b. Oct. 15, 1829, m. Aug. 1857, Rosanna Baldwin, of Berea, Ohio, a grad. of Oberlin College. They have 1 son. He was prepared for College, at the Mexico Academy, N. Y., and at Oberlin, O., where he united with the Cong. ch.; entered Oberlin Coll., in Aug. 1851, and completing the 4 yrs. course in 3 yrs., was graduated in 1854. He entered the New York Theo. Seminary, Aug. 1854, was grad. May, 1857, and immediately ord. and settled as Pastor, in Lodi, N.J., resigning his charge June 1, 1860. He rem. in 1860, to Rockville, Ct., and has charge of the Cong. ch.

1328. II. Ida,[8] b. Dec. 4, 1834, d. Dec. 8, ae. 4 days.

Chil. of Hon. JESSE WALKER,[7] [649] of Buffalo, N. Y.

1329. I. Eliza Coe,[8] b. about 1840.

1330. II. Jessie M.,[8] b. about 1844.

Chil. of SAMUEL T. WALKER,[7] [651] of Whiting, Vt.

1331. I. George S.,[8] b. Dec. 27, 1823, m. July, 1860, Maria Needham, of Whiting, Vt. He is a farmer, in W., has a well cultivated mind, is Justice of the Peace, and has been Superintendent of the Schools.

Chil. of Rev. LEVI WALKER,[7] [654] of Clarion, Ill.

1332. I. Levi,[8] b. Jan. 23, 1830, is a farmer in Clarion.

1333. II. MARTHA,[8] b. Feb. 6, 1832, in Hebron, N.Y., m. June 3, 1850, E. W. Winslow, of Clarion, Ill.

1334. III. GEORGE B., b. Sept. 21, 1835, is a farmer, in C.

1335. IV. MARY,[8] b. May 19, 1838, in Hanover, N. H.

CHIL. OF FRANKLIN WALKER,[7] [659] OF CLARION, ILL.

1336. I. WILLIAM,[8] b. July 11, 1842, d. July 16.

1337. II. WILLIAM F.,[8] b. Sept. 12, 1843, d. Aug. 7, 1851.

1338. III. CHESTER B.,[8] b. Aug. 25, 1846, d. March 12, 1847.

1339. IV. SUSAN L.,[8] b. March 27, 1848, d. Aug. 8, 1851.

1340. V. FRANCES E.,[8] b. Jan. 10, 1853.

CHIL. OF TIMOTHY M. WALKER,[7] [661] OF HUBBARDTON, VT.

1341. I. NANCY MARIE,[8] b. in Whiting, July 17, 1823, m. Feb. 1841, George Dickerman, of Hubbardton, Vt. He is a farmer, in H. No chil.

1342. II. TIMOTHY MILLER,[8] (1844) b. in W., March 24, 1825, m. 1848, Caroline Hall, of Rochester, Vt., and has 2 chil. He is a farmer, in Waukan, Winnebago Co., Wis.

1343. III. EPHRAIM MOULTON,[8] (1846) b. in W., Oct. 9, 1828, m. Fanny Peters, of Hubbardton, Vt., and has 1 son. He is a farmer, formerly in H., and now in Waukau, Wis.

1344. IV. SARAH J.,[8] b. in W., about 1837, m. July 3, 1857, David Ingalls, Jr.

CHILDREN OF AMOS E. WALKER,[7] [662] OF WHITING, VT.

1345. I. MELZAR,[8] b. April 15, 1832, in W., m. June 1, 1859, Julia, dau. of Artemas and Louisa Hall. He is a farmer in W.

1346. II. DEE BARZILLAI,[8] b. Sept. 19, 1833. Farmer, and unm.

1347. III. JOHN ASHLEY,[8] b. Nov. 14, 1834. Farmer, and unm.

1348. IV. ELIZABETH,[8] b. Sept. 17, 1839, in Whiting.

1349. V. EVELINE,[8] b. July 25, 1846, in Brandon, Vt.

1350. VI. ALBERT ELMORE,[8] b. July 13, 1849, in Brandon, Vt.

CHIL. OF RICHARD HART WALKER,[7] [666] OF WHITING, VT.

1351. I. JOSEPH MILLER,[8] b. Feb. 12, 1834, m. Nov. 24, 1859, in Kingston, Wis., Mary Ann Sample.

1352. II. JERUSHA,[8] b. March 25, 1835.

BY 2d MARRIAGE.

1353. III. MARTIN ALLEN,[8] b. July 9, 1843, d. Aug. 6, 1844.

1354. IV. ALBERT MARTIN,[7] b. June 26, 1845.

1355. V. CHESTER,[8] b. Aug. 30, 1848.

1356. VI. HERBERT HART,[8] b. Jan. 16, 1853.

1357. VII. ANDRE,[8] b. Oct. 2, 1855, d. July 12, 1858.

BY 3d MARRIAGE.

1358. VIII. CARRIE ELIZA,[8] b. April 12, 1859.

CHIL. OF DAN'L M. WALKER,[7] [669] OF SWANTON CENTRE, VT.

1359. I. CORNELIA HELEN,[8] b. Oct. 5, 1831. She is m. Bap. ch. and unites fine mental gifts with uncommon christian excellence.

1360. II. SARAH JANE,[8] b. May 8, 1833, m. Oct. 7, 1856, Wm. H. Jennison. Both m. Cong. ch. They have—

(1) *Minnie E.*, b. Feb. 25, 1859.

1361. III. HENRY OLIN,[8] b. Oct. 15, 1835, is m. Bap. ch. He was grad. at the Literary and Scientific School, in Fairfax, Vt., July, 1860, and in Sept. 1860, entered the Theo. Seminary, at Newton, with a view to the ministry.

BY 2d MARRIAGE.

1362. IV. LUCINDA,[8] b. Feb. 25, 1839, is m. Bap. ch.

1363. V. MARY ANN,[8] b. Jan. 24, 1841, d. Nov. 30, 1855, in S.

CHIL. OF SAMUEL BENT WALKER,[7] [674] OF CHICAGO, ILL.

1364. I. CHASTINA BUSWELL,[8] b. Sept. 11, 1829, in Hubbardton, Vt.

1365. II. FRANCES ELLEN,[8] b. July 26, 1831, d. Aug. 9, 1834.

1366. III. SARAH JANE,[8] b. Aug. 18, 1840, d. Feb. 7, 1841.

1367. IV. EVELYN MARIETTA,[8] b. July 30, 1842, in Chicago.

1368. V. ELLA MARIA,[8] b. Dec. 6, 1849, in Chicago.

CHIL. OF MARTIN O. WALKER,[7] [675] OF CHICAGO, ILL.

1369. I. MARTIN TIFFANY,[8] b. April 26, 1851, d. Sept. 1, 1853.

1370. II. SAMUEL OTIS,[8] b. Dec. 22, 1852.

1371. III. EDWARD STOW,[8] b. Sept. 11, 1854.

CHIL. OF JOHNSON WALKER,[7] [682] OF WILLISTON, VT.

1372. I. WILLIAM W.,[8] b. July 12, 1823, d. ae. 31 yrs.

1373. II. JANE ELIZABETH,[8] b. March 8, 1830, m. March 8, 1850, William Con?

1374. III. JOHN J.,[8] b. June 27, 1836.

1375. IV. SOLOMON,[8] b. Feb. 15, 1838.

1376. V. SARAH,[8] b. 1840.

1377. VI. HANNAH,[8] b. Sept. 21, 1844.

CHIL. OF PHILIP FIELD WALKER,[7] [685] OF FAYETTE, MO.

1378. I. OSCAR L.,[8] b. Oct. 31, 1828, d. June 8, 1848.

1379. II. ORVILLE,[8] b. May 21, 1830, d. Oct. 15, 1830.

1380. III. ADELA A.,[8] b. Feb. 4, 1832, d. Jan. 26, 1851.

1381. IV. LINDA M.,[8] b. Feb. 19, 1834.

1382. V. HELEN E.,[8] b. June 29, 1836, d. April 17, 1837.

1383. VI. DAU., d. Oct. 27, 1840.

CHIL. OF FREEBORN WALKER,[7] [699] OF PROPHETSTOWN, ILL.

1384. I. ALMARY,[8] b. about 1840.

1385. II. LORAINE, b. about 1843.

1386. III. CHILD,[8] d. young.

1387. IV. GEORGE,[8] b. about 1849.

1388. V. CATHARINE,[8] b. about 1852.

1389. VI. CHILD,[8] b. about 1854.

CHIL. OF HON. ZURIEL WALKER,[7] [707] OF FERRISBURGH, VT.

1390. I. OBADIAH J.,[8] (1847) b. Jan. 6, 1828, m. June, 1852, Mary White, of Burlington, Vt., formerly of Buffalo, N. Y., and has 3 chil. He is in the firm of Van Sicklen & Walker, commission merchants, and wholesale dealers in produce, in Burlington. He is m. Meth ch., and highly esteemed for moral and christian worth.

1391. II. HENRY HOBART,[8] b. Sept. 20, 1829, is a merchant in the firm of Flack & Walker, Michigan City, Ind. He is m. Meth. ch. and sustains an unblemished character.

1392. III. WILLIAM WIRT,[8] b. Aug. 6, 1831, was fitted for Coll., in Vergennes, Vt., was grad. at Middlebury Coll., in 1853, then took charge of a family school in Palo Alto, N. C., and in 1855, became Principal of an Academy in Swansboro', N. C. He is now an Attorney and Counsellor at Law, in Burlington, Vt.

1393. IV. HIRAM,[8] b. Feb. 8, 1833, is one of the firm of Shedd & Walker, merchants in Burlington, Vt, and is a young man of talent and energy.

1394. V. EDWARD,[8] b. Dec. 31, 1834, is a clerk, in B.

1395. VI. SOLOMON,[8] b. Jan. 10, 1838.

1396. VII. JAMES OTIS,[8] b. Jan. 28, 1840.

1397. VIII. MARY MALVINA,[8] b. Feb. 19, 1849.

1398. IX. MARTHA ANN,[8] b. Oct. 6, 1844.

1399. X. MARIA AGNES,[8] b. Aug. 15, 1846.

CHIL. OF OBADIAH WALKER,[7] [710] OF VERGENNES, VT.

1400. I. CHARLES,[8] b. after 1841.

CHIL. OF SOLOMON WALKER,[7] [711] OF BURLINGTON, VT.

1401. I. ALMARY,[8] b. 1843.

By 2d Marriage.

1402. II. John Ensign,[8] b. Jan. 1849.

Chil. of HARRY G. WALKER,[7] [714] of Canton, N.Y.

1403. I. Hiram N.,[8] b. July 20, 1818, in Canton, N.Y. He entered Vermont Univ., in 1842, and left, on account of ill health, in 1844, while a member of the Sophomore class. After a year of rest, his health was regained, and he was on the point of returning to Coll., in 1845, but was prevailed upon to commence the study of medicine, under Dr. Darius Clark. He received his diploma, Oct. 6, 1849, and commenced professional practice. He was appointed Hospital Surgeon of the 15th Brigade of the N.Y. State militia, Dec. 3, 1855; is Justice of the Peace, Superintendent of the Schools, and has also been elected Associate Judge of Franklin Co. He is a physician of acknowledged ability, and has been very successful. Res. Hogansburgh, N.Y.

1404. II. Theresa P.,[8] b. July 4, 1820, m. 1844, Moses Folson, a farmer and Universalist. Res. Indiana. Chil.—

(1) *Lucy M.*, b. Jan. 12, 1845. (2) *Hartwell W.*, b. May 16, '55.

1405. III. Chauncey D.,[8] b. June 4, 1823, is a mechanic. Res. Elyria, O.

1406. IV. Sarah E.,[8] b. April 17, 1825, m. July 4, 1849, John Hubbard, a farmer. She is a Universalist. Chil.—

(1) *Mary E.*, b. May 1, 1851. (2) *Walter G.*, b. March 29, '53. (3) *Francis W.*, b. Sept. 22, '55.

1407. V. Solomon,[8] b. May 16, 1829, m. June 23, 1853, Elizabeth ———, of Ohio. He is a farmer, and Universalist. Child—

(1) *Clara A.*, b. March 14, 1855.

1408. VI. Lydia,[8] b. Aug. 3. 1832. Res. Wisconsin.

Chil. of FERDINAND C. WALKER,[7] [716] of Quincy, Ill.

1409. I. Daniel,[8] b. Dec. 12, 1848.

1410. II. Electa J.,[8] b. July 6, 1850.

1411. III. Ferdinand,[8] b. Feb. 11, 1852.

[illegible] MARRIAGE.
[illegible] Jan. 18[illegible]

[illegible] C. WALKER [illegible]

[illegible] 18[illegible] [illegible] N. Y.

[illegible] son [illegible]

[illegible]

[illegible] SARAH [illegible]

[illegible]

1408. [illegible]

[illegible] C. WALKER, [illegible]

[illegible] DAN[illegible], b. Dec. 12, 18[illegible]
[illegible] J[illegible] 1850.
[illegible] FERNAND[illegible], b. Feb. [illegible], 18[illegible].

Hiram h. Walker

CHIL. OF JOSEPH B. WALKER,[7] [722] OF CENTREVILLE, IA.

1412. Neither number nor names are reported.

CHIL. OF WILLIAM WALKER,[7] [723] OF WEST CANAAN, O.

1413. He had 6 chil., but their names are not reported.

CHIL. OF SOLOMON WALKER,[7] [730] OF CENTREVILLE, IOWA.

1419. I. WM. MONTGOMERY,[8] b. Nov. 23, 1846, in Ohio.

1420. II. ZURIEL BONAPARTE,[8] b. Aug. 8, 1848, in Ohio.

1421. III. ALVIRA LUCINDA,[8] b. Jan. 15, 1850, in Ohio.

1422. IV. GEO. BYRON,[8] b. May 24, 1852, in C., Ia.

1423. V. SOLOMON,[8] b. Nov. 22, 1855, in C., Ia.

1424. VI. JOSEPHINE BEALL,[8] b. Aug. 23, 1857, in C., Ia.

1425. VII. NANCY CAPTOLIA,[8] b. June 26, 1859, in C., Ia.

CHIL. OF ALBERT WALKER,[7] [732] OF WAUPUN, WIS.

1426. I. WILLIAM NATHAN,[8] b. April 17, 1835, in Clarke, C. W.

1428. II. JOHN ALEXANDER,[8] b. June 7, 1837, in Newfane, N. Y.

1429. III. ELIZA JANE,[8] b. Aug. 13, 1839, in Whitby, C. W.

1430. IV. NANCY ANN,[8] b. Feb. 2, 1841, in Whitby, C. W.

1431. V. ALBERT WASHINGTON,[8] b. Aug. 23, 1844, in Whitby.

1432. VI. GEO. THOMAS,[8] b. March 24, 1847, in Waupun, Wis.

1433. VII. HARRIET LUCINDA,[8] b. Dec. 4, 1850, in Trenton, Wis.

1434. VIII. MARGARET ELIZABETH,[8] b. July 7, 1855, d. Jan. 19, 1857.

CHIL. OF LEVI WALKER,[7] [733] OF WAUPUN, WIS.

1435. I. HARRIET AMELIA,[8] b. May 26, 1838, in Clarke, C. W.

1436. II. GEO. WASHINGTON,[8] b. April 15, 1840, in West Canaan, O.

1437. III. GIDEON TUPPER,[8] b. Sept. 17, 1841, in Newburgh, O.

1438. IV. Nathan Seymour,[8] b. April 7, 1843, in Newburgh, O.

1439. V. Levi Joseph,[8] b. Sept. 29, 1844, in Newburgh, O.

1440. VI. Charles Henry,[8] b. Aug. 8, 1846, in Newburgh, O.

Chil. of GEORGE W. WALKER,[7] [739] of Lyndon, Wis.

1441. I. Mary Eliza,[8] b. Sept. 1856.

1441.[1] II. Child.

Chil. of CHITTENDEN WALKER,[7] [744] of Eddyville, Ky.

1442. I. Elizabeth,[8] b. about 1842.

1443. II. Reuben Ebenezer,[8] b. about 1844.

Chil. of SAM'L TUPPER WALKER,[7] [746] of Lyon Co., Ky.

1444. I. William,[8] b. June 6, 1854.

1445. II. Amanda,[8] b. Aug. 3, 1856.

Chil. of TRUMAN C. WALKER,[7] [750] of Eddyville, Ky.

1446. I. James K.,[8] b. July 6, 1848.

By 2d Marriage.

1447. II. Mary Electa,[8] b. March 11, 1857.

Children of ALVIN WALKER,[7] [755] of Sparta, Wis.

1448. I. Dau.,[8] d. in infancy.

1449. II. Elvira,[8] m. Frederick Waldrath, and lost 1 child.

1450. III. Thomas.[8]

1451. IV. Lucy Ann.[8]

1452. V. Albert.[8]

Chil. of LUTHER B. WALKER,[7] [757] Johnsonsburgh, N.Y.

1453. I. Sophia,[8] b. Jan. 14, 1828, m. May, 1853, Lyman Williams. He is a carriage maker. Res. ———.

1453.[1] II. RHUA A.,[8] b. July 27, 1830, d. April 14, 1842.

1454. III. BENJAMIN F.,[8] b. Aug. 27, 1832, m. July 5, 1858, Euphemia Williams, dau. of Hiram, of Java, N. Y.

1455. IV. WILLIAM F.,[8] (1850) b. Aug. 27, 1832, twin, m. June 13, 1858, Lucy Coburn, dau. of Cyrus, of Orangeville, N. Y., and has 1 dau.

CHIL. OF ETHIEL C. WALKER,[7] [759] OF JACKSONVILLE, IA.

1456. I. CAROLINE,[8] m. ———, name not reported.

1457. II. ANN.[8]

1458. III. SON,[8] d. young.

1459. IV. SON,[8] d. young.

1460. V. SON,[8] d. young.

1461. VI. ELIAS.[8]

1462. VII. PHILETUS.[8] }

1463. VII. PHILEMON.[8] }

1464. VIII. DAU.[8]

CHILDREN OF ASA WALKER,[7] [761] OF LENOX, N. Y.

1465. I. ANDREW,[8] b. Dec. 27, 1835, m. July 4, 1856, Lodice Harden. He is a farmer. Both m. Meth. ch. Res. ——.

1466. II. CHARLOTTE,[8] b. May 30, 1837, m. May 27, 1855, Daniel Petrie, and has 1 child, b. 1856.

1467. III. CHRISTOPHER,[8] b. Dec. 1, 1839.

CHILDREN OF URIAL WALKER,[7] [762] OF CHICAGO, ILL.

1468. I. HELEN,[8] b. about 1840.

1469. II. FRANCES,[8] b. about 1844.

1470. III. HENRIETTA,[8] b. about 1847.

1471. IV. ABRAM CLINTON,[8] d. ae. 6 mos.

CHIL. OF BENJ. CUSHMAN WALKER,[7] [764] OF TEXAS.

1472. I. DAU.,[8] and probably other chil. also.

CHIL. OF WM. GREEN WALKER,[7] [765] OF KING'S MILLS, ILL.

1473. I. NATHAN,[8] dec'd.
1474. II. ANTOINETTE,[8] dec'd.
1475. III. BENJAMIN,[8] drowned.
1476. IV. CLARISSA.[8]
1477. V. JANE.[8]
1478. VI. MARY LOVE.[8]

CHIL. OF ANSON WALKER,[7] [767] OF CANANDAIGUA, N.Y.

1479. I. JOHN ACKLEY,[8] b. May 29, 1831, d. March 15, 1837.

1480. II. ELIZABETH,[8] b. Sept. 22, 1833, m. Oct. 31, 1855, Vincent Luther, in Canandaigua. They have—

(1) *Amelia M.*, b. Aug. 3, 1857, in Lenawee, Ill.

1481. III. REBECCA MELVINA,[8] b. Jan. 7, 1836.

1482. IV. AMELIA PAMELIA,[8] b. June 1, 1838.

1483. V. OLIVE,[8] b. Nov. 28, 1840.

1484. VI. MINERVA URETTA,[8] b. Jan. 27, 1843, d. May 12, 1857.

1485. VII. BENJAMIN EVERETT,[8] b. Jan. 27, 1843.

1486. VII. FRANCIS MARION,[8] b. May 26, 1845.

1487. VIII. LOIS ALICE,[8] b. Dec. 1, 1847.

1488. IX. MARY JANE,[8] b. Nov. 28, 1849.

1489. X. EDNA ROSE,[8] b. May 2, 1852.

1490. XI. VIRGIL ANSON,[8] b. Oct. 8, 1854.

CHIL. OF NELSON WALKER,[7] [768] OF KING'S MILLS, ILL.

1491. I. JANE N.[8]
1492. II. MARTIN EUGENE.[8]
1493. III. A. JOSEPHINE ELMIRA,[8] dec'd.
1494. IV. CECILIA V.[8]
1495. V. THO'S H. BENTON.[8]

1496. VI. Elvira L.,[8]
1497. VII. Franklin P.[8]
1498. VIII. Louis P.[8]

Children of ABEL WALKER,[7] [769] of Pecatonia, Ill.

1499. I. Chester.[8]
1500. II. Charles.[8]
1501. III. Calista C.[8]
1502. IV. George R.[8]
1503. V. Robert A.[8]
1504. VI. Julius A.[8]
1505. VII. Emma C.[8]

Children of HIRAM WALKER,[7] [770] of Manistee, Mich.

1506. I. Silas.[8]
1507. II. Amelia.[8]

Chil. of Hon. WM. P. WALKER,[7] [786] of Lenox.

1508. I. Lucy F.,[8] b. Jan. 6, 1808, m. Nov. 22, 1836, Julius Rockwell, Esq., of Pittsfield, who was b. in Colebrook, Ct. He was graduated at Yale College in 1826, studied Law at New Haven, and began his professional practice in P., where he has resided ever since. He was Representative in the State Legislature from 1834 to 1838, and again in 1858,—Speaker of the House 2 yrs., 1836 and 1837—has been Bank Commissioner of the State 3 yrs., mem. of the Constitutional Convention, Representative in Congress from 1843 to 1851, and U. S. Senator by Gubernatorial appointment, after Mr. Everett's resignation. He has shown himself equal to the labors and responsibilities of all these offices. He was a prominent candidate before the Whig State Conventions, 1853 and '54. He was the Republican candidate for Gov. in 1855, at a time when the disruption of parties afforded little hope of his election, but he came out of the contest, with a large vote, although beaten, and with increased popularity. In May, 1859, he was appointed a Judge of the Superior Court, and maintains a high rank as a jurist. As a man and lawyer, he has a character worthy of the highest respect, and even as a politician, is irreproachable.

He possesses a clear and original mind, and unites fine taste with high literary attainments. Though grave, he has great enthusiasm, and a vein of rich humor. Chil.—

(1) *William*, b. July 28, 1839. (2) *Cornelia*, b. Oct. 3, '41. (3) *Francis W.*, b. May 26, '44. (4) *Alice G.*, b. Jan. 19, '46, d. Feb. 21, '50. (5) *Robert C.*, b. Aug. 28, '48.

1509. II. WILLIAM,[8] (1851) b. July 26, 1810, m. July 8, 1833, Harriet W. Collins, dau. of Dan'l Swan, of Norwich, Ct., and widow of Dr. Ethan S. Collins, of Granby, Ct. She d. in Poughkeepsie, Oct. 26, 1858, ae. 46 yrs. He was a merchant, in Ohio, but is now engaged in the iron and coal business in Scranton, Penn. He is a man of sound judgment, and excellent business qualities. He has 1 dau.

1510. III. GEORGE,[8] (1852) b. Sept. 17, 1812, d. March, 1860. He m. June 25, 1845, Harriet, dau. of Hon. and Lieut. Gov. George Hull, of Sandisfield, and had 2 chil. She d. June 2, 1851, ae. 31 yrs. Res. Lenox.

1511. IV. SARAH W.,[8] b. Sept. 4, 1814, m. Oct. 30, 1838, Hon. David Davis, of Bloomington, Ill., who was b. in Cecil Co., Md. He was graduated at Kenyon Coll., O., studied Law in Lenox, with Judge Bishop, and at the Law School, in New Haven. He is now Judge of the Circuit Court, (the office being elective,) and upon the 2d term of 7 yrs. He has great wealth, unusual energy, and a high order of talents. Chil.—

(1) *George P*, b. June 5, 1842. (2) *Mercer*, b. Oct. 27, '45, d. Sept. 3, '46. (3) *Lucy A.*, b. Jan 5, '50, d. Aug. 31, '50. (4) *Sarah W.?*

1512. V. FRANCES M.,[8] b. June 23, 1817, m. Dec. 30, 1841, Daniel R. Williams, Esq., of Stockbridge. No chil. He is Cashier of the Housatonic Bank in S.; a man of excellent character and highly respected in his business relations. She is m. ch.

1513. VI. CHARLES,[8] b. June 21, 1819, d. Feb. 4, 1820.

1514. VII. JOHN A.,[8] (1854) b. Jan. 7, 1821, m. Oct. 14, 1847, Margaret E. Magee, dau. of Charles E., of Boston. They have 4 chil. He was graduated in 1840, at Williams Coll., with one of the highest honors of his class, "The Philosophical Oration;" studied Theology one yr., at Andover, 1841-42; was Tutor in Williams Coll., 1844 and '45; studied Law at New Haven, and with Judge Bishop, of Lenox, and was admitted to the Bar in 1848. He rem. from Lenox to Pittsfield, Oct., 1853; in Dec., 1855, was appointed Special Justice, in Oct., 1858, Standing Justice of the Police Court in Pittsfield, which office he resigned in 1859. He was Rep. in the State Legislature, 1859, a member of the Com. on the revision of the Statutes, the same yr., and in April, 1860, was elected Sec. & Treas. of the Berkshire Mutual Fire Insurance Co. He is m. Cong. ch., and is highly esteemed for ability and integrity.

1515. VIII. CORNELIA,[8] b. Feb. 22, 1823, m. July 13, 1843, (3 ? Scranton Genealogy,) Joseph Hand Scranton, Esq., of Augusta, Georgia, a descendant of John Scranton, of Guilford, Ct. See Memorial of the Scranton Family. They have 5 chil. He was formerly a merchant in Augusta, and now Agent and Superintendent of the Iron Works in S. He is largely engaged in the iron and coal business, and is a man of superior energy and capability. Chil.—

(1) *William W.*, b. April 4, 1844, in A. (2) *Walter*, b. Aug. 12, '49, in S., Pa. (3) *Frances*, b. Nov. 20, '51, in S., Pa. (4) *Alice*, b. '54, in S., Pa. (5) *Arthur*, b. Jan. '60.

1516. IX. RICHARD H.,[8] b. Feb. 4, 1826, m. Feb. 7, 1854, Charlotte E. Goodrich, who is dec'd. He m. 2d, Nov. 28, 1855, Annie G. Perry, and is a farmer in Lenox. No chil.

CHIL. OF CALEB R. WALKER,[7] [793] OF PLYMOUTH, MICH.

1517. I. HULDAH C.,[8] b. ——, m. Joseph Pawlett, of Milwaukie, Wis., and is dec'd.

1518. II. SARAH,[8] b. ——, m. Wm. Packard. Res. Plymouth, Mich., till 1844, when they rem. to Tuscola ? Livingston Co., Mich.

1519. III. LYDIA,[8] b. ——, m. Geo. Dickinson, of West Mich.

1520. IV. SON,[8] d. y.

1521. V. SON,[8] d. y.

CHILDREN OF CALEB WALKER,[7] [794] OF SEEKONK.

1522. I. ABBY,[8] b. March 14, 1821, m. July 4, 1842, John Wing, and has had 3 chil., 2 dec'd. Res. Smithfield, R. I.

1523. II. LEWIS,[8] m. Lydia Greenfield, of Mansfield, who is dec'd. He is a machinist. Res. Providence, R. I.

1524. III. ANNE M.,[8] m. Samuel Wing, bro. of John, (No. 1522) and has 3 chil. Res. Cranston, R. I.

CHILDREN OF WILLIAM WALKER,[7] [795] OF ATTLEBORO'.

1525. I. FANNY D.,[8] b. April 12, 1821, d. March, 1849. She m. March 1, 1842, Nelson Smith. Res. Attleboro'. Chil.—

(1) *Francis.* (2) *Josephine.* (3) *Jane.*

1526. II. WILLIAM,[8] b. March 2, 1824, is a jeweler, unm., in A.

1527. III. ESTHER JANE,[8] b. about 1827, is unm.

1528. IV. LOUISA,[8] b. about 1830, m. 1852, James Bowen, of Attleboro'. Res. A.

1529. V. ALBERT,[8] b. June, 1834, m. Aug. 14, 1855, Clara Sweet, of Attleboro'. He is a jeweler. Res. A.

CHIL. OF ZECHARIAH WALKER,[7] [797] OF PROVIDENCE, R. I.

1530. I. EZRA,[8] (1857) b. April 4, 1827, in Warwick, R. I., m. Aug. 10, 1853, Margaret Lambert, dau. of Wm. and Sarah, and b. 1830. He is a carriage painter, and has 2 chil. Res. Providence.

1531. II. SARAH M., b. 1828, is unm., in P.

1532. III. JAMES I.,[8] b. April 14, 1830. Res. San Francisco, Cal., unm.

1533. IV. EMILY J.,[8] b. about 1832, is unm., in P.

1534. V. ADELINE B.,[8] b. 1833 or '34, is unm.

1535. VI. DUDLEY,[8] b. 1835 or '36, is a silver smith in No. Attleboro', unm.

1536. VII. LYDIA,[8] b. about 1839.

1537. VIII. REBECCA K.,[8] b. May 11, 1843.

CHIL. OF CHAUNCEY WALKER,[7] [801] OF BRIGHTON, N. Y.

1538. I. OSCAR A.,[8] (1859) b. Dec. 19, 1819, d. Jan. 13, 1848, in Rochester. N. Y. He m. Mary Eliza Heather, Aug. 12, 1843, who d. Sept. 1848, in R. Both were m. Meth. ch. He was a farmer, and had 3 chil.

1539. II. SARAH A.,[8] b. Dec. 5, 1821, in Brighton, N. Y., m. Aug. 12, 1843, Rufus Robinson, a joiner and farmer. Both m. Bap. ch. Res. Nunda, (East Hill,) Livingston Co., N. Y. Chil., all b. in N.—

(1) *Wm. Chauncey*, b. June 9, 1844. (2) *Geo. Rufus*, b. March 8, '46. (3) *Franklin Augustus*, b. Aug. 23, '48. (4) *Edward Everett*, b. May 25, '52. (5) *Emma Louisa*, b. Aug. 30, '54. (6) *Herbert Walker*, b. March 13, '56.

1540. III. EMILY A.,[8] b. Sept. 5, 1823, m. 1845, Charles L. Street, a farmer. Both m. Bap. ch. Res. Benton, Eaton Co., Mich. Chil.—

(1) *Orson De Loss*, b. Jan. 27, 1846. (2) *Adaline*, b. Sept. 24, '48, is m. Pres. ch. (3) *Lura A.*, b. Feb. 28, '51. (4) *Byron E.*, b. Aug. 27, '53? (5) *Frances A. M.*, b. Aug. 13, '57.

BY 2d MARRIAGE.

1541. IV. FRANCES JANE,[8] b. March 2, 1828, m. about 1849, John Howell, a farmer. Res. North Chili, Monroe Co., N. Y. Chil.—

(1) *Carrie*, d. in infancy. (2) *Carrie Frances*, b. about July, 1854. (3) *Dau.*, b. '56.

CHIL. OF ANSEL W. WALKER,[7] [802] OF DETROIT, MICH.

1542. I. LOUISA,[8] b. June 1, 1826, m. Nov. 2, 1847, Wm. Langley, a mason. Res. Detroit. Chil.—

(1) *Clara L.*, b. Nov. 18, 1848. (2) *William P.*, b. May 27, '51. (3) *Kittie J.*, b. Oct. 3, '55. (4) *Minnie Walker*, b. May 27, [26?] '58.

1543, II. NAOMI Z.,[8] b. Nov. 5, 1830, m. Nov. 16, 1855, David Barrows, a cabinet maker. Res. Detroit. Chil.—

(1) *Ida*, b. Jan. 17, '57, (2) *Charles*, b. Aug. 19, '58. (3) *Wm. Henry*, b. Nov. 22, '59.

1544. III. GEORGE O.,[8] b. Nov. 6, 1831, is a carpenter and joiner, in D., unm.

1545. IV. RICHARD J.,[8] b. Feb. 13, 1834, is a mason in D.

1546. V. JAMES EDWIN,[8] (1861) b. Jan. 1, 1837, m. Aug. 17, 1858, Fanny Rogers. He is a joiner, and and has 1 son, Res. D.

1547. VI. JULIA E.,[8] b. April 2, 1840. Res. D.

1548. VII. ANSEL W.,[8] b. Aug. 28, 1844.

1549. VIII. CHARLES W.,[8] b. Oct. 28, 1846.

CHIL. OF GEORGE WALKER,[7] [803] OF ROCHESTER, N. Y.

1550. I. EDWARD H.,[8] b. Nov. 6, 1826, is a bookbinder in N.Y. City.

1551. II. JOHN E.,[8] b. Sept. 27, 1830, is an ornamental painter and gilder, in N. Y. City.

1552. III. HENRY S.,[8] b. Oct. 13, 1832, is a printer in N.Y. City.

1553. IV. ADELINE A. M.,[8] b. Jan. 30, 1835. Res. Meriden, Ct.

CHIL. OF THOMAS J. WALKER,[7] [806] OF DETROIT, MICH.

1554. I. LUTHER C.,[8] b. 1837. Res. Olivet, Mich.

1555. II. ARVILLA M.,[8] b. 1839. " " "

1556. III. MELINDA Z.,[8] b. 1841. " " "

1557. IV. WILLIAM H.,[8] b. 1844. " " "

1558. V. WELLS W.,[8] b. 1845. " " "

Two of these sons were drowned March, 1859.

CHILD OF EDWIN WALKER,[7] [807] OF MARSHALL, MICH.

1559. I. DELIA,[8] b. in the autumn of 1833.

CHIL. OF WILLIAM H. WALKER,[7] [808] OF CHICAGO, ILL.

1560. I. CORNELIA A.,[8] b. about 1837.

1561. II. HENRY,[8] b. about 1840.

CHILDREN OF EPHRAIM WALKER[7], [811] OF SAVOY.

1562. I. ESTHER A.,[8] b. Jan. 4, 1827, m. May 14, 1848, Ezra, son of Ephraim Leonard, of Savoy. He is an overseer in a woollen mill in North Adams. Both m. Meth. ch. Chil.—

(1) *Cassius E.*, b. Feb. 2, 1850. (2) *Abby L.*, b. Dec. 26, '53.

1563. II. CANDACE M.,[8] b. Jan. 5, 1829, d. Feb. 16, 1850.

1564. III. EPHRAIM J.,[8] b. June 19, 1831, m. March 13, 1859, Mary Bishop, of Readsboro', Vt.

1565. IV. SON,[8] d. May 9, 1833.

1566. V. DANIEL L.,[8] b. March 22, 1835, d. Oct. 16, 1858.

CHIL. OF ALVAH WALKER,[7] [817] OF OSWEGO, N. Y.

1567. I. ABEL,[8] b. June 27, 1822, d. July 7, 1822.

1568. II. VESTA A.,[8] b. Oct. 9, 1823, m. Nov. 24, 1847, Willet R. Worden, a cooper, who was b. Nov. 15, 1821. She is m. Meth. ch. Res. Minetto, N. Y. Child—

(1) *Byron W.*, b. Oct. 21, 1852.

1568.[1] III. AURORA B.,[8] b. Sept. 21, 1825, m. Dec. 27, 1848, Lyman Coates, a farmer. She is m. Meth. ch. Res. Oswego, N. Y. Child—

(1) *Vesta L.*, b. Nov. 4, 1851.

1568.[2] IV. LUNA,[8] b. Feb. 24, 1827, m. Oct. 20, 1846, Wickham Griswold, a farmer, who was b. June 28, 1821. She is m. ch. Res. Oswego, N. Y. Chil.—

(1) *Charles W.*, b. June 27, 1848. (2) *Aurora W.*, b. Feb. 8, 1851. (3) *Julia A.*, b. May 2, 1853. (4) *Alvah Orley*, b. Nov. 5, 1856.

1569. V. CYNTHIA M.,[8] b. Nov. 13, 1828, d. Feb. 20, 1849.

1570. VI. MARY E.,[8] b. Nov. 26, 1832, in Oswego, N. Y., m. Nov. 19, 1855, Albert E. Miller, M. D., of Oswego, N. Y. They rem. to Rome, N. Y., immediately after marriage, and are both engaged in the practice of medicine. She early manifested an ardent love for intellectual pursuits, and from the age of 18 was engaged for some time in teaching, in order to obtain the means for prosecuting her studies. She was offered the assistance she needed, on the condition of entering the Missionary field, but although inclined to such a work, she was unwilling to involve herself in any obligations, and declined the aid. Struggling with pecuniary difficulties, she however, at the age of 22, after 3 yrs. of study in a Medical Coll., was grad. with honor, as an M. D., and at once begun professional practice in Columbus, O. She is passionately devoted to her profession, and though a wife, does not cease to be a physician, and also retains her maiden name, Walker, as her surname. She is a zealous advocate of "Woman's Rights," and has devoted her life and talents, to the support of the principles of that movement. She advocates and wears the Bloomer costume, as adapted to her active habits, in discharge of the duties of her profession.

1571. VII. ALVAH H.,[8] b. Dec. 26, 1833, m. March 10, 1856, Sarah J. Miller, in Oswego, N. Y.

Children of ABEL WALKER,[7] [824] of Elgin, Ill.

1572. I. Charles A.,[8] b. Dec. 13, 1836, d. April 7, 1849.

1573. II. Abel H.[8] b. Jan 4, 1840, d. Dec. 13, 1840.

1574. III. James H.,[8] b. Jan. 24, 1843, d. July 14, 1844.

1575. IV. Mary E.,[8] b. Nov. 4, 1848.

Child of THOMAS P. WALKER,[7] [820] of Greenwich.

1576. I. Ezra Elansford,[8] b. June 15, 1840.

Chil. of JAMES HERVY WALKER,[7] [829] of Hardwick.

1577. I. Fanny Priscilla,[8] b. Sept. 27, 1855.

1578. II. Wm. Hervy,[8] b. Nov. 30, 1857.

Chil. of WILLIAM WALKER,[7] [832] of New York City.

1579. I. Isabella Steel,[8] b. June 27, 1829, m. Dec. 19, 1850, James William McCulloh, Jr., who was b. in Baltimore Co., Md., March 19, 1827. Chil.—

(1) *Caroline*, b. Feb. 16, 1852. (2) *Henry Mayer*, b. Dec. 24, '53.

1580. II. Thomas,[8] b. March 31, 1831, d. Feb. 3, 1834.

1580.[1] III. Louisa Buloid,[8] b. March 30, 1833, m. Nov. 9, 1854, Ashbel Green, son of James S. Green, and Isabella McCulloh, and b. in Princeton, N. J., Dec. 17, 1825.

1581. IV. William,[8] b. Oct. 4, 1835, d. March 22, 1841.

1582. V. Eliza Corning,[8] b. March 8, 1838—is unm.

1583. VI. Robert Steel,[8] b. June 27, 1840, d. March 27, 1842.

1584. VII. James Henry,[8] b. Jan. 8, 1844.

1585. VIII. Edwin Field,[8] b. Feb. 4, 1846.

1586. IX. Caroline Steel, b. Dec. 5, 1848.

1587. X. William Hunter,[8] b. Jan. 25, 1851.

CHIL. OF HON. THOMAS R. WALKER,[7] [834] OF UTICA, N.Y.

1588. I. LOUISA JOHNSON,[8] b. Feb. 26, 1831, d. Dec. 29, 1834.

1589. II. ANNIE BREESE,[8] b. Jan. 29, 1833, m. Aug. 4, 1856, Henry Stanley Dexter, of San Francisco, Cal., and they went abroad, spending two years in Europe. Chil.—

(1) *Stanley Dexter*, b. Oct. 3, 1857, in London, Eng. (2) *Arthur Breese*, b. April 10, '59, in San Francisco.

1590. III. SUSAN LOUISA,[8] b. Sept. 7, 1834, m. Henry W. Smith, of N.Y. City, a merchant, son of Wm. H. They have—

(1) *Walker Breese*, b. Aug. 31, 1858, in N.Y. City.

1591. IV. MARY SEYMOUR,[8] b. July 10, 1845.

CHILDREN OF GEORGE WALKER,[7] [835] OF UTICA, N.Y.

1592. I. WILLIAM MERVINE,[8] b. Sept. 7, 1850.

1593. II. THOMAS EATON,[8] b. Sept. 10, 1852.

1594.[1] III. GEORGE HATTON,[8] b. Jan. 9, 1854, d. Oct. 17, 1854.

CHIL. OF DEAN WALKER,[7] [839] OF ROCKVILLE, MEDWAY.

1594. I. HORACE DEAN,[8] (1862) b. Sept. 15, 1815, in Framingham, m. Jan. 21, 1844, Mercy Adams Mason, of Medway, dau. of Horatio and Julia (Adams,) and b. in M., Feb. 18, 1823. She was educated at the Female Seminary in Charlestown. In 1842, she made a profession of religion, and united with the 1st ch. in Medway. They have had 7 chil. He was graduated at Yale Coll. in 1841, and pursued his Theological studies with Rev. Dr. Ide, of Medway, and at the Theo. Seminary, Bangor, Me. He was ordained and installed pastor of the Cong. church in East Abington, Feb. 15, 1844, and has labored there nearly 17 yrs. Several of his sermons have been published. He is an able and impressive preacher, and a highly esteemed and useful pastor.

1595. II. WILLIAM,[8] b. Sept. 7, 1817, d. April 7, 1819.

1596. III. WILLIAM F.,[8] b. Nov. 12, 1819, d. Dec. 11, 1822.

1597. IV. AUGUSTUS,[8] (1869) b. Oct. 30, 1822, m. Oct. 16, 1852, Eliza Mary Harding, dau. of Rev. Sewall and Eliza (Wheeler) Harding, and b. Dec. 25, 1826. They have had 3 chil. He was graduated at Yale Coll., in 1849, pursued his professional studies 1 yr., at the Theo. Sem. in Bangor, Me., and 2 yrs. at the Theo. Sem. in Andover, graduating at A., in 1852. He was ord. Oct. 16, 1852, and sailed for Turkey, Jan. 7, 1853. He is a Missionary of the A. B. C. F. M., at Diarbekir, Turkey.

1599. V. JOHN SAVAGE,[8] (1872) b. Sept. 4, 1824, m. June 20, 1850, Ellen M. Hoyt, who was b. Jan. 30, 1824, and d. Dec. 9, 1851. He m. 2d, April 28, 1853, Melinda G. Whipple, who was b. March 5, 1831. He has 2 chil., and is a manufacturer in Medway.

1600. VI. REBECCA ELMIRA,[8] b. Dec. 9, 1827, m. Jan. 19, 1853, Rev. Edwin A. Buck, of Bethel, Me., son of Ja's Buck and Lydia (Treat) of Bucksport, Me., and b. May 31, 1824. He is a grad. of Yale Coll. and Bangor Theo. Seminary. Having preached 1 yr. at Pownal, Me., he was ord. and settled as Pastor, at Bethel, May 31, 1854, and in 1859? installed over the Cong. ch. in Slatersville, R. I. They have had 4 chil.—

(1) *Eliza Harding*, b. Nov. 12, 1853. (2) *Alice Lydia*, b. Aug. 6, '55. (3) ——. (4) ——. Names not given.

1601. VII. ARABELLA,[8] b. Dec. 8, 1830, in M., m. June 19, 1860, Frederick L. Church, of Boston.

1602. VIII. ISABELLA,[8] b. Dec. 8, 1830, twin, is unm. Res. M.

CHILDREN OF CLARKE WALKER,[7] [840] OF MEDWAY.

1602. I. SARAH,[8] b. Aug. 9, 1820, m. May 18, 1848, Augustus Bassett, of (Dayville) Killingly, Ct., who was b. June 21, 1821. Chil.—

(1) *Annie Lovering*, b. Sept. 7, 1849. (2) *Freddie Eugene*, b. June 3, [27?] '53. (3) *Charlie Warren*, b. Jan. 1, '56.

1603. II. TIMOTHY CLARKE,[8] (1874) b. May 22, 1823, m. June, 1852, Mary Smith, of Gardiner, Me., and has 1 son. He is a Sea-captain. Res. G.

1604. III. ELLEN FRANCES,[8] b. Aug. 14, 1835.

1605. IV. ANNIE AUGUSTA,[8] b. Nov. 11, 1839, d. July 18, 1850.

CHIL. OF DEA. TIMOTHY WALKER,[7] [842] OF HOLLISTON.

1606. I. GEORGE FREDERIC,[8] b. May 31, 1825, m. Jan. 1, 1852, Esther Amelia Ballard, dau. of Samuel, Esq., of Holliston, and b. Sept. 8, 1833. He was fitted for Coll., at Leicester Academy, and was graduated at Amherst, in 1849. He commenced teaching at Holliston, immediately, where he built the Mt. Hollis Seminary, and was its Principal. He then became associated in the River Side Institute, a boarding school for boys, at Auburndale. Studying Theology under the instruction of Rev. J. T. Tucker, of H., he received a licensure to preach, from the Mendon Association, in 1853. He is now Agent of the Turret and Marine Clock Co., of Boston.

1607. II. LOUISA A.,[8] b. April 21, 1834.

CHIL. OF WM. ROBINSON WALKER,[7] [851] OF AMESVILLE, O.

1608. I. JULIA HOWE,[8] b. Nov. 19, 1826, m. March 26, 1850, Rev. William Steele Beard, who was b. in Rockbridge Co., Va., 1820, and d. April 30, 1854. He was graduated at Lexington Coll., Va., studied Theology at Union Seminary, Prince Edward Co., Va. He was a Presbyterian clergyman, and having preached 8 yrs., d. after 18 days' illness with the pneumonia. Dr. Brown, of Charlestown, Va., wrote of him, just before his marriage:—" His standing in Coll. and at the Seminary, I know, was always very good. He was regarded as a promising young man; his talents and his acquirements were good, and he exhibited more than ordinary energy and prudence." She returned to O., and lives in A. They had—

(1) *Wm. Douglas*, b. April 1, 1851, who, after his father's death, received his father's name, Wm. Steele.

1609. II. PERSIS PUTNAM,[8] b. Jan. 15, 1828, is unm., in A.

1610. III. DOUGLAS WEBSTER,[8] (1875) b. Aug. 3, 1829, m. May 23, 1854, Sarah Elizabeth Miller, and has 1 child. He is a portrait painter, with decided genius.

1611. IV. LUCY,[8] b. June 11, 1832, d. April 20, 1833.

1612. V. EDWARD PAYSON,[8] b. May 24, 1834, was graduated in July, 1856, at Marietta Coll, O., having the first honor of his class, " The Valedictory Oration," and also winning the $70 prize. Serving as Tutor awhile in M. Coll., he entered the Theo. Seminary at Andover, was grad. 1860, and immediately accepted the appointment to a Professorship of Rhetoric and English Lit. in Marietta Coll.

By 2d Marriage.

1613. VI. Henry Martyn,[8] b. Feb. 12, 1838, had a collegiate and professional education in view, but is unable to study, on account of an injury to one of his eyes.

Chil. of ARCHIBALD B. WALKER,[7] [852] of Athens, O.

1613. I. Laura A.,[8] b. Feb. 17, 1827, m. Aug. 27, 1850, James Ballard, from Framingham. He is a merchant and salt manufacturer. Res. Athens, O. Chil.—

(1) *Frank Otis*, b. March 22, 1852. (2) *Effie Belle*, b. Dec. 14, '54.

1614. II. Joanna Lee,[8] b. Nov. 3, 1828, d. Oct. 15, 1835.

1615. III. Mary Augusta,[8] b. Sept. 24, 1830. Res. A., unm.

1616. IV. Louisa Jane,[8] b. July 11, 1832, d. March 7, 1834.

1617. V. Charles Manning,[8] b. Dec. 25, 1834, was graduated at the Ohio University, (Athens,) 1853. He has since been a Teacher, and for several yrs., Principal of the State Institute for the Blind, in Indianapolis, Ind. He is also studying Law, with a view to the legal profession.

1618. VI. Alice,[8] b. June 10, 1837.

1619. VII. Ezra Lee,[8] b. April 6, 1839, entered the Ohio University in 1855.

1620. VIII. Helen Ames,[8] b. June 27, 1841.

Chil. of EZRA WALKER,[7] [853] of Charlestown, Va.

1621. I. Kate.[8]

1622. II. Ezra,[8] b. after the death of his father.

Chil. of Prof. R. M. WALKER,[7] [855] of Westerville, O.

1623. I. Abigail Cornelia,[8] b. Nov. 7, 1837, is m. ch.

1624. II. Ellen Louisa,[8] b. Jan. 21, 1839, " " "

1625. III. Archibald Ralph,[8] b. Feb. 17, 1845, d. Sept. 11, 1847.

1626. IV. EDWIN GRISWOLD,[8] b. Feb. 9, 1850.

1627. V. RALPH MANNING,[8] b. Sept. 19, 1853.

CHIL. OF HENRY D. WALKER,[7] [858] OF CHARLESTON, S. C.

1628. I. ANN CATHARINE,[8] b. Nov. 23, 1836.

1629. II. HENRY CALEB,[8] b. Dec. 1, 1838.

1630. III. MARIA EDGERTON,[8] b. Aug. 12, 1840, d. March 1, 1844.

1631. IV. ROBERT STEWART,[8] b. Nov. 18, 1842.

1632. V. CLARA,[8] b. March 5, 1845, d. Nov. 10, 1846.

1633. VI. CAROLINE JANE,[8] b. Sept. 26. 1849.

CHIL. OF COMFORT WALKER,[7] [865] OF CENTRAL VILLAGE, CT.

1634. I. AARON THOMAS,[8] b. April, 1835, is a mason.

1635. II. HENRY FENNER,[8] b. Oct. 15, 1837.

1636. III. WILLIAM OLNEY,[8] b. March 31, 1840.

1637. IV. ANN ELIZA,[8] b. Feb. 13, 1843.

1638. V. ALBERT COMFORT,[8] b. July 4, 1850.

CHIL. OF THO'S MOWRY WALKER,[7] [866] OF MORAVIA, N.Y.

1639. I. MARY M.,[8] b. April 26, 1842.

1640. II. JAMES FITCH,[8] b. Oct. 31, 1846.

1641. III. ELLEN,[8] b. July 29, 1849.

CHILDREN OF CALEB WALKER,[7] [871] OF GREENWICH.

1642. I. ABIGAIL R.,[8] b. April 26, 1845, in Belchertown.

1643. II. EBENEZER C.,[8] b. July 26, 1846, d. Aug. 29, 1847.

1644. III. MARTHA H.,[8] b. Jan. 2, 1848, in B.

1645. IV. AMBROSE E.,[8] b. Oct. 20, 1849, in G.

1646. V. WILLIAM S.,[8] b. March 2, 1851, " "

1647. VI. Sarah M.[8] b. Jan. 2, 1853, in G.

1648. VII. Fanny L.,[8] b. Oct. 20, 1854' " "

Chil. of EZRA S. WALKER,[7] [872] of Belchertown.

1649. I. Washington D.,[8] (1876) b. March 27, 1830, in Willington, Ct., m. ———, and has 1 son. Res. Belchertown.

1650. II. Emily H.,[8] b. Feb. 10, 1834, in Belchertown.

1651. III. Mary A.,[8] b. June 17, 1837, in B.

1652. IV. Sarah H.,[8] b. July 12, 1839, in B.

1653. V. William,[8] b. Dec. 6, 1841.

1654. VI. Susan L.,[8] b. March 12, 1842, twin.

1655. VII. Samuel E.,[8] b. " " " "

Chil. of EBENEZER WALKER,[7] [873] of Belchertown.

1656. I. Hannah J.,[8] b. Sept. 30, 1843. Res. B.

Children of HORACE WALKER,[7] [880] of Greenwich.

1657. I. Adeline M.,[8] b. July 31, 1843, in Belchertown.

1658. II. Huldah L.,[8] b. May 27, 1845, in B.

1659. III. Almira E.,[8] b. June 4, 1850, in G.

Children of WILLIAM C. WALKER,[7] [881] of Sutton.

1660. I. Eliza Q.,[8] b. March 6, 1834, in Uxbridge, m. July 22, 1850, ——— Cox, a shoemaker, and has 2 chil.

1661. II. Isabel V.,[8] b. Aug. 20, 1835, in Sutton, m. Aug. 12, 1856, Wm. H. Howard, of S., a shoemaker. Res. S.

1662. III. William H.,[8] b. Dec. 7, 1836, in Northbridge, m. Aug. 3, 1859, Lauretta Houghton. He is a shoemaker. Res. S.

1663. IV. 'Alonzo V.,[8] b. Nov. 19, 1838, in Oxford, is a shoemaker.

1664. V. Adelaide,[8] b. Nov. 29, 1840, in Oxford.

1665. VI. Sydney W.,[8] b. Aug. 28, 1842, was drowned in Millbury, Aug. 8, 1850.

1666. VII. CLARENDON,[8] b. Aug. 5, 1844, in Webster.

1667. VIII. GEORGIETTA,[8] b. Aug. 20, 1846, in Millbury, d. March 7, 1847.

1668. IX. EMMA A.,[8] b. Sept. 20, 1848.

CHILDREN OF LEMUEL WALKER[7], [882] OF VESTAL, N. Y.

1669. I. SILAS L.,[8] b. April 18, 1836. Res. Vestal, N. Y.

1670. II. SYLVIA E.,[8] b. Oct. 11, 1840.

CHILDREN OF ABNER C. WALKER,[7] [885] OF DUDLEY.

1671. I. SUSAN A. H.,[8] b. Feb. 10, 1847, in D.

1672. II. JANE D.,[8] b. Oct. 16, 1848, " "

1673. III. HARRIET M.,[8] b. Oct. 30, 1850, " "

1674. IV. HUDSON R.,[8] b. Nov. 30, 1853, " "

NINTH GENERATION.

CHILD OF TIMOTHY WALKER,[8] [886] OF NEWTON CENTRE.

1675. I. SAMUEL ALPHEUS,[9] b. Feb. 23, 1837, in Bellingham.

CHILD OF GEO. LA FAYETTE WALKER,[8] [891] PAWTUCKET.

1676. I. CHILD,[9] b. in the autumn of 1852.

CHIL. OF SAMUEL WALKER,[8] [898] OF MARGARETTA, O.

1677. I. CHANCY B.,[9] b. April 30, 1836, is a farmer.

1678. II. THEODORE PERRY,[9] b. Jan. 6, 1838, is a farmer.

1679. III. MARY ELIZA,[9] b. March 18, 1841.

1680. IV. ADELAIDE L.,[9] b. July 19, 1843.

1681. V. EMMA ANN,[9] b. Dec. 4, 1846.

1682. VI. MELISSA MARIA,[9] b. Aug. 16, 1849.

CHIL. OF JOHN B. WALKER,[8] [899] OF MARION, IOWA.

1683. I. ALMIRA,[9] b. Dec. 30, [11 ?] 1838, in Margaretta, O.
1684. II. WILLIAM HENRY,[9] b. March 21, 1840, in " "
1685. III. CYNTHIA ANN,[9] b. March 1, 1843, in Marion, Ia.
1686. IV. JAMES HIEL,[9] b. June 18, 1845, " " "
1687. V. MYRON,[9] b. July 21, 1850, " " "
1688. VI. HARRIET ELIZA,[9] b. Aug. 27, 1855, " " "
1689. VII. JASPER O.,[9] b. Aug. 28, 1858, " " "

CHIL. OF GAMALIEL WALKER,[8] [901] OF LYTTLETON, IOWA.

1690. I. CHILD,[9] b. Aug. 12, 1844, d. Aug. 26, 1844.
1691. II. CLARK,[9] b. Dec. 2, 1846.
1692. III. CHARLOTTE,[9] b. Dec. 12, 1849.
1693. IV. SIMEON,[9] b. April 22, 1852, d. March 22, 1854.
1694. V. SIMON,[9] b. Dec. 28, 1854.
1695. VI. THEODORE,[9] b. May 20, 1857, d. July 8, 1858.

CHIL. OF WM. RUSSELL WALKER,[8] [925] OF PAWTUCKET.

1696. I. GEORGE CLIFTON,[9] b. Nov. 7, 1853.

CHILD OF LEONARD WALKER,[8] [940] OF WRENTHAM.

1697. I. ELIZA FRANCES,[9] b. May 29, 1850, in Taunton.

CHIL. OF GEORGE E. WALKER,[8] [954] OF DEXTER, MICH.

1698. I. DWIGHT C.,[9] b. Nov. 25, 1855.
1699. II. SARAH G.,[9] b. Aug., 1857.
1700. III. FRANK M.,[9] b. 1859.

CHIL. OF GEORGE B. WALKER,[8] [1000] OF LYNDON, VT.

1701. I. FRANK K.,[9] b. July 6, 1858.
1702. II. MARTHA JANE,[9] b. Nov. 25, 1859.

Chil. of LEWIS S. WALKER,[8] [1011] of Grafton, Vt.

1703. I. Corona C.,[9] b. Feb. 29, 1852.
1704. II. Edwin L.,[9] b. Feb. 22, 1859.

Chil. of SAMUEL M. WALKER,[8] [1013] of Grafton, Vt.

1705. I. Baxter,[9] b. July 1, 1849.
1706. II. Romanzo,[9] b. April, 1851.

Chil. of ORVAL C. WALKER,[8] [1014] of Wyoming, Ill.

1707. I. Aronell,[9] b. Jan. 3, 1851.
1708. II. Charles,[9] b. Feb. 1853.
1709. III. Samuel Lewis,[9] b. March, 1855.

Child of ALDEN WALKER,[8] [1015] of Grafton, Vt.

1710. I. Samuel J.,[9] b. Oct. 31, 1858.

Child of JOHN C. WALKER,[8] [1022] of No. Stratford, N.H.

1711. I. William L.,[9] b. Sept. 12, 1858.

Children of JESSE B. WALKER,[8] [1041] of Gates, N. Y.

1712. I. Eben,[9] b. Oct. 1, 1838, d. Sept. 8, 1840.
1713. II. Ellen,[9] b. Oct. 17, 1843.
1714. III. Albert E.,[9] b. April 10, 1846, d. Dec. 8, 1852.

Child of HARVEY I. WALKER,[8] [1050] of Gates, N. Y.

1715. I. Truman,[9] b. March 25, 1857.

Chil. of STEPHEN H. WALKER,[8] [1053] of Orwell, Pa.

1716. I. Eliza,[9] b. April 25, 1849.
1717. II. John,[9] b. Sept. 23, 1853.
1718. III. Elizabeth,[9] b. Feb. 1, 1857.

CHIL. OF WILLIAM N. WALKER,[8] [1056] OF SWEDEN, N. Y.

1719. I. JAMES M.,[9] b. Dec. 7, 1843, in Alabama, N. Y.

1720. II. JUDSON L.,[9] b. Jan. 3, 1845, in " "

1721. III. WALLACE S.,[9] b. Sept. 18, 1851, in Ridgway, N. Y.

1722. IV. BYRON A.,[9] b. Jan. 31, 1856, in " "

CHILD OF URI WALKER,[8] [1057] OF BERGEN, N. Y.

1723. I. MARY E.,[9] b. Aug. 7, 1853.

CHIL. OF AMASA WALKER,[8] [1072] OF UNION, N. Y.

1724. I. GEORGE WINFIELD,[9] b. Jan., 1843.

1725. II. MARYETTE,[9] b. 1845.

1726. III. ELEANOR,[9] b. 1847.

1727. IV. HARRISON A.,[9] b. 1849.

1728. V. JEANETTE,[9] b. 1854.

CHIL. OF PHILIP HALL WALKER,[8] [1118] OF ROXBURY, N.Y.

1729. I. JOHN B.,[9] b. ———.

1730. II. LUCY ESTHER,[9] b. ———, m. Samuel Runyan, and has 1 child—

(1) *William.*

1731. III. CLARISSA JANE,[9] b. ———, m. Alfred R. Dotey, and has 2 chil.—

(1) *George Ransler.* (2) *Orison Lafayette.*

CHIL. OF IRA CASWELL WALKER,[8] [1119] CAMPVILLE, N.Y.

1732. I. EDWARD.[9]

1733. II. FISHER.[9]

1734. III. MARTHA.[9]

1735. IV. SARAH JANE.[9]

} All efforts to obtain information respecting these, have failed.

CHILDREN OF EZRA WALKER,[8] [1120] OF NO. BRANCH, N. Y.

1736. I. CYNTHIA,[9] b. June 8, 1828, m. April 21, 1847, Henry Morse, of Roxbury, N. Y., a farmer and dairyman in R. Chil.—

(1) *Amanda M.* (2) *Nancy J.* (3) *Joseph P.*

1737. II. IRA C.,[9] b. Aug. 4. 1832, m. Jan. 10, 1856, Rebecca Keator. He is a mechanic and teacher of music. Res. Roxbury, N. Y.

1738. III. JOHN S.,[9] (1877) b. March 27, 1835, m. July 9, 1854, Lydia P. Tubbs, of Wis., and has 1 dau. He is a miller, and resides near Ripon, Wis.

1739. IV. JAMES WILSON,[9] b. March 31, 1838.

1740. V. STEPHEN PHILIP,[9] b. Aug. 23, 1841.

BY 2d MARRIAGE.

1741. VI. EZRA FERDINAND,[9] b. Nov. 13, 1847.

1742. VII. ADAM,[9] b. Aug. 20, 1849.

1743. VIII. DANIEL EDWARD,[9] b. March 21, 1851.

1744. XI. HENRY M.,[9] b. Jan. 22, 1853.

1745. X. JOSEPH C.,[9] b. March 13, 1856.

1746. XI. MARYETTE,[9] b. May 10, 1859.

CHILD OF JOHN S. WALKER,[8] [1122] OF CHEMUNG CO., N. Y.

1747. I. HANNAH SALOME,[9] b. ——.

CHIL. OF LIBERTY S. WALKER,[8] [1128] OF SHELBY CO., IND.

1748. I. JOHN S.,[9] b. Aug. 10, 1839, in Butler Co., O., d. Oct. 16, 1841.

1749. II. ELIZABETH,[9] b. Sept. 24, 1840, in Butler Co., O., m. Sept. 25, 1856, John B. Hill, b. in Bartholomew Co., Ind., April 7, 1834. He is a farmer.

1750. III. NABBY,[9] b. March 24, 1842.

1751. IV. ZILPHA A.,[9] b. Oct. 23, 1843.

1752. V. MARY M.,[9] b. June 16, 1845, d. Nov. 25, 1846.

1753. VI. TAYLOR,[9] b. March 7, 1847.

1754. VII. MISSOURI CAROLINE,[9] b. June 11, 1849.

1755. VIII. THOMAS SULLIVAN,[9] b. July 29, 1851.

1756. IX. NANCY EMMA,[9] b. Sept. 28, 1853, in Shelby Co.

1757. X. SARAH FLORENCE,[9] b. Sept. 28, 1855, in Shelby Co.

CHIL. OF DANIEL L. WALKER,[8] [1129] MARGARETTVILLE, N.Y.

1758. I. MARY D.,[9] b. March 13, 1831, m. April, 1853, Henry T. Hewitt. Res. Middletown, (Margarettville,) Delaware Co., N.Y. Chil.—

(1) *Everett S.*, b. Feb. 1854. (2) *Clarence F.*, b. Dec. 1, 1855. Twin. (3) *Florence B.*, b. Dec. 1, 1855. Twin.

1759. II. CHARLES T.,[9] b. Nov. 16, 1832. Res. La Porte, Ind.

1760. III. GEO. W.,[9] b. Sept. 18, 1835.

1761. IV. EDWARD B.,[9] b. May 30, 1837, m. 1859, Jane Frazier. Res. Middletown, (Clark's Factory,) Delaware Co., N. Y.

1762. V. FRANCES B.,[9] b. Feb. 26, 1839.

1763. VI. MARGARET E.,[9] b. March 1, 1842. Res. Clark's Factory.

1764. VII. CHILD,[9] d. in infancy.

1765. VIII. " " " "

1766. IX. " " " "

BY 2d MARRIAGE.

1767. X. SUSAN O'CONNOR,[9] b. July 25, 1855.

CHIL. OF HENRY L. WALKER,[8] [1132] OF ROXBURY, N. Y.

1768. I. THOMPSON,[9] b. March 22, 1849.

1769. II. EVA,[9] b. Oct. 18, 1854.

CHILDREN OF ERIE WALKER,[8] [1133] OF WEBSTER.

1770. I. ARNOLD B.,[9] b. Dec. 24, 1843, in Cumberland, R. I.

1771. II. GEORGE A.,[9] b. Nov. 20, 1847, in " "

1772. III. MARY E.,[9] b. March 22, 1850, in Webster.

1773. IV. ELBRIDGE E.,[9] b. June 26, 1853, in "

CHIL. OF ISRAEL WALKER,[8] [1134] OF PROVIDENCE, R. I.

1774. I. SILAS A.,[9] b. July 8, 1843, d. May 5, 1845.

1775. II. HERBERT A.,[9] b. May 21, 1848, in P.

1776. III. WILLIAM H.,[9] b. Feb. 5, 1850, d. Feb. 16, 1851.

1777. IV. ISAAC N.,[9] b. Oct. 23, 1853, in P.

1778. V. EDWARD E.,[9] b. Feb. 13, 1856, d. Oct. 18, 1856.

CHILD OF MASON WALKER,[8] [1135] OF STERLING, CT.

1779. I. IRVING M.,[9] b. June 28, 1855, in S.

CHILD OF CHARLES WALKER,[8] [1137] OF PROVIDENCE, R.I.

1780. I. ADELAIDE F.,[9] b. Jan. 31, 1856.

CHILDREN OF ISAAC WALKER,[8] [1140] OF COVENTRY, R. I.

1781. I. BYRON,[9] b. Sept. 6, 1854.

1782. II. EZRA MATTESON,[9] b. Feb. 17, 1856.

CHIL. OF HENRY WALKER,[8] [1148] OF WARWICK, R. I.

1783. I. ELIZA JANE,[9] b. Oct. 23, 1846.

1784. II. STEPHEN HENRY,[9] b. July 18, 1848.

1785. III. GEORGE EDWIN,[9] b. Sept. 5, 1850.

1786. IV. MARIA EVELINE,[9] b. March 29, 1853.

1787. V. FANNY ESSTELLE,[9] b. Feb. 17, 1855.

CHIL. OF NATH'L L. WALKER,[8] [1173] OF PAWTUCKET.

1788. I. SARAH,[9] b. Nov. 10, 1853, twin.

1789. II. ELLEN,[9] b. " " " "

CHIL. OF ORSAMUS WALKER,[8] [1176] OF MACOMB, ILL.

1790. I. MARIA,[9] b. Feb. 26, 1826, in Barre, Vt., m. Jan. 17, 1849, Abram Rowe, of Cohoes, N.Y., who was b. in Burlington, Vt. He is a daguerrean in Macomb, Ill. Chil.—

(1) *Alice*, b. Nov. 3, 1849, d. June 22, '51. (2) *Adaline R.*, b. Feb. 19, '53.

1791. II. CHARLES C.,[9] b. Aug. 20, 1827. Farmer in Kanzas.

1792. III. HARRIET A.,[9] b. May 11, 1829, m. Nov. 29, 1848, Adam Southworth, in Cohoes, N.Y. He d. Aug. 17, 1849. She m. 2d, March 21, 1850, Rufus McElwane, in Saratoga, N.Y. Chil.—

(1) *Alice*, b. June 29, 1851. (2) *Nancy*, b. July, '54.

1793. IV. LUCIUS E.,[9] b. April 1, 1833. Res. Portage City, Wis.

1794. V. WILLARD,[9] b. Feb. 12, (3?) 1837, d. April 16, 1847.

1795. VI. GERRY R.,[9] b. July 13, 1842.

CHIL. OF BENJ. F. WALKER,[8] [1179] OF CHICAGO, ILL.

1796. I. ELIZABETH,[9] b. July 24, 1834, in Barre, Vt., m. Sept. 1855, Wm. Hinchman, a merchant of Savannah, Mo.

1797. II. EMMA H.,[9] b. Sept. 18, 1836, in Barre, Vt.

1798. III. CLARA M.,[9] b. May 3, 1849, in Barre, Vt.

CHIL. OF EDWIN R. WALKER,[8] [1181] OF PROVIDENCE, R.I.

1799. I. KATIE G.[9]

1800. II. ELISHA B.[9]

CHIL. OF DANIEL H. WALKER,[8] [1182] OF ALTON, ILL.

1801. I. EDWIN J.,[9] b. 1850, in Macomb, Ill.

1802. II. LOUISA,[9] b. 1851, in Alton, Ill.

CHIL. OF LEMUEL F. WALKER,[8] [1187] OF PLATTSBURGH, N.Y.

1803. I. CORDELIA E.,[9] b. 1828.

1804. II. ELIZA R.,[9] b. 1835.

1805. III. EMMA M.,[9] b. 1837.

1806. IV. HANNAH M.,[9] b. 1842.

CHIL. OF BENJ. R. WALKER,[8] [1189] OF KEESEVILLE, N. Y.

1807. I. FRANCIS,[9] b. 1844, in N. Y.

1808. II. ELIZBETH,[9] b. 1847, " "

1809. III. CHARLES W.,[9] b. 1850, " "

CHILD OF SAMUEL N. WALKER,[8] [1192] WATERTOWN, WIS.

1810. I. JEREMIAH E.,[9] b. 1848.

CHIL. OF CLARK E. WALKER,[8] [1193] OF NORTH BANGOR, N.Y.

1811. I. GEORGE C.,[9] b. 1846, in N.Y.

1812. II. ELLEN M.,[9] b. 1850, " "

CHIL. OF WM. H. WALKER,[8] [1198] OF GRASS LAKE, MICH.

1813. I. AURORA M.,[9] b. Dec. 13, 1836.

1814. II. DANIEL,[9] b. Feb. 27, 1849.

CHIL. OF ALLEN C. WALKER,[8] [1203] OF BARRE ? VT.

1815. I. EDGAR A.,[9] b. Feb. 25, 1851.

1816. II. ABBY J.,[9] b. May 27, 1853, d. Aug. 27, 1854.

CHIL. OF LONDUS B. WALKER,[8] [1204] OF CHICAGO, ILL.

1817. I. CELIA HARRINGTON,[9] b. April 23, 1843.

1818. II. STEPHEN L.,[9] b. about 1851.

CHILDREN OF OTIS F. WALKER,[8] [1205] OF BARRE, VT.

1819. I. CELIA,[9] b. Nov. 1847, in B.

1820. II. JOHN N.,[9] b. Aug. 8, 1853, in B.

CHIL. OF JOHN N. WALKER,[8] [1206] OF MONTPELIER, VT.

1821. I. HENRY C.,[9] b. 1844, d. Aug. 23, 1845.

1822. II. ABERTA,[9] b. May 15, 1848.

1822.[1] III. ADELBERT H.,[9] b. Aug. 26, 1850.

CHILDREN OF BENJ. H. WALKER,[8] [1208] OF LAKEVILLE.

1823. I. PHEBE E.,[9] b. July 29, 1850.

1823.[1] I. GEORGE B.,[9] b. Jan. 5, 1853.

CHIL. OF HENRY C. WALKER,[8] [1221] OF BUFFALO, N. Y.

1824. I. SARAH ELLEN,[9] b. Oct. 7, 1840, in Conneaut, O.

1825. II. CATHARINE JUDSON,[9] } b. April 17, 1845, d. Mar. 1847.

1826. III. ELIZA SMITH,[9] } b. April 17, 1845, d. July, 1845.

1827. IV. GEORGE JUDSON.[9] b. Nov. 20, 1848, in Milan, O.

1828. V. CHARLES HENRY,[9] b. May 19, 1851, in B.

CHIL. OF ISAAC C. WALKER,[8] [1224] OF BUFFALO, N. Y.

1829. I. HENRY STEPHEN,[9] b. May 28, 1847, in Milan, O.

1830. II. JOHN JAY,[9] b. Nov. 4, 1850, " " "

1832. III. WILLIAM I.,[9] b. July 17, 1852, " "

1833. IV. FREDERICK ALBERT,[9] b. Oct. 21, 1854, in B.

CHIL. OF LEWIS E. WALKER,[8] [1233] OF WARSAW, N.Y.

1834. I. WILLIAM ABNER,[9] b. July 24, 1855.

1835. II. JOHN FRANKLIN,[9] b. Nov. 24, 1858.

CHIL. OF CHARLES R. WALKER,[8] [1257] OF BUFFALO, N. Y.

1836. I. JARED LAKE,[9] b. July 27, 1847, d. Aug. 25, 1849.

1837. II. CHARLES RUDD,[9] b. Aug. 2, 1850, d. Oct. 24, 1853.

1838. III. STEPHEN,[9] b. Oct. 25, 1854.

CHIL. OF LOUIS M. WALKER,[8] [1297] OF CLARENDON, VT.

1839. I. ADAH A.[9]
1840. II. JULIA C.[9]
1841. III. LEWIS ARNOLD,[9] b. Feb. 7, 1856.

CHILD OF LUCIUS W. WALKER,[8] [1314] OF URBANA, ILL.

1842. I. EVA M.,[9] b. July 16, 1851.

CHILD OF REV. AVERY S. WALKER,[8] [1327] OF ROCKVILLE, CT.

1843. I. JOHN BALDWIN,[9] b. Jan. 15, 1860.

CHIL. OF TIMOTHY M. WALKER,[8] [1342] OF WAUKAN, WIS.

1844. I. GEO. DICKERMAN.[9]
1845. II. CARRIE,[9] b. May, 1856.

CHILD OF EPHRAIM M. WALKER,[8] [1343] OF WAUKAN, WIS.

1846. I. MILLER T.,[9] b. Sept. 1857.

CHIL. OF OBADIAH J. WALKER,[8] [1390] OF BURLINGTON, VT.

1847. I. JOHN HENRY,[9] b, May 15, 1853.
1848. II. FREDERICK WM.,[9] b. Sept. 6, 1855.
1848.[1] III. CHARLES EDWARD,[9] b. Nov. 15, 1856.

CHIL. OF SOLOMON WALKER,[8] [1407] OF ———.

1849. I. CLARA A.,[9] b. March 14, 1855.
1849.[1] II. One or two more, whose names are not known.

CHILD OF WM. F. WALKER,[8] [1455] OF JOHNSONSBURGH, N. Y.

1850. I. RHUA L.,[9] b. March 16, 1859.

CHILD OF WILLIAM WALKER,[8] [1509] OF SCRANTON, PA.

1851. I. FRANCES S.,[9] b. Aug. 3, 1835, m. Nov. 12, 1855, Cyrus Swan, of Poughkeepsie, N.Y., a Lawyer. Res. P. They have a dau., b. July 14, 1857, in Sharon, Ct.

CHILDREN OF GEORGE WALKER,[8] [1510] OF LENOX.

1852. I. FRANCES M.,[9] b. Jan. 17, 1847.

1853. II. EMMELINE D.,[9] b. Jan. 6, 1849.

CHIL. OF HON. JOHN A. WALKER,[8] [1514] OF PITTSFIELD.

1854. I. WM. PERRIN,[9] b. June 25, 1849.

1855. II. MARY MAGEE,[9] b. Dec. 4, 1852.

1856. III. ELLIOT,[9] b. Sept. 27, 1855.

1856.[1] IV. LOUISA HUNTINGTON,[9] b. April 16, 1858.

CHIL. OF EZRA WALKER,[8] [1530] OF PROVIDENCE, R. I.

1857. I. ELLEVA C.,[9] b. Oct. 10, 1854.

1858. II. SARAH L.,[9] b. March 20, 1857.

CHIL. OF OSCAR A. WALKER,[8] [1538] OF ROCHESTER, N.Y.

1859. I. CHAUNCEY OTIS,[9] b. May 16, 1844, d. April 21, 1848.

1860. II. FRANCES JANE,[9] b. May 18, 1846.

1860.[1] III. OSCAR,[9] b. Sept. 1848.

CHILD OF JAS. EDWIN WALKER,[8] [1546] OF DETROIT, MICH.

1861. I. MARCUS A.,[9] b. Dec. 6, 1859.

CHIL. OF REV. HORACE D. WALKER,[8] [1594] OF E. ABINGTON.

1862. I. WILLIAM MASON,[9] b. March 9, 1845, in A.

1863. II. HORACE DEAN AUSTEN,[9] b. Aug. 6, 1847, d. Oct. 24, 1848.

1864. III. ANNA MATILDA,[9] b. Jan. 2, 1850, d. Jan. 10, 1852.

1865. IV. ELLEN AUSTEN,[9] b. Nov. 22, 1851.

1866. V. PHILIP AUGUSTUS,[9] b. Sept. 8, 1853, d. Aug. 22, 1854.

1867. VI. SOPHIA ANTOINETTE,[9] b. June 22, 1855.

1868. VII. EDWARD AUGUSTUS,[9] b. June 22, 1860.

CHIL. OF REV. AUG. WALKER,[8] [1597] OF DIARBEKIR, TURKEY.

1869. I. SEWALL HARDING,[9] b. Oct. (14?) 16, 1854, d. Jan. 7, 1856.

1870. II. FREDERICK WILLIAMS,[9] b. Jan. 10, 1858.

1871. III. DEAN AUGUSTUS,[9] b. Feb. 1860.

CHILDREN OF JOHN S. WALKER,[8] [1599] OF MEDWAY.

1872. I. DEAN HOYT,[9] b. May 20, 1851.

1873. II. ELLEN M.,[9] b. June 3, 1854.

CHILD OF TIMOTHY C. WALKER,[8] [1603] OF GARDINER, ME.

1874. I. CHARLES,[9] b. March, 1853.

CHILD OF DOUGLAS W. WALKER,[8] [1610] OF AMESVILLE, O.

1875. I. MARIA TERESA,[9] b. June 2, 1855.

CHILD OF WASHINGTON D. WALKER,[8] [1649] BELCHERTOWN

1876. I. EZRA D.,[9] b. Nov. 26, 1856, in B.

TENTH GENERATION.

CHILD OF JOHN S. WALKER,[9] [1738] OF FON DU LAC CO., WIS.

1877. I. DAU.[10]

SAMUEL WALKER,

OF REHOBOTH.

IN the Metcalf Genealogy, contributed by Dr. Luther M. Harris, of Jamaica Plain, to the Genealogical Register, 1852, 172 pp., there is an abstract of the will of Michael Metcalf, of Dedham, dated 15: 9, 1664. In it, he made this bequest: "To my daughter, Joane Walker, 40s." There were other chil., sons and daus. Joane was the 10th child, b. March 24, 1632, and m., the Genealogy states, Samuel (?) Walker, of Rehoboth. The will, however, does not give Mr. W.'s christian name. There is no Samuel, of so early a date, in any Old Colony Record, either town or county, and every Walker (except one since 1800,) who is mentioned in the Records of Rehoboth, Seekonk and Attleboro', (parts of the old township of Rehoboth,) and also in Bristol Co. Rec., has a place in the Genealogy of Philip Walker and his descendants. There is strong circumstantial proof, that there was no Samuel Walker in R. so early.

May not the compiler of the Metcalf Genealogy have mistaken Samuel for Philip. Philip's wife's name was Jane. The dates also will justify this theory. Besides, Philip had a son Michael. May not his name have been derived from the grandfather Michael. This is the only instance in which the name occurs among nearly 1900 Walkers, descendants from Philip, and as he had a son Samuel, it is probable, that tradition has confounded the names, and led the compiler of the Metcalf Genealogy into error.

With no other proof of the existence of a Samuel Walker in Rehoboth, at this period, except the Metcalf Genealogy, it is very much less probable, that "he died and left no sign," and no descendant, than that there was no such SAMUEL WALKER.

1. WILLIAM WALKER, (2)

Of Eastham,

AND HIS DESCENDANTS.

The earliest notice of any William Walker in this country, is found in the Proprietors' Records of the town of Hingham. He received a grant of land in 1636, among the first settlers of H. And it is highly probable, that he is the William mentioned in Savage's Gleanings, with Richard, James and Sarah embarking for New England, in the Elizabeth, in April, 1635; (see 4th p. of this Genealogy;) 1st, because several of those who received grants in Hingham at this time, afterward went to Taunton, where James and Sarah were, and several to Rehoboth, where James Walker's mother and brother Philip settled. In addition to this, the date of his grant, harmonizes with that of his leaving England. Furthermore, there is no trace of a William Walker in any other town of the Old Colony, at so early a period. And this mention of a grant of land to him in Hingham, is the only one in the records of H. concerning him. He then disappears. These circumstances favor the conjecture, that the William in H. in 1636, and the William afterward in Eastham, were the same person. Only 16 years of age when in Hingham, if we suppose him to have been the William of the Elizabeth, from London, the dates respecting William Walker of Eastham, do not make the theory at all improbable; they rather confirm it, inasmuch as these were the only William Walkers in the Old Colony, of whom there is any record.

In an article by S. G. Drake, Esq., in the N. E. Hist. & Gen. Reg., Oct. 1860, on "The Founders of New England," is the following, copied by him, from a small parchment vol. in the Rolls Office, Chancery Lane, London :—

"May the 11th, 1637. The examinaction of John Gedney of Norwich, in Norff......to passe for New England with his wife Sarah, ageed 25 yeares......Lediah, Hannah and John; mo[r] 2 Seruants; William Walker, ageed......Burges ageed 26 yeares are desirous to passe for Salam."*

He may have been the William, of whom the Mass. Col. Records, Vol. IV., Part II., 66 p., (1662) give the following memorial:—

"In ans[r] to the petition of Willjam Walker, seaman, now a prisoner for the breach of ye law abt making suite to a servant majd wthout the masters consent first obteyned, &c., the Court, considering he was a strainger, & not knowing the lawe, that he hath lyen in prison neere a moneth, judged meet to graunt his request & dischardg him, he paying the chardge of the prison."

As John Gedney came to Salem, his "Seruant William Walker" belonged to the Mass. Colony, and there being no trace or record of a William Walker in the Colony, except the preceding, he may have been the unfortunate person whose matrimonial aspirations received such unfriendly treatment from the master of the "servant majd," but whose ignorance of the lawe, enlisted the lenity of the Government. Whether one and the same, or not, neither of them could have been the William in Hingham, 1636, and without doubt, neither, was the William of Eastham. These, though few, are all the instances of the name in the ancient records, except such as are known to relate to William of E.†

There can be little doubt that the William emigrating in the Elizabeth, April, 1635, and 15 years of age, was the William of H., in 1636, and though there is no positive proof that he went to E., yet, as there is no trace of him in H. after 1636, it may be presumed, that he was the one who settled in E., and was the father of the Eastham Walkers. He was not related to the other Walkers of the Old Colony, or if so, only remotely, being of the same age as James of Taunton, who came in the same ship with him. As his name is associated in the certificate of conformity, with "Richard ae. 24 yrs.," who went to Lynn, it is more probable they were more or less nearly related.

William Walker of Eastham, b. 1620, m. Jan. or Feb., (Feb. 25, Plym. Col. Rec.,) 1654, Sarah Snow, dau. of Nicholas,‡ of E., had 6 chil., and d. at an advanced age. His will was proved, 1703.

---

* The same may be found in Savage's Gleanings, Mass. Hist. Coll., 4th series, vol. 1.

† Wm. Walker imbarqued 17 Februarij, 1634, from ye Porte of London in ye Hopewell, for the Barbadoes. (See Gen. Reg. 1860, 348p)

‡ He was a man of considerable note in the Colony. He was Deputy, Select-man 7 yrs., and Town Clerk 16 yrs. He d. 1671.

His name is in the list of those able to bear arms in 1643, but the time of his settlement in E., is unknown. He was propounded June 8, 1655, and admitted to freedom, June 3, 1656. He was chosen to take up the excise, in 1664 and '67, and to take notice of what liquors were brought into the Gov., and the following is evidence, that he was not neglectful of the duties of his office, nor indifferent to the welfare of the town:—

"Trustrum Hull, of Barnstable, brought a barrell of rum to the town of E., and sold it, but gave noe account of it to either of us, and we thought it good to giue the Court notice of it. June 9, 1655."

Willam Walker,
John Done.

He was surveyor of highways, 1668, '69, '78 and '79, and constable in 1682.

"May 3, 1653, there were agitations about and conserning a warr with the Duch, in these ptes of America,....and messengers sent by comissioners to the Munhatoes,....and preperacõn was made, viz., warrants issued for the pressing of 60 men; Eastham to furnish 3. Morouer two barkqes were alsoe pressed to attend the expedition, ...the barkqe in which Richard Knowles sayleth, with him, the master thereof was pressed for the same purpose with John Younge and Willam Walker, and all things nessearie for their vse belonging to the said barkqe." Plym. Col. Rec., 3d vol., 30, 31 pp.

Ralph Smith was fined, in 1662–3, for striking and thrusting over a boat thought Willam Walker. Samuel Smith was fined, for saying he "could find in his hart to stick a pen into Willam Walker."

They may have had some provocation, for the Col. Rec. show, that as a man, he was not altogether blameless.

Plym. Col. Rec. 6th vol., 170th p., June 2, 1685. "William Walker, haueing 2 naturall sons in the training band, and 1 killed in the warrs, and some weakness and infirmitye of body, the Court orders that hee, the said William Walker, from hence forward shall be excused from training."

Grants of land were made to him, as follows, viz.:—

"A parcel of land granted to Wm. Walker, lying upon * * * * * * containing 20 acres, more or less. Lying on the southwest side of the pond; and bounded at each corner by 4 several trees marked, leaving a sufficient passage between his land and the pond, as the trees are marked, the tree upon the southwest corner being upon a * * * *. April 27, 1659.

A parcel of meddow granted to Wm. Walker. Lying at Silver Spring meddow, and containing 3 acres and ¾, more or less, bounded by Jonathan Sparrow's bounds, at the beach by a marked tree, and by Nicholas Snow by a marked tree, and a stake in the marsh. April 27, 1659.

A parcell of upland, granted to William Walker adjoining to his house lott on the southern side, containing two acres more or less, bounded by 3 trees marked. March 6, 1663.

Granted to William Walker, Senior, for (convenience?) to sett his house where his new dwelling house now stands, a small parcell of upland and swamp, containing one acre, more or less, bounded by the swamp side, toward John Mayo's, &c., &c., &c. Feb. 23, 1683.

Granted to Wm. Walker, Senior, a small bitt of land, at the westerly end of his land next the meeting house, that is to say, so much as to make his fence straite from the corner of his land, next Samuel Freeman's, to the corner of his own fence, at the brow of the hill above said Walker's barne—this grant is allowed of by the major part of the men appointed by the Town, to have a negative note in disposing of lands, in the Town of Eastham. Recorded April 30, 1699." THO. PAINE, Town Clerk.

Another grant of two acres is made, same date, and described in vol. 1st, 106 p., of Eastham Records of land and meadow. Tradition says he lived on the North bank of the Great Pond, about 500 yds., west of his father-in-law, Nicholas Snow. There have been houses on the place to this day, and it has been in possession of the Walkers till the purchase lately, by Philip Smith.

His descendants have not been numerous. Living on the sea shore, a considerable number have been engaged in maritime pursuits, and exposed to their perils, some died in early manhood, and others with few or no children.

SECOND GENERATION.

CHILDREN OF WILLIAM WALKER,[1] [1] OF EASTHAM.

2. I. JOHN,[2] b. Nov. 24, 1655, He, with 3 others, was killed in the Indian assault upon Eastham, in 1676.

3. II. WILLIAM,[2] b. Oct. 12, 1657, d. before Aug. 16, 1859.

4. III. WILLIAM,[2] (8) b. Aug. 2, 1659, d. Jan. 1743–4. He m. ———, and had several chil. Res. Eastham.

5. IV. SARAH,[2] b. July 30, 1662, was not mentioned in her father's will, (proved 1703,) and probably d. unm.

6. V. ELIZABETH,[2] b. Sept. 28, 1664, is called by her maiden name in her father's will, and probably d. unm.

7. VI. JABEZ,[2] (12) b. July 8, 1668, d. 1742. He m. Elizabeth ———, and had 8 chil. His will was made July 11, 174–, and proved Oct. 1742. He made his mark. Inv'y, £13, 10, 3. Res. Eastham.

THIRD GENERATION.

CHILDREN OF WILLIAM WALKER,[2] [4] OF EASTHAM.

8. I. WILLIAM,[3] (20) b. 1692 or '93, d. Feb. 15, 1780, in 88th yr. He m. Oct. 24, 1717, Anne Young. His will was made in 1772, and proved March, 1780, He had 5 sons and 4 daus., according to Eastham Rec., though his will gives the names of only 3 sons and 2 daus., married. He bequeathed "to grandson Nathaniel, his gun; to grandson David, his silver buckles." Res. Eastham.

9. II. MEHETABLE,[3] m. John Knowles, pub. March 25, 1721. The compiler infers that this Mehetable, and John, No. 10, and Susanna, No. 11, were the chil. of Wm., (though having no positive proof,) because there was no other, except Jabez, to be their father, and the names of Jabez' children are given in his will and the town records.

10. III. JOHN,[3] (29) b. ——, m. ——, and had 6 chil., according to his will, made 1754, and proved Feb. 30, 1760. Res. Eastham, in the part which is now Wellfleet.

11. IV. SUSANNA,[3] m. June 7, 1716, Jonathan Collins.

CHILDREN OF JABEZ WALKER,[2] [7] OF EASTHAM.

12. I. RICHARD,[3] (35) b. June 12, 1695, m. Joanna Tomlin, of Needham, pub. Feb. 13, 1719–20. He was living 1741 or '42, and had, according to Eastham Rec., 2 sons and 1 dau. Res. Eastham, in the part which is now Orleans.

13. II. REJOICE,[3] b. May 13, 1697, m. Nov. 9, 1732, Joseph Leven, of Plymouth.

14. III. MARY,[3] b. Sept. 14, 1699, m. March 9, or 19, 1748, John Berry, of Yarmouth.

15. IV. JEREMIAH,[3] (38) b. Sept. 17, 1702, d. 174–, and before Oct. 1742. He m. Esther Tomlin, pub. Sept. 12, 1724, who survived him. They had 3 sons and 1 dau., whose names are given by a grandson.

16. V. MERCY,[3] b. Nov. 1704, m. Jan. 3, 1733, Nathaniel Smith, of Harwich, and was living in 1742.

17. VI. JABEZ,[3] (42) b. ——, m. July, 1748, Sarah Atwood, of Provincetown, and had 2 sons and 1 dau. He was in E., in 1743, in Provincetown, after 1748, and nothing more is known of him.

18. VII. SARAH,[3] b. ——, m. Aug. 7, 1729, Nathaniel Higgins, as 2d wife, and had 2 sons.

19. VIII. PATIENCE,[3] m. Oct. 15, 1747, Wm. Chase, in Harwich.

FOURTH GENERATION.

CHILDREN OF WILLIAM WALKER,[3] [8] OF EASTHAM.

20. I. SUSANNA,[4] b. Oct. 5, 1718, m. Elkins Snow, pub. Sept. 24, 1637. They had 4 chil., and he d. before the birth of the last. She m. 2dly, Aug. 1, 1754, Jonathan Collins, of Truro. Her chil. were—

(1) *Margaret*, b. Aug. 2, 1738. (2) *Susanna*, b. Aug. 26, '41. (3) *Priscilla*, b. Dec. 9, '43. (4) *Elkins*, b. Dec. 28, '45.

21. II. PRISCILLA,[4] b. March 6, 1719–20, m. Silvanus Cole, pub. Sept. 12, 1741, and was living in 1772. She had 6 chil., 1743—1755.

22. III. NATHANIEL,[4] b. Jan. 17, 1721–2, d. bef. 1772. He m. Miriam Hatch, of Falmouth, pub. Oct. 1, 1748. Res. Eastham, the part which is now Orleans. All efforts have failed to find any descendants.

23. IV. HANNAH,[4] b. Sept. 25, 1724, d. bef. 1772, probably childless, if not unm., and in youth.

24. V. ANNE,[4] b. Dec. 18, 1726, d. bef. 1772, and probably in youth.

25. VI. ANDREW,[4] (45) b. June 29, 1728, m. Nov. 14, 1754, Sarah Doane, of Eastham, who d. May 30, 1761. They had 4 chil. He m. 2d, Dorcas Paine, pub. Jan. 1, 1763, and had 5 chil. He was a cooper, in E.

26. VII. WILLIAM,[4] (54) b. Sept. 15, 1730, d. in Eastham, 1815, or '16. He m. Nov. 17, 1757, Hannah Hinckley, of Truro, and had 4 chil. Res. Eastham, on his father's homestead.

27. VIII. DAVID,[4] (58) b. Sept. 30, 1732, d. before 1772. He m. Thankful Brown, pub. May 20, 1758. The name of one son only

is given in the Eastham records, but no success has attended repeated endeavors to ascertain what became of him, and where his descendants are.

28. IX. ELEAZER,[4] (59) b. March 22, 1734–5, m. Sarah Snow, pub. Oct. 4, 1760, and had 4 sons and 6 daus. He rem. from Eastham to Deer Island, Me., where he had trouble about his claim,—thence to Orphan's Island, Me., in Penobscot River, opposite Bucksport, and thence to Hampden, Me., where he d., about 1826. She d. about 1828.

CHILDREN OF JOHN WALKER,[3] [10] OF EASTHAM.

29. I. SAMUEL,[4] (69) m. Rebecca Freeman, dau. of Samuel, pub. Jan. 23, 1741–2, and had 9 chil. He m. 2dly, Mrs. Sarah Hopkins, and had 3 chil. Res. Eastham, now Wellfleet.

30. II. JOSHUA,[4] b. ——. He was m. in Eastham, the part which is now Wellfleet, in 1743, and living in 1754. Nothing more is known of him. [A Joshua Maker, or Walker, (the record is obscure,) m. Sept. 7, 1754, Leurah Covel, or Cowel.]

31. III. JOHN,[4] (81) b. ——, d. bef. 1754. Res. Eastham, now Wellfleet. [J. W. Jr., m. Hannah Remick, pub. June 12, 1744. J. W. Jr., and wife Phebe, had Phebe, b. Aug. 3, 1745. Was Hannah or Phebe, the wife of this John ?]

32. IV. MERCY,[4] m. Barnabas Cook, pub. July 21, 1746.

33. V. SARAH,[4] m. Jan. 30, 1752, Jesse Knowles, and had 6 chil., 1753—1765. Res. Eastham.

34. VI. MEHETABLE,[4] was living in 1754.

CHILDREN OF RICHARD WALKER,[3] [12] OF EASTHAM.

35. I. ELIZABETH,[4] b. Sept. 20, 1722.
36. II. NATHANIEL,[4] b. March 8, 1724–5.
37. III. MATTHEW,[4] b. Sept. 12, 1727.

} All efforts to learn more of these and their descendants have been fruitless

CHILDREN OF JEREMIAH WALKER,[3] [15] OF EASTHAM.

38. I. JEREMIAH,[4] (82) d. 1811. He m. April 19, 1756, Elizabeth Small, of Harwich. He m. 2d, Jan. 11, 1810, Rebecca

Gould, of H., who d. about 1820. He had 4 sons and 2 daus. His will was made 1807, and presented Oct., 1811. His son Benjamin, was the executor. He was a millwright and farmer, and a somewhat noted and influential man in the town. Res. Eastham.

39. II. BENJAMIN,[4] (88) d. 1816, in Monson, about 90 yrs. old. He m. Marsylvia? or Sylvia Keith of Bridgwater, who d. near 90 yrs. of age, in 1822. They had 9 chil. He was a ship carpenter, rem. from B., to South Brimfield, now Wales. They lived there many yrs., but d. in Monson. Though living to a great age, they retained their mental faculties unusually well.

40. III. JAMES,[4] d. ae. 8 or 9 yrs.

41. IV. BETSEY,[4] m. Nath'l Eldredge, of Harwich, and had chil.

CHILDREN OF JABEZ WALKER,[3] [17] OF PROVINCETOWN.

42. I. JABEZ,[4] b. Dec. 7, 1749, d. unm. in Provincetown. Adm'n on his estate, Jan. 23, 1799.

43. II. JAMES,[4] b. Dec. 5, 1752, in Provincetown, perhaps d. early or had gone from P., as David Young was adm'r of Jabez, (No. 42) in 1799.

44. III. JOANNA,[4] b. ——, m. David Young, and had—

(1) *Joanna Walker*, b. July 18, 1783.

FIFTH GENERATION.

CHILDREN OF ANDREW WALKER,[4] [25] OF EASTHAM.

45. I. ANNA,[5] b. March 23, 1756, d. ae. 90 yrs. She m. Josiah Linckhorneal, (called Lincoln since 1810,) pub. March 1, 1777, and had 8 chil., who all lived to be over 50 yrs. of age. Res. Eastham. Chil.—

(1) *Joshua*, b. abt. 1778, m. Tamsen Doane, of E. Res. E. Chil.—1, Joshua W., m. Mercy Chipman, and 2d, Hannah Smith, and had 5 chil. 2, Laertes. 3, Tamsen. 4, Betsey.

(2) *Dawson*, m. Mrs. Rachel Doane, of E., settled in Me., and had 2 sons and 1 dau.

(3) *Doane*, m. Ruth Ward, of Wellfleet. Res. E. Chil.—1, Dawson W., 2, Timothy W., d. 1857. He m. 2dly, Mrs. Ruth Ward, of E., and had 1 dau., 3, Ruth, who m. Samuel Nickerson, Jr., of E.

(4) *Andrew W.*, m. Sarah Ann Kennedy, of Henrietta, N. Y., settled in Pennfield, Monroe Co., N. Y. Chil.—1, Andrew W. 2, Charlton. 3, Josiah. 4, Harriet. 5, Sarah. He is an extensive and wealthy Flour manufacturer.

(5) *Josiah*. Res. E., unm. (6) *Anna*. (7) *Dorcas*. Res. E., unm. (8) *Sarah D*. Res. E., unm.

46. II. NATHANIEL,[5] b. Nov. 25, 1757, d. at sea, it is supposed. He was engaged to a young lady in Bermuda, when last heard from. He and his brother Joshua, were in Capt. Isaiah Higgins' Co. of Provincials, at Boston, 1 mo., from June 17, 1776.

47. III. JOSHUA,[5] b. July 11, 1759, d. at sea, unm.

48. IV. SARAH,[5] b. May 24, 1761, d. June 14, 1761.

BY 2d MARRIAGE.

49. V. SARAH,[5] b. Oct. 20, 1763, d. 1844, ae. 83? yrs. She m. March, 1814, as 4th wife, Elkanah Linnell, of Orleans. No chil.

50. VI. PETER,[5] (97) b. Dec. 28, 1764, d. Feb. 1837. He m. Abigail Brown, of Truro, pub. Oct. 17, 1789, and had 3 sons and 8 daus. He m. 2d, about 1831, Mrs. Susanna (Knowles) Thomas. He was a blacksmith. Res. Eastham.

51. VII. MERCY,[5] b. Jan. 3, 1770, d. Jan. 5, 1816. She was pub. April 26, 1794, to Benjamin Higgins, (See No. 78,) of Eastham, who was b. Sept. 23, 1767. They had 10 chil. Res. Eastham. Chil.—

(1) *John W.*, b. about 1798, m. 1835, Mary S. Taylor, of Wellfleet. Res. E. He is a farmer, and highly esteemed. Chil.—1, Fanny K., a successful school teacher. 2, Peter.

(2) *Elkanah*, m. 1825, Hannah King, of W. He was master of a ship, and d. in Cuba, 1828, ae. 31. They had 1 child, Zephaniah, lost at sea, 1846.

(3) *Dorcas*, m. 1821, Capt. Barnabas Higgins, of Orleans, and d. 1837. She had Barnabas N. G., who was lost at sea, 1846, in same vessel with Zephaniah, his cousin.

(4) *Ben*, m. 1826, Hannah Higgins, of Wellfleet. Res. Eastham. He has—1, Mary Jane, m. Nathan M. Hatch, of E., a blacksmith. Res. Chatham. 2, Mercy Ann, m. Elijah Young, of C., a brickmaker. Res. Barnstable. 3, Daniel. Res. Albion, Cal. 4, Corinda. 5, Benjamin. 6, Eldad.

(5) *Phebe H.*, m. 1835, Sam'l S. Taylor, of Wellfleet, who d. ae. about 52 yrs. Res. Gloucester. Chil.—1, Benj'n, d. Aug. 25, 1858, ae. 25 yrs. and 6 days, of injury to his back by falling upon a barrel. He was a great sufferer. 2, William, lost at sea, Feb. 1858, on the passage from Newfoundland. 3, John, b. about 1842.

(6) *Andrew W.*, m. Rebecca Atkins, of Orleans. Res. E. Chil.—1, Cordelia, m. 1855, Theophilus Newcomb, of Wellfleet. She d. Jan. 1858. 2, Atkins. He m. 2d, 1837, Chloe Whelden, of Barnstable, has—3, Isaac H. and 4, Andrew.

(7) *Bartlett*, m. 1833, Lucy Higgins, of Wellfleet, and d. 1847, a shoemaker. Chil.—1, Sarah Ann, m. 1852, Alfred Freeman, of W. 2, John G., m. 1856, Lucinda R. Newcomb, of W.

(8) *Anna J. D.*, m. Dec. 1, 1831, James Chapman, Jr., of Dennis, who d. Oct. 10, '56. Res. Barnstable. She rem. to Plymouth, in 1856. Chil.—1, Mary Ann, b. Nov. 2, 1832, m. Aug. 17, 1852, Isaac J. Lucas, of Plymouth, who d. Oct. 17, 1858. They had—[Jane H., b. May 14, 1856.] 2, James Henry, b. Nov. 21, 1834, m. Mary B. Diman, of Plymouth, and has—[Mary B., b. Nov. 8, 1859.] 3, Hannah Walker, b. May 31, 1836. 4, Bennett Wing, b. Sept. 3, 1838, d. July 25, '39. 5, John Franklin, b. May 22, '40. 6, Martha Green, b. Feb. 26, '42. 7, Mercy Joy, b. Nov. 26, '44. 8, Phebe Higgins, b. Nov. 21, '46. 9, Pamelia Baker, b. March 9, '49, d. Jan. 9, '55. 10, Sarah Eliz'th, b. Aug. 6, '52. 11, Catharine Lucas. 12, Twin son, (still-born,) Feb. 21, '55.

(9) *Justus*, m. 1835, L—— Hickman, of W., and has had 5 chil.—1, Sarah L. 2, Lewis H. 3, Benj'n. 4, Bartlett. 5, Justus.

(10) *Mercy*, m. 1835, Franklin Smith, of E. Res. Orleans. Chil.—1, Lucy B. 2, Mercy. 3, Thomas.

52. VIII. ANDREW,[5] b. Jan. 3, 1771, d. at sea, unm.

53. IX. JOHN,[5] b. Oct. 16, 1775, d. at sea, 1797, ae. 23? unm.

CHILDREN OF WILLIAM WALKER,[4] [26] OF EASTHAM.

54. I. PRISCILLA,[5] b. Feb. 19, 1759, was pub. May 9, 1778, to John Mayo, of Eastham. They settled in E., and had 12 chil.

55. II. HANNAH,[5] b. Sept. 9, 1762, was pub. Jan. 10, 1801, to David Snow, of Orleans. No chil.

56. III. DAVID,[5] (108) b. April 19, 1765, d. 1842, in West Boylston. He m. Susannah Higgins, dau. of Elkanah, and had 10 chil. She d. 1826. They rem. to West Boylston, in 1814, where they died.

57. IV. PHEBE,[5] b. April 21, 1773, d. 1816. She was pub. Nov. 5, 1796, to Joseph Linkhorne, (Lincoln) of Eastham, son of Joseph and Ann, and b. July 26, 1770. They had 9 chil.

CHILD OF DAVID WALKER,[4] [27] OF EASTHAM.

58. I. DAVID,[5] b. Feb. 6, 1759. It is thought he emigrated to Maine, but none of the kindred can tell the town or county.

CHILDREN OF ELEAZER WALKER,[4] [28] OF EASTHAM.

59. I. AARON,[5] b. Sept. 14, 1761, d. Nov. 30, 1764.

60. II. ZEBIAH,[5] b. Sept. 25, 1763, d. Nov. 28, 1816. She m. March, 1790, Col. Andrew Grant, who d. Feb. 8, 1854. He was Col. in the 2d Regiment in the War of 1812; was in the Battle at Hampden; a good officer and worthy citizen. He was a farmer. Both m. Meth. ch. Res. Hampden, Me. Chil.—

(1) *Daniel*, b. Aug. 10, 1792, m. Jan. 17, 1819, Ruth Thompson, who d. Oct. 10, 1840. He d. June, 1827. Res. H. Chil.—1. Joel T., b. Sept. 20, 1820. 2, Zebiah W., b. Aug. 5, '23· 3, Hannah S., b. March 26, '26·

(2) *Lucy*, b. Oct. 8, 1794, m. 1814, Wm. H. Reed, who d. March 31, '58· She d. April 12, '58· Both m. Meth. ch. He was a mechanic, and had 8 chil.

(3) *Ruth*, b. April 28, 1798, m. Daniel Smith, a mechanic, and has 4 chil. Res. H.

61. III. RACHEL,[5] b. Aug. 5, 1765, d. 1840. She m. about 1777, Eleazer Webber, a farmer, who d. 1842. Res. Hermon, Me. Chil.—

(1) *Sally*, b. Sept. 1, 1779, m. Aug. 10, 1811, Cha's Page. He was b. Aug. 22, 1788, and d. June.1840. Res. Hampden. Both m. Meth. ch. Chil.—1, Wm., b. July 27, 1812, m. Octavia Kempton. Farmer in Frankfort, Me., and has [Lemuel and Mary F.] 2, Charles, b. March 12, 1815, m. Joan Inman. Farmer in H., and has [Charles T., b. Dec, 23, '42· Albion W., b. Sept. 23, '44· Eugene A., b. May 17, '46· Zuinglius, b. Jan. 19, '48· Felix, b. Sept. 12, '51. Levi, b. Nov. 28, '53· Ann D. and Abby D., b. Oct. 28, '55. George J., b. Sept. 6, '57.] 3. James, b. May 9, 1817, m. Betsey Clark. Farmer in Newburg, Me. No chil. 4, Truxton, b. Sept. 7, '20, m. Angeline Keser. Lumberman in Howland, Me., and has [Mary A., b. April 22, '45· Josephine E., b. May 9, '47.] 5, Benj., b. March 13, '22, m. Lucinda Higgins. Farmer in Hampden, and has [Isadora, b. May, '57.] 6, Julia A., b. Sept. 5, '25, d. June, '57· 7, Samuel, b. Jan. 2, '28, m. Mary Pratt. Manufacturer in Medway, Mass. 8. Jefferson, b. March 23, '30, is a farmer in Hampden, and unm.

(2) *Betsey*, b. June, 1781, m. Stephen Emerson, and has 1 son. Res. Hermon, Me. Both m. Meth. ch.

(3) *Polly*, b. April, 1783, m. Seth Cole, who is dec'd. Both m. Meth. ch. They had 7 chil. Res. Frankkort, Me.

(4) *Eleazer*, b. 1785, m. Polly Patten. He is a farmer, and has 7 chil. Res. Hermon.

(5) *Daniel*, b. Aug. 1787, m. Sarah Goodell, of Hampden. Res. Hermon. He is a farmer, and has 7 chil.

(6) *Rachel*, b. Dec., 1789, m. Jeremiah Holmes, a farmer, and has 4 chil. Both m. Meth. ch. Res. Newburg, Me.

(7) *Isaac*, b. June, 1791, m. Polly Goodell, had 2 chil., and d. 1835. Res. Hermon.

(8) *Louisa*, b. Sept. 1793, m. Jan. 1827, Obed Knowles, a farmer, and has 8 chil. Both m. Meth. ch. Res. Hampden.

(9) *Maria*, b. Sept. 1793, twin, m. Thornton Emerson, a farmer, and has 6 chil. Res. Hermon.

(10) *Lucy*, b. 1795, m. Aug. 1839, Solomon York, b. 1792, and d. Oct. 1855. She had 4 chil., and d. June, 1856. Res. Hermon.

62. IV. SUSANNA,[5] b. Aug. 5, 1765, twin, d. 1835. She m. Eliphalet Perkins. Res. Augusta, Me. Chil.—

(1) *Nathaniel*, m. Lucy Tuttle. Res. Mercer, Me. (2) *Eliphalet*, m. Lucy Jacobs. Res. Orono, Me. (3) *Eunice*, m. Melvill Wade, of Smithfield, Me. (4) *Benj.*, m. Hannah Page, of Frankfort, Me. Res. Mass. 7 chil. (5) *Jerusha*, m. Knowles Rogers. Res. So. Orrington, Me. (6) *Charity*, m. Jonathan Perkins. (7) *Zebiah*, d. unm. in 1857. (8) *Lydia*, m. Jeremiah Nye. Res. So. O.

63. V. AARON,[5] (118) b. Oct. 12, 1767, in Eastham, d. Sept. 27, 1836, ae. 69. He m. Sept. 12, 1793, Betsey Knowles, dau. of Freeman, and b. in E., March 25, 1772. They had 2 sons and 9 daus. She resides in Hampden, Me. He rem. with his father to Deer Island, Me., and thence to Orphan's Island, and thence to Hampden, Me.

64. VI. LUCY,[5] b. Oct. 6, 1769, d. 1772.

65. VII. ELEAZER,[5] b. Oct. 16, 1771, probably d. young, as nothing is known of him by any of his kindred.

66. VIII. LUCY,[5] b. Oct. 20, 1773, d. several yrs. since. She m. Elijah Wentworth, lived in Hampden, Me., a few yrs., and then rem. to Chicago, Ill. Mr. W. was a man of some note. He kept a public house and was Postmaster, in C., at one time. Chil.—

(1) *Elijah*. (2) *Hiram*, and several b. in Ill.

67. IX. BENJAMIN,[5] (130) b. Nov. 2, 1775, d. April 23, 1848, ae. 72 yrs. He m. Ruth Knowles, dau. of Freeman, b. 1781, and d. June 11, 1853, ae. 72 yrs. She was sister of Betsey. (See No. 63.) They had 3 sons and 6 daus. He was a farmer, and m. Meth. ch. Res. Hampden, Me.

68. X. JERUSHA,[5] b. Oct. 21, 1778, d. 1852. She m. Samuel Cone, of Mercer, Me., who served in the Revolutionary War, and d. 1840. No chil. Res. Hermon, Me.

CHILDREN OF SAMUEL WALKER,[4] [29] OF EASTHAM.

69. I. SAMUEL,[5] b. Nov. 22, 1743, d. May 1, 1744.

70. II. MERCY,[5] b. Oct. 22, 1744, was pub. Nov. 1764, to Joseph Pepper, of Eastham, and had 3 chil.

71. III. SUSANNAH,[5] b. April 4, 1747, d. about 1820. She m. John Knowles, of Eastham, and had 7 sons and 3 daus.

72. IV. LYDIA,[5] b. Aug. 28, 1749, m. Asa Cole. Res. Wellfleet. She m. 2dly, Samuel Waterman, Attorney at law.

73. V. REBECCA,[5] b. Sept. 15, 1751, d. bef. 1764.

74. VI. MEHETABLE,[5] b. March 18, 1754, was pub. July 6, 1776, Joel Doane, of Eastham, and had—

(1) *Dorcas*, b. Oct. 12, 1778, m. Rev. Philander Shaw, of E.. who d about 1798. She m. 2dly, Col. Elisha Cobb, of E., who d. about 1810.

75. VII. SARAH,[5] b. Sept. 11, 1756, m. Daniel Myrick, and 2dly, Samuel Harding, of Gorham, Me.

76. VIII. JOHN,[5] b. Dec. 23, 1759, d. y.

77. IX. REBECCA,[5] b. Jan. 26, 1764, m. John Atwood, and had 1 son, Samuel. Res. Wellfleet.

BY 2d MARRIAGE.

78. X. HANNAH,[5] b. 1767, d. March 18, 1842, ae. 75 yrs. She m. Feb. 19, 1817, Benj. Higgins, of Eastham. He m. previously, Mercy. [See No. 51.]

79. XI. JOHN,[5] (139) d. about 1802, ae. about 28 yrs. He m. Deliverance Atwood, of Eastham. He was a mariner, captured by the Algerines and made a slave. After 3½ yrs. of slavery, he was redeemed, and returned to E. about 1798. Obtaining a divorce from his wife, he rem. to Boston, and m. again. He d. abroad or at sea.

80. XII. JESSE,[5] d. in West Indies, ae. about 18 yrs.

CHILDREN OF JOHN WALKER,[4] [31] OF EASTHAM.

81. I. PHEBE,[5] b. Aug. 3, 1745, (See No. 31,) m. Sept. 29, 1767, Edward Knowles, Jr., of Eastham. They had 1 dau., perhaps others.

CHILDREN OF JEREMIAH WALKER,[4] [38] OF HARWICH.

82. I. JEDIDAH,[5] b. 1757 or 8, d. about 1836. She m. Isaac Eldredge, of Harwich, and had 10 chil.

83. II. PHILENA,[5] b. about 1760, d. young.

84. III. BENJAMIN,[5] (141) b. Sept. 28, 1762, d. 1818. He m. between April, 1792 and April, 1793, Thankful Robbins, of Harwich, who was b. Aug. 13, 1768. They had 8 chil. He was a housewright. Res. Harwich.

85. IV. JAMES,[5] (149) b. 1763 or '64, d. 1847, ae. 83. He m. Mary Cahoon, of Harwich, who d. short time before her husband. They had 3 sons and 5 daus. Res. H.

86. V. JEREMIAH,[5] (157) b. 1766, d. April, 1846. He m. 1787, (pub. Dec. 3,) Lydia Small, dau. of Elijah and Barbara Godfrey, b. July 15, 1767, and d. Dec. 10, 1830. They had 5 chil. He m. 2d, Aug. 11, 1831, Mrs. Polly Phipps, dau. of John Allen, of H. He m. 3d, March 17, 1833, Mrs. Susanna Hunt, of H., sis. of 2d w. He was a shipwright and a merchant, and had considerable influence in town affairs. Res. Harwich.

87. VI. SETH,[5] (162) b. Dec. 31, 1768, m. Mercy Bassett, of Chatham, who was b. July, 1768. He was a wheelwright. Both living in Harwich, in 1855, very aged. They had 7 chil.

CHILDREN OF BENJAMIN WALKER,[4] [39] OF WALES.

88. I. JAMES,[5] b. about 1751, d. 1847, ae. 96. He m. Chloe Leach, of Bridgwater. No chil. Res. Wales.

89. II. MARSYLVIA,[5] b. ——, d. in Wales, 1795. She m. March 16, 1798, Capt. Edson. Both were of Bridgwater, when married. They settled in Brimfield, now Wales, and had 5 chil., who are dec'd.

90. III. MARSHALL,[5] (169) b. June 20, 1757, d. Feb. 1816. He m. Oct. 7 or 9, 1776, Hannah Dunbar, who was b. May 20, 1760, and d. Feb. 1816. Both were of Bridgwater, when married. He served in the War of the Revolution, with his brother James, from May, 1776 to 1777. He was a farmer. Res. South Brimfield, now Wales. He had 10 chil., 9 of whom had from 10 to 15 chil. each. They have been an industrious and respectable people, and most of them professors of religion. All of his family were religious, except-

ing one, and most of them lived to a great age. They were all large men and women. Most of the men weigh 200 lbs. and upwards.

91. IV. ANNE,[5] b. about 1761, d. 1804, in So. B., unm.

92. V. BETHANIA,[5] b. about 1763, d. in Monson, July 4, 1854, ae. 91 yrs. She m. James Dorman, and had 9 chil., b. 1784— He was one of Burgoyne's men. Res. M.

93. VI. JOSEPH,[5] (179) b. about 1767, d. June 13, 1844, ae. 77 yrs. He m. Susan Needham, and had 2 chil. He m. 2d, Thankful Robbins, of Harwich, dau. of Eleazer, and had 4 chil. He was a ship-carpenter. Res. Wales and Monson.

94. VII. SARAH,[5] b. Jan. 10, 1769, in Bridgwater, and d. in Wales, June, 1839, ae. 70 yrs. She m. Aug. 10, 1788, Jonathan Cady Richmond, who was b. in Killingly, Ct., March 13, 1763, and d. Feb. 10, 1816. Res. So. Brimfield. Chil.—

(1) *Chloe*, b. Oct. 21, 1788 or '89, m. 1800, Cyrus Dunbar, had 10 chil., and d. Oct. '58, ae. 69 yrs. (2) *James*, b. Oct. 6, '90, m. March, 1818, Olive Moulton, dau. of Daniel, of Monson, and had 5 chil. Res. M.

95. VIII. BENJAMIN,[5] (185) b. June 8, 1773, was drowned in Bloomfield, Ct., March 9, 1836, ae. 63 yrs. He was pub. July 15, 1798, to Susanna Crowell, of Harwich, who was b. Oct. 17, 1779, and d. in Hartford, Ct., Oct. 28, 1854. He was a ship-carpenter, and had 10 chil. Res. many yrs. in Hartford, Ct.

96. IX. LINUS,[5] (196) b. Dec. 3, 1776, d. Dec. 10, 1836. He m. Dec. 30, 1798, Hannah Philips, of Harwich, sister of Huldah, (See No. 162,) who was b. Jan. 22, 1778. They had 8 chil. He was insane the 25 yrs. before his death. Res. Constantia, N. Y. She lives, (1858,) in Brewerton, N. Y., and is m. ch.

SIXTH GENERATION.

CHILDREN OF PETER WALKER,[5] [50] OF EASTHAM.

97. I. HANNAH C.,[6] d. y.

98. II. DIANA,[6] b. Jan. 10, 1792, d. 1819. She m. David Brown, of Eastham, 1817. Chil.—

(1) *James*, m. Betsey Chipman. Res. Charlestown. (2) *Son*, d. y.

99. III. SARAH,[6] b. Sept. 19, 1794, m. 1818, Carmi Higgins, of Orleans, pub. Dec. 14, 1818. No chil. Res. Eastham.

100. IV. HANNAH C.,[6] d. 1845. She m. 1818, Heman Linnell, of Orleans, and had 3 chil. who d. young.

101. V. MERCY,[6] b. July 3, 1798, d. March 18, 1800.

102. VI. JOHN,[6] b. Jan. 9, 1800, d. March 19, 1800.

103. VII. PETER B.,[6] b. July 9, 1801, d. at sea, 1827.

104. VIII. MERCY,[6] b. Aug. 17, 1804, m. Joshua W. Nickerson, of Eastham. Chil.—

(1) *Abigail B.*, b. Aug. 18, 1830, m. Abel Shattuck, and has 1 son, Carmi. Res. Orleans. (2) *Joshua W.*, b. March 3, '33. (3) *Sarah H.*, b. Sept. 18, '34. (4) *William H.*, b. July 6, '36, d. '40. (5) *Laura A.*, b. Sept. 8, '38. (6) *William H.*, b. July 11, '41. (7) *John D.*, b. Feb. '43. (8) *Hannah R.*, b. May 19, '44. (9) *Mercy A.*, b. Oct. 26, '46.

105. IX. RUTH,[6] b. Jan. 10, 1806, m. William Smith, of Eastham. Res. E. Chil.—

(1) *Diana B.*, b. May 3, 1832, m. Warren May. Res. E. (2) *Lydia*, b. Jan. 30, '34, d. Dec. 25, '47. (3) *Ruth A.*, b. March 20, '37.

106. X. JOHN,[6] (203) b. May 10, 1808, m. 1831, Hannah Linnell, of Orleans, pub. Dec. 10, and has had 5 chil. Res. Eastham. This is now the only family of Walkers in E.

107. XI. ABIGAIL, d. in infancy.

CHILDREN OF DAVID WALKER,[5] [56] OF WEST BOYLSTON.

108. I. JAMES S.,[6] b. Aug. 1793, was drowned at sea by falling overboard, ae. 17 yrs.

109. II. LYDIA,[6] b. Aug. 1795, d. 1835, in W. B.

110. III. PRISCILLA,[6] b. 1797, m. Nov. 27, 1817, Vickery Baker, and has had 7 sons and 6 daus. Res. Brookfield, Vt.

111. IV. WILLIAM,[6] (208) b. Aug. 13, 1799, d. March, 1853. He m. 1822, Mary Rugg, of Leominster, and had 10 chil., 7 of whom d. young. Res. Clinton, the last 4 or 5 yrs.

112. V. JOHN K.,[6] b. Feb. 14, 1801, d. 1829, in W. B.

113. VI. NATHANIEL,[6] b. Nov. 3, 1803, was drowned, 1805.

114. VII. JEDIDAH,[6] b. May 8, 1805, m. Asa Rice, a soap manufacturer, and has 5 chil. Res. Ware Centre.

115. VIII. DAVID,[6] b. Jan. 23, 1807, d. 1826, in W. B.

116. IX. SYLVANUS,[6] (218) b. Dec. 11, 1808, m. Nov. 14, 1831, Caroline M. Reed, dau. of William, of Sterling, and b. July 23, 1809. He has had 8 chil. Res. S.

117. X. SUSANNA,[6] b. 1811, d. June, 1851, unm.

CHILDREN OF AARON WALKER,[5] [63] OF HAMPDEN, ME.

118. I. SARAH,[6] b. May 28, 1794, d. Aug. 9, 1834. She m. Sept. 12, 1813, Asa Porter, of Hampden, Me. She was m. Meth. ch. Res. H. Chil.—

(1) *Mary Ann*, b. Dec. 24, 1815, m. Capt. Obadiah Doane, of Wellfleet, and has 4 chil. Res. W.

(2) *Julia*, b. Dec. 7, 1817, m. James M. Becket, of Boston. Res. Melrose. No chil.

(3) *Sarah*, b, Nov. 14, 1819, m. Jan. 8, '39, Royal Bachelor, and has 4 sons. Res. Troy, Me.

(4) *Abigail*, b. Jan. 17, 1821, m. Nathaniel Allen, and has 2 chil. Res. Boston.

119. II. CHARLOTTE,[6] b. June 12, 1796, d. in infancy.

120. III. CHARLOTTE P.,[6] b. Jan. 30, 1798, m; June 5, 1826, John Pomroy, a farmer, of Hampden, Me. No chil. Res. H.

121. IV. FREEMAN,[6] b. Feb. 30, 1800, d. in infancy.

122. V. ZERUAH,[6] b. March 25, 1802, d. June 15, 1842. She m. May 20, 1830, Ezra Mayo, of Hampden, Me., and had 1 dau.

123. VI. RUTH,[6] b. Feb. 11, 1804, d. Feb. 19, 1838. She m. June 15, 1824, William Smith, of Hampden, Me., who d. in Ill., June, 1851. She was m. Meth ch. Chil.—

(1) *William B.* He is a teacher in Lexington, Miss., and has 2 chil. (2) *Lydia D.*, d. Sept. 1839. (3) *Aaron W.*, m. Eliza Luce, and has 2 chil. Res. H. He is a sea captain, and a worthy man. (4) *Joseph*, d. in infancy. (5) *Charles*, d. '54, at sea. (6) *Esther A.*, m. Andrew Emery, Sept. '56, a mechanic, in H.

124. VII. BETSEY,[6] b. Aug. 16, 1806, d. Dec. 20, 1841. She m. Sept. 18, 1828, Hiram Knowles, of Hampden, Me., a sea captain, who d. 1842. She was m. Meth. ch. No chil. Res. H.

125. VIII. PAULINA,[6] b. Oct. 10, 1808, m. Sept. 26, 1826, Jabez Gould, a farmer. Both m. Meth. ch. Res. Hampden, Me. Chil.—

(1) *Laura H.*, b. Nov. 11, 1828, m. Nov. 29, '55, Joseph Day, of Melrose, a boat maker. (2) *Lucy W.*, b. Oct. 5, '32, m. May 2, '54, Sam'l A. Foster,

farmer. Res. H. (3) *Amasa W.*, b. Nov. 3, '34, is a sailor, unm. (4) *Robert J.*, b. Sept. 24, '36, is a sailor, unm. (5) *Elizabeth*, b. Oct. 28, '38, unm. (6) *Charlotte P.*, b. April 9, '41. (7) *John P.*, b. April 9, '43. (8) *Lemuel A.*, b. Nov. 17, '44. (9) *David W.*, b. Sept. 15, '46, d. June 12, '50. (10) *Clara V.*, b. Aug. 12. '49. (11) *Isadora F.*, b. Nov. 17, '53.

126. IX. URSULA,[6] b. Jan. 12, 1811, d. Sept. 8, 1827.

127. X. ESTHER M.,[6] b. June 1, 1814, m. Oct. 5, 1846, Dan W. Heath, of Mass., a farmer. Res. Easton. Chil.—

(1) *Henry Wilmarth*, b. Nov. 9, 1847. (2) *Ella F.*, b. Oct. 10, '49. (3) *Lucy Ann*, b. '51. (4) *Eliz'th*, b. Nov. 12, '53. (5) *Arabella G.*, b. Sept. 5, '55. (6) *Charlotte P.*, b. July 22, '57.

128. XI. AMASA K.,[6] (226) b. Dec. 12, 1817, m. March 10, 1840, Mary Ann Cobb, of Hampden, Me., who was b. Aug. 22, 1818. He has had 6 chil. Both m. Meth. ch., and he for 25 yrs. He was Lieutenant of an Independent Company in the Aroostook War, and afterward held the office of Colonel. He has been Select-man 3 yrs., and was Representative in the State Legislature, 1854 and '55. Res. Hampden, Me.

129. XII. MEHITABLE S.,[6] b. March 29, 1820, m. David W. Swett. No chil. Res. Hampden, Me.

CHIL. OF BENJAMIN WALKER,[5] [67] OF HAMPDEN, ME.

130. I. IRAD,[6] (232) b. Oct. 18, 1809, m. Oct. 25, 1829, Emeline Peabody, who was b. June 17, 1811. He is a farmer, and has had 13 chil. Res. Hampden, Me.

131. II. VILINTA,[6] b. Nov. 11, 1811, d. June, 1844. She m. David Kendall, a farmer, of Hampden, Me. They rem. several yrs. since to Minnesota. Chil.—

(1) *Henry C.* (2) *John.* (3) *Elizabeth.* (4) *David.* (5) *Llewelyn.*

132. III. ABIGAIL,[6] b. Oct. 15, 1813, m. July 20, 1833, Eldridge G. Wing, a farmer. Res. Hampden, Me. Chil.—

(1) *Martin V.*, b. Aug. 14, 1834. (2) *Martha H.*, b. Feb. 14, '36, m. July '58, Elkanah Knowles. (3) *Ferdinand*, b. Dec. 10, '38. (4) *Elbridge G.*, b. March 22, '40. (5) *Sarah W.*, b. March 28, '42, d. June 18, '46. (6) *Augustus C.*, b. Dec. 26, '44. (7) *Aravesta*, b. Aug. 16, '46. (8) *Franklin R.*, b. April 15, '48. (9) *George E.*, b. Feb. 18, '50.

133. IV. AARON,[6] (245) b. March, 1815, m. Olive Palmer. He is a farmer, and has 4 chil. Res. Hampden, Me.

134. V. SUSAN,[6] b. June, 1818. Res. H., unm.

135. VI. SARAH,[6] b. Aug. 1820, d. 1844, m. Meth. ch.

136. VII. LUCY,[6] b. 1822, d. Sept. 1856. She m. Nathaniel Myrick, a mechanic. She was m. Meth. ch. Res. Hampden, Me. Chil.—

(1) *Frederick*, b. June, 1850. (2) *Ada*, b. Aug. '52

137. VIII. EPHRAIM,[6] b. 1824, d. 1828.

138. IX. MINERVA,[6] b. 1826, d. Feb. 6, 1854, unm.

CHILDREN OF JOHN WALKER,[5] [79] OF EASTHAM.

139. I. ABIGAIL,[6] m. Capt. Reuben Higgins, and rem. to Me.

140. II. JESSE,[6] was a seaman, and d. unm., 1812. The administration of his property states that a sister Sally was his only legitimate heir. Relatives say his only sister was named Abigail.

CHILDREN OF BENJAMIN WALKER,[5] [84] OF BREWSTER.

141. I. ISAAC,[6] b. March 30, 1794, d. May 12, 1794.

142. II. SUSAN,[6] b. Aug. 11, 1795. Res. B., unm.

143. III. JANE,[6] was pub. Aug. 7, 1819, to Elnathan Eldredge, 3d, of Harwich. She was killed on the way to Utah. Chil.—

(1) *Ziba*. (2) *Elnathan*. (3) *George S.* (4) *James B.*

144. IV. ENOCH,[6] b. April 3, 1799, d. April 3, 1818.

145. V. BENJAMIN,[6] (249) b. Nov. 5, (16) 1800, d. Jan. 29, 1850. He m. 1824, Desire Welch, of Dennis, and had 7 chil. Res. Brewster.

146. VI. JEDIDAH,[6] m. Lyman Dexter, and 2d, Sylvanus Perry. Chil. by 1st marriage—

(1) *Clark*. (2) *Eliza*.

147. VII. THANKFUL,[6] m. Nathaniel Sears, a fisherman, and had 10 chil., only 4 living. She m. 2d, ———, of Dennis, a farmer, and has 1 child. Chil. by 1st marriage—

(1) *Nath'l*. (2) *Henry*. (3) *Jedidah*. (4) *Greene*.

148. VIII. JEREMIAH,[6] (256) b. 1810, m. 1829, Aurilla Cash, of Dennis. He is a farmer, in Brewster, and has 10 chil., all living in 1856.

Children of JAMES WALKER,[5] [85] of Harwich.

149. I. Molly,[6] b. 1788, m. 1818, Seth Chase, of Harwich. No chil.

150. II. Samuel,[6] was lost in Labrador straits, unm.

151. III. Sally,[6] b. about 1791, m. March 7, 1811, Freeman Doane, of Chatham, and had 1 son. Both are dec'd.

152. IV. Rhoda,[6] m. Nov. 20, 1823, David Rogers, of Harwich, and has chil. Res. H.

153. V. James,[6] (265) m. Bethiah Hambleton, of Chatham, (pub. Dec. 29, 1814,) and had 1 son. He was a seaman. Res. Harwich.

154. VI. William,[6] (266) m. Oct. 13, 1816, Hannah Chase, of Harwich. He m. 2d, April 11, 1822, Hannah Robbins, of H. He was a mariner, and lost at sea.

155. VII. Abigail,[6] m. Nov. 3, 1823, Jonathan Eldredge, of Chatham, a fisherman, and had 2 chil. She m. 2d, —— Clark, a seaman.

156. VIII. Fanny,[6] m. Oct. 16, 1827, Timothy Coombs, of Vinal Haven, Me., a seaman, and has a large family. Res. Harwich.

Children of JEREMIAH WALKER,[5] [86] of Harwich.

157. I. Anna,[6] b. March 24, 1789, d. 1819. She m. May 24, 1807, (1808?) Capt. Edward Nickerson, Jr., of H., a seaman, and had 2 chil. She m. 2d, —— Philips, and rem. to Constatia, N. Y., where she died. Chil.—

(1) *Lydia*, b. Sept. 1809, d. June, '47. (2) *Grafton*, b. 1811. Drowned at sea, April, '40. He m. Miss Baker, and had 3 chil.

158. II. Betsey,[6] b. Oct. 14, 1793, m. Aug. 22, 1812, Capt. Sam'l Tripp, of H., a sea captain, who d. about 1842. Both m. Bap. ch. Res. Harwich. Chil.—

(1) *Samuel*, b. 1814, d. '44. (2) *Deborah*, b. '16, d. '35. (3) *Alonzo*, b. '18, m. '41, Abigail Baker, dau. of Capt. David, of South Dennis, and has had 9 chil., 5 dec'd. In early life he was a sailor, and before 18 yrs old passed through all the grades from a cabin boy to commander. He then traveled extensively in Europe, the West Indies, British Am. and U. S. After his marriage he began teaching, 1st in charge of the South Yarmouth

Academy, and with great success; then as Principal of Union Sem., No. Fairhaven; then visited Europe to inspect the educational institutions of E., and on his return took charge of the Village Sem., in Hyannis. He published an account of his European tour, entitled, "Crests from the Ocean World," which had an unprecedented sale of 11 editions, and was highly eulogized by the Am. and English Press. He is also the author of "The Fisher Boy," a Cape Cod tale, published in '56. which was well received. Since '55 he has been Principal of the Highlands Institute, Roxbury, a select Boarding and Day school for young ladies. (4) *Barbara W.*, b. '21, d. '38. (5) *Betsey J.*, b. '28, m. Dec. 5, '47, Martin L. Chase, and d. '48. (6) *Anna*, b. '33, m. Aug. 15, '52, Wm. Brown, who was lost at sea, '57. (7) *Orlando*, b. '35. Teacher in Tremont, Ill.

159. III. MARSHALL,[6] (267) b. Sept. 29, 1796. He m. Oct. 3, 1819, Rebecca Burgess, of H., and has had 11 chil. He was formerly a seaman, and now a farmer, in Harwich.

160. IV. BARBARA,[6] b. July 29, 1800, d. 1805.

161. V. ALVAN,[6] b. Jan. 16, 1805, [1804 ?] d. Jan. 28, 1857. He m. Dec. 3, 1829, Hepzibah D. Snow, dau. of Osborn, of H., and b. Dec. 1807. He was a farmer, and held the office of constable. He was proved a man of unbending integrity, preferring to sacrifice pecuniary advantage rather than moral principle. Res. H.

CHILDREN OF SETH WALKER,[5] [87] OF HARWICH.

162. I. DAVID,[6] b. about 1789, m. April 25, 1811, m. Huldah Philips, of Harwich, who is dec'd. (See No. 96.) He is a miller in H. No. chil.

163. II. JOHN,[6] (278) b. May 31, 1792, m. 1814, Ruth Rogers, of Orleans, dau. of Hezekiah, and b. Aug. 6, 1790. He is a seaman, and has had 7 chil. Res. So. Orleans.

164. III. NATHAN,[6] (285) b. Oct. 17, 1795, d. March 6, (5 ?) 1839, ae. 44 yrs. He m. Jan. 11, 1821, Lucy Moody, of Harwich, who was b. May 1, 1799, and d. June 8, 1842. He is m. Bap. ch., and has had 8 chil.

165. IV. JONATHAN,[6] (293) b. March 22, 1799, m. Oct. 8, 1822, Jane Gage, dau. of Seth, of Harwich, and has 9 chil. He has led a chequered and adventurous life, has been a farmer, sailor, shipwright, carpenter and doctor, residing in Harwich, New Bedford, Florida, and now in Linden, Sheboygan Co., Wis.

166. V. PHILINDIA,[6] b. Dec. 24, 1801, m. May 15, 1827, Samuel Snow, of Middleboro', and rem. to Taunton, 1823, living there in 1856. He is a housewright. She is m. Bap. ch. Chil.—

(1) *Samuel*, b. March 26, 1828, m. Feb. 3, '51, Ann Maria Walker, dau. of Richmond, of Exeter, R. I., and has 2 chil. (See Taunton Branch, No. 600, 113 p.) (2) *James H.*, b. Jan. 15, '31, m. Jan. 16, '54, Ruth, dau. of John Walker, of Orleans. (See No. 281.) (3) *Ezekiel*, b. June 2, '33. (4) *Benj. Walker*, b. May 16, '36. (5) *Lois H.*, b. Sept. 22, '40.

167. VI. ESTHER,[6] b. 1805, m. Nov. 13, 1828, Heman Eldredge, of Chatham, a pilot. No chil, Res. Nantucket.

168. VII. BETSEY,[6] d. 1842, ae. about 32. She m. Elbridge G. Clark, of Kingston. She was m. Bap. ch. Chil.—

(1) *Elizabeth*, b. Nov. 29, 1835. (2) *Infant*, d. without name.

CHILDREN OF MARSHALL WALKER,[5] [90] OF WALES.

169. I. ENOS,[6] (302) b. March 11, 1777, d. March, 1856, in ——, Susquehannah Co., Pa. He had a large family of chil.

170. II. DAVID,[6] (304) b. Aug. 1779, d. since 1847. Res. unknown. He m. and rem. to ——, Penn., where his wife died. He m. 2d, and rem. to New Jersey. He had a large family.

171. III. ISAIAH,[6] (305) b. March 14, 1782, in S. Brimfield, now Wales. He m. Jan. 3, 1808, Mary Aldrich, of Killingly, Ct., b. April 1, 1786. They had 6 chil. He resides in Wales, on the farm bought by his grandfather, on his removal to W. Though 78 yrs. old, he manages his farm alone, mowing his grass and taking care of his stock.

172. IV. HANNAH,[6] b. July 5, 1784, m. Jan. 6, 1805, Wm. Young, a shoemaker, b. Nov. 1783. Res. Wales. They had 10 chil., and only 3 are living. Chil.—

(1) *Wm. G.*, b. April 19, 1809, m. Nancy Town, formerly of Thompson, Ct., and has 3 chil., [1, Edward H., b. Aug. 7, '35, is a book-keeper in W. 2, Susan Richmond, b. Nov. '39. 3, Wm. Deforest, b. Aug. 11, '43?] Res. Wales. (2) *Elbridge G.*, b. May 11, '11. (3) *Sabrina*, b. March 21, '13, m. Preston F. Wight, of Wales. Res. W., and has 4 chil., [1, Wm. H., a Methodist clergman at Bellows Falls, Vt. 2, Henry Kirk. Res. Wilbraham. 3, Dau., ae. 19. 4, Dau., ae. 17 yrs. in 1859.] (4) *Susan R.*, b. May 23, '15. (5) *John S.*, b. May 19, '17. (6) *James Thompson*, b. June 27, '20. Res. Utica, N. Y.

173. V. MARSHALL,[6] b. March 12, 1787, d. young.

174. VI. ARNOLD,[6] (309) b. 1790. Res. South Gibson, Pa. He m. and has had a large family, but every appeal for information respecting them has been disregarded.

175. VII. DIANA,[6] b. April 5, 1793, in W., m. Jan. 16, 1812, Jonas Moulton, who was b. in Monson, June 17, 1782, and d. there a few yrs. since. She has had 11 chil., and lives in M.

176. VIII. CADY R.,[6] (310) b. Feb. 5, 1796, m. Electa Sparks, has had 14 chil., and 2 only are dec'd. He is a wealthy farmer, in Friendship, N. Y. Both are m. Bap. ch.

177. IX. MARSHALL KEITH,[6] (324) b. April 27, 1799, m. Sept. 17, 1818, Ann Hawley, who was b. June 2, 1802. She is m. Meth. ch. He is a farmer, and has had 10 chil. Res. Salem, Wayne Co., Pa.

178. X. SUBINUS,[6] (334) b. Aug. 5, 1801, m. and had chil. He is a successful merchant, and has been Postmaster. Res. Limestone, Cattaraugus Co., N. Y.

CHILDREN OF JOSEPH WALKER,[5] [93] OF MONSON.

179. I. HORACE,[6] (335) m. —— Smallage, of Union, Ct., and had 2 sons and 2 daus. He m. 2d, Mrs. —— Walker, of Union. Res. Plainfield, Otsego Co., N. Y.

180. II. JAMES,[6] d. in infancy.

BY 2d MARRIAGE.

181. III. JOSEPH,[6] (339) m. Hannah Peck, of Monson, and had a large family. He m. 2d, ———. Res. Stafford, Ct.

182. IV. LINUS,[6] (347) b. about 1797, m. Vienna Skinner, of Monson, and had several chil. Res. Springfield, Bradford Co., Pa.

183. V. ELEAZER R.,[6] (350) b. about 1799, m. Eliza Moulton, of Monson, and has had 2 sons. Res. M.

184. VI. CHILD,[6] d. in infancy.

CHIL. OF BENJAMIN WALKER,[5] [95] OF HARTFORD, CT.

185. I. LEVI,[6] (352) b. Jan. 19, 1799, m. 1833, Elizabeth Young, of Laurens, S. C. He was a merchant, in Unionville, S. C., and was lost in the Steam Packet Home, which was wrecked off Cape Hatteras, Oct. 7, 1837, in the passage from N. Y., to Charleston. He left a wife and dau., who have since died.

186. II. SUSAN,[6] b. Aug. 24, 1801, m. 1821, Algernon S. Cowles, a machinist. Res. Hartford, Ct. Chil.—

(1) *Ephraim*, Res. E. Windsor. (2) *Frances A.*, m. Wm. Hubbard. Res. Springfield. (3) *Sarah H.*, m. Solomon Brown. Res. Ridgefield, O. (4) *Lorin S.* Res. H. (5) *Mary A.*, m. Daniel P. Bates. Res. H. (6) *George A.* Res. H. (7) *Lester W.* (8) *Benj. L.* (9) *Jane L.* (10) *Child*, d. y.

187. III. LYMAN,[6] (353) b. Aug. 24, 1804, d. May 4, 1836. He m. Nancy Alexander, of Greenville, N. C., and had 1 son. She is dec'd. Res. G. He was a house carpenter, and d. of consumption at St. Augustine, Fla.

188. IV. SARAH,[6] b. Aug. 14, 1806, d. Dec. 8, 1832. She m. 1831, John Hatfield, a shoe dealer. No chil. Res. H.

189. V. LORIN,[6] b. Oct. 23, 1808, d. unm. He was a house carpenter. Res. Charleston, S. C. He was lost on the passage from St. Augustine, Fla., to C., Aug. 6, 1837.

190. VI. MARY,[6] b. April 11, 1811, m. July, 1833, James T. Hinsdale, a merchant tailor, who d. May 9, 1838. Res. Hartford, Ct. Chil.—

(1) *Mary*, is dec'd. (2) *James T.* Res. H.

191. VII. AMOS C.,[6] b. June 12, 1814, d. unm., at Unionville, S. C., March, 1837, of consumption.

192. VIII. EMELINE S.,[6] b. March 22, 1817, m. May, 1839, Wm. H. Miller, and d. of consumption, Dec. 2, 1840. No chil.

193. IX. JULIA A.,[6] b. Feb. 25, 1820. Res. Hartford, Ct., unm.

194. X. JANE B.,[6] b. Sept. 21, 1822, m. 1846, Fayette Brown. Res. Hartford, Ct. Chil.—

(1) *William.* (2) *Charles.* (3) *Henry.* (4) *Jennie.*

195. XI. LOUISA M.,[6] b. Nov. 14, 1824, m. 1846, Moses Church. He is a telegraphic operator. Res. Worcester. Chil.—

(1) *Edward.* (2) *Howard.* (3) *Mary.*

CHILDREN OF LINUS WALKER,[5] [96] OF CONSTANTIA, N. Y.

196. I. LEWIS,[6] b. July 2, 1800, d. May 12, 1826.

196.[1] II. SYLVIA,[6] b. July 26, 1802. She m. Augustus Miller, of Wales, and had 10 chil. He is a mason. She has obtained a divorce, and m. 2d ——. Res. Stafford, Ct.

197. III. ALENDER,[6] (354) b. March 4, 1804, m. March 4, 1830, Sophia Warner, of Onondaga, and has 8 chil. Both m. Meth. ch. Res. Onondaga, N. Y.

198. IV. SALLY,[6] b. April 27, 1806, m. March 4, 1830, Eben'r Philips, of Constantia, N. Y., a farmer, and has had 9 chil.

199. V. SAREPTA,[6] b. Sept. 19, 1808, m. Dec. 25, 1828, John B. Kathan, of Cicero, N. Y., and has had 6 chil. He is a farmer and land speculator.

200. VI. GEORGE,[6] b. Feb. 13, 1810, d. March 19, 1828.

201. VII. BROCK,[6] (362) b. April 19, 1813, d. Nov. 27, (1845?) 1846. He m. 1838, Catharine Butler, of Constantia, N. Y., and had 2 chil. She m. 2d, Geo. Turner, of ——.

202. VIII. BENJAMIN,[6] b. July 25, 1813, is unm.

SEVENTH GENERATION.

CHILDREN OF JOHN WALKER,[6] [106] OF ORLEANS.

203. I. SARAH,[7] b. Sept. 15, 1833.

204. II. PETER B.,[7] b. April 28, 1835, was lost at sea, April 6, 1848.

205. III. JOHN F.,[7] b. Sept. 9, 1837, d. Oct. 23, 1838.

206. IV. JOHN F.,[7] b. Oct. 4, 1840.

207. V. ABSALOM L.,[7] b. Dec. 3, 1841.

CHILDREN OF WILLIAM WALKER,[6] [111] OF CLINTON.

208. I. AUGUSTUS,[7] (364) b. 1823, m. about 1856, in Vt., and has had 2 chil. He is a painter in ——, Vt.

209. II. ALLEN,[7] (366) b. 1825, m. about 1848, Lydia Piper, of Hancock, Vt., and has had 4 chil. She d. about 1854. He is a boot maker. Res. Malden.

210. III. AURELIA,[7] b. 1828, m. D. F. Chaffin, of Leominster, a painter, who d. March 8, 1859. They had 3 chil., 2 d. y. Res. Clinton.

211. IV. ABIGAIL,[7] d. young.

212. V. DAVID,[7] d. young.

213. VI. SUSAN,[7] d. young.

214. VII. MARIA,[7] d. young.

215. VIII. LEONARD,[7] d. young.

216. IX. GEORGE,[7] d. young.

217. X. CHILD,[7] d. young.

CHILDREN OF SYLVANUS WALKER,[6] [116] OF STERLING.

218. I. MANDANA M.,[7] b. Jan. 5, 1833.

219. II. EDWARD P.,[7] b. Feb. 24, 1835, d. April 12, 1835.

220. III. GEORGE S.,[7] b. June 6, 1837, d. July 28, 1837.

221. IV. LEONARD T.,[7] b. May 4, 1839, d. March 9, 1840.

222. V. JANE E.,[7] b. Aug. 17, 1841, d. Sept. 11, 1841.

223. VI. WM. SERENO,[7] b. Oct. 17, 1842.

224. VII. S. BURTON,[7] b. June 4, 1844.

225. VIII. CREON K.,[7] b. June 4, 1850, d. July 23, 1850.

CHIL. OF COL. AMASA K. WALKER,[6] [127] OF HAMPDEN, ME.

226. I. CHARLES L.,[7] b. Dec. 19, 1840.

227. II. WILLIAM F.,[7] b. April 12, 1843.

228. III. ANDREW M.,[7] b. April 13, 1845, d. Oct. 28, 1846.

229. IV. MARY E.,[7] b. July 30, 1848.

230. V. SARAH N.,[7] b. Aug. 17, 1851.

231. VI. EVA DELIA,[7] b. March 4, 1859.

CHILDREN OF IRAD WALKER,[6] [130] OF HAMPDEN, ME.

232. I. BENJAMIN,[7] b. Dec. 30, 1829.

233. II. CORDELIA,[7] b. Aug. 16, 1831, m. July, 1857, Henry C. Gay, a boot maker. Res. Medway.

234. III. EMMA,[7] b. Oct. 1, 1832, m. Oct. 25, 1857, Rob't M. Laury, a seaman. Res. Thomaston, Me.

235. IV. MARY M.,[7] b. May 14, 1834, is unm., (1859.)

236. V. RUTHA A.,[7] b. Dec. 21, 1835, is unm., "

237. VI. IRAD,[7] b. Sept. 28, 1837, is unm., "

238. VII. WILLIAM H.,[7] b. Sept. 21, 1829, is unm., "

239. VIII. MELVILL M.,[7] b. July 19, 1841, is unm., "

240. IX. AMANDA M.,[7] b. Sept. 28, 1843, is unm., "

241. X. HARRIET A.,[7] b. Aug. 16, 1845, d. May 25, 1849.

242. XI. SANNOK S.,[7] b. Oct. 14, 1847.

243. XII. GUSTAVUS W.,[7] b. Nov. 13, 1849.

244. XIII. MARCELLO L.,[7] b. Oct. 19, 1851.

CHILDREN OF AARON WALKER,[6] [133] OF HAMPDEN, ME.

245. I. OLIVE,[7] b. June, 1851.

246. II. AARON,[7] b. Oct. 1853.

247. III. MATILDA,[7] b. Oct. 1855.

248. IV. JOHN,[7] b. April, 1857.

CHILDREN OF BENJAMIN WALKER,[6] [145] OF BREWSTER.

249. I. BENJAMIN,[7] (370) b. Jan. 22, 1831, d. Feb. 16, 1859. He m. ———, and had 2 chil. Res. Brewster.

250. II. JOSEPH,[7] b. Aug. 25, 1833, m. Betsey Cash, and is a fisherman. Res. Brewster.

251. III. EDMUND,[7] b. Nov. 17, 1835, m. ——— Cash, and is a fisherman.

252. IV. Keziah,[7] b. Aug. 31, 1838. She m. Samuel Walker, and has 3 chil. (See No. 266.)

253. V. Susannah,[7] b. Sept. 18, 1841, m. Timothy Clark.

254. VI. George,[7] b. Oct. 15, 1844, is a fisherman.

255. VII. Almira,[7] b. May 22, 1847.

Children of JEREMIAH WALKER,[6] [148] of Brewster.

256. I. Reuben,[7] (372) b. May 4, 1829, m. Ann, and has 1 son. He is a sailor. Res. Brewster.

257. II. Seth,[7] (373) b. March 19, 1831, m. Olive Bassett, and has 4 chil. Res. Brewster.

258. III. Jane,[7] b. Jan. 22, 1833, m. Charles ——, of Harwich.

259. IV. Jeremiah,[7] (377) b. Nov. 16, 1835, m. Matilda Case, and has 2 chil. He is a farmer in B.

260. V. Mary,[7] b. Nov. 10, 1837, m. Cyrus Cahoon, of Harwich.

261. VI. Anna,[7] b. Nov. 10, 1839, m. James Chase, of Yarmouth, a sailor.

262. VII. Daniel,[7] b. Feb. 25, 1842.

263. VIII. Isaac,[7] b. June 1, 1845.

264. IX. Ziba,[7] b. Oct. 8, 1847.

264.[1] X. Enoch,[7] b. Feb. 11, 1851.

Child of JAMES WALKER,[6] [153] of Harwich.

265. I. James,[7] b. about 1820, m. ——, in New Bedford?

Children of WILLIAM WALKER,[6] [154] of Harwich.

266. I. Samuel,[7] (380) m. Keziah Walker, (See No. 252,) and has 3 chil. Res. Brewster.

266.[1] II. William,[7] (383) m. Mercy Dean, and has 3 chil. Res. B.

CHILDREN OF MARSHALL WALKER,[6] [159] OF HARWICH.

267. I. JOSHUA,[7] b. April 1, 1820, d. ae. 2 yrs.

268. II. HANNAH,[7] b. Dec. 3, 1821, m. David Howes, Jr., of Dennis, and has had 3 chil., 1 dec'd. He is a seaman. Res. D.

269. III. JEREMIAH,[7] (379) b. about 1824, m. Sarepta Nickerson, of Harwich, and has had 1 child. Res. H.

270. IV. REBECCA,[7] m. Lorenzo Doane, of H., a seaman, and has had 2 chil., 1 dec'd.

271. V. LYDIA S.,[7] b. 1829, d. Aug. 16, 1856. She m. about 1849, Freeman Nickerson, of H., and had 2 chil.

272. VI. MARY,[7] b. about 1831. She m. Feb. 11, 1851, Alpheus M. Eldredge, of H., a mason, and has 2 chil.

273. VII. SUSAN,[7] b. about 1833, was unm., in 1856.

274. VIII. BARBARA,[7] b. about Dec. 1837, m. July 22, 1856, Ensign R. Raymond, of H., a seaman.

275. IX. HARRIET,[7] b. Sept. 1840. Res. Harwich.

276. X. HENRY,[7] b. 1843. Res. Harwich.

277. XI. ELEANORA F.,[7] b. April, 1846, d. April, 1852.

CHILDREN OF JOHN WALKER,[6] [163] OF ORLEANS.

278. I. REBECCA,[7] b. Nov. 3, 1814, m. Dec. 14, 1837, Eleazer Rogers, Jr., son of Eleazer, and Elizabeth, and b. Feb. 1, 1815. Res. South Orleans. He is a mariner. Chil.—

(1) *Sarah W.*, b. April 26, 1839, m. Francis W. Rogers. (2) *Rebecca F.*, b. Nov. 3, '40. (3) *George*, b. Aug. 23, '42. (4) *Tamesin*, b. July 21, '45.

279. II. NANCY R.,[7] b. Sept. 8, 1816, m. Dec. 17, 1835, Yates Rogers, of Orleans, a seaman, and has had 5 chil. Res. O.

280. III. SARAH M.,[7] b. Sept. 13, 1819, m. Jan. 21, 1839, Wm. Sparrow, of Orleans, a mariner, and has 2 chil.

281. IV. RUTH,[7] b. Sept. 15, 1821, d. July 29, 1854, ae. 33 yrs. She m. Jan. 16, 1854, James H. Snow, of Taunton, her cousin, and son of Philindia. (See No. 166.)

282. V. SETH,[7] (386) b. Aug. 17, 1823, d. Aug. 31, 1855, in Port Aux Prince. He m. April 30, 1848, Phebe S. Mayo, of Orleans, and had 3 chil.

283. VI. MEHETABLE R.,[7] b. Oct. 5, 1826, m. June 24, 1847, Elisha Hopkins, Jr., of Orleans, a mechanic, and had 2 chil. Res. O.

284. VII. JOHN W.,[7] (389) b. July 15, 1830, m. Nov. 13, 1851, Susan Thomas, of Labrador, British America, and has 1 dau. He is a mariner. Res. Labrador.

CHILDREN OF NATHAN WALKER,[6] [164] OF HARWICH.

285. I. BETSEY M.,[7] b. Dec. 16, 1821, d. unm., Sept. 28, 1841.

286. II. SAMUEL,[7] b. Nov. 17, 1823, d. Oct. 11, 1824.

287. III. SEREDA L.,[7] b. Aug. 8, 1825, d. April 16, 1848, in Nantucket. She m. 1843, Ebenezer B. Gould, in N. No chil.

288. IV. MERCY,[7] b. Sept. 15, 1827, m. June 1, 1850, Benj'n Matthews, Jr., of Yarmouth. Res. Y.

289. V. NATHAN,[7] (390) b. Dec. 25, 1829, m. Jan. 3. 1850, Fanny H. Eldredge, of Harwich, and has had 1 child. He is a seaman in Harwich.

290. VI. LUCY ANN,[7] b. Feb. 27, 1832, m. Jan. 23, 1856, Wm. M. Rogers, of Harwich. Res. H.

291. VII. SAMUEL,[7] b. June 30, 1835. Res. Orleans, unm.

292. VIII. JONATHAN,[7] b. Nov. 19, 1838, d. June 30, 1839.

CHIL. OF JONATHAN WALKER,[6] [165] OF LINDEN, WIS.

293. I. JOHN B.,[7] (391) b. May 13, 1823, m. Eliza A. Philips, and had 2 chil. He m. 2d, Daty Chase? and has 2 chil. Res. Port Washington, Washington Co., Wis., 1860.

294. II. ALTEMERA,[7] b. Jan. 13, 1827, m. Allen Chase, of Harwich, a seaman, and has had 9 chil., 1 dec'd. Res. H.

295. III. NANCY C.,[7] b. Jan. 7, 1828, m. Lewis Berry, a seaman, and has 4 chil. Res. South Dartmouth.

296. IV. SAVIAH J.,[7] b. March 11, 1830, m. Zadock K. Chase, a seaman, and has had 3 chil., 1 dec'd. Res. West Harwich.

297. V. MARY,[7] b. April 8, 1832, m. J. B. Lucas, in Plymouth, and has 3 chil. Res. Linden, Sheboygan Co., Wis.

298. VI. MARIA C.,[7] b. July 18, 1841, in Pensecola, Fla.

299. VII. LLOYD G.,[7] b. July 18, 1841, " " "

300. VIII. WILLIAM W.,[7] b. May 13, 1843.

301. IX. GEORGE F.,[7] b. Feb. 13, 1848.

CHILDREN OF ENOS WALKER,[6] [169] OF ——, PENN.

302. I. WARREN R.,[7] (392) m. and has chil. Res. So. Gibson, Pa.

303. II. WILLARD,[7] (393) " " "

There are other sons or daus., but it has been impossible to learn any thing concerning them.

CHILDREN OF ISAIAH WALKER,[6] [171] OF WALES.

305. I. MARY,[7] b. July 25, 1809, m. Davis B. Nelson, a farmer. Res. Wales.

305.[1] II. BENSON D.,[7] b. Jan. 9, 1811, d. April 5, 1814.

306. III. ELIZA,[7] b. Feb. 26, 1813, m. Orin Foskett, a moulder. Res. Worcester.

307. IV. CAROLINE,[7] b. July 9, 1815, m. Joseph C. Hunter, a shoemaker. Res. Brimfield.

308. V. MALORA,[7] b. July 31, 1822. She m. Edward W. Potter, a blacksmith. Res. Brimfield.

308.[1] VI. EMELINE,[7] b. June 1, 1827, d. March 7, 1829.

CHIL. OF ARNOLD WALKER,[6] [174] OF SOUTH GIBSON, PA.

309. I. Some are in S. G., some in Mich., and several in California. The compiler could obtain no details.

CHIL. OF CADY R. WALKER,[6] [176] OF FRIENDSHIP, N. Y.

310. I. ELMIRA,[7] b. Aug. 3, 1814, m. S. C. Cotton, of Friendship, N. Y.; a farmer, and has 3 chil. He has been High Sheriff. Res. F.

311. II. DENNIS E.,[7] b. May 10, 1816, m. Lucy Godfrey. He is a farmer, in Lima, N. Y.

312. III. ELBRIDGE G.,[7] b. May 19, 1818, m. Matilda Wood, and is a farmer, in Lake Mills, Wis.

313. IV. ELECTA,[7] b. May 29, 1820, m. Jefferson Hosley, a farmer. Res. Hinsdale, N. Y.

314. V. CADY,[7] b. July 12, 1822, d. Dec. 3, 1841.

315. VI. LYMAN LEE,[7] b. Nov. 9, 1824, m. Lucinda Dunn. He is a farmer in Hinsdale, N. Y.

316. VII. LAURA P.,[7] b. Sept. 1, 1826, m. George Scott, a farmer. Res. Oshkosh, Wis.

317. VIII. SAREPTA,[7] b. June 12, 1829, m. Harrison Gillett, a cooper. Res. F.

318. IX. MELITA,[7] b. Oct. 10, 1831, m. —— Gilbert, a cooper. Res. Cuba, N. Y.

319. X. MELISSA,[7] b. March 13, 1834, m. James Wisner, a farmer. Res. F.

320. XI. PHILO DUNBAR,[7] b. March 24, 1836, m. Cara Matthews. He is a farmer in Oshkosh, Wis.

321. XII. MARCIA,[7] b. June 3, 1838, d. Oct. 13, 1860. She m. Daniel H. Smith, a farmer. Res. Berlin Heights, O.

322. XIII. JOSEPHINE,[7] b. Oct. 5, 1840, m. William Burt. Res. Decatur, Mich.

323. XIV. ADDISON,[7] b. Feb. 4, 1843, is unm. Res. F.

CHIL. OF MARSHALL K. WALKER,[6] [177] OF SALEM, PA.

324. I. JOHN B.,[7] (394) b. June 13, 1820, m. Oct. 26, 1843, Elmira Tiffany, who was b. June 2, 1825, and d. June 28, 1853. He m. 2d, Jane Hollister. He is m. Meth. ch., and a farmer, and has had 6 chil.

325. II. SABINUS,[7] (400) b. Dec. 24, 1821, m. July 11, 1844, Delancy Carpenter. He is a farmer, in Salem, Pa., and has had 6 chil.

326. III. GEORGE W.,[7] (406) b. Feb. 17, 1824, m. Dec. 30, 1844, Eunice Packer, who was b. Nov. 21, 1827. He is a merchant, in South Gibson, Pa., and has 3 chil.

327. IV. ALANSON B.,[7] (409) b. April 30, 1826, m. March 30, 1849, Laura A. Hollister, who was b. Oct. 26, 1825. He is a merchant, in Salem, Pa., and has 2 chil.

328. V. BETSEY ANN,[7] b. May 21, 1828, m. March, 1851, Charles M. West, who was b. April 2, 1817. Both m. ch. Chil.—
(1) *Charles Nelson*, b. April 3, 1852. (2) *Arthur Legrand*, b. March 3, '56. (3) *Wm. J.*, b. June 25, '58.

329. VI. MYRA C.,[7] b. May 23, 1833, m. Oct. 20, 1859, Geo. W. Geer, M. D., who was b. Aug. 4, 1835. She is m. Meth. ch. He is a Physician, in Salem, Pa.

330. VII. SOLOMON TAYLOR,[7] (411) b. Aug. 8, 1835, m. Aug. 15, 1856, Melissa Jones. He is a farmer, in Salem, Pa., and has 1 dau.

331. VIII. IRA TAYLOR,[7] b. May 22, 1838, m. Nov. 16, 1859, Oralia A. Barnes, who was b. Nov. 11, 1839. He is a Methodist Clergyman. Res. Lynn, Pa.

332. IX. NELSON L.,[7] b. Aug. 28, 1841, is a Teacher, in Salem.

333. X. HARRIET M.,[7] b. May 3, 1848. Res. Salem, Pa.

CHIL. OF SUBINUS WALKER,[6] [178] OF LIMESTONE, N. Y.

334. I. All efforts to learn about them have failed.

CHIL. OF HORACE WALKER,[6] [179] OF PLAINFIELD, N. Y.

335. I. Two SONS,[7] and 2 DAUS.,[7] names not reported.

CHIL. OF JOSEPH WALKER,[6] [181] OF STAFFORD, CT.

339. I. He has a large family—not reported.

CHIL. OF LINUS WALKER,[6] [182] OF SPRINGFIELD, PA.

347. I. He has several chil., but the compiler has been unable to learn even their names.

CHILDREN OF ELEAZER R. WALKER,[6] [183] OF MONSON.

350. I. SON,[7] d. about 1838.

351. II. SON,[7] m. Trask? d. about 1858, ae. about 30 yrs.

CHILD OF LEVI WALKER,[6] [185] OF UNIONVILLE, S. C.

352. I. SARAH,[7] d. since 1837.

CHILD OF LYMAN WALKER,[6] [187] OF ——.

353. I. ALEXANDER,[7] d. young.

CHIL. OF ALENDER WALKER,[6] [197] OF ONONDAGA CO., N.Y.

354. I. LYMAN,[7] b. after 1830, is a school teacher.

355. II. WILLIAM,[7] is a farmer.

356. III. LEWIS,[7] is a cooper.

357. IV. CHARLOTTE,[7] m. 1855, Albert Potter, rem. West and has 1 son.

358. V. WILLARD.[7]

359. VI. ALBERT.[7]

360. VII. CICERO.[7]

361. VIII. ELLEN.[7]

CHIL. OF BROCK WALKER,[6] [201] OF CONSTANTIA, N. Y.

362. I. SALLY MARIA,[7] d. ae. 5 mos.

363. II. MELVIN W.?[7] b. about 1843.

EIGHTH GENERATION.

CHILDREN OF AUGUSTUS WALKER,[7] [208] OF ——, VT.

364. I. Two CHIL.,[8] names not reported.

CHILDREN OF ALLEN WALKER,[7] [209] OF MALDEN.

366. I. FOUR CHIL.,[8] names not reported.

CHILDREN OF BENJAMIN WALKER,[7] [249] OF BREWSTER.

370. I. OLIVE,[8] b. about 1855.

371. II. MARY,[8] b. about 1857.

CHILD OF REUBEN WALKER,[7] [256] OF BREWSTER.

372. I. REUBEN,[8] b. July 6, 1852.

CHILDREN OF SETH WALKER,[7] [257] OF BREWSTER.

373. I. SETH,[8] b. Oct. 8, 1852.

374. II. OLIVE,[8] b. Oct. 20, 1853.

375. III. CYRUS,[8] b. Aug. 1855.

376. IV. LUCY ANN,[8] b. Sept. 1856.

CHILDREN OF JEREMIAH WALKER,[7] [259] OF BREWSTER.

377. I. JEREMIAH,[8] b. Jan. 1857.

378. II. AURILLA,[8] b. Aug. 1858.

CHILD OF JEREMIAH WALKER,[7] [269] OF HARWICH.

379. I. EUSELIA,[8] b. 1851, d. Dec. 29, 1851.

CHILDREN OF SAMUEL WALKER,[7] [266] OF BREWSTER.

380. I. ——,[8] b. about 1853.

381. II. SAMUEL,[8] b. about 1856.

382. III. EDMUND,[8] b. Sept. 21, 1859.

CHILDREN OF WILLIAM WALKER,[7] [266[1]] OF BREWSTER.

383. I. HANNAH?[8] b. about 1852.

384. II. WILLIAM,[8] b. about 1855.

385. III. TIMOTHY,[8] b. about 1858.

CHILDREN OF SETH WALKER,[7] [282] OF ORLEANS.

386. I. ARTHUR E.,[8] b. Sept. 16, 1849.
387. II. ELBRIDGE M.,[8] b. Jan. 2, 1852.
388. III. PHEBE A.,[8] b. July 9, 1855.

CHILD OF JOHN W. WALKER,[7] [284] OF LABRADOR.

389. I. ELIZA T.,[8] b. Jan. 9, 1853.

CHILD OF NATHAN WALKER,[7] [289] OF HARWICH.

390. I. CHILD,[8] d. y.

CHIL. OF JOHN B. WALKER,[7] [293] OF PORT WASHINGTON, WIS.

391. I. Two SONS[8] and 2 DAUS., whose names are not reported.

CHIL. OF WARREN R. WALKER,[7] [302] OF SO. GIBSON, PA.

392. I. ——— ———. No report.

CHIL. OF WILLARD WALKER,[7] [303] OF SO. GIBSON, PA.

393. I. ——— ———. No report.

CHILDREN OF JOHN B. WALKER,[7] [324] OF SALEM, PA.

394. I. FRANCIS E.,[8] b. Oct. 21, 1844, d. Oct. 12, 1846.
395. II. EMMA F.,[8] b. Aug. 6, 1848.
396. III. JOHN F. E.,[8] b. July 14, 1851, d. Aug. 30, 1853.
397. IV. ALMIRON C.,[8] b. June 18, 1853, d. Sept. 14, 1853.
398. V. ASA EUGENE,[8] b. July 3, 1856.
399. VI. ANNA I.,[8] b. Jan. 20, 1858.

CHILDREN OF SABINUS WALKER,[7] [325] OF SALEM, PA.

400. I. GEORGE W.,[8] b. April 22, 1845.
401. II. DANIEL WEBSTER,[8] b. Oct. 11, 1846, d. Aug. 24, 1847.
402. III. MANNING D.,[8] b. Aug. 8, 1848.
403. IV. JANE E.,[8] b. Nov. 25, 1850.
404. V. EMMA D.,[8] b. March 21, 1852.
405. VI. LILLIAN,[8] b. Jan. 8, 1854.

CHILDREN OF GEO. W. WALKER,[7] [326] OF SO. GIBSON, PA.

406. I. CHARLES,[8] b. May 27, 1847.
407. II. DELLA,[8] b. June 8, 1854.
408. III. CARRIE MALVINA,[8] b. May 20, 1859.

CHIL. OF ALANSON B. WALKER,[7] [327] OF SALEM, PA.

409. I. VICTORINE VIOLA,[8] b. April 28, 1850.
410. II. WM. MARSHALL,[8] b. Aug. 7, 1852.

CHILD OF SOLOMON T. WALKER,[7] [330] OF SALEM, PA.

411. I. LINDA,[8] b. Jan. 23, 1858.

1. JOHN WALKER,[1] (2)

OF MARSHFIELD,

AND HIS DESCENDANTS.

HIS origin, and the date of his birth, and of his emigration to this country, are unknown. He first appears in 1643, and his name is in the list of those able to bear arms at that time. Only the scantiest details have been gleaned by the most diligent search for information respecting him. There is no indication of any relationship between him and the other Walkers of the Old Colony. He occupied no prominent position, and was entrusted with no public services. His life was brief. Dying in the prime of his manhood, there was little opportunity, even if his abilities qualified him, to participate in public affairs, so as to have his name conspicuous in the records of the town or Colony. He was on the grand inquest in 1654, and took the oath of fidelity in 1657.

He m. Oct. 20, 1654, Lydia Reed, of Marshfield, dau. of Mrs. Margaret (Reed) Howland, who m. 2d, Arthur Howland, Sen., of M. He had 1 son and 3 daus., and d. or was buried Dec. 11, 1663. In'y, £57: 9: 9. Mr. Howland was a zealous Quaker, and it is probable that, John Walker, his son-in-law, adopted the same religious opinions. Many of his descendants, some in every generation, to the present time, have been members of the Society of Friends. There is a burying ground of this people on the ancient Howland estate, where the early families, bearing these names, Walker and Howland, were buried. As the discipline of this Society did not until lately, allow of memorial stones, no data can be gathered respecting those whose dust is deposited there.

The descendants of John Walker have not been numerous. The family is a small one. The earlier and present generations have been characterized by industry, economy and cheerfulness, and have belonged, with scarcely an exception, to the mechanical and agricultural classes. They have been long-lived and some have reached a great age.

SECOND GENERATION.

CHILDREN OF JOHN WALKER,[1] [1] OF MARSHFIELD.

2. I. LYDIA,[2] b. Sept. 30, 1655, m. March 17, 1684, Wm. Fisher.

3. II. JOHN,[2] (6) b. Oct. 26, 1657, d. 1747, in his 90th yr. Whom he married is unknown. He was a blacksmith, lived in Marshfield, and was a member of the Soc. of Friends. An abstract of his will, made July 13, 1747, is as follows. "To my son, Isaac, improvement of homestead, and meadow land and wood land, in M., and at my decease, the same to go to my gd. son Isaiah and heirs, they paying to heirs of my son John, £100. To gd. son Isaac, all my lands in Pembroke. To gd. son, John, my silver whistle. After debts, funeral charges are paid, all my moveable estate remaining, I give to my gd. chil. My son, Isaac, and gd. son, Isaiah, to be executors." He made his mark, and his will was proved, Aug. 8, 1747. In'y £1376: 14s.

4. III. MARTHA.[2] Nothing is known concerning her.

5. IV. MARY,[2] m. Jan. 29, 1684–5, John Howland, of Duxbury.

THIRD GENERATION.

CHILDREN OF JOHN WALKER,[2] [3] OF MARSHFIELD.

6. I. ISAAC,[3] (8) d. 1750. He m. Oct. 3, 1715, Bethiah Norcut, and had 5 chil. He was a blacksmith and lived in Marshfield. His will was proved Feb. 4, 1750. The In'y of his widow was taken Oct. 7, 1763. He was a Friend.

7. II. JOHN,[3] (13) d. before 1747. (See will of his father, No. 3.) He m. and had chil. or "heirs," probably a son John, to whom was bequeathed the "silver whistle," and others perhaps. There is no record of this John in Marshfield or Plymouth Co. The compiler several yrs. ago found a John Walker, in Dartmouth Rec., as early as 1721, but knew nothing of his origin. Tracing his descendants and finding them mostly members of the Society of Friends, it occurred to him recently, that this John may have rem. to D. On examination it was found that John of D. d. 1742, which harmonizes with John's

(No. 3) will;—he was a blacksmith and a Quaker, and such were this John's father and ancestry. He had a son John, and so had John, of M., for the "gd. son John," in the will, must be his son,—Isaac, his only brother, having no son John. In the list of his 5 chil. in D. Rec., he is called John Jr. His will was proved Oct. 19, 1742. The same name, same religious faith, same occupation, with dates concurring, leave no room for doubt, that this John Jr., removed to Dartmouth. His descendants, with few exceptions, have been members of the Soc. of Friends.

FOURTH GENERATION.

Children of ISAAC WALKER,[3] [6] of Marshfield.

8. I. Isaac,[4] (18) b. Aug. 8, (25?) 1716, d. 1813, ae. 97 yrs. He m. Abigail Saunders, dau. of John, and had 7 chil. He was a blacksmith and having inherited lands in Pembroke by the will of his grand father, in 1747, he rem. there, as early as 1753. He was the ancestor of the Pembroke Walkers and a Friend. His will was proved June 7, 1813. In'y $3881, 87 cts. The tradition among his descendants in Pembroke, that he was b. in England, is without any foundation, as the ancient wills and deeds show.

9. II. Abraham,[4] (25) b. Feb. 6, 1718, d. 1800. He m. 1750, Betsey Simmons, of Duxbury, whose will was proved, Sept. 7, 1802. In'y $1201. He was a blacksmith, and had 4 chil. Res. Marshfield. The appraisers of his estate were appointed Dec. 23, 1800.

He was quite a noted Tory, and piloted the British troops (who were stationed in Marshfield by Gen. Gage, prior to the Revolution,) to a place suitable for embarkation on Marshfield beach, where a vessel from Boston was in the offing waiting to receive them. This occurred when the news of the battle at Lexington reached M. He with 2 sons, Zara and Benjamin joined the Loyalists at Boston. The sons went away with the British in their evacuation of the town. The father, while fishing near Boston light, for the loyal party, was taken prisoner by a rebel craft, and carried to Springfield jail for safe keeping, he having been one of the 23 Tories who returned thanks to Gen. Gage and Admiral Graves, "for their ready and kind interposition in sending troops to protect them from the threatened insults of their neighbors," meaning the Whig or Revolutionary party. This very party on account of his family, petitioned for his release from prison, and restoration to his family, on the usual conditions which the times demanded. His confession of past bad conduct and promise of good for the future, with that of 11 others, is entered on the books of the town, under date of July 14, 1777.

An old gentleman, Isaac Thomas, living in M., 1858, about 94 yrs. of age, who was present when the repentant Tory returned and met his family, could give quite a graphic description of the scene. It is presumed that the Messrs. Walkers proved true friends to their country, after their recantation of Tory sympathies and principles.

10. III. BETHIAH,[4] b. Jan. 19, 1720, m. before 1763, —— Mosur, (probably Mosher.) Nothing is known of them or their descendants.

11. IV. LYDIA,[4] b. March 13, 1721, m. Elisha Sherman? of Marshfield, and had 3 chil., or perhaps m. 1st, —— Barker, 2d, Jeremiah Crooker, and 3d, John Chubbuck.

12. V. ISAIAH,[4] (30) b. Aug. 12, 1724, d. 1793. Appraisers were appointed May 22, 1793. In'y £394. He m. April 5, 1750, Bathsheba Sherman, who was b. May 18, and d. — 20, 1811, ae. 78 yrs. They were Friends, and had 9 chil. He was a blacksmith, and settled on a portion of the ancient homestead in Marshfield. His house is still standing, owned and occupied by his descendants. He was a Loyalist and refugee in the Revolution, but at length returned to M., and made a confession July 17, 1777, with 9 others including the Rev. Atherton Wales, of the Second Parish in M. This confession is preserved in the Town Records.

CHIL. OF JOHN WALKER,[3] [7] OF MARSHFIELD & DARTMOUTH.

13. I. MARY,[4] b. Nov. 16, 1721, was pub. Sept. 22, 1750, to Job Manchester, of Tiverton, R. I., and had 1 dau. Res. New Bedford.

14. II. HANNAH,[4] b. Jan. 7, 1722–3, m. David Bennett, of Tiverton, R. I., and had chil.

15. III. JOHN,[4] (39) b. April 12, 1725, (Dartmouth Rec.) April 23, 1726, (Old Fam. Bible,) d. in Stillwater, N. Y., July 4, 1804, ae. 78 yrs., 2 mos. and 11 days. He m. Margaret, dau. of Joseph and Mehetable Mosher, b. in Bristol, March 25, 1725, and d. April 8,

1801, ae. 76 yrs., 14 days. They had 7 chil. He was a blacksmith, inheriting the occupation of his father and ancestors. He early rem. from Dartmouth to Stillwater, N. Y.

16. IV. GENEVRA,[4] b. June 12, 1728–9, m. Gifford. Res. Monument, near Sandwich. Nothing more is known of them.

17. V. KEZIAH,[4] b. Sept. 16, 1730, d. Aug. 8, 1818, in 88th yr. She m. Seth Russell, of New Bedford, who d. 1821, ae. 92. She was a Quakeress, and a woman of uncommon excellence. He was a wealthy, prominent and honored merchant of N. B. No man did more business, or was more influential in securing commercial importance to New Bedford. He held all the town offices, was Select-man in the time of the Revolution, and went on board of the English man of war, to confer with the officers in regard to the destruction of the town. Chil.—

(1) *Seth*, m. Elizabeth Swain, dau. of Thaddeus of Nantucket, and was an active merchant in N. B. Chil., 1, Meribah, m. Cyrus Keith, of Charleston, S. C., 2d, Geo. Tyson, of Boston, and d. in Baltimore. 2, Sarah, d. unm. 3, Benj., m. Hannah Howland, of N. B. Res. N. B., (1857.) 4, George, m. Alice Butler, dau. of Peter. Res. Cincinnati, O. 5, Seth, m. Maria Haskell, dau. of Eli, and d. at Panama, of cholera, about 1849. 6, Eliza, d. unm. 7, Anna, m. Capt. Caleb Anthony, of N. B., where they live. 8, Child, d. in infancy. 9, Child, d. in infancy.

(2) *Charles*, m. Martha Tillinghast, of Newport, R. I., and d. in Albany, N. Y., on a visit to a dau. Chil., 1, John Summers, m. 1826, Lydia Macy, of N. B. He was a grad. of Harv. Coll., and a lawyer in Taunton, and a partner of Theophilus Parsons, Esq. He was also a Quaker, and d. in N. B. 2, Abby T., m. Capt. Alexander H. Campbell, of Boston, and d. early in N. B. 3, Mary, m. Peter Van O. Linda, M. D., of Albany. Res. A. 4, Martha, m. James Allen, Esq., of Richmond, Va., and is dec'd. 5, Keziah, m. Ezra Bassett, Esq., of N. B., a lawyer, and 2d, Capt. Benj. Price, of N. B., who d. suddenly, 1859, ae. 67 yrs. 6, Child, d. in infancy. 7, Child, d. in infancy.

FIFTH GENERATION.

CHILDREN OF ISAAC WALKER,[4] [8] OF PEMBROKE.

18. I. JOHN,[5] (46) b. Feb. 28, 1743, d. 1809. Appraisers were appointed Dec. 20. He m. Deborah Rickard, and had 3 chil. Res. Pembroke. In'y, $1054.

19. II. SAUNDERS,[5] b. Dec. 2, 1745, d. in P., a sailor, and unm.

20. III. LYDIA,[5] m. Joshua Winslow, and rem. from Pembroke to place unknown.

21. IV. MARY.[5] Not mentioned in her father's will.

22. V. ABIGAIL SAUNDERS,[5] m. after 1790, Silas Veazie, and had 4 daus. Res. Pembroke.

23. VI. GEORGE,[5] d. ae. about 90 yrs., and unm.

24. VII. ISAAC,[5] (49) d. about 1848, ae. about 100 yrs. He m. Lydia Dawes, of Marshfield, and had 1 dau. Res. Pembroke.

CHILDREN OF ABRAHAM WALKER,[4] [9] OF MARSHFIELD.

25. I. CARDIS,[5] b. July 2, 1752, d. unm., in Readfield, Me., at an advanced age.

26. II. BENJAMIN,[5] (50) b. March 25, 1754, d. ae. 72 yrs. He m. about 1780, Hannah Bunce, dau. of Zebediah, of Long Island. She was m. Pres. ch., and d. ae 77 yrs. He, with his father, brother and cousin, joined the Loyalists in the Revolution. He was proscribed and banished in 1778; and went away with the British, in their evacuation of Boston, but after a time, returned to Marshfield, and became a good Whig and patriot. In early life, he was a coaster, and visited L. I., where he married. Living in M. several yrs., he rem. about 1810, to Smithtown, L. I. He had 12 chil., was a farmer, and m. Meth. ch.

27. III. ZARA,[5] b. April 12, 1756, joined the Loyalists, and was proscribed and banished in 1778. He and his cousin Gideon, (No. 30,) went away with the British troops, in their evacuation of Boston, and never returned. His end is unknown.

28. IV. BETTY,[5] b. Nov. 24, 1760, d. before April 15, 1803. She m. John Kent, and had several chil. They rem. to Readfield, Me., about 1800.

29. V. JOEL,[5] b. Oct. 9, 1765, d. May 11, 1836. He m. Sally Turner, of Scituate, who d. March, 1853, ae. 82, or in 82d yr. No chil. Res. Duxbury.

CHILDREN OF ISAIAH WALKER,[4] [12] OF MARSHFIELD.

30. I. GIDEON,[5] b. Dec. 20, 1750, m. Ruth ——. He joined the Loyalists in the Revolution and was proscribed and banished in 1778. He went away with the British troops, and d. in early manhood. An appraisal of his estate was ordered Feb. 19, 1784. He was a blacksmith. She m. 2d, Joshua Winslow, of Duxbury.

31. II. Bathsheba,[5] b. Dec. 7, 1752, m. 1772, John Holmes, and had 1 son and 3 daus.

32. III. Isaiah,[5] b. March 3, 1755, d. sometime in the Revolution.

33. IV. Bethiah,[5] b. Nov. 15, 1757, m. Peleg Thomas, and had 1 son and 3 daus.

34. V. Daniel,[5] (62) b. July 15, 1760, m. May 6, 1764, Experience Fuels, dau. of Barnabas and Experience, b. April 12, 1762, and d. Aug. 12, 1846. They rem. from M., July 4, 1804, to Knox, Me., where some of his descendants still reside. He was a farmer and had 5 chil.

35. VI. Asa,[5] (67) b. May 21, 1763, d. April 8, 1820, in his 57th yr. He m. Nov. 28, 1792, Abigail Baker, dau. of Charles, of Marshfield. She d. April 8, 1812, ae. 42 yrs. He m. 2d, April 15, 1813, Lydia Thomas, dau. of Zenas, of M. She d. March 19, 1858, ae. 81 yrs. He was a farmer in M., and had 8 chil.

36. VII. Levi,[5] (75) b. July 9, 1766, d. Dec. 20, 1854, ae. 88 yrs. (Ins.) He m. Ruth, only child of Ezra and Ruth (Winslow) Cushman, of Marshfield. She d. May 27, 1789, ae. 21, leaving one dau. He m. 2d, Zeruiah Holmes, dau. of Ephraim, of Kingston, b. Jan. 20, 1771, and d. April 12, 1857, (Fam. Rec.,) April 5, 1857, (Ins.) He had 7 chil., and was a farmer. Res. M.

37. VIII. Sarah,[5] b. May 22, 1769, d. March 16, 1854, ae. 84 yrs. She m. Thomas Bourn, who d. Oct. 20, 1807, ae. 47 yrs.

"Aunt Bourne," as she was familiarly termed in M., was a woman of much usefulness. Left a widow with a young family, and but small property, she took up the occupation of nursing, in which business she became distinguished, and did not vacate her office till about eighty years of age. She retained, till her decease, measurably, the fashion of the costume worn by her in the prime of her life, never dropping the full boned stays, or the bright scarlet cloak, fashionable at that period of her earthly existence. Her funeral services were performed by Rev. Mr. Alden, Pastor of the 1st Cong. Ch., whose text on the occasion, was Gen. 35th ch., 8th v., viz., "Deborah, Rebekah's nurse, died, and she was buried beneath Bethel, under an oak." Chil.—

(1) *Thomas*, m. Mary Holmes, and d. May 9, 1831, ae. 26. No chil. (2) *Betsey*, b. Feb. 11, 1796. Res. M., unm. (3) *Abigail*, b. Jan. 20, 1800, m. James Sprague. Res. M. (4) *Lucy*, b. April 21, 1803, m. Nathaniel Stevens, and d. June 13, 1839.

38. IX. James,[5] (82) b. Oct. 7, 1771, d. May 23, 1844. He m. July 19, 1795, Alice Sherman, who was b. Dec. 26, 1773, and d. Sept. 20, 1800. They rem. from Marshfield, to Readfield, Me. He m. 2dly, Sept. 16, 1801, Betsey Barrell, dau. of Wm., b. in Scituate, Aug. 11, 1782, and d. Oct. 3, 1806. They rem. from R. to Knox, Me., where he commenced clearing a farm and building a small house in the woods. The first season, he carried all his provision on his back, from R. to K., a distance of 40 miles. The next winter, he hauled his provision to the south part of Montville, the nearest point he could reach by road, at that time, and from M., carried them on his back 8 miles. The 2d summer, he raised corn and carried it to and from the mill on his back, a distance of 6 miles. In 1804, he sold his farm in K. and settled in Montville. He m. 3dly, Jan. 6, 1807, Lucinda, sister of his 2d w., who was b. Jan. 11, 1784. He lived in M., on the farm he cleared, till 1834, when he emigrated to Jefferson Township, Richland Co., O. He made a profession of religion in connection with the Freewill Bap. ch., in 1800, and illustrated his profession by a consistent christian life, till his death. He was an Elder in the church for many years, and was always deeply interested in religious services and affairs. His religious character and office in the church secured him an extensive acquaintance and high esteem as a man and christian. He had 14 chil.

Children of JOHN WALKER,[4] [15] of Dartmouth.

39. I. Mehitable,[5] b. May 12, 1748, in Dartmouth, d. Jan. 27, 1811, ae. 62 yrs., 8 mos., 15 days, in Peru, Clinton Co., N. Y., unm.

40. II. Walter,[5] (96) b. Dec. 10, 1749, d. in Macedon, Wayne Co., N. Y., March 26, 1844, in 95th yr. He m. Thankful, dau. of Jabez and Anna Wing, of Smithfield, who d. Oct. 1825. He was a blacksmith, and had 7 chil. He removed from Smithfield, R. I., to Macedon, N. Y., where he lived many yrs. He was m. of the Soc. of Friends.

41. III. Sarah,[5] b. Jan. 30, 1751, d. April 19, 1843, ae. 92. She m. David Shepard, of New Bedford, and had 9 chil. He was a wagon maker and farmer. About 1791, they rem. to Saratoga, N. Y., where they died.

42. IV. Nathaniel,[5] (103) b. Jan. 30, 1754, d. May 19, 1838, in Macedon, Wayne Co., N. Y., ae. 84. He m. Oct. 10, 1788, Martha, dau. of Stephen and Mary Aldrich, of Northbridge, Mass., and b. Aug.

7, 1763. They rem. in 1802, to Saratoga Co., N. Y., thence to Palmyra, now Macedon, N. Y. He had 7 chil., was a carpenter, and m. of the Society of Friends.

43. V. JOHN,[5] (110) b. Aug. 29, 1757, in Dartmouth, d. Aug. 7, 1845, ae. 87 yrs., 11 mos., and 9 days, in Stillwater, N. Y. He m. about 1777, Lydia Smith, of Scituate, R. I., dau. of Caleb. She was b. in Holliston, Aug. 23, 1757, and d. March 28, 1837, in S. They had 3 chil. He rem. from Smithfield, R. I., to Saratoga, N. Y., in 1794, and to Stillwater, April 7, 1800, upon a farm, where the Battle of Saratoga was fought. He was a blacksmith, and maintained through a long life, an exemplary character. Both were consistent members of the Soc. of Friends.

44. VI. ISAAC,[5] (113) b. May 17, 1759, d. May 6, 1813, in Peru, Clinton Co., N. Y., (1812? ae. 53 yrs., 11 mos., and 19 days, Fam. Rec.) He m. Abigail Harris, of Smithfield, R. I., and was a clock maker, and had 1 son.

45. VII. MARY,[5] b. May 11, 1768, d. March 4, 1842. She m. Nicholas Barker, of Peru, Clinton Co., N. Y., a farmer. No chil.

SIXTH GENERATION.

CHILDREN OF JOHN WALKER,[5] [18] OF PEMBROKE.

46. I. JOHN,[6] (114) b. Sept. 7, 1769, d. about 1837, ae. about 60 yrs. He m. Aug. 1792, Lydia Joyce, of Marshfield, dau. of Seth and Abigail (Thomas,) and b. March 6, 1772. He was a mariner 30 yrs., also a blacksmith, and had 11 chil. Res. Pembroke.

47. II. MARY,[6] d. before 1814. She m. Elijah Glover, and had 3 chil. Res. Pembroke.

48. III. SAUNDERS,[6] (125) d. June 5, 1803. He m. Hannah Walker, (See No. 49,) dau. of Isaac, of Pembroke, and had 1 dau. Res. P.

CHILD OF ISAAC WALKER,[5] [24] OF MARSHFIELD.

49. I. HANNAH,[6] b. about 1784, m. Saunders Walker, her cousin, (See No. 48,) and had 1 dau. She m. 2d, James Bates, of Pembroke, and had 4 chil. Res P.

CHIL. OF BENJAMIN WALKER,[5] [26] OF SMITHTOWN, L. I.

50. I. BENJAMIN,[6] (126) b. June 26, 1781, d. Dec. 13, 1841, ae. 62? yrs. He m. Oct. 27, 1808, Hannah Bunce, his cousin, only child of Theodore, of L. I., b. Oct. 17, 1791, and d. April 26, 1848, ae. 57 yrs. They had 6 chil. Res. Smithtown, L. I., village of Hauppaughs.

51. II. ZEBEDIAH,[6] b. Aug. 15, 1783, d. in infancy.

52. III. BETSEY,[6] b. Dec. 19, 1785, m. Thomas Ripley, of Sag Harbor, L. I., a merchant, who is dec'd. She lives in S. H. Chil.—

(1) *Ann Maria.* (2) *Thomas*, a merchant, in S. H. (3) *Mary E.* (4) *John*, a merchant, in S. H.

53. IV. ABRAHAM,[6] b. March 24, 1787, d. in infancy.

54. V. HANNAH BUNCE,[6] b. Nov. 5, 1788, m. Melancthon Wheeler, a mechanic. Res. Smithtown, L. I. Chil.—

(1) *Benj. P.*, b. Dec. 22, 1812, d. ae. 9 yrs. (2) *Lyman Beecher*, b. July 24, '14, m. Nov. 1, '38, Frances M. Wheeler. (3) *Dau.*, b. April 7, '16. (4) *Deborah V.*, b. Feb. 22, '17? m. May 5, '41, Sam'l Hammond. (5) *Edmund*, b. July 29, '19, m. Dec. 4, '43, Mary Norton. (6) *Hannah M.*, b. June 24, '22, m. Dec. 6, '43, Edmund Smith. (7) *Charles C.*, b. Aug. 2, '25, m. Oct. 19, '48, Ann M. Walker. (No. 134.) (8) *Harvey*, b. Feb. 3, '28, m. '55, Phebe Richmond, of Brooklyn, N. Y. (9) *Elizabeth R.*, b. Sept. 1, '30, m. '53. (10) *Wickham Havens*, b. Aug. 26, '33, m. '56, Abigail Sammis.

55. VI. DAU,[6] b. 1790, d. in infancy.

56. VII. ABIGAIL,[6] b. June 10, 1791, m. Adam Darling, of Smithtown, L. I., and both d. before 1840. Chil.—

(1) *Joel W.*, m. Emeline Golden, and is a mechanic in N. Y. City.

(2) *Nath'l H.*, m. Almira A. Fowler, and is " " " "

(3) *Charles W.*, is unm. Res. N. Y., " " " " "

(4) *Sarah*, m. Wickham S. Havens, now a retired Shipmaster, and has 10 chil. Res. Sag Harbor, L. I.

57. VIII. NATHANIEL,[6] b. June 16, 1793, was lost at sea when about 18 yrs. of age.

58. IX. BETHIAH,[6] b. Feb. 24, 1795, m. Rev. Charles W. Carpenter, of N. Y. City, a Methodist clergyman, who d. aged about 60 yrs. He was educated in N. Y. city, was preacher in charge there and in Brooklyn several times, and a few yrs. before his death

was settled in Newburgh, N. Y. He possessed superior abilities, and held a high rank in his denomination. She resides in Sag Harbor, L.I. They had—

(1) *Ann Maria*, who d. ae. 1 yr.

59. X. THEODORE,[6] (134) b. April 29, 1797, m. dau. of Nathaniel Havens, of Huntington, and has 2 daus. He was a merchant tailor in N. Y. City, and now resides in Michigan Bay City.

60. XI. HARVEY,[6] (136) b. Sept. 8, 1799, m. Mary Macy, of Smithtown, whose parents rem. from Nantucket. He is a merchant and has 2 chil. Res. Smithtown, L. I.

61. XII. JOEL,[6] b. July 3, 1804, d. in infancy.

CHILDREN OF DANIEL WALKER,[5] [34] OF KNOX, ME.

62. I. EXPERIENCE,[6] b. Oct. 11, 1786, m. May 11, 1806, Wm. Leonard, and has had 2 sons and 3 daus.

63. II. BATHSHEBA,[6] b. Nov. 26, 1789, d. Nov. 20, 1803.

64. III. DANIEL LEWIS,[6] (138) b. Aug. 30, 1798, m. June 9, 1820, Hannah Whiller, who d. Aug. 12, 1835. They had 3 chil. He m. 2d, Feb. 12, 1838, Irene Sprowl, who d. Nov. 18, 1849. He m. 3d, Jan. 9, 1851, Louisa Hearin, and is a blacksmith, in East Knox, Me.

65. IV. PROCTER SAMPSON,[6] (141) b. Oct. 21, 1800, m. March 12, 1824, Sophia E. Wentworth, and has 2 chil. He is a farmer and blacksmith, and rem. from Knox to Hermon, Me., Jan. 2, 1856.

66. V. NANCY,[6] b. Nov. 24, 1805, m. April 12, 1827, Stephen Wentworth.

CHILDREN OF ASA WALKER,[5] [35] OF MARSHFIELD.

67. I. LUCY,[6] b. June 7, 1794, m. June 7, 1813, Thomas O. Sylvester, of Quincy, a blacksmith, and has had 8 chil. Res. North Abington. Chil.—

(1) *Lucy Walker*, b. Feb. 10, 1814. (2) *Roxanna Thomas*, b. Feb. 13, '16. (3) *Jane Lewis*, b. Nov. 9, '18. (4) *Son*, d. (infant) April 25, '21. (5) *Deborah Walker*, b. May 19, '22. (6) *Marcia Ann*, b. Feb. 14, '24. (7) *Mary Ann Hatch*, b. Dec. 20, '29. (8) *Sarah Augusta*, b. March 29, '33.

68. II. Deborah,[6] b. June 24, 1798, m. Jan. 30, 1831, Edward Stevens, of Pembroke, who d. Feb. 26, 1859, ae. 74 yrs., 11 mos., 15 days. Res. Hanson. Chil.—

(1) *Lucy Walker*, b. March 3, 1832, d. Dec. 5, '43, ae. 11 yrs., 9 mos., and 2 days. (2) *Albert Wilmot*, b. Jan. 5, '35, m. May 25, '56, Rosanna O. Fish, who d. April 25, '59, ae. 26 yrs., and has 1 child,—Sarah E.

69. III. Charles,[6] (143) b. Aug. 30, 1800, d. Sept. 26, 1852. He m. Ann M. Reed, dau. of Col. Jesse, and had 4 chil. Res. No. Marshfield.

70. IV. Welthea,[6] b. Nov. 28, 1802, m. Horatio Reed, of Scituate. Res. S. Chil.—

(1) *Horatio Gates*, b. April 12, 1828. (2) *Welthea Maria*, b. Feb. 25, '33. (3) *Ellen Louisa*, b. June 15, '39. (4) *Mary Fobes*, b. Jan. 5, '41.

71. V. Julia Ann,[6] b. Jan. 19, 1805, d. in Middleboro', June 22, 1834, ae. 29 yrs., and 5 mos. She m. Alexander Feltis, and d. soon after. He resides in Quincy. Child—

(1) *Asa W.*, b. June 14, 1834.

72. VI. Abigail Baker,[6] b. July 23, 1807, (1806?) She m. Dean Randall, of Weymouth, who d. Dec. 9, 1852. Res. East Weymouth. Chil.—

(1) *Dau.*, b. March 21, 1830. (2) *Davis Dean*, b. Feb. 20, '31, m. Emily Sweet. (3) *Otis Howard*, b. Oct. 14, '33, m. Henrietta Niles. (4) *Andrew J.*, m. Mary Eliza Newton. (5) *Angeline Mott*.

By 2d Marriage.

73. VII. Olive,[6] b. Dec. 17, 1814, m. Oct. 22, 1837, Martin S. Bates, and has had 2 chil. Res. Hanover. Chil.—

(1) *Robert M.*, b. Jan. 9, 1845, d. Sept. 4, '45. (2) *Emma J.*, b. April 9, '49.

74. VIII. Asa,[6] (147) b. July 6, 1817, m. Huldah, dau. of Israel Carver, and b. Oct. 27, 18—. He is a nailor, has 5 chil., and resides in the ancient home in Marshfield, and owns a remnant of the landed estate of his ancestors.

Children of LEVI WALKER,[5] [36] of Marshfield.

75. I. Ruth Winslow,[6] b. April 29, 1787, m. Capt. Wm. Bourn, and rem. to Knox, Me., many yrs. since, where they reside. No chil.

BY 2d MARRIAGE.

76. II. SARAH HOLMES,[7] b. Feb. 19, 1793, m. Charles Porter, of Marshfield, and d. soon after. Child—

(1) *Sarah Ann*, m. David Lakin, and d. April 27, 1855, ae. 36.

77. III. REBECCA OLIVER,[6] b. Oct. 11, 1796, m. Daniel Baker, of Knox, Me., who is dec'd. Res. Knox. Chil.—

(1) *Daniel*. (2) *William*. (3) *Ruth*. (4) *James*, dec'd.

78. IV. ZERUIAH BRYANT,[6] b. Sept. 12, 1799, m. Daniel Baker, of Duxbury. Res. D., near Marshfield. Chil.—

(1) *Daniel D.*, is a shipmaster. Res. M. (2) *Adeline*, m. Wm. Jameson, of Plymouth, who d. April 27, 1853, ae. 33. She d. June 29, '56, ae. 27. (3) *Edward*, is a shipmaster. Res. M. (4) *Levi*.

79. V. LEVI,[6] (152) b. Feb. 22, 1802, m. March 27, 1827, Ruth Stetson, of Pembroke, and has 3 chil. He is a farmer in Marshfield.

80. V. EPHRAIM HOLMES,[6] (155) b. June 11, 1805, m. Sarah Thayer Hunt, of Milton, and has had 3 chil. He is a master builder. Res. Marshfield.

81. VI. ISAIAH,[6] (158) b. June 11, 1805, m. Feb. 5, 1827, Emily Wadsworth, of Duxbury, and has had 7 chil. He is a blacksmith. Res. D., till about 1837, whem he rem. to Pembroke, his present residence.

CHILDREN OF JAMES WALKER,[5] [38] OF MONTVILLE, ME.

82. I. NANCY,[6] b. May 26, 1796, d. Sept. 11, 1800.

83. II. JAMES,[6] (165) b. April 2, 1798, m. 1824, Sally Smart, dau. of Robert, and has 5 chil. He emigrated to Ohio in 1833, and lives in Bellville, Richland Co.

84. III. ALICE,[6] b. March 22, 1800, d. Sept. 3, 1800.

85. IV. WILLIAM,[6] (170) b. Feb. 7, 1803, in Knox, Me. He m. 1826, Nancy, dau. of Thomas Foster, of Montville, Me., b. Sept. 1804, and d. Sept. 1831, leaving 1 child. He m. 2d, 1832, Persis Holmes, and had 4 chil. He was bred a farmer, and has also been engaged in trade. Res. Bedford, Taylor Co., Iowa.

86. V. REBECCA,[6] b. Sept. 17, 1804, in Montville, Me., m. 1821, Nathaniel Files, son of Wm. of Gorham, Me. They emigrated to O., 1835. He is shoemaker and farmer. Res. Jefferson Township, O. Chil.—

(1) *Hannah*, b. March, 1822, m. 1841, S. J. Devol, house joiner, and res. in Mt. Vernon, O. Chil. [1, Elzada, b. 1842. 2, J. W., b. '44. 3, J. A., b. '46. 4, J. B., b. '48, d. '50. 5, Mary B., b. '50. 6, Almeda, b. '52. 7, S. E., b. '55. 8, Celinda, b. '59.]

(2) *Wm. Sewall*, b. June, 1824, m. '49, Martha Ewers. Chil. [1, Zorada. V., b. '50. 2, O. W., b. '52. 3, E. O., b. '54. 4, E. T., b. '56. 5, A. B., b. '58.]

(3) *Betsey Ann*, b. Feb. 1827, d. April, '50. (4) *George A.*, b. Feb. 1829, d. March, '29. (5) *George A.*, b. April, 1830, m. 1851, Barbara Strawsbaugh. Chil. [1, Mary, b. '51. 2, Rebecca, b. '54.] (6) *Abigail*, b. Feb. '34, m. '59, Josiah Armstrong. (7) *James A.*, b. Feb. '37. Res. O. (8) *Nath'l G.*, b. Feb. '39. Res. O. (9) *Lucinda A.*, b. Dec. '44. Res. O.

87. VI. LEVI,[6] (176) b. Sept. 22, 1806, in Montville, Me. He m. Feb. 1831, Lucy B. Foster, who was b. March, 1810, dau. of Thomas, and has 3 chil. He is a farmer, rem. to Ohio, in the Autumn of 1835, and resides in Jefferson Township, Richland Co.

88. VII. ISAAC,[6] (179) b. Oct. 17, 1807, in Montville, Me., d. July 11, 1857. He m. 1829, Dorothy, dau. of Robert Smart, and had 9 chil. Res. Bellville, O.

89. VIII. BETSEY,[6] b. Oct. 21, 1809, d. 1845. She m. 1835, Geo. C. Howard, son of Samuel of Montville, Me. Res. Bellville, O. Chil.—

(1) *Louisa*, b. 1835, in O., m. '55, Oliver Gurney, son of Samuel who emigrated from Waldo, Me. She has 1 son, Worth.

(2) *Sarah E.*, b. 1836, m. '54, Geo. W. Bull, and has chil., 1, Louisa E., b. '55. 2, Rebecca, b. '59.

(3) *Charles A.*, b. 1839. (4) *Ralph*, b. and d. '41. (5) *William*, b. '42. (6) *Lucy Ann*, b. '44.

90. IX. LUCINDA,[6] b. Jan. 4, 1812. She m. 1851, Wm. P. Crain, a farmer in Jefferson Township, O., and has—

(1) *Wm. L.*, b. 1853. (2) *Geo. E.*, b. 1855.

91. X. ASA,[6] b. May 4, 1814, d. Nov. 12, 1814.

92. XI. JOEL,[6] (188) b. Oct. 7, 1815, m. Dec. 22, 1842, Mary B. Gallagher, and has 6 chil. He is a carpenter, wagon maker and farmer, and emigrated to Iowa, in Fall of 1854, and is Justice of the Peace. Res. Bedford, Taylor Co., Ia.

93. XII. BATHSHEBA,[6] b. July 1, 1818, m. Johnson Howard, son of Samuel of Montville, Me. He is farmer in Jefferson Township, O. Chil.—

(1) *Olive M.*, b. March, 1837, m. '55, Simon Young, a farmer. Chil., [1, B. Young, b. '56. 2, Ada, b. May, '58.] (2) *Hollis B.*, b. Aug. '38. (3) *Lewis E.*, b. April, '40, d. Sept. '44. (4) *Otis*, b. May, '42, d. '44. (5)

James, b. July, '44. (6) *Ira J.*, b. Feb. '46. (7) *Isaiah W.*, b. Dec. '48. (8) *Bathsheba Rosilla*, b. Aug. '50. (9) *Lucinda C*, b. July, '52. (10) *Alice May*, b. '57.

94. XIII. ISAIAH,[6] (194) b. Jan. 7, 1821, in Montville, Me., m. June 5, 1849, Huldah Montgomery, 2d dau. of Jonathan, b. March 7, 1829, and has 1 dau. He emigrated with his father to Ohio, in 1834, and settled in Richland Co. Attending the common schools, excepting in the winter, till 1845, he became a clerk at Newville. In 1846, he entered the Academy at Ashland, and was there 3 summers. He commenced reading Law with J. W. Rankin, at A., in 1848, while attending school. After his marriage, he suspended the study of Law partially, worked on the farm, as a carpenter, and in various other employments, teaching every Winter but one, from 1840 to 1857. He has served as deputy Auditor of Richland Co., was deputy Clerk of Probate in 1857 and '58, admitted to the Bar, May, 1858, rem. to Rochester, Fulton Co., Ind., May, 1859, and purchased the Printing establishment of the "Rochester Sentinel," Nov. 14, 1859, of which he is now publisher and principal editor.

95. XIV. RUTH WINSLOW,[6] b. June 30, 1823, d. Aug. 22, 1825.

CHIL. OF WALTER WALKER,[5] [40] OF MACEDON, N. Y.

96. I. ABRAHAM.[6] His relatives know nothing of him.

97. II. MARGARET,[6] m. —— Pratt, and 2d, Barnabas Wilcox.

98. III. SUMMERS.[6] (194) Res. Hammond, St. Lawrence Co., N. Y.

99. IV. ANNA,[6] m. Joseph Baker, of Farmington, N. Y., and had 9 chil., who have all rem. West. Res. Hartland, Niagara Co., N. Y.

100. V. WING.[6] No information can be got respecting him.

101. VI. ELIZABETH,[6] b. 1789, d. 1832. She m. 1813, in Macedon, N. Y., Barnabas I. Curran, who was b. 1775, on the Atlantic Ocean, in the passage of his mother from Ireland to this country. He was a shoemaker, and d. Aug. 25, 1832. Res. Macedon. Chil.—

(1) *Esther*, b. June 7, 1815, m. about '35, Henry Slater, of Mich., a farmer.

(2) *James W.*, b. June 22. '17, is unm., and deranged for the last 22 yrs.

(3) *Mary Ann*, b. April 21, '19, m. March 3, '41, James D. Galloway, who was b. Aug. 7, 1807. Chil., 1, John A., b. June 27, '42. 2, Mary Isabel, b. July 25, '47. 3, Ellen Augusta, b. May 14, '49.

102. VII. PHEBE,[6] m. Thomas Lake, and 2d, Gerrit Lake. She had 2 daus., one of whom lives in Macedon, N. Y.

CHIL. OF NATHANIEL WALKER,[5] [42] OF MACEDON, N. Y.

103. I. CYNTHIA,[6] b. Aug. 21, 1789, d. Sept. 18, 1820. She m. Thomas Bills, from New Jersey, a tanner, and m. Soc. of Friends. They had 1 son and 2 daus.

104. II. SARAH,[6] b. March 4, 1792, d. June 3, 1839. She m. John Arnold, of New Jersey, a tailor, and had 3 sons and 6 daus. He has been Justice of the Peace and Town Clerk, several yrs. Res. Seneca, Lenawee Co., Mich.

105. III. RUTH,[6] b. Nov. 23, 1795, m. Isaac Jackson, from New Jersey, a farmer, and m. Soc. of Friends, who d. 1858. No chil.

106. IV. KEZIAH,[6] b. Aug. 4, 1797, m. John Cook, who was b. in Vt., and has had 4 chil. He is a farmer, m. Soc. of Friends, and has held several town offices. Res. Martin, Alleghany Co., Mich.

107. V. JOHN,[6] b. April 28, 1799, d. unm. June 26, 1834.

108. VI. STEPHEN,[6] (195) b. Aug. 26, 1801. He m. Lydia White, dau. of David and Thankful, b. in Cheshire Co., N. H., Nov. 1, 1801. He is a farmer and Friend, and has 5 chil. Res. Fairfield, Lenawee Co., Mich.

109. VII. MARY,[6] b. Oct. 26, 1804, d. Dec. 27, 1804.

CHIL. OF JOHN WALKER,[5] [43] OF STILLWATER, N. Y.

110. I. ROBERT,[6] (200) b. Oct. 19, 1778, in Scituate, R. I., d. Oct. 29, 1854, ae. 76, in Stillwater. He m. 1809, Judith Mead, of Saratoga, who was b. Feb. 7, 1780, and d. May 4, 1814. He m. 2d, Nov. 25, 1814, Patience Mosher, of Saratoga, who was b. May 27, 1787. He was a farmer, and had 10 chil. Res. Stillwater, N. Y.

111. II. JOSEPH,[6] (210) b. July 21, 1780, in Scituate, R. I., d. in Stillwater, N. Y., April 18, 1854. He m. Nov. 28, 1805, Lydia Walker, who was b. in S., April 8, 1787, and is living there. They had 9 chil., all b. in S. (Her father Archibald was b. in Argyleshire, Scotland.) He was a blacksmith and farmer, industrious, honest and persevering. Res. S. Most of the Battle of Oct. 7, 1777 was fought on his farm.

112. III. LUCY,[6] b. Nov. 9, 1783, in Smithfield, R. I., m. Jan. 4, 1832, John Wing, who was b. in Dover, Dutchess Co., N. Y., Sept. 5,

1779, and d. April 30, 1858, having no chil. He was a farmer and carriage maker. He held the offices of Town Clerk, and Commissioner of deeds. For many years, he was Clerk of the monthly and quarterly meetings of the Society of Friends. Res. Washington, Dutchess Co., N. Y.

CHILD OF ISAAC WALKER,[5] [44] OF PERU, N. Y.

113. I. HARRIS,[6] b. 1783, m. it is thought, —— Dexter, and lived in Smithfield or Providence, R. I. Res. now unknown.

SEVENTH GENERATION.

CHILDREN OF JOHN WALKER,[6] [46] OF PEMBROKE.

114. I. ISAAC,[7] (219) b. Oct. 4, 1793, m. about 1820, Betsey, dau. of Levi Ramsdell, of Hanson. He was accidentally shot in Marshfield, Nov. 20, 1821. He was an anchor-smith. Res. H.

115. II. SETH,[7] (220) b. Oct. 31, 1794, m. 1816, Abigail Ford, of Pembroke, dau. of William. She d. Sept. 12, 1849. He settled in Hanson, and rem. about 1825, to Providence, R. I. He is a blacksmith, and has had 12 chil. Res. P.

116. III. KOHADAD,[7] d. in infancy.

117. IV. SYLVANUS WESTON,[7] (232) b. May 12, 1798, m. Polly Johnson, of Bridgwater, pub. July 3, 1819. He is an anchor-smith, and has had 6 chil. Res. B.

118. V. JOHN THOMAS,[7] (238) b. July 12, 1800, m. Aug. 1823, Sarah Waldron, who was b. May, 1793. He is a machinist, and has had 8 chil. Res. Providence, R. I.

119. VI. SOLOMON DEXTER,[7] (245) b. Feb. 12, 1802, was drowned in West Duxbury, Sept. 15, 1854. He m. Jan. 20, 1833, Dorothy Joice, of Marshfield, dau. of Seth and Dorothy (Samson,) and b. Aug. 10, 1796. They had 2 chil. Res. W. D.

120. VII. SAUNDERS,[7] (247) b. July 1, 1805, m. Mary Ann Chandler, of Duxbury, and has 9 chil. Res. Pembroke.

121. VIII. Abigail D.,[7] b. July 1, 1805, twin, m. Jan. 29, 1832, Harvey Stetson, Jr., of Pembroke, a shipwright Chil.—

(1) *Isaac H.*, b. Jan. 8, 1834. (2) *William T.*, b. Feb. 26, '35, d. Jan. 12, '41. (3) *Abby*, b. May 19, '37, d. Feb. 13, '41. (4) *Sylvanus*, b. June 21, '42, d. Sept. 13, '48, twin. (5) *William*, b. June 21, '42, twin. (6) *John W.*, b. June 7, '44.

122. IX. Ward,[7] d. in infancy.

123. X. Olivia P.,[7] b. April 23, 1811, d. Nov. 27, 1848. She m. Oct. 27, 1833, Judah Harlow, of Marshfield, a farmer, son of Eleazer and Alathea (Thomas,) b. Jan. 27, 1811. Res. M. Chil.—

(1) *Julia M.*, b. Oct. 17, 1834. (2) *Sarah J.*, b. Jan. 24, '37. (3) *Abbie T.*, b. March 1, '39. (4) *Judah*, b. Dec. 14, '41. (5) *Briggs H.*, b. March 29, '44, d. Sept. 30, '46.

124. XI. Rebekah Sprague,[7] b. Nov. 14, 1814, m. Nov. 12, 1837, Wm. H. Jackson, of Plymouth, b. Aug. 25, 1813, son of Salsbury and Sally (Goodwin) and gd. son of Wm. H. and Deborah Salsbury. He is a harness maker. Res. P. Chil.—

(1) *William Hall*, b. April 20, 1842. (2) *Rebecca*, b. June 7, '49.

Children of SAUNDERS WALKER,[6] [48] of Pembroke.

125. I. Bethiah S.,[7] b. Sept. 9, 1800, m. David Ramsdell, a shoemaker, and has had 3 sons and 4 daus. Res. Pembroke.

Chil. of BENJAMIN WALKER,[6] [50] of Smithtown, L. I.

126. I. Hannah Eliza,[7] b. Oct. 19, 1809, m. Sept. 11, 1829, Dr. Elias S. Nichols, of Smithtown, L. I., son of Paul, and b. Sept. 23, 1801. In 1819 or '20, he rem. to N. Y. City, and was engaged 3 yrs., in teaching and study. In 1824, he commenced the study of Medicine, passed through the medical course in the N. Y. University, and was graduated in 1827. Since that time he has been constantly engaged in the practice of his profession, and is highly esteemed and successful as a physician. Chil.—

(1) *Mary Jane*, b. June 5, 1833, m. Wm. J. Lyon, a merchant, and has—1, Laura. (2) *Julius*, b. Aug. 3, '35. Res. N. Y. City. Physician.

127. II. Benjamin H.,[7] b. Oct. 13, 1811, d. April 9, 1812.

128. III. Jane Maria,[7] b. Jan. 13, 1813, d. Feb. 12, 1813.

129. IV. BETHIAH C.,[7] b. Dec. 29, 1814, m. Dec. 12, 1835, Lebbeus Barnes, son of the late Rev. Allen Barnes, of Middletown, Ct. He is a manufacturer. Res. Watertown, Iowa. Chil.—

(1) *Theodore P.*, b. May 14, 1837. (2) *Frances Helen*, b. Oct. 4, '38. (3) *Clarendon W.*, b. Oct. 21, '41. (4) *Edwin W.*, b. Sept. 9, '48.

130. V. THEODORE B.,[7] b. May 9, 1817, d. Dec. 30, 1830.

131. VI. MARY ALMIRA,[7] b. June 29, 1819, m. April, 1839, Platt A. Nichols, a farmer, son of Paul. Res. Queens, Queens Co., L. I. Chil.—

(1) *Benj. A.*, b. about 1841. (2) *Merriville H.*, b. about '43. (3) *Hannah E.*, b. about '45. (4) *Elliot M.*, b. about '47. (5) *Leverett C.*, b. about '50.

132. VII. FRANCES E.,[7] b. Sept. 13, 1821, m. Sept. 18, 1848, Edwin A. Hoyt, a merchant. No chil. Res. Queens, Queens Co., L. I.

133. VIII. REBECCAH J.,[7] b. Sept. 20, 1825, m. June 9, 1857, Owen E. Westlake, son of Ellis, who was b. in Orange Co., N. Y., Feb. 29, 1825. He is an Attorney at Law, in Watertown, Floyd Co., Iowa. Has—

(1) *Josephine J.*, b. Aug. 19, 1859.

CHIL. OF THEODORE WALKER,[6] [59] OF DETROIT, MICH.

134. I. ANN MARIA,[7] b. about 1830, m. Oct. 19, 1848, Charles Carpenter Wheeler, her cousin, (No. 53,) and has had 4 chil. Res. Michigan Bay City.

135. II. REBECCA,[7] m. —— Jarvis, and rem. to St. Louis, where she d. 1858.

CHIL. OF HARVEY WALKER,[6] [60] OF SMITHTOWN, L. I.

136. I. EDWARD HARVEY,[7] b. about 1830, is unm.

137. II. EMILY,[7] b. about 1837, m. Hamilton Jayne, son of Eben'r of Smithtown, L. I., and has 1 dau.

CHIL. OF DANIEL L. WALKER,[6] [64] OF EAST KNOX, ME.

138. I. EXPERIENCE,[7] b. June 24, 1824, d. Aug. 8, 1825.

139. II. NANCY ANN,[7] b. July 12, 1827, m. Feb. 14, 1853, Wm. B. Baker.

140. III. CHARLES ALBERT,[7] (256) b. Dec. 24, 1829, m. July 20, 1851, Adaline B. Merrill, and has 1 son. He is a farmer in K.

CHIL. OF PROCTER S. WALKER,[6] [65] OF HERMON, ME.

141. I. FREEMAN W.,[7] (257) b. Nov. 18, 1827, m. March 10, 1847, Louisa Wentworth, and has 4 chil. He is a farmer.

142. II. BENJ. E.,[7] (261) b. Oct. 15, 1834, m. Oct. 20, 1852, Elizabeth Charles, and has 1 dau. He is a painter. Res. Bangor, Me.

CHIL. OF CHARLES WALKER,[6] [69] OF NO. MARSHFIELD.

143. I. MATILDA ANN,[7] b. May 22, 1830, m. Jas. L. Damon.

144. II. CHARLES HOWARD,[7] (262) b. April 25, 1832, m. Deborah Sherman, and has 1 son. Res. No. Marshfield.

145. III. EDMUND DEAN,[7] b. March 16, 1834, is unm.

146. IV. ALMEDA,[7] b. Jan. 29, 1842, m. Jan. 13, 1859, Zenas T. Ewell. Res. No. Marshfield.

CHILDREN OF ASA WALKER,[6] [73] OF MARSHFIELD.

147. I. HULDAH AMANDA,[7] b. March 27, 1842, d. Sept. 19, 1845.

148. II. MARIA L.,[7] b. March 26, 1844.

149. III. SARAH A.,[7] b. Aug. 31, 1846.

150. IV. LIZZIE B.,[7] b. Feb. 19, 1850.

151. V. ELLA C.,[7] b. Feb. 17, 1854.

CHILDREN OF LEVI WALKER,[6] [79] OF MARSHFIELD.

152. I. CHARLES ANDREW,[7] b. Sept. 22, 1829, is a carpenter, unm.

153. II. HENRY,[7] b. Sept. 12, 1831, is a farmer, unm.

154. III. MARY JANE,[7] b. April 23, 1827, m. Jan. 9, 1857, Nahum Stetson, Jr., of Hanson, a housewright. Res. Abington.

CHIL. OF EPHRAIM H. WALKER,[6] [80] OF MARSHFIELD.

155. I. SARAH THAYER,[7] b. Nov. 3, 1835, m. John H. Bourne. Res. M.

156. II. EPHRAIM,[7] b. March 23, 1838, d. July 9, 1838.

157. III. EPHRAIM,[7] b. Nov. 15, 1840.

CHILDREN OF ISAIAH WALKER,[6] [81] OF DUXBURY.

158. I. EMILY J.,[7] b. Oct. 1829, m. Nov. 25, 1850, Briggs Ford, of Pembroke, a moulder. Res. P. Chil.—

(1) *Permelia M.*, b. Sept. 20, 1853. (2) *Briggs H.*, b. Sept. 14, '55.

159. II. PERSIS W.,[7] b. June 15, 1831, m. June 26, 1848, Edward D. Maglathlin, of Duxbury, a shipwright. Res. East Boston. Chil.—

(1) *Edward B.*, b. May 15, 1852. (2) *Sidney E.*, d. Aug. 17, '53, ae. 4 yrs. (3) *Persis D.*, d, Dec. 30, '56, ae. 15 mos. (4) *Abbott* d. Oct. 16, '59, ae. 13 mos.

160. III. ISAIAH,[7] b. Nov. 29, 1833, is a blacksmith in D., unm.

161. IV. SAMUEL W.,[7] b. 1836, is a caulker in D., unm.

162. V. SOPHIA H.,[7] b. 1838, m. Jan. 31, 1857, Adam S. Smalley, of St. George, Me., a seaman. No chil. Res. Pembroke.

163. VI. ALPHEUS,[7] b. 1840, is a mason in D., unm.

164. VII. BATHSHEBA,[7] b. 1843, m. Jan. 1, 1860, John H. Harding, of Chelsea, a caulker.

CHILDREN OF JAMES WALKER,[7] [83] OF BELLVILLE, O.

165. I. JAMES WINSLOW, (263) b. Dec. 1824, m. Feb. 1849, Catharine Nelson, dau. of John, and b. Oct. 1824. Res. Bellville, O. He is a carpenter, and has had 5 chil.

166. II. ASA,[7] b. 1828, d. 1832.

167. III. BENJAMIN,[7] b. 1832.

168. IV. MARY ANN,[7] b. 1835.

169. V. DANIEL,[7] b. 1837.

CHIL. OF WILLIAM WALKER,[6] [85] OF BEDFORD, IOWA.

170. I. LOVINA B.,[7] b. March, 1829, d. 1835.

BY 2d MARRIAGE.

171. II. CORDELIA E.,[7] b. 1833, m. ———, a Lawyer. Res. Bedford, Iowa.

172. III. CLARISSA O.,[7] b. 1836, d. 1837.

173. IV. FRANKLIN,[7] b. 1837, is a tinsmith. Res. Bedford.

175. V. FRANCIS,[7] b. 1840, is a printer in B.

CHILDREN OF LEVI WALKER,[6] [87] OF JEFFERSON, O.

176. I. GEORGE WASHINGTON,[7] b. 1832, in Me., m. 1859, Calista Warren. He was graduated at Oberlin Coll., O., Aug. 1859. He is m. Pres. ch., and has the ministry in prospect, but is now, (1860,) Principal of a High school in Geneva, O., his wife assisting him as teacher.

177. II. ANDREW JACKSON,[7] b. Oct. 5, 1833, in Me., m. Oct. 5, 1859, Martha King, in Clarinda, Page Co., Iowa. He has been a farmer and school teacher, and is now a clerk in the Treasury and Recorder's office of Page Co. Res. C.

178. III. THOMAS FOSTER,[7] b. March 1837, is a farmer in J., unm.

CHILDREN OF ISAAC WALKER,[6] [88] OF BELLVILLE, O.

179. I. ISAAC HOWARD,[7] (268) b. 1830, m. ———, and has 1 son. He is a County Judge and also Judge of Probate. Res. Clarinda, Page Co., Iowa.

180. II. NANCY PAUL,[7] b. May, 1832, d. June, 1844.

181. III. OLIVER,[7] b. March 1835, d. Feb. 1838.

182. IV. ZORADA,[7] b. May 1838, d. 1845.

183. V. SILAS,[7] b. May, 1840, d. 1848.

184. VI. SALATHIEL,[7] b. April, 1842, d. 1849.

185. VII. VIOLA,[7] b. 1846, d. 1847.

186. VIII. MATILDA,[7] b. 1848, d. 1849.

187. IX. MILLER MOODY,[7] b. 1852.

CHILDREN OF JOEL WALKER,[6] [92] OF BEDFORD, IOWA.

188. I. VALEDIA ORINDA,[7] b. May 31, 1844.

189. II. LUCINDA,[7] b. March, 1846, is dec'd.

190. III. LEWIS EDWIN,[7] b. May 27, 1849.

191. IV. LEON ALBERT,[7] b. May 25, 1853.

192. V. CORA ALICE,[7] b. April 23, 1855.

193. VI. MARY EMMA,[7] b. Feb. 5, 1858.

CHILDREN OF ISAIAH WALKER,[6] [94] OF ROCHESTER, IND.

194. I. DAU.,[7] b. Sept. 1, 1851.

CHIL. OF STEPHEN WALKER,[6] [108] OF FAIRFIELD, MICH.

195. I. MARTHA,[7] b. Sept. 1, 1826, in Hartland, N.Y., m. Dec. 5, 1844, Joel Johnson, from Ohio, a farmer, and has had 2 chil. Both m. ch. Chil.

(1) *Cynthia*, b. Dec. 1845, d. in infancy. (2) *Warren*, b. Jan. '49.

196. II. DAVID,[7] (269) b. July 15, 1828, m. Jan. 1852, Melissa Gray, dau. of Addison, of Lenawee Co., Mich., and has 1 dau. He is a wagon maker. Res. Ronald, Ionia Co., Mich.

197. III. JOHN M.,[7] (270) b. March 15, 1831, in H., m. Almira, dau. of Job T. Reynolds, of Jackson, Mich., and has 2 chil. He is a wagon maker. Res. Ronald, Mich.

198. IV. NATHANIEL,[7] (272) b. Feb. 19, 1836, in Fairfield, Mich., m. Nov. 1856, Elvira, dau. of Job Reynolds, and has 2 daus. He is a farmer in Fulton, Gratiot Co., Mich.

199. V. RANSOM,[7] b. Sept. 21, 1840, is unm. Res. Fairfield.

CHIL. OF ROBERT WALKER,[6] [110] OF STILLWATER, N. Y.

200. I. JOHN,[7] b. July 13, 1810, d. May 31, 1838, unm.

201. II. JAMES,[7] (274) b. Oct. 24, 1811, m. Sept. 1, 1838, Sarah B. Main, of Guilderland, Albany Co., N. Y., who was b. Oct. 15, 1815. He has had 1 dau. Res. Stillwater, on the homestead.

202. III. SMITH,[7] b. Feb. 17, 1813, d. Aug. 1838, in Naples, Ill. He m. Rebecca Laten, (Leighton?) No chil.

203. IV. DAVID,[7] (275) b. April 8, 1814, m. June 25, 1841, Emma Ann Davis, of Saratoga, and has 1 dau. Res. Queensburg, Warren Co., N. Y.

204. V. DEBORAH,[7] b. Aug. 18, 1815, m. June 5, 1832, Oliver K. Bishop, of Saratoga, who was b. Jan. 5, 1806. He is a farmer and has 6 chil. Res. Stillwater.

205. VI. STEPHEN M.,[7] b. Feb. 13, 1817, d. May 12, 1838.

206. VII. CHARLES R.,[7] b. Jan. 12, 1819' d. Aug. 27, 1835.

207. VIII. LYDIA S.,[7] b. April 20, 1821, m. Jan. 31, 1850, Stephen Henry Winne, a farmer, who was b. Dec. 29, 1822, in Saratoga. She has had 7 chil. Res. S.

208. IX. PHEBE,[7] b. Feb. 28, 1823, m. Jan. 5, 1846, Kellion Davis, a farmer. No chil. Res. Stillwater.

209. X. HANNAH,[7] b. May 22, 1829, is unm. Res. Stillwater.

CHIL. OF JOSEPH WALKER,[6] [111] OF STILLWATER, N. Y.

210. I. BETSEY W.,[7] b. Nov. 28, 1806, m. 1824, Abraham Leggett, a farmer, who was b. in West Farms, Westchester Co., N. Y., 1798. They have had 7 chil. Res. Schuylerville, N. Y.

211. II. MELISSA,[7] b. Aug. 27, 1808, m. 1828, Elijah Munger, of Stillwater, a farmer. No chil. Res. S.

212. III. SARAH,[7] b. Aug. 3, 1810, d. Nov. 4, 1834, unm.

213. IV. MARY B.,[7] b. July 6, 1812, m. Nov. 9, 1831, Wm. H. Van Buren, of Easton, Washington Co., N. Y., a farmer, and b. June 29, 1807. She has had 6 chil. Res. Easton.

214. V. JUDITH,[7] b. Aug. 31, 1814, d. Oct. 22, 1817.

215. VI. RHODA L.,[7] b. Nov. 6, 1816, m. Sept. 25, 1839, Josiah S. Scofield, of Hadley, N. Y., and b. May 28, 1812. Res. Waterford, Saratoga Co., N. Y. He is Ticket and Freight Agent of Albany, Vt. & Canada R. R., and has had 5 chil.

216. VII. MERIBAH R.,[7] b. Sept. 29, 1819, d. May 26, 1850, unm.

217. VIII. LUCY JANE,[7] b. March 18, 1822, d. April 10, 1858, in Easton, N. Y. She m. June 26, 1849, John W. Quackenbush, a painter, and has 3 chil. Res. E.

218. IX. SETH RUSSEL,[7] (276) b. Aug. 2, 1825, m. Oct. 12, 1847, Harriet E. Sherman, of Stillwater, N. Y., who was b. May 22, 1830, and d. Oct. 24, 1853. They had 2 chil. He m. 2d, Nov. 25, 1854, Ruth Clements, who was b. Nov. 7, 1821, and has 1 child. Res. Stillwater, N. Y., on the homestead of his father and grandfather.

EIGHTH GENERATION.

CHILD OF ISAAC WALKER,[7] [114] OF PEMBROKE.

219. I. BETSEY,[8] b. March, 1822, m. Aaron Thomas, and has 4 daus. and 1 son. Res. South Abington.

CHILDREN OF SETH WALKER,[7] [115] OF PROVIDENCE, R. I.

220. I. HIRAM RICKARD,[8] (279) b. Dec. 31, 1816, m. Dec. 1842, Mary Ann Davis, and has had 3 chil. She d. 1851. Res. N. Y.

221. II. BITHIA SAUNDERS,[8] b. Jan. 12, 1819, m. Sept. 19, 1844, Chandler Ford, a farmer, of Marshfield, who d. Aug. 19, 1850. Res. Worcester.

222. III. SETH JOICE,[8] (282) b. Nov. 23, 1821, m. March, 1842, Harriet E. Peirce, who d. July 11, 1856. He is a moulder, has 4 chil., and res. in ———, N. Y.

223. IV. ISAAC,[8] b. Aug. 31, 1823, d. ae. about 2 yrs.

224. V. ABBY LOUISE,[8] b. Sept. 20, 1825, m. Jan. 1844, Joseph E. Dispeau. Res. Pawtucket.

225. VI. THOMAS DEXTER,[8] b. Sept. 1, 1827, d. y.

226. VII. PHEBE ANNE,[8] b. Aug. 29, 1828, d. ae. about 1 yr.

227. VIII. PHEBE FORD,[8] d. March 3, 1830, " " " " "

228. IX. DELIA EDDY,[8] b. Nov. 26, 1831, d. April 18, 1855. She m. Dec. 1851, Wm. Briggs, and left 1 child.

229. X. MARY OLIVIA,[8] b. Nov. 26, 1833, d. Nov. 18, 1853. She m. Henry Sampson, of Worcester.

230. XI. Rebecca Jackson,[8] b. March 26, 1838. She m. Nov. 27, 1857, Ezra L. Robbins, a machinist.

231. XII. Gilbert,[8] b. Aug. 1840.

Chil. of SYLVANUS W. WALKER,[7] [117] of Bridgwater.

232. I. Mary T.,[8] b. July 21, 1820, d. July 22, 1821.

233. II. Lucy,[8] b. Nov. 27, 1821, m. B. Dennis Clifford, a mason. No chil. Res. Bridgwater.

234. III. George Augustus,[8] b. Aug. 15, 1824, d. Oct. 11.

235. IV. Mary Jane,[8] b. Nov. 24, 1825, m. Charles T. Hall, an anchor smith, and has 2 chil. Res. Bridgwater.

236. V. Hannah B.,[8] b. Nov. 9, 1827, m. John Dean, of Dedham. No chil.

237. VI. Marcia C.,[8] b. Aug. 15, 1834, m. James Fairbanks, of Dedham, and has 1 son.

Chil. of JOHN T. WALKER,[7] [118] of Providence, R. I.

238. I. Nathan C.,[8] b. Sept. 1, 1824, d. Oct. 15, 1824.

239. II. Lydia A. T.,[8] b. Oct. 15, 1825, m. Nov. 3, 1846, James D. Cook, who was b. Aug. 6, 1821, and is a jeweller in Providence, R. I. She has had 3 chil., all dec'd.

240. III. Margaret J.,[8] b. Oct. 10, 1827, d. Jan. 28, 1828.

241. IV. Mary R.,[8] b. June 20, 1829, d. Oct. 10, 1831.

242. V. George T.,[8] b. Aug. 20, 1831, d. June 4, 1833.

243. VI. Sarah V.,[8] b. Nov. 15, 1833, d. March 11, 1836.

244. VII. John Thomas,[8] b. Dec. 25, 1836, d. Sept. 1, 1837.

Chil. of SOLOMON D. WALKER,[7] [119] of West Duxbury.

245. I. David P.,[8] b. July 1, 1834, is a shoemaker, in W. D.

246. II. John Thomas,[8] d. Aug. 30, 1839, in Providence, R. I.

Children of SAUNDERS WALKER,[7] [120] of Pembroke.

247. I. Lydia A.,[8] b. Dec. 22, 1832, m. Robert Hunt, of Duxbury, a shoemaker. Res. West Duxbury.

248. II. Rebecca S.,[8] b. Aug. 30, 1835, m. Horace Waterman, of Kingston, an anchor-smith in K.

249. III. Mary A.,[8] b. Jan. 19, 1838, m. George P. Weston, of Marshfield, a blacksmith in M.

250. IV. William F.,[8] b. Jan. 4, 1840, is unm.

251. V. Sarah V.,[8] b. May 2, 1842, " "

252. VI. Cordelia,[8] b. April 9, 1844, " "

253. VII. John T.,[8] b. June 22, 1846, " "

254. VIII. Lysander C.,[8] b. Jan. 3, 1850, " "

255. IX. Charles T.,[8] b. Jan. 1, 1852, " "

Child of CHA'S ALBERT WALKER,[7] [140] of Knox, Me.

256. I. Charles W.,[8] b. Aug. 20, 1854.

Chil. of FREEMAN W. WALKER,[7] [141] of Hermon, Me.

257. I. Nancy W.,[8] b. Jan. 15, 1848.

258. II. John R. M.,[8] b. Dec. 19, 1850.

259. III. Lucinda H.,[8] b. Dec. 15, 1852.

260. IV. Daniel P.,[8] b. Sept. 8, 1857.

Child of BENJ. E. WALKER,[7] [142] of Bangor, Me.

261. I. Mary E.,[8] b. Dec. 22, 1855.

Child of CHA'S H. WALKER,[7] [144] of No. Marshfield.

262. I. Son,[8] —— ——.

JAMES W. WALKER,[7] [165] OF

WILLIAM H.,[8] b. Jan. 1850.

. JOHN M.,[8] b. May, 1852, d. July, 1

I. ELIZABETH A.,[8] b. Oct. 1853.

ʼ. SARAH ELLEN,[8] b. Nov. 1855.

. ALMA ANN,[8] b. Feb. 1858.

HON. ISAAC WALKER,[7] [179] OF

SON.[8]

F DAVID WALKER,[7] [196] OF

CHLOE,[8] b. Oct. 1853.

JOHN M. WALKER,[7] [197] OF

RANSOM DEWITT,[8] b. Sept. 1857.

CHIL. OF SETH R. WALKER,[7] [218] OF STILLWATER, N. Y.

276. I. HELEN FRANCES,[8] b. Oct. 15, 1849, d. Oct. 24, 1853.

277. II. JOSEPH CONKLIN,[8] b. Aug. 10, 1852, in Georgia.

278. III. EDWARD WILSON,[8] b. Jan. 8, 1856, in Stillwater.

NINTH GENERATION.

CHIL. OF HIRAM R. WALKER,[8] [220] OF ——, N. Y.

279. I. THREE CHIL.,[9]——names not reported.

CHIL. OF SETH J. WALKER,[8] [222] OF ——, N. Y.

282. I. FOUR CHIL.,[9]——names not reported.

†

JOHN WALKER,

OF MARSHFIELD.

The jury appointed "to view the dead body of John Walker, seruant to Robert Latham of this towne," gave their verdict the last of Jan. 1654. This may be found in the 3d vol. of Plym. Col. Rec.

"Att the Generall Court holden att New Plymouth the sixt day of March, 1654, Robert Latham was indited for fellonious crewelty done vnto John Walker, his seruant, aged about 14 yeares, by vnreasonable conection, by withholding necessary food and clothing, and by exposing his said servant to extremitie of seasons, whereof the said John Walker languished and immediately died, the 15th day of January, anno., 1654."

"A pettye jury was impannelld and sent forth vpon the case. These found the said Robert Latham guilty of manslaughter by chaunc medley. Where vpon the prisoner desired the benefitt of law, viz: a psalue of mercye, which was graunted him, and sentence was further pronownsed against him, which was, that the said Robert Latham should bee burned in the hand, and his haueing noe lands, that all his goods are confiscate vnto his highnes, the Lord Protector; and that the said sentance should bee forthwith executed, which accordingly was pformed the 4th of March, 1654."

FRANCIS WALKER,

OF MIDDLEBORO'.

He m. between 1650 and 1668, Elizabeth Soule, dau. of Geo. Soule, the 35th signer of the compact in the May Flower, and one of Richard Warren's Company in the assignments of lands. Nath'l Warren, son of Richard, m. Sarah Walker, 1645, and Nath'l her son, settled in Mid'o. It is a natural conjecture that Francis and Sarah Walker were related. Their origin is unknown. He was one of the proprietors of land in Duxbury, 1672, was living in M., in 1668, and as late as 1673. There is no evidence in the Mid'o', Duxbury, or any Old Colony Records, that he had any descendants, unless the following be such. In the 77th division of land in Mid'o', July 6, 1789, Francis Walker and John Haskell had the 4th and 5th lots. Over 100 yrs. intervene, with not even a link to establish a connection.

THOMAS WALKER,

Of Bristol, R. I.,

AND HIS DESCENDANTS.

1\. I. Thomas Walker,[1] (2) was one of the founders of Bristol, in 1681, with the distinguished Capt. Church. His origin is unknown. There is no proof that he was related to the other Walkers of the Old Colony. He was propounded a freeman, and took the oath of fidelity, June 6, 1682. He was a tanner, and owned a windmill or cornmill, "rate free from tax." He filled a prominent place in the affairs of the town, and was honored with various civil offices. In 1702 he was a constable, an assessor in 1682 and '94, on the jury, 1696 and 1707, and tithing-man, 1716. He held the office of Select-man, 1686–7, '92, '98, 1701, 2, 3, 4, 5, 7. He was also a member of the Com., "to agree with Mr. Woodbridge about salary." He m. Nov. 4, 1684, Elizabeth Parris, and had 2 sons and 2 daus. His will was made, 1721–2, when he was "aged and infirm," and was proved 1724. To his wife Eliz'th, who survived him, he bequeathed his "negro boy, Peleg." In'y £133. Her will was made 1735, and proved, April 8, 1743. All that is now known of his participation in public affairs, and the civil distinctions conferred upon him, is given here, and is creditable to his abilities and moral worth. He had few descendants, and his name, it is supposed early became extinct.

SECOND GENERATION.

Children of THOMAS WALKER,[1] [1] of Bristol, R. I.

2\. I. John,[2] b. Oct. 1, 1685, is not mentioned in father's or mother's will, and probably d. unm, or without issue.

3\. II. William,[2] (7) b. Aug. 5, 1687, d. 1735. He m. Hannah ——, who d. May 2, 1774, ae. 82. They had 4 chil. He was a tanner, held the office of constable, 1714–15, and was also a captain. His will was proved July 13, 1735, in which he bequeathed his "negro man Peleg," to his wife Hannah. His in'y was £2982.

4. III. THOMAS,[2] (11) d. probably before 1721–2, as his name is not mentioned in his father's will, but his dau. is a legatee. He m. Frances ——, of Christ church, Barbadoes, and had 1 dau.

5. IV. MARY,[2] m. Nov. 7, 1717, Edward Little, and had 4 sons and 4 daus, 1718—1737. Res. Bristol.

6. V. ELIZABETH,[2] m. —— Bowen, and had 4 chil. Res. B.

THIRD GENERATION.

CHILDREN OF WILLIAM WALKER,[2] [3] OF BRISTOL, R. I.

7. I. JOHN,[3] (12) b. May 17, 1714–15, d. April 3, 1773, ae. 59. He m. Aug. 18, 1746, Mrs. Patience Coggeshall, of Bristol, R. I., and had 5 chil. He was a tanner, and Town Clerk of B. in 1743 and '44.

8. II. RACHEL,[3] b. Oct. 24, 1716. A Rachel Walker m. Jan. 31, 1762, Simeon Munro. Was it this?

9. III. ELIZABETH,[3] b. Feb. 15, 1720–1, d. March 15, 1786, ae. 66. She m. Stephen Rawson, of Bristol, pub. March 29, 1745, and had 4 chil. He was son of Wilson, and gd. son of Rev. Grindal Rawson, also uncle of Priscilla. (See No. 98, Rehoboth Branch, 135 p.) He was b. April 2, 1722, and d. March 14, 1773, in 50th yr. He settled in Providence, R. I., was mem. of the Legislature, 1760, and Dea. of the 2d Cong. ch. His funeral sermon, preached by his pastor, Rev. Joseph Snow, Jr., was from the text, Acts, 8th chap., 2d v., "And devout men carried Stephen to his burial, and made great lamentation over him;" a very appropriate text, inasmuch as the Deacons of the several religious societies in P. officiated as pall-bearers. Hon. James Burrill, of R. I., Attorney General many yrs., Chief Justice of the Supreme Judicial Court, and U. S. Senator, distinguished for splendor of genius and purity of life, was her gd. son. For further information respecting his ancestry and her descendants, see Rawson Genealogy, and Gen. Reg., vol. 3d, 1849.

10. IV. MARY,[3] b. Oct. 23, 1722, m. Oct. 2, 1743, Elisha Weaver, and had 3 sons.

FOURTH GENERATION.

CHILDREN OF THOMAS WALKER,[3] [4] OF BRISTOL, R. I.

11. I. JANE,[4] was in Barbadoes in 1721–2, unm.

CHILDREN OF JOHN WALKER,[3] [7] OF BRISTOL, R. I.

12. I. WILLIAM,[4] b. July 25, 1748, d. Dec. 6.

13. II. ELIZABETH,[4] b. Dec. 20, 1750.

14. III. JOHN.[4] b. Oct. 28, 1753.

15. IV. ABIGAIL,[4] b. March 16, 1758.

16. V. REBECCA,[4] b. Nov. 6, 1759, d. Oct. 29, 1765, ae. 6 or 7.

17. VI. ANNA.[4]?

Mrs. May of B., b. 1762, says, (1859) that she remembers John Walker and his 2 daus., and that their names were Betsey and Anna, not Abigail. Perhaps Abigail died, and another dau. Anna may have been born after her, whose name is not given with the others in the Town Rec. She has no recollection of any son John. Several other very aged persons in B., who knew the family, have no recollection of any son. If John, No. 14, d. unm., or without issue, this Bristol Family of Walkers is extinct, having no male descendants after the 4th generation.

APPENDIX.

To show how abundantly the race of Walkers was early planted in the soil of New England, brief notices of those of the Mass. Colony, and other sections of N. E., who were here before 1700, are introduced. There were 14 of the name in the country, even before 1650, not including those of the Old Colony, nor those related to each other.

ARCHIBALD WALKER, OF PROVIDENCE, R. I.

He emigrated from Scotland, and settled in Providence. He was tailor, and tradition reports him to have been a worthy man.

He was in P., 1700, m. Mary Gardner, and had chil.—(1) *Charles*, b. May 6, 1691, m. May 22, 1719, Alice Mitchell, both of P. (2) *Susanna*, b. 1695. (3) *Abigail*, b. 1699, m. Jonathan Aldrich, March 13, 1725–6. (4) *Hezekiah*, b. 1701. (5) *Nath'l*, b. 1704. (6) *Anne*, b. 1709. His descendants settled in Scituate, R. I., and the name is there yet.

AUGUSTIN WALKER, OF CHARLESTOWN.

He came, it is supposed, from Old Sarum, Eng. to Charlestown, about 1640. He was a shipmaster and died in Bilboa, Spain. In'y, Oct. 1653. He and his w. Hanna were m. ch. Chil.—(1) *Hanna*, b. Sept. 12, 1640. (2) *Samuel*, b. Oct. 11, [1 ?] 1642. (It has been thought that he m. Sarah Reed, 1662, and settled in Woburn. This is an error. It was Sam'l, Jr., b. June or Sept. 28, 1643.) (3) *Augustin*, b. Dec. 14, 1646. (4) *James*, b. July 25, 1647 ? ('48.)

BENJAMIN WALKER, OF BOSTON.

He was one of the founders of Brattle St. Church. He m. Patsey ——. The record of chil. is from an Old Testament in possession of Dr. Joshua Green, of Groton, viz.,—(1) *Eliz'th*, b. July 13, 1673. (2) *Jane*, bapt. May 8, 1676. (3) *Benj.* b. Dec. 28, 1677–8, all in London, Eng. (4) *Benj.* 2d, b. Jan. 24, 1679–80, in Boston, and living 1753. (5) *Eliz'th*, b. April 29, 1682. (6) *John*, b. March 18, 1684, living 1753. (7) *Eben'r*, b. May 23, 1687. Boston Rec. confirm the last 3 dates.

DORCAS WALKER, OF ROXBURY.

She was buried April 17, 1640. "Possibly she was mother of John, (says Mr. Savage) and too wise to partake of his heresy, and too old to go to R. I., with him."

GEORGE WALKER, OF NEW HAVEN.

He was married, and in 1645 "was licensed to retail spirits."

GEORGE WALKER, OF READING.

He was one of the early settlers, and probably, says Mr. Savage, a son of an earlier one, or it may be a mistake for Walkup. If Walker, perhaps it was Geo., of Portsmouth, who m. 1689, and d. 1741, ae. 86.

GEORGE WALKER, OF NEW HAMPSHIRE.

His name is in "the humble addresse of the inhabitants and train soldiers of ye Province of N. H.," to the Governor of Mass., for protection, Feb. 20, 1689. Perhaps this was the Capt. Geo. of Portsmouth.

HENRY WALKER, OF GLOUCESTER.

He was in G., 1647, m. Sept. 26, 1662, Mrs. Mary Brown, and d. 1693. He was made freeman Oct. 8, 1672. Perhaps he was the Henry of Ipswich, 1651.

HENRY WALKER, OF IPSWICH.

He was one of the first settlers, or first appeared in I., in 1651.

ISAAC WALKER, OF BOSTON.

He m. Sarah, and 2d or 3d Susan, wid. of Henry Symonds, who d. Sept. 30, 1646. He m. Susanna ——, and d. Oct. 19, 1688. He was made freeman 1646, m. Old South ch. 1674. He was a proprietor of Lancaster, but did not rem. there. He had 6 or 7 chil., who died young, except Nicholas, b. 1651, and Stephen, b. 1656, and perhaps Isaac.

ISABEL WALKER, OF LANCASTER.

She d. April 3, 1669. Nothing more is known of her.

JAMES WALKER, OF CHELMSFORD.

Perhaps he was the son of Augustin. He m. Eliz'th, and had—(1) *Zechariah*, b. Jan. 14, 1659. (2) *Eleazer*, b. Nov. 9, 1660.

JOHN WALKER, OF R. I.

He m. Hannah, dau. of Capt. Edward Hutchinson. Both m. ch. in Roxbury. He was admitted a freeman, 1634, rem. to Boston, where he was disarmed, Nov. 1637. He went with Wm. Coddington and other sympathizers of the famous Mrs. Ann Hutchinson, to Aquedneck, R. I., was in Portsmouth, R. I., 1638, and had grant of 100 acres in P. Feb. 1639. Nothing more is known of him.

JOHN WALKER, OF CHARLESTOWN.

He m. Ann, and had—(1) *John*, b. May 13, 1667. (2) *Richard*, b. Jan. 4, 1668. (3) *Sam'l*, b. Feb. 12, 1670. (4) *Anna*, b. March 15, 1672, d. March 20, 1671–2. He m. 2d, Aug. 1, 1672, Hannah Mirricke, dau. of John. Chil.—(5) *Joseph*, bap. Oct. 17, 1675. (6) *Anne*, bap. April, 1676. (7) *Benj.*, b. June 3, 1678, d. June 7, 1678. (8) *Lydia*, bap. June, 1680. (9) *Benj.*, bap. 1681. She was a wid. June, 1681.

JOHN WALKER, OF BEVERLEY.

He m. Eliz'th Woodbury, dau. of Humphrey, and had daus.—(1) *Sarah*. (2) *Eunice*.

JOHN WALKER, OF ——.

He was a soldier in Capt. Turner's Company, and killed in King Philips War, May 19, 1676, in "The Fall Fight," at what is now Turner's Falls. He had no descendants in 1731.

JOHN WALKER, OF NEW HAVEN, CT.

He was one of those who entered into and subscribed to "the fundamental agreement of the free planters," 1639; also one of those who drew lots, 1641, "on ye banke side and by ye west creeke," and became freeman 1644. He m. Grace ——, and d. early. His inv'y was taken April 22, 1652. Chil.—(1) *Mary*, bap. March, 1641, m. Jan. 1, 1661, John Brown. (2) *Hannah*, bap. 1646, m. May 6, 1668, Sam'l Hall.

JO. WALKER, OF ——.

He was one of those to be transported to Virginia, embarqued in the Eliz'th, Aug. 1, 1635, ae. 16.

JOSEPH WALKER, OF PORTSMOUTH, N. H.

He was one of many petitioners, 1655.

JOSEPH WALKER, OF BOSTON.

"Mr. J. W." was in B., 1679. See Lane Fam. Papers, (Gen. Reg. 1857, 233d p.) Was he son of Robert or had Robert's son rem. to Conn.? A Jos. W. and w. Abigail had Joseph, b. Dec. 8, 1674, Joanna, b. May 5, 1677. See 405th p., 33d line.

MATTHEW WALKER, OF ——.

"May 26, 1680, M. W., aged about 63, died very suddainly, none yt time in ye room wth him. He was well a few minutes before." (Journal of Rev. Simon Bradstreet, New London, Ct.)

OBADIAH WALKER, OF READING.

He was one of the early settlers. (Eaton.) Nothing more is known of him, except that he had—(1) *Sarah*, in R., b. Aug. 2, 1674, d. Aug. 18, 1674.

NATHANIEL WALKER, OF BOSTON.

He obtained a grant of 240 acres in right of Morrill, of Roxbury, May 27, 1668. It was near S. W. "of Groaten towne, beyond Nashaway River."

RICHARD WALKER,[1] OF LYNN.

He was b. in 1593. He came to this country in 1630, settled in Lynn, spent several yrs. in Reading, was Rep. 1650, went back to L., and was buried May 16, 1687, ae. 95 yrs. He was a captain and prominent man. He had 2 sons and 2 daus.? Chil.—

(1) *Richard*,[2] b. 1611, came to this country 1635. (See 4th p.) He was "a man endowed with faith, and of a courageous spirit," and leader of the Band of Reading men against the Indians. He lived in Reading and was Rep. 1660 and '73.

(2) *Samuel*,[2] removed to Reading. He d. 1684. (Wob. Rec.) The Reading Records give names of his chil., thus—

1, Samuel,[3] b. June or Sept. 28, 1643, m. Sept. 10, 1661, (1662?) Sarah Reed, of Woburn, and d. Jan. 18, 1703, ae. 61. He lived in Woburn, was Representative and had 7 chil., viz:— 1, Edward,[4] b. 1663, d. 1690. 2, John,[4] b. 1665. 3, Sam'l,[4] b. 1667. 4, Sarah,[4] b. 1670. 5, Timothy,[4] b. 1672. 6, Isaac,[4] b. 1677. 7, Ezekiel,[4] b. 1679.

2, Joseph,[3] b. 1645, m. Dec. 15, 1669, Sarah Wyman, dau. of Lieut. John, of Charlestown. He was Rep., and lived in Billerica. Chil.—1, Joseph,[4] b. 1670. 2, Joseph,[4] b. 1673. 3, Sarah,[4] b. 1675. 4, Eliz'th, b. 1675. 4, Hannah,[4] b. 1679.

3, Hannah,[3] b. 1647, d. 1648. 4, Hannah,[3] b. June 28, 1648, twin, m. James Thompson, of Woburn.

5, Israel,[3] b. June 28, 1648, m. Susanna, and had 4 sons— 1, Israel.[4] 2, Henry.[4] 3, Nath'l.[4] 4, Israel,[4] and 5, Daus.[4]

6, John,[3] b. Feb. 14, 1649, m. Mary Pierce, and had—1, Benj.[4] 2, John.[4] 3, Mary.[4] Res. W.

7, Benj.,[3] b. 1651, d. 1653.

(3) *Tabitha*,[2] b. 1647, m. March 11, 1662–3, Dan'l King, Jr., and had 5 chil.

(4) *Eliz'th*,[2] b. March 2, 1663–4, Ralph King, and had 5 chil.

May not the last two have been chil. of Richard, Jr., instead of Richard, Sen.?

RICHARD WALKER, OF ——.

His name is in the list of such persons as shipt at town of Hampton, in the James of London, of iijc tonnes, Wm. Cooper, Master, vs.: New Eng., in and about 6 of April, 1635. The record found by Mr. Savage in Eng. is—"Richard Walker, shomaker, late of Marlborough."

RICHARD WALKER, OF BOSTON.

He was perhaps the "shoemaker" who came in the James, in 1635. He m. 1637, Anne, wid. of Robert Bolton. She was cast out of the church, because of intemperance and other misdemeanors, and sentenced to the whipping-post. He was in B., 1650. No chil.

RICHARD WALKER, OF SALEM.

He had a grant 1637. Persis, who joined the ch., in S., in 1639, may have been his dau. He may have been the Richard of Manchester, and father of Richard of Ipswich, 1671 and 1700.

RICHARD WALKER, OF IPSWICH.

He was admitted freeman, May 31, 1671.

RICHARD WALKER, OF LONG ISLAND.

He was one of the pioneer settlers and first purchasers of Middleburg or Newtown, near Flushing, L. I., about 1652.

RICHARD WALKER, OF NEW LONDON, CT. 1695.

ROBERT WALKER,[1] OF BOSTON.

He was b. about 1606, and d. May 29, 1687. He was a "linen webster," came from Manchester, Eng., settled in B., and was one of the founders of the Old South Ch. Sewall says he was "a very good man." His w. d. Dec. 21, 1695. Chil.—(1) *Elishua*,[2] b. 1635, m. Benj'n Thurston. (2) *Zechariah*,[2] b. 1637, d. Jan. 20, 1699–1700. He m. Susanna, dau. of Dr. Bryan Rossiter, of Guilford, Ct. He was a Pres. minister at Jamaica, L. I., and then in Stratford, now Woodbury, Ct. He had 1 son, Zechariah, and 2 daus. (3) *John*,[2] b. 1639, d. 1652. (4) *Sarah*,[3] b. 1641, d. 1643. (5) *Jacob*,[3] b. 1644, m. 1670, Mrs. Eliza Blackman, [Blakeman ?] settled in S., and had 3 sons, Sam'l, Moses, John and 3 daus. (6) *Joseph*,[3] b. 1646, m. Nov. 14, 1667, Mary, dau. of Rev. Peter Prudden, settled in Ct., and had Robert and 3 others. The sons of Robert[1] settled in Conn., and their descendants lived mostly in Stratford, Woodbury and Killingworth, Ct. (7) *Thomas*,[3] and (8) *Mary*,[3] twins, b. 1649. (9) *Eliakim*,[3] b. 1652, d. 1654. (10) *Mary*,[3] b. 1654. (11) *John*,[3] b. 1656, d. 1657.

SAMUEL WALKER, OF BOSTON.

He was a merchant in B. 1654, and m. Sarah, dau. of Joshua Scottow, who gave him an estate in B. 1672. Nothing more is known of him. Perhaps he was the Sam'l with w. Sarah, of Boston, who had Sarah, Dec. 10, 1679, Mercy, July 5, '81, Sam'l, April 25, '83, Wm., Dec. 8, '84, Mary, Oct. '86, Eliz'th, Nov. 16, '88.

SAMUEL WALKER, OF EXETER, N. H.

Farmer says he was in E. 1639. He took the oath of freeman in E., April 17, 1644. Perhaps this was Sam'l of Reading.

SARAH WALKER, OF ——.

She m., 2d wife, Nov. 19, 1683, Benj. Lombard, of Barnstable ——, and had (1) *Bathshua*, b. May 4, 1687. (2) *Sarah*, b. Oct. 29, 1688. (3) *Mary*, b. June 17, 1688? (4) *Sam'l*, b. Sept. 15, 1691. She d. Nov. 6, 1693.

SHUBAEL WALKER, OF LYNN.

He m. May 29, 1666, at L., Patience Jewett, and was buried Jan. 24, 1689. He was a Captain, and lived at Swampscott Farms; in L. 1650, and in Haverhill, Nov. 28, 1677. He was also of Rowley, and early a Town Clerk, at one time, in Reading, living in what is now called Bradford. He was one of the select-men of B. Reading Rec. give names of his chil. (1) *Richard*, b. June 8, 1667. (2) *Mary*, b. Oct. 30, 1619. The name of his son confirms the conjecture, that he was son of Richard, of Lynn.

THOMAS WALKER, OF BOSTON.

He m. Anne, and d. July 2, 1659. He was a brick-burner. His w. survived him. Chil.—(1) *Elizabeth*, b. 1650. (2) *John*, b. 1652. (3) *Ann*, b. 1654, d. 1655. (4) *Sam'l*, b. 1656. (5) *Ann*, b. 1659. *Thomas* was perhaps oldest, and probably rem. to Sudbury. He was adm'r of his father's estate.

THOMAS WALKER, OF BOSTON.

He m. March 25, 1662, Susanna Collins, dau. of John, of B. Chil.—(1) *Susanna*, b. 1662. (2) *Thomas*, b. 1665. (3) *Mary*, b. 1667. (4) *John*, b. 1668. (5) *Joseph*, b. 1670. (6) *Eliz'th*, b. 1673. (7) *Mercy*, b. 1677.

THOMAS WALKER, OF SUDBURY.

He was probably son of Thomas and Ann, of Boston. He m. Mary, taught school in S. 1664, and in 1672, kept an ordinary. Will proved, 1697. Chil.—(1) *Mary*, b. 1661. (2) *Thomas*, b. 1664, m. Martha Howe, 1687, and had 7 sons and 3 daus. Res. Sudbury. (3) *William*, b. 1666, m. 1686, Sarah Goodenow, and had 4 sons and 3 daus. (4) *Hannah*, b. 1668, d. young. (5) *Hannah*, b. 1669. (6) *Daniel*, b. 1674. (7) *Sarah*, b. 1677. (8) *Abigail*, b. 1679. (9) *John*, d. y. (10) *Eliz'th*, d. y.

WILLIAM WALKER, OF SALEM.

He came with John Gedney. (See 331st p.)

WILLIAM WALKER, OF ——.

He was "imprisoned for making suite to a servant majd." (See 332d p.) Perhaps these were the same persons.

WILLIAM WALKER, OF PORTSMOUTH, N. H.

He d. 1720? very old and decrepit for many yrs. He m. Alice, and was living 1685 near the Sagamore Creek. He m. 2d, 1695? Mary, wid. of Wm. Brookin. She was then 85 yrs. old. His son? Joseph, m. 1670? Hannah Philbrook, of Hampton. Res. P. (Com. by A. W. Brown, Esq., E. Rockport, O.)

As many of the emigrants to Virginia, Barbadoes and other islands, found their way to New England, the following is added :—

Wm. Walker,	21,	imbarqued for the	Barbadoes,		17 Februarij,	1634.
Joseph "	18,	"			24 Aprilis,	1635.
Grace "	34,	"			2° Maij,	"
Matthew "	19,	"	" St. Christopher's,		21° "	"
James "	30,	"	"	"	2° "	"
Tho. "	19,	"	"	"	2° Octobris,	"

The statistics of the present extent of the name in our cities, may fitly follow the list just given, of the Walkers who settled in N. Eng. before 1700. These are gleaned from the business directories of 1857, '58, '59 or '60, in most cases. The numbers do not, of course, include more than half of those bearing the name, resident there, the chil., and many single persons being omitted. Doubtless many of these are of foreign birth. The compiler found this to be the fact in Providence, R. I. A very few, only, of Old Colony descent, are included in these numbers—these are in Providence, Detroit, and Chicago. There is only one in Boston, one in Phil., and none in N. Y. City. The London Directory of 1855, had 234 of the name.

1860.	Philadelphia,	217	1860.	Covington, Ky.,	13
"	New York City,	203	1857.	Memphis, Tenn.,	12
1858.	Boston,	88	1859.	Augusta, Ga.,	12
"	Baltimore,	69	1860.	Cambridge,	11
"	Brooklyn, N.Y.,	65	1857.	San Francisco,	9
"	Pittsburg, Pa.,	60	"	Milwaukie,	9
1859.	Chicago,	61		Kingston, Canada,	9
1860.	Cincinnati,	60	1859.	Portland,	8
"	Buffalo, N. Y.,	39	1856.	Syracuse,	8
1858.	Washington,	39	1857.	Quebec,	8
1860.	New Orleans,	30	1858.	Newark, N. J.,	7
1857.	Rochester, N. Y.,	26	"	Fort Wayne,	7
1859.	Detroit,	25	"	Columbus, O.,	7
"	Charleston, S.C.,	21	1857.	Jersey City,	7
1858.	Hamilton, Canada,	20	1858.	Schenectady,	7
1859.	Montreal, "	20	1852.	Norfolk,	6
1856.	Toronto, "	21	1856.	Wheeling,	6
1860.	Roxbury,	17	1858.	Georgetown,	6
"	Louisville, Ky.,	17	1859.	New Albany,	5
"	Worcester,	16	1858.	Dayton,	5
1855.	Richmond, Va.,	15	1859.	Poughkeepsie,	5
1859.	Lowell,	14	1860.	Hartford,	4
1857.	Utica, N. Y.,	13	1859.	Savannah,	4

Walkers who were Tories in the Revolution.

Only 5 persons of this name in Mass. were proscribed and banished in 1778, viz., Adam, of Worcester; John of Shrewsbury; and Gideon, Benjamin and Zara, of Marshfield.

Walkers in the Pension list of Mass.

In the Pension list for 8 months' service in 1775, there are the names of 46 Walkers; 40 in Mass., and 6 in Maine. Six of these belonged to the Old Colony. There were nearly 100 of the name in Mass. who took part, more or less, in the Revolution.

Members of Congress named Walker.

SENATORS.

John	Walker,	Ga.	1790–91.
John	"	Va.	1790–90.
George	"	Ky.	1814–15.
Freeman	"	Ga.	1819–21.
Robert J.	"	Miss.	1836–47.

REPRESENTATIVES.

Francis Walker,	Va.	1793–95.
Benj'n "	N. Y.	1801–03.
David "	Ky.	1817–20.
Felix "	N. C.	1817–23.
William A. "	N.Y.	1853–55.
Percy "	Ala.	1855–57.

There should be added to the list of U. S. Senators, John W. Walker, from Ala. 1819–22, and Isaac P. Walker, from Wis. 1843–55. There were no Walkers in the Old Congress. There had been previous to 1835, no Governors, nor Commanders in Chief, of states, and territories, bearing the name.

GRADUATES OF COLLEGES NAMED WALKER.

Harv. Coll. has graduated before yr. 1858, 18; Yale Coll., before 1861, 14; Dartmouth Coll., bef. 1858, 12; Amherst Coll., bef. 1861, 7; Brown Univ., bef. 1861, 6; Williams Coll., bef. 1841, 3; Middlebury Coll., bef. 1854, 3; all of Old Colony descent. Bowdoin Coll., 1; Univ. Vt., bef. 1846, 1. Of the 65 graduates of N.E. Colleges, 12 belong to the Taunton and Rehoboth Branches. Of the 30 grad. at Colleges out of N. E., bef. 1844, 6 may be found in this Genealogy; 4 have been grad. since. About ¼ of the whole number of graduates in the U. S. are the descendants of Widow Walker, of Rehoboth.

There have been 6 connected with the Theo'l Sem. at Andover, 3 of whom are of Old Colony descent.

GRADUATES OF COLLEGES INCLUDED IN THIS GENEALOGY.

TAUNTON BRANCH.

Rev. Elnathan,	Brown Univ., was grad.	1803.	See No. 139,	p.	55.
" William,	" " "	1842.	" " 327,	"	91.
" Geo. Clinton,	Ham. Lit. & Theol. Inst.	1838.	" " 432,	"	98.
" James B. R.,	Brown Univ., was grad.	1841.	" " 436,	"	101.

REHOBOTH BRANCH.

Hon. Edward Carey,	Yale Coll., was grad.	1842.	See No. 624,	p.	219.
" DeWitt C.,	Mid. " "	1834.	" " 639,	"	222.
" Jesse,	" " "	1833.	" " 649,	"	225.
Rev. Levi,	Ham. Lit. & The. Inst.	1828.	" " 654,	"	227.
Hon. Wm. Perrin,	Williams Cl. was grad.	1798.	" " 786,	"	243.
" Thos. Read,	Ham. " "	1824.	" " 834,	"	252.
James,	Union " "	1833.	" " 836,	"	252.
Ezra,	Ohio Univ., "	1826.	" " 853,	"	257.
Prof. Ralph M.,	West Res., "	1832.	" " 855,	"	257.
Rev. Edwin S.,	Roch. Univ., "	1856.	" " 1322,	"	292.
" Avery S.,	Oberlin Coll., "	1854.	" " 1327,	"	293.
Wm. Wirt,	Mid. " "	1853.	" " 1392,	"	297.
Hon. John A.,	Williams " "	1840.	" " 1514,	"	304.
Rev. Horace D.,	Yale " "	1841.	" " 1594,	"	311.
" Augustus,	" " "	1849.	" " 1597,	"	312.
" Geo. Fred.,	Am. " "	1849.	" " 1606,	"	313.
Prof. Edward P.,	Marietta " "	1856.	" " 1612,	"	313.
Chas. Manning,	Ohio Univ., "	1853.	" " 1617,	"	314.

Those who entered Coll., but did not complete the course.

REHOBOTH BRANCH.

Leonard,	Am. Coll.,	ent. 1846.	See No. 940, p. 265.
Alvan C.,	Mid. "	" ——	" " 1209, " 283.
Geo. W.,	Oberlin "	" ——	" " 1238, " 286.
Hiram N.,	Vermont Univ.,	" 1840.	" " 1403, " 298.

Ministers now living in the U. S., (1860) bearing the name.

There are of Meth., 17; Bap., 14; Cong., 8; Epis., 6; Pres., O. S., 5; Pres., N. S., 5; Free Will Bap., 5; Cumberland Pres., 4; United Pres., 2; Ref. Synod Pres., 1; (Pres. in Nova Scotia, 1; Pres. in Canada, 3; viz: in connection with ch. of Scotland, 1; Canada, 1; United Pres., 1; not a complete list;) Unitarian, 1; Universalist, 1; Evangelical Lutheran, 1; Spiritualist, 1; Catholic, 3; making in all 78, of whom only 8 are of Old Colony descent.

Authors named Walker.

These are not given with any idea that there is any connection between them and the families in this work, but as a part of the history of the name.

George Walker, Batch. of Divinity. "This learned person was b. at Hawkeshead in Tournifalls in Lancashire, educated at St. John's Coll., in the Univ. of Cambridge where he was esteemed an excellent logician, Orientalian and Divine. He was at this time Minister in Watling St., in London, where he was ready upon all occasions, to encounter with any learned Catholic priest. On the last of May, 1623, was a set and solemn disputation between him and one that went by the name of Smith. It was published for the satisfaction of both parties, with this title, "The sum of a Disputation between Mr. Walker, Pastor of St. John the Evang., &c., and a popish priest, calling himself Mr. Smith," but indeed Norris, printed 1623. In the year following, he, the said W., had to do with the Father, John Fisher, the Jesuit, as being Dr. Dan. Featly's second, and thereupon published, "Fisher's Folly unfolded, or the vaunting Jesuit's challenge answered," Lond. 1624. Afterwards, when another Walker who was a severe Puritan, beheld the profanation of the Lord's Day as he took it, he preached against this, and other Practices and Opinions, which procured him trouble, and 2 yrs. imprisonment, as he said. After the Tory Parliament began, he preached against the King and his followers, and published several things, which before, he was not permitted to do, among which were; (1) Socinianism in the fundamental point of justification, discovered and confuted, &c., London Oct. 1641. (2) The Doctrine of the Holy weekly Sabbath, &c. Lond., 1641. In the yr. 1643 he was chosen one of the assembly of Divines, preached sometimes before the members of Parliament and had his sermons made public, one of which is entitled, "Fast sermon before the House of Commons, Jan. 29,

1644, on Ps., 58 chap., 9th v., London, 1645, qu. He hath also other things extant, as, "God made visible in all his works, &c., printed 1641, qu., &c., which for brevity's sake, I now pass by and only tell you, that he died in 1651, ae. about 70, and was buried in ch. of St. John Evang., before mentioned. In Arch. Laud's annual account of his Province, to the King, for the yr. 1635, at the end of his Troubles and Tryal, p. 535, the Reader may find him thus mentioned:"

"Mr. W., of St. John, the Evang., in London, (a Peculiar of mine,) who hath at this time been a disorderly and peevish man, and now of late, hath very forwardly preached against the Bish. of Ely's Book, concerning the Lord's Day Act, and by authority. But upon a canonical admonition given him to desist, he hath recollected himself, so also in the said history of the Troubles and Tryal of Arch. Laud, Cap. 23, p. 237, George Walker, for preaching Factious matters was imprisoned by the Council Table, and afterwards upon some carriage of his, there censured by the Court of the Star Chamber." (Wood's Fasti.)

NICHOLAS WALKER, D.D., archdeacon of Bedford, appointed 1629, d. or resigned 1631. He was author of "The Life of King Alfred the Great, in 3 books." This was translated into Latin, by the care of Obadiah Walker, Master of Univ. Coll., (see below,) who published large and learned notes thereon, and illustrated it with many cuts. Oxon, 1678, fol.

CLEMENT WALKER, b. in Cliffe, Dorsetshire, author of "The Compleat Hist. of Independency," and is said to have been educated at Christ Ch., Oxford. He was in good repute for his hatred of the Puritans, while he lived at Charterhouse. But he soon after changed his mind. Says Wood, when the Puritans or Pres. were like to carry all before them, he closed with them, and was elected member of Parliament. He was a curious observer and diligent inquirer, well read, also, and notably versed in the Liberties and Privileges of Parliament, and Statute Law of the kingdom. He became a zealous Covenanter. He was a voluminous author. His principal works were "The Mystery of two Juntos, Presbyterianism and Independency, Lond. 1647; Hist. of Independency, Lond. 1648; Appendix to do., Lond. 1648; Parallel between Argyle and Cromwell; Anarchia Anglicana, or Hist. of Independency, 2d part, Lond. 1649. The High Court of Justice, or Cromwell's Slaughter House, being 3d part of Hist. of Ind'y, 1651." When the 2d part of his Hist. of Independency was pub. in 1649, he was discovered to be the author, and imprisoned by Cromwell. He d. in the Tower, Oct. 1651.

OBADIAH WALKER, a divine, son of Wm., b. at Worsperdate in the West Riding of Yorkshire, in 1616, entered Univ. Coll., Oxford, 1631, took holy orders, and became a noted Tutor. In 1648, he was ejected, went abroad, and is supposed to have been reconciled to the ch. of Rome. He might have been elected Master of his Coll., on the death of Dr. Thos. Walker, 1665, but refused, though he accepted the headship in 1676. At Accession of James I., he avowed himself a Cath., had mass said in the Coll., and published books against the Protestants. At the Restoration, he was deposed from his Coll., sent to the tower, and arraigned for treason, but soon after released. He d. 1699, [1698?] and was buried in Old St. Pancreas' ch. yard. He published various works, one of which was a violent pamphlet against Luther. He was a very learned and able man, and a voluminous author.

WILLIAM WALKER, grad. of Trin. Coll., Cambridge, took degree of D. D., became master of public school in ——, in Lincolnshire, then Rector of Colsternorth, and at length master of Free School at Grantham, where he d. Jan. 1684. Very useful in his day, and author of several works.

GEORGE WALKER, an Irish divine, b. of Eng. parents, in Co. of Tyrone, and ed. at Glasgow. He became Rector of Donoughmore, where he raised a regiment, when King James landed in that kingdom, defended Londonderry against him with great prudence and valor, after it had been abandoned by the governor, and held out, till the siege was raised, July 30, 1689, by Major Gen. Kirk. For this bravery he received the thanks of the House of Commons, great honor at court of Wm. III., and was created Doct. of Divin. at Oxford. He was killed at the battle of the Boyne, July, 1690. He pub., (1) A true account of the siege and famous defence of Londonderry. (2) Vindication of true account.

JOHN WALKER, b. in Devonshire, ed. at Exeter Coll., Oxford, took degree of A. M., in 1699, was Rector of the parish, St. Mary's the More in E. In 1714, he pub. a folio book with the title of "An attempt Towards Recovering an Account of the Numbers and Sufferings of the Clergy of Church of Eng., who were Sequester'd, Harass'd, &c., in the late Times of the Grand Rebellion. Occasioned by the Ninth chap. of Dr. Calamy's abridgement of the Life of Baxter." Fol. Lond., 1714, pp. 220. For this performance he received the deg. of D. D., from Univ. of Oxford. He d. in 1725. He made the entire number of Epis. clergy, who were imprisoned, banished, and sent a starving, to have amounted to seven or eight thousand.

SIR EDWARD WALKER, an historian and herald of arms by the title of Chester, 2d son of Edward of Roobersin, b. at Netherstowey, in Somersetshire. He was Sec. of Earl of Arundel, Earl Marshall of Eng. in the Expedition to Scotland, in 1639, and he then became known to Charles I., followed him, 1641, into North of Eng., was with him at Edghill fight, and was made Sec. at War, and in June, 1644, clerk extraordinary of the privy council. In 1645, he received the honor of Knighthood. After the execution of his royal Master, he fled to Chas. II., whom he attended in his exile, and was appointed by him Garter at arms. He d. 1676–7. He wrote (1) Iter Carolinum or an account of the Marches, &c. of King Chas. I., from 1641 to '48. (2) The acts of the Knights of the Garters in the Civil Wars, also Military Discourses and Hist. Discourses. He is mentioned by Lord Clarendon, whom he is said to have assisted in the part of his (Lord C's) history, which relates to military transactions.

JOHN WALKER, of Christ Church, was curate for Dr. Geo. Hooper, at Woodhay, in Hampshire, and author of "The antidote; a seasonable discourse on Rom., 13th ch., 1st v., shewing necessity and reasonableness of subjection to higher Powers; with an account of the Divine right or origin of Gov't." Lond. 1684.

DR. WALKER wrote a book on the English particles. The following pun was perpetrated: "Here lie Walker's Particles."

WILLIAM WALKER, a learned divine of the 17th century, b. in Lincolnshire, ed. at Trinity Coll., Cambridge, d. 1684. Newton was one of his scholars. He was author of several useful works on grammar, logic, &c.

SAMUEL WALKER, a pious divine, b. in Exeter, 1714, became a travelling tutor. On entering orders, he became curate of Truro, in Cornwall, and resided there many yrs. He d. 1761. His sermons and lectures on the Catechism were published.

JOHN WALKER, a philological writer, b. at Barnet, in Middlesex, 1732, went on the stage, left it 1767, then lectured on elocution. Brought up a Pres., he became a Cath., d. Aug. 1, 1807, and was buried in St. Pancreas. He was author of a "Pronouncing Dictionary of the Eng. Language," and several other works.

GEORGE WALKER, Mathematician, F. R. S. b. about 1734, at Newcastle on Tyne, went to Univ. of Edinburgh; from E., he went to Glasgow, for study of Theology and Philosophy, and settled about 1756, at Durham as a dissenting minister, thence to Yarmouth,—in 1772 to Warrington as mathematical tutor, pub. in 1775, "Doctrine of the sphere," and d. near Liverpool, 1807. He published sermons, also the 1st part of a "Treatise of Conic Sections," which was worthy of his mathematical reputation.

On a petition for recognising Am. Independence drawn up by him, Mr. Burke declared that he would rather have been the author of that piece, than of all his own compositions.

ADAM WALKER, philosophical lecturer, b. in Westmoreland, and brought up a weaver. While thus employed he amused himself in constructing models of mills, and devoted so much time to reading, that at the age of 15, he was qualified to be an usher in a school. He next became a writing master, and accomptant at Macclesfield, and settled in London where he met with great encouragement. He invented the transparent orrery and various useful engines. He pub. various important works, and d. 1821, in 90th yr.

"SIR HOVENDEN WALKER was the naval commander of the Great Expedition against Canada, which sailed from Boston, N. E., 1710, but which proved a complete failure, owing, it was said, to the unskilfulness of the pilots, by which eight ships and nearly a thousand men were lost in the St. Lawrence. Great blame was attached to Sir Hovenden, and he published this account in his own defence."—Nichol's Lit. Anec. vol. i. 178. It is entitled "A Journal of the Late Expedition to Canada, 8vo." London, 1720.

ROBERT WALKER, an eminent minister in Scotland, author of Practical Sermons, 3 vols.

COOPER WALKER, author of "Hist. Memoirs of the Irish Bards." Lond. 4to., p. 141, 1786.

RICHARD WALKER, author of "Memoirs of Medicine," 8vo. Lond. 1799.

GEORGE WALKER, author of "The Vagabond, a Tale." Boston, 1800.

A. WALKER, author of Life of Gen. Jackson, 12mo., N. Y.

G. S. WALKER, edited Corpus Latinorum, containing Catullus and Horace, 1 vol., 8vo. Lond.

T. WALKER, author of "The Original," 8vo. Lond. 1836.

REV. S. A. WALKER, author of "Christian Missions in Western Africa." 350 pp. 1845. Dublin.

TIMOTHY WALKER, L. L. D. Judge, b. in Wilmington, grad. of Harv., rem to Cincinnati, was author of a "Treatise on Geometry," which was a Text Book in the schools, also of "Introduction to Am. Law," 4th ed., 8vo., Boston.

REV. JAMES B. WALKER, of Sandusky, O., author of the "Philosophy of the Plan of Salvation," &c.

JAMES P. WALKER, editor of Book of Raphael's Madonnas, Royal, 8vo., 104 p., 1859. Leavitt & Allen, N. Y.

REV. JOSEPH R. WALKER, of Beaufort, S. C., is author of "Spiritual Riches of Clergy." Prot. Epis. Soc., N. Y.

—— WALKER, author of a work on Manly Exercises, 9th Lond. Ed. Reprint in Phil. 1856.

ALEXANDER? WALKER, author of a work on Beauty and Physiology.

INVENTORS.

The 1st real printing press was made by the Earl of Stanhope, Eng., assisted by a skillful mechanic named Walker. It was an improvement of Blaew's machine, invented about 1620. Instead of using the old *wooden* screw and *wooden* frame, which had been employed in all previous inventions, he made a press of iron and combined the screw with the bent lever, and also contrived a movable carriage for holding the forms of type. He also arranged the spring, so that as soon as the impression was given, it caused the platen to fly up. This press was at once adopted in Eng. and Am., and for a long time, maintained its supremacy over all others.

JOHN WALKER, in Stockton upon Tees, Eng., d. May 18, 1860, ae. 78. He was a chemist, and said to be the inventor of Lucifer Matches, in 1827.

SUMMARY.

The following Tables classify and condense some interesting facts respecting the families and individuals included in this Genealogy. The first gives the number in each Generation of each Branch, who married and had chil., and whose chil. are here enumerated. The Table does not include those females, named Walker, and persons of other names, whose marriages are given, but whose chil. have not been reported.

NUMBER OF FAMILIES IN EACH BRANCH AND EACH GENERATION.

Taunton Branch.	1st Gen.	2d G.	3d G.	4th G.	5th G.	6th G.	7th G.	8th G.	9th G.	Totals.
Named Walker,	Wid. W.	James	2	7	11	16	40	48	5	131
Having other names,		Sarah	5	11	15	15	42	81	29	199
Rehoboth Branch.										
Named Walker,	Wid. W.	Philip	3	12	28	71	159	72	1	347
Having other names,			2	10	14	54	171	96	6	353
Eastham Family.	1st Gen.	2d G.	3d G.	4th G.	5th G.	6th G.	7th G.	8th G.		Totals.
Named Walker,	William	2	5	8	13	31	20			80
Having other names,				2	10	35	5			52
Marshfield Family.										
Named Walker,	John	1	2	4	11	21	18	2		60
Having other names,				1	3	17	16			37
Bristol Family.	Thomas	1	2							4
Mass. Colony Walkers.	37	4	4							45
										1308

The Tables below, give the entire number of persons in each Generation of each Branch, bearing the name of Walker, or other names.

DESCENDANTS OF "WIDOW WALKER," NAMED WALKER. TAUNTON BRANCH.

1st Gen.	2d G.	3d G.	4th G.	5th G.	6th G.	7th G.	8th G.	9th G.	10th G.	Total.
Wid. W.	James	5	17	32	62	117	219	205	7	666

DESCENDANTS OF "WID. WALKER," HAVING OTHER NAMES. TAUNTON BRANCH.

1st Gen.	2d G.	3d G.	4th G.	5th G.	6th G.	7th G.	8th G.	9th G.	10th G.	Total.
Wid. W.		8	35	58	99	70	222	276	57	825

DESCENDANTS OF "WIDOW WALKER," NAMED WALKER. REHOBOTH BRANCH.

1st Gen.	2d G.	3d G.	4th G.	5th G.	6th G.	7th G.	8th G.	9th G.	10th G.	Total.
Wid. W.	Philip	10	29	87	192	569	795	208	1	1892

DESCENDANTS OF "WID. WALKER," HAVING OTHER NAMES. REHOBOTH BRANCH.

1st Gen.	2d G.	3d G.	4th G.	5th G.	6th G.	7th G.	8th G.	9th G.	10th G.	Total.
		13	52	73	381	876	356	18		1769

DESCENDANTS OF WM. WALKER. OF EASTHAM, NAMED WALKER.

1st Gen.	2d G.	3d G.	4th G.	5th G.	6th G.	7th G.	8th G.	9th G.	10th G.	Total.
William	6	12	25	52	106	166	70			438

DESCENDANTS OF WM. WALKER, HAVING OTHER NAMES.

1st Gen.	2d G.	3d G.	4th G.	5th G.	6th G.	7th G.	8th G.	9th G.	10th G.	Total.
William			4	44	167	29				244

DESCENDANTS OF JOHN WALKER, OF MARSHFIELD, NAMED WALKER.

1st Gen.	2d G.	3d G.	4th G.	5th G.	6th G.	7th G.	8th G.	9th G.	10th G.	Total.
John	4	2	10	28	68	105	60	7		282

DESCENDANTS OF JOHN WALKER, HAVING OTHER NAMES.

1st Gen.	2d G.	3d G.	4th G.	5th G.	6th G.	7th G.	8th G.	9th G.	10th G.	Total.
John			2	20	71	57				150

DESCENDANTS OF THOMAS WALKER, OF BRISTOL, NAMED WALKER, 17

MASS. COLONY WALKERS. 152

The whole number of families is 1308, and the whole number of persons included in these families is 6435, of whom 3447 are named Walker, and 2988 have other names.

The following Table gives the number of those in each Generation and each Family who have attained the greatest age.

	TAUNTON FAM.			REHOBOTH FAM.			EASTHAM FAM.			MARSHF'D FAM.			
	From 70 to 80 yrs.	From 80 to 90 yrs.	From 90 to 100 yrs.	From 70 to 80 yrs.	From 80 to 90 yrs.	From 90 to 100 yrs.	From 70 to 80 yrs.	From 80 to 90 yrs.	From 90 to 100 yrs.	From 70 to 80 yrs.	From 80 to 90 yrs.	From 90 to 100 yrs.	100 yrs
1st Gen.								1					
2d "	James						1	1			1		
3d "	1							1					
4th "	5	3		2	4			2	1	1	2	1	
5th "	2	3		7	9		8	2	4	3	6	3	1
6th "	5	6	2	32	31	1	1			3			
7th "	3	3		1	2								
	17	15	2	42	46		10	7	5	7	9	4	1

The Marshfield Family has had the only centenarian. The Rehoboth Branch has 1 in the 6th generation living at the age of 98 yrs. 9 mos., and bidding fair to reach her century. (See No. 215.) She has descendants (not traced in this work) of the 5th gen., who are therefore of the 11th gen. from Wid. Walker. The whole number of Walkers who lived beyond 70 yrs., is 166. Quite a large number are now living, who have passed that age.

The Table which follows, gives the earliest birth and latest death, in each Branch and each Generation, and shows the duration of each.

Taunton Branch.	1st Gen.	2d G.	3dG	4thG	5thG	6th G.	7th G.	8th G	9th G.	10th G
Earliest Birth, Walkers,	Wid. W.	1620	1646	1674	1703	1728	1753	1790*	1816	1854
" " not "		1618	1642	1681	1696				1781	1844
Latest Death, "		1691	1724	1770	1808	1856				
" " not "		1676	1731							
Duration of each Generation,		73yrs	89	96	112	128				
Rehoboth Branch.										
Earliest Birth, Walkers,	Wid.	Phil.	1655	1682	1707	1742	1774	1801	1820	1855
" " not "						1730	1768	1797	1826	1845
Latest Death, "		1679	1740	1799	1835	living†				
Duration of each Generation,			85y.	117	128	118				
Eastham Family.		1st G	2dG	3dG	4 G.	5th G.	6th G.	7th G.	8th G.	9th G.
Earliest Birth, Walkers,		1620	1655	1692	1718	1756	1777	1800	1825	*
" " not "						1738				
Latest Death "		1703	1742	1780	1826	Livi'g.	No. 87	in 1855	& per-	haps
Duration of each Generation,		83yrs	87	88	108	117				now.
Marshfield Family.										
Earliest Birth, Walkers,		John	1665	1690	1716	1743	1769	1793	1816	1843
Latest Death, "		1663	1747	1750	1813	1848	Livi'g.			
Duration of each Generation,			88	60	97	105	91			

* There are chil., but not reported. † Nos. 163, ae. 86, 165, ae. 80, 215, ae. 98, 301, ae. 83.

The earliest births and latest deaths in each Branch and in each Generation have been almost uniformly those named Walker, and not those whose mothers were Walkers. The Rehoboth Branch alone, has several of the 6th gen. living ——. The generations of the Eastham and Marshfield Families do not correspond in time with those of the Rehoboth and Taunton Families, these having an earlier ancestress in Widow Walker. This should be kept in mind in a comparison. Accordingly the 1st gen. of E. and M. Families, are put in line with the 2d gen. of the T. and R. Families, as they were contemporaneous generations, and the same order holds with all the others. The generations of the Rehoboth Branch have been of longest duration, and it has the oldest member living.

Of the Taunton Branch the 9th gen. was b. 2 yrs. before the 5th died, and the 10th was b. 27 yrs. before the death of the 6th. Of the Rehoboth Branch the 8th gen. was b. 2 yrs. before the death of the 4th, and the 9th b. 15 yrs. before the death of the 5th. The 6th generation is living yet, once contemporaneous with the 3d, and now with the 11th, and as the earliest of the 3d was b. 1655, those of the 6th now living, stand on an eminence looking before and after, over a period of 205 yrs.

Of the Eastham family, the 6th was contemporaneous with the 3d, and some of them are now living. The 8th gen. was b. before the 4th and the 9th before the 5th.

Additions and Explanations.

TAUNTON BRANCH.

James Walker was not one of the 1st purchasers of Taunton in 1638, but of Rehoboth, and an early settler of T. 5 yrs. after its purchase.

Baylies in his Mem. of Plym. Col., Part III., p. 54th, giving a history of Philip's War, says, "Philip being driven to desperation, effected his escape from the Pocasset swamp, in the night of the last day of July (1675) and fled to the Nipmuck country. A part of his force spread themselves into the wilderness about Taunton, where they succeeded in burning the houses of John Tisdill, and James Walker. Tisdill was killed, and two other soldiers, viz: John Knolles and Samuel Atkins of Eastham." (Plym. Col. Records, give June 27, 1675, as the date of John Tisdill's death.) Their "houses in the wilderness" confirm the supposition that James Walker lived in the South part of Taunton, (3 miles from the village,) where lands were granted to him, and where his descendants have lived ever since. This was on the route of the Indians from Pocasset swamp to Taunton. Probably, after the destruction of his house, he removed to the village, and lived "near the ancient meeting house." (See 8th p. and 18th line.) Baylies says he was re-elected deputy in 1654, but the Plym. Col. Rec. state this as his 1st election.

P. 14. Assonate Neck was divided, 1680, among the proprietors who purchased it, viz.: Rev. Geo. Shove, Jas. Walker and John Tisdill, &c.

P. 18. John Tisdill of Duxbury, propounded for freedom, Sept. 7, 1642, was admitted March 7, 1642–3. He was constable in Taunton, June 8, 1655. (Plym. Col. Rec. vol. 3d, p. 78,) one of the purchasers of Assonate Neck, 1659, and Select-man in T., 1773 and '74.

P. 20, 4th line from foot. Phillip is the name, as spelt in Town Rec.

P. 20, No. (4) 3, Mary, m. Feb. 11, 1707–8, Joseph Winslow.

P. 23, No. 7, Joseph Wood m. Abigail Paul, Oct. 16, 1697.

P. 38, No. 67, after Dec. 7, insert (12 Fam. Rec.)

P. 48, No. 114. He could have been only 86 yrs. old. Having no record, he called his age 1 yr. too much. The Town. Rec. is more trustworthy than his memory.

P. 51, No. 122. Geo. Walker, Esq., who knew him well, says he was not in the Rev. service. If so, who was the Benj. of Taunton in Capt. Blake's Co.?

P. 52, No. 127. (4) His chil. were born—1, *Eliza*, b. Aug. 5, 1814, d. June 26, 1834. 2, *Jacob A.*, b. March 1, 1816, is a cotton merchant in N. Y. City. 3, *Charlotte F.*, b. Aug. 31, 1818, d. May 15, 1834.

P. 55, No. 139. He m. Oct. 24, 1811, A. King, dau. of Geo. of East Windsor, Ct.

P. 64, No. 162. His wife d. in Dighton, Sept. 15, 1860, ae. 76 yrs. 5 mos.

P. 68, No. 187. John (362.) The reference No. (362) is useless, as the compiler could obtain no report of his chil.

P. 70, No. 202. He has also 2 daus.

P. 83, No. 270. He spent his youth with his uncle, Wm. King, in Seneca, N. Y., and made a profession of religion at the age of 17. He attended school 2½ yrs. in Lansingburgh, N. Y., went thence to N. Y. City, studied the French and German languages, thence to Wheeling, Va., where he taught school, and began the study of the Spanish and Hebrew languages. He then travelled in Georgia, Ky., and N. Y. Returning to Baker Co., Ga., he taught school 2 yrs., pursuing his studies during the time, and went thence to Princeton, N. J., to complete his Theo'l studies. He left Little Britain ch., in autumn of 1850, and was stated supply at Eufala and Fort Gains, about 2 yrs., residing at La Fayette.

P. 87, No. 303. Mr. and Mrs. Horton and their 2 daus. are m. ch.

P. 102, No. 440, (6) Emily R., d. Aug. 28, 1860.

P. 103, No. 451. Geo. E. has another son, Earnest Clifford, b. Aug. 26, 1860, whose No. is 655.

P. 111, No. 564. Edwin A., m. Dec. 19, 1860, Jane Paul of Taunton. Res. T.

P. 115, No. 638. She m. July 20, 1859, Josiah W. Crocker, of No. Raynham.

REHOBOTH BRANCH.

"The Widow Walker" is the only female signer of the "combination" or compact, "entered into by all the inhabitants of Seakunk," (Rehoboth.)

The following persons of the Rehoboth Branch were soldiers in the R. I. Regiment in the Revolutionary War. Elijah, (No. 89.) Calvin, (No. 143.) Nath'l, (No. 226.) Chas. P. (No. 232.) (Thos. Walker was gunner. Who was he ?)

P. 133, No. 86. His w. Eliz'th d. Nov. 10, 1781.

P. 136, No. 108. Gideon had great force of character and large power of endurance. His w. possessed indomitable energy and firmness, with superior mental endowments. They made large sacrifices, both pecuniary and personal, for their country's independence.

P. 147, No. 167, (3) had also a dau. Lucy, who d. unm.

P. 149, No. 178. He d. Oct. 19? 1857, and she d. March, 1858.

P. 150, No. 187. His w. b. Dec. 1, 1768, in East Haddam, Ct., d. Dec. 1, 1790? (Error, Goodwin's Notes.) She was 7th child of Stephen Nott, 1st of Middletown, Ct., then of Saybrook, E. Haddam, and Ashford. He m. 1749, Deborah Selden, of Lyme, Ct.

P. 156, No. 228. (5) All of Col. Borden's chil. are m. Cong. ch.

P. 189, No. 386. (1) Ferdinand, m. May 13, 1849, Martha T. West, who was b. Dec. 18, 1826. Chil.—1, *Fredrika*, b. June 23, '50. 2, *Evelyn*, b. April 22, '53. 3, *Georgianna*, b. Dec. 17, '55. 4, *Charles*, b. May 21, '57. 5, *Martha*, b. Jan. 10, '60.

P. 191, No. 407. Nath'l C. has a dau. b. in Spring of '57 or '58, and her No. is 989.

P. 204, No. 522, for "Living, 1854," read Living, in 1860.

P. 217, No. 619. (3) Elmira Smith, m. Dec. 13, 1860, Hamilton Bigelow, M. D., of Pontiac, Mich. Res. P.

P. 227, No. 655, Abel. He was Rep. to the Legislature from Whiting, in 1860.

P. 229, No. 670, for Juliett, read Juliaet R., and her dau. (1) is *Juliette Emory*.

P. 237, No. 733. Levi, should be Levi Osgood.

P. 238, No. 734. Chittenden Walker, has had 7 chil., viz.:—1, *Levi*. 2, *Daniel*. 3, *Averill*. 4, *George*. 5, *Christine*. 6, *Wealthy*, d. ae. 9 yrs. 7, *Adeline*. Res. Hope, Newcastle district, C. W. Their place in the Genealogy would have been next to 1440.

P. 238, No. 736. Levina J. Powers, had 2 sons, who d. y.

P. 238, No. 737. Selina J. Averill, d. Feb. 18, 1860, in Coburg, C. W. She had 3 chil., viz:—1, *Wm.*. dec'd. 2, *Wealthy Jane*. 3, ——.

P. 238, No. 738. Caroline A. Powers, has 7 chil., 1860. viz.:—(1) *Freeman Nathan*, ae. 19. (2) *Selina Jane*, ae. 17. (3) *Hartwell Abner*. (4) *Joseph Walker*. (5) *Levi*. (6) *Caroline Laura*, ae. 6. (7) *Geo. W.*, b. Aug. 4, 1860.

P. 238, No. 739. Geo. m. Mary Ann Webster, and has now 3 chil. Res. Keldare, Juneau Co., Wis., P. O., Lyndon Station.

P. 243, No. 786. Judge Walker was Chief Justice of the Court of Sessions 4 yrs. (Mass. Reg.) Postmaster in Lenox, from 1820 to 1848, when he resigned, and was for many yrs., a Mem. of the Board of Trustees of Williams Coll.

P. 252, No. 835. George, has a 4th child, Mary Sturges, b. April 13, 1859. (No. 1594.)

P. 259, No. 866. Thos. M., d. Aug 13, 1860. His w. was b. Nov. 12, 1818.

P. 263, No. 914. Harriet Jane, b. June 13, 1834, m. Aug. 5, 1860, Joseph E. Morrison, son of Joseph M., of Rockville, Ct., and b. March 26, 1837. He is a housewright. She is m. Cong. ch. Res. R.

P. 283. No 1208, has 2 chil., and should have Ref. No., (1823,) and for Taunton read Lakeville.

P. 291, No. 1318. For Martha, read Martha M., of Franklin, Mass.

P. 292, No. 1322. Rev. Edwin S. became pastor of the 1st Bap. Church in Ripon, Wis., in Jan. 1861.

P. 298, No. 1403. Hiram N., m. 1860, Mary E. Babcock, dau. of James M., of Hogansburgh, N. Y.

P. 298, No. 1408. Lydia, m. —— Stout, since 1856. Res. Canton, N. Y.

P. 299, No. 1429. Eliza J., m. Sept. '58, Louis Eaton, and has—1, *Mary Agnes*, b. June '59.

P. 300, No. 1441-1, is named Warren Adelbert, and b. May 12, 1858.

P. 300, No. 1441-2, (to be added,) Selina Ann, b. May 19, 1860. These two live in Kildare, Juneau Wis., P. O., Lyndon Station.

No. 1557, Wm. H., b. March 4th, was drowned March 4, 1859, ae. 15 yrs.

No. 1558, Isaac Wells, (not Wells W.,) " " " " ae. 13 yrs.

No. 1559. For Delia, read Delia E.

P. 310, No. 1579. The following completes Mrs. McCulloh's family record. (2) *Henry Mayer*, d. Jan. 11, 1856. (3) *Charles Sears*, b. July 1, '56. (4) *Allan*, b. Aug. 31, '60. She resides in ——, New Jersey.

P. 310, No. 1580. Louisa B., has—(1) *William Walker*, b. Aug. 9, '55. (2) *Louisa*, b. May 13, '57. (3) *Sarah*, b. April 8, '59.

P. 311, No. 1589. Mr. Dexter is a civil engineer.

P. 312, No. 1600, has 2 more chil., viz.:—1, *Mary Rebecca*, b. July 18, '57. 2, *Nancy Eveline*, b. March 2, '60. Rev. Mr. Buck was grad. at Yale, 1849, Bangor Theo'l Sem., 1852, left Bethel, Me., March, 1859, and was installed in Slatersville, March 30, '59.

EASTHAM FAMILY.

P. 334, 17 to 21 line. This tradition contradicted by the grants of land to Wm. Walker, Sen., has been proved to apply not to Wm. the ancestor of the Eastham Family, but to his gd. son Wm., No. 8, p. 335. Wm. the Sen. lived on the farm now occupied by Seth Knowles, which corresponds with the grants as recorded in the Prop. Rec. (See 333–4 pp.)

P. 334, No. 2. John Walker was killed March 26, 1676, in "Pierce's Fight," in Pawtucket. This Fight was by far the severest disaster which befell the Colony in King Philip's War. Rev. Mr. Newman in his letter the day after, to Rev. Mr. Cotton, giving an account of the slain, states that 4 soldiers of Eastham, among whom he mentions John Walker, were killed.

P. 338, No. 39. Benj., a shipwright, was in Taunton, 1752, and bought land in Raynham. He bought land in Kingston, and "work-house, near wharf," &c., 1765. This was his homestead and was sold Sept. 8, 1767. He was in Bridgwater, in 1765. In 1785, he was a shipwright in Somers, Ct., and sold 4 parcels of land to Polycarpus Edson, 2 in Raynham, and 2 in South west corner of Bridgwater, in Titicut. Jas. Walker, witness.

P. 339, No. 51, (6) m. Nov. 26, Rebecca R. Atkins, and 2d, April 23, 1837, Mrs. Chloe Whelden. Res. Wellfleet.

P. 344, No. 88. James was pub. to Chloe Leach, both of Bridgwater, Sept. 23, 1775. He was a husbandman in B., and sold land in Raynham, Feb. 19, 1781.

P. 349, No. 147. Thankful by 1st marriage had 8 chil., m. 2d, Sylvester Spindle, and had 1 child, m. 3d Alvin? Howland. Res. Dennis.

P. 350. No. 154. Wm. had by 2d w. 6 chil. viz.:—No. 265–1, *Jerusha*. No. 265–2. II. *Wm*. No. 266. III. *Samuel*. No. 266–2. IV. *Timothy*. No. 266–3. V. *Barbara A*. No. 266–4. VI. *Mary*.

P. 353, No. 179. *Horace*, b. Aug. 28, 1789, m. 2d, Mrs. Phebe Perrin. He has 4 chil. by 1st marriage and 1 by 2d marriage, viz.:

P. [363, No. 335, I. *Austin*, b. Dec. 29, 1812, in Monson, m. Dorcas Burdick, and has chil., whose place in the Genealogy is No. 412, viz., I. *Billings*, 413, b. about 1836, is married. II. *Charles*, 414. III. *George*, 415. IV. *Oliver*, 416. V. *Alexander*, 417. VI. *Napoleon*, 417. VII. *Mary L*., 418. He is a trader. Res. Geneva, Walworth Co., Wis.

P. 363, No. 336. II. *Susan*, b. in M., Feb. 12, 1819, m. Maxon Simmons, a farmer. Res. Brookfield, Madison Co., N. Y.

P. 363, No. 337. III. *Mary*, b. in M., Dec. 1, 1821, d. Dec. 20, 1841, in B., unm.

" " " 338. IV. *Henry*, b. Dec. 1, 1824, in Exeter, N. Y., m. Diana Smith, and has 9 chil., whose place in the Genealogy is No. 419. I. *Albert*, b. about 1843. 420. II. *Olive*. 421. III. *Jane*. 422. IV. *Laura*. 423. V. *Phebe*. 424. VI. *Mary*. 425. VII. *Sarah*. 426. VIII. *Anna*. 427. ——. He is a laborer. Res. Remsen, Oneida Co., N. Y.

P. 363, No. 338. V. *James*, by 2d marriage, b. Oct. 16, 1836, in Monson, m. Mrs. Lovisa Washburn, and has—428. I. *James*, b. about 1857. He is a laborer. Res. Plainfield, N. Y.]

P. 357, No. 251. *Edmund*, m. Maria Cash.

P. 358, No. 256, *Reuben*, m. Aug. 6, 1851, Ann Hopkins, of Brewster, and has 1 son, Reuben Henry. (No. 372.)

P. 365, No. 374. For Olive read Olivia F——.

" " " 380, is named Barbara.

" " " 382, " ". Edmund Atwood.

" " " 383, " " Hannah Emma.

P. 363. The chil. of Linus are—No. 347. I, *Thomas*, is boatman on N. Y. and Erie Canal. 348. II. *William*, b. about 1842. 349. III. *Ruby*, b. about 1844. These 2 live in Leonard Hollow, Springfield, Pa. 349-1. IV. *Child*, b.about 1848. Res. S. 349-2. V. *Kate*, b. about 1853. Res. S. Two others. 349-3 and 349-4, live in Suffield, Ct., with their mother.

MARSHFIELD FAMILY.

P. 369, No. 3, *John*. Perhaps he is the John who m. July 26, 1684, Mary Knowles. See p. 421.

P. 382, No. 98. *Summers*, (194.) The Ref. No. (194) is useless, as no report of his family could be obtained.

P. 402, 29th line. James of C. was not son of Augustin, as Augustin's James was b. 1647 or '48. (See 401st p.)

P. 403, 28th line, for "He was 1 of many petitioners, 1655," read, He with the Select-men and others, in 1665, protested against the petitions of sundry inhabitants complaining of the Gov't.

P. 408, last line. For 1836–'47, read '45. His term expired in 1847, but he was Secretary of the Treasury from 1845 till 1849, and was Governor of Kansas in 1857.

The following statement, will show the completeness of this work, as a Genealogy of the Walkers of the Old Colony, and how few families, either of the males or females, have not been included. This feature of the work, is especially observable in regard to the Taunton and Rehoboth Families, and to the males who alone perpetuate the name.

Every male line has been traced with the following exceptions:

TAUNTON BRANCH.—Nos. 59, James,[6] of N. Y. city. 187, John,[7] of Wis., now living.

REHOBOTH BRANCH.—89, Elijah,[5] of Providence, R. I. 115, Stephen.[5] 116, Levi,[5] both b. in Rehoboth. 135, Peter.[6] 199, Joseph.[6] 200, John,[6] both b. in Ashford, Ct. 207, James.[6] 249—252, Wm.[6] Theadon.[6] Walter.[6] Worden,[6] all in Canada. 551, Caleb.[7] 552, Joseph.[7] 1732, Edward.[9] 1733, Fisher.[9] Doubtless some of these had no descendants, and have baffled all inquiries, because dying young or without issue. The following have chil., whose names are not reported. 546, Joseph,[7] of Penn. 722, Joseph B.,[7] of Centerville, Ia. 723, Wm.[7] 727, Nathan.[7] 728, Daniel.[7] These are all living and the last 3 in West Canaan, O.

EASTHAM FAMILY.—Nos. 24, Nath'l.[4] 30, Joshua.[4] 36, Nath'l.[4] 37, Matthew.[4] The following have descendants whose names have not been reported. Nos. 58, David,[5] of Me. 178, Subinus,[6] of Limestone, N. Y. 181, Joseph.[6] 208, Augustus,[7] of Vt. 209, Allen.[7] 302, Warren R.[7] 303, Willard,[7] both of South Gibson, Pa. These are living except No. 58.

MARSHFIELD FAMILY.—Nos. 27, Zara,[5] (Tory banished.) 96, Abraham.[6] 98, Summers,[6] of Hammond, N.Y. 100, Wing.[6] 113, Harris.[5] Of the males who have baffled all search and inquiry, there are only 2 in the Taunton Branch, 15 in the Rehoboth, 4 in the Eastham, and 5 in the Marshfield, making 26 out of about 3300.

The chil. of all the females named Walker, and intermarried with persons of other names, (and in many cases their gd. chil. and gt. gd. chil.) are given with the following exceptions:

TAUNTON BRANCH.—Nos. 40,[5] 45,[5] 96,[6] 117.[6] Perhaps they had no chil. Nos. 126,[7] 334,[8] 336,[8] 359,[8] 359,[8] 360,[8] 361,[8] have had chil., but their names are not reported and the number only is stated.

REHOBOTH BRANCH.—Of Nos. 78,[5] 105,[5] 117,[5] 118,[5] 201,[6] 202,[6] 206,[6] 208,[6] 212,[6] (253,[6] 254,[6] 255,[6] in Canada,) 1734,[9] 1735,[9] nothing is known.

Nos. 140,[5] 214,[6] 720,[7] 721,[7] 725,[7] 731,[7] 1456,[8] 1517,[8] 1518,[8] 1519,[8] married, but many have had no chil.

Nos. 79,[5] 106,[5] 138,[6] 177,[6] 345,[7] 475,[7] 476,[7] 481,[7] 482,[7] 547,[7] 548,[8] 1086,[8] 1121,[8] 1239,[8] 1240,[8] 1466,[8] 1524,[8] 1660,[8] all had chil., but their names have not been reported.

EASTHAM FAMILY.—Nothing is known in regard to No. 35.[4]

Nos. 9,[3] 11,[3] 13,[3] 14,[3] 16,[3] 19,[3] 32,[4] 75,[5] married, but may have had no chil.

One of the 3d gen., 3 of 4th, 8 of 5th, 8 of 6th, 28 of 7th, had chil., but their names have not been obtained. Most of those of the 6th or 7th generations are now living.

MARSHFIELD FAMILY.—Nos. 2,[2] 5,[2] 10,[4] 97,[6] married, but may have had no chil.

Three of 4th gen., 6 of 5th, 9 of 6th, 13 of 7th, married and had chil., whose names have not been reported. Most of those of the 6th and 7th generations are now living.

The names of chil., whose mothers were Walkers, are given therefore in all cases, with the exception of 11 Families, in the Taunton, 42 in the Rehoboth, 48 in the Eastham, and 36 in the Marshfield Branch. Undoubtedly some of these had no chil., or they would have been ascertained.

MISCELLANEOUS.

NAMES OF WALKERS IN THE OLD COLONY WHICH THE COMPILER CANNOT TRACE TO THE PROPER RELATIONSHIPS.

The three following, are from a record of marriages, solemnized by Major Thomas Leonard, of Taunton, between 1684 to 1713. The manuscript is still extant.

John Walker and Mary Knoles were married 22d of July, 1684. This may have been John, No. 3, of the Marshfield Branch. There is no trace of any descendants in Taunton.

John Paul and Dorothy Walker married May 26, 1692.

Benj. Jones and Hannah Walker married April 8, 1695.

James Walker, of Dartmouth, was sergeant in Capt. Dan'l Egrey's Co., under Col. Timothy Danielson in Rev. War. (Coat Rolls.)

Elizabeth Walker, d. 1718, ae. 42 yrs. (Ins. in Seekonk Cemetery.) This was probably 2d w. of Sam'l, No. 2, p. 122. She m. 2d, John Smith, and her 1st married name was doubtless put upon the stone by her chil.

Enos Walker and Levina Hoyt m. July 19, 1840. (Seekonk Rec.)

Jedidah Walker and Lyman Dexter m. Nov. 5, 1822. " "

John Thompson of Seekonk and Charlotte Walker were pub. Oct. 16, 1820. (Attleboro' Rec.)

Joseph Walker, of Pawtucket, R. I. In'y, $1342, 1847–8. Dan'l Rounds, adm'r.

Deborah, m. Wm. Smith, Oct. 3, 1728, and had 1 dau. (Eastham Rec.)

Lydia, m. Feb. 20, 1728–9, Caleb Cook. and had 4 chil. " "

Elizabeth Maker or Walker, m. Jesse Brown, 14th Aug. 1729, and had 4 chil. (Eastham Rec.)

Elizabeth, m. Aug. 3, 1753, Nath'l Ellis, both of Harwich. (Eastham Rec.)

Sarah Walker, m. Nov. 19, 1645, Nath'l Warren, and had chil. " "

Susanna Walker, m. Jan. 19, 1769, John Knowles, and had 2 sons. (Eastham Rec.)

Jonathan Hatch, b. May 16 or 17, 1652, m. at Barnstable, Abigail, (Falmouth Rec.,) Sept. 4, 1676; or Eliza Walker, (Barn. Rec.,) Dec. 4, 1676. (Gen. Reg., 1860, 198th p., Hatch Family.)

Isaac Walker, late of town of Woodbridge, in Co. of Middlesex, East New Jersey, now of Little Compton, R. I., sold land in Middleboro', 1702.

Isaac Walker, of Swansey, March, 1704-5, sold land he owned in Mid'o. Eph'm and Sarah Little, witnesses.

Isaac Walker, of Shawamett, of Town of Swansey, 1716.—There are no Walkers mentioned in the Swansey Rec.—Was he a descendant of Francis of Mid'o? See p. 397.

Francis Walker and John Haskell, in the division of the 77th lot in Mid'o, had 4th and 5th lots, July 6, 1789. The name indicates descent from Francis, of Mid'o, in 1670, but there is no other instance of name, birth, marriage or death, deed or will, in the town or county records, to connect the widely distant periods, and prove relationship.

Ruth Green Walker in M., before 1800.

Thomas Walker, in Duxbury, 1771, owning 40 acres of land.

Dr. Rufus Walker, m. Dec. 11, 1814. Olive M. Mitchell, of Bridgwater, and d. in Raynham, Sept. 29, 1820, without chil. He was from Livermore, Me., and descended from John, b. in Hopkinton, 1749. His wid. m. Lieut Isaac Fobes, of Wareham. Nov. 1822.

Olney Walker, of Mid'o, and Lydia B. In'y, Nov. 1840, $895.

ERRATA.

TAUNTON BRANCH.

P. 2, 26th line, for *her's* read *hers*.
P. 7, 31st line, *at that time* is superfluous.
P. 8, 15th line of notes, omit the comma after Taunton.
P. 9, 5th line of notes, put a period after blameless.
P. 12, 37th line of notes, for *Frances* Smith read *Francis* Smith.
P. 13, 26th line of notes, for *pers* read *lers*, meaning letters.
P. 23, 2d line should follow Taunton. in 3d line, or 2d and 3d lines should be transposed.
P. 24, 10th line from foot, for (4) Sarah read (3) Sarah.
P. 30, No. 31, 10th line, for *Elakim's* read *Eliakim's*.
P. 33, No. 38, (9) "These emigrated to Vt.," refers not to chil. of Amaziah, but to chil. of Mary, brothers and sisters of Amaziah.
P. 34, No. 45, for *Macrh* read *March*.
P. 38, No. 67, between this and 66, insert—By 2d marriage.
P. 47, No. 101, for *in 44th yr.* read *in 49th yr.*
P. 47, No. 102, for *in 74th yr.* read *in 73d yr.*
P. 49, No. 120, 15th line, for 1831 read 1833.
P. 59, No. 141, 4th line, for *She m. ch. Cong.* read *She was m. Cong. ch.*
P. 62, No. 152, for *Muston* C. Luce read *Marston* C. Luce.
P. 70, No. 201, 4th line, for *Has 2 sons*, read *Has 2 sons and 2 daus.*
P. 69, No. 193, (1) should read, b. July 10, 1824, m. Oct. 12, 1845, Betsey, who was b. Oct. 12, 1825.
P. 69, No. 194, for Chil. of Nathaniel Walker, [102] read [100.]
P. 74, No. 288, for Elisha (433) read (431.)
P. 76, No. 229, 19th line, for *Saving's* read *Savings*.
P. 87, No. 299, for Chil. of William Walker, (154) read (155)
P. 88, No. 309, (4) for *Keyhoe* read *Kehoe*.
P. 96, No. 377, (4) for *Clarillar* read *Clarilla*.
P. 102, No. 437, Mr. Davenport is descended (6th generation) from Thomas Davenport, of Dorchester, who was probably descended from the same family in England, as Rev. John Davenport.
P. 102, No. 437, (5) for *Frances* Whiting read *Francis* Whiting.
P. 112, No. 590, for Chil. of Wm. Walker, [333] read Chil. of Wm. H. Walker.
P. 116, No. 655, for *b. Nov.* 9, 1859, read *b. Sept.* 9, 1858.

REHOBOTH BRANCH.

P. 120, Note, last line, for June 27, 1676, read June 27, 1675. See 18th p. 20th line.
P. 121, 30th line, after *true*, substitute a comma for the period.
P. 128, No. 43, (4) Sarah was b. Dec. 11, 1737, not 1837.
P. 144, No. 150, (1) for 1799 read 1797.
P. 144, No. 150, (5) should be transposed with (4.)
P. 149, No. 178, d. Oct. 29, '57. (Gen. Reg.) Another says Oct. 19.
P. 154, No. 219, for *they* read *then*.
P. 158, 5th line, for *all his* read *and his*.
P. 167, No. 264, for ref. No. (682) read (684.)
P. 177, No. 304, for ref. No. (829) read (838.)
P. 178, No. 305, the ref. No. for his chil. is (847.)
P. 178, No. 305, 15th line, for 1832 read March or April, 1833.
P. 203, No. 514, 4th line, for *Mashapang* read *Mashapaug*.
P. 210, No. 576, has no chil. and ref. No. (1063) is useless.
P. 213, No. 596, for *Marine Mills* read *Marine*.
P. 213, No. 603, for *Porter* read *Porter E.*

P. 246, No. 806, for Res. *Oivet*, read Res. *Olivet.*
P. 254, No. 841, Tamar is *not* deceased.
P. 256, No. 851, 3d line, for *Belfre* read *Belpre.*
P. 285, No. 1224, should have ref. No. (1829.)
P. 297, No. 1397, Mary Malvina, for Feb. 1849 read 1842.
P. 298, No. 1407, should have ref. No. (1849.)
P. 310, No. 1576, for Child of Thomas P. W. (820) read (826.)
P. 304, No. 1558, (1) for *William* read *William W.*

EASTHAM FAMILY.

P. 334, No. 3, for Aug. 16, 1859, read Aug. 16, 1659.
P. 337, No. 30, for *He was m. in Eastham*, read *He was in E.*
P. 356, No. 226, for Chil. of Col. Amasa, [127] read [128.]

MARSHFIELD FAMILY.

P. 374, No. 37, (1) Thomas was youngest, and should have been numbered (4.)
P. 387, No. 147, for Chil. of Asa, [73] read [74.]

P. 405, 31st line, for (4) Sarah,[3] read (4) Sarah,[2]—substitute 2 for 3 over the names below, so as to read thus,—(5) Jacob.[2] (6) Joseph.[2] (7) Thomas.[2] (8) Mary.[2] (9) Eliakim.[2] (10) Mary.[2] (11) John.[2]
P. 407, 2d line from foot, for *none* read *two.*

INDEX.

PART FIRST of this Index, contains the christian names of all the Walkers embraced in this volume, excepting those who died under 12 yrs. of age. Of these, there are 68 of the Taunton, 265 of the Rehoboth, 55 of the Eastham, 46 of the Marshfield, and 2 of the Bristol Family, making an aggregate of 436, out of 3447.

Part Second contains the names of persons who have married Walkers, or their descendants. The names of the parents of those who have married Walkers and descendants of Walkers, are to a considerable extent, given in the Genealogy, but they are not indexed, as their surnames appear in Part II.

The number on the right of a name refers to the page. Two or more references to the same person, are included in a parenthesis. The figure on the left of a name, indicates the generation of the person. The letters on the left of the figures, denote the Branch of the Family to which the person belongs; thus T. is for Taunton, R. for Rehoboth, E. for Eastham, M. for Marshfield, B. for Bristol, and A. denotes the Walkers of the Mass. Colony mentioned in the Appendix.

If any reference should prove incorrect, the name may be found upon the page following the one referred to.

PART I.—NAMES OF WALKERS.

PART II.—PERSONS ALLIED TO WALKERS, OR THEIR DESCENDANTS, BY MARRIAGE.

THOSE WHO MARRIED WALKERS, AND WHOSE SURNAMES ARE NOT KNOWN.

ADDITIONS AND ERRATA. (SUPPLEMENT.)

P. 70, No. 197, Nathaniel d. bef. March, 1860.
P. 90, No. 321, (2,) Augustina F. d. Jan. 11, 1861.
P. 131, No. 60, for *Jemima (Walker) Bishop* read *Jemima (Bishop) Walker.*
P. 185, No. 343, for *Glacier* read *Glazier.*
P. 195, No. 434, Wm. H. d. Jan. 17, 1861, of malignant erysipelas.
P. 210, No. 579, Capt. Lewis Walker d. Feb. 9, 1861, ae. 72 yrs.
P. 226, No. 651, for Sally *Swiss* read Sally *Twiss.*
P. 245, No. 794, for *Kesiah* read *Keziah.*
P. 276, No. 1127, for *Zadok* read *Zadock.*
P. 288, No. 1263, (2,) Sarah d. Jan. 1, 1861, of diptheria.
P. 298, No. 1404, for *Folson* read *Folsom.*
P. 310, No. 1579, for *McCulloh* read *M'Culloh.*
P. 343, No. 71, Susannah m. 1769. (See 422d p.)
P. 348, No. 132, for *Eldridge* read *Elbridge.*
P. 349, No. 146, m. L. Dexter. (See 421st p.)
P. 423, 42d line, for Sarah was *b.* read Sarah was *bapt.*
P. 424, the 8th line is incorrect. See last two lines but one of 418th p.
P. 442, Geer Geo. W. read 363.
P. 442, Gilbert for 363 read 362.

(See 423d and 424th pp. for Errata.)

CPSIA information can be obtained
at www.ICGtesting.com
Printed in the USA
BVHW090721021118
531944BV00016B/205/P

9 781332 02264